MACROECONOMICS
Fifth Edition

MACROECONOMICS

Fifth Edition

Edwin G. Dolan
George Mason University

David E. Lindsey
Deputy Director
Division of Monetary Affairs
Board of Governors of the Federal Reserve System

The Dryden Press
Chicago   New York   San Francisco   Philadelphia   Montreal   Toronto   London   Sydney   Tokyo

Acquisitions Editor: Elizabeth Widdicombe
Developmental Editor: Rebecca Ryan
Project Editor: Karen Vertovec
Design Director: Alan Wendt
Production Manager: Barb Bahnsen
Permissions Editor: Doris Milligan/Cindy Lombardo
Director of Editing, Design, and Production: Jane Perkins

Copy Editor: Nancy Maybloom
Indexer: Leoni McVey
Compositor: York Graphic Services, Inc.
Text Type: 10/12 Plantin Light

Library of Congress Cataloging-in-Publication Data

Dolan, Edwin G.
  Macroeconomics / Edwin G. Dolan, David E. Lindsey. — 5th ed.

    p. cm. Includes bibliographies and index.
  1. Macroeconomics. I. Lindsey, David Earl. II. Title.
HB172.5.D65 1988   338.5—dc 19   87-33033
ISBN 0-03-020409-7

Printed in the United States of America
890-032-987654321

Address orders:
111 Fifth Avenue
New York, NY 10003

Address editorial correspondence:
One Salt Creek Lane
Hinsdale, IL 60521

The Dryden Press
Holt, Rinehart and Winston
Saunders College Publishing

Cover Source: Wassily Kandinsky, *Shaking Balancement*, 1925, The Tate
            Gallery, London. Copyright Artists Rights Society,
            Inc., New York/ADAGP 1987.

The Dryden Press Series in Economics

Asch and Seneca
Government and the Marketplace

Breit and Elzinga
The Antitrust Casebook

Breit and Ransom
The Academic Scribblers, *Revised Edition*

Campbell, Campbell, and Dolan
Money, Banking, and Monetary Policy

Dolan and Lindsey
Economics, *Fifth Edition*

Dolan and Lindsey
Macroeconomics, *Fifth Edition*

Dolan and Lindsey
Microeconomics, *Fifth Edition*

Eckert and Leftwich
The Price System and Resource Allocation, *Tenth Edition*

Gardner
Comparative Economic Systems

Hyman
Public Finance: A Contemporary Application of Theory to Policy, *Second Edition*

Johnson and Roberts
Money and Banking: A Market-Oriented Approach, *Third Edition*

Kaufman
The Economics of Labor Markets and Labor Relations

Kidwell and Peterson
Financial Institutions, Markets, and Money, *Third Edition*

Lindsay
Applied Price Theory

Link, Miller, and Bergman
Econograph: Interactive Software for Principles of Economics

Nicholson
Intermediate Microeconomics and Its Application, *Fourth Edition*

Nicholson
Microeconomic Theory: Basic Principles and Extensions, *Third Edition*

Pappas and Hirschey
Fundamentals of Managerial Economics, *Second Edition*

Pappas and Hirschey
Managerial Economics, *Fifth Edition*

Puth
American Economic History, *Second Edition*

Rukstad
Macroeconomic Decision Making in the World Economy: Text and Cases

Welch and Welch
Economics: Theory and Practice, *Second Edition*

Yarbrough and Yarbrough
The World Economy: Trade and Finance

Preface

Change Is the Only Constant

It has been a decade and a half since the authors first collaborated on an economics text. Those years have shown that in economics, change is the only constant.

Since our first effort to set forth the principles of economics for beginning students, economists have gained a better understanding of both the world at large and their own discipline. In macroeconomics, more is known about the dynamics of inflation and disinflation, the role of expectations in shaping economic behavior, and the interaction of the domestic economy with the world economy. In microeconomics, the contributions of public choice theory have lent a new perspective to many policy issues, the work of the modern Austrian school has brought new emphasis to the role of entrepreneurship, and long-established fields of economics such as antitrust policy, human resources, and income distribution have taken on new life.

But the economy has not stood still in the face of economists' improved understanding. Events have continued to pose new questions. Economists still disagree on such matters as the effects of the federal deficit, the proper strategy for monetary policy, the sources of volatility in securities prices and exchange rates, the reasons for differences in men's and women's average pay, and the effects of antipoverty policies, to name just a few areas of controversy.

The rapid pace of change in economic theory and reality makes teaching economics a challenge. Meeting that challenge requires a textbook that changes too. First, the book must bring the latest policy issues and theoretical topics into the classroom and explain them clearly. Second, the book must emphasize the ways of thinking that all economists use to attack new problems, even where they do not ultimately agree. Finally, the book must reflect ongoing innovation in pedagogical techniques so that the complexities of economics are made accessible to the beginning student.

This fifth edition of *Macroeconomics* responds to the need for change with these major innovations:

1. **Feature: Integrated international economics.** Topics in international theory and policy are covered in special sections of chapters that discuss related domestic theory and policy—for example, balance of payments accounts together with national income accounts and foreign exchange operations of the Fed together with its domestic open market operations. Because these sections are self-contained, however, those who wish to follow the traditional option of a single international unit at the end of the course may still do so. The special international sections are designated by a world map logo.
   Purpose: To show how domestic economic events and policy can best be understood in the context of an integrated world economy.
   Benefit: Crucial international issues are no longer crowded into the last days before the final exam.

2. **Feature: One-model macro option.** The macro chapters now offer a one-model option for teaching the theory of income determination. This permits Keynesian and classical theory, fiscal and monetary policy, and the dynam-

ics of inflation and unemployment all to be taught in an aggregate supply and demand framework. The income-expenditure model is covered in an optional chapter, Chapter 10, and an optional section of Chapter 11 for those who prefer to follow the traditional two-model approach. The accelerationist model of inflation, using inflation-adjusted Phillips curves, is found in Chapter 19, which is self-contained and also optional.

Purpose: To unify the teaching of macroeconomics within a single theoretical framework.

Benefit: Less time spent developing models, more time spent on issues and applications, including international topics.

3. **Feature: State-of-the-art pedagogy.** Enhanced teaching and learning aids and a new generic organization of boxed cases mean that the fifth edition of *Macroeconomics*, like past editions, defines the state of the art in pedagogy.

Purpose: To help students see the forest as well as the trees.

Benefit: Students who understand economics as a way of thinking rather than just a grab bag of models retain more of what they learn in the principles of economics course.

Keeping a textbook like this up to date is not simply a matter of adding new material. Selective pruning is also necessary. In deciding what to eliminate, our overriding aim has been to focus on a few key models and concepts that will unify the student's way of thinking about economics. Input from many reviewers, users, and students has helped us in this task. In some cases, topics have been deleted when they were found repetitive or were used by only a minority of instructors. Other topics no longer appear as separate chapters but are grouped with related topics elsewhere.

Edwin G. Dolan and David E. Lindsey have collaborated on every edition of this book. In this edition, Lindsey has returned to the status of full coauthor. His wide knowledge of macroeconomic theory and insider's view of the policy process complement Dolan's experience in the classroom and as a government analyst. Of course the views expressed in this book are those of the authors and do not necessarily reflect the views of the Board of Governors of the Federal Reserve System or other members of its staff. The following pages outline the approach of this book to the changing world of economics in more detail.

Organization of the Book

The Introductory Chapters

The book begins with a set of chapters that provide an overview of economics and the economy. As a group, these five chapters provide the background that students need to proceed with either a macro-first or micro-first course sequence.

Chapter 1, "What Economics Is All About," focuses on scarcity and choice as the issues that define the discipline of economics. It gives an idea of how economists, as people, think, confront disagreement, and work in academic, business, and government careers. Chapter 2, "Exchange and Production," looks at the central problems of what, how, and for whom that every economy faces. Chapter 3, "Supply and Demand," presents the basic model on which both micro and macro chapters build, stressing reactions to disequilibrium as well as equilibrium. Chapter 4, "The Role of Business: The Firm, Financial Markets, and Corporate Control," looks at current issues, such as takeovers and insider trading, as well as traditional material relating to the organization of the firm. Chapter 5, "The Role of Government: Market Failures, Rent Seeking, and Privatization," uses the concept of market failure to discuss such topics as provision of public goods and control of externalities and uses the concept of rent seeking to explain why government failures also sometimes occur.

Core Chapters

Integration of International Economics

The traditional structure of the macro course calls for teaching fiscal and monetary theory in a closed-economy context and then adding international topics at the end as time permits. In terms of the logic of step-by-step model building, this approach has some appeal. However, it also has a drawback: Increasingly, any newspaper article or TV news report that mentions monetary policy or the budget deficit is likely to mention the balance of payments and exchange rates in the same breath.

But if an instructor wants to bring international policy issues into the course from the beginning, the student needs an early introduction to the linkages between the domestic economy and the rest of the world. Six of the macro chapters contain special sections that serve this aim. A section in Chapter 6, "The Circular Flow of Income and Product," uses the circular flow model to show the basic linkages between the domestic and world economies. A new section in Chapter 7, "Measuring National Income and Product," outlines the balance of payments accounts as a natural extension of the domestic national income accounts. Chapter 10, "The Income-Expenditure Model," includes a section on the net export component of planned expenditure and shows how imports affect the expenditure multiplier. Chapter 13, "Central Banking and Money Creation," adds a section on the activities of the Fed's foreign exchange market operations as a follow-up to the usual discussion of its open market operations. The impact of interest rate changes on international capital flows is covered in a new section of Chapter 14, "The Supply of and Demand for Money." A section of Chapter 15, "An Integrated View of Monetary and Fiscal Policy," briefly discusses international implications of fiscal policy. These sections provide a series of stepping stones to Chapter 20, "Foreign Exchange Markets and International Monetary Policy."

Some instructors may, of course, prefer the traditional sequence in which international topics are covered at the end of the macro course. For this reason, the international sections of the various macro chapters are self-contained and clearly identified by a world map logo placed in the margin. It is possible to skip over these sections as the chapters are covered with no loss of continuity. The whole set can then be covered as a unit after Chapter 19 and before proceeding to Chapter 20.

The One-Model Option

For many years, textbooks relied on a single model for determining the level of real income: the Keynesian income-expenditure model, also known as the "Keynesian cross" or the "45° model." When the issue of inflation rose to importance in the 1970s, it became popular to supplement the income-expenditure model with a flexible-price aggregate supply and demand (AS/AD) model. The Lindsey/Dolan *Basic Macroeconomics* of 1974 was one of the first principles texts to do this. But today an increasing number of instructors take the view that two models for determining real income is one too many. For one thing, it is difficult to give a clean reconciliation of the two models at the principles level. Also, time spent teaching a second income determination model is time taken away from other course objectives, such as integrating international economics more closely into the course.

Unfortunately, almost all texts to date have been written in such a way that the instructor has no choice but to use both models. Not so with this fifth edition of *Macroeconomics*. This text takes the logical next step in the evolution of the principles course *by using AS/AD as the core model for macro theory while treating the income-expenditure model as an optional supplement*. The basic income-expenditure model is presented in an optional chapter, Chapter 10. This chapter first presents the standard fixed-price version of the model and then allows prices to vary in order to show the relationship of the income-expenditure and AS/AD models. In addition, an optional section of Chapter 11 applies the income-expenditure model to fiscal policy. In both cases, the income-expenditure material is entirely self-contained. It can be taught in sequence as it appears, preserving the traditional course outline, or omitted without loss of continuity.

But what about the historical importance of Keynes and his work? Taking the one-model option in no way downplays Keynes's contributions to macroeconomic theory and policy. Quite the contrary. Chapter 9 of this edition provides a fuller discussion of the Keynesian and classical views of economic stabilization than was given in previous editions. This discussion, presented in the framework of the AS/AD model, presents Keynes's ideas as set forth in his *General Theory* more accurately than the conventional approach used in other texts. By the time students have completed Chapter 9 they will have all the tools they need, including an understanding of the expenditure multiplier, to move directly to the discussion of fiscal policy in Chapter 11.

Continuing Features

Not everything in the macroeconomics chapters is new. Many features that found favor with users of previous editions remain. One is the use of the circular flow model to introduce key macroeconomic concepts and relationships (Chapter 6). Another is the blending of monetary theory, financial institutions, and practical policy issues in Chapters 12 through 15. Still another is the optional, chapter-length treatment of the accelerationist model of inflation (Chapter 19 in this edition). Along the way, many favorite case studies have been retained and a number of new ones added.

Pedagogy

Many innovative features of earlier editions of *Macroeconomics* have become industry standards. An example is multilevel vocabulary reinforcement, with boldface terms, marginal definitions, and an end-of-book glossary. While others play catch-up, the process of innovation and refinement continues in this new edition of Dolan/Lindsey.

Bracketing

One of the most solidly established techniques of effective pedagogy is that of *bracketing*. Every good classroom lecturer uses bracketing in the form of "Here's what we are going to say; here it is in detail; here is what we just said." The textbook equivalent is chapter preview and review. Sheer volume of preview and review material counts for less than do the care with which the two are tied together and what comes between. Here are the key bracketing techniques used in *Macroeconomics:*

- Each chapter opens with a set of *learning objectives* posed in the form of issues to be addressed in the chapter. These are then used in question form to organize the *chapter summary.*

- A list of *key terms from previous chapters* appears at the beginning of each chapter. This is balanced by a list of *newly introduced terms* at the end of the chapter.

- Each chapter begins with a *lead-off case* and ends with a *case for discussion.* The first item in the *problems and topics for discussion* at the end of the chapter asks students to apply what they have learned to issues raised in the lead-off case. The case for discussion is followed by its own set of questions. (Answers to these questions are given in the *Instructor's Manual.*)

Generic Organization of Boxed Cases

Since its first edition, *Macroeconomics* has been a leader in the use of case studies as a teaching and learning tool. In addition to the lead-off cases and cases for discussion used to bracket each chapter, numerous *boxed cases* appear within each chapter. An innovative feature of this edition is the organization of these cases into four generic categories, each with a specific purpose:

1. **Economics in the News.** Illustrates an abstract concept raised in the chapter with an actual quoted or paraphrased news item. Example: "Consumer Switch to Chicken Brings Change to Beef Industry" (Chapter 3).

2. **Applying Economic Ideas.** Uses a tool learned in the chapter for solving a problem drawn from real life. Example: "The Opportunity Cost of a College Education" (Chapter 1).

3. **Who Said It? Who Did It?** Highlights the contribution of an economist of the past or present to a key idea discussed in the chapter. Example: "Adam Smith on the Invisible Hand" (Chapter 1).

4. **Perspective.** Takes a look at a controversial issue or adds additional detail to a point raised in the chapter. Example: "A Junk Job Explosion?" (Chapter 8).

The Package

A complete support package provides instructors and students with everything they need to teach and learn economics.

Test Bank

Written by Louis Amato and Irvin B. Tucker III, both of the University of North Carolina at Charlotte, in collaboration with Edwin G. Dolan, the *Test Bank* includes more than 1,000 items. The authors have fully class-tested each item, guaranteeing a comprehensive, "teacher-friendly" selection. The *Test Bank* contains the following features.

Number and Type of Questions

The *Test Bank* offers over 1,000 multiple-choice and true/false questions. It also contains many graphical questions.

Distribution of Questions by Chapter

- Each chapter has an appropriate number of questions based on its content and length. This varies from 40 questions for the first, introductory chapter to 120 for some of the core concept chapters.

- Some questions appear in alternate forms to permit reuse.

- Questions are arranged in the approximate order of the chapter coverage of each topic.

Categorization and Coding

All questions are coded according to level of difficulty and cognitive learning type. These are E (easy), M (moderate), D (difficult), DF (definition or fact), SA (simple analysis), and CI (complex interpretation). This allows the instructor to select a spectrum of questions for testing both recall learning and concept comprehension.

Graphing Emphasis

Many questions ask students to work directly on graphs. Questions are formatted to follow the "hands-on" sample items in the *Study Guide*.

Recordkeeping Aid

The *Test Bank* contains marginal recordkeeping space for the instructor to personalize it with the date each question is used and the percentage of students who correctly answer each question.

Additional Exam and Essay Problems

The *Instructor's Manual* contains two exam and essay problems for each chapter with which to supplement tests. Exam and essay problems typically serve as excellent extra-credit test questions for more proficient students. Answers are included.

Computerized Version

The *Computerized Test Bank* (available for the Apple® IIe, IBM® PC, IBM® PC-XT, and mag tape) allows the instructor to create tests tailored to particular requirements. By using the questions stored on disk, both short quizzes and full-length exams can be quickly and easily constructed.

The *Computerized Test Bank* allows instructors to

- preview questions on the computer screen

- edit publisher-supplied questions and create personalized questions

- select exam questions manually or randomly

- create exam headings and determine the amount of space to be allotted each question
- scramble questions to create multiple versions of the same test
- print exams with answer keys and student answer sheets
- store exams created for future use
- produce partial hard copy of most graphs that appear in the *Test Bank*.

"Sticky-paper" versions of all graphs are also available for placement on the master copy.

Direct Service Hotline
For instructors who have any technical difficulties with the *Computerized Test Bank*, The Dryden Press/TEC offers a direct service number: 516-681-1773, 9 a.m. to 5 p.m. EST.

Instructor's Manual

The *Instructor's Manual* for *Macroeconomics* is intended to help new instructors prepare their first principles course and experienced instructors retailor their course to mesh optimally with the text. With these aims in mind, the *Instructor's Manual* includes the following features.

What's Different Here and Why
This section, found at the beginning of each chapter, helps convert the course outline and lecture notes from other texts to *Macroeconomics*, fifth edition. Changes from the fourth edition of *Macroeconomics* are noted. This section also provides technical information on the theoretical models that underlie the book.

Instructional Objectives
All elements of the *Macroeconomics* package—text, *Study Guide*, *Test Bank*, and *Instructor's Manual*—are coordinated by means of specific instructional objectives listed in each chapter of the *Instructor's Manual*. In the text, they are listed for students at the beginning of each chapter. Questions covering every topic on the list of instructional objectives are included in the *Test Bank*.

EconoGraph II
An important element of the *Macroeconomics* package is *EconoGraph II*, a computer-aided instruction program featuring interactive graphical exercises and simulations. It consists of nine computer-based lessons divided between micro- and macroeconomic topics. A special section in the corresponding chapters of the *Instructor's Manual* discusses the use of *EconoGraph II*.

Lecture Notes and Suggestions
Each chapter of the *Instructor's Manual* contains a section of lecture notes in outline form. The pages are perforated and three-hole punched to facilitate their integration with the instructor's own lecture notes. The lecture notes cover the optional appendixes as well as the chapters. In addition, they list transparency acetates that are available for use with the text. The use of the transparencies is more fully discussed in a separate transparency guide.

Examination Problems and Essays

Each chapter contains two or three suggestions for examination problems and essays. These are valuable supplements to the multiple-choice and true/false questions contained in the *Test Bank* where the teaching situation permits grading of problems and essays.

Answers to Selected Problems and Topics for Discussion

Answers are given to selected items from the "Problems and Topics for Discussion" sections of the text as well as the "Case for Discussion" sections in each chapter. Items that involve library research or ask questions that pertain to students' personal or community situation are omitted.

Course Planning Guide

In addition to these chapter-by-chapter features, the introductory section of the *Instructor's Manual* contains extensive suggestions on course planning to fit a wide variety of course calendars.

Study Guide

The *Study Guide* for *Macroeconomics* provides students with hands-on applications and self-testing opportunities. It reinforces the text and prepares students for exams. The *Study Guide* contains the following features.

Where You're Going

All parts of the *Macroeconomics* package are tied together by a numbered set of learning objectives for each chapter. These learning objectives, which also appear in the text and the *Instructor's Manual,* are given in the "Where You're Going" section of each chapter of the *Study Guide*. A list of terms introduced in the chapter is also provided.

Walking Tour

The "Walking Tour" section is a narrative summary of the chapter and incorporates questions on key points. Students work through this material, answering the questions as they go along. Answers to the questions are given in the margins.

Hands On

This section contains graphical and numerical exercises that give students hands-on experience in working with the concepts covered in the chapter. It is particularly helpful to students who require extra work in order to master difficult graphical material. Complete solutions, including graphs, are given at the end of the chapter.

Economics in the News

Each of these sections takes the form of a brief news item with questions that relate the item to concepts covered in the chapter. Answers are found at the end of the chapter. These items are particularly valuable in preparing for essay-type exam questions. This feature is the *Study Guide* version of the case study approach used in the text and links economics to the real world.

Self Test

This section consists of 15 multiple-choice questions, which are similar in structure to those in the *Test Bank* and act as a final checkpoint before an exam. Annotated answers to the self-test items are given at the end of the chapter.

Don't Make This Common Mistake

These are special boxes, strategically placed throughout the *Study Guide*, that caution students against certain common mistakes made by successive generations of economics students. All of these mistakes are easy to avoid if the student is alerted to them.

Careers in Economics

A unique feature of the *Study Guide* is the "Careers in Economics" section. This section, written by Keith Evans of California State University, Northridge, has been updated for the fifth edition. This material should appeal to students considering a major in economics.

EconoGraph II

Created by Charles Link, Jeffrey Miller, and John Bergman of the University of Delaware, *EconoGraph II* is a computer software package for principles of economics. It consists of nine interactive tutorial lessons. These lessons include the topics students find most difficult to master, including

- supply and demand
- money expansion
- AS/AD
- Keynesian cross analysis
- cost functions
- supply under perfect competition
- monopoly.

EconoGraph II is designed for use with IBM PCs with at least 128K of memory, DOS 2.0, and a color graphics card (use with IBM compatibles is possible but not guaranteed). Features include:

1. Intensive instruction in the use of graphs, which are critical in economics.
2. Self-contained 10- to 40-minute lessons.
3. Diagnostic questions and problems in which the computer tells students what they did right or wrong.
4. Graphical manipulations in which students can plot lines and shift curves.
5. Graphs constructed in stages so that each stage can be explained and important aspects highlighted.
6. Self-paced instruction to allow for repetition and review.

GraphPac

A completely new concept in student study aids, *GraphPac* is the first graph note-taking device available to economics students. Each *GraphPac* tablet contains reproductions of all major graphs in the text with additional graph-ruled margins. *GraphPac* allows students to take notes on key graphs without having to sketch transparency acetates, masters, or basic chalkboard drawings. The marginal graph rules provide space for students to reproduce additional graphs drawn by the instructor during a lecture. This is especially useful when the student wants to capture the effect of a shift or change in a basic graph.

GraphPac is free to students upon adoption of the text. It can be ordered by submitting the request number when placing a textbook order.

GraphPac is unique to the fifth edition of *Macroeconomics*.

Transparency Acetates

The transparency acetates are two color and computer generated. This provides maximum accuracy and readability. For complete pedagogical consistency, the color used in the graphics matches that in the text. There are more than 160 acetates of graphs from the text. Each transparency has a complete teaching note to help instructors integrate the transparency into their lectures.

Some Words of Thanks

We wish to thank the following people for their help in revising this edition:

Jack Adams, *University of Arkansas*
Charles Bennett, *Gannon University*
Thomas Bonsor, *East Washington University*
David Brasfield, *Murray State University*
Donald Bumpass, *Texas Technical University*
William Carlisle, *University of Utah*
James Clark, *Wichita State University*
Avi Cohen, *York University*
C. M. Condon, *College of Charleston*
James Cover, *University of Alabama*
J. R. Cowart, *Mobile College*
Kenneth DeHaven, *Tri-County Technical College*
Mary Deily, *Texas A&M University*
Howard Elder, *University of Alabama*
Charles Ellard, *Pan American University*
Michael Erickson, *Eastern Illinois University*
Christopher Fiorentino, *West Chester University*
David Fractor, *California State University, Northridge*
Gary Galles, *Pepperdine University*
Lynne Gillette, *Texas A&M University*
Robert Gillette, *Texas A&M University*
Fred Graham, *University of Texas, Arlington*
Harish Gupta, *University of Nebraska*
James Hamilton, *University of Virginia*
Oskar Harmon, *University of Stamford*
Charles Hegji, *Auburn University, Montgomery*

John Holland, *Iona College*
R. James, *James Madison University*
Robert Jerome, *James Madison University*
James Jonish, *Texas Technical University*
Ebrahim Karbassioon, *Eastern Illinois University*
Bruce Kaufman, *Georgia State University*
Calvin Kent, *Baylor University*
James Kyle, *Indiana State University*
Luther Lawson, *University of North Carolina, Wilmington*
Stephen Lile, *Western Kentucky University*
Joseph Lin, *Louisiana State University*
Raymond Lombra, *Pennsylvania State University*
Don Losman, *National Defense University, Washington*
J. L. Love, *Valdosta State College*
David MacPherson, *Pennsylvania State University*
Jay Marchand, *University of Mississippi*
Benjamin Matta, *New Mexico State University*
John Mbaku, *Kennesaw College*
Eugene McKibbin, *Fullerton College*
Shah Mehrabi, *Mary Washington College*
Joseph Mesky, *East Carolina University*
Don Meyer, *Louisiana Tech University*
Steve Meyer, *Francis Marion College*
Jefferson Moore, *Louisiana State University*
J. M. Morgan, *College of Charleston*
John Murdoch, *Northeast Louisiana University*

Kenneth Nowotny, *New Mexico State University*
James O'Neill, *University of Delaware*
Pat Papachristou, *Christian Brothers College*
Carl Pearl, *Cypress College*
Thomas Peterson, *Central Michigan University*
John Piscotta, *Baylor University*
J. M. Pogodzinski, *Georgia State University*
David Rees, *Mesa College*
Michael Rendich, *Westchester Community College*
D. Rogers, *LeMoyne College*
Donald Schaefer, *Washington State University*
Bruce Seaman, *Georgia State University*
Frank Slesnick, *Bellarmine College*
Phillip Smith, *Gainesville Junior College*

Ken Somppi, *Auburn University*
David Spenser, *Brigham Young University*
Henry Thomasson, *Southeastern Louisiana University*
Timothy Tregarthen, *University of Colorado, Colorado Springs*
David Tuerck, *Suffolk University*
Arienne Turner, *Fullerton College*
Steven Ullmann, *University of Miami*
K. T. Varghese, *James Madison University*
Thomas Vernon, *Clarion University of Pennsylvania*
Michael Watts, *Purdue University*
William Weber, *Illinois State University*
Don Williams, *Kent State University*
Eugene Williams, *Northwestern State University*
Ernie Zampelli, *Catholic University of America*

In addition, we would like to thank the staff of The Dryden Press for making this edition possible. They are a truly dedicated, tireless group of professionals.

Edwin G. Dolan
Great Falls, Virginia

David E. Lindsey
Arlington, Virginia

December 1987

About the Authors

Edwin G. Dolan grew up in a small town in Oregon. He attended Earlham College and then Indiana University, earning a B.A. degree from Indiana. After staying at Indiana to earn an M.A. in economics, he completed his Ph.D. at Yale University. Dolan spent the next few years teaching economics at the University of Connecticut, Dartmouth College, and the University of Chicago. He has served as a specialist in transportation regulation, both in the antitrust division of the U.S. Department of Justice and at the Interstate Commerce Commission. For the last ten years, he has taught economics at George Mason University.

David E. Lindsey comes from the university town of West Lafayette, Indiana. He received his B.A. from Earlham College and his Ph.D. from the University of Chicago, where he studied under Milton Friedman. Lindsey taught economics for several years at Ohio State University and Macalester College. He began his long-running collaboration with Dolan on their principles text while at Macalester. Since 1974 he has been on the staff of the Board of Governors of the Federal Reserve System, where he now serves as Deputy Director of the Division of Monetary Affairs.

Contents in Brief

Chapter 20   **Foreign Exchange Markets and International Monetary Policy**   484

                    Dictionary of Economic Terms   515

                    Index   523

5total chapters

Contents

---

*Indicates optional international section.

An Overview of the Market Economy

Part One

1 What Economics Is All About

After reading this chapter, you will understand . . .

- What economics is all about.
- How the need to choose is related to the concept of cost.
- The roles that households, business firms, and government units play in the economy.
- What markets are and how they work.
- Who worries about unemployment, inflation, and economic growth and why.
- Why economists sometimes disagree.
- How ethics and value judgments enter into economics.

How to Cope with a Teacher Shortage

"There's a limit to how much good you're doing serving tea and Coke. I identify more with being a third-grade teacher than I ever did with being a flight attendant." So says Kendall Hagerty, a former American Airlines flight attendant, recently retrained in a program devised by the city of Dallas to meet an acute teacher shortage. In Maine, a lobsterman and a blueberry farmer are among those enrolled in a new mid-career teacher training program. Delaware is converting people with chemical-industry backgrounds into science teachers, and Texas is training laid-off oil geologists.

The armed forces are particularly ripe for teacher recruiting. Military

Teaching economics

personnel retire early, get generous pension benefits to supplement a teacher's pay, and are experienced in discipline and leadership. So the University of West Florida now offers teacher training on nearby Navy and Air Force bases, and Arizona State University targets the military in a new mid-career program.

These efforts reflect a shrinking supply of teachers in the face of strong demand. Between 1972 and 1982, enrollment in teacher education programs fell by 50 percent. Women and minority-group members, the traditional groupings from which teachers emerged, now have wider opportunities in higher-paying fields. Also, more teachers are retiring or quitting.

One result of the shortages: After many years of indifferent, even contemptuous treatment in the job market, teachers are being fawned over and catered to by recruiters who scour the country for prospects.

At one job fair, Prince George's County, Maryland, gave away book bags, balloons, and apples to lure teachers to its table, where it told them about all the goodies they would get if they signed on—including a month's free rent and cut-rate car loans.

Bad form, competitors complained. Tough, says a spokesman for the district. "It's a cutthroat market out there. Teachers deserve to be competed for,"

3

he adds. Helped by a recent 21 percent salary raise as well as the balloons, the county was swamped with 4,000 applications for 400 jobs.

Source: Francis C. Brown III, "Recruiting Drive: Shortage of Teachers Prompts Talent Hunt by Education Officials," *The Wall Street Journal*, January 15, 1987, 1. Reprinted by permission of *The Wall Street Journal*, © Dow Jones & Company, Inc. 1987. All Rights Reserved. Photo Source: © Chris Paganelli.

Scarcity
A situation in which there is not enough of a resource to meet all of everyone's wants.

THE balloons and book bags are symptoms of the efforts of Prince George's County officials to cope with a universal economic problem: scarcity. **Scarcity** is a situation in which there is not enough of some resource to meet everyone's wants. In this case, the scarce resource is people. School administrators across the country want people to serve as teachers to educate the children entering their classrooms. But there are not enough people to do everything at once; thus, school administrators are taking actions to attract flight attendants, lobstermen, and oil geologists to change careers. In another situation, the scarce resource might be fresh water. In order to be available for household use, water might have to be diverted from farming. In still another, the scarce resource might be time. In order to find time to devote to studying, hours spent satisfying other wants, such as sports, might have to be cut back. Scarcity is something that is encountered in thousands of forms every day.

Economics
The study of the choices people make and the actions they take in order to make the best use of scarce resources in meeting their wants.

The concept of scarcity is central to economics. In fact, **economics** can be defined as the study of the choices that people make and the actions they take in order to make the best use of scarce resources in meeting their wants. The above example illustrates the actions and choices of two groups of people. First are the school officials who are making choices and taking actions that they hope will attract the teachers they want. Second are the people who are making the choice of whether to devote their limited working years to teaching or to some other career.

In this book, we will meet scarcity in hundreds of situations. As we do so, we will see how the discipline of economics provides a framework for analyzing actions and choices that are directed toward fulfilling people's wants.

Scarcity and Choice

In a world of scarcity, we constantly encounter trade-offs between one goal and another. If we spend more on lunch, we may have less left to spend on dinner. If we live in the country, we may have to commute farther to work. On a national level, if we spend more on defense, other federal programs may have to be cut back. The number of such trade-offs is limitless.

Goods
All things that people value.

Services
The valued acts that people perform for one another.

One trade-off highlighted in the opening article in this chapter is that between goods and services. **Goods** are simply all the things that people value—blueberries, lobsters, oil, or whatever. **Services** are the valued acts that people perform for one another—teaching school, serving meals on an airplane, providing insurance, and so on.

Education is an example of a service. In the long run, getting an education may help you achieve a higher standard of living, but in the short run, it means sacrifice. To finish college—or even high school—you may have to spend your savings, postpone getting a full-time job, or live at home longer than you would like. Further, education entails trade-offs not just for one person but for the economy as a whole. Resources must be devoted to building classrooms rather than factories or airports. Teachers and school staff cannot work at producing other things at the same time. Finally, while students who graduate may eventually contribute more to the economy than they would had they shortened their education, they will contribute less during the time they are in school.

The Production Possibility Frontier

Economists are fond of using graphs to illustrate key concepts. We will use many graphs in this course.[1] As an introduction to the use of graphs in economics, we will use a simple graph to illustrate the concept of scarcity.

The actual U.S. economy is complex. It produces thousands of different goods and services. To facilitate our first illustration of scarcity, we will envision a simpler economy in which just one service is produced, education, and just one good, cars. Exhibit 1.1 shows the trade-offs between education and cars for such an economy. The horizontal axis measures the quantity of education in terms of the number of high school graduates "produced" per year; the vertical axis measures the production of cars. Any combination of education and cars can be shown as a point in the space between the two axes. For example, production in some year of 10 million high school graduates and 5 million cars would be represented by point E.

In drawing this figure, we assume given supplies of the basic inputs known as **factors of production.** There are three of these. **Labor** consists of the productive contributions made by people working with their minds and muscles. **Capital** consists of all the productive inputs created by people, including tools, machinery, structures, and intangible items such as computer programs. **Natural resources** include everything that can be used as a productive input in its natural state, such as farmland, building sites, forests, and mineral deposits. The factors of production used to produce education include labor in the form of teachers and staff; capital in the form of buildings, desks, and computers; and natural resources in the form of building sites and fuel with which to heat buildings. The figure also assumes a certain state of technology for the production of both cars and education.

Exhibit 1.1 shows that even if all factors of production were devoted to education, there would be a limit to the quantity of education that could be produced. To illustrate, suppose that the limit is 20 million graduates per year. The extreme possibility of producing 20 million graduates and nothing else is shown by point A in Exhibit 1.1. As the figure is drawn, the maximum output of cars if no resources whatever are put into education is 18 million, shown by point B. Between these two extremes is a whole range of possible combinations of education and other goods. These intermediate possibilities are shown by points such as C and D, which fall along a smooth curve. This curve is called a **production possibility frontier.** It is called a "frontier" because it is a boundary between the combinations of education and cars that can be produced and those that cannot given the available technology and factors of production.

Points A, B, C, and D, which lie directly on the curve, stand for the combinations of education and cars that can be produced. Combinations inside the

Factors of production
The basic inputs of labor, capital, and natural resources used in producing all goods and services.

Labor
The contributions to production made by people working with their minds and muscles.

Capital
All means of production that are created by people, including tools, industrial equipment, and structures.

Natural resources
Anything that can be used as a productive input in its natural state, such as farmland, building sites, forests, and mineral deposits.

Production possibility frontier
A graph showing the possible combinations of goods that can be produced in an economy given the available factors of production and technology.

---

[1] Readers who would like to review the basic techniques of graphing may refer to the appendix to this chapter.

Exhibit 1.1   Production Possibility Frontier

This figure shows possible outputs of cars and education in a simple economy where these are the only two products. Technologies and the available supplies of factors of production are assumed to be fixed. If all factors are devoted to education, 20 million high school graduates can be "produced" each year (point A). If all factors are devoted to making cars, 18 million cars can be made each year (point B). If the factors are divided between the two products, combinations such as those at points C and D are possible. The curve connecting A, B, C, and D is called a *production possibility frontier*. The slope of the frontier shows the opportunity cost of education in terms of cars. For example, between points C and D, producing an extra graduate requires giving up two cars. Points inside the frontier, such as E, are also possible and can be reached even if not all factors are used or some are used inefficiently. Points outside the frontier, such as F, cannot be reached with the available resources.

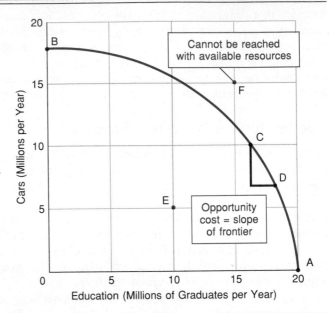

frontier, such as E, are also possible and do not require the full use of all available factors. But a combination represented by a point outside the frontier, such as F, cannot possibly be produced given the scarcity of factors of production and the available technology. It can be produced only if new factors of production become available (say, through growth of the labor force) or if new technologies permit more output per unit of the currently available factors.

Opportunity Cost

At any point along the frontier, there is a trade-off between education and cars. Given the scarcity of factors of production, choosing to produce more of one must mean choosing to produce less of the other. For example, suppose we begin at point C, where 16 million students are graduating from high school each year and 10 million cars are being made. If we want to increase the output of graduates to 18 million per year, we must give up some cars and use the freed-up factors of production to build and staff classrooms. In moving from point C to point D, then, we will be trading off production of 4 million cars for the extra 2 million graduates; that is, over this range of the frontier, each extra graduate will cost us about two cars.

Cost is a central concept in economics. In a world of scarcity, it is rare to get something for nothing. Typically we must bear costs in order to obtain benefits. In ordinary conversation, laypeople tend to use the term *cost* rather loosely; economists, however, are more cautious. The key cost concept in economics is that of **opportunity cost**—the cost of doing something as measured in terms of the value of the lost opportunity to pursue the best alternative activity with the same time or resources. In Exhibit 1.1, opportunity cost is shown by the slope of the production possibility frontier. For example, in moving from point C to point D, we sacrificed two cars for each additional graduate. Thus, in this range of the frontier, the opportunity cost of one graduate is two cars.

Opportunity cost
The cost of a good or service measured in terms of the lost opportunity to pursue the best alternative activity with the same time or resources.

In real life, we cannot refer to a handy book of production possibility frontiers to measure opportunity costs. Often prices stated in dollars and cents give an accurate picture of opportunity costs. For example, if a hamburger costs $3 and a bratwurst $1, we can say that the cost of eating a hamburger is the lost opportunity to eat three bratwursts. In other cases, time is a more appropriate measure of opportunity cost than is money. For example, the cost of spending an hour studying economics is the loss of the opportunity to spend the same hour studying math. In still other cases, such as that discussed in "Applying Economic Ideas 1.1," both time and money are involved in the calculation of opportunity cost.

We will find many applications for the concept of opportunity cost in this course. Economics, after all, is about scarcity and choice. Because time and resources are scarce, we must choose to give up one opportunity in order to take advantage of another many times each day.

What Economists Do

We now know a little about the subject matter of economics: It deals with scarcity and choice. What, however, do economists *do?* It is highly unlikely that they just sit around bemoaning the opportunities they passed up when they entered their chosen profession. In the broadest sense, as we have said, they study the ways in which people deal with the problem of scarcity. But it will be useful, as a preview of this course, to take a closer look. We will begin with the distinction between *microeconomics* and *macroeconomics*.

Microeconomics

The prefix *micro* comes from a Greek word meaning "small." **Microeconomics** is the branch of economics that deals with the choices made by small economic units—households, business firms, and government units.

Microeconomics
The branch of economics that deals with the choices and actions of small economic units—households, business firms, and government units.

Units of Analysis
In economics, a *household* is a group of people who pool their incomes, own property in common, and make economic decisions jointly. People who do not belong to such a group are counted as one-person households. Households supply factors of production and consume the goods and services that are produced.

Business firms are the second basic unit of microeconomic analysis. Firms buy factors of production from households and use them to produce goods and services. Firms come in many shapes and sizes. According to census data, there are more than 16 million business firms in the United States, ranging from small stores and family farms to huge corporations. Chapter 4 discusses the role of business firms in more detail.

Microeconomics also analyzes the actions of *government units* such as Congress, the courts, and regulatory agencies. As we will see throughout this book, units of government have a major impact on the economic lives of firms and households; their decisions, in turn, are affected by events in the economy. Chapter 5 examines the relationship between government and business in the U.S. economy.

The Opportunity Cost of a College Education

How much does it cost you to go to college? If you are a resident student at a typical four-year private college in the United States, you can answer this question by making up a budget like the one shown in Table A. This can be called a budget of *out-of-pocket costs*, because it includes all the items—and only those items—for which you or your parents actually must pay in a year.

Table A   Budget of Out-of-Pocket Costs

Tuition and fees	$ 5,800
Books and supplies	400
Transportation to and from home	400
Room and board	2,900
Personal expenses	700
Total out-of-pocket costs	$10,200

Your own out-of-pocket costs may be much higher or lower than these averages. Chances are, though, that these are the items that come to mind when you think about the costs of college. As you begin to think like an economist, you may find it useful to recast your college budget in terms of *opportunity costs*. Which of the items in Table A represent opportunities that you have forgone in order to go to college? Are any forgone opportunities missing? To answer these questions, compare Table A with Table B, which shows a budget of opportunity costs.

Table B   Budget of Opportunity Costs

Tuition and fees	$ 5,800
Books and supplies	400
Transportation to and from home	400
Forgone income	8,000
Total opportunity costs	$14,600

Some items are both opportunity costs and out-of-pocket costs. The first three items in Table A show up again in Table B. In order to spend $5,800 on tuition and fees and $400 on books and supplies, you must give up the opportunity to buy other goods and services—say, to buy a car or rent a ski condo. In order to spend $400 getting to and from school, you must pass up the opportunity to travel somewhere else or to spend the money on something other than travel. But not all out-of-pocket costs are also opportunity costs. The last two items in the out-of-pocket budget are examples. By spending $3,600 a year on room, board, and personal expenses during the year, you are not really giving up the opportunity to do something else. Whether or not you were going to college, you would have to eat, live somewhere, and buy clothes. Because these are expenses you would have in any case, they do not count as opportunity costs of going to college.

Finally, there are some items that are opportunity costs without being out-of-pocket costs. Thinking about what you would be doing were you not going to college suggests a major item that must be added to the opportunity cost budget but does not show up at all in the out-of-pocket budget. Had you not decided to go to college, you probably would have taken a job and started earning money soon after leaving high school. As a high school graduate, your earnings would be about $8,000 during the nine months of the school year. (You could work during the summer even if you were attending college.) Because this potential income is something you would have to forgo for the sake of college, it is an opportunity cost even though it would involve no monetary outlay.

Which budget you use depends on the kind of decision you are making. If you have already decided to go to college and are doing your financial planning, the out-of-pocket budget will tell you how much you will have to raise from savings, parents' contributions, and scholarships in order to make ends meet. But if you are making the more basic decision between going to college and taking up a career that does not require a college degree, the opportunity cost of college is what counts.

Markets

Microeconomists are interested not only in the actions of households, firms, and government units but also in how those actions are coordinated. In an economy such as that of the United States, markets play a key role in coordination.

A **market** is any arrangement that people have for trading with one another. Some markets, such as the New York Stock Exchange, are highly visible and organized. Others, such as the word-of-mouth networks that put teenage baby-sitters in touch with people who need their services, do their work informally and behind the scenes. Whether visible or not, markets play a key role in the job of putting scarce resources to their best uses in meeting people's wants and needs. Markets accomplish this by performing three essential tasks.

The first task is to transmit information. In order to put resources to their best possible uses, the people who make decisions must know which resources are the most scarce and which uses for them are best. Markets transmit information about scarcity and resource values in the form of prices. If a good becomes more scarce, its price is bid up. The rising price signals buyers to cut back on the amount of that good that they buy and alerts producers to find new sources of supply or substitute less costly resources. As a good becomes more abundant, its price tends to fall. The falling price signals users to favor that good over more costly ones.

The second task that markets perform is providing incentives. Knowing the best use for scarce resources is not enough unless people have an incentive to use them in that way. Markets offer many kinds of incentives. Consumers who are well informed and spend their money wisely achieve a higher standard of living with their limited budgets. Workers who stay alert to job opportunities and work where they can be most productive earn the highest possible incomes. Profits motivate business managers to improve production methods and tailor their goods to consumers' needs. The importance of the market as a source of incentives led Adam Smith to call it an "invisible hand" that nudges people into the roles they can play best in the economy (see "Who Said It? Who Did It? 1.1").

The third task of markets is to distribute income. People who supply factors of production—their own labor skills, capital, or natural resources—receive high incomes if they put them to the best possible use. People with fewer skills or resources to sell receive lower incomes, even if they make an equal effort to use what they have wisely. Businesspeople who take risks and guess right make large profits; those who take risks and guess wrong suffer losses. In short, the market distributes income according to the value of each person's contribution to the production process—which is not always in proportion to the effort expended in making that contribution.

The Microeconomist's Job

To say that microeconomists study households, firms, and markets is one way to describe what microeconomists do. But the question can also be answered in terms of what microeconomists do for a living, that is, the kinds of jobs they hold.

Many microeconomists are employed in private firms. For example, an insurance company might hire an economist to study the impact of economic trends on the insurance industry and help design new kinds of insurance policies to meet changing customer needs. An electric utility might employ an economist to help prepare proposals for rate changes. A trade association representing the natural-gas industry might employ an economist to analyze the impact of changes in government regulations. In these examples, the economist is employed by the business as a specialist. In other cases, people trained in microeconomics rise to positions at the firm's general management level.

Market
Any arrangement that people have for trading with one another.

WHO SAID IT? WHO DID IT?   1.1

Adam Smith on the Invisible Hand

Adam Smith was the founder of economics as a distinct field of study. He wrote only one book on the subject—*The Wealth of Nations*, published in 1776. Smith was 53 years old at the time. His friend David Hume found the book such hard going that he doubted many people would read it. But Hume was wrong—people have been reading it for more than 200 years now.

The wealth of nations, in Smith's view, was the result not of accumulating gold or silver, as many of that time

[a] Adam Smith, *The Wealth of Nations* (1776), Book 1, Chapter 2. Photo source: Library of Congress.

believed, but of ordinary people working and trading in free markets. To Smith, the remarkable thing about the wealth produced by a market economy is that it does not result from any organized plan; rather, it is the unintended outcome of the actions of many people, each of whom is pursuing the incentives the market offers with his or her own interests in mind:

> It is not from the benevolence of the butcher, the brewer, or the baker that we expect our dinner, but from their regard to their own interest. . . . Every individual is continually exerting himself to find out the most advantageous employment for whatever capital he can command. . . . By directing that industry in such a manner as its produce may be of the greatest value, he intends only his own gain, and he is in this, as in many other cases, led by an invisible hand to promote an end which was no part of his intention.[a]

Much of the discipline of economics as it has developed over two centuries consists of elaborations of ideas found in Smith's work. The idea of the "invisible hand" of market incentives that channels people's efforts in directions that are beneficial to their neighbors remains one of the most durable of Smith's contributions.

Thousands of microeconomists are employed by government. Government regulation of business is the source of many such jobs. The economists who work for insurance companies, electric utilities, gas companies, and the like find government economists working on the other side of every issue. Government economists often work closely with lawyers in cases involving regulation, equal opportunity, international trade disputes, and other issues. While the lawyer interprets the laws that apply to the case, the economist analyzes the effects on prices, markets, incomes, and jobs.

Finally, many economists work for colleges, universities, and research institutes. Most of them teach either full or part time and devote the rest of their time to research on problems of economic theory. Academic economists do quite a bit of applied research, too. Businesses, law firms, and government agencies often hire them as consultants rather than employing full-time, in-house economists.

The chapters on antitrust law and regulation, labor relations, poverty, the environment, and international trade in this book provide many other examples of the kinds of work microeconomists do.

Macroeconomics
The branch of economics that deals with large-scale economic phenomena, particularly inflation, unemployment, and economic growth.

Macroeconomics

The prefix *macro* comes from a Greek word meaning "large." Thus, **macroeconomics** refers to the study of large-scale economic phenomena, particularly inflation, unemployment, and economic growth. These phenomena result from the combined effects of millions of microeconomic choices made by households, firms, and government units. A review of the performance of the U.S. economy in the years since World War II will serve us as a preview of the subject matter of macroeconomics.

Unemployment

One of the key indicators of an economic system's health is its ability to provide a job for anyone who wants one. The economy's performance in this area is measured by the **unemployment rate**—the percentage of people in the labor force who are not working but are actively looking for work. (People who are not actively looking for work—full-time students, retired people, and so on—are not counted as members of the labor force and thus are not included in the unemployment rate.)

Even in the best of times the unemployment rate does not fall to zero. In a healthy, changing economy, it is normal for a certain number of people to be out of work for a short time when they first enter the labor force or when they have quit jobs in order to look for better ones. There is some disagreement as to what the "normal" or "natural" unemployment level is. A generation ago, it was thought that an unemployment rate of 4 percent was a reasonable goal. Given the structure of today's economy, many economists think that an unemployment rate of 6 to 6.5 percent indicates a healthy job market. We will look at this issue in some detail in later chapters.

Exhibit 1.2 shows the U.S. unemployment record since 1950 with the 4 to 6.5 percent range highlighted for reference. During the 1950s and 1960s, the unemployment rate generally stayed within this range. There were higher rates of unemployment in some years than in others, but these episodes were brief. In the 1970s and 1980s, the performance of the job market deteriorated, even taking into account changing views of the acceptable upper limit for the unemployment rate. In 1975, the rate jumped to 8.3 percent—at that time, the highest since the Great Depression—and in 1982, it averaged nearly 10 percent. From 1975 to 1986, the rate dropped below 6.5 percent in only two years. Macroeconomics explores the reasons for increases in the unemployment rate as well as some proposals for dealing with them.

Unemployment rate
The percentage of people in the labor force who are not working but are actively looking for work.

Inflation

Inflation means a sustained increase in the average level of prices of all goods and services. Price stability—that is, the absence of inflation—is a second major sign of an economy's health. True price stability means no increase at all in the average price level. However, many economists and policymakers find moderate rates—3 percent per year or less—acceptable.

Exhibit 1.3 shows trends in inflation in the United States since 1950. Until the late 1960s, inflation stayed more or less within the safe range. In fact, for the entire century from the Civil War to the mid-1960s, inflation averaged only about 2 percent per year; higher inflation rates occurred mostly in wartime.

The inflation of the late 1960s was related in part to the Vietnam War. During the 1970s, the inflation rate varied widely and stayed above the 3 percent benchmark for the entire decade. Then, in the early 1980s, the inflation rate fell abruptly—far more so than many economists had expected. However, the inflation of the 1970s and the fear of its return have had a lasting impact on the U.S. economy.

Inflation
A sustained increase in the average prices of all goods and services.

Exhibit 1.2   Unemployment in the United States Since 1950

There is no one unemployment rate that is universally accepted as best for the U.S. economy. A zero rate is never reached, because there are always people who are out of work while changing jobs or looking for first jobs. A generation ago, a rate of 4 percent was thought to be a reasonable target, and such rates were sometimes reached in the 1950s and 1960s. Today unemployment rates of 6 or even 6.5 percent are seen as consistent with a healthy economy. In the 1970s and early 1980s, however, there were many years in which unemployment was excessive even by this standard.

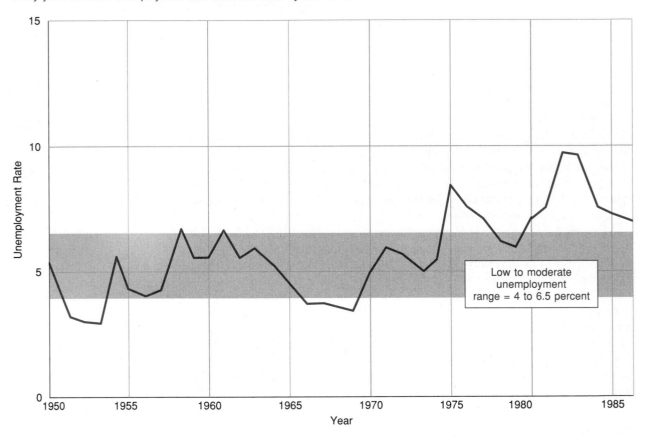

Source: *Economic Report of the President* (Washington, D.C.: Government Printing Office, 1987), Table B-35.

Gross national product (GNP)

A measure of the economy's total output of goods and services.

Economic Growth

Economic growth is a third major sign of economic health. The economy must grow in order to provide jobs for new workers and permit everyone a rising standard of living.

The most often used measure of the economy's total output is **gross national product,** or **GNP.** In order to be meaningful as a measure of economic growth, changes in GNP over time must be adjusted for the effects of inflation. Suppose we want to see how much the U.S. economy grew from 1972 to 1986. In 1972, GNP was about $1,200 billion. In 1986, it was a little over $4,200 billion—3.5 times as high. However, this does not mean that people's standard of living was 3.5 times as high in 1986. Much of the increase in GNP can be explained by

Exhibit 1.3   Inflation in the United States Since 1950

True price stability means no increase at all in the average price level. However, many economists believe that an inflation rate of 3 percent per year or less is acceptable. As the chart shows, such low inflation rates were the rule during the 1950s and early 1960s. Inflation soared in the 1970s and returned to moderate levels in the mid-1980s. In this figure, the inflation rate is measured in terms of the consumer price index, which is a weighted average of the prices of products that consumers typically buy.

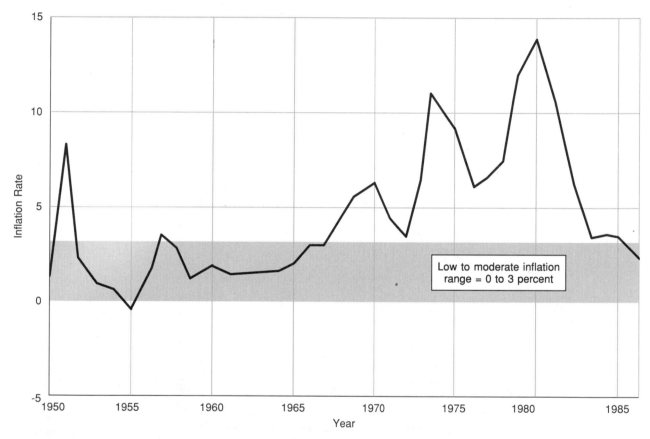

Source: *Economic Report of the President* (Washington, D.C.: Government Printing Office, 1987), Table B-58.

higher prices; in fact, the price level was 2.5 times as high at the end of 1986 as it was in 1972. In order to get an accurate comparison with the 1972 GNP, the 1986 GNP must be divided by 2.5 to account for the change in the price level.

Economists use the term **nominal** to refer to data that have not been adjusted for the effects of inflation. The term **real** is used to refer to data that have been adjusted for inflation. In the above example, we can say that in 1986 *nominal GNP* was $4,200 billion and *real GNP* (relative to 1972) was $1,680 billion ($4,200 billion divided by the more than 2.5-fold increase in prices over the 1972 to 1986 period).

From 1950 to 1986, the growth rate of real GNP in the United States varied around a trend of about 3 percent per year, which most economists consider

Nominal
In economics, a term that refers to data that have not been adjusted for the effects of inflation.

Real
In economics, a term that refers to data that have been adjusted for the effects of inflation.

Exhibit 1.4   Economic Growth in the United States Since 1950

This chart shows the growth of the U.S. economy since 1950. It shows real gross national product for each year (that is, gross national product adjusted for inflation) and a trend line for real-GNP growth over the whole period. A growth rate of 3 percent per year or more is considered healthy. As the figure shows, real GNP sometimes rises above the trend and sometimes falls below it.

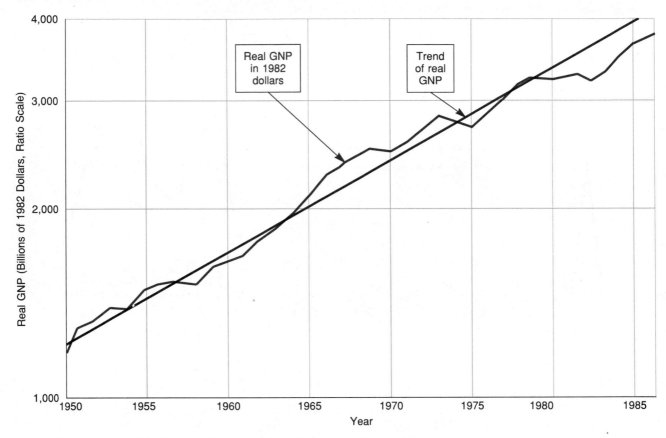

Source: *Economic Report of the President* (Washington, D.C.: Government Printing Office, 1987), Table B-2.

quite satisfactory (see Exhibit 1.4). However, it did not follow this trend smoothly. In some years output fell below the trend, and in others it rose above it. The reasons for these fluctuations in the level of real GNP and for its trend over time are a major focus of macroeconomics.

The goals of full employment, price stability, and economic growth are closely linked. When real output falls, the unemployment rate tends to rise. When real output rises, the rate of inflation sometimes—but not always—tends to speed up. These are two of many linkages among economic phenomena. Macroeconomics studies these linkages in detail, along with others involving interest rates, the money supply, consumption and investment levels, and the international value of the dollar.

The Macroeconomist's Job

Having looked at the subject matter of macroeconomics, we will close with a brief look at some of the jobs held by macroeconomists. Like their micro colleagues, macroeconomists hold jobs in business, government, and academic institutions.

Business macroeconomists are hired to advise managers on the impact of economic trends on their firms. This is often crucial to the firms' survival. Take, for example, the home-building industry. People's ability to buy houses depends on their incomes and on the interest rates at which they can obtain mortgage loans. Firms in every part of the home-building industry—construction, lumber, and other building supplies—can benefit from information on economic trends and policies. As we will see shortly, it is not easy to forecast economic trends. But even when reliable forecasts are impossible, economists can help managers make plans based on a set of "what-if" projections. The example of the housing industry can be extended to others, from consumer goods to banking to transportation. Businesses that do not employ economists often hire consulting firms to advise them on macroeconomic trends.

Government agencies also employ macroeconomists to aid in planning and forecasting. In addition, thousands of economists are employed by government units in charge of macroeconomic policy. The Federal Reserve System, which guides monetary policy, is a major employer of macroeconomists. The U.S. Treasury is another. The Office of Management and Budget and the Council of Economic Advisers, which advise the President, also have large economic staffs. Still other macroeconomists are found in the Congressional Budget Office and on the staffs of congressional committees.

Finally, many macroeconomists are employed by colleges, universities, and research institutes. Like academic microeconomists, they divide their time among teaching, research, and consulting.

Why Economists Sometimes Disagree

George Bernard Shaw once complained that if you took all the economists in the world and laid them end to end, they wouldn't reach a conclusion. Harry Truman begged for a "one-armed economist" because those with two arms kept saying, "On the one hand, . . . and then on the other hand, . . . " But one could argue that economists are no worse than other professionals. Physicists disagree about the origin of the universe. Doctors disagree about treatments for heart disease. Teachers disagree about methods of teaching math. So why are economists singled out for jokes?

The idea that economists can't agree results partly from the fact that disagreement makes the news while agreement doesn't. In fact, economists present a united front on a wide range of issues. For example, one survey found that more than 90 percent of economists concur with the following statements:[2]

---

[2] J. R. Kearl, Clayne L. Pope, Gordon C. Whiting, and Larry T. Wimmer, "A Confusion of Economists?" *American Economic Review* (May 1979): 30. It is worth noting that the survey revealed widespread disagreement on certain other matters, such as the economic power of labor unions and the optimal level of spending for national defense.

- Tariffs and import quotas reduce general economic welfare.
- A ceiling on rents reduces the quantity and quality of housing available.
- Increased government spending or a tax cut is likely to speed recovery from a recession.

But the jokes about disagreement among economists have deeper roots than the newsworthiness of controversy. In the remainder of this chapter, we will discuss some of the chief causes of these disagreements in the contexts of theory versus reality, forecasting, and positive versus normative economics.

Theory and Reality

One reason suggested for economists' disagreements is that they are unrealistic. For example, they are said to make too many simplifying assumptions, such as that people are motivated only by greed, and perform calculations based on information they cannot possibly have.

Indeed, economic theory *is* full of "unrealistic" assumptions. It has to be for the simple reason that economic reality is complex. To take just one example, suppose an economist is asked what effect a tax cut will have on consumers' total spending. There are hundreds of millions of consumers. Their manner of spending depends on their moods, hopes, fears, and health; on the weather; on interest rates, bank regulations, and new products on the market; on wages, fringe benefits, and lottery winnings. The list is endless.

Model
A simplified representation of the way in which facts are related.

But economists do not try to make a complete list of the things that influence consumer spending. Instead, they try to identify the factors that have the greatest influence and use them as the basis for a theory or—to use an expression favored by economists—a model. A **model** is an attempted representation of the way in which facts are related. Models can be—and often are—expressed in ordinary English, but they are also often presented in graphical or mathematical form.

As an example, consider the question of tax cuts and their effects on consumer spending. One widely accepted economic model says that the change in consumer spending depends on how much the tax cut raises consumers' after-tax incomes and on how long consumers expect the tax cut to remain in effect. In proposing such a model, economists don't deny that other things affect consumer spending; they simply say that of all the things that matter, these two are the most useful. In much the same way, engineers who build model aircraft to be tested in wind tunnels are careful to represent the shape of the wings accurately but do not bother to round out their models with tiny seats equipped with armrests and magazine racks.

Clearly, however, this approach contains the seeds of many disagreements. One economist's model of consumer spending might take only the above two factors into account. Another's might also consider whether the tax cut affects mainly upper-income or middle-income consumers. Which model is better? One approach to testing competing theories is to see which one better fits statistical data from the past relating to the phenomenon in question. But such tests are not always conclusive. Data on past events may be unreliable. One model may better explain the events of one period and the other those of a different one. Before the dispute is resolved, someone else may propose a third theory that challenges both models.

Forecasting

An economic model is considered good if it correctly explains the relationships of two or more key facts. Such models often help us understand past economic events. For example, macroeconomics presents models that provide useful insights into the causes of the Great Depression of the 1930s or the high inflation rates of the late 1970s. But even the best economic models are limited in their ability to help us foretell the future.

At best, economic models allow us to make statements that take the following form: "If A, then B, other things being equal." Most economists would agree with the statement "If income taxes are lowered, consumers will spend more provided that the many other factors that affect spending don't change in the meantime." It is a short step from this type of statement to a **conditional forecast,** which is simply an "if-then" statement about the future. For example, an economist might say that if income tax rates are cut by 10 percent in July 1989, total consumer spending will rise by $100 billion in 1989, $120 billion in 1990, and $145 billion in 1991, other things being equal.

Why are economic forecasts such a source of controversy? One obvious reason is that forecasters are often wrong. They have sometimes missed major turning points in the economy. They also often disagree among themselves. It is not uncommon for one forecaster to predict recession while another predicts continued expansion.

But the problem does not lie entirely with forecasters. Part of it is due to the way forecasts are reported to the public. On television and in the newspapers, forecasts are often reported in the unconditional form "This is how it will be" rather than in the conditional form "If A, then B, other things being equal" that the forecaster intended. In addition, it is not always made clear that even forecasts that are reported as simple numbers are really statements about probabilities. For example, it may be reported that a certain economist has predicted that a tax cut will add $100 billion to consumer spending when the proper way of putting it would be that there is a 90 percent probability that the tax cut will add between $80 billion and $120 billion to spending.

Most economists take the view that forecasts, for all their faults, are a better basis for making business decisions and public policy than whims and guesswork. For example, a maker of building supplies might ask a forecaster, "If the economy grows as much in the second half of the year as it did in the first, how will the demand for new houses be affected?" The answer might be: "A 3 percent rate of economic growth will cause housing demand to rise by somewhat more than 3 percent if interest rates remain the same. However, each percentage point rise in the mortgage interest rate will cause about a 5 percent drop in the demand for housing." Getting an answer like this isn't as good as having a crystal ball, but it is better than nothing.

At the same time, economists caution against overrelying on forecasts. In the 1970s, many forecasters projected higher oil prices throughout the 1980s. Many oil companies, banks, and even national governments got in trouble when they relied too heavily on these forecasts, which turned out to be wrong. This issue of how much government policymakers should rely on forecasts is especially controversial, because so much is at stake when major policy decisions are made.

Conditional forecast
A prediction of future economic events, usually stated in the form "If A, then B, other things being equal."

Positive versus Normative Economics

Economists, as we have seen, sometimes disagree over issues of theory. They disagree even more often when they try their hands at forecasting. But nothing produces as much disagreement as issues of economic policy. Should the government try to prop up the price of wheat and corn? Should automobile imports be restricted? Should taxes be raised in order to cut the federal budget deficit? Questions like these tend to bring economists out of their corners ready to fight.

However, before the sparks start to fly, it is worth noting the chain of reasoning on which policy decisions are based. There are three steps:

1. If policy X is followed, outcome Y will result.

2. Outcome Y is a good (or bad) thing.

3. Therefore, let us adopt (or not adopt) policy X.

The first step in this chain of reasoning is a conditional forecast. Forecasts are examples of **positive economics,** that is, the portion of economics that is limited to making statements of fact and relationships among facts.

Positive economics
The part of economics concerned with statements about facts and the relationships among them.

Disputes are common in positive economics. Economists may disagree over whether facts are accurate, how they are related, and how they are likely to unfold in the future. But these disputes can—at least in principle—be resolved by scientific methods. Repeated measurement, statistical tests of theories, and comparison of forecasts with actual events are a few of the ways in which the area of disagreement on matters of positive economics can be narrowed.

But positive statements of the type "If policy X, then outcome Y" do not tell us whether policy X is desirable. In order to make a policy decision, one must also decide whether outcome Y is good or bad. Statements of the type "Outcome Y is good" are examples of **normative economics**—the part of economics that is devoted to making judgments about which economic policies or outcomes are good and which are bad.

Normative economics
The part of economics devoted to making judgments about which economic policies or conditions are good or bad.

Most economists do not think of themselves as experts in philosophy or ethics. Yet economists who want to influence policy are in a better position to do so if they can point to some general principles on which their views are based. Those who base their opinions of a policy on whim or prejudice are less likely to be listened to than those who speak in terms of well-thought-out values. Calling your opponent a racist or a fascist may win cheers from those who already agree with you and boos from those who are already against you. But name calling is far less likely to win uncommitted people to your side than is an articulate explanation of your reasons for thinking that your opponent's policies will have undesirable outcomes. With this in mind, let us now look at some basic concepts of normative economics.

Efficiency and Fairness

One standard by which economic policies can be judged is *efficiency*. In economics, as elsewhere, this means doing something with a minimum of waste, effort, and expense. (A more precise definition of economic efficiency will be given in Chapter 2.) But a policy that is merely efficient may not be good; other standards must be applied. Among the most important of these is fairness.

Fairness can play two roles in relation to efficiency. First, it may be used to complement efficiency when the choice is between two or more equally efficient policies—for example, those that differ only in terms of which groups of people bear costs or receive benefits. In such a case, we might reason as follows:

1. Policies X and Y are equally efficient, but they will distribute benefits to different groups.

2. The distribution of benefits under policy X is fairer.

3. Therefore, we should follow policy X.

Second, the standard of fairness may be used to override that of efficiency. Many people believe that efficiency should not be pursued at the expense of fairness. If both goals cannot be reached at once, efficiency should be sacrificed in the name of fairness. In such a case, our reasoning might run as follows:

1. Policy X would be inefficient, but it would be more fair than policy Y.

2. Efficiency is desirable, but fairness is more important.

3. Therefore, if there is no policy that is both efficient and fair, choose policy X.

In whatever manner it is used, the standard of fairness plays a major role in policy analysis. However, it also raises a problem that the standard of efficiency does not, namely that fairness means different things to different people. Rational debate on matters of economic policy is difficult when people attach different meanings to the same term and fail to make those meanings clear. With this problem in mind, let's look at two concepts of fairness that often arise in discussions of economic policy.

The Egalitarian Concept of Fairness

One widely held view equates fairness with equitable distribution of income.✳ The phrase "from each according to ability, to each according to need" reflects this viewpoint. This concept of fairness is based on the idea that all people, by virtue of their shared humanity, deserve a portion of the goods and services turned out by the economy.

There are many versions of this concept. Some people believe that all income and wealth should be distributed equally. Others think that people have a right to a "safety net" level of income but that any surplus beyond this may be distributed according to other standards. Still others think there are certain goods, such as health care, food, and education, that should be distributed equally but it is all right for other goods to be distributed unequally.

In policy debates, the egalitarian view of fairness often takes the form "What effect will this policy have on the poor?" Consider the debate over rent control for city apartments. Some people favor ending these controls on the grounds that they discourage new-housing construction and upkeep of existing housing. Others oppose ending rent controls because they believe that higher rents would cause hardship for consumers in the lowest income groups. Chapter 3 will provide an economic analysis of this policy problem.

The Libertarian Concept of Fairness

A second widely held view links fairness to people's right to live their lives according to their own values, free from threats and coercion. This concept of fairness stems from a long tradition in Western political thought, especially the idea of liberty as stated by such philosophers as John Locke and Thomas Jefferson.

The libertarian view of fairness puts economic rights, such as the rights to own property and to make exchanges with others, on a par with the basic rights of free speech, free press, and free worship. From this viewpoint, efforts to promote fairness should stress equality of opportunity. Attempts to redistribute income by placing a penalty on economic success or giving people unequal access to markets are seen as unfair whether or not they lead to equality of income.

In policy debates, proponents of the libertarian point of view often argue that competition and economic freedom lead to a general prosperity that is good for everyone. For example, libertarian economists have led the fight to end regulations protecting business firms from competition. They have argued that when new, small airlines are allowed to compete with larger, more established ones, when savings and loan associations are allowed to compete with banks, and when natural-gas producers are allowed to compete with oil producers in an open market, the firms that best serve the consumer will be the ones to prosper.

Why the Distinction?

Distinguishing between positive and normative economics and among different meanings of normative terms like "fairness" will not settle all policy disputes. Still, viewing policy analysis as a three-step process in which both positive and normative elements play a role makes policy debates more rational in three ways.

First, the distinction between positive and normative analysis makes it clear that there are two kinds of disagreement on policy questions. We can disagree as to whether policy X is good or bad because we disagree on the positive issue of whether it will cause outcome Y, which we both desire. Alternatively, we can agree that policy X will cause outcome Y but disagree on the normative issue of whether Y is a good thing. Once the source of the disagreement is clear, the argument can be more focused.

Second, when positive statements are mixed with normative ones, they may not be judged on their merits. Reactions to value judgments tend to be much stronger than reactions to statements of fact or theory. Consider tax policy. There has been much debate in recent years about the effects of tax cuts and increases on the federal budget deficit, interest rates, and economic growth. Many issues of fact and theory need to be resolved. But economists operating in the positive mode often find it hard to get the attention of policymakers who are distracted by charges and countercharges of "soaking the rich" or "milking the poor."

Third, it is important to make the distinction in order to be aware of the ways in which normative considerations influence the conduct of positive research. At one time it was thought that a "purely" positive economics, completely untainted by normative considerations, could be developed. Within this framework, all disputes could be resolved by reference to objective facts. Today this notion is less widely held; instead, it is recognized that normative considerations influence positive research in several ways. The most significant is simply the selection of the topics that are considered important enough to investigate. Also, normative views are likely to influence the ways in which data are collected, ideas about which facts can be taken as true, and so on.

This book will raise many controversial issues as it tours the subject of economics. For the most part, we will focus on the positive economic theories that bear on these issues, but we will touch on normative considerations as well. However, a textbook can provide no more than a framework for thinking about public issues and policies. Your job will be to blend positive theories and normative judgments within this framework to reach your own conclusions.

Summary

1. **What is economics all about?** *Economics* is the study of the choices people make and the actions they take in order to make the best use of scarce resources in meeting their wants. Resources are said to be *scarce* when people do not have enough of them to meet all their wants. At all times and in all societies, everyone faces the scarcity problem in some form.

2. **How is the need to choose related to the concept of cost?** Because resources are scarce, when people choose to use them in one way, they must forgo the opportunity to use them in another. The cost of doing something, measured in terms of the forgone opportunity to do the next best thing with the same time or resources, is called *opportunity cost*. Opportunity cost can be illustrated by the slope of a *production possibility frontier*.

3. **What roles do households, business firms, and government units play in the economy?** *Microeconomics* is the branch of economics that deals with the choices made by small economic units—households, business firms, and government units. Households supply the basic factors of production, namely labor, capital, and natural resources. Business firms buy the factors of production from households and transform them into goods and services. Government units—including Congress, the courts, regulatory agencies, and others—influence the economic choices made by households and firms. In turn, all of these are influenced by events in the economy.

4. **What are markets, and how do they work?** A *market* is any arrangement people have for trading with one another. Markets play a key role in putting resources to their best uses. In so doing, they perform three tasks. First, they transmit information, in the form of prices, that helps households and firms decide which of the possible ways of using scarce resources are most valuable. Second, they provide incentives, especially in the form of profits. Third, they distribute income according to the value of each person's contribution to the production process.

5. **Who worries about inflation, unemployment, and economic growth, and why?** The branch of economics that studies large-scale economic phenomena, particularly unemployment, inflation, and economic growth, is known as *macroeconomics*. The *unemployment rate* is the percentage of people in the labor force who are actively looking for work but are unable to find it. *Inflation* is a sustained increase in the average price level of all goods and services; it is measured by the consumer price index. Economic growth is measured by the rate of increase in real *gross national prod-*

uct. (The term *real* refers to economic quantities that have been adjusted for inflation. Quantities that have not been adjusted for inflation are known as *nominal* quantities.)

6. **Why do economists sometimes disagree?** Economists, like other professionals, sometimes disagree about how the world works. They construct *models* in an attempt to explain relationships among facts, but they may disagree about which aspects of reality should be emphasized in a given model. They use their models to make *conditional forecasts*, that is, "if-then" statements about the future. But because the future cannot be known with certainty, these forecasts are themselves a source of disagreement. The portion of economics that is devoted to constructing models and making forecasts is known as *positive economics*.

7. **How do ethics and value judgments enter into economics?** The part of economics that is devoted to making judgments about whether economic policies or events are good or bad is called *normative economics*. The concepts of efficiency and fairness are important in such policy decisions. Judging the value of an economic policy requires both a positive analysis of the policy's likely effects and a normative judgment of the desirability of those effects.

Terms for Review

- scarcity
- economics
- goods
- services
- factors of production
- labor
- capital
- natural resources
- production possibility frontier
- opportunity cost
- microeconomics
- market
- macroeconomics
- unemployment rate
- inflation
- gross national product (GNP)
- nominal
- real
- model
- conditional forecast
- positive economics
- normative economics

Questions for Review

1. How are the terms *scarcity* and *economics* related? Can you think of any resources that are not scarce?

2. How can cost be measured in terms of forgone opportunities? Illustrate the concept of opportunity cost with a production possibility frontier.

3. Which of the following are microeconomic issues? Which are macroeconomic issues?
   a. How will an increase in the cigarette tax affect smoking habits?
   b. What caused the rate of inflation to fall so rapidly between 1980 and 1984?
   c. Does a high federal budget deficit tend to slow the rate of real economic growth?
   d. How would quotas on steel imports affect profits and jobs in industries that use steel as an input, such as automobiles and construction?

4. What is a market? What three tasks do markets perform? Describe the arrangements by which people buy and sell houses, football tickets, and haircuts. Are all of these markets?

5. Compare the 1960s and the 1970s in terms of inflation, unemployment, and growth in the U.S. economy. How do the 1980s look by comparison so far?

6. What is an economic model? Why do economists use theories and models instead of limiting themselves to verbal descriptions of economic events? In what ways does the use of models lead to disagreements among economists?

7. Why is it important to distinguish between positive and normative economics? What are the roles of efficiency and fairness in making policy decisions?

Problems and Topics for Discussion

1. **Examining the lead-off case.** A "shortage" means that there is less of something available *at the current market price* than buyers want. (This term will be defined formally in Chapter 3.) On the basis of information given in this case, is Prince George's County facing a teacher shortage? Is there reason to think it was previously facing a teacher shortage? What role do the three functions of markets play in helping to overcome shortages? Is "shortage" a synonym for "scarcity"? Does the fact that after the 21 percent salary increase 4,000 applications were received for 400 jobs mean that there is no longer a teacher shortage?

2. **Scarcity for millionaires.** Suppose you won $1 million in a lottery. Would this remove all problems of scarcity and choice from your life? Would time still be a scarce resource for you? What other things might still be scarce? Can you imagine anyone who would face no economic problems of any kind?

3. **The production possibility frontier.** A farmer has four fields spread out over a hillside. He can grow either wheat or potatoes in any of the fields, but the low fields are better for potatoes and the high ones are better for wheat. Here are some combinations of wheat and potatoes that he can produce:

Number of Fields Used for Potatoes	Tons of Potatoes	Tons of Wheat
4	1,000	0
3	900	400
2	600	700
1	300	900
0	0	1,000

Use these data to draw a production possibility frontier for wheat and potatoes. What is the opportunity cost of wheat, stated in terms of potatoes, when the farmer converts the highest field into wheat production? What happens to the opportunity cost of wheat as more and more fields are switched to wheat?

4. **The nature of your household.** To what kind of household do you belong? How large is the group of people with whom you pool income and share decision making? Are you a member of a one-person household for some purposes and of a larger household for others? How are economic decisions made in your household?

5. **The market for video games.** After a boom in the early 1980s, the video game industry ran into trouble. Consumer interest in these games leveled off, and competition forced prices and profit margins down. Some firms left the industry; others seriously considered doing so. How does this example illustrate the three functions of markets?

6. **Your role in the market for education.** As a student, you are a buyer in the market for education. What price signals affected your decision to go to college? What market incentives, if any, made you decide as you did? How do you think your education will affect your future position in the distribution of income?

7. **Macroeconomic indicators.** Exhibits 1.2, 1.3, and 1.4 give data on unemployment, inflation, and economic growth, respectively, through the end of 1986. Extend the charts using the most recent available data. For annual data, a good source is the *Economic Report of the President,* published each January or February. For current-year data, check business news sources such as *The Wall Street Journal* or *Business Week.* Two

government publications, the *Survey of Current Business* and the *Federal Reserve Bulletin,* are also useful sources of data. The government releases information on the unemployment rate and the consumer price index each month and information on the growth of real GNP every three months.

8. **Nominal and real salaries.** Professor Alvarez began teaching economics at State University in 1967. In that year, she earned a salary of $9,500. Sixteen years later, her salary had risen to $26,000. Meanwhile the price level had risen to 2.98 times its 1967 value. How much did her real income grow or shrink?

Case for Discussion
Public Policy and Auto Safety

Whether or not the government should require cars to be equipped with airbags has been a matter of debate for years. The following editorial on this subject appeared in Business Week:

Transportation secretary Elizabeth H. Dole will issue by July 11 a final ruling as to whether or not auto manufacturers must start including airbags as required equipment in cars. This issue is hotly controversial, and Secretary Dole will rule on it in a climate of renewed concern over drunk driving. She will probably issue mandatory accident-safety standards that can be met either by airbags or automatic seat belts. If so, this shows a commendable degree of flexibility. What the Secretary should not do is flatly order airbags in all automobiles.

Airbag enthusiasts say the device will save lives. But the safety issue is not airbags vs. nothing at all—in that case, the airbag would win hands down—but airbags vs. the shoulder-lap harness, which is cheaper and less risky. Estimates are that the airbag will add anywhere from $300 to $500 to the cost of a car. Regular seat belts add about $60 to a car's cost, automatic seat belts about twice that. As to the far more important issue of reliability, the airbag is an electronic device subject to failure. The chances that it might not inflate when needed or inflate at the wrong time are small but real, and in either case could produce injury or death. Neither problem arises with seat belts, which are highly effective when used.

The catch, of course, is that only 10 percent to 15 percent of drivers use belts. A state law requiring their use will probably make many people buckle up. Automatic belts are a good idea. Auto makers, insurance companies, and safety organizations should work harder to promote seat belt use. Over time, though, it is likely that the new attack on drunk driving by raising the national drinking age to 21 will save more lives than making airbags mandatory in everybody's car.

Question
Analyze this editorial in terms of the three steps of policy analysis. Which statements of positive economics are used to support the argument? What normative judgments are made or implied? What role does the standard of efficiency play in the argument? What view of fairness underlies the argument? Is there any way to tell from this editorial?

Appendix to Chapter 1   Working with Graphs

How Economists Use Graphs

Students at one well-known college have their own names for each course. They call the astronomy course "Stars," the geology course "Rocks," and the biology course "Frogs." Their name for the economics course is "Graphs and Laughs." This name choice demonstrates two things. First, it shows that the students think the professor has a sense of humor. Second, it shows that in their minds economics is a matter of learning about graphs in the same way that astronomy involves learning about stars, geology about rocks, and biology about frogs.

However, economics is not about graphs; it is about people. It focuses on how people make choices, use resources, and cooperate in their attempts to overcome the universal problem of scarcity. But if economics is not about graphs, why are there so many of them in this book? The answer is that economists use graphs to illustrate their theories of people's economic behavior in order to make those theories more vivid and memorable. Everything that can be said in the form of a graph can also be said in words, but saying something in two different ways is an established learning aid. The purpose of this appendix is to show how to make the best use of this tool.

Pairs of Numbers and Points

The first thing to master is how to use points on a graph to represent pairs of numbers. The table in Exhibit 1A.1 presents five pairs of numbers. The two columns are labeled "x" and "y." The first number in each pair is called the *x value* and the second the *y value*. Each pair of numbers is labeled with a capital letter. Pair A has an x value of 2 and a y value of 3; pair B has an x value of 4 and a y value of 4; and so on.

The diagram in Exhibit 1A.1 contains two lines that meet at the lower left-hand corner; these are called *coordinate axes*. The horizontal axis is marked off into units representing the x value and the vertical axis into units representing the y value. In the space between these axes, each pair of numbers from the table can be shown as a point. For example, point A is found by going two units to the right along the horizontal axis and then three units straight up, parallel to the vertical axis. This represents the x value of 2 and the y value of 3. The other points are located in the same way.

Exhibit 1A.1   Pairs of Numbers and Points

Each lettered pair of numbers in the table corresponds to a lettered point on the graph. The x value of each point corresponds to the horizontal distance of the point from the vertical axis; the y value corresponds to its vertical distance from the horizontal axis.

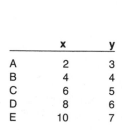

	x	y
A	2	3
B	4	4
C	6	5
D	8	6
E	10	7

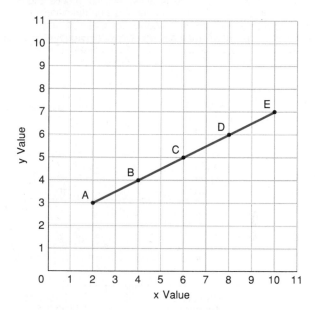

The visual effect of a graph usually can be improved by connecting the points with a line or a curve. By doing so, it can be seen at a glance that as the x value increases, the y value also rises.

Common Economic Graphs

Exhibit 1A.2 shows three typical economics graphs. Each type of graph will appear many times in this book. Part a of Exhibit 1A.2 shows the relationship between the price of a subway token and the number of people who ride the subway each day at any given price. The corresponding table shows that as the price of tokens goes up, fewer people ride the subway. The graph shows the same thing. In economics, when a graph involves both money values and quantities, the vertical axis is usually used to measure the money values (here the price of tokens) and the horizontal axis to measure the quantities (here the number of riders per day).

Part b of Exhibit 1A.2 uses quantities on both axes. Here the purpose is to show the various combinations of milkshakes and hamburgers that can be bought at the local carry-out when milkshakes cost $.50 each, hamburgers cost $.50 each, and the buyer has exactly $2.50 to spend. The table shows that the possibilities are five burgers and no shakes, four burgers and one shake, three burgers and two shakes, and so on. The graph gives a visual representation of this "menu." The points are drawn in and labeled, and a diagonal line is used to

Exhibit 1A.2 Three Typical Economic Graphs

This exhibit shows three graphs typically used in economics. Part a shows the relationship between the price of tokens and the number of riders per day on a city subway system. For a graph that shows the relationship between a price and a quantity, it is conventional to put the price on the vertical axis. Part b shows the possible choices for a person who has $2.50 to spend on lunch and can buy hamburgers at $.50 each or milkshakes at $.50 each. Part c shows how a graph can be used to represent change over time.

	Price of Subway Tokens	Number of Riders per Day (Millions)
A	$.50	6
B	.40	7
C	.30	8
D	.20	9
E	.10	10

	Number of Hamburgers	Number of Milkshakes
A	5	0
B	4	1
C	3	2
D	2	3
E	1	4
F	0	5

Year	Unemployment Rate (Nonwhite Males, 16–19 Years Old)
1969	21.4%
1970	25.0
1971	28.9
1972	29.7
1973	26.9
1974	31.6
1975	35.4
1976	35.4
1977	37.0
1978	34.4

Source: Part c is from President's Council of Economic Advisers, *Economic Report of the President* (Washington, D.C.: Government Printing Office, 1979), Table B-30.

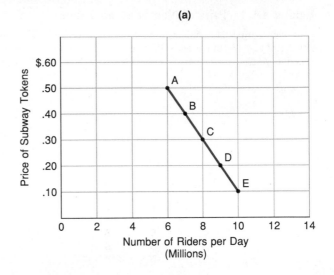
(a)

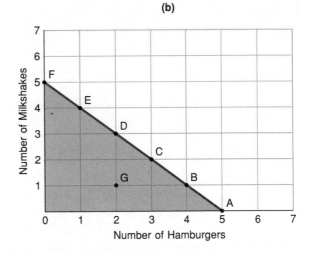
(b)

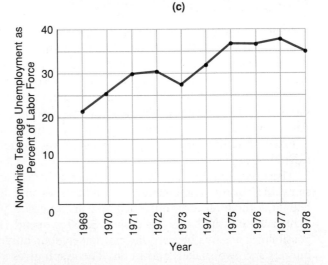
(c)

connect them. If the purchase of parts of hamburgers or milkshakes is allowed, the buyer can choose among all the points along this line (for example, 2.5 burgers and 2.5 shakes). A buyer who wants to have some money left over can buy a lunch shown by a point within the shaded area, such as G (which stands for two burgers and one shake and costs just $1.50). But unless the buyer gets more money, points outside the shaded area cannot be chosen.

Part c of Exhibit 1A.2 shows a third kind of graph that is often used in economics—one that indicates how a magnitude varies over time. This example shows what happened to the unemployment rate of nonwhite teenage males over the years 1969 to 1978. The horizontal axis represents the passage of time; the vertical axis shows the percentage of nonwhite teenage males who were unemployed. Graphs such as this are good for showing trends. Although teenage unemployment has had its ups and downs, the trend in the 1970s was clearly upward.

Slopes

When discussing graphs, it is convenient to describe lines or curves in terms of their slopes. The *slope* of a straight line between two points is defined as the ratio of the change in the y value to the change in the x value between the points. In Exhibit 1A.3, for example, the slope of the line between points A and B is 2. The y value changes by six units between these two points, whereas the x value changes by only three units. The slope is the ratio 6/3 = 2.

When a line slants downward such as the one between points C and D in Exhibit 1A.3, the x and y values change in opposite directions. Going from point C to point D, the y value changes by −1 (that is, decreases by one unit) and the x value changes by +2 (increases by two units). The slope of this line is the ratio

Exhibit 1A.3   Slopes of Lines

The slope of a straight line drawn between two points is defined as the ratio of the change in the y value to the change in the x value between them. For example, the line between points A and B in this exhibit has a slope of +2, whereas the line between points C and D has a slope of −½.

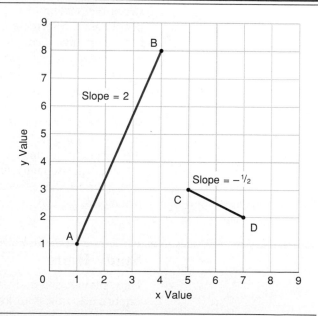

Exhibit 1A.4   Slopes of Curves

The slope of a curve at any given point is defined as the slope of a straight line drawn tangent to the curve at that point. A tangent line is one that just touches the curve without crossing it. In this exhibit, the slope of the curve at point A is 1 and the slope of the curve at point B is −2.

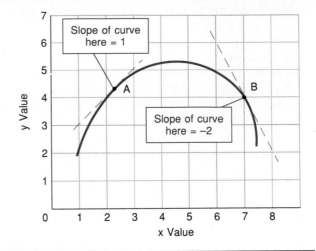

−1/2. A downward-sloping line such as the line between C and D is said to have a *negative slope*.

The slope of a curved line, on the other hand, varies from one point to the next. The slope of a curve at any given point is defined as the slope of a straight line drawn tangent to the curve at that point. (A *tangent* line is one that just touches the curve without crossing it.) In Exhibit 1A.4, the slope of the line at point A is 1 and the slope at point B is −2.

Abstract Graphs

In all the examples given so far, there have been specific numbers for the x and y values. But sometimes we know only the general nature of the relationship between two magnitudes. For example, we might know that when incomes rise, people tend to increase their meat consumption. The increase is rapid at first, but at very high incomes meat consumption levels off. If we want to show such a relationship without worrying about the precise numbers involved, we can draw a graph such as that in Exhibit 1A.5. The vertical axis is the quantity of meat consumed per month, with no specific units. The horizontal axis is income, also with no specific units. The curve, which rises rapidly at first and then levels off, shows the general nature of the relationship between income and meat consumption: When income goes up, meat consumption rises, but not in proportion to the change in income.

We will use many such abstract graphs in this book. In contrast to graphs with numbered axes, which present specific information, these express general principles.

Study Hints

How should you study a chapter that is full of graphs? The first—and most important—rule is to avoid trying to memorize graphs. In every economics class, at least one student comes to the instructor after failing an exam and

Exhibit 1A.5   An Abstract Graph

When we know the general form of an economic relationship but do not know the exact numbers involved, we can draw an abstract graph. Here we know that as people's incomes rise, their consumption of meat increases rapidly at first, then levels off. Because we do not know the exact numbers for meat consumption or income, we have not marked any units on the axes.

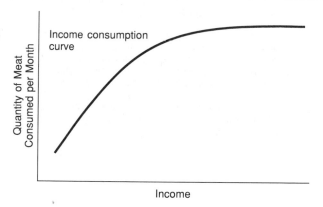

exclaims, "But I learned every one of those graphs! What happened?" The usual reply is that the student should have learned economics instead of memorizing graphs. Following are some hints for working with graphs.

After reading through a chapter that contains several graphs, go back through the graphs one at a time. Cover the caption accompanying each graph, and try to put the graph's picture into words. If you cannot say as much about the graph as the caption does, reread the text. Once you can translate the graph into words, you have won half the battle.

Next, cover each graph and use the caption as a guide. Try to sketch the graph on a piece of scratch paper. If you understand what the words mean and can go back and forth between the caption and the graph, you will find that the two together are much easier to remember than either one separately.

Making Your Own Graphs

For some students, the hardest kind of test question to answer is one that requires an original graph as part of an essay. Here are some hints for making your own graphs:

1. Write down the answer to the question in words. If you cannot, you might as well skip to the next question. Underline the most important quantities in your answer, such as "The larger the *number of students* who attend a college, the lower the *cost per student* of providing them with an education."

2. Decide how you want to label the axes. In our example (Exhibit 1A.6), the vertical axis is labeled "cost per student" and the horizontal axis "number of students."

3. Do you have specific numbers to work with? If so, the next step is to construct a table showing what you know and use it to sketch your graph. If you have no numbers, you must draw an abstract graph. In this case, all you know is that the cost per student goes down when the number of students goes up. Sketch in a downward-sloping line such as the one in Exhibit 1A.6.

4. If your graph involves more than one relationship between quantities, repeat steps 1 through 3 for each relationship you wish to show. When constructing a graph with more than one curve, pay special attention to points at which you think the curves should intersect. (This happens whenever the

Exhibit 1A.6   Constructing a Graph

To construct a graph, first put down in words what you want to say: "The larger the *number of students* at a university, the lower the *cost per student* of providing them with an education." Next, label the coordinate axes. Then, if you have exact numbers to work with, construct a table. Here we have no exact numbers, so we draw an abstract graph that slopes downward to show that cost goes down as the number of students goes up. For graphs with more than one curve, repeat these steps.

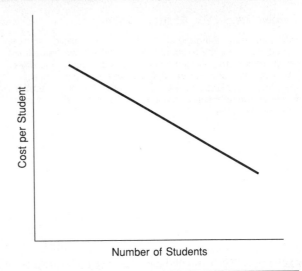

x and y values of the two relationships are equal.) Also note the points at which you think two curves ought to be tangent (which requires that their slopes be equal).

5.   When your graph is finished, try to translate it back into words. Does it really say what you want it to?

A Reminder

As you read this book and encounter the various kinds of graphs, turn back to this appendix now and then. Do not memorize graphs as meaningless pictures; if you do, you will get lost. If you can alternate between graphs and words, each one's underlying point will be clearer than if you rely on either one alone. Keep in mind that the primary focus of economics is people and the ways in which they deal with the challenge of scarcity.

2 Exchange and Production

After reading this chapter, you will understand . . .

- The ways it is decided what goods and services the economy is to produce.
- The roles of efficiency, investment, and entrepreneurship in the decision on how goods and services will be produced.
- The impact of positive and normative economics on the decision on for whom goods and services will be produced.
- The principle that guides the division of labor within an economy and among nations.
- How capitalist and socialist economies differ in their approach to the questions of what, how, and for whom.

Before reading this chapter, make sure you know the meaning of . . .

- Factors of production
- Production possibility frontier
- Opportunity costs
- Capital
- Markets
- Positive economics
- Normative economics

Muddy Cars Draw Tickets in Moscow

Traffic patrolman in the Soviet Union

MOSCOW, USSR. In spring, as the sun comes out, the temperature inches past freezing and the snow begins to melt, is not the time to own a car in the Soviet Union.

The problem is mud. At the end of winter, Russia turns to mud. It leaps from the puddles and melting mounds of dirty snow, coating vehicles that venture past.

Dirty cars, however, are against the law in the Soviet Union. Traffic police, bored on the beat, can wave over a mud-splattered car and either fine the driver as much as 30 rubles (about $45 at the official exchange rate) in some cities, tell him to proceed directly to a car wash, or confiscate his license until the entire car has been inspected for flaws.

Nicks, dents and scratches on the body of a car also are against the law. Drivers of unsightly cars can be fined or have their licenses confiscated. Bald tires, bad paint jobs—even flashy paint jobs—are considered violations of traffic esthetics and reason enough to harass the auto owner.

Car owners here often find themselves between a rock and a hard place. One recounted the following exchange with a huffy traffic policeman:

"You can't drive with tires like that."

"What am I supposed to do? The wait for new tires is 20 months right now."

"That's hardly my problem."

Top on a Soviet driver's list of priorities are spare parts, which are not necessarily here when you need them. One Soviet traveling in Australia used the occasion to buy a camshaft for his Soviet-made car, according to a newspaper report. Foreigners owning Soviet cars here get their spare parts from Finland, and pay import duties on them.

The problem is partly explained by a miscalculation by the Soviet automobile industry, which at one point assumed that the life span of a Soviet car would be seven years. In reality, 31 percent of the 11 million cars on the roads are more than 11 years old, which creates an unplanned strain on the system.

Faced with shortages and poor service, car owners compensate as best they can. Some simply steal what they need, which is why most Soviet drivers remove windshield wipers and side mirrors and lock them up whenever they leave their cars on public streets.

One Soviet driver recalled a road trip through the western Soviet Union on the way back from Eastern Europe. "When someone stole our windshield wipers, we knew we were home again."

Source: Celestine Bohlen, "Muddy Cars Draw Tickets, and Dents Are a Nyet-Nyet," *The Washington Post*, March 17, 1987, A20. Reprinted with permission. Photo Source: © 1987 Phyllis Woloshin.

T HE troubles of Moscow's drivers bring us back to the central problem of economics: dealing with scarcity. In this chapter we take a closer look at that problem. We begin with three basic questions that every economic system must answer:

1. *What* should be produced given limited supplies of labor, capital, and natural resources? (How many tires? How much bread? How many airplanes?)

2. *How* should goods and services be produced? (Should tires be made of synthetic or natural rubber? Should they be brought to market by truck, rail, or air? Should the stores that sell them have many clerks using adding machines or fewer clerks aided by computers?)

3. *For whom* should goods and services be produced? (For ordinary people shopping in ordinary stores? For stores that cater to the elite? For export?)

Examining these questions in detail will clarify the economic problem and the tools economists use to understand it.

This chapter has another purpose. Moscow's car situation highlights the questions of what, how, and for whom. But it also shows that different societies deal with the problem of scarcity in different ways. The Soviet economic system answers the questions of what, how, and for whom quite differently than does that of the United States—and these are only two of the world's many economic systems. Although we will deal primarily with the U.S. economy, we must not lose sight of the fact that the basic problems of economics are universal.

The Economic Problem

Scarcity means that we cannot have enough of everything to satisfy all our wants; instead, we must choose. The questions of what, how, and for whom highlight three key choices that must be made in every economy.

What to Produce?

Soviet drivers' search for tires and windshield wipers illustrates the question of what should be produced. If more good tires were produced, they would be more widely available, but there would be an opportunity cost in that the factors of production used to produce the extra tires would be unavailable for use in the production of other goods and services. In Chapter 1, we used a production possibility frontier to illustrate the problem of what to produce using the example of cars and education. The same approach can be used for the choice between tires and bread, guns and butter, and any other alternatives.

The choice of what to produce is sometimes illustrated by Robinson Crusoe's shipwreck on an uninhabited island. Crusoe wakes up hungry in the morning. But what should he eat? He can spend the day fishing and eat poached grouper, or he can spend the day hunting and dine on roast pheasant. If we drew a production possibility frontier illustrating Crusoe's choice between fish and game, we would notice one important aspect of the problem of what to produce: the fact that once the production possibility frontier is reached, more of one good can be produced only at the cost of giving up the opportunity to produce some quantity of another good. But this example skirts another important aspect of the problem—namely that in a modern economy producers and consumers are not interchangeable. The choice of which goods to produce is made by firms, while the choice of which goods to consume is made by households. Thus, there must be some way to tell producers what consumers want.

In Chapter 1, we noted that markets play this signaling role in the U.S. economy. They are the primary channel of communication between firms and households. Firms put goods on the market; consumers tell them yes or no by buying or not buying. This is sometimes called the principle of **consumer sovereignty.** In the Soviet as well as some other economies, markets play a smaller role in communicating consumers' wants to producers. We will return to the question of alternative ways of organizing the economy later in the chapter.

Consumer sovereignty
A system under which consumers determine which goods and services will be produced by means of what they decide to buy or not to buy.

How to Produce?

How goods and services should be produced is a second key question that must be answered in every economy. This too is a question that Crusoe would face on his island. Should he fish with a line or a net? Should he hunt with a gun or snares? Let's look at three aspects of the question of how to produce.

Efficiency in Production
One aspect of the question concerns the choice of the best method of producing a given output with given factor supplies and technology. For example, consider the trade-off between clean air and other consumer goods, represented by the production possibility frontier in Exhibit 2.1. Suppose that we are at point A on this frontier. Starting from there, making the air a little cleaner will require forgoing the opportunity to produce some other goods.

However, there is more than one way to clean up the air. For instance, suppose we want to reduce the pollution from electric power plants. These plants can be made cleaner by either switching to low-sulfur coal or installing stack scrubbers that clean the gases emitted by high-sulfur coal. Which choice is better depends on where the plant is located relative to coal sources, the age of the plant, and so on. If the right choice of technique is made, the economy will slide down the production possibility frontier from A to, say, B. If the wrong choice is made, more other goods will have to be given up in order to attain the same level of clean air. That will leave the economy at a point inside the production possibility frontier, such as C.

Economists say that points lying on the frontier, such as A and B, are characterized by **efficiency in production.** By this they mean that starting from

Efficiency in production
A situation in which it is not possible, given available technology and factors of production, to produce more of one good or service without forgoing the opportunity to produce some of another good or service.

Exhibit 2.1 Efficiency in Production: Cleaning Up the Air

This production possibility frontier shows the trade-off between clean air and other goods. Suppose that we are at point A. Starting from here, the air cannot be made cleaner without some sacrifice of other goods. If efficient pollution control techniques are chosen, the economy can slide down the frontier to another efficient point, such as B. If inefficient techniques are chosen, the economy may end up at a point such as C. Moving from A to C sacrifices more than the amount of other goods necessary for achieving a given increase in clean air.

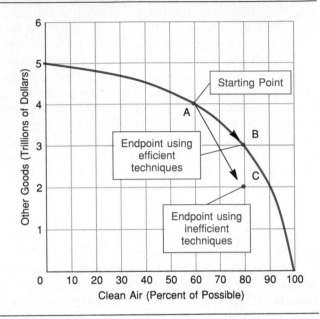

point A or B it is impossible, given the available technology and factors of production, to produce more of one good or service without forgoing the opportunity to produce another good or service. Point C, in contrast, is *inefficient;* that is, it represents an ill-chosen set of pollution control techniques. Starting from that point, it would be possible to have more other goods and services without sacrificing clean air by changing to more appropriate means of control, such as using cheap low-sulfur coal rather than expensive stack scrubbers.

Investment

A production possibility frontier is drawn on the assumptions of given supplies of factors of production and given technologies. The question of how to produce, then, is in part a matter of using the available factors efficiently so that the economy will not fall inside the frontier. If the assumptions are relaxed, the production possibility frontier can be used to illustrate other aspects of the question of how to produce.

Let us return to the case of Robinson Crusoe. The simplest way for Crusoe to catch fish is to stand on the shore and use a hook and line; with this technique, he could catch enough fish to live on. However, he could also use another method: He could stop fishing for a few days and use the time to weave a net and build a boat; then, using the boat and net, he could catch many more fish per hour spent fishing. His new equipment would let him have as many fish as before and give him extra time in which to hunt birds; have more fish and the same number of birds; or have more of both.

Construction of the boat and net is a simple form of investment. **Investment** is the process of accumulating capital. The boat and net are capital because they are durable means of production made by people. The act of building them is an investment by Crusoe just as building a new continuous-casting mill would be an

Investment
The act of increasing the economy's stock of capital, that is, its stock of means of production made by people.

Exhibit 2.2 Expansion of the
Production Possibility Frontier

Production possibility frontiers assume given supplies of
factors of production and a given state of knowledge. In the
short run, the economy can increase the output of capital
goods only by decreasing the output of consumer goods. In
the long run, however, accumulation of capital will expand
the frontier, as shown here. Population growth, discoveries
of new natural resources, and innovation by entrepreneurs
are other things that can cause the frontier to expand.

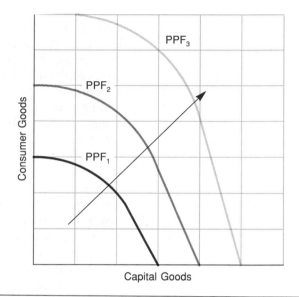

investment by a steel company. Once the investment has been made, the range
of production possibilities expands.

Similarly, the production possibility frontier of a modern economy expands
over time as the result of capital accumulation; this is shown in Exhibit 2.2. In
this version of the production possibility frontier, the vertical axis measures the
output of consumer goods and the horizontal axis measures the output of capital
goods.

In the short run, the economy is confined to movements along a fixed frontier such as PPF_1. Given the factors of production and technology assumed in
drawing this frontier, the economy would have to produce fewer consumer
goods such as cantaloupes and ski vacations in order to produce more capital
goods such as tractors and ski lift equipment. Such a shift in output would be
shown by a movement down and to the right along PPF_1.

Over time, however, increased output of capital goods would increase the
economy's productive capacity. With better farm equipment, more cantaloupes
could be grown per acre of land; with faster ski lifts, the same number of lift
operators could transport more skiers to the top of the mountain. The productive capacity of capital-goods-producing industries could also be increased: Ro-
bots could be used to produce tractors, better machine tools could increase
output of ski lifts, and so on. In the long run, then, accumulation of capital
allows the whole production possibility frontier to shift outward from PPF_1 to
PPF_2 and beyond. As this expansion takes place, the economy can expand along
a path such as that shown by the arrow, on which output of both capital and
consumer goods can be increased.

Capital accumulation is not the only way for the economy to grow. Increased
supplies of other factors of production—for example, labor—would also expand
the frontier. The discovery of new natural resources would do the same thing,

although the depletion of known natural resources would inhibit the expansion. Additional investment—substituting capital for natural resources—would be required in order to overcome this slowdown.

Entrepreneurship

Entrepreneurship
The process of looking for new possibilities—making use of new ways of doing things, being alert to new opportunities, and overcoming old limits.

Increasing the quantities of factors of production is one way to expand the production possibility frontier, but it is not the only way. There is still another aspect of the question of how to produce that we have not explored. **Entrepreneurship,** as economists call it, is the process of looking for new possibilities: finding new ways of doing things, being alert to new opportunities, and overcoming old limits. It is a dynamic process that breaks out of the static constraints set by given technology and factor supplies.

In the world of business, entrepreneurship is often linked with the founding of new firms. When a Henry Ford sets out to launch a whole new industry, there are few givens to deal with. New production processes must be invented. The constraints of existing sources of supply must be overcome. Consumers are encouraged to satisfy wants and needs to which they gave little thought before because there were no products that could satisfy them. This kind of exploring and experimenting is the essence of entrepreneurship.

But entrepreneurship is not limited to founding new firms. The manager of a Ford plant may be less of an entrepreneur than the founder, but the manager's work is not entirely routine. Unexpected problems arise that must be solved somehow—often by figuring out a new way of doing things.

Entrepreneurship does not have to mean inventing something, although it sometimes does. It can take other forms as well. It may mean finding a new market for an existing product—for example, convincing people in New England that tacos, long popular in the Southwest, make a quick and tasty lunch. It may mean taking advantage of differences in prices between one market and another—for instance, buying hay at a low price in Pennsylvania, where growing conditions are good in a certain year, and reselling it in Virginia, where a drought has damaged the hay crop.

Consumers can be entrepreneurs too. They do not simply repeat the same patterns of work and leisure every day. They seek variety—new jobs, new foods, new places to visit. Each time you try something new, you are taking a step into the unknown. In this respect, you are playing the role of entrepreneur.

For Whom to Produce?

The final part of the economic problem is the question of for whom goods should be produced. At first, this might seem primarily a normative question, one involving the equitable division of a given quantity of output. Family fights, lawsuits, and even wars have touched on different views of what constitutes a fair distribution of the goods and services an economy produces. However, some basic principles of positive economics apply here too.

Efficiency in Distribution

The positive economics behind "for whom" can best be seen when production has already occurred and there is a fixed supply of goods and services. Suppose that 30 students get on a bus to go to a football game. Bag lunches are handed out. Half the bags contain a ham sandwich and a root beer; the other half contain a tuna sandwich and a cola. What happens when the students open the bags?

They don't just eat whatever they find—they start trading. Some swap sandwiches; others swap drinks. Maybe there isn't enough of everything to give each person his or her first choice. Nevertheless, the trading makes at least some people better off than they were when they started. Further, no one ends up worse off, because if some don't want to trade, they can always eat what was given to them in the first place.

This example shows that the "for whom" question is partly about efficiency: Starting from any given distribution of goods, the allocation can be improved through trades until it fits people's preferences. So long as it is possible to trade in a way that permits some people to better satisfy their wants without making others worse off, we can say that **efficiency in distribution** can be improved even while the total quantity of goods remains fixed. The federal food stamp program illustrates this principle in action. How many food stamps, if any, a family should get is a subject of debate. But once that question has been settled, each family should be allowed to choose the mix of foods it prefers.

Incentives in Distribution and Overall Economic Efficiency

Efficiency in production and efficiency in distribution are two aspects of the broader concept of economic efficiency. Overall **economic efficiency** means a state of affairs in which it is impossible to satisfy one person's wants more fully by altering either the pattern of production or the pattern of distribution without causing another person's wants to be satisfied less fully.

When this broad notion of economic efficiency is taken into account, the application of positive economics is not restricted to situations in which the total amount of goods is fixed in advance. This is because the rules for distribution are likely to affect the pattern of production. One reason is that the rules for distribution are likely to affect the quantities of labor and other factors of production supplied. Most people earn their incomes by providing labor and other factors of production to business firms. Therefore, when we speak of the system of distribution, we mean the overall system that sets wages, salaries, and returns to the owners of capital. Another reason is that the rules for distribution will affect incentives for entrepreneurship. Some people may work hard to discover new ways of doing things even if they expect no material reward, but that is not true of everyone.

In short, if the system of distribution rewards hard work and careful use of resources, there will be more goods available for distribution. If goods are distributed in a way that is irrelevant to people's efforts and choices, less will be produced. Finally, still less will be produced if the distribution system rewards people for wasting scarce resources.

This is not to say that incentives are the only thing that counts in deciding for whom goods and services should be produced. Almost everyone would agree that fairness should be kept in mind too (although not everyone would concur on the meaning of "fairness"). We will return to the issues of distribution, incentives, and fairness at many points in this book.

Efficiency in distribution
A situation in which it is not possible, by redistributing existing supplies of goods and services, to satisfy one person's wants more fully without causing some other person's wants to be satisfied less fully.

Economic efficiency
A state of affairs in which it is not possible, by changing the pattern of either distribution or production, to satisfy one person's wants more fully without causing some other person's wants to be satisfied less fully.

Exchange and Comparative Advantage

As we have seen, some aspects of the economic problem can be found in a one-person economy such as that of Robinson Crusoe alone on his island. But a one-person economy cannot hold our attention for long. The questions of what, how, and for whom to produce are, in practice, *social* ones—questions concerning the proper way to cooperate in the tasks of production and distribution. In this section, we look at one of the most powerful principles guiding cooperation in production.

Comparative Advantage and Cooperation: An Example

Jim and Bill have agreed to spend their Saturdays helping a local political candidate prepare mailings of campaign literature. There are two steps in preparing a mailing. One consists of stuffing envelopes with several pieces of literature and sealing them; the other is typing address labels and sticking them on the envelopes. The steps can be performed in either order.

Bill has excellent clerical skills; he can stuff 300 envelopes an hour and type 100 labels an hour. Jim is a bit fumble-fingered; he can stuff only 100 envelopes an hour and type only 50 labels an hour.

The first Saturday, they sit down to work at 8:00 a.m. with a list of 1,200 people who are to get that week's mailing. They begin with stuffing. At 400 an hour (100 for Jim and 300 for Bill), this part of the job takes them 3 hours. Then they start typing and sticking on labels. At 150 per hour (50 for Jim and 100 for Bill), the labels take them another 8 hours. At 7:00 p.m.—11 hours after they started—they are done. Hard work, but it was all for a good cause.

On the second Saturday, Jim takes a look at the 1,200 envelopes piled on the table and fears it will be another long day. "Look," he says to Bill, "you're a lot better at this kind of thing than I am. Let me do the stuffing—that's the easy part. Save yourself for the typing, which takes most of the time." At first this strategy looks promising. Since Jim can stuff as quickly as Bill types, they work through the pile at a rate of 100 envelopes per hour. By the end of the day, though, the job has taken them 12 hours—an hour longer than the first week.

The third Saturday rolls around. This time Bill has an idea. "Stuffing those envelopes took you all day last week," he says. "Let me do that part. You start out typing, and when I'm finished stuffing I'll help you finish up the labels." Bill swiftly gets to work, and in four hours he has stuffed the whole pile of envelopes. Meanwhile, Jim, to his embarrassment, has managed to type a paltry 200 labels, and 1,000 remain. But with Bill joining in the typing, they go through the pile at 150 per hour, completing the remaining labels in 6 hours and 40 minutes. They finish at 6:40 p.m. after a total workday of 10 hours and 40 minutes—their best record yet.

It took three weeks for Bill and Jim to find the best pattern of cooperation. Is there a way they could have found it immediately, without the trial and error? There is. The key lies in the notion of opportunity cost. In this case, the opportunity cost of typing one address label is measured by the number of envelopes that could have been stuffed in the same amount of time. Bill can stuff 300 envelopes an hour or type 100 labels an hour; for him, the opportunity cost of typing 1 label is stuffing 3 envelopes. Jim can stuff 100 envelopes an hour or type 50 labels an hour; for him, the opportunity cost of typing 1 label is stuffing only 2 envelopes. The reason the work goes fastest when Jim spends all his time typing is that the opportunity cost of typing is lower for him than it is for Bill.

Comparative advantage
The ability to produce a good or service at a lower opportunity cost than another person or country.

Because the opportunity cost of typing is less for Jim than for Bill, Jim is said to have a **comparative advantage** in typing. Bill, on the other hand, has a comparative advantage in stuffing. The opportunity cost of stuffing an envelope is one-third of an address label for Bill and one-half of a label for Jim.

David Ricardo and the Theory of Comparative Advantage

David Ricardo, the greatest of the classical economists, was born in 1772. His father, a Jewish immigrant, was a member of the London stock exchange. Ricardo's education was rather haphazard, and he entered his father's business at the age of 14. In 1793, he married and went into business on his own. These were years of war and financial turmoil. The young Ricardo developed a reputation for remarkable astuteness and quickly made a large fortune.

In 1799, Ricardo read Adam Smith's *The Wealth of Nations* and developed an interest in political economy (as economics was then called). In 1809, his first writings on economics appeared. These were a series of newspaper articles on "The High Price of Bullion," which appeared the following year as a pamphlet. Several other short works

Art Source: Bettmann Archives

added to his reputation in this area. In 1814, he retired from business to devote all his time to political economy.

Ricardo's major work was *Principles of Political Economy and Taxation*, first published in 1817. This work contains, among other things, a pioneering statement of the principle of comparative advantage as applied to international trade. With a lucid numerical example, Ricardo showed why it is to the mutual advantage of both countries for England to export wool to Portugal and import wine in return even though both products can be produced with less labor in Portugal.

But international trade is only a sidelight of Ricardo's *Principles*. The book covers the whole field of economics as it then existed, beginning with value theory and progressing to a theory of economic growth and evolution. Ricardo held that the economy was growing toward a future "steady state." In this state, economic growth would come to a halt and the wage rate would be reduced to the subsistence level.

Ricardo's book was extremely influential. For more than half a century thereafter, much of economics as written in England was an expansion of or a commentary on Ricardo's work. The most famous economist influenced by Ricardo's theory and method was Karl Marx (see "Who Said It? Who Did It? 2.2"). Although Marx eventually reached conclusions that differed radically from any of Ricardo's views, his starting point was Ricardo's theory of value and method of analyzing economic growth.

The principle to be drawn from this example is that the cost of producing a given output is minimized if each party involved specializes in the task in which he or she has a comparative advantage. It is important to note that the principle of comparative advantage works even when one party (Bill, in this case) is, in an absolute sense, better at everything. It is Jim's typing skill compared to his own stuffing skill that counts, not his typing skill versus Bill's. Although somewhat of a klutz at clerical tasks, Jim contributes more by typing than by stuffing.

International Applications

Wider applications of comparative advantage abound. The first application of this principle was not to the division of labor within a country but to trade among countries (see "Who Said It? Who Did It? 2.1"). The most basic principle of international trade is that two countries can both raise their living standards through a pattern of trade that follows comparative advantage.

Suppose, for example, that in the United States a tractor can be produced with 100 hours of labor and a pair of shoes with 2, while in China the same products require 500 and 5 labor hours, respectively. Can each country gain by trading? Yes—if each follows the principle of comparative advantage.

Who has the comparative advantage in which product? Consider tractors first. Under U.S. conditions, shifting enough labor from shoes to produce 1 more tractor (100 hours) requires giving up the opportunity to produce 50 pairs of shoes. In China, shifting enough labor from shoes to produce 1 more tractor (500 hours) means giving up 100 pairs of shoes. Thus, the opportunity cost of tractors in terms of shoes is lower in the United States than in China. Similarly, shifting enough labor from tractors to make 100 pairs of shoes (200 hours) will require giving up 2 tractors in the United States. In China, shifting enough labor from tractors to shoes to make 100 pairs of shoes (500 hours) will require giving up only 1 tractor. Hence, China has a comparative advantage in shoes.

Next, suppose that initially each country produces 1 million tractors and 100 million pairs of shoes a year. Now each shifts production in the direction of the product in which it has a comparative advantage. The United States adds, say, 100,000 tractors to its output by shifting 10 million labor hours from shoes. Shoe output thus drops by 5 million pairs. Meanwhile, China steps up its shoe output by 7 million pairs by shifting 35 million labor hours from tractor building. Chinese tractor output drops by 70,000.

As a result of these changes, world output of both goods has increased. Tractor output is up 100,000 in the United States and down only 70,000 in China for a net gain of 30,000 tractors. Shoe output is up 7 million pairs in China and down only 5 million pairs in the United States for a net gain of 2 million shoes. Clearly there has been a gain in terms of efficiency in production. But the fruits of the increase in production are not well distributed. The U.S. is awash in tractors but actually has fewer shoes than before even though world shoe output has increased. Similarly, China is flooded with shoes but has fewer tractors even though world tractor output has increased. To draw an analogy with an earlier example, it is as though the person who packed the bag lunches for the bus trip put several cans of soda and no sandwiches in some bags and several sandwiches but no drinks in others.

In order to benefit from the increase in world output made possible by specialization according to comparative advantage, the gains in productive efficiency must be redistributed by trade. The United States must export some of its tractors in exchange for some of China's shoes. Negotiators must get together and strike a bargain that benefits both countries. A possible bargain—one that divides the gain in world production equally between the two countries—is shown in Exhibit 2.3. Under the terms of trade established there, the United States exports 85,000 tractors to China in exchange for 6 million pairs of shoes. This leaves both countries with more of both products than they started with. By means of international trade and comparative advantage, then, there have been gains in both the productive and distributional aspects of economic efficiency.

Market Prices and Comparative Advantage

Much more will be said about the organization of production and international trade in later chapters. The examples given here are highly simplified. Nonetheless, as more details are added to models of trade and production, it will still be true that efficiency gains are realized when the principle of comparative advantage is respected.

Exhibit 2.3 Gains from Trade: An Example

In this example, it is assumed that in the United States it takes 100 hours to build a tractor and 2 hours to make a pair of shoes, while in China it takes 500 and 5 hours, respectively. Before trade, each country is assumed to produce 1 million tractors and 100 million pairs of shoes. The United States then steps up tractor output by 100,000 at the expense of 5 million pairs of shoes. China steps up shoe output by 7 million pairs at the expense of 70,000 tractors. These actions increase total world output of tractors by 30,000 units and total world output of shoes by 2 million pairs. Tractors are then exchanged for shoes, with the United States exporting 85,000 tractors and importing 6 million pairs of shoes. The result, as the following table shows, is that both countries end up with more of both shoes and tractors.

	United States	**China**
A. Before Trade		
Tractors	Produced: 1,000,000 Consumed: 1,000,000	Produced: 1,000,000 Consumed: 1,000,000
Shoes	Produced: 100,000,000 Consumed: 100,000,000	Produced: 100,000,000 Consumed: 100,000,000
B. After Trade		
Tractors	Produced: 1,100,000 Exported: 85,000 ⟶ Consumed: 1,015,000	Produced: 930,000 Imported: 85,000 Consumed: 1,015,000
Shoes	Produced: 95,000,000 Imported: 6,000,000 ⟵ Consumed: 101,000,000	Produced: 107,000,000 Exported: 6,000,000 Consumed: 101,000,000

But this raises a question: How do people know whom to hire for which jobs and from whom to buy various goods and services? The answer is that they depend on information transmitted to them via market prices. In competitive markets, prices tend to reflect opportunity costs. (This is a central concept of microeconomic analysis that will be developed over several chapters.) Comparative advantage requires that one buy where opportunity costs are lowest; for the most part, this simply means buying where prices are lowest. When Bill and Jim compete in the market for clerical services, we can count on Bill to submit the lower bid on stuffing services and Jim the lower bid on typing services.[1] When competing in world markets, China will usually be able to underbid the United States on shoes and the United States will usually be able to underbid China on tractors. Neither labor markets, international markets, nor any other markets work perfectly at all times. But as long as competition tends to keep market prices close to opportunity costs, markets will do a remarkably good job of organizing production and exchange.

---

[1] What if Bill turns in the lower bid on both typing and stuffing services? This might happen at first, but if it does, Bill will be swamped with work and Jim will have nothing to do. Bill will then tend to raise his rates and Jim to cut his until each gets some of the work. Of course, since Bill is more productive at both tasks, he will probably end up earning a higher income. There is no rule of markets saying that people will earn equal incomes—but that is a story for another chapter.

Economic Systems

The questions of what, how, and for whom are all parts of an economic problem that apply to the economies of the United States, the Soviet Union, Crusoe's island, and all other economies, real or fictional. But although all economies are alike in the problems they face, they differ in the way decisions are made. The U.S. economy, as we have mentioned, relies heavily on markets and the price system to guide decisions. But there are other approaches to decision making. In this section, we make some brief comparisons.

Ownership and Economic Decision Making

To *own* something means to have the right to use it and prevent others from using it. If you own something, you are an economic decision maker. You decide who uses it and how it is used. Because owners are decision makers, ownership of business firms is a key feature of any economic system.

In the United States, most firms are controlled by the people who own the firms' capital, that is, their buildings, production equipment, inventory, and so on. Depending on the exact legal form of ownership, these people may be small-business proprietors, partners, or corporate stockholders. Chapter 4 will discuss these three forms of ownership in more detail. The point here is that whatever the legal details, a system in which control of business firms rests with the owners of capital is called **capitalism.**

Not all firms—even in the United States—are owned and controlled by capitalists. For instance, mutually or cooperatively owned firms are owned by the people who work in them or use their services. Examples include mutual insurance companies and savings banks, agricultural and consumer cooperatives, private colleges and universities, and not-for-profit publishers such as the organization that puts out *Consumer Reports*. Other firms are owned by the government, such as the Tennessee Valley Authority, the U.S. Postal Service, and, until recently, Conrail. Mutual, cooperative, and government ownership are all forms of *social* ownership. A system in which social ownership prevails is called **socialism.**

However, in the real world there are no purely capitalist or socialist systems; rather, all existing systems are mixtures of the two forms. In the United States, Canada, Western Europe, and Japan, the newly industrialized countries such as Brazil, South Korea, and Taiwan, and some less developed countries, capitalism prevails. Nevertheless, mutual, cooperative, and government-owned firms exist in all these economies.

In the Soviet Union, Eastern Europe, China, and many other less developed countries, social ownership prevails. The theories on which these economies are based can be traced to the writings of the nineteenth-century economist Karl Marx (see "Who Said It? Who Did It? 2.2"). Following Marx's precepts, almost all industry in these countries is government owned, but some private ownership can be found in farming, retail trade, and services. One country—Yugoslavia— has its own home-grown brand of cooperative ownership and control.

However, our purpose here is not to list the world's economic systems but to show that different forms of ownership place authority for decision making in the hands of different groups of people. Under capitalism, the owners of capital are the managers and entrepreneurs. Under mutual and cooperative ownership,

Capitalism
An economic system in which control of business firms rests with the owners of capital.

Socialism
An economic system in which firms are owned and controlled by the people who work in them or by the government acting in their name.

Karl Marx: Economist and Socialist

Karl Marx—German philosopher, revolutionary, and patron saint of socialism—was also a well-known economist. From the age of 31, he lived and worked in London. His thinking was strongly influenced by the British classical school of economics, especially the writings of David Ricardo. But while economists of the classical school were, for the most part, sympathetic to the capitalist system, Marx took the tools of classical economics and turned them against capitalism.

The cornerstone of classical economics was the *labor theory of value*—the doctrine that the values and relative prices of various goods are determined mainly by the number of labor hours that go into their production. For Marx, the labor theory of value was more than a mere description of how prices are determined. He went on to argue that if labor is the source of all value, workers should receive the whole product of their labor. He viewed it as unjust that under capitalism a large part of the product was paid to owners of land and capital in the form of rent, interest payments, and profit—in his terms, "surplus value."

In his massive work *Capital*, Marx tried to show that capitalism was headed for collapse and would be followed by a socialist revolution. All of his life he worked with revolutionary groups to prepare for that day. Following the revolution, he envisioned an economy based on collective ownership and economic planning. He gave the name *communism* to the highest form of socialism, toward which the revolution would strive and in which the principle of "from each according to his ability, to each according to his need" would govern production and distribution. Today "communism" is used to describe the economic systems of the Soviet Union, Eastern Europe, and other countries that follow Marxist principles, even though these are not pure communism in the Marxist sense of the term.

Marx was not the first socialist, nor are all of today's socialists followers of Marx. Nevertheless, he must be regarded as the most influential thinker in the history of socialism and one of the most important economists of all time.

Photo Source: Library of Congress

---

managers are chosen by workers, consumers, or some other group. Under forms of socialism that feature government ownership, managers are public employees.

Styles of Decision Making

No less important than differences in who makes economic decisions are differences in how those decisions are made. Broadly speaking, there are three styles of decision making: market decision making, regulation, and planning.

Markets

Chapter 1 discussed the role of markets in decision making. Markets perform three tasks: (1) They transmit information on the values of resources to firms and households; (2) they set incentives for workers, traders, and entrepreneurs; and (3) in the process of doing these things, they determine the distribution of income. Beginning with Chapter 3, the remainder of this book will be devoted primarily to the ways in which markets do all three.

Although the role of markets in decision making is greatest in capitalist systems, most socialist economies also use markets. Take cars in the Soviet

Union. Cars are produced by a government-owned firm and sold in a government-owned store. Nevertheless, the choice of what to buy—a car, furniture, airline tickets, or whatever—is a market decision; that is to say, this decision is governed, at least in part, by the prices of available goods. Quite recently the use of markets by Soviet motorists has been extended. Private automobile repair shops, which previously operated "underground," have been allowed to emerge in the public marketplace to compete with inefficient government-run repair shops.

Other socialist countries use markets much more extensively. In Poland, the bulk of the farm sector relies on markets. China uses markets heavily in light industry and services. Hungary and Yugoslavia use market incentives throughout their economies—in fact, systems such as theirs are often called *market socialism*.

Regulation

No economic system leaves all decisions to the market. Even in the most strongly capitalist systems, the government plays a major role in the decisions of what, how, and for whom. Its activities in this area are known as **regulation.** The U.S. Food and Drug Administration's regulation of prescription drugs affects *what* pharmaceutical firms produce. The Environmental Protection Agency's rules on air and water pollution affect *how* firms produce their outputs. Laws such as the federal minimum wage law and the Davis-Bacon Act determine levels of pay for many workers and thus affect *for whom* goods and services are produced. We will discuss many kinds of regulation in later chapters.

Planning

The governments of many countries go beyond regulation and engage in **economic planning.** This can be defined as systematic intervention in the economy with the goal of improving coordination, efficiency, and growth.

Because planning and regulation differ mainly in degree, there is no sharp line between them. The most comprehensive planning is found in socialist economies such as that of the Soviet Union. There each firm, be it a tire factory, auto parts plant, or distillery, is required to follow a plan governing its level of output, production methods, sources of supply, and so forth. As the article that opens this chapter illustrates, planning mistakes may take years to correct or never be corrected at all.

Other socialist countries engage in more limited planning. They try to coordinate the work of the largest firms and set a framework for economic growth, but they leave more detailed decisions to each firm's managers. Some countries in which capitalist ownership prevails have tried this style of planning too; France is a notable example. The United States probably has the smallest degree of national economic planning in the world.

Looking Ahead

This is not a book on comparative economics; most of its examples are based on the American economic system. Still, it is worthwhile to keep the variety of economic systems in mind. The basic problems of what, how, and for whom are universal ones that have many possible solutions. Further, even within the U.S. economy, a great many competing forms of ownership and decision-making approaches coexist.

Regulation
Government intervention in the market for the purpose of influencing the production and distribution of particular goods and services.

Economic planning
Systematic government intervention in the economy with the goal of improving coordination, efficiency, and growth.

Summary

1. **How is it decided what goods and services the economy is to produce?** Scarcity means that we cannot have enough of everything to satisfy all our wants. Therefore, it must somehow be decided what, among all possible combinations of goods and services, is to be produced. This means that there must be some way for consumers to tell producers what they want. In the U.S. economy, markets are the principal channel through which consumers communicate with producers.

2. **How do efficiency, investment, and entrepreneurship enter into the decision of how goods will be produced?** For given factors of production and technology, the range of goods and services from which an economy can choose can be represented by a production possibility frontier. If production is organized *efficiently*, the economy will be on its production possibility frontier. In that case, it will be impossible to more fully satisfy one want without less fully satisfying some other. The economy cannot move outside the frontier with a given supply of factors, but *investment*— that is, the accumulation of additional capital—can expand the frontier. The frontier can also be expanded through *entrepreneurship*, which is the process of looking for new ways to do things, being alert to new opportunities, and overcoming old limits.

3. **How do positive and normative economics bear on the question of for whom goods will be produced?** The question of for whom goods will be produced is partly a normative question, that is, one of fairness. However, the question has positive aspects as well. For one thing, a given output of goods and services must be efficiently distributed so that one person's wants cannot be better satisfied without less fully satisfying someone else's. For another, positive economics can be used to analyze the way in which the choice of goods distribution will affect incentives and, hence, the quantity and selection of output.

4. **What principle guides the division of labor within an economy and among nations?** When people cooperate in production, efficiency requires that the division of labor follow the principle of *comparative advantage*. A person who is able to produce a good or service at a lower opportunity cost than someone else is said to have a comparative advantage in producing that good or service. Trade among nations, as well as the division of labor within an economy, will be most efficient when it follows the principle of comparative advantage.

5. **How do capitalist and socialist economies differ in their approaches to the questions of what, how, and for whom?** A *capitalist* economy is one in which control of business firms rests with owners of the firm's capital. Such economies rely heavily on markets to guide the decisions of what, how, and for whom. A *socialist* economy is one in which firms are controlled by the people who work in them or by the government acting in the workers' name. Such economies tend to rely more extensively on planning. In practice, all economies use a widely varying mixture of markets, planning, and regulation.

Terms for Review

- consumer sovereignty
- efficiency in production
- investment
- entrepreneurship
- efficiency in distribution
- economic efficiency
- comparative advantage
- capitalism
- socialism
- regulation
- economic planning

Questions for Review

1. In what sense do markets serve as a channel of communication between consumers and producers in a capitalist economy?

2. Under what conditions will an economy operate inside its production possibility frontier? How can the frontier be expanded?

3. Why does the question of for whom to produce raise both normative and positive economic questions?

4. Why can it be said that everyone has a comparative advantage in something even if there is nothing a person can do that someone else cannot do better?

5. Give examples of social forms of ownership in the United States and capitalist forms of ownership in the Soviet Union and Eastern Europe. Give examples of markets, regulation, and economic planning as methods of decision making in various countries.

Problems and Topics for Discussion

1. **Examining the lead-off case.** Compare the situation faced by Soviet and U.S. motorists in terms of the roles of markets, regulation, and planning. What useful purpose, if any, do you think is served by regulations requiring cars to be clean, neatly painted, and so on? Would you favor such a regulation in the United States? Why or why not?

2. **Pollution and growth.** Exhibit 2.2 shows an expanding production possibility frontier. Relabel the horizontal axis of this figure so that it represents "clean air" as in Exhibit 2.1. If the economy followed the path of the arrow in the diagram, it would be possible to enjoy both more material goods and cleaner air. Yet, at least in some locations, the air has become dirtier as output of other goods has expanded over time. Does this mean that the production possibility frontier is not expanding as shown in the exhibit? Does it mean that growth must be stopped if we want to keep the air from getting dirtier? Or does it mean that during the expansion the economy is following a different path than the one shown in the exhibit? Illustrate your answer with a diagram. Discuss the issue of clean air versus other goods in an expanding economy from the viewpoint of both positive and normative economics.

3. **Efficiency and the production possibility frontier.** Turn back to problem 3 from Chapter 1. Note that the accompanying table assumes that the farmer switches his highest field first from potatoes to wheat. What would happen if instead he grew potatoes in the three highest fields and wheat in the two lowest? How would that point be represented in relation to the production possibility frontier? How would you describe such a situation? Now compare the opportunity cost of producing wheat in the top field with that in the bottom field. Which field has a comparative advantage in producing wheat? Which has a comparative advantage in producing potatoes? In using the highest fields first for wheat, is the farmer following the principle of comparative advantage? Why or why not?

4. **Comparative advantage.** Suppose you learned that the great pianist Vladimir Horowitz was also an amazing typist. Knowing this, would it surprise you to discover that he hired a secretary to type his correspondence even though he could do the job more quickly himself? How does this relate to comparative advantage?

5. **International trade.** In the United States, a car can be produced with 200 labor hours, while a ton of rice requires 20 labor hours. In Japan, it takes 150 labor hours to make a car and 50 labor hours to grow a ton of rice. Which country has a comparative advantage in cars? In rice? Show that both countries can have both more cars and more rice by trading at a rate of five tons of rice per car. If trade that follows the principle of comparative advantage is beneficial to both parties, why do you think the United States limits the import of Japanese cars while Japan restricts the import of U.S. rice? Discuss.

6. **Efficiency in distribution and the food stamp program.** The federal food stamp program leaves low-income families free to choose their preferred mix of foods. However, instead it could give them a ticket book with so many bread coupons, so many milk coupons, so many meat coupons, and so on. Which plan do you think would be more efficient for a given cost to the government? Would it be still more efficient if low-income families were allowed to trade their food stamps for cash? (Such trading does happen, but it is restricted by law.) Or perhaps low-income families should be given cash in the first place and allowed to spend it on whatever they want. Discuss this issue, taking both positive and normative economics into account.

Case for Discussion
Growing Rich in Wenjiang County

Chinese peasant farmers

Wu Xiangtin, a farmer in Wenjiang County, is growing rich—at least by Chinese standards—off the so-called "responsibility system." This is a program in which plots of land have been turned over to farmers for up to 15 years to use in producing goods for consumer markets. Wu earns about $15 a day by selling the eggs produced by his 200 chickens. Last year, he claims, his total income was about 10,000 yuan, or roughly $4,800.

The newly affluent Wu has purchased a new house, a new chicken coop, and a TV set. His next project is to raise rabbits, ducks, and geese. He notes that duck and goose eggs command higher prices than chicken eggs.

Wu's projects are typical of the entrepreneurial energy that was bottled up by Chairman Mao's policies. In 1966, at the start of the Cultural Revolution (a campaign to shape Chinese society along more purely socialist lines), Wu was working as a veterinarian at a nearby commune. The political turmoil made it impossible for him to remain at that job, so he began raising pigs. Local socialist activists, known as Red Guards, denounced him as an "exploiter" and warned,

"You will be taking the capitalist road if you raise ducks or chickens."

Wu becomes indignant at the suggestion that the Communist party might someday take away his chickens. "It's the policy of the party," he says. "The party will never take away my 10,000 yuan."

Maybe not. For the time being, local party officials, far from denouncing Wu, are showing him off to foreign visitors as a success story of the new China. Moreover, they say that because of the responsibility system, the average income of the 1,300 people in Wu's production brigade has more than doubled since 1978.

But there are problems that could hinder further change. The most obvious is inequality of income, which could trigger a backlash. Take Wu's neighbor, Li Xiaochuan, who lives in a cramped and dirty house. Li has only four pigs, six chickens, and an income about one-tenth of Wu's. At some point, he and other poor peasants may come to resent their "rich" neighbor and seek a return to what they see as more egalitarian policies.

Source: David Ignatius, "China's Capitalistic Road Is Uphill from Here," *The Wall Street Journal*, May 4, 1984, p. 30. Reprinted by permission of *The Wall Street Journal*, © Dow Jones & Company, Inc. 1984. All Rights Reserved. Photo Source: Reuters/Bettmann Newsphotos.

Questions

1. In what ways does Wu fit the definition of an entrepreneur?

2. How does this story illustrate the three functions of markets? How does it illustrate the use of markets in a socialist society?

3. What examples are given in this story of the what, how, and for whom decisions that every economy faces?

4. Discuss the tension between the Maoist belief that pure socialism should strive for equality above all and the desire of China's current leaders to make the economy more efficient and productive.

Suggestions for Further Reading

Defoe, Daniel. *The Adventures of Robinson Crusoe.* London, 1719.

The examples used in this chapter are only fancifully related to this classic novel. However, try reading it with an eye to understanding the economic problems faced by Crusoe and, later, by Crusoe and Friday together.

Goodman, John C., and Edwin G. Dolan. *The Economics of Public Policy*, 3d ed. St. Paul, Minn.: West, 1985.

Chapter 2 uses the issue of the military draft versus the volunteer army to illustrate the concepts of opportunity cost and the production possibility frontier. Chapter 3 compares the U.S. and British methods of deciding who receives medical treatment.

Wiles, P. J. D. *Economic Institutions Compared.* New York: Wiley, 1977.

This book compares the methods used by different economic systems to solve the problems they all face. Chapter 6, which deals with cooperatives, communities, and communes, is of particular interest.

3 Supply and Demand

After reading this chapter, you will understand . . .

- How the price of a good or service affects the quantity demanded by buyers.
- Other market conditions that affect demand.
- How the quantities of goods and services that producers supply are affected by prices and other market conditions.
- How supply and demand interact to determine the market price of a good or service.
- Why market prices and quantities change in response to changes in a variety of market conditions.
- How price supports and price ceilings affect the operations of markets.

Before reading this chapter, make sure you know the meaning of . . .

- Markets and their functions (Chapters 1 and 2)
- Real and nominal values (Chapter 1)
- Opportunity cost (Chapter 1)
- Comparative advantage (Chapter 2)
- Entrepreneurship (Chapter 2)

Are the Fakes Real or the Real Ones Fake?

A cubic zirconia can easily pass for a diamond.

Marylou Whitney—Mrs. Cornelius Vanderbilt Whitney—is well aware that there are a lot of fake diamonds around these days. She wears them much of the time.

"I'm delighted with fake jewelry," says Whitney, who can certainly afford the real thing. She explains: "I would like to wear real, but it isn't safe." And when she does wear real, she says, she passes it off as fake, saying that she is amused "that people who don't have the real thing pretend their fakes are real, and people like me pretend the real is fake."

Marylou Whitney's fakes and many others are CZs, made from a substance called cubic zirconia. CZs have about the same refractive index (brilliance) as diamonds and more light-dispersion (fire) than the real thing. They can be very convincing. In 1983 reporter John Stossel of the TV show "20/20" embarrassed the jewelry industry by taking a CZ and a $50,000 diamond to New York's jewelers' row. Half the jewelers he visited thought the CZ was a diamond.

But there is one big difference between diamonds and CZs: price. CZs sell for $15 to $150 a carat, compared to $2,000 to $20,000 a carat for diamonds. Why? Supply and demand, of course. About 200 million carats of CZs are made every year, compared to about 9 million carats of jewelry-quality diamonds. And although CZs are pretty, there is no demand for them for nonjewelry uses. CZs are too soft to make cutting tools, and they are no help in laser technology. So if you want to sparkle like a Whitney, CZs could be your best friend.

Source: Joan Kron, "If Diamonds Can Be a Girl's Best Friend, CZs Are Good Pals," *The Wall Street Journal*, June 15, 1984, p. 30. Reprinted by permission of *The Wall Street Journal*, © Dow Jones & Company, Inc. 1984. All Rights Reserved. Photo Source: © 1987 Phyllis Woloshin.

As we have seen, a key function of markets is that of transmitting information in the form of prices. Prices give buyers and sellers signals regarding the opportunity costs of goods and services. Buyers' and sellers' responses to these signals, in turn, determine what is produced, how it is produced, and for whom it is produced.

The role of prices is so central to the functioning of a market economy that the field of microeconomics is sometimes referred to as "price theory." This chapter introduces the theory of prices. The centerpiece of the chapter is a set of tools that show how supply and demand affect the prices of CZs, chicken, dental services, beef, and just about everything else. Once these tools are clearly understood, it becomes difficult to pick up the business page of a newspaper without noticing "supply" and "demand" between the lines of every story.

Demand

Just a few years ago, compact disk players carried price tags of $1,000 and up. At that price, they were a plaything for the rich audiophile—the person who just had to have the best available sound even if it cost the equivalent of a Caribbean vacation. Today discounters sell CD players for as little as $100, and that same flawless sound can be heard booming out of dormitory windows on any campus in the country. Is it surprising that when the price fell more CD players were sold? Hardly—it was simply the law of demand in action.

Law of demand
The principle that, other things being equal, the quantity of a good demanded by buyers tends to rise as the price of the good falls and to fall as its price rises.

The **law of demand** can be stated formally as follows: In any market, other things being equal, the quantity of a good or service that buyers demand tends to rise as its price falls and to fall as its price rises. We expect this to happen for two reasons. First, if the price of one good falls while the prices of other goods stay the same, people are likely to substitute the cheaper good for goods they would have bought otherwise. (When chicken is on sale and beef is not, people have chicken for dinner more often.) Second, when the price of one good falls while incomes and other prices stay the same, people feel a little richer. They use their added buying power to buy a bit more of many things, including a little more of the good whose price went down. In many cases, as we will see, these two factors combine to boost sales of goods whose prices fall and cut sales of goods whose prices rise.

Behind the Law of Demand

While the formal law of demand satisfies common sense, three of its elements are worth clarifying.

Quantity Demanded

It is important to understand what is meant by *quantity demanded*. This is the quantity that buyers are willing and able to buy over a given period, such as a month or a year. Quantity demanded is not the same thing as quantity wanted or needed. I might *want* a Porsche, but the last time I checked, the sticker price was over $40,000. At that price I would have to give up too much else to buy one, so I choose not to. The quantity of Porsches I demand at the going price is zero.

On the other hand, I might *need* dental surgery to avoid losing my teeth. But suppose I am poor. If I cannot pay for the surgery or find a benefactor to pay my way, I am out of luck. The quantity of dental surgery I demand therefore is zero, however great my need.

Other Things Being Equal

The phrase *other things being equal* means that a change in the price of a product is only one of a number of things that affect the quantity people are willing to buy. If real incomes go up, people are likely to buy more of many goods even if their prices do not drop. If tastes change, people will buy more of some goods and less of others even if prices do not change. Other factors can affect demand even when prices remain fixed.

For example, "other things being equal" means that the prices of other goods are assumed to remain the same as buyers respond to a change in the price of any one good. As economists put it, *relative prices* are what count.

It is important to distinguish between changes in relative prices and changes in nominal prices—the number of dollars actually paid per unit—during periods of inflation. If the price of eggs goes up 10 percent at the same time that consumers' nominal incomes and the prices of muffins, butter, and all other goods rise by 10 percent, we should not expect any change in the quantity of eggs demanded. The opportunity cost of buying eggs does not change in this situation. As before, buying a dozen eggs means giving up the opportunity to buy three muffins, a jar and a half of jam, or whatever. The law of demand does not apply to this situation because other things are not equal as the price of eggs climbs.

During a period of inflation, the relative price of a good may fall even though its nominal price is going up. For example, from 1974 to 1978, the nominal price of gasoline rose, but at a less rapid rate than the rate of inflation. People responded to the lower relative price of gasoline by buying more. In 1979 and 1980, the nominal price of gasoline went up faster than the prices of other goods. People responded to the increase in the relative price by buying less.

The Demand Curve

The law of demand states a relationship between the quantity of a good that people intend to buy, other things being equal, and the price of that good. This one-to-one relationship can be shown in a table or a graph, as in Exhibit 3.1.

Look at the table that forms part a of the exhibit. The first line shows that when the price of chicken is $.64 a pound, the quantity demanded per year is 1.4 billion pounds. Reading down the table, we see that as the price falls, the quantity demanded rises. At $.60 per pound, buyers plan to purchase 1.5 billion pounds per year; at $.56, they plan to buy 1.6 billion pounds; and so on.

Part b of Exhibit 3.1 presents the same information in graphic form. The graph is called a **demand curve** for chicken. Suppose we want to use the demand curve to find out what quantity of chicken will be demanded at a price of $.40 per pound. Starting at $.40 on the vertical axis, we move across, as shown by the arrow, until we reach the demand curve at point A. Continuing to follow the arrow, we drop down to the horizontal axis. Reading from the scale on that axis, we see that the quantity demanded at $.40 per pound is 2 billion pounds per year. This is the quantity demanded in line A of the table in part a.

Demand curve
A graphic representation of the relationship between the price of a good and the quantity of it that buyers demand.

Movements along the Demand Curve

The effect of a change in the price of chicken, other things being equal, can be shown as a movement from one point to another along the demand curve for chicken. Suppose the price drops from $.40 to $.20 per pound. In the process,

Exhibit 3.1   A Demand Curve for Chicken

Parts a and b show the quantity of chicken demanded at various prices. For example, at a price of $.40 per pound, buyers are willing and able to purchase 2 billion pounds of chicken per year. This price-quantity combination is shown by line A in part a and point A in part b.

(a)	
Price of Chicken (Dollars per Pound)	**Quantity of Chicken Demanded (Billions of Pounds per Year)**
.64	1.4
.60	1.5
.56	1.6
.52	1.7
.48	1.8
.44	1.9
A .40	2.0
.36	2.1
.32	2.2
.28	2.3
.24	2.4
B .20	2.5
.16	2.6

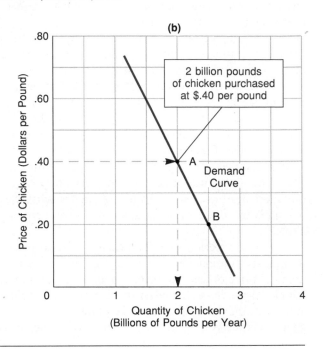

the quantity that buyers plan to purchase rises. The point corresponding to the quantity demanded at the new, lower price is point B (corresponding to line B of the table). Because the quantity demanded increases as the price decreases, the demand curve has a negative slope.

Economists speak of a movement along a demand curve as a **change in quantity demanded.** Such a movement represents buyers' reaction to a change in the price of the good in question, other things being equal.

Shifts in the Demand Curve

Demand curves such as the one in Exhibit 3.1 are always drawn on an "other things being equal" basis. They assume that as the price of chicken changes other factors, such as consumers' incomes, consumers' tastes, and the prices of other goods, remain fixed. If any of these other factors changes, the quantity of chicken that consumers are willing and able to buy will change even if there is no change in the price of chicken. We must then draw a new demand curve. The new curve, like the old one, will have a negative slope, following the law of demand, but it will be shifted to the right or the left.

Economists speak of a shift in the demand curve as a **change in demand.** Such a shift represents a change in buyers' plans caused by some factor other than the price of the good in question. Several sources of changes in demand are worth looking at. Among the most important are changes in the prices of other

Change in quantity demanded
A change in the quantity of a good that buyers are willing and able to purchase that results from a change in the good's price, other things being equal; a movement from one point to another along a demand curve.

Change in demand
A change in the quantity of a good that buyers are willing and able to purchase that results from a change in some condition other than the price of that good; a shift in the demand curve.

goods, changes in consumers' incomes, changes in expectations, and changes in tastes.

Changes in the Prices of Other Goods

The demand for a good may be affected by changes in the prices of related goods as well as by changes in the price of the good in question. Exhibit 3.2 shows demand curves for lettuce and cabbage, either of which can be used to make salad. People's decisions about whether to eat tossed salad or cole slaw depend on the prices of both lettuce and cabbage.

Suppose that the price of lettuce starts out at $.70 a pound and then rises to $1.00 a pound. The effect of this change is shown in part a of Exhibit 3.2 as a movement along the lettuce demand curve from point A to point B. With the price of lettuce higher than before, consumers will tend to buy more cabbage than they would otherwise (part b). Now suppose the price of cabbage is $.50 a pound. Before the price of lettuce went up, consumers would have bought 20 million pounds of cabbage a week (point A' on cabbage demand curve D_1). After the price of lettuce has gone up, they will buy 26 million pounds of cabbage a week at the same price (point B' on cabbage demand curve D_2). Thus, an

Exhibit 3.2 Effects of an Increase in the Price of Lettuce on the Demand for Cabbage

An increase in the price of lettuce from $.70 to $1.00 per pound, other things being equal, results in a movement from point A to point B on the lettuce demand curve. This is called a decrease in the quantity of lettuce demanded. With the price of cabbage unchanged at $.50 per pound, consumers will substitute cabbage for lettuce. This will cause an increase in the demand for cabbage, which is shown as a shift in the cabbage demand curve from D_1 to D_2.

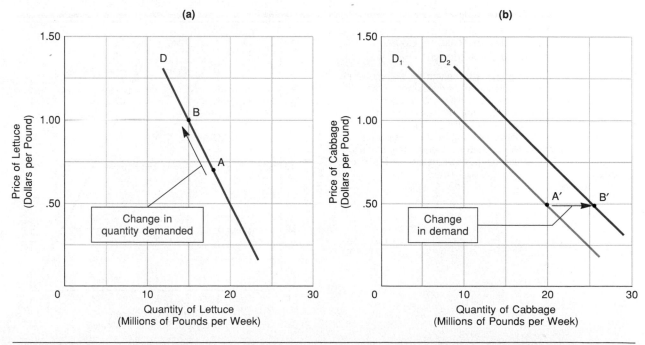

increase in the price of lettuce causes a *movement along* the lettuce demand curve and, at the same time, a *shift* in the cabbage demand curve.

People tend to buy more cabbage when the price of lettuce goes up because they use one in place of the other in their salads. Economists call such pairs of goods **substitutes** because an increase in the price of one causes an increase in the demand for the other—a rightward shift in the demand curve. In effect, when the price of lettuce goes up, the opportunity cost of cabbage—that is, the amount of lettuce consumers must give up in order to buy a given amount of cabbage—falls.

Consumers react differently to price changes when two goods tend to be used together. One example is tires and gasoline. When the price of gasoline goes up, people drive less; thus, they buy fewer tires even if there is no change in their price. An increase in the price of gasoline hence causes a movement along the gasoline demand curve and a simultaneous leftward shift in the tire demand curve. Pairs of goods that are related in this way are known as **complements.** In effect, when the price of gasoline goes up, the opportunity cost of using tires—including the amount that must be spent on gasoline to drive a given distance—rises.

Changes in Consumer Income

Another key factor affecting the demand for a good is consumer income. When their incomes rise, people tend to buy larger quantities of many goods, assuming that their prices do not change.

Exhibit 3.3 shows the effect of a rise in consumer income on the demand for chicken. Demand curve D_1 is the same as that shown in Exhibit 3.1. According to this curve, the quantity demanded at a price of $.40 per pound is 2 billion pounds and the quantity demanded at $.20 per pound is 2.5 billion pounds.

Substitutes
A pair of goods for which an increase in the price of one causes an increase in demand for the other.

Complements
A pair of goods for which an increase in the price of one results in a decrease in demand for the other.

Exhibit 3.3   Effect of an Increase in Consumer Income on the Demand for Chicken

Demand curve D_1 in this graph is the same as that shown in Exhibit 3.1. It assumes a given level of consumer income. If their incomes increase, consumers will want to buy more chicken at any given price, other things being equal. This will shift the demand curve to the right to, say, D_2. At $.40 per pound, the quantity demanded will be 3 billion pounds (B) rather than 2 billion (A); at $.20 per pound, the quantity demanded will be 3.5 billion pounds (D) instead of 2.5 billion (C); and so on.

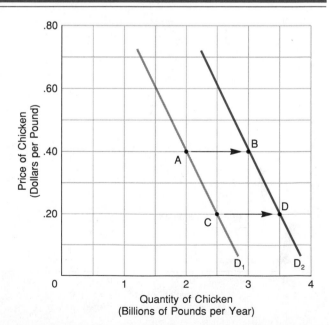

Consumer income was one of the items covered by the "other-things-being-equal" condition when this demand curve was drawn.

Suppose, however, that consumer incomes rise. With higher incomes, people will want to eat more protein than before, including chicken, at any given price. Suppose that consumers are now willing to buy 3 billion pounds of chicken instead of 2 billion at a price of $.40 per pound. This change is shown as a move from point A to point B in Exhibit 3.3. Given the new, higher income, even more chicken would be bought if the price were $.20. Instead of 2.5 billion pounds, as shown by D_1, buyers now might plan to purchase 3.5 billion pounds. This corresponds to a move from point C to point D.

In both cases, the effects of a change in consumer income at a given price are shown by a movement off the original demand curve, D_1. Points B and D are on a new demand curve, D_2. Thus, the increase in income has shifted the demand curve for chicken to the right. If the price of chicken later changes while income remains at the new, higher level, the effects will appear as movements along the new demand curve.

In sum, there is a demand curve for every possible income level. Each represents a one-to-one relationship between price and quantity demanded *given* the assumed income level.

In the above example, we assumed that an increase in income would cause an increase in the demand for chicken. Experience shows that this is what normally happens. Economists therefore call chicken a **normal good,** meaning that when consumers' incomes rise, other things being equal, people will buy more of it.

There are some goods, however, of which people will buy less if their incomes rise, other things being equal. For example, your classmates with higher incomes are likely to go out for pizza more often than those with lower incomes; this implies that the demand for dorm food falls as income rises. Similarly, people who do their cooking at home tend to buy less flour when their incomes rise and buy more baked goods instead. People tend to buy fewer shoe repair services when their incomes rise; instead, they buy new shoes. Also, they tend to ride intercity buses less often, since they would rather fly or drive. Goods such as dorm food, flour, shoe repair services, and intercity bus travel are called **inferior goods.** When consumers' incomes rise, the demand curve for an inferior good shifts to the left instead of to the right.

Changes in Expectations

Changes in buyers' expectations are a third factor that can shift demand curves. If people expect the price of a good to rise relative to the prices of other goods or expect the opportunity cost of acquiring the good to increase in some other way, they will step up their rate of purchase before the change takes place.

In a classic case of this type, consumers rushed to buy cars in December 1986 before a new tax law went into effect. After January 1987, car buyers expected to be unable to deduct the sales tax on a new car from their federal income taxes. Depending on the state and the car's price, the change in tax treatment could easily have equaled a price increase of $200 to $300. After running well above normal in December, new-car sales fell in January. Because more cars were sold in December than would have been sold at the same price had consumers not expected the tax law to change, buyers' behavior in December could be properly interpreted as a temporary rightward shift in the demand curve for cars.

Normal good
A good for which an increase in consumer income results in an increase in demand.

Inferior good
A good for which an increase in consumer income results in a decrease in demand.

Changes in Tastes

Changes in tastes are a fourth source of changes in demand. Sometimes these happen rapidly, as is the case in such areas as popular music, clothing styles, and fast foods. The demand curves for these goods and services shift often. In other cases, changes in tastes take longer to occur but are more permanent. For example, in recent years consumers have been more health conscious than in the past; as a result, they have reduced their demand for high-cholesterol foods such as beef, eggs, and whole milk. Such changes can disrupt whole industries, as "Economics in the News 3.1" indicates.

Supply

Supply curve
A graphic representation of the relationship between the price of a good and the quantity of it supplied.

We now turn from the demand side of the market to the supply side. As in the case of demand, we can construct a one-to-one relationship between the price of a good and the quantity of it that sellers intend to offer for sale. Exhibit 3.4 shows such a relationship for the chicken market.

The upward-sloping curve in Exhibit 3.4 is called a **supply curve** for chicken. Like demand curves, supply curves are based on an "other-things-being-equal" condition. The supply curve for chicken shows how producers

ECONOMICS IN THE NEWS   3.1

Consumer Switch to Chicken Brings Change to Beef Industry

GREELEY, COLORADO. Rhonda Miller is building a better steak.

Donning rubber boots, a white coat and a hard hat in Monfort of Colorado Inc.'s chilly packing plant, she mixes up a secret recipe of shredded beef and seaweed extract and pushes it through a stainless steel extruder to make logs of meat.

After the meat binds together in a cooler, she slices it into perfectly shaped, lean strip steaks and seals them in individual packages. "My husband loves these because they're so convenient," says Miller, the company's research director.

The new, tender steak is a radical departure from the unpopular, fatty chuck roasts that roll down conveyor belts

at Monfort's plants. Cattlemen are praying that the refabricated steak and other new, easy-to-fix Monfort products will halt the decline in the cattle business.

But beef has lost its central place on the American dinner plate, forcing a wrenching shrinkage in the nation's cattle herds to a 23-year low. Consumers, who have eaten more chicken each year for two decades, are clearly indicating that many of them have begun to prefer it to beef. One reason is the way the chicken industry has quickly capitalized on chicken's more healthful image, which it acquired when many medical researchers began warning that consumption of too much red meat could contribute to heart disease, strokes, and possibly cancer.

Desperately seeking to avoid being trampled further, some beef packers are struggling to go beyond their traditional cost-cutting to create new products to win back consumers. At stake is the economic survival of packers, Midwestern farm feedlots and hundreds of small communities dependent on livestock sales. Cowboys are being forced off the range, and millions of acres of Western grasslands are lying idle.

Exhibit 3.4 A Supply Curve for Chicken

Parts a and b of this exhibit show the quantity of chicken supplied at various prices. As the price rises, the quantity supplied increases, other things being equal. The higher price gives farmers an incentive to raise more chickens, but the rising opportunity cost of doing so limits the supply produced in response to any given price increase.

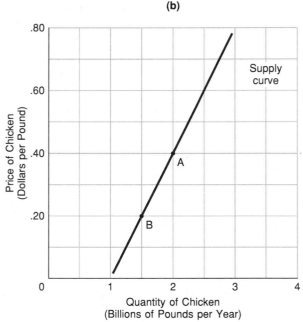

(b)

(a)

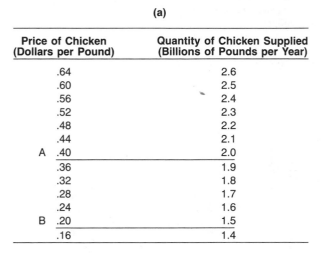

	Price of Chicken (Dollars per Pound)	Quantity of Chicken Supplied (Billions of Pounds per Year)
	.64	2.6
	.60	2.5
	.56	2.4
	.52	2.3
	.48	2.2
	.44	2.1
A	.40	2.0
	.36	1.9
	.32	1.8
	.28	1.7
	.24	1.6
B	.20	1.5
	.16	1.4

change their plans in response to a change in the price of chicken assuming that there are no changes in the prices of other goods, in production techniques, in input prices, or in any other relevant factors.

Movements along the Supply Curve

Why does the supply curve have a positive slope? Why do sellers, other things being equal, plan to supply more chicken when the price that prevails in the market is higher than they will be when the prevailing market price is lower? Microeconomics courses give a detailed discussion of what lies behind the supply curve, but a preliminary answer, based on the concept of opportunity cost, can be given here.

Part a of Exhibit 3.5 shows a production possibility frontier for chicken in an imaginary rural county. Here the most attractive alternative to raising chickens is growing tomatoes. The production possibility frontier, like those we have seen earlier, is a curve that becomes steeper as the quantity of chicken produced increases. This happens because not all farms or farmers are alike. Some, because of the nature of their land or skills, have a comparative advantage in raising chickens. As we saw in Chapter 2, this means that they can raise chickens at a relatively low opportunity cost, measured in terms of the quantity of tomatoes they would otherwise be able to grow. Other farmers have a comparative advantage in growing tomatoes. For them the opportunity cost of raising chickens is comparatively high.

Exhibit 3.5   Opportunity Cost and
the Supply of Chicken

Part a of this exhibit shows a production possibility frontier for chicken and tomatoes in a
hypothetical rural county. The slope of the frontier at any point shows the opportunity cost of
producing an additional pound of chicken measured in terms of the quantity of tomatoes
that could have been produced using the same factors of production. The frontier curves
because some operators have a comparative advantage in producing tomatoes and others a
comparative advantage in producing chicken. Because the curve gets steeper as more
chicken is produced, the opportunity cost rises, as shown in part b. The supply curve slopes
upward because in order to shift factors of production from tomatoes to chicken, an
incentive—in the form of a higher price—is needed to overcome the rising opportunity cost
of chicken.

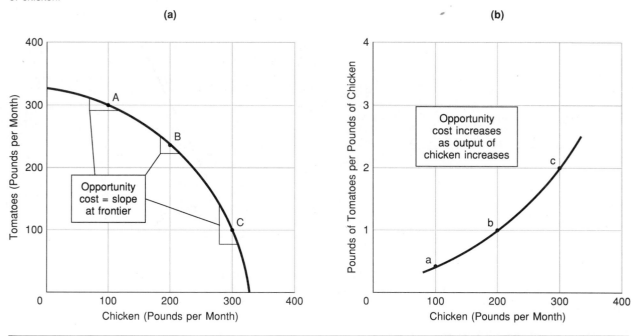

When chicken farming is introduced in the county, those operators with a
comparative advantage in raising chickens are the first to enter the market. At
point A on the frontier, for example, the opportunity cost of an additional pound
of chicken, shown by the slope of the frontier, is about a half-pound of tomatoes.
As chicken output rises, farmers further along the frontier are drawn into the
market. At point B, the opportunity cost has risen to one pound of tomatoes per
pound of chicken. To increase output still more, even those who are comparatively best at growing tomatoes will have to switch to chickens. Thus, at point C
the opportunity cost of chickens has risen to two pounds of tomatoes.

Part b of Exhibit 3.5 graphs the opportunity cost of producing an additional
pound of chicken beyond the quantity already being produced. The height of
each point (a, b, and c) on the opportunity cost curve of part b corresponds to
the slope of the frontier (at points A, B, and C) in part a. Now we can see why
the supply curve has a positive slope: The price of chicken must rise (in this
case, relative to the price of tomatoes) in order to provide the incentive needed to
draw in factors of production whose comparative advantages lie less and less
strongly in the direction of chicken raising.

Shifts in the Supply Curve

As in the case of demand, the effects of a change in the price of chicken, other things being equal, can be shown as a movement along the supply curve for chicken. This is called a **change in quantity supplied.** A change in some factor other than the price of chicken can be shown as a shift in the supply curve. This is referred to as a **change in supply.** Four sources of change in supply are worth noting. Each is related to the notion that the supply curve reflects the opportunity cost of producing the good or service in question.

Technological Change

A supply curve is drawn on the basis of a particular production technique. From time to time, changes in technology reduce opportunity costs of production. Producers will then plan to sell more of the good than before at any given price. Exhibit 3.6 shows how such an event would affect the chicken supply curve. Supply curve S_1 is the same as the one shown in Exhibit 3.4. According to S_1, farmers will plan to supply 2 billion pounds per year at a price of $.40 per pound (point A).

   Now suppose that new factory-farming techniques reduced the quantity of labor used in raising chickens. In terms of Exhibit 3.5, the technological change would stretch the production possibility frontier to the right; its intercept with the horizontal axis would move to the right but its vertical intercept would not change. The opportunity cost, which is indicated by the slope of the curve, would be lower for each given quantity of chicken. Using the new techniques, farmers would be willing to supply more chicken than before at any given price. They might, for example, be willing to supply 2.6 billion pounds of chicken at $.40 per pound (point B). The move from A to B would be part of a shift in the entire supply curve from S_1 to S_2. Once the new techniques were established, an increase or decrease in the price of chicken, other things being equal, would result in a movement along the new supply curve.

Change in quantity supplied
A change in the quantity of a good that producers are willing and able to sell that results from a change in the good's price, other things being equal; a movement along a supply curve.

Change in supply
A change in the quantity of a good that producers are willing and able to sell that results from a change in some condition other than the good's price; a shift in the supply curve.

Exhibit 3.6 Shifts in the Supply Curve for Chicken

Several kinds of changes can cause the supply of chicken to increase or decrease. For example, a new production method that lowers costs will shift the curve to the right from S_1 to S_2. An increase in the price of inputs, other things being equal, will shift the curve to the left from S_1 to S_3. Changes in sellers' expectations or in the prices of competing goods can also cause the supply curve to shift.

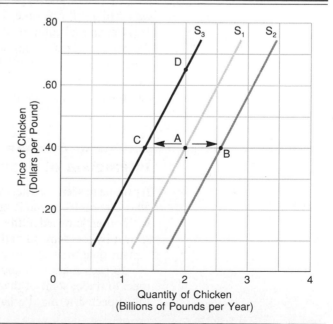

Changes in Input Prices

Changes in input prices are a second item that can cause supply curves to shift. An increase in input prices, other things being equal, raises the opportunity cost of producing the good in question and, hence, tends to reduce the quantity of it that producers plan to supply at a given price. Refer again to Exhibit 3.6. Suppose that starting from point A on supply curve S_1, the price of chicken feed increases and no other, offsetting changes occur. Now, instead of supplying 2 billion pounds of chicken at $.40 per pound, farmers will supply, say, just 1.4 billion pounds at that price (point C). The move from A to C is part of a leftward shift in the supply curve, from S_1 to S_3.

If the price of feed remains at the new level, changes in the price of chicken will cause movements along the new supply curve. For example, farmers could be induced to supply the original quantity of chicken—2 billion bushels—if the price rose enough to cover the increased cost of feed. As you can see in Exhibit 3.6, that would require the price to rise to $.64 per pound (point D).

Changes in Prices of Other Goods

Changes in the prices of other products can also produce a shift in the chicken supply curve. Suppose that the price of tomatoes rises while the price of chicken stays at $.40. If this happens, the opportunity cost of raising chickens, in terms of forgone tomato profits, increases even though there is no change in the opportunity cost measured in physical quantities. The change in the price of tomatoes thus gives farmers—even some who have only a weak comparative advantage in tomatoes—an incentive to shift from chickens to tomatoes. The effect of an increase in the price of tomatoes can thus be shown as a leftward shift in the chicken supply curve.

Changes in Expectations

Changes in expectations can cause supply curves to shift in much the same way that they cause demand curves to shift. Again we can use farming as an example. At planting time, a farmer's selection of crops is influenced not so much by current prices and opportunity costs as by the prices and opportunity costs expected at harvest time. Long-term expectations also affect supply. Each crop requires special equipment and know-how. We have just seen that an increase in the price of tomatoes gives farmers an incentive to shift from chicken to tomatoes. The incentive will be stronger if the increase in the price of tomatoes is expected to be long-lasting. If it is, farmers are more likely to buy the special equipment needed for that crop.

Interaction of Supply and Demand

As we have seen, markets transmit information, in the form of prices, to people who buy and sell goods and services. Taking these prices into account, along with other knowledge they may have, buyers and sellers make their plans. As shown by the demand and supply curves, buyers and sellers plan to buy or sell certain quantities at any given price.

In each market, many buyers and sellers make different plans. When they meet to trade, some of them may be unable to carry out their plans according to the expected terms. Perhaps the total quantity that buyers plan to purchase is greater than the total quantity suppliers are willing to sell at the given price. In that case, some would-be buyers must change their plans. Or perhaps planned sales exceed planned purchases at the given price. In that case, some would-be sellers will be unable to carry out their plans.

Sometimes no one is surprised: The total quantity buyers plan to purchase exactly matches the total quantity producers plan to sell. When buyers' and sellers' plans mesh when they meet in the marketplace, no one needs to change plans. Under these conditions, the market is said to be in **equilibrium.**

Equilibrium
A condition in which buyers' and sellers' plans exactly mesh in the marketplace so that the quantity supplied exactly equals the quantity demanded at a given price.

Market Equilibrium

Supply and demand curves, which reflect buyers' and sellers' plans, can be used to give a graphical demonstration of market equilibrium. Exhibit 3.7 uses the same supply and demand curves as before, but this time both are drawn on the same diagram. If the quantity of planned sales at each price is compared with the quantity of planned purchases at that price (either the table or the graph can be used to make the comparison), it can be seen that there is only one price at which the two sets of plans mesh. This price—$.40 per pound—is the equilibrium price. If all buyers and sellers make their plans with the expectation of a price of $.40, no one will be surprised and no plans will have to be changed.

Shortages

But what will happen if, for some reason, buyers and sellers see a price of chicken other than $.40 a pound and make their plans accordingly? Suppose, for example, that they base their plans on a price of $.20. Exhibit 3.7 shows that at a price of $.20, buyers will plan to purchase chicken at a rate of 2.5 billion pounds per year but farmers will plan to supply only 1.5 billion pounds. When the quantity demanded exceeds the quantity supplied, as in this example, the difference is an **excess quantity demanded** or, more simply, a **shortage.** In Exhibit 3.7, the shortage is 1 billion pounds of chicken per year when the price is $.20 per pound.

Shortages and Inventories

In most markets, the first sign of a shortage is a drop in **inventories,** that is, in the stocks of the good that have been produced and are waiting to be sold or used. Sellers plan to hold a certain quantity of goods in inventory to allow for minor changes in demand. When they see inventories dropping below the planned level, they change their plans. Some may try to rebuild their inventories by increasing their output, if they produce the good themselves, or by ordering more from the producer. Some sellers may take advantage of the strong demand for their product to raise its price. Many sellers will do a little of both. If sellers do not take the initiative, buyers will—they will offer to pay more if sellers will supply more. Whatever the details, the result will be an upward movement along the supply curve as price and quantity increase.

As the shortage puts upward pressure on price, buyers will change their plans too. Moving up and to the left along their demand curve, they will cut back on their planned purchases. As both buyers and sellers change their plans, the market moves toward equilibrium. When the price reaches $.40 per pound, both the shortage and the pressure to change plans will disappear.

Excess quantity demanded (shortage)
A condition in which the quantity of a good demanded at a given price exceeds the quantity supplied.

Inventory
Stocks of a finished good awaiting sale or use.

Exhibit 3.7   Equilibrium in the Chicken Market

Parts a and b of this exhibit show the same supply and demand curves for chicken presented earlier. The demand curve shows how much buyers plan to purchase at a given price. The supply curve shows how much producers plan to sell at a given price. At only one price—$.40 per pound—do buyers' and sellers' plans exactly match: the equilibrium price. A higher price causes a surplus of chicken and puts downward pressure on price. A lower price causes a shortage and puts upward pressure on price.

(a)

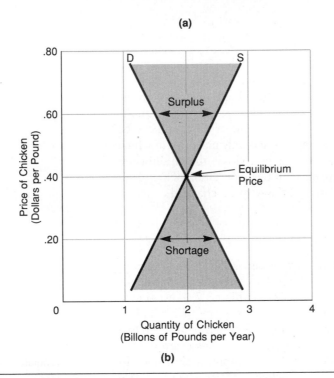

Quantity of Chicken
(Billons of Pounds per Year)

(b)

Price per Pound (1)	Quantity Supplied (Billions of Pounds) (2)	Quantity Demanded (Billions of Pounds) (3)	Shortage (Billions of Pounds) (4)	Surplus (Billions of Pounds) (5)	Direction of Pressure on Price (6)
.64	2.6	1.4	—	1.2	Downward
.60	2.5	1.5	—	1.0	Downward
.56	2.4	1.6	—	0.8	Downward
.52	2.3	1.7	—	0.6	Downward
.48	2.2	1.8	—	0.4	Downward
.44	2.1	1.9	—	0.2	Downward
.40	2.0	2.0	—	—	Equilibrium
.36	1.9	2.1	0.2	—	Upward
.32	1.8	2.2	0.4	—	Upward
.28	1.7	2.3	0.6	—	Upward
.24	1.6	2.4	0.8	—	Upward
.20	1.5	2.5	1.0	—	Upward
.16	1.4	2.6	1.2	—	Upward

Shortages and Queues

In the markets for most goods, sellers have inventories of goods ready to be sold. There are exceptions, however. Inventories are not possible in markets for services—haircuts, tax preparation, lawn care, and the like. Also, some goods, such as custom-built houses and machine tools tailored to a specialized need, are not held in inventories. Sellers in these markets do not begin production until they have a contract with a buyer.

In markets in which there are no inventories, the sign of a shortage is a "queue" of buyers. The queue may take the form of a line of people waiting to be served or a list of names in an order book. The queue is a sign that buyers would like to purchase the good at a faster rate than producers have planned to supply it. However, some plans cannot be carried out—at least not right away. Buyers are served on a first-come, first-served basis.

The formation of a queue of buyers has much the same effect on the market as a fall in inventories. Sellers react by increasing their rate of output, raising their prices, or both. Buyers react to the rising price by reducing the quantity they plan to purchase. The result is a movement up and to the right along the supply curve and, at the same time, up and to the left along the demand curve until equilibrium is reached.

Surpluses

Now suppose that for some reason buyers and sellers see a price of chicken that is higher than the equilibrium price—say, $.60 per pound—and base their plans accordingly. Exhibit 3.7 shows that farmers will plan to supply 2.5 billion pounds of chicken per year at $.60, but their customers will plan to buy only 1.5 billion pounds. When the quantity supplied exceeds the quantity demanded, there is an **excess quantity supplied,** or a **surplus.** As Exhibit 3.7 shows, the surplus of chicken at a price of $.60 per pound is 1 billion pounds per year.

Surpluses and Inventories

When there is a surplus of a product, sellers will be unable to sell all they had hoped at the planned price. As a result, their inventories will begin to grow beyond the level they had planned to hold in preparation for normal changes in demand. Sellers will react to the inventory buildup by changing their plans. Some will cut back their output. Others will cut their prices in order to reduce their extra stock. Still others will do a little of both. The result of these changes in plans will be a movement down and to the left along the supply curve.

As unplanned inventory buildup puts downward pressure on the price, buyers change their plans too. Finding that chicken costs less than they had expected, they buy more of it. This is shown as a movement down and to the right along the demand curve. As this happens, the market will be restored to equilibrium.

Surpluses and Queues

In markets in which there are no inventories, surpluses lead to the formation of queues of sellers looking for customers. Taxi queues at airports are a case in point. At least at some times of the day, the fare for taxi service from the airport to downtown is more than enough to attract a number of taxis equal to the demand. In some cities, drivers who are far back in the queue try to attract riders with offers of cut-rate fares. More often, though, there are rules against fare cutting. The queue then grows until a surge of business shortens it again.

Excess quantity supplied (surplus)
A condition in which the quantity of a good supplied at a given price exceeds the quantity demanded.

Changes in Market Conditions

On a graph, equilibrium looks like an easy target. In real life, however, it is a moving target. Market conditions—all the items that lie behind the other-things-being-equal contingency—change frequently. When they do, both buyers and sellers must revise their plans as the point of equilibrium shifts.

Response to a Shift in Demand

Let's first consider a market's response to a shift in demand. The decline in demand for beef described in "Economics in the News 3.1" (page 58) provides a good example. Exhibit 3.8 interprets this case in terms of the supply and demand model. As the figure is drawn, the market initially is in equilibrium at E_1. There the price is $.50 per pound (quoted on a live-weight basis as at stockyard auctions) and the quantity produced is 25 billion pounds per year. Now the changed dietary habits of U.S. consumers cause the demand curve to shift to the left from D_1 to D_2. This is a *shift* in the demand curve, because it is caused by a change in tastes—one of the things covered by the other-things-being-equal assumption that lies behind the curve. What will happen next?

If the price does not change—that is, if it remains at $.50 per pound—there will be a surplus of beef. The supply curve indicates that at that price, ranchers will plan to produce 25 billion pounds per year. However, according to the new demand curve, D_2, consumers will no longer buy that much beef at $.50 per pound. Instead, given their new tastes, they will buy only 15 billion pounds at that price.

However, the price does *not* stay at $.50. As soon as the demand curve begins to shift and the surplus starts to develop, beef inventories rise above their planned levels, putting downward pressure on the price. As the price falls, ranchers revise their plans. They move down and to the left along their supply curve, reducing the quantity supplied as the price drops. This is a *movement*

Exhibit 3.8   Effects of a Decrease in Demand for Beef

This exhibit shows the effects of a decrease in demand for beef caused by a shift in tastes away from high-cholesterol foods. Initially the market is in equilibrium at E_1. The change in tastes causes a shift in the demand curve. At the original equilibrium price of $.50 per pound, there is a temporary surplus of beef. This causes inventories to start to rise and puts downward pressure on the price. As the price falls, producers move down along their supply curve, as shown by the arrow, to a new equilibrium at E_2. There both the price and quantity of beef are lower than before the shift in demand.

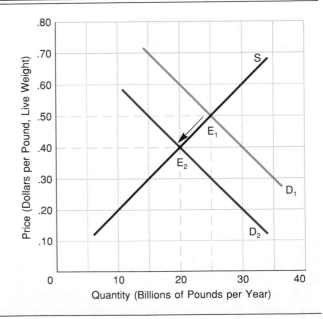

along the supply curve, not a shift, because the ranchers are responding to a change in the price of beef. Nothing has happened, as far as we know, to change the other-things-being-equal conditions, such as technology, input prices, and so on. Thus, nothing has happened to cause the supply curve to shift.

As ranchers move down along their supply curve in the direction shown by the arrow in Exhibit 3.8, they eventually reach point E_2, where their plans again mesh with those of consumers. At this point, the price has fallen to $.40 per pound and production to 20 million pounds. Although health-conscious consumers would not have bought that much beef at the old price, they will do so at the new, lower price. E_2 is thus the new equilibrium.

Entrepreneurship and Equilibrium

If producers reacted passively to changes in market conditions, this would be the end of the story. As "Economics in the News 3.1" relates, however, cattle producers are not passive folks. They are not happy with the change in market conditions, so they fight back. Rhonda Miller, for example, fought back by trying to invent a better steak that would be both lean and tender. Other examples of new beef products are precooked London broil, premixed meatloaf, and pastrami packed in individual foil pouches. These are *entrepreneurial* responses to the decline in demand for beef. By developing new products and creating new opportunities, beef industry entrepreneurs hope to change consumer tastes back in favor of beef. If successful, they will push the demand curve back to the right. As demand rises, the price will rise and producers will be able to move back up along their supply curve.

The constant activity of entrepreneurs keeps economics from being a ho-hum exercise in curve pushing. Supply and demand analysis gives us a way to describe what entrepreneurs are trying to do. In this case, they are attempting to stimulate demand by developing new beef products. In another case, they might be trying to push costs down, thus shifting the supply curve. Supply and demand analysis also gives us a way to make conditional predictions of markets' reactions to changes brought about by entrepreneurs in the same way that it allows us to predict changes effected by forces beyond their control. In this case, the reaction to a shift of the demand curve back to the right would be more beef produced and a higher price. But supply and demand analysis cannot predict exactly what entrepreneurs will try next or whether they will succeed. The only thing we can be certain about in a market economy is that the future will bring surprises—new ways of doing things that no one has ever thought of before.

Applications of Supply and Demand

In the study of economics—both macro and micro—we will encounter a great many applications of supply and demand. While each situation is unique, each to some extent draws on ideas developed in this chapter. This section gives only an inkling of the possible range of applications.

Changing Market Conditions: The Case of Dentists

The examples given so far in this chapter concern markets for goods, but the same tools apply to markets for services. In this case, we look at the market for dental services. As "Economics in the News 3.2" tells us, this market has under-

ECONOMICS IN THE NEWS   3.2

What's Good for America Isn't Necessarily Good for the Dentists

When Dr. Murray Helfman set up his practice 25 years ago, fortune seemed to smile on him. Dentistry, which began as a sideline for barbers, had become a respected profession. Rich-dentist jokes were the rage. By the early 1970s dentists' incomes were finally approaching those of physicians.

But after a quarter-century in practice, Helfman, who lives in Rochester, New York, is hardly a rich man. He doesn't drive a Mercedes and owns no country home. If his wife didn't help out by managing his office, he would have trouble making ends meet. He moans: "I have three kids in college and a house that I couldn't afford to live in if I hadn't bought it 13 years ago."

The American Dental Association claims the average dentist nets $59,530 a year, but that average covers a lot of grief. Adjusted for inflation, this figure has been shrinking since it peaked some dozen years ago. Dentists' real net incomes are no higher now, on average, than they were in the early 1960s.

The problems are particularly intense among younger practitioners. Older dentists went into business when demand was rising and entry costs were relatively low, but consider the obstacles that confront a dentist starting out in the world. Four years in a decent dental school can easily cost $50,000. And unless Daddy is affluent, that's all debt.

Then try to set up a practice. The expenses are astronomical. Operating room equipment will run about $24,000; office supplies and reception area, $10,000; a modern X-ray machine, $5,000. Add the incidentals, and today, an average office costs something like $60,000.

In all this, the federal bureaucracy has, as usual, done the wrong things. In the late 1960s federal officials decided Americans were getting inadequate dental care, and the government began spending to encourage dental education. Old dental schools expanded, while new ones opened. The result was too many dentists.

On top of this, there are fewer patients coming through the door. Are Americans neglecting their teeth? Hardly. The basic difficulty is simple. Cavity-filling has always been the bread-and-butter business for most dentists. But cavities are going the way of smallpox and polio in the United States. Tooth decay has declined by about 50 percent since the mid-1960s. According to the ADA, one out of three people of college age has never had a cavity. Army dentists, who see a cross section of society, used to tell horror stories about mouths full of rotten teeth. Now they see lots of cavity-free mouths. The reason for this? Better nutrition, for one thing. And fluoridation of drinking water is an even bigger factor.

For many dentists, then, the dream of affluence is fading. Instead of a BMW, a Toyota. Instead of striving for wealth, many young dentists now settle for the security of salaried dentistry. Says Dr. Thomas Ciuchta, a 20-year-old Temple University School of Dentistry graduate: "I see friends who have their own practices sitting idle two days a week with their expenses building up. I like the security of knowing exactly what I'm making."

Ciuchta gets his regular paycheck from a clinic called Dentalworks located in the Hess's department store in Allentown, Pennsylvania. At such facilities, which are often franchises owned by nondentists, 40-hour weeks, including Saturdays, are the rule and starting salaries are often under $30,000.

Source: Richard Greene, "What's Good for America Isn't Necessarily Good for the Dentists," *Forbes*, August 13, 1984, 79–84.

---

gone major changes in recent years. Let's see how this story looks when told in terms of the supply and demand model.

A Shift in Supply
According to the news item in "Economics in the News 3.2," the late 1960s saw government encouragement of dental school expansion. The effect can be represented as a rightward shift of the supply curve for dentists as shown in part a of Exhibit 3.9. The supply curve shifts because students were willing to fill the new vacancies in dental schools and thus add to the supply of dental services *given* dentists' prevailing earnings—$40,000 per year in 1967 dollars, as the figure is

Exhibit 3.9   Changing Conditions in the
Market for Dental Services

This exhibit shows the impact on the market for dental services of two changes in market
conditions. Part a shows the effect of government efforts to increase the number of students
going to dental school. This action shifts the supply curve to the right and, by itself, would
move the market from E_1 to E_2. At the same time this government policy is increasing the
supply of dentists, however, improvements in dental health are reducing the demand for
their services. The effect of the improvement in dental health is shown as a shift in the
demand curve in part b. Taking the changes in both educational policy and dental health
into account, the market moves to a new equilibrium at E_3, where S_2 and D_2 intersect. Had
the demand shift occurred with no change in policy regarding dental schools, the market
would have moved to E_4, where D_2 intersects S_1.

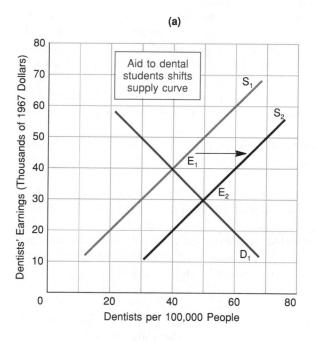

(a)

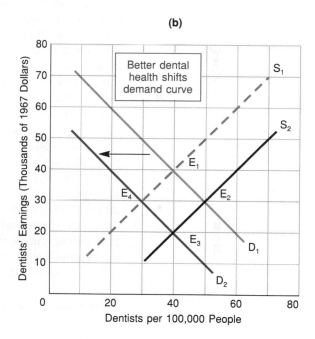

(b)

drawn. By itself the expansion of dental schools would have been sufficient to
create a surplus of dentists. The surplus would have put downward pressure on
dentists' earnings. As earnings fell, other things being equal, the market would
have reached a new equilibrium at E_2, where supply curve S_2 intersects demand
curve D_1.

Compare part a of Exhibit 3.9 with Exhibit 3.8. In Exhibit 3.8, which shows
the market for beef, a fall in price is caused by a shift in the demand curve. The

market moves along its supply curve to a point at which both the equilibrium price and quantity are lower. In part a of Exhibit 3.9, the fall in dentists' earnings is caused by a shift in the supply curve. The market moves along demand curve D_1 to point E_2, where the equilibrium price is lower and the equilibrium quantity is greater.

Adding a Shift in Demand

If the world were run for the convenience of economics professors and their students, things would happen one at a time. A market would be hit with either a shift in demand or a shift in supply, thus keeping diagrams tidy. But reality is far less cooperative. In the case of dental services, as "Economics in the News 3.2" makes clear, the expansion of dental schools was only part of the story. In addition, at the same time dental schools were expanding, there was an improvement in dental health that acted on the demand side of the market. Because people were suffering fewer cavities, they tended to make fewer visits to the dentist at any given price. This improvement in dental health can be represented by a leftward shift in the demand curve as shown in part b of Exhibit 3.9. This shift in the demand curve increased the surplus of dentists and added to the downward pressure on price. Together the two changes in market conditions moved the equilibrium point to E_3. Dental earnings fell by more than they would have as a result of dental school expansion alone.

Exhibit 3.9 shows that supply and demand analysis can be applied to complex changes in market conditions where more than one thing happens at once. The key to considering such cases—which are common in the real world—is to break things down into those forces that act on the supply side of the market and those that act on the demand side. In this case, the dental school expansion shifted the supply curve because more students were then willing and able to train to become dentists at any given earnings level. With no change in the incidence of cavities, this alone would have moved the market to E_2. At the same time, the improvement in dental health shifted the demand curve to the left. Had dental schools not expanded, this alone would have depressed earnings, moving the market to E_4, where S_1 intersects D_2. Taken together, however, the two shifts moved the market to E_3, where S_2 and D_2 intersect.

Entrepreneurial Reactions

Before leaving the market for dental services, it is worth noting that here, as in the case of the market for beef, there were entrepreneurial responses to changing market conditions. Dentists did not react passively, simply dropping their prices and continuing the same old style of solo practice. Instead, they tried to attract new customers by such means as setting up dental clinics in shopping centers. These "doc-in-a-box" clinics have attracted many patients who never—or rarely—made the effort to make appointments in traditional dental offices. The innovations in dental services moderated the decline in demand caused by fluoridation, better nutrition, and so on.

Price Supports: The Market for Milk

In our earlier example of the market for beef, a decrease in demand caused a surplus, which in turn caused the price to drop until the surplus was eliminated. Markets are not always left free to respond to prices in this manner, however. A case in point is the market for milk.

Exhibit 3.10 shows the market for milk in terms of supply and demand curves. Suppose that initially the market is in equilibrium at point E_1. The wholesale price of milk is $13 per hundredweight, and production is 110 million hundredweight per year. A trend in taste away from high-cholesterol foods—the same trend that hit the market for beef—then shifts the demand curve for milk to the left. As in the case of beef, the result is a surplus, as shown by the arrow in Exhibit 3.10.

Here, however, the similarity between the beef and milk markets ends. In the beef market prices are free to fall in response to a surplus, but in the milk market they are not. Instead, an elaborate set of government controls and subsidies sets a support price for milk. As the exhibit is drawn, the government agrees to pay $13 per hundredweight for all milk that cannot be sold at that price on the open market. With the demand curve in position D_1, there is no surplus; thus, the government need not buy any milk. But with the demand curve in position D_2, there is a surplus of 40 million hundredweight per year. Under the price support law, the government must buy this surplus and store it in the form of cheese, butter, and other products with long shelf lives. Over the years, the government has accumulated vast stores of such products at a cost of billions of dollars. Dairy farmers have been happy to sell the extra milk, but the cost to consumers and taxpayers has been high.

Without price supports, the shift in demand would cause the price of milk to fall to the new equilibrium price of $10 per hundredweight. But when price supports are applied to a product at a level higher than the equilibrium price, the result is a lasting surplus condition. This happens because the support price sends conflicting messages to consumers and producers. To consumers the $13 price says, "Milk is scarce. Its opportunity cost is high. Hold your consumption down." To producers it says, "All is well. Incentives are unchanged. Feel free to continue using scarce factors to produce milk." A drop in the price to $10 would send a different set of messages. Consumers would hear, "Milk is cheaper and

Exhibit 3.10 Price Supports for Milk

Suppose that initially the market for milk is in equilibrium at E_1. A shift in tastes away from high-cholesterol foods then shifts the demand curve to D_2. If the price were free to fall, there would be a temporary surplus that would push the price down to a new equilibrium at $10 per hundredweight. In practice, the government maintains a system of price supports for milk at a level shown here as $13 per hundredweight. Because the price cannot fall, the surplus is permanent. The government must buy the surplus milk, in the form of butter and cheese, in order to keep the price from falling.

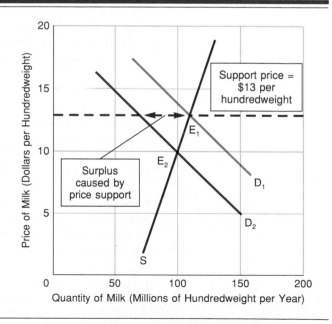

more abundant. Although it is not cholesterol free, you might consider drinking more of it.'' Producers would hear, ''The milk market isn't what it once was. Look at your opportunity costs. Is there perhaps some better use for your labor, capital, and natural resources?''

From time to time, the government has tried to eliminate the milk surplus by shifting the supply curve to the left so that it would intersect the demand curve at the support price. In recent years, for example, dairy farmers have been encouraged to sell their cows for beef, thus reducing the size of their herds. But these programs have failed to eliminate the milk surplus. The chief reason has been dairy farmers' entrepreneurial response to the high price of milk. In particular, the government's efforts to cut herd size have been largely offset by increased output per cow as a result of genetic improvement and better farm management practices. Thus, the government's vast stocks of butter and cheese continue to grow.

Price Ceilings: The Case of Rent Control

In the milk market, the government maintains a support price that is above the equilibrium price. In other markets, a price ceiling that is below the equilibrium price is maintained. An example of this type of market intervention is rent control in housing markets.

Rent control in one form or another exists in several major U.S. cities, including New York, Washington, D.C., San Francisco, and Los Angeles. The controls vary across cities, but the essential common feature—at least for some categories of apartments—is that maximum rents are established by law. In all cases, the purpose is to aid tenants by preventing landlords from charging ''unreasonably'' high rents. What is unreasonably high is determined by the relative political strengths of landlords and tenants rather than by supply and demand.

Intended Effects

Exhibit 3.11 interprets the effects of rent control in terms of supply and demand. For simplicity, it is assumed that the rental housing stock consists of units of equal size and rental value. Part a of the figure shows the effects of rent control in the short run. Here the short run means a period of time that is too short to permit significant increases or decreases in the stock of rental housing; thus, the short-run supply curve is a vertical line.

Under the conditions shown, the equilibrium rent per standard housing unit is $500 per month on each of the 100,000 units in the city. A rent ceiling of $250 is then imposed. This results in a gain to tenants of $250 per unit per month, or $25 million per month in total, and an equal loss to landlords. This sum is shown by the shaded rectangle. The benefit to tenants at the expense of landlords is the principal intended consequence of rent control.

Unintended Short-Run Effects

Rent control, like many government policies, has unintended as well as intended effects. In the short run, when the stock of apartments is fixed, the unintended consequences stem from the apartment shortage created by the controls. The shortage occurs because the quantity demanded is greater at the lower ceiling price than at the higher equilibrium price.

The increased quantity demanded has several sources. First, people who would otherwise own a house or condominium may now want to rent. Second,

Exhibit 3.11   Effects of Rent Control

Part a shows the short-run effects of rent control. In the short run, the supply of rental apartments is considered to be fixed. The equilibrium rent is $500 per month. A rent ceiling of $250 per month is then put into effect. One possible outcome is that landlords will charge disguised rent increases, raising the true price back to $500 per month. If such disguised increases are prohibited, there will be a shortage of 50,000 units at the ceiling price. Part b shows the long-run effects when there is time to adjust the number of units in response to the price. If the ceiling price is enforced, landlords move down their supply curve to E_2. The shortage then becomes even more severe than in the short run.

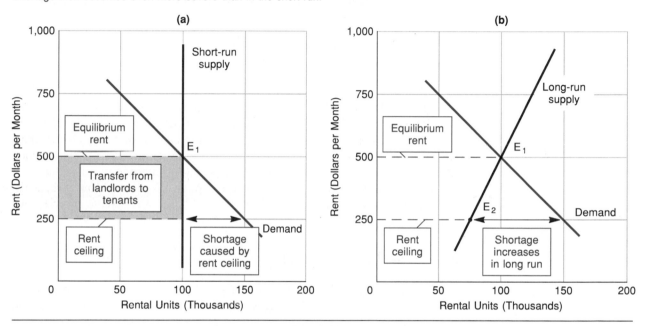

people who would otherwise live in noncontrolled suburbs may now seek rental units in the city. Third, each tenant may want more space, which means a demand for more of the standardized units shown in Exhibit 3.11.

The shortage creates a problem for both landlords and tenants: How will the limited supply of apartments be rationed among those who want them? Both landlords and tenants devise a number of creative—or, as an economist would say, entrepreneurial—responses.

One response on the part of landlords is to seek disguised rent increases. These may take the form of large, nonrefundable "key deposits" or security deposits. Alternatively, they may take the form of selling old, used furniture or drapes at high prices as a condition for renting apartments. Finally, certain maintenance or security services for which landlords might otherwise have paid may be transferred to tenants.

Tenants too may get into the act. When they decide to move, they may sublet their apartments to other tenants rather than give up their leases. Now it is the tenant who collects the key money or sells the old drapes to the subtenant. The original tenant may have moved to a distant city but maintains a bank account and a post office box for use in paying the rent. The subtenant is instructed to play the role of a "guest" if the landlord telephones. The charade may get very elaborate and go on for decades in cities such as New York, where rent control is a long-established tradition.

Rent control advocates view these responses as cheating and often try to outlaw them. If prohibitions are enforced, the landlord will face many applicants for each vacant apartment. In that case, the landlord must decide to whom to give the apartment. In his book *Rent Control: The Perennial Folly,* Charles W. Baird describes the effects in these terms:

> People with unconventional life styles will be told to look elsewhere. Families without children will be favored over families with children. Tenants without pets will be favored over tenants with pets. . . . Families whose heads have histories of steady employment will be favored over families whose heads are just beginning employment or frequently change jobs. Landlords know from experience that people with steady employment histories tend to be more dependable in paying their bills.

If a landlord has two applicants for a vacancy who are alike as far as family and job considerations are concerned, he or she will tend to pick the applicant whose noneconomic characteristics—for example, race or religion—are most appealing. The other applicants will be put on the waiting list and sent to look elsewhere. People who make decisions based solely on economic considerations are often accused of being crass, materialistic, and uncaring. However, when people are forbidden to make decisions on the basis of economic criteria, they may well use other criteria that are even more uncharitable.[1]

Unintended Long-Run Effects

In the long run, rent control has other unintended effects. The long run in this case means enough time for the stock of rental units to grow through construction of new units or shrink through abandonment of old ones or their conversion to condominiums. Other things being equal, the higher the rent, the greater the rate of construction, and the lower the rent, the greater the rate of abandonment and/or conversion. This is reflected in the positively sloped long-run supply curve in part b of Exhibit 3.11.

If rent controls are enforced so that there are no disguised charges, the stock of rental units shrinks and the market moves from E_1 to E_2. At E_2, the unintended effects that appeared in the short run become more pronounced. The number of people subject to housing discrimination increases relative to the short-run case. The number of people potentially subject to discrimination equals the difference between the number of units available and the number sought by renters. Graphically, this is the horizontal gap between the supply and demand curves at the ceiling price. In the short run, there was a shortage of 50,000 units; in the long run, this increases to 75,000 units.

Rent controls are often defended as being beneficial to the poor. But when all of the unintended effects of rent control are taken into account, it seems questionable whether poor families really benefit. In cases where disguised rent increases are possible, the true cost of rental housing is not really decreased. Further, it is hard to believe that landlords' tendency to discriminate against minority group members, single-parent families, and tenants with irregular

---

[1] Charles W. Baird, *Rent Control: The Perennial Folly* (Washington, D.C.: The Cato Institute, 1980), 60–61.

work histories will benefit the poor. The most likely beneficiaries of rent control are stable, middle-class families who work at the same jobs and live in the same apartments for long periods.

Looking Ahead

As the great economist Alfred Marshall once put it, nearly all of the major economics problems have a "kernel" that reflects the workings of supply and demand (see "Who Said It? Who Did It? 3.1"). This chapter covered the basics of the supply and demand model and illustrated it with some applications. Many more applications will be found in both the macro- and microeconomics courses. In macroeconomics, the supply and demand model is applied to financial markets, labor markets, and the problem of determining the rates of inflation and real output for the economy as a whole. In microeconomics, the model is applied to product markets, factor markets, and policy issues ranging from pollution to farm policy to international trade.

A detailed look at the underpinnings of the model in the microeconomics course will show that the model fits some kinds of markets more closely than

---

WHO SAID IT? WHO DID IT?   3.1

Alfred Marshall on Supply and Demand

Alfred Marshall, considered by many the greatest economist of his day, was born in London in 1842. His father was a Bank of England cashier who hoped the boy would enter the ministry. Young Marshall had other ideas, however. He turned down a theological scholarship at Oxford to study mathematics. He received an M.A. in mathematics from Cambridge in 1865.

While at Cambridge, he joined a philosophical discussion group. There he became interested in promoting the broad development of the human mind. He was soon told, however, that the harsh realities of economics would prevent his ideas from being carried out. Britain's productive resources, it was said, could never allow the masses sufficient leisure for education. This disillusioning episode appears to have triggered Marshall's fascination with economics.

Photo Source: The Granger Collection, New York.

At the time, British economics was dominated by the classical school founded by Smith and Ricardo. Marshall had great respect for the classical writers. Initially he saw his own work as a simple application of his mathematical training to strengthen and systematize the classical system. Before long, however, he was breaking new ground and developing a system of his own. By 1890, when he brought out his famous *Principles of Economics*, he had laid the foundation of what we now call the *neoclassical* school.

In an attempt to explain the essence of his approach, Marshall included this passage in the second edition of *Principles:*

> In spite of a great variety in detail, nearly all the chief problems of economics agree in that they have a kernel of the same kind. This kernel is an inquiry as to the balancing of two opposed classes of motives, the one consisting of desires to acquire certain new goods, and thus satisfy wants; while the other consists of desires to avoid certain efforts or retain certain immediate enjoyment . . . in other words, it is an inquiry into the balancing of the forces of demand and supply.

Marshall's influence on economics—at least in the English-speaking world—was enormous. His *Principles* was the leading text for decades, and today's student can still learn much from reading it. As a professor at Cambridge, Marshall taught a great many of the next generation's leading economists. Today his neoclassical school continues to dominate the profession. It has received many challenges but so far has weathered them all.

others. The fit is best for markets in which there are many producers and many customers, the goods sold by one producer are much like those sold by others, and all sellers and buyers have good information on market conditions. Markets for farm commodities, such as wheat and corn, and financial markets, such as the New York Stock Exchange, are examples that meet these standards. However, even in markets that do not display all of these features, the fit is often close enough to enable the supply and demand model to provide useful insights into what is going on. Thus, the supply and demand model serves a precise analytical function in some cases (for example, the supply of and demand for wheat) and a broader, metaphorical function in others (such as the supply of and demand for clean air). It is this flexibility that makes the model one of the most useful items in the economist's tool kit.

Summary

1. **How does the price of a good or service affect the quantity of it that buyers demand?** According to the *law of demand*, in any market, other things being equal, the quantity of a good that buyers demand tends to rise as the price falls and to fall as the price rises. For any given market, the law of demand sets up a one-to-one relationship between price and quantity demanded. This relationship can be shown by a downward-sloping *demand curve*.

2. **How do other market conditions affect demand?** A change in any of the items covered by the other-things-being-equal clause of the law of demand causes a shift in the demand curve, known as a *change in demand*. Examples include changes in the prices of goods that are *substitutes* or *complements* of the given good; changes in consumer incomes; changes in expectations; and changes in tastes.

3. **How are the quantities of goods and services supplied by producers affected by prices and other market conditions?** In most markets, an increase in the price of a good will increase the quantity that producers are willing to supply. This relationship can be shown as an upward-sloping *supply curve*. The higher price gives producers an incentive to supply more, but rising opportunity costs set a limit on the amount they will supply at any given price. A change in any of the items covered by the other-things-being-equal assumption underlying the supply curve will shift the curve. Examples include changes in technology, in input prices, in the prices of other goods that could be produced with the same factors of production, and in expectations.

4. **How do supply and demand interact to determine the market price of a good or service?** In a market with an upward-sloping supply curve and a downward-sloping demand curve, there is only one price at which the quantity that producers plan to supply will exactly match the quantity that buyers plan to purchase. This is known as the *equilibrium* price. At any higher price there will be a *surplus* and at any lower price a *shortage*.

5. **Why do market prices and quantities change in response to changes in a variety of market conditions?** A change in any market condition that shifts the supply or demand curve will change the equilibrium price and quantity in that market. For example, the demand curve may shift to the right as the result of a change in consumers' incomes. This causes a shortage at the old price, and the price begins to rise. As the price rises, suppliers move up along the supply curve to a new equilibrium. Alternatively, better technology may shift the supply curve to the right. In that case, there is a surplus at the old price and the price starts to fall. As it does, buyers will move down along their demand curve to a new equilibrium.

6. **How do price supports and price ceilings affect the operation of markets?** A price support prevents the market price from falling when the demand curve shifts to the left or the supply curve shifts to the right. The result is a permanent surplus. The government may have to buy and store the surplus to maintain the price, as in the case of milk. A price ceiling prevents the price from rising to its equilibrium level. The result is a permanent shortage. The total quantity supplied will be less than buyers would like to purchase at the ceiling price or even at the equilibrium price.

Terms for Review

- law of demand
- demand curve
- change in quantity demanded
- change in demand
- substitutes
- complements
- normal good
- inferior good
- supply curve
- change in quantity supplied
- change in supply
- equilibrium
- excess quantity demanded (shortage)
- inventory
- excess quantity supplied (surplus)

Questions for Review

1. How does the concept of demand differ from the concepts of want and need?

2. What conditions are covered by the "other-things-being-equal" clause in the law of demand? What effect does a change in any of these conditions have on buyers' plans?

3. Using an example from agriculture or industry, explain why we normally expect the supply curve for a good to slope upward. Give examples, other than those used in the text, of events that can cause a supply curve to shift.

4. How do inventories put upward or downward pressure on prices when markets are not in equilibrium? How is equilibrium restored in markets in which there are no inventories of finished goods?

5. Describe each of the following in terms of shifts in or movements along supply and demand curves: (a) a market's reaction to a shift in supply; (b) a market's reaction to a shift in demand.

6. Will a price support that is lower than the equilibrium price lead to a surplus, a shortage, or neither? What about a price ceiling that is higher than the equilibrium price?

Problems and Topics for Discussion

1. **Examining the lead-off case.** Make a sketch of the markets for CZs and diamonds. You know the approximate equilibrium price and quantity from the opening case in this chapter, but you must guess at the slopes of the demand and supply curves. Do you think the demand curves for these goods slope downward in the usual way? Why or why not? Do you think the supply curves slope upward? Why or why not?

Now suppose there is a breakthrough in mining technology that lowers the cost of producing natural diamonds. Use your diagram to show what will happen in the diamond market. Will the supply curve shift? Will the demand curve shift? Will the new equilibrium price be higher or lower than the original price? What about the new equilibrium quantity? What will happen in the CZ market? Will the supply curve, the demand curve, or both shift? In which direction will the equilibrium price and quantity of CZs move?

2. **A shifting demand curve.** A vending machine company has studied the demand for soft drinks sold in cans from machines. Consumers in the firm's territory will buy about 2,000 cans of soda at a price of $.50 on a 70-degree day. For each $.05 rise in price, the quantity sold falls by 200 cans per day; for each 5-degree rise in the temperature, the quantity sold rises by 150 cans per day. The same relationships hold for decreases in price or temperature. Using this information, draw a set of curves showing the demand for soft drinks on days when the temperature is 60, 70, and 85 degrees.

3. **Demand and the relative price of motor fuel.** In 1979 and 1980, the nominal price of motor fuel rose more rapidly than the general price level, pushing up the relative price of motor fuel. As we would expect, the quantity sold decreased. In 1981 and 1982, the relative price leveled off and then began to fall; however, the quantity sold did not increase but continued to fall. Which one or more of the following hypotheses do you think best explains the behavior of motor fuel sales in 1981 and 1982? Illustrate each hypothesis with supply and demand curves.

   a. In the 1970s, the demand curve had the usual downward slope. However, in 1981 and 1982, the demand curve shifted to an unusual upward-sloping position.

   b. The demand curve sloped downward throughout the period. However, the recession of 1981 and 1982 reduced consumers' real incomes and shifted the demand curve.

   c. The demand curve has a downward slope at all times, but the shape depends partly on how long consumers have to adjust to a change in prices. Over a short period, the demand curve is fairly steep because few adjustments can be made. Over the long term, it has a somewhat flatter slope because further adjustments, such as buying more fuel-efficient cars or moving closer to work, can be made. Thus, the decreases in fuel sales in 1981 and 1982 were delayed reactions to the 1979 and 1980 price increases.

4. **Shortages, price controls, and queues.** In 1974 and again in 1979, shortages in the world oil market caused long lines of motorists to form at gas stations in the United States but not in European countries. Do you think this had anything to do with the fact that the United States had price controls on gasoline but European countries did not? Back up your reasoning with supply and demand curves.

5. **Eliminating queues through flexible pricing.** You are a member of the Metropolitan Taxi Commission, which sets taxi fares for your city. You have been told that long lines of taxis form at the airport during off-peak hours. At rush hours, on the other hand, few taxis are available and there are long lines of passengers waiting for cabs. It is proposed that taxi fares from the airport to downtown be cut by 10 percent during off-peak hours and raised by 10 percent during rush hours. How do you think these changes would affect the queuing patterns of taxis and passengers? Do you think the proposal is a good one from the pas-

sengers' point of view? From the cabbies' point of view? From the standpoint of efficiency? Discuss.

6. **Rent control.** Turn to part b of Exhibit 3.11 (page 73), which shows the long-run effects of rent control. If the controls are enforced and there are no disguised rent charges, landlords move down the supply curve to E_2. Buildings are abandoned or converted because of the low rent they bring in. Now consider some alternative possibilities:

    a. Suppose the controls are poorly enforced so that landlords, through key deposits, furniture sales, or some other means, are able to charge as much as the market will bear. What will be the resulting equilibrium price and quantity taking both open and disguised rental charges into account?

    b. Now suppose the controls are enforced against landlords so that they really cannot collect more than $250 per month. However, the controls are not enforced against tenants who sublet. What will be the equilibrium quantity and the equilibrium price, including both the rent paid to landlords and the disguised rental payments made by subtenants to their sublessors?

Case for Discussion
Good News and Bad News for the Coal Industry

There is good news and bad news for the coal industry. The bad news is that the drop in oil prices has sent coal prices into a tailspin. The good news is that given time, new technology is on the way that could make coal more competitive with oil than ever in the electric utility market.

First the bad news. After 1970, the U.S. coal industry rode high. It can thank OPEC for that. For a quarter of a century after World War II, coal prices hovered around $5 per ton. After 1970, when OPEC came to power, coal prices rose in tandem with oil prices, peaking at $28. But now oil prices are dropping. Switching back to oil has already begun. In April 1986, when electric power production rose more than 1 percent, the quantity of coal burned went down more than 5 percent.

Coal miners checking in after a shift.

Now the good news. A big barrier to selling more coal to electric utilities is the pollution that results when coal is burned. Adding stack scrubbers to remove the pollution is so expensive that many utilities use oil instead. Now a new technology is on the horizon: fluidized bed combustion of coal. This improvement in the technology of burning coal to generate electricity could make the cost of burning coal less than that of burning oil for many utilities, even if oil prices stay low.

Source: James Cook, "Coal Comfort," *Forbes*, August 11, 1986, 62–63. Excerpted by permission of *Forbes* magazine. © Forbes Inc., 1986. Photo Source: Russell Lee, 1946. Records of the Solid Fuels Administration for War.

Questions

1. Are coal and oil complements or substitutes? How can you tell from this article?

2. Draw a supply and demand diagram showing the effect on the coal market of the increase in oil prices caused by OPEC in the 1970s.

3. Draw a pair of supply and demand diagrams, one representing the market for coal and the other the market for electric power. How will the development of fluidized bed combustion affect the market for electric power? Will the supply curve shift? Will the demand curve shift? Will both shift? Explain why. How will the new technology affect the market for coal in terms of shifts in the supply and/or demand curves? Show equilibrium in each market before and after the introduction of the new technology. (Assume that oil prices are constant in this part of the problem.)

Suggestions for Further Reading

Baird, Charles W. *Rent Control: The Perennial Folly*. Washington, D.C.: The Cato Institute, 1980.

This book describes the history and recent practice of rent control in the United States and elsewhere.

Breit, William, and Roger L. Ransom. *The Academic Scribblers*, 2d ed. New York: Holt, Rinehart and Winston, 1982.

Chapter 3 is an essay on Alfred Marshall, the founder of modern supply and demand analysis. Chapters 1 and 2 provide useful background.

Campbell, Colin D., ed. *Wage and Price Controls in World War II: United States and Germany*. Washington, D.C.: American Enterprise Institute, 1971.

This book provides vivid descriptions and insightful analyses of what happens when governments overrule the law of supply and demand.

Marshall, Alfred. *Principles of Economics*, various editions.

First published in 1891, this book remains remarkably amenable to browsing even by beginning students.

4 The Role of Business: The Firm, Financial Markets, and Corporate Control

After reading this chapter, you will understand . . .

- Why business firms exist in so many different sizes and organizational forms.
- Why all the business in an economy cannot be handled by one big firm.
- What can be learned by looking at a firm's balance sheet.
- The role that financial markets play in the economy.
- What lies behind headlines dealing with corporate control, takeovers, and insider trading.

Before reading this chapter, make sure you know the meaning of . . .

- Markets and their functions (Chapters 1 and 2)
- Entrepreneurship (Chapter 2)
- Supply and demand (Chapter 3)

Chrysler to Buy American Motors

Lee A. Iacocca

MARCH 10, 1987. Chrysler Corporation yesterday announced plans to buy American Motors Corporation for a total of more than $1.5 billion in a deal that would reduce to three the number of homegrown U.S. car manufacturers.

The buyout proposal is contained in a letter of intent signed by Chrysler and French auto maker Regie Nationale des Usines Renault, which owns 46.1 percent of AMC.

The agreement is contingent upon approval by the boards of directors of the two companies and by AMC stockholders. Because Renault is government-owned and because of American antitrust laws, the French and U.S. governments must also approve the deal.

"This is an agreement in principle. Much work remains to be done before the deal is complete," said Chrysler Chairman Lee A. Iacocca, who steered his own company away from the brink of bankruptcy eight years ago.

"But we believe our decision to acquire American Motors is right for both companies, for the immediate future and the long haul. It'll strengthen both of us in what's already become a tough market," Iacocca said.

AMC, which has lost a total of $856.6 million since 1980, was too short of cash and product lines to survive much longer, according to auto industry analysts and officials. The firm's strength has been in its Jeep products—four-wheel drive sports-utility vehicles such as the Jeep Wrangler and Wagoneer, and pickups like the Comanche. But the Japanese are zeroing in on those models also, leaving AMC desperate for new ammunition and the kind of undisputed marketing savvy exhibited by Iacocca's Chrysler.

"It's a reasonable deal all around," said David Healy, an analyst with Drexel Burnham Lambert Inc. in New York. "Chrysler needs the additional capacity that AMC has to offer, and Chrysler certainly could use AMC's Jeep products."

Source: Warren Brown, "Chrysler to Buy American Motors," *The Washington Post*, March 10, 1987, p. 1. Reprinted with permission. Photo Source: Courtesy of Chrysler Corporation.

CLOSE reading of this news item raises a number of questions about the role of business firms in the U.S. economy. What exactly is a corporation? Who owns and controls giant corporations such as Chrysler? Where do these firms get the billions of dollars they need to do business? Why do some firms grow to be giants, while others prosper on the small scale of a corner store? These and other questions will be addressed in this chapter.

At the same time, the item raises questions about the role of government. Why is it that the vast bulk of goods and services in the United States are produced by private firms rather than by government-owned firms such as France's Renault? What is the government's role in regulating business transactions? If the government plays only a minor role in the production of goods and services, what does it do with all the billions that it collects in taxes? We will look at these questions in Chapter 5. Together this chapter and Chapter 5 will establish themes that will be developed in detail throughout the macro- and microeconomics courses.

Forms of Business Organization

Business firms vary widely in terms of their size and scope of operations. They also differ in terms of their form of organization. In this section we discuss the three most common types of firms—sole proprietorships, partnerships, and corporations—and briefly examine a few less common ones.

The Sole Proprietorship

Sole proprietorship
A firm that is owned and usually operated by one person, who receives all the profits and is responsible for all of the firm's liabilities.

A **sole proprietorship** is a firm that is owned and operated by a single person who receives all of its profits and is personally responsible for all of its liabilities. Sole proprietorships are very common. As Exhibit 4.1 shows, more than three-quarters of U.S. firms take this form. However, they are usually small. Together proprietorships account for less than 10 percent of total business receipts. Proprietorships are common in farming, construction, and wholesale and retail trade but far less so in other sectors of the economy.

Advantages of Proprietorships

Proprietorships have a number of advantages that make them well suited to small firms. Perhaps the biggest one is that they are easy to form. Starting a proprietorship requires little more than registering the firm's name. Proprietorships are also easy to dissolve: The owner simply stops doing business, and the firm ceases to exist.

A second advantage of the proprietorship is the fact that its owner receives all the profits (if any) directly. Income from a proprietorship is subject only to the personal income tax.

Finally, proprietors have the advantage of working for themselves without being accountable to employers or other owners. Many people value this independence so highly that they are willing to run their own businesses in return for lower incomes than they could earn working for someone else.

Disadvantages of Proprietorships

Proprietorships have certain drawbacks that limit their usefulness for large ventures. One is the owner's unlimited liability. Just as the owner receives all the

Exhibit 4.1   Forms of Business Organization

These charts show the distribution of firms in the United States according to form of ownership. Proprietorships are by far the most numerous. They are the main form of ownership in agriculture and are also common in retail trade and construction. However, most proprietorships are small; in terms of total receipts, they are overshadowed by corporations. The corporate sector, in turn, is dominated by the small number of firms (some 418,000 in 1980) that have reported receipts of $1 million or more.

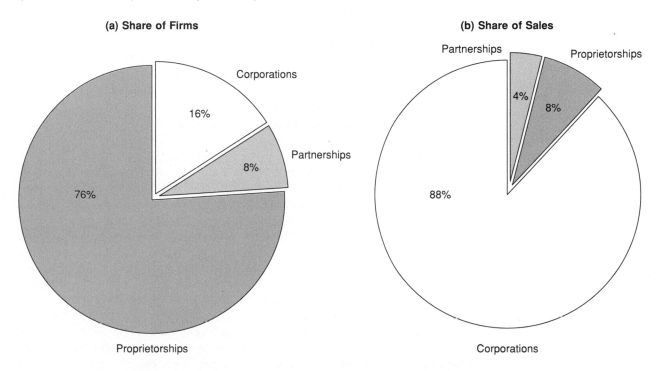

Source: U.S. Department of Commerce, *Statistical Abstract of the United States: 1984,* 104th ed. (Washington, D.C.: Government Printing Office, 1984), Tables 887, 888.

profits, he or she must bear any losses. Any liabilities that the firm incurs, such as business debts, lawsuits, or damages for breach of contract, are borne by the proprietor. Thus, a bankrupt proprietorship means a bankrupt owner.

The fact that a proprietorship cannot be separated from its owner is another drawback. The firm's growth may require more capital than the owner can purchase with his or her own funds, and it is difficult for a proprietorship to tap outside sources of funds. Also, the legal life of a proprietorship comes to an end upon the proprietor's death.

The Partnership

A **partnership** is an association of two or more people who operate a business as co-owners. Partnerships are the least common of the three major forms of business organization. They account for only about 7 percent of all U.S. firms and less than 4 percent of all business receipts. Partnerships are most often found in professions, such as law, medicine, and accounting. In these fields, state laws

Partnership
An association of two or more people who operate a business as co-owners by voluntary legal agreement.

restrict the use of the corporation by groups of professionals. Some of these laws have been relaxed in recent years, however, and professional corporations are becoming more common.

Advantages of Partnerships

Forming a partnership is one way for a proprietorship to grow. Two or more partners can pool their skills and financial resources to create a firm that is larger and stronger than either could support alone. Also, in certain situations partnerships have tax advantages over corporations.

Disadvantages of Partnerships

Offsetting these advantages are some serious drawbacks. One is the partners' unlimited liability. In terms of liability, a partner is worse off than a proprietor because he or she bears the liabilities of the entire firm. If the firm fails, a partner can lose far more than was put into it. A partner in a professional partnership may even be held liable for damages awarded in suits against other firm members.

Continuity is another serious problem for partnerships, since the death of any partner ends the firm's legal life. A partner's withdrawal can also create problems. If a partner wants to leave the firm, someone—either a new partner or the existing ones—must be willing to buy his or her interest in the firm. Until a buyer is found, the partner's investment may be "frozen," that is, unable to be withdrawn as cash or invested in another business.

Limited Partnerships

For some purposes, such as real estate ventures, a special kind of partnership called a *limited partnership* is used in order to avoid the problem of unlimited liability. A limited partnership includes one or more general partners who are in charge of running the firm and have much the same status as the co-owners of an ordinary partnership. It also includes one or more limited partners who put in funds and share profits but whose liability can never exceed the amount they have invested. A limited partnership has many of the advantages of a corporation in terms of raising funds with which to acquire capital. At the same time, it retains the tax advantages of a partnership.

The Corporation

Corporation
A firm that takes the form of an independent legal entity with ownership divided into equal shares and each owner's liability limited to his or her investment in the firm.

The **corporation** is the third major form of business organization. A corporation is a business that is organized as an independent legal entity, with ownership divided into shares. The corporation is the dominant form of organization for large firms. Only about 14 percent of all U.S. firms are corporations, but they account for more than 85 percent of all business receipts. Exhibit 4.2, which lists the 25 largest industrial corporations in the United States, contains many familiar names. Small corporations are also common, however; one-quarter of all corporations report receipts of less than $25,000 a year.

Advantages of Corporations

The usefulness of the corporate form for large businesses stems from two facts: (1) The corporation is a legal entity apart from its owners, and (2) the owners have limited liability.

The legal independence of the corporation makes it stable and long-lived.

Exhibit 4.2   The 25 Largest U.S. Industrial Corporations

Each year *Fortune* magazine publishes a list of the 500 largest industrial corporations in the United States, ranked by sales. This list of the top 25 contains many familiar names.

Rank	Company	Sales ($ thousands)	Net Income ($ thousands)
1	General Motors	102,813,700	2,944,700
2	Exxon	69,888,000	5,360,000
3	Ford Motor	62,715,800	3,285,100
4	International Business Machines	51,250,000	4,789,000
5	Mobil	44,866,000	1,407,000
6	General Electric	35,211,000	2,492,000
7	American Telephone and Telegraph	34,087,000	139,000
8	Texaco	31,613,000	725,000
9	E.I. du Pont de Nemours	27,148,000	1,538,000
10	Chevron	24,351,000	715,000
11	Chrysler	22,513,500	1,403,600
12	Philip Morris	20,681,000	1,478,000
13	Amoco	18,281,000	747,000
14	RJR Nabisco	16,998,000	1,064,000
15	Shell Oil	16,833,000	883,000
16	Boeing	16,341,000	665,000
17	United Technologies	15,669,157	72,727
18	Procter & Gamble	15,439,000	709,000
19	Occidental Petroleum	15,344,100	181,100
20	Atlantic Richfield	14,585,802	615,116
21	Tenneco	14,558,000	−39,000
22	USX	14,000,000	−1,833,000
23	McDonnell Douglas	12,660,600	277,500
24	Rockwell International	12,295,700	611,200
25	Allied-Signal	11,794,000	605,000

Source: *FORTUNE* 500; © 1987 Time Inc. All rights reserved. Reprinted by permission.

Stockholders can enter or leave the firm at will. Creditors and customers have only one legal entity to deal with rather than a number of partners. Further, the firm can own property and enter into contracts in its own name rather than just in its owners'.

Limited liability means that stockholders cannot suffer a loss greater than the sum they have invested in the business. This is the stockholder's most important protection. A person can own shares in dozens of corporations without ever facing the risks that a partner or proprietor does.

Together these two features make the corporation ideal for raising large sums from many small investors. We will discuss some of the ways in which this is done later in the chapter.

Disadvantages of Corporations

Corporations also have some disadvantages. (If they didn't, every firm would be a corporation.)

One disadvantage is the relative cost and difficulty of forming or dissolving a corporation. Although each state has its own laws in this area, forming a corporation usually requires the services of a lawyer and the payment of fees. These costs make the corporation poorly suited to many small or temporary business ventures.

Corporations also have a major tax disadvantage in that corporate income is taxed twice. When earned, it is subject to corporate income taxes; when paid out to stockholders as dividends, it is subject to the personal income tax. This double taxation can be very costly. If state and federal taxes take 40 percent of a firm's profit when earned and personal income taxes take 40 percent of the remainder when paid out as dividends, the firm's owners receive only $.36 of each dollar earned.

Not-for-Profit Firms

In addition to profit-seeking proprietorships, partnerships, and corporations, the private sector contains many *not-for-profit firms*. These include churches, colleges, charities, labor unions, country clubs, and the like. Like profit-seeking firms, these organizations participate in markets, produce goods and services, and provide jobs.

Most not-for-profit firms are corporations. Unlike profit-seeking corporations, however, they have no stockholders. They are run by independent boards of trustees whose members are chosen under rules set forth in the organization's bylaws. In a typical private college, for example, the trustees are elected by alumni, faculty, and sometimes students.

Some not-for-profit firms depend on donations for their income. Many also receive income from fees and sales of goods and services, as is the case with not-for-profit hospitals, publishers, and theater groups. If a not-for-profit firm takes in more donations and sales revenues than it spends, it is required by law to plow the surplus back into the business.

Cooperatives are closely related to not-for-profit firms. They are formed by consumers, farmers, and sometimes factory workers to run a business for their mutual benefit. Unlike not-for-profit firms, however, cooperatives may distribute any surplus they earn to their members. For example, the surplus of a co-op supermarket might be distributed to members at the end of the year on the basis of each member's total purchases during that period.

Unlike ordinary corporations, however, cooperatives do not always have profits as their main goal. Other benefits of forming a cooperative include consumers' chance to pool their purchasing power and buy at wholesale prices and farmers' opportunities to control the marketing of their crops.

The Firm as Coordinator

Whatever their form of organization, all business firms have one thing in common: They coordinate economic activity. They are responsible, in large part, for deciding what goods are made, who makes them, and how they are made. They do this by means of two types of coordination, which we will call *market coordination* and *managerial coordination*.

Coordinating the work of many people requires a system of incentives. It also requires a means by which people can communicate with one another. **Market coordination** uses the price system both as a means of communication

Market coordination
A means of coordinating economic activity that uses the price system to transmit information and provide incentives.

and as a source of incentives. As prices change in response to supply and demand, buyers are led to substitute lower-priced goods and services for higher-priced ones. At the same time, changing prices create new profit opportunities for entrepreneurs who expand their output of goods whose prices have been bid up by strong consumer demand. All this is done in a decentralized fashion; no central authority makes decisions or issues commands.

However, there are large areas of economic activity in which market coordination is not used. Take, for example, the coordination of work in a television factory. Workers do not decide on their own, in response to price changes, that they will spend the day making portables rather than cabinet models. Instead, they make portables because their boss tells them to. This is an example of **managerial coordination,** which is based on directives from managers to subordinates. The subordinates follow the directives because they have agreed to do so as a condition of employment.

Managerial coordination
A means of coordinating economic activity that uses directives from managers to subordinates.

Coordination within the Firm

In a well-known essay on the nature of the firm, Ronald Coase posed a question about these two ways of coordinating economic activity[1] (see "Who Said It? Who Did It? 4.1"). If the market works as well as economists say it does, Coase asked, why is managerial coordination used at all? Why must workers in a television factory take orders from a boss? If market coordination were used everywhere, all TV cabinets and picture tubes would be built by independent firms working on contract. Changes in the relative prices of various components would keep the right number of workers on each job and the right amounts of goods flowing to consumers.

Coase found an answer to his question. He said that market coordination is not used in every case where coordination is needed because it entails transaction costs. **Transaction costs** are incidental costs incurred by buyers and sellers in the process of making a transaction. They include the costs of gathering information about market conditions; the costs of negotiating contracts, writing invoices, and making payments; and the costs of straightening things out when contracts are not carried through.

Transaction costs
Incidental costs to buyers and sellers of making a transaction, including the costs of gathering information, making decisions, carrying out trades, writing contracts, and making payments.

Transaction costs limit the use of the market as a means of coordination. Imagine that you had to negotiate with each person who helped build a TV set that you wanted—the one who built the cabinet, the one who put the finish on, the one who installed the picture tube, and so on. The transaction costs of all these dealings would make buying a TV set a very expensive proposition. To avoid these costs, you might have a local shop build a set from scratch. But then the benefits of large-scale production would be lost, and the set would still cost a lot. When a firm like Magnavox acts as an intermediary between you and all the people who build the set, thousands of transactions are avoided. You can buy your TV set in a store, and the job of building it is coordinated within the firm through the issuing of directives that workers carry out.

Coase realized, though, that in answering one question he had raised another, namely, if managerial coordination works so well, why use the market at all? Why not run the entire economy as one big firm, with all people acting as employees and a single, central manager running the whole show? Then coordination would be a matter not only of giving TV or autoworkers instructions for

[1]Ronald H. Coase, "The Nature of the Firm," *Economica* (November 1937): 386–405.

WHO SAID IT? WHO DID IT?   4.1

Ronald Coase: Interpreter of Economic Institutions

Economists are sometimes charged with expressing their models in such abstract mathematical or graphical form that they lose all touch with real-world economic institutions. But not Ronald Coase. Through his own writings and work as editor of the *Journal of Law and Economics*, Coase has fostered a cross-fertilization between analytic and institutional economics. In the approach Coase favors, one selects an economic institution and poses two related questions:

Photo Source: Courtesy of the University of Chicago Law School Publications; Photographer: David Joel.

1. What are the effects of this particular institution on the allocation of resources?

2. How can one account for the evolution and continued existence of the institution in terms of an analysis of its effects on resource allocation?

Coase, who was born and educated in London, began his studies of economic institutions early in his career. His paper on the nature of the firm was published in 1937 and brought him international recognition. He came to the United States in 1951 to teach first at the University of Buffalo, then at the University of Virginia, and finally at the University of Chicago. In 1961, his most famous paper, "The Problem of Social Cost," appeared in the *Journal of Law and Economics*. At that time, the journal was new and the study of law and economics hardly existed as an independent specialty within either profession. Coase's probing analysis of the nature of the law as an economic institution sparked so much interest among both economists and lawyers that economic analysis of law soon became one of the most exciting fields of study available. Within a little over a decade, all leading law schools had economists on their staffs and were offering courses in the new approach.

the day but also of giving high school graduates orders concerning whether to become technicians or welders. Not only would the question of how many portables and how many cabinet-model TVs be answered by managerial coordination, such questions as how many factories should be in each industry and where they should be located would be answered as well.

However, managerial coordination has its own costs. Under managerial coordination, the person who actually does a job need not know all the reasons for doing it—and that is a saving. But offsetting this is managers' need to learn a great deal about all the jobs they coordinate. Sometimes the costs of giving information to a central decision maker are greater than those of giving information to people close to the job. Once central managers get the information they need to make decisions, they must transmit clear instructions back to middle managers and then to workers. The further central managers are from the workers doing the job, the more costly is the coordination process, the longer are the delays, and the greater is the chance of error. At some point, the costs of managerial coordination become so great that it loses its advantage over market coordination.

Limits of the Firm

Coase saw that the two coordinating mechanisms we have discussed are the key to understanding the nature of the firm and its role in the economy. A firm, he said, uses managerial coordination for its internal activities. It uses the market to coordinate its activities with those of people on the outside. Each firm finds it worthwhile to expand its operations only to the point at which the managerial costs of organizing one more task within the firm equal the transaction costs of organizing the same task outside the firm through the market.

In some cases, this principle leads to very large firms. Magnavox, for example, is a large firm in itself. It is also part of the Philips organization, one of the 50 or so largest firms in the world. Such a firm coordinates a vast number of activities. It builds hundreds of different products, makes parts in one plant for products that will be assembled in another halfway around the world, and so on. But even a firm like Philips does not do everything for itself. If it wants to ship goods by rail, it does not build a railroad. Some jobs are so big that even the largest firms find it more efficient to use outside specialists.

In other cases, Coase's principle leads to firms that are very small. Bullard's Welding of Chelsea, Vermont, is an example from the millions of small business firms in the U.S. economy. Bullard does a few things for himself that most firms of that size would not do. For example, he built his own furnace to heat his shop. But he does not make the parts for the diesel engines he repairs or set up a rolling mill to make the sheet steel he needs or hire a lawyer as an employee. Instead, he finds it cheaper to buy those goods and services on the market.

In Bullard's case, as in Philips', allowing each firm to expand to its optimal size while leaving coordination among firms to the market keeps total coordination costs down when both the transaction costs of market coordination and the managerial costs of coordination within firms are taken into account. The concept of the firm as a means of making economic coordination more efficient should be kept in mind throughout the study of economics.

Financing Private Business

The Balance Sheet

Regardless of their size or legal form, all private firms need financial resources in order to purchase capital and carry on their operations. One way to understand how a firm obtains and uses financial resources is to look at its **balance sheet**—a financial statement that shows what the firm owns and what it owes. Exhibit 4.3 shows a balance sheet for an imaginary firm, Great Falls Manufacturing Inc. (GFMI).

The left-hand column of the balance sheet lists the firm's **assets,** which are all the things to which it holds a legal claim. GFMI's assets include $10 million in cash and accounts receivable; $15 million in inventory; and $100 million in property, plant, and equipment. Its assets thus total $125 million.

The right-hand column of the balance sheet lists the firm's liabilities and net worth. A firm's **liabilities** are all the legal claims that outsiders hold against it. For GFMI, these include $5 million in accounts payable; $15 million in short-term loans from banks; and $55 million in long-term debts, such as mortgages on its property. The final item on the right-hand side of the balance sheet is the firm's **net worth,** also known as **owners' equity,** which is the difference between total assets and total liabilities. The firm's net worth represents its owners' claims against its assets. The fact that GFMI's net worth is $50 million means that if its owners closed it down, sold all its assets at the values listed on the balance sheet, and paid off all its liabilities, they would have $50 million left over.

Balance sheet
A financial statement showing a firm's or household's assets, liabilities, and net worth.

Assets
All the things to which a firm or household holds legal claim.

Liabilities
All the legal claims against a firm by nonowners or against a household by nonmembers.

Net worth (owners' equity)
A firm's or household's assets minus its liabilities.

Exhibit 4.3   Balance Sheet of Great Falls Manufacturing Inc.

A firm's balance sheet gives a snapshot of its financial position. The left-hand side lists the firm's assets—all the things to which it holds legal claim. The right-hand side lists the firm's liabilities—claims against it by nonowners—and its net worth, or owners' equity. According to the accounting equation, assets always equal liabilities plus net worth.

Assets (Millions)		Liabilities and Net Worth (Millions)	
Cash and accounts receivable	$ 10	Accounts payable	$ 5
Inventory	15	Short-term debt	15
Property, plant, and equipment	100	Long-term debt	55
		Total liabilities	$ 75
		Net worth	50
Total assets	$125	Total liabilities plus net worth	$125

The balance sheet gets its name from the fact that the totals of the two columns always balance. This follows from the definition of net worth. Because net worth is defined as assets minus liabilities, liabilities plus net worth must equal assets. In equation form, this basic rule of accounting reads as follows:

$$\text{Assets} = \text{Liabilities} + \text{Net worth}.$$

As a firm grows, so do the entries on its balance sheet. A growing firm will need more plant and equipment and a larger inventory. It will also need more cash, and its accounts receivable will increase as it does business with more workers, customers, and suppliers.

According to the accounting equation, the firm's liabilities, net worth, or both must grow along with its assets. If the firm is profitable, it can obtain funds for growth by plowing profits back into the business. If it does this, its assets will grow without a corresponding increase in its liabilities; therefore, by definition, its net worth will grow. Thus, by plowing profits back into the business, owners increase their stake in the firm. If the firm does not make enough profits to finance its own growth, it must turn to outside sources of funds.

Broadly speaking, there are two outside sources of funds to which the firm can turn. One is to bring in more owners—new partners for a partnership, new stockholders for a corporation, or new members for a cooperative. The funds raised from these new owners are entered on the firm's balance sheet as additions to its net worth. The alternative is to borrow funds from individuals, banks, or other lenders. If the firm does this, its liabilities will increase.

Financial Markets

Financial markets
Markets through which borrowers obtain funds from savers.

The markets in which a firm obtains funds are known as **financial markets.** A basic understanding of these markets is useful, since they play key roles in both macro- and microeconomics.

Exhibit 4.4 gives an overview of financial markets. Such markets serve as a link between economic units that are *net savers* (those that spend less than they earn) and units that are *net borrowers* (those that spend more than they earn). Some households are net borrowers, but the total saving of all households exceeds their total borrowing. Therefore, the household sector is shown in Exhibit

Exhibit 4.4   Financial Markets

This chart shows how financial markets channel investment funds from households (net savers) to nonfinancial businesses (net borrowers). Two types of financing are shown. Direct financing is the sale of claims against firms (such as stocks or bonds) directly to households. Indirect financing channels the funds through financial intermediaries—firms that gather funds from households and use them as a basis for making loans to other firms. The chart shows flows of funds as solid arrows and flows of financial claims issued in exchange for funds as dotted arrows.

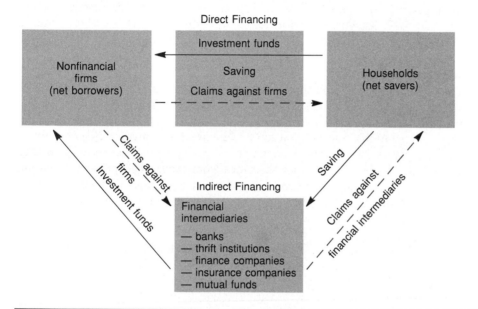

4.4 as a source of funds for financial markets. Some nonfinancial firms take in more funds than they use and thus are net savers, but the total borrowing of nonfinancial business firms exceeds their total saving. Thus, the nonfinancial business sector is shown as a user of funds provided through financial markets.

Direct Financing

One way for a firm to raise funds is to approach net savers—households or other nonfinancial firms—directly. This process is called **direct financing.** In exchange for the funds they provide, these net savers receive claims against the firm. These claims take several forms, the most common of which are bonds and stocks.

A **bond** is a promise, given in return for borrowed funds, to make interest payments at an agreed-upon rate over a set period, plus a final payment equal to the amount borrowed. Most bonds are issued in denominations of $1,000 for periods of 10 to 30 years. Suppose that GFMI wanted to raise $1 million to buy some new injection-molding equipment. It could sell 1,000 bonds with a face value of $1,000 each, promising to pay the lenders, say, $150 a year for 30 years and to repay the $1,000 at the end of that period.

Instead of borrowing funds by selling bonds, GFMI could raise the $1 million by selling stock. A share of **common stock** is a certificate of part ownership in the firm. In return for their funds, the new stockholders become co-owners

Direct financing
The process of raising investment funds directly from savers.

Bond
A promise, given in return for borrowed funds, to make a fixed annual or semiannual payment over a set number of years plus a larger final payment equal to the amount borrowed.

Common stock
A certificate of part ownership in a corporation that gives the owner a vote in the selection of the firm's directors and the right to a share of dividends, if any.

with all other stockholders. Unlike bondholders, though, common stockholders are not promised a fixed return on their investment. Instead, they expect to be rewarded for their investment through dividends or capital gains. *Dividends* are payments to stockholders that are made out of profits. *Capital gains* are sums that are realized when and if stockholders are able to sell their shares at a higher price than they paid for them. Firms also sometimes issue *preferred stock*, which is stock that has guaranteed dividends but no voting rights.

Stocks and bonds are only two of a great many types of financial instruments that firms issue. Others include *commercial paper* (similar to bonds but scheduled for repayment in a year or less) and *convertible bonds* (bonds that can be exchanged for stock at a set price). A detailed discussion of these securities is beyond the scope of this book.

Indirect Financing

Direct financing is by no means the only source of funds for a firm such as GFMI. Instead of approaching households directly, a firm can turn to financial intermediaries such as banks, savings and loan associations, insurance companies, mutual funds, and pension funds. **Financial intermediaries** gather funds from net savers and pass them along to net borrowers by either making loans or buying stocks, bonds, or other securities from them. The process of raising funds through financial intermediaries is known as **indirect financing.** Indirect financing accounts for about two-thirds of all funds raised by nonfinancial sectors in U.S. financial markets.

Suppose that GFMI needs $100,000 to build a new warehouse. Instead of seeking the funds directly from households or other nonfinancial firms, it applies to the Great Falls National Bank for a mortgage loan. In return for the funds, GFMI gives the bank a mortgage note promising to repay the $100,000, with interest, over a period of 15 years. If it fails to make the payments, the bank can take possession of the warehouse.

Where does the bank get the funds it needs to make the loans? It gets them by accepting checking and savings deposits from the citizens of Great Falls. As Exhibit 4.4 shows, indirect financing involves a double exchange of funds and claims. Households give their funds to the bank in return for claims against it, and the bank passes the funds along to GFMI in return for a claim against the new warehouse.

Indirect financing has a number of advantages over direct financing. First, it is more flexible. A bank could, for example, lend a retail store a few thousand dollars for 90 days to finance an inventory buildup for the Christmas season. Selling securities for this purpose would be impractical for a small firm. Second, indirect financing can be used by small firms, including proprietorships and partnerships. Because these firms are not widely known and do not always have high credit ratings, they may find it difficult to sell stocks or bonds. Finally, financial intermediaries perform a useful service by matching the needs of borrowers and lenders. For example, the Great Falls National Bank would be able to give GFMI a 15-year mortgage loan for $100,000 even though none of its depositors may have that much in savings or want the savings tied up for such a long period.

Not all indirect financing takes the form of loans. Sales of stocks, bonds, or other financial instruments to financial intermediaries also count as indirect financing. Pension funds, mutual funds, and insurance companies have large holdings of corporate financial instruments.

Financial intermediaries
Financial firms, including banks, savings and loan associations, insurance companies, pension funds, and mutual funds, that gather funds from net savers and provide funds to net borrowers.

Indirect financing
The process of raising investment funds via financial intermediaries.

Secondary Financial Markets

The financial markets shown in Exhibit 4.4 are called **primary financial markets** because they are markets in which newly issued claims against firms are exchanged for new investment funds. There are also many **secondary financial markets,** in which firms and households buy and sell previously issued bonds, stocks, and other securities. The best known of these secondary markets is the New York Stock Exchange. Stocks and bonds are also traded in so-called *over-the-counter* markets, which are networks of dealers who do business by telephone or computer hookup.

The prices of stocks and other securities traded in secondary markets vary hour by hour and day by day as buyers and sellers revise their expectations regarding general economic conditions and profits of individual firms. Each day financial newspapers publish multipage reports on the latest prices of stocks, bonds, and other securities. Averages of the prices of selected stocks, such as the Dow Jones Industrial Average, are widely reported on radio and television as well as in newspapers.

Secondary markets allow shareholders who become disillusioned with their firms' management to sell out and invest elsewhere. As we will see in the next section, these markets play a key role in determining who controls corporate policy.

Primary financial markets
Markets in which newly issued stocks, bonds, and other securities are sold.

Secondary financial markets
Markets in which previously issued bonds, stocks, and other securities are traded among investors.

Corporate Control, Takeovers, and Insider Trading

Because corporations contribute such a large share of the total output of the U.S. economy, the question of who controls these firms is important. For example, the news article that opens this chapter refers to "Lee Iacocca's Chrysler Corporation." In what sense is it "his" company? Who makes decisions such as Chrysler's takeover bid for American Motors? Who decides whether such bids succeed? This section looks briefly at these important issues.

Stockholders' Rights

One of the advantages of the corporation is that it can raise funds from many thousands of people, none of whom need invest much in any one firm. In most corporations, the stockholders have the legal power to control the firm by electing its board of directors, who in turn appoint its top managers. In such a corporation, the stockholders are the *principals* in whose interest the firm is supposed to be run. Directors and managers—the Lee Iacoccas—are the stockholders' *agents*. It is their legal duty to serve the stockholders' interests, particularly their interest in earning a return on the funds they have invested.

In practice, however, many corporations' stockholders exercise little day-to-day power over the firm's policies. This is especially true when ownership is divided among many stockholders, none of whom holds a significant percentage of the total stock. Typically, stockholders own shares in many different corporations; this is true of both individual stockholders and institutional stockholders such as pension funds and insurance companies. If they disapprove of the policies of one firm's managers, they can simply sell that stock and buy stock of another company rather than voicing their concerns via shareholder meetings and election of directors.

However, many observers have asked, if stockholders take this attitude, what guarantee exists that directors and managers will act in stockholders' interests? What will keep them from turning corporations into private fiefdoms in which they rule from lavish penthouse suites, gad about in corporate jets, and pay themselves extravagant bonuses while the business goes to pot?

Incentives and Bonuses

One way to keep manager-agents working in the interests of their stockholder-principals is to set incentives and bonuses that are tied to the firm's profitability. A common type of profit-sharing plan is the stock option, which gives a manager the right to buy a certain number of shares of the firm's stock at a set price before a specified date. Suppose that in July 1987 a manager is given the option to buy 1,000 shares of the firm's stock at any time until 1992 at the 1987 price of $25. If the manager does a good job of running the firm, the price of the stock is likely to rise. If it rises to, say, $45 by 1992, the option to buy 1,000 shares at $25 is worth $20,000. This is a nice reward for a job well done. But if the company is poorly managed and the stock's price falls below $25, the option will be worthless.

Takeovers

An even more powerful incentive for managers to heed stockholders' interests is the threat of a takeover. We have noted that when stockholders do not like a firm's policies, they are likely to sell their shares and buy shares in another firm. If many stockholders decide to sell at the same time, the price of the stock is driven way down. The firm then may be subject to a *takeover* bid, that is, a bid by a new owner to buy a block of shares large enough to control election of the firm's directors.

Sometimes takeovers are friendly, such as the one between Chrysler and American Motors discussed in the article that opens this chapter. In such cases, managers see mutual interests in a merger. But other takeovers are not friendly. If the price of its stock sags, the firm may face the prospect of a hostile takeover, in which the buyer—if successful—will throw out the present management team and install its own.

A hostile takeover bid may be made by an individual, a group, or, most often, another corporation. One tactic is to make a *tender offer,* meaning an offer to buy a controlling interest in the firm's stock at a stated price, usually well above the stock's current market price. Another tactic is to ask stockholders for *proxies,* that is, promises to vote for a new board of directors at the next stockholder meeting. In either case, if the takeover succeeds, the new management will do its best to raise profits. When investors realize this, the price of the firm's stock will be bid up and the takeover group will reap handsome gains.

Some economists have argued that it is the right to sell out to a raider staging a takeover, rather than attendance at stockholder meetings, that is the true basis of stockholders' power to discipline management. Together with stock options and other profit-sharing devices, takeovers act as carrots and sticks to keep managers from straying too far from their duty of earning profits for their stockholders. However, not all observers share this view. The debate as to whether takeovers are good for the economy revolves around three principal sets of issues: debt, defensive strategies, and short-run bias.

Debt versus Equity

In order to persuade stockholders to sell out, raiders offer to buy a company's shares at a price substantially higher than its current market value. They finance the purchases with borrowed money. As a result, after the takeover the company has more debt in relation to its net worth than before. Economists critical of takeover practices say that all that debt makes the firm financially weak. The reason debt makes a company financially weak is that a firm has a legal obligation to make payments to its bondholders or to banks from which it has borrowed whether or not it is earning a profit. These fixed-payment obligations can force a firm into bankruptcy in a period when its sales and profits have slipped. In contrast, equity funding gives the corporation more flexibility. The firm has no legal obligation to make dividend payments to its stockholders each year. Omitting dividends during hard times can give the firm the breathing space it needs to work its way back to profitability in the long run.

Critics worry that the tendency to replace owners' equity with debt will weaken the corporate sector as a whole and reduce its ability to survive an economic downturn. In the period 1984 to 1986 alone, more than $300 billion of owners' equity was exchanged for debt through a variety of financial restructuring methods. However, raiders—and those economists who side with them—say not to worry: The debt can be repaid with higher earnings once the old management is replaced by a stronger one. Also, some of the debt can be paid off by selling real estate, subsidiaries, and other assets that the corporation has been using inefficiently.

Defensive Strategies

Critics claim that fear of takeover prompts managers to adopt defensive strategies that hurt the company. They may sell off the firm's "crown jewels"—its most profitable assets or divisions. They may load up the firm with debt to make it less attractive. They may design "poison pills"—complex financial traps that they hope would-be raiders will choke on. They may pay "greenmail"—huge ransoms to raiders who agree to go away—that leaves the firm impoverished.

Defenders of the takeover mechanism agree that these tactics can be harmful. They see them as an expression of contempt for shareholders on management's part. If raiders can oust such managers, the sooner the better.

Short-Run Bias

The threat of takeover, say economists who are critical of certain widely used tactics, forces managers to stress the short run over the long run. Managers do everything they can to keep short-term profits up, hoping that this will boost their firms' stock prices and keep them from becoming takeover targets. In so doing, they allegedly slight research and development and pass over risky but potentially profitable long-term projects.

However, many economists tend to be skeptical of this argument. It assumes that stockholders systematically overvalue the stocks of firms that pursue short-sighted goals and undervalue those of companies that invest in long-term profitability. In fact, the very things that managers must do to resist a takeover—restructure, sell assets they cannot manage well, and so on—are more likely to strengthen than weaken the firm in the long run.

Takeovers and Insider Trading

Although many economists defend takeovers on the grounds that they improve efficiency by replacing bad managers with good ones, the people who actually play the takeover game are not in it to make the world a better place. They are in it to make money. Because the sums of money involved in a major corporate merger such as Chrysler/AMC are enormous, the issue of takeovers has become entangled with another controversy: *insider trading*. The explosive mixture of takeovers and insider trading has led to some of the most spectacular headlines to come out of Wall Street; "Economics in the News 4.1" provides a case in point.

The Mechanics of Insider Trading

First we must understand why insider trading is so profitable. Let Ace Corporation be a poorly run, plodding dog of a company with much greater potential than its current managers have been able to extract. On the basis of current management performance, its stock is trading at $15 per share. Now comes Zeus Corporation, a go-go outfit that employs teams of researchers to identify firms like Ace. Zeus's management figures that by selling off some of Ace's timber holdings, revamping its line of women's shoes, and doing some heavy-duty cost cutting, it can so boost profitability that Ace's stock will rise to a market value of $25. Having planned how to turn Ace around, Zeus will go into the stock market on June 1 with a public tender offer, bidding $20 per share for any or all of Ace's

---

ECONOMICS IN THE NEWS   4.1

Another Wall Street Insider Pleads Guilty

FEBRUARY 14, 1987. Martin A. Siegel, one of Wall Street's premier investment bankers, pleaded guilty yesterday to criminal charges that he participated in an illegal information swapping and stock trading scheme with high-ranking executives of Goldman, Sachs & Co. and Kidder, Peabody & Co.

Siegel agreed to pay the government more than $9 million to settle charges that he violated federal securities laws. He also pleaded guilty to income-tax evasion charges.

The 38-year-old investment banker also was charged yesterday by the Securities and Exchange Commission with selling secret information about corporate takeovers to stock speculator Ivan F. Boesky, who used the tips to make more than $33 million in the stock market.

For the illegal stock tips, Boesky paid Siegel $700,000, which was delivered by aides who handed over briefcases containing cash after exchanging secret passwords with Siegel in public places, the SEC said.

Source: David A. Vise and Michael Schrage, "Another Wall Street Guilty Plea," *The Washington Post*, February 14, 1987, p. A1. Reprinted with permission.

Siegel resigned yesterday from his multimillion-dollar-a-year job as cohead of the merger department at Drexel Burnham Lambert Inc. An executive at Kidder for 15 years before he joined Drexel last year, Siegel helped arrange more than 500 corporate takeovers and helped develop novel takeover defense strategies for corporations, including Martin Marietta Corp. Drexel said that all of the charges against Siegel involve activities that took place before he joined the firm.

"I swapped material, nonpublic information with Robert Freeman of Goldman, Sachs, for the mutual benefit of Goldman, Sachs and Kidder, Peabody," Siegel replied when U.S. District Judge Robert J. Ward asked what he had done. Ward then asked Siegel if he knew what he had done was wrong. "Yes, your honor," Siegel replied, after he wiped tears from his cheeks.

Siegel, dressed in a dark suit, light blue shirt and red tie, stood alongside other defendants who were pleading guilty to crimes ranging from drug-pushing to assault. He faces up to 10 years in prison on information swapping and tax evasion charges. He was released on his own recognizance after the hearing.

10 million outstanding shares. Zeus hopes that Ace's present stockholders will be happy with a $5 capital gain. If its hunch that better management will boost the stock price to $25 is right, the additional $5 a share will give Zeus a fat profit from the takeover. All this is honorable, ethical, and legal—exactly how the system is supposed to work.

Now comes Dwight the Insider. Dwight is a lawyer who works for the law firm that represents Zeus. When asked to draw up a set of legal papers in conjunction with the coming tender offer, he sees an opportunity. Borrowing $1.75 million from a friendly banker (with whom he perhaps shares his tip), Dwight buys 100,000 shares of Ace during the month of May. His trading boosts demand for the stock enough to push up its price, making him pay an average of $17.50 a share. Even so, when Zeus makes its tender offer, Dwight sells out at $20 and clears a cool quarter-million, less brokerage commissions and interest on the loan.

The Case against Insider Trading

Dwight's actions are illegal. If detected by the Securities and Exchange Commission, he can be forced to forfeit his profits and possibly serve a jail term as well. What has he done to deserve such harsh treatment?

The case against insider trading rests on the view that every player in the stock market should have an equal chance of profiting from an upward or downward move in a stock's price. The insider who trades on information not yet available to the public is seen in the same light as a blackjack dealer who plays with marked cards. In our example Dwight, by buying Ace's stock at $17.50, can be seen as robbing the sellers of a chance to profit from Zeus's coming tender offer.

In Support of Insider Trading

Not everyone, however, is persuaded that insider trading is reprehensible. If the stock market is viewed as a mechanism for using information in the service of efficient resource allocation, it is not so clear that Dwight's actions are damaging.

For one thing, there are winners as well as losers among the people with whom the insider trades. The case against insider trading assumes that someone— let's say Ellen—who owns Ace stock would have held it until June 1 had Dwight not come along. But stock in every company is bought and sold every day. What about Margaret, who needed to sell her Ace holdings by May 31 in order to meet her daughter's college tuition bill? Thanks to Dwight, she sells at $17.50 instead of $15.

The important thing, say defenders of insider trading, is that such trading moves stock prices in the right direction—right from an efficiency point of view, that is. In a well-functioning stock market, the price of each share should reflect each firm's true long-term earning potential. In this case, Zeus has discovered a defect in the constellation of prices. Ace stock is underpriced, due to the clumsy practices of its present managers. From the standpoint of efficiency, the sooner the price goes up, the better.

. . . But Not All Insider Trading

The above arguments suggest that Dwight the Insider may have helped as many people as he hurt and probably improved the efficiency of stock prices. Does this mean he did nothing wrong? Even among those who see insider trading as beneficial, there is one disturbing element in the story. Dwight is an attorney employed by Zeus to help with its takeover attempt. But by running up the stock price prematurely, Dwight is potentially damaging his client. With the stock's price already on the rise, Zeus's $20 tender offer may not look so good after all; it may have to bid $21, or $22, or $24.75. Thus, it appears that in the end Dwight has acted unethically. However, the real victim is not Ellen, the innocent bystander, but Zeus, his client.

It is easy to see that our fictional case of Dwight the Insider has elements in common with the case of Martin A. Siegel reported in "Economics in the News 4.1." Whether or not the deals Siegel cut with Ivan Boesky and others moved stock prices in the "right" direction, critics charge that Siegel stole from his employer and the clients that hired the firm to conduct their merger business. Trading on information obtained through abuse of a position of trust, the critics say, is little different, ethically speaking, from pocketing $5 bills from the cash register at the corner gas station.

Looking Ahead

As you continue your study of economics, you will draw on the material in this chapter at many points. Both macroeconomics and microeconomics deal frequently with financial markets. Firms' ability to attract funds with which to invest in new capital is crucial to their own performance and to the growth of the economy as a whole. The balance sheet concepts of assets, liabilities, and net worth are necessary for understanding the operation of the banking system (a part of macroeconomics) and of individual firms (a part of microeconomics). Sometimes economists deal with simplified models in which firms are treated as identical, interchangeable units. However, you should keep in mind that behind those models lies a real world in which business firms come in all sizes, shapes, and legal forms.

Summary

1. **Why do business firms exist in so many different sizes and organizational forms?** Different forms of business organization suit different firms depending on their size and scope of operations. The most common type of firm is the *sole proprietorship*. Small firms often choose this form because of its flexibility and the complete control it gives the owner. However, limited liability and continuity make the *corporation* a more suitable form of organization for large firms. In between, some firms, especially those in the professions, assume the *partnership* form of organization.

2. **Why cannot all business in the economy be handled by one large firm?** Business firms play a major role in solving the economic problems of what, how, and for whom. They do so by means of both market and managerial coordination. *Market coordination* uses the price system as a means of communication and a source of incentives. *Managerial coordination* relies on directives from managers to subordinates. Each form

of coordination entails certain costs that limit its usefulness. Firms tend to expand their operations to the point at which the managerial costs of organizing one more task within the firm equal the *transaction costs* of organizing the same task through the market. This is what sets an upper limit on the efficient size of firms.

3. **What can be learned by looking at a firm's balance sheet?** A firm's *balance sheet* is a financial statement that shows what it owns and what it owes. The firm's *assets*—all the things to which it holds a legal claim—are listed on the left-hand side of the balance sheet. Its *liabilities*—all the claims that outsiders hold against it—are listed on the right-hand side. The right-hand side of the balance sheet also lists *net worth (owners' equity)*, which is the difference between total assets and total liabilities. Owners' equity represents owners' claims against the firm according to a relationship known as the accounting equation: Assets = Liabilities + Net worth.

4. **What role do financial markets play in the economy?** *Financial markets* are the markets in which firms obtain funds for operations and investment. They serve as a link between savers and borrowers. With *direct financing*, firms borrow directly from or sell securities directly to households or other nonfinancial firms. With *indirect financing*, they deal with households or other nonfinancial firms via *financial intermediaries* such as banks, insurance companies, and pension funds. Markets in which newly issued securities are sold are called *primary financial markets;* those in which previously issued securities are traded are called *secondary financial markets.*

5. **What lies behind headlines dealing with corporate control, takeovers, and insider trading?** Stockholders have the legal power to control the corporations they own. Their main channel of control is the right to elect the firm's board of directors. However, in practice managers have a good deal of day-to-day independence from stockholders. Stockholders get into the corporate control act in a major way only when the firm is faced with a takeover bid. Takeovers are controversial because of their questionable effects on the economy and their links to insider trading scandals.

Terms for Review

- sole proprietorship
- partnership
- corporation
- market coordination
- managerial coordination
- transaction costs
- balance sheet
- assets
- liabilities
- net worth
- owners' equity
- financial markets
- direct financing
- bond
- common stock
- financial intermediaries
- indirect financing
- primary financial markets
- secondary financial markets

Questions for Review

1. List the main advantages and disadvantages of the sole proprietorship, the partnership, and the corporation.

2. What are the advantages of market coordination? Give an example of a situation in which transaction costs

limit its use. In what way do the costs of managerial coordination limit the firm's size?

3. What kinds of items would be listed as assets of a typical manufacturing firm? As its liabilities? What is the relationship among the firm's assets, liabilities, and net worth?

4. Distinguish between direct and indirect financing. List some common types of financial intermediary, and explain their role in financial markets.

5. What are the main mechanisms through which stockholders exercise control of corporations? Why is their control often less than complete?

Problems and Topics for Discussion

1. **Examining the lead-off case.** What benefits does each corporation hope to realize from the proposed merger of AMC and Chrysler? How does the secondary market in AMC stock make it possible for AMC's stockholders to share in these benefits? How might Chrysler president Lee Iacocca personally benefit from bringing about the merger?

2. **Types of business organization.** Look around your community for businesses organized as proprietorships, partnerships, corporations, and not-for-profit firms. Do you think each firm has chosen the most appropriate form of organization? Why or why not?

3. **Examining a corporate balance sheet.** Obtain a copy of a corporation's annual report. (You may find one in your library. If not, you can get one by writing or telephoning the corporation, or you can borrow one from a friend or relative who is a corporate stockholder.) At the back of the report, you will find the firm's balance sheet. Compare this balance sheet with the one given in Exhibit 4.3. What similarities do you see? What differences?

4. **A personal balance sheet.** Howard Winters is a graduate student in economics at Catatonic State University. He owns a 1974 Chevrolet worth about $800; a $1,000 stereo system; and about $500 worth of other personal possessions. He has $420 in his checking account and no other financial resources. Over the past seven years he has borrowed $8,700 under a student loan program, which he plans to pay back after he has received his degree and landed a job. He also owes $125 on a credit card account.

   Draw up a personal balance sheet for Winters. Which items go on the right-hand side? On the left-hand side? What is his net worth? Which of his "assets" (not listed on his balance sheet) have made it possible for him to borrow so much money?

5. **Secondary financial markets in the news.** Each day for one week, look at the stock and bond market re-

ports in a newspaper with a good financial section. (*The Wall Street Journal* has the most complete reports, but any big-city paper will do.) Also, look for stories that discuss increases or decreases in the prices of stocks and bonds traded in secondary financial markets. What reasons for the price changes are given?

6. **Mergers and acquisitions in the news.** Scan recent issues of business magazines like *Business Week*, *Fortune*, or *Forbes* for a story about a merger that has recently taken place or is being considered. What reasons for the merger are given? Do you think the merger makes sense in terms of Coase's theory of the firm? Is this a "friendly" merger, in which the acquired company's management is cooperating or a hostile takeover that management is trying to resist? What controlling role, if any, are the acquired firm's stockholders expected to play in the merger?

Case for Discussion
A Bill of Rights for Corporate Shareholders

Harrison J. Goldin

Kings of corporate management beware: Your once loyal and passive subjects have declared their independence by adopting the Shareholder Bill of Rights.

No longer will your biggest stockholders stand idly by as you take away their right to vote on questions as crucial as who will rule the corporate kingdom. Gone are the days when shareholders will watch silently as top executives adopt antitakeover devices that entrench management and depress stock prices.

Instead, with the Shareholder Bill of Rights as its guide and more than $160 billion in assets as its economic weapon, the Council of Institutional Investors is preparing to launch a campaign in support of shareholder democracy.

"We have done something very important, even revolutionary," said Harrison J. Goldin, comptroller of New York City and cochairman of the council.

The first demand in the Bill of Rights is that each share of common stock have an equal vote. "The right to vote is inviolate and may not be abridged," the Bill of Rights says.

The bill's "one-share, one-vote" rule is violated by some public companies, which have different classes of common stock with unequal voting rights. Unequal voting rights is the most effective antitakeover device in existence, because it typically is used to give control of a company to friends of management, who own stock that may have 10 votes per share, while stock owned by the public has only one vote per share.

"A share of stock without a vote is truly a crippled instrument," said Roland Machold, who directs $16 billion in pension assets for 380,000 state and municipal policemen, teachers, firemen, judges and public employees in New Jersey. He said the fundamental problem in many public companies is that the interests of shareholders and top management differ. If top management owns relatively little stock in the company, it usually will favor two classes of voting stock and any other device that deters takeovers and preserves its jobs. But shareholders, including pension funds, are interested in getting the highest price for their stock. Thus, shareholders typically favor the generous takeover bids that managements oppose.

The Bill of Rights also charges that corporate managements are making too many critical decisions without consulting shareholders. The bill calls on corporations to allow shareholders to vote on greenmail payments, the sale of significant corporate assets, the lucrative compensation arrangements for executives known as golden parachutes, and poison-pill provisions—corporate devices that can be activated to make a company less attractive—which many managements have adopted recently to deter takeovers.

Source: David A. Vise, "'Bill of Rights' Seeks to Boost Power of Shareholders," *The Washington Post*, April 13, 1986, p. F-1. Reprinted with permission. Photo Source: Courtesy of Office of the Comptroller, New York City.

Questions

1. According to this news item, why do the interests of shareholders and managers diverge? What does each party want?

2. You have your choice between buying two kinds of stock in XXX corporation: Class A stock, with 1 vote, and Class B stock, with 10 votes. Each share will pay equal dividends and represents an equal fraction of ownership in every other respect. For which will you pay more? Why?

3. Do you think there should be a law to enforce one-share, one-vote and other provisions of the Shareholder Bill of Rights? Or do you think that because no one is forced to buy stock in a company with policies that violate the bill the matter can safely be left to the parties involved?

4. Some critics of takeovers say that raiders do not really improve the management of the firms they acquire—they just make a quick buck at the expense of the firms' long-term profit prospects. If this is true, would you expect the price of a firm's stock to rise or to fall after implementing antitakeover measures like unequal voting rights?

5. Why would incompetent managers be able to persuade their "friends" to buy and hold large blocks of stock in the firms they are mismanaging? Wouldn't this be asking a lot of their friends? Discuss.

Suggestions for Further Reading

Galbraith, John Kenneth. *The New Industrial State.* Boston: Houghton Mifflin, 1967.

In this unorthodox book, Galbraith suggests that the market plays little or no role in coordinating the U.S. economy and that corporations are run not by their stockholders but by something called the technostructure.

Gordon, Scott. "The Close of the Galbraithian System," *Journal of Political Economy* 76 (July/August 1968): 635–644.

A critique of Galbraith's view of the economy and the corporation.

Keating, Barry P., and Maryann O. Keating. *Not for Profit.* Glen Ridge, N.J.: Thomas Horton and Daughters, 1980.

An analysis of the not-for-profit sector of the U.S. economy. Covers government as well as private not-for-profit firms.

Malkiel, Burton G. *A Random Walk Down Wall Street.* New York: Norton, 1975.

A readable and informative introduction to the stock market.

5 The Role of Government: Market Failures, Rent Seeking, and Privatization

After reading this chapter, you will understand . . .

- How large the government sector of the U.S. economy is.
- Why government action is needed to control pollution.
- Why the Army, Navy, and Air Force are not private firms.
- Why the government does not leave the questions of what, how, and for whom entirely to the market.
- Why some government programs seem designed to enrich private firms and individuals rather than promote the goals of efficiency and fairness.
- Which government roles might be better turned over to the private sector.

Before reading this chapter, make sure you know the meaning of . . .

- Opportunity costs (Chapter 1)
- Entrepreneurship (Chapter 2)
- Supply and demand (Chapter 3)
- Price ceilings and supports (Chapter 3)

Jails—Public or Private?

PANAMA CITY, FLORIDA. The nation's fledgling private corrections companies have a lot riding on the county jail here.

In October, 1985, the Bay County jail, then faced with two state corrections department lawsuits that included charges of overcrowding, fire safety violations and inadequate medical care and staffing, became the first large maximum-security jail to be turned over to a private company, Corrections Corp. of America. The

Bay County Jail in Panama City, Florida

Nashville, Tennessee, company's managers, most of whom learned the corrections business in the state systems whose bureaucratic clumsiness they now disparage, say they can do a better job when they aren't manacled by government red tape.

In Florida, as in some other states, the county sheriff normally operates the county jail and hires and fires its staff. So when the Bay County Commission decided to take control of the jail away from the sheriff, it immediately became a volatile political issue. County Commissioner Helen Ingram says that for her the issue wasn't politics, but saving money. Construction of a new jail work camp and other renovations blur comparisons, but the bottom line is this: The county was able to budget $700,000 less for the jail under CCA than it estimates it would have if the sheriff were still in control.

CCA is making major renovations to the existing jail building. Extra staff has been added and there is better medical care. The inmates are seeing lots of little amenities, such as new mattresses and sheets and new color television sets in cell pods.

Most of the sheriff's jail staff stayed on to work for CCA and they are taking home bigger paychecks. They have learned to call their charges "residents," and they have traded in their traditional deputy uniforms for brown blazers that sport the CCA logo. Stephen Toth, the jail's former administrator who stayed on to become the jail's security chief under CCA, has adopted the company's businesslike perspective on treatment of inmates. "You want to do the right thing. Lawsuits cost a lot of money."

Some prisoner-rights advocates fear companies like CCA will become a forceful lobby for more prisons and harsher sentences to keep the cells full. But so far, the most vocal opposition to privately run prisons has come from public employee unions concerned about losing turf. Bay County employees weren't unionized, but Florida sheriffs almost succeeded in persuading the legislature to completely ban private jails. The legislature did make it harder for counties to turn over their jails to private companies by requiring a four-fifths majority vote of county commissioners to do so. But that may have only helped slow the push. Already, several other Florida counties are talking to private companies.

Source: Ed Bean, "Private Jail in Bay County, Fla., Makes Inroads for Corrections Firms, but the Jury Is Still Out," *The Wall Street Journal*, August 29, 1986, p. 38. Reprinted by permission of *The Wall Street Journal*, © Dow Jones & Company, Inc. 1986. All Rights Reserved. Photo Source: Courtesy of Corrections Corporation of America.

WE are used to the idea of a division of labor between private business and government. It seems natural that cars be made by private firms and jails run by government. But a closer look at things shows that the division of labor is by no means as clear-cut as we might expect. The article that opened Chapter 4 noted that American Motors, before Chrysler's takeover bid, was largely owned by the French government. The story did not note that Lee Iacocca, a vociferous advocate of free enterprise, rescued his own Chrysler Corporation from bankruptcy only with the help of a massive infusion of funds from the U.S. government. Having noted the government's involvement in the automobile industry, we now find that private firms are involved in the running of jails. The division of labor between business and government, it turns out, is not so clear-cut after all.

This chapter gives an overview of the role of government in the U.S. economy. We begin with a general description of government in terms of its size and finances. Next, we look at two theories that have been advanced to explain the scope of government activity. Finally, we examine the issue of *privatization*—the process of moving government functions to the private sector—as exemplified in the case of the Bay County jail.

Government in the U.S. Economy

The government sector of the U.S. economy consists of federal, state, and local units. Of the nearly $1.5 trillion spent by all government levels in 1986, the federal government accounted for just under 70 percent, with state and local governments making up the rest. For purposes of economic analysis, the three levels of government are often combined. Therefore, unless specific reference to government level is being made, we will assume that "government" includes the federal, state, and local levels.

The Growth of Government

Exhibit 5.1 shows how government in the United States has grown since 1955. Two different measures are used to show the size of federal, state, and local governments in relation to the economy as a whole.

Exhibit 5.1   Growth of Government in the United States, 1955–1986

This chart shows the growth of the federal, state, and local governments combined using two measures. In terms of government purchases of goods and services, the government sector stayed roughly steady at 20 percent of GNP over the period. When transfer payments are taken into account, however, the government sector grew from about one-quarter to over one-third of GNP.

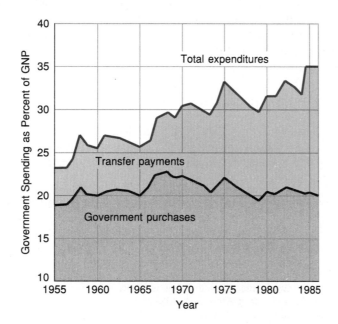

Source: *Economic Report of the President* (Washington, D.C.: Government Printing Office, 1987), Table B-77.

The first measure is **government purchases of goods and services,** or simply **government purchases.** It includes all the goods bought by governments—from submarines to typewriter ribbons—plus the cost of hiring the services of government employees and contractors—from the President to the courthouse janitor. As Exhibit 5.1 shows, purchases by federal, state, and local governments have remained roughly constant at about 20 percent of GNP for over 30 years. **Transfer payments,** on the other hand, have grown a great deal. These include all payments by governments to individuals that are not made in return for current services, for example, social security benefits, unemployment compensation, and welfare. Until 1967, transfer payments by all government levels were about 5 percent of GNP; since then, they have grown to almost 15 percent.

Which is a better measure of government growth—government purchases or total expenditures, including transfers? The answer depends on what we are trying to measure. Government purchases measure the percentage of GNP that is "used up" by government; they represent real resources that are shifted from satisfying private wants to satisfying public wants. According to this measure, government has grown little—if at all—since the mid-1950s. Transfer payments, in contrast, are funds that flow through the government without being used up. Even after they have been collected (through taxation) and paid back out, they are available for the satisfaction of private wants.

Government purchases of goods and services (government purchases)
Purchases of finished goods by government plus the cost of hiring the services of government employees and contractors.

Transfer payments
Payments by government to individuals that are not made in return for goods and services currently supplied.

Nevertheless, total expenditures, including transfers, are in some ways a better measure of government growth than are government purchases alone. The reason is that although transfer payments do not use up resources, the transfer process determines who uses them and how they are used. Total government spending thus measures the share of the economy for which government decision making replaces market decision making. In terms of this measure, government has continued to grow.

However, even though the economic role of government in the United States is expanding, it is still modest by world standards. In Sweden, government expenditures exceed 60 percent of GNP; in Norway and the Netherlands, they are over 50 percent; and in West Germany and the United Kingdom, they exceed 40 percent.

Patterns of Expenditure

Exhibit 5.2 shows what the federal, state, and local governments buy with their expenditures. Part a shows the pattern of federal government expenditures. The biggest category is income security; this includes social security, unemployment

Exhibit 5.2   Government Expenditures by Program

These charts compare federal government expenditures with those of state and local governments by program. Income security, which includes social security, unemployment benefits, public welfare, and so on, is the largest federal item, followed by national defense. Because of high interest rates and extensive federal borrowing, interest on the national debt has grown rapidly. Education is the largest item for state and local governments, followed by public welfare, highways, health and hospitals, and police and fire protection.

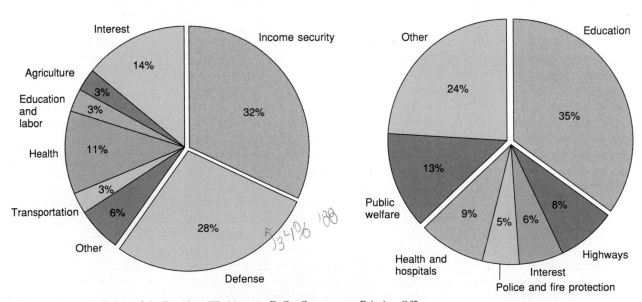

(a) Federal

(b) State and Local

Sources: *Economic Report of the President* (Washington, D.C.: Government Printing Office, 1987), Table B-74; U.S. Department of Commerce, *Statistical Abstract of the United States: 1987*, 107th ed. (Washington, D.C.: Government Printing Office, 1987), Table 446.

compensation, public assistance (welfare), and federal employee retirement and disability benefits. Income security has been the largest category of federal expenditures only since 1974. Before then, national defense, now in second place, took a larger share of the budget. As recently as 1968, national defense accounted for 40 percent of federal spending. By 1980, its share had fallen to 20 percent. Under the Reagan administration, it has grown again, to 28 percent.

Although defense outlays have commanded an increasing share of the federal budget under the Reagan administration, they have not been the most rapidly growing category. Because of large federal deficits, interest payments on the national debt grew from 9 to 14 percent of the budget during the 1980 to 1986 period. Still faster-growing categories during this period were health, including medicare (from 6 to 11 percent), and agricultural subsidies (from about 1.5 to more than 3 percent).

Part b of Exhibit 5.2 shows the pattern of state and local government spending. State governments have accounted for about two-fifths of this. By far, the largest item in state and local government budgets has been education, followed by highways, welfare, police and fire protection, and hospitals and health programs.

Financing the Public Sector

The other side of government budgets concerns sources of funds. These are shown in Exhibit 5.3. Part a shows the sources of funds for the federal government for the 1986 budget year. Personal income taxes were the largest source of revenue, closely followed by social security taxes paid by employers and employees. Corporate income taxes, excise taxes, and items such as customs receipts accounted for another 14 percent. The remaining 22 percent was raised by borrowing.

Part b of Exhibit 5.3 gives similar information for state and local governments. For state governments, sales taxes were the largest source of revenue, and property taxes were the largest source for local governments. Personal and corporate income taxes and other sources, such as fees and charges for services, were also significant. The federal government contributed substantially to state and local funds through a variety of programs, including highway and sewage treatment grants, medicaid, income security programs, and general revenue sharing. The data on which the exhibit is based do not reflect the operations of liquor stores, utilities, and pension trust funds of state and local governments. Some state and local units relied on borrowed funds during the period for which data are given, but the state and local government sector as a whole showed a small budget surplus for that period.

The Economic Role of Government: Externalities and Other Market Failures

The preceding section gives some idea of government size and the kinds of programs government undertakes. We now turn to the question of why the government does certain things and not others, that is, to the economic justification of government functions. This section is devoted to a theory according to which the role of government is to compensate for market failures. **Market failures** are instances in which markets fail to meet accepted standards of effi-

Market failure
An instance in which a market fails to meet accepted standards of efficiency or fairness in performing its functions of transmitting information, providing incentives, and distributing income.

Exhibit 5.3   Sources of Government Funds

These charts show the sources of funds for federal, state, and local governments. The personal income tax is the largest federal item, followed by employer and employee social security contributions. In 1986, 22 percent of federal spending was financed by borrowing. Individual and corporate income taxes are less important at the state and local levels. Sales taxes are the largest source of revenue for state governments and property taxes the largest source for local governments. The federal government has provided a large share of state and local funds through revenue sharing and other programs. State and local governments have had a modest budget surplus; thus, borrowing does not appear as a source of funds.

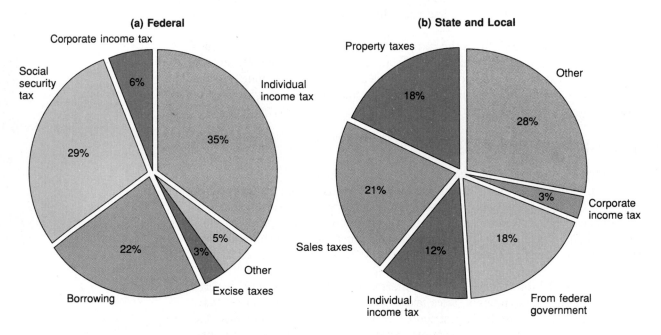

Sources: *Economic Report of the President* (Washington, D.C.: Government Printing Office, 1987), Table B-74; U.S. Department of Commerce, *Statistical Abstract of the United States: 1987*, 107th ed. (Washington, D.C.: Government Printing Office, 1987), Table 446. The data for state and local governments do not reflect the activities of state utilities and liquor stores or those of state and local trust funds and pension funds.

ciency or fairness in performing their functions of transmitting information, providing incentives, and distributing income. The next section looks at a different theory of government known as the theory of *rent seeking*. The final section looks at private-sector alternatives to government action.

Externalities

The first instance of market failure we will examine concerns a failure of the market to perform its function of transmitting information about scarcity in the form of prices. In order for markets to perform their job efficiently, the prices they transmit should reflect the opportunity costs of producing the goods or services in question.

Ordinarily, market prices do reflect at least a reasonable approximation of opportunity costs. As we saw in the discussion of the supply curve in Chapter 3, producers of a good or service normally must receive a price at least equal to opportunity costs or they will employ their factors of production elsewhere. However, situations arise in which producers' actions (and consumers') have effects on *third parties*, that is, people other than the buyer and seller who carry out a transaction. These third-party effects, which are not reflected in prices, are known as **externalities.** When externalities are present, the price system fails to transmit accurate information. Let us consider some examples.

Externality
An effect of producing or consuming a good whose impact on third parties other than buyers and sellers of the good is not reflected in prices.

Pollution

The classic example of an externality is pollution. Suppose that a steel mill burns coal in its blast furnaces. The costs of fuel, capital, and labor come to $100 per ton of steel produced. These are called *internal costs* because they are borne by the steel mill itself. These costs are reflected in market transactions—payments to coal producers, workers, stock- and bondholders, and so on. Internal costs are part of the opportunity cost of making steel because they represent the forgone opportunities of using the same natural resources, capital, and labor in some other industry. In order to stay in business, the mill must receive a price of at least $100 per ton, that is, a price at least equal to the internal opportunity costs.

But the internal costs are not the only costs of making steel. In the process of burning coal, the mill spews out clouds of sulphur dioxide, soot, and other pollutants. The pollution damages health, kills trees, and ruins paint in areas downwind of the plant. These effects are *external* costs of generating electricity because they are borne by third parties—people who are neither buyers nor sellers of steel or any of the inputs used in making it. External costs are also part of the opportunity cost of making steel in that they represent the value of the factors destroyed by the pollution (dead trees, workers in firms other than the steel producer taking sick leave) or required in order to repair its effects (repainting houses, treating pollution-related diseases).

Suppose that pollution damage of all kinds comes to $20 per ton of steel produced. Added to the $100 in internal costs, the $20 of external costs makes the overall opportunity cost of steel $120 per ton. This figure reflects the value of the factors of production used directly by the mill plus those destroyed or diverted from other uses by the pollution.

If the price of steel is set by supply and demand in a competitive market, it will tend toward the level of $100 per ton that just covers internal costs. But this sends a false signal to steel users: It tells them that producing a ton of steel puts a smaller drain on the economy's scarce factors of production than is really the case. Thus, steel users will use more steel than they should. They will be less inclined to find substitutes for steel, recycle steel, design products so as to use less steel, and so on. In short, the market will fail to achieve efficient resource allocation because prices will have sent users the wrong information.

Crowding

Another common type of externality results from crowding of common property. By **common property** economists mean property that is open to use by all members of a community. Ocean fishing grounds, parks, and city streets are examples of common property.

Common property
Property to which all members of a community have open access.

Consider the case of ocean fishing grounds. In order to enter the fishing business, an operator must bear a number of internal costs, including the capital costs of a boat, crew members' pay, the cost of fuel, and so on. These costs are fully reflected in transactions between boat owners and their suppliers. When many boats compete, fish prices are set by supply and demand at a level that reflects these internal costs.

However, when the fishing ground reaches a certain level of crowding, there begin to be external costs as well. When fishing strains the ability of the fish population to reproduce, the total catch of all boats will fall as more boats enter the fleet. With more boats going after fewer fish, the costs per ton of fish and the market price of fish rise.

The effects of crowding are a type of externality in which the third parties on whom the external costs fall are other participants in the activities—in this case, other fishing boats. The measure of the external costs is the amount by which the entry of an additional boat reduces the daily catch of the boats already there and hence raises the cost per ton of fish they catch. Thus, the true opportunity cost of adding one boat to the fleet is greater than the internal costs of capital, wages, fuel, and so on that the new entrant bears. As the fishing grounds become increasingly crowded, consumers must pay an ever higher price for fish in order to insure that each boat will continue to earn enough to cover internal costs.

External Benefits

Pollution and crowding generate external costs, that is, effects that harm third parties. However, some externalities are beneficial. For example, a person who raises bees to produce honey benefits the owners of neighboring orchards by improving pollination. If the price of honey does not reflect the value of the pollination services, the price overstates the opportunity cost of producing honey, resulting in too little honey produced and consumed. This too can be considered a market failure.

The examples of steel, fish, and honey all relate to externalities of production. There are also externalities of consumption, both harmful and beneficial. Exhaust pollution from cars is an example of a harmful externality of consumption; so is a noisy party in a quiet neighborhood. A commuter using a crowded highway generates an externality of consumption in the form of crowding. Raising flowers in one's yard, on the other hand, produces an external benefit for neighbors and passersby.

The Role of Government

Market failures resulting from externalities are widely believed to require corrective action by government. There are many possible kinds of corrective action. Take the case of steel mill pollution. One option is to require the mill to use stack scrubbers and other pollution abatement equipment. Another is to place a tax (in this case, of $20 per ton) on steel so that users will bear the full opportunity cost. Still another is to allow those injured by pollution to seek redress from the mill through federal or state courts. The objective in each case is the same: By imposing the cost of buying pollution control equipment, a tax, or the cost of lawsuits, the external costs will be "internalized," that is, brought to bear on the parties involved in the transaction that is the source of the externality. A closer study of pollution and its remedies is part of the microeconomics course.

In addition to taking action against external harms such as pollution, some see a role for government in cases of external benefits. Beekeepers might be paid a subsidy; property owners might be subject to laws requiring them to keep their property presentable; and so on.

Private Action to Internalize Externalities

Although externalities are often seen as calling for government action, sometimes private alternatives exist. Problems of externalities are closely linked to the nature of property rights (Ronald Coase pointed this out in his article on social costs; see "Who Said It? Who Did It? 4.1," page 88). Contracts among private property owners can sometimes internalize externalities that would otherwise require government action. For example, in many residential developments, private covenants among property owners control both beneficial and harmful externalities associated with property upkeep, subdivision of lots, type of construction, and so on. Beekeepers often contract with fruit growers to bring their hives to the orchard at blossom time. The owners of private amusement parks, private fishing lakes, and so on are able to control crowding through fees that they can raise during periods of peak demand.

Public Goods

A second category of market failure that is widely held to call for government action occurs in the case of *public goods*. In the terminology of economics, **public goods** are goods and services that cannot be provided for one person without being provided for that person's neighbors and that, once provided for one person, can be provided for others at no extra cost.

> **Public good**
> A good or service that (1) cannot be provided for one person without also being provided for others and (2) once provided for one person can be provided for others at zero added cost.

Perhaps the closest thing to a pure public good is national defense. One person cannot be protected against nuclear attack without the protection being extended to everyone. Also, it costs no more to protect a single resident of an area than to safeguard an entire city or region. Police and fire protection are public goods in part (police and fire departments also provide many individual services). Some people think the space program and even the national parks are public goods too. The idea is that people everywhere get satisfaction from reading or hearing about them even if they themselves do not take a ride in orbit or a hike in the mountains.

It is difficult for private firms to make a profit selling products that, once provided to one customer, become available to others at no additional cost. The reason is that people who do not pay their share of the cost of the good cannot be excluded from enjoying its benefits. To see why the market may fail in such cases, imagine that someone tries to set up a private missile defense system, Star Wars Inc., to be paid for by selling subscriptions to people who want protection from a nuclear attack. If my neighbors subscribed and got their houses protected, I would not need to subscribe myself; instead, knowing that their homes' protection would be my home's as well, I would be tempted to become a "free rider."

However, my neighbors would probably reason the same way. They would not subscribe, hoping that I would; then they could be the free riders. If some of them were willing to pay their fair share, that would not be enough to cover the whole cost. Those few public-spirited people would have to pay far more than their fair share to keep the service from going bankrupt. In short, it is unlikely that a private missile defense firm would ever get off the ground.

The free-rider problem, which is always present in the case of public goods, means that government may have to provide those goods if they are to be provided at all (we say "may" because, as "Applying Economic Ideas 5.1" illustrates, some things that have the characteristics of public goods are provided by private firms). However, it should be noted that many goods and services provided at public expense are not public goods in the sense that the term is used in economics. Take education, for example. The primary beneficiaries of public education are students. It is not impossible to exclude students from the schools. Only a few schools, public or private, operate on an "open admission" basis. Others select their students according to neighborhood, or ability to pay, or scholastic achievement. Nor can students be added to the schools at no expense. The more students a school has, the more teachers, classrooms, laboratories, and so on it needs. Thus, education does not fit the definition of a public good. It may, however, have certain external benefits in the form of promoting good citizenship. As we saw in the preceding section, such external benefits would—in some people's eyes, at least—justify a government role in education whether or not it is a true public good.

Insufficient Competition

Still another source of market failure that many economists think justifies government action is insufficient competition. As we have seen, market prices should reflect opportunity costs if they are to guide resource allocation efficiently. In the case of harmful externalities, market failure occurs because prices fall below opportunity costs. Where competition is insufficient, however, market failure can occur because prices are too *high*.

As an extreme case, consider a market in which there is only a single seller of a good or service—that is, a *monopoly*. Public utilities such as residential electric and telephone service are a frequently cited example. Suppose, for instance, that Metropolitan Electric can generate power at an opportunity cost of $.10 per kilowatt hour. Selling power to customers at that price would guide them in making efficient choices between electricity and other energy sources, such as oil or coal, and in undertaking energy-saving investments, such as home insulation and high-efficiency lighting.

If homeowners could buy electricity from anyone they wanted, as they can eggs or gasoline, the forces of competition, acting through supply and demand, would push the market price toward the level of opportunity costs. The utility would not sell power for less than the opportunity costs because doing so would put it out of business (we assume that appropriate government policies would internalize any externalities of pollution). Further, in a competitive market, any one seller that tried to raise prices much above the opportunity costs would be undercut by others seeking to take its customers away.

However, utilities do not compete in sales to residential customers. Every home, after all, is connected to only one set of power lines. In this case a utility, left to its own devices, could substantially increase its profits by charging a price higher than the opportunity costs. Of course, raising the price would mean that less power would be sold as customers moved up and to the left along their demand curves. But up to a point, the greater profit per kilowatt hour sold

APPLYING ECONOMIC IDEAS   5.1

Private Marketing and the Public Goods Problem:
The Case of Computer Software

To a substantial degree, computer software has the properties of a public good. Once a game program, word processing system, or spreadsheet system has been provided for one user, others are likely to make copies for their own use. Further, the cost of copying many kinds of software is near zero. Yet despite these traits, the writing and selling of computer software is a multi-million-dollar private business. How do firms do it?

One technique is to "copy protect" software before it is sold. A program that cannot be copied no longer resembles a public good. Lotus Development Corporation, creator of the popular *1-2-3* spreadsheet program for personal computers, uses this strategy. However, copy protection has its drawbacks. For one thing, the codes used to protect the software can be broken and the means for doing so spread quickly along the computer user grapevine. Also, copy-protected software is somewhat less convenient to use, a fact that gives competitors an advantage.

For these reasons, other major software suppliers sell their programs in a form that can be easily copied. Buyers are required as part of their purchase contract to pledge that they will not copy the program except to make extra copies for their own convenience. However, there is no barrier to copying by dishonest users. Ashton-Tate, which sells the *MultiMate* word processing program, is an example of a firm that permits copying only by contract. The fact that thousands of users pay several hundred dollars for the firm's programs rather than using pirated copies attests to the fact that most are honest.

A third approach to the free-rider problem relies even more directly on user honesty: the Freeware™ approach developed by Headlands Press of Tiburon, California. This firm does not sell its popular program *PC-Talk* through computer stores or other retail channels. Instead, a message encoded in the program invites new users to make copies of the program and distribute them to their friends in return for a modest contribution to Headlands Press. This unusual business strategy has earned tens of thousands of dollars (he won't say exactly how much) for computer author Andrew Fluegelman, Freeware's inventor. This example shows that despite the marketing challenges it creates, the free-rider problem is not an absolute barrier to the private marketing of products with the properties of a public good.

would more than outweigh the effect on overall profit of the reduction in quantity demanded. (The microeconomics course explores the profit-maximizing calculus of the monopolist in detail.)

If too high a price is charged, homeowners will get a false message regarding the opportunity cost of electricity. They may make substitutions that are not economically justified. For example, they may switch from electricity to oil for heat even in regions where cheap hydroelectric power is available or from electric air conditioning to gas air conditioning even in areas where the opportunity cost of electricity is below that of gas.

Many economists think that market failures due to insufficient competition are not limited to the extreme case of monopoly. As the microeconomics course explains, they think that competition among a small number of firms may also lead to higher prices, especially if the firms collude with one another to keep prices high.

Several kinds of government actions aim to prevent market failures due to insufficient competition. In some cases, the government may assume ownership of monopoly public utilities, as does the Tennessee Valley Authority. In others, the utilities remain in private hands but are subject to price regulation. In other markets, *antitrust policy* is used to insure a reasonable number of competing firms in each market. For example, although the government normally permits mergers between nondominant firms such as Chrysler and American Motors, it would oppose a merger of Ford and General Motors. Even given competition from imports, it would be feared that there would be insufficient competition in the auto industry following a merger of two such dominant firms. Antitrust laws and monopoly regulation are covered in greater detail in the microeconomics course.

Income Distribution

In the cases of externalities, public goods, and insufficient competition, the market fails in that it does not achieve an efficient resource allocation. In terms of the economic questions of Chapter 2, mistakes are made with respect to *which* outputs are produced and *how* they are produced. In addition, many observers feel, the market may fail to achieve a fair distribution of income; in other words, its answer to the question of *for whom* goods are to be produced is unacceptable.

As pointed out in Chapter 1, opinions differ as to what constitutes a fair distribution of income. Some ideally would like to do away with almost all inequality of income. Others would be satisfied with a system that guaranteed an adequate minimum income. Still others think that there are certain **merit goods,** such as education and health care, that should be distributed more or less equally, whereas other goods and services, such as cosmetics or airline travel, matter less. These are all variations of the egalitarian view of fairness. As Chapter 1 also pointed out, some people take a libertarian point of view, under which they see fairness as applying mainly to freedom and equality of opportunity rather than to a particular income distribution.

Those who believe the market fails to achieve a fair distribution of income favor a variety of government remedies. Transfer payments, from social security to food stamps, are one type of cure. Free or below-cost provision of merit goods, such as education, is another. Programs intended to raise the earnings of low-income workers, including the federal minimum wage, are still another possibility. These programs also are given more detailed treatment in the microeconomics course.

Merit good
A good to which all citizens are entitled regardless of ability to pay.

The Macroeconomic Role of Government

All of the market failures mentioned so far are microeconomic in nature. However, many economists see yet another role for government in correcting macroeconomic failures of the market economy. In their view, a capitalist economy is inherently unstable, subject to cycles of inflation alternating with periods of high unemployment and slow or negative economic growth.

The macroeconomics course looks at the policy tools that the government has available for promoting macroeconomic stability. These include federal tax and expenditure policies and policies related to control of money, interest rates, and financial markets. The macroeconomics course also examines the views of economists who think that the private economy is not so unstable after all. In their eyes, much of the inflation and unemployment experienced in the past was caused by policy mistakes on the part of officials who might better have taken a hands-off approach.

The Rent-Seeking Theory of the Government's Economic Role

The market failure theory of the role of government is largely a *normative* theory. As such, it attempts to define the role that government ought to play in the economy: The government should promote efficient allocation of resources; insure a fair distribution of income; and do all it can to stabilize the macroeconomy.

But when we look at what government actually does rather than what it ought to do, we find many programs that poorly fit the categories of market failure. In fact, some programs seem designed to promote inefficiency and inequality in markets that would function reasonably well without government intervention. Consider, for example, price supports for farm products. As we saw in Chapter 3, these hold farm prices above equilibrium levels, thus causing huge surpluses. This is hardly efficient. Further, although some benefits go to farmers in financial difficulty, thus serving the goal of fairness, most of the subsidies, as "Economics in the News 5.1" points out, go to farmers who are financially well off.

It appears, then, that at least some government programs cannot be adequately explained in terms of the market failure theory of government. Gordon Tullock of George Mason University and others have advanced a theory of *rent seeking* as an alternative.[1]

The Nature of Economic Rents

In everyday language, a *rent* simply means a payment made for the use of something, say, an apartment or a car. Economists use the term in a more specialized sense, however. An **economic rent** is any payment to a factor of production in excess of its opportunity costs. The opportunity cost of supplying a factor of production, in this case, means its value in its best alternative use. The concept is broad and can apply to any factor of production. For example:

Economic rent
Any payment to a factor of production in excess of its opportunity costs.

- Ralph Singer owns two fields, one flat and one hilly, on which he grows hay worth $50 a year net of growing costs. The opportunity cost of the fields (that is, the payment needed to bid them away from hay growing) is $50 a year. A youth club agrees to pay $100 per year to rent the flat field for playing baseball. Of the $100 received for the flat field, $50 covers its opportunity cost and the remaining $50 is economic rent.

- Billingham Pharmaceuticals Inc. holds a patent on a lotion claimed to cure baldness. The lotion costs only $1 a jar to produce, but since it has no competition, it can be sold for $8 per jar. Of the $8, $7 can be considered economic rent.

- Joe Zmud is an autoworker with 20 years' seniority. Ford Motor Company pays him $20 an hour. Given his age and specialized skills, the best alternative job he could get would probably pay only half his cur-

[1]For a representative collection of papers on the theory of rent seeking, see James M. Buchanan, Robert D. Tollison, and Gordon Tullock, eds., *Toward a Theory of the Rent-Seeking Society* (College Station, Tex.: Texas A&M Press, 1980).

·ECONOMICS IN THE NEWS   5.1

Farm Subsidies Often Benefit the Strong

In Hollywood and Washington, there is a sharp image of the American farm problem: a family enterprise, passed down from one hard-working generation to the next, now threatened by low prices but ready to rise strong and healthy once more if only given a helping hand. However, the reality is more complex. Certainly there are many farms that fit the classic family-farm description. But of the $26 billion a year that the federal government spends on farm subsidies (as of 1986), much of it misses farmers in need and ends up in other pockets. Items from the news:

- To evade a $50,000-per-farmer cap on government payments, a California rice farm was leased to 56 tenants, each of whom qualified for the top payment and then split the $1.5 million income with the landlord. At least eight of the tenants were related to the owner.

- To benefit corn growers by increasing the demand for their crop, the government subsidizes the production of gasohol, a blend of ethanol distilled from corn and gasoline. In 1986, $29,230,000 was paid to Archer Daniels Midland, a huge, Illinois-based agribusiness that reported record profits that year. This sum represented 54 percent of total government payments under the program, which critics have christened "corporate food stamps."

- Mohammed Aslam Khan grows rice in Butte City, California. He is a U.S. citizen, but four relatives, passive investors in the farm, are not—they live in Faisalabad, Pakistan. Uncle Sam paid the four $152,010 for Khan's 1984 crop.

- In Vincennes, Indiana, Dennis Carnahan's family has pushed corn production costs so low that they could probably turn a profit if the farm program were abolished. But the 33-year-old farmer figures that the program is "the best ball game in town." The Carnahans expect to collect $81,180 from the government for the corn grown on their 3,800-acre farm this year.

The *Des Moines Register* is considered the most influential newspaper in the farm belt. What does it think of the government's programs? "American farm policy is a colossal hoax. It is a hoax on the countryside as well as on urban taxpayers," says the *Register*. Noting that less than one dollar in three spent on farm subsidies goes to a farmer in need, it suggests limiting payments to a safety net for small and medium-size farms. Under current policy, "Never before have Americans spent so many tax dollars on agriculture, and never have the results been more destructive to the kind of rural life that Americans profess to want."

Sources: Ward Sinclair, "Loophole Allows Extra Farm Subsidies," *Washington Post*, January 20, 1987, A3; Michael Isikoff, "Ethanol Producer Reaps 54 Percent of U.S. Subsidy," *Washington Post*, January 29, 1987, A14; Wendy L. Wall and Charles F. McCoy, "New Farm Law Raises Federal Costs and Fails to Solve Big Problems," *The Wall Street Journal*, June 17, 1986, 1; "Sacred Farmers," *The Wall Street Journal*, March 5, 1987, 28. The quotations from the *Des Moines Register* are as given in "Sacred Farmers."

rent wage. Thus, he can be considered as earning $10 per hour in economic rent.

As the above examples show, rents are very nice for those who receive them. However, they are not always easy to come by. Ralph Singer was just lucky to have inherited one of the few flat fields in his hilly county. Billingham had to spend millions on research and thousands more on patent lawyers to secure its position as the sole maker of baldness lotion. Zmud and his predecessors at Ford staged many bitter strikes before attaining the current wage scale.

Moreover, rents not only are hard to come by but are under constant threat in the form of competition. Someone else might lease a baseball field more cheaply. A competitor might come up with a different baldness formula and undercut Billingham's price. Buyer preference for Toyotas and Yugos might force Zmud to seek work selling shoes.

In short, a rent is something that must be first won and then defended. The process of obtaining and defending rents is known as **rent seeking.**

Rent seeking
The activity of obtaining and defending rents.

The Process of Rent Seeking

One way to seek and defend rents is through entrepreneurship. As competition forces prices toward opportunity costs, rents are eroded. They can be reestablished by exploring new opportunities, finding new ways of doing things, and inventing means of satisfying consumer wants. Rents earned by entrepreneurs as the reward for creating new value are commonly called *profits*. But business firms are not the only ones who earn rents as a reward for entrepreneurship. In labor markets, the first workers to move into a fast-growing region or a new specialty often earn rents in the form of higher wages than they could obtain in older, more crowded labor markets. These entrepreneurial types of profit seeking and rent seeking are an essential part of the market process in a capitalist economy.

However, instead of taking the entrepreneurial route, firms, workers, and resource owners may turn to government in their search for rents. A rent earned through a government program that raises prices or cuts costs is just as good, dollar for dollar, as a rent that is won in the marketplace. In some cases it may even be better, because government can not only create rents but shield them from erosion by competition.

Agricultural price supports are an example of rents obtained through government action. As "Economics in the News 5.1" points out, the bulk of farm subsidies go to farmers who are not in trouble. This reflects the fact that whether the price is set by the market or by the government, most farmers will receive enough to cover their opportunity costs. Those with better than average land or managerial skills will receive rents even at the market price, although the rent will be even higher if the government sets a price above the market price. In a period when production costs are rising or demand for the product is falling, some farmers with average or below-average land and skills will be unable to cover their costs and will be in financial difficulty, but this will not happen to all farmers at once.

According to the rent-seeking model of government, the reason farm programs are not more narrowly targeted is that broad-ranging programs that generate rents for all farmers will draw much wider political support. Without the political support of the relatively prosperous farmers who draw the bulk of the subsidies, say the rent-seeking theorists, programs for troubled farmers would not get the votes they need in Congress. This line of reasoning is discussed in detail in the microeconomics course under the heading of *public choice theory*.

Subsidies are one important tactic of rent seeking, but not the only one. Restrictions on competition are another way of generating rents. We have seen that competition from other producers—especially from those who can produce at lower costs—tends to erode rents in a free market. Such rents can be protected by laws that restrict competition.

Restrictions on imports are a leading example. Tariffs and import quotas on clothing, cars, sugar, steel, and other products shield domestic firms and their employees from competition. The firms are thus able to earn rents in the form of higher profits and the employees to earn rents in the form of higher wages.

From the standpoint of the rent-seeking theory of government, a policy such as import quotas on automobiles is perfectly understandable in view of the political power of the firms and their unions. However, it is more difficult to reconcile with the market failure theory. It clearly does not promote efficiency, since it interferes with specialization according to comparative advantage. Also, it is questionable whether it promotes equity in view of the fact that automakers' stockholders and unionized employees have higher average incomes than the typical auto buyer.

Examples of government restrictions on competition can be found within the domestic economy as well. Banking regulations prohibit commercial banks from competing with investment banks in the securities business. Licensing fees and examinations restrict the number of competitors who can enter such professions as law and medicine and often even such occupations as manicuring and hair styling. The article that leads off this chapter notes that public employee unions in Florida tried, with partial success, to get the state legislature to block competition from private prisons. Also, recently tightened immigration control has generated rents for some U.S. citizens by reducing the supply of competing immigrant workers.

Ironically, even successful rent seekers do not always come out ahead. A major reason is that the activity of seeking rents is itself costly. Firms sometimes spend millions on lawyers, lobbyists, and public relations firms in the hope of winning an arms contract, television license, or offshore drilling site. Expenditures on rent seeking are sometimes seen as a major waste of resources.

Rent Seeking and the Concept of Government Failure

Much work on the theory of market failure aims to identify cases in which government action could, if properly carried out, enhance efficiency or fairness. However, it is important to realize that government programs themselves may fail to work efficiently. Rent seeking is one major reason.

For examples, we can run right down the list of programs designed to correct market failures. Let's start with national defense. Defense is a public good and might well be inadequately supplied by private firms. But the defense budget is also a major source of rents for defense contractors, communities hosting military bases, and so on. Each year the U.S. defense department itself publishes a "Pentagon pork" list of billions of dollars' worth of unwanted bases that it is forced to keep open and ineffective weapons that it is made to buy because they generate rents in the home district of some powerful member of Congress.

Next, consider pollution control. Government regulations often frustrate private firms' efforts to reduce pollution at the lowest cost. For example, regulators have forced some utilities to use "stack scubbers" to clean the sulphur dioxide from coal smoke rather than the cheaper method of burning low-sulphur Western coal to begin with. The reason: rent seeking by politically powerful producers of high-sulphur Eastern coal.

Regulation of monopolies may also fall victim to rent seeking. In some cases, regulated firms manage to "capture" regulatory agencies. The agencies then end up protecting the rents of producers rather than insuring low prices and efficient service for consumers. The relationship between the Interstate Commerce Commission and the trucking industry prior to the regulatory reforms of the early 1980s is a case in point.

Even programs designed to redistribute income to the poor are distorted by rent-seeking behavior. For instance, in the 1970s and early 1980s a program designed to encourage construction of low-cost housing became a multi-billion-dollar tax shelter for wealthy doctors, lawyers, and stockbrokers.

The point of these examples is not that government always makes a mess of things or that the market always functions perfectly; rather, they demonstrate that both the market and government are imperfect institutions. In deciding whether to transfer a function to government from the market, the possibilities of government failure must be weighed against those of market failure. As the next section reveals, these types of comparisons often lead to the conclusion that some functions of government should be moved to the private sector.

Privatization

Privatization means the turning over of government functions to the private sector. In part, privatization is the opposite of nationalization. *Nationalization,* once popular in many countries, means the transfer of private firms in communications, transportation, heavy industry, and finance to government ownership. Under privatization, such firms are now being returned to private ownership in many countries. Privatization can also mean contracting with private firms to provide services for which the government continues to pay. The private jail in Bay County, Florida, described at the beginning of this chapter is an example of this alternative form of privatization.

Privatization
The turning over of government functions to the private sector.

Privatization in Action

Privatization is a worldwide phenomenon. As the following examples indicate, privatization is underway in advanced industrial nations, the Third World, and even the Soviet Union and other socialist countries. In the United States, steps toward privatization have been taken at all government levels.

The United Kingdom under Prime Minister Margaret Thatcher is, in many respects, the world leader in privatization. Major state-owned industries sold to the public include British Telecom (the telephone company), British Airways, and, biggest of all, the $7.9 billion British Gas. France is not far behind, having recently sold the large glassmaker Saint-Gobain and Paribas, a major bank. In the British and French styles of privatization, shares are sold to individual investors; for example, 1.5 million French investors bought shares in Saint-Gobain and 4.5 million Britons bought shares in British Gas. By widely distributing shares, the governments hope to maximize political support for the programs. Industrial countries outside Europe are also privatizing. Japan, like the United Kingdom, has sold its national telephone company and is planning to sell its railway system and airline. Israel and Canada have also taken privatization steps.

Privatization is not limited to the advanced industrial countries. State-owned telephone and telegraph companies are being sold in Bangladesh, Mexico, Thailand, South Korea, Malaysia, and Sri Lanka; state-owned airlines in Thailand, Singapore, Bangladesh, Malaysia, and South Korea; state-owned banks in Chile, South Korea, Bangladesh, the Philippines, and Taiwan; and sugar refineries in Jamaica and Uganda.[2]

---

[2]Peter Young, "Privatization around the Globe: Lessons for the Reagan Administration," *Policy Report No. 120* (Dallas: National Center for Policy Analysis, January 1986).

Privatization is even underway in some socialist countries, with farming and service industries the main focus. China under Deng Xiaoping has privatized much of its vast farm sector. Private restaurants and retail shops are now common. State-owned housing has been sold to tenants in China, as is also being done in Cuba. In Eastern Europe, Hungary sports the only private hotel in the Soviet Bloc. The Soviet Union under Gorbachev has been cautious, but some small-scale private service businesses, such as automobile and shoe repair, have been permitted.

In the United States, state and local governments have moved ahead of the federal government. In Farmington, New Mexico, a private firm runs the airport control tower. Chandler, Arizona, buys sewage treatment services from a private firm. In Virginia, a private firm wants to build a 10-mile toll road through rapidly growing Louden County, and another wants to build a rapid transit system to link Dulles Airport to the Washington, D.C., subway system. And, of course, there is that private jail in Florida.

At the federal level—despite some pro-privatization claims by the Reagan administration—there have been few major actions. This is partly because the U.S. government has never become as involved in ownership of transportation, communications, and heavy industry as have the governments of European countries. The one major privatization step taken was the sale of Conrail, the dominant railroad in the Northeast. After an aborted plan to sell Conrail to Norfolk Southern, the government sold shares to the public following the British and French models.

Perceived Benefits of Privatization

The perceived benefits of privatization vary among countries and industries. However, there are some common elements.

Political and Ideological Motives
In some cases, political and ideological motives are behind privatization. For example, the conservative governments of Britain and France hope that the millions of shareholders in newly privatized industries will feel they have a stake in the capitalist system and thus vote conservative in future elections. One of the most effective moves reportedly has been the sale of hundreds of thousands of British public housing units to current tenants.

Improved Administration
A more widespread motivation for privatization is the hope of improved administration. Government bureaucracies are not designed for the creativity and quick reactions needed for managing a modern business. The hallmarks of bureaucracy are caution, job security, and decisions by the book. There is no "bottom line" to spur government managers to better performance.

Cost Savings through Competition
With large-scale European-type privatization, it is hoped that cost savings will be realized once subsidies are cut off and firms are exposed to competition in the international marketplace. In the kind of privatization practiced by state and local governments in the United States, the savings come through competitive bidding for contracts to collect garbage, repair transit equipment, and so on. As

the article that opens this chapter notes, Bay County, Florida, turned to a private prison operator largely because this would save $700,000 a year.

Suppression of Rent Seeking

As we have seen, one of the reasons many government undertakings are inefficient is that they become the focus of rent seeking. For example, in cities whose sanitation and transit workers are public employees, wage scales have been pushed far above private-sector levels and restrictive work rules have sharply cut productivity in contrast to private contractors. Both employees and managers of government programs may practice a form of rent seeking in which power, prestige, and salary are enhanced by maximizing the number of people who work in an agency rather than by minimizing costs.

Improved Service Quality

Private firms often are able not only to supply services at lower costs than government agencies but to improve service quality as well. Anyone who has compared the process of getting a driver's license with that of getting a haircut knows the difference. In the Soviet Union and Eastern Europe, better service quality is seen as the most important benefit of privatization.

Potential Limitations of Privatization

Despite privatization's current popularity, it is unlikely that government participation will disappear. Privatization has inherent limitations. Some of these stem from the notion of market failure discussed earlier in the chapter. There is no practical way to supply some public goods at a profit. In these cases, the government may contract with private operators to provide services but continue to foot the bill.

Even where public goods are not involved, there is the problem that some government enterprises are too unprofitable to attract private buyers. The French automaker Renault is an example, at least for the time being. In the United States, the government rail passenger system Amtrak provides a case in point. Conrail could be sold because as an all-freight operation, it can be run at a profit. Amtrak, on the other hand, shows little promise of doing the same.

Finally, rent seeking can become a problem even when government is involved as a buyer of privately supplied services. The opening article to this chapter mentions the fear that private jailers will campaign for harsh prison sentences in order to keep their cells full. This is a small-scale variant of the notorious rent-seeking activities of the private arms makers who comprise the so-called military industrial complex in the United States.

In the final analysis, then, drawing the line between government and private sectors of the economy will always be a matter of balancing the imperfections of one set of institutions against those of the other.

Summary

1. **How large is the government sector of the U.S. economy?** The government sector of the U.S. economy consists of federal, state, and local units. The federal government accounts for about 70 percent of total government expenditures and state and local governments for the remainder. *Government purchases*

of goods and services at federal, state, and local levels combined equal about 20 percent of GNP. When *transfer payments* are added, total government expenditures rise to over one-third of GNP.

2. **Why is government action needed for controlling pollution?** According to one theory, the role of government is to compensate for *market failures. Externalities*—the effects of an economic activity on third parties—are one important source of market failure. Pollution is a case in point. If producers do not have to limit pollution or pay for the damages it causes, the price system will transmit distorted information about opportunity costs and efficiency will suffer. Crowding of *common property* is another example of an externality.

3. **Why are the Army, Navy, and Air Force not private firms?** National defense is an example of a *public good*— a good or service that cannot be provided to one person without being provided to that person's neighbors and that once provided to one person can be provided to others at no extra cost. Public goods often cannot be sold at a profit by private firms because "free riders" who use the goods but do not help pay for them cannot be excluded from enjoying their benefits. Providing public goods is thus seen as a government role.

4. **Why does the government not leave the questions of what, how, and for whom entirely to the market?** Market failures associated with externalities, public goods, and insufficient competition result in inefficient allocation of resources. These market failures represent defects in the market's method of handling the questions of what and how. Many government programs are designed to compensate for such market failures and, in so doing, improve efficiency. In addition, many people think that the market distributes income unfairly, that is, offers an unacceptable answer to the question of for whom goods and services will be produced. Transfer payments are designed to address this problem. Finally, the government also attempts to control inflation, unemployment, and economic growth, although not always successfully.

5. **Why do some government programs seem designed to enrich private firms and individuals rather than to promote the goals of efficiency and fairness?** Some government policies, such as farm price supports and import restrictions, rate poorly in terms of efficiency and fairness. Some economists think that such programs can be explained as the result of *rent seeking* by private firms and individuals. An *economic rent* is any payment to a factor of production in excess of its opportunity costs.

6. **Which of the roles of government might be better turned over to the private sector?** In the 1980s, there has been a global movement toward *privatization*, meaning the turning over of government functions to the private sector. One type of privatization is the sale of government-owned business firms to private owners; examples are the sale of British Gas, the Japanese telephone system, and the U.S. railroad Conrail. Another form of privatization involves contracts with private firms to provide services for which the government continues to pay; examples include the operations of jails, airports, garbage collection, and transit services.

Terms for Review

- government purchases of goods and services (government purchases)
- transfer payments
- market failure
- externality
- common property
- public good
- merit good
- economic rent
- rent seeking
- privatization

Questions for Review

1. As a measure of the size of government, what is revealed by the share of government purchases in GNP? By the share of government expenditures, including transfer payments?

2. What is an externality? Give five examples of externalities other than those mentioned in the chapter, including at least one beneficial externality.

3. Is police protection a public good? If so, in whole or in part? Consider police actions aimed at (a) reducing the level of street crime and (b) releasing the kidnapped child of a rich industrialist.

4. Why may the prices charged by a monopolist fail to reflect the opportunity costs of the good or service produced?

5. Give three examples, other than those mentioned in the chapter, of government programs that you think reflect rent seeking.

Problems and Topics for Discussion

1. **Examining the lead-off case.** Why do you think jails are usually run by the government? Is this govern-

ment activity better explained by the market failure approach or the rent-seeking approach—or do both theories fit the case of jails to some degree?

2. **Growth of government.** Using the latest *Economic Report of the President* or other source, update the information given in Exhibit 5.1. Has government grown more rapidly or more slowly than GNP over the past year?

3. **Externalities of traffic congestion.** Some cities are testing a new technology to reduce traffic congestion in downtown areas. A special device called a "transponder" is attached to the license plate of every car registered in the area. When a transponder-equipped car drives over wires embedded in the pavement along certain busy streets and highways, a computer records the license number. At the end of the month, the car's owner receives a bill reflecting how often he or she used the busy streets. The charge is higher if the car passed the detector during rush hour. How would this technology "internalize" externalities of traffic congestion? Do you think it would improve efficiency? Would it be a fair way to pay for street repair, police patrol, and so on? If the technology proved successful, would it become possible to privatize city streets by selling or leasing them to private firms that would regulate traffic, make repairs, and collect fees? Discuss.

4. **Economics of education.** A variety of arguments have been advanced in support of public funding for primary and secondary education. Some claim that education is a public good. Others say that education has beneficial externalities. Still others say that education is a merit good. What do you think? Do you believe that the same arguments apply to college education?

5. **Superstar rents.** Luciano Pavarotti reputedly is a very accomplished chef as well as one of the world's greatest opera tenors. Suppose that by running a restaurant he earns, say, $100,000 per year as opposed to $1 mil-

lion during a season of singing operas and recitals. What part of his earnings as a singer is economic rent? Do you think Pavarotti's rent is threatened by competition? Can the high earnings of superstars in other areas be explained in terms of the concept of rent? Discuss.

6. **Rent controls as a form of rent seeking.** Review the discussion of rent controls in Chapter 3. Of the monthly rental payments received by landlords for apartments, which portion represents economic rent? Is the answer the same in a long-run context as in a short-run context? We saw that some tenants benefit from rent control, especially those who live in rent-controlled apartments for an extended period. In what sense, if any, are the gains of such tenants analogous to economic rents? Should political support of rent control by tenant groups be considered a form of rent seeking?

7. **Private versus public universities.** In the field of higher education, private colleges and universities compete with government-run institutions. Write a short essay either in favor of or in opposition to privatization of public universities. First, consider the possibility that private firms are hired to run the schools but ownership remains in government hands and tuition is kept at the current level. Second, consider the possibility that universities will be sold outright to private operators who will cover all costs through tuition or alumni contributions. Would you feel differently about privatization of state universities if the private organizations that took them over from government were not-for-profit firms rather than profit-seeking corporations? If you attend a public college or university, are any university services privatized or are all the service providers employees of the school? What about cafeteria services? Custodial services? Security services? If none of these are privatized at your school, do you think they should be?

Case for Discussion
Backdoor Spending

You might think that, with huge federal budget deficits, Congress would be stymied. The deficits clearly make big new spending programs or tax cuts more difficult. How, then, can members of Congress do something for their constituents? Don't worry. The solution is to create new government benefits and make someone else pay for them.

Politically, the logic is powerful. A shrewdly designed program focuses benefits on a selected constituency while spreading costs across a large population

Since 1986, the Democrats do most of the "backdoor spending."

that won't realize it's paying. The economic logic is less compelling. At best, these programs simply redistribute society's wealth from A to B. At worst, they create pressures that make noninflationary economic growth more difficult. Everyone loses.

Although the political charms of backdoor spending appeal to both Republicans and Democrats, the Democrats—having regained control of Congress in 1986—are mainly responsible for its new-found importance. It allows them to create a legislative agenda without busting the budget. Consider:

- Sen. Edward Kennedy (D-Massachusetts) wants to raise the minimum wage $1 an hour or more over the current $3.35, with the increase spread over three or four years. Automatic annual changes would then keep the minimum at 50 percent of average hourly earnings.

- Sen. Tom Harkin (D-Iowa) and Rep. Richard A. Gephart (D-Missouri) would improve farmers' incomes by having the government restrict the size of crop plantings. Higher food prices would then raise farmers' profits.

- Many southern members of Congress—Republicans as well as Democrats—propose tighter import restrictions on textiles and apparel. Other industries will also probably seek relief.

- Rep. Patricia Shroeder (D-Colorado) and Sen. Christopher Dodd (D-Connecticut) would require most businesses to give parents four and a half months of unpaid leave on the birth of a child. The bill also requires unpaid leave for workers to care for sick children or family members.

Source: Robert J. Samuelson, "Backdoor Spending," *The Washington Post*, February 25, 1987, F1. Reprinted with permission.

Questions

1. Discuss each of the programs mentioned. Is the program justified as a government action for correcting market failure? If so, what kind of a failure? Or is the program better understood as an example of rent seeking? Could a program possibly fit both theories of the role of government?

2. Compare the Harkin-Gephart plan of crop restrictions with the support price program for milk discussed in Chapter 3. What are the similarities? What are the differences? Who would benefit from the crop restriction program—just farmers in need or all farmers? If plantings were to be restricted, would you favor an equal cutback in production by all farmers or giving proportionately larger allotments to the most efficient farmers or those farmers in greatest financial need? Discuss the pros and cons of each choice.

Suggestions for Further Reading

Buchanan, James M., Robert D. Tollison, and Gordon Tullock, eds. *Toward a Theory of the Rent-Seeking Society*. College Station, Tex.: Texas A&M Press, 1980.

A collection of papers by several authors applying the theory of rent seeking in various areas.

Coase, Ronald. "The Problem of Social Cost," *Journal of Law and Economics* 3 (1960).

A classic discussion of the problem of externalities and their relationship to property rights.

Goodman, John C. *Privatization*. Dallas: National Center for Policy Analysis, 1985.

A collection of papers on privatization, including several on the British experience. Includes an appendix on privatization at the state and local levels in the United States.

Hyman, David N. *Public Finance*, 2d ed. Hinsdale, Ill.: The Dryden Press, 1987.

Public finance is the name of the economics field devoted to the role of government. This is a comprehensive textbook on the subject.

Introduction to Macroeconomics

Part Two

6 The Circular Flow of Income and Product

After reading this chapter, you will understand . . .

- How households and firms are linked by incomes and expenditures.
- How income is related to money.
- How the concepts of supply and demand can be applied to the economy as a whole.
- How the various pieces of the economy—households, firms, government, and financial markets—fit together.
- How the U.S. economy is linked to the rest of the world.

Before reading this chapter, make sure you know the meaning of . . .

- Factors of production (Chapter 1)
- Gross national product (Chapter 1)
- Real and nominal values (Chapter 1)
- Equilibrium (Chapter 3)
- Inventories (Chapter 3)
- Financial markets (Chapter 4)
- Balance sheet, asset, and liability (Chapter 4)
- Government purchases of goods and services (Chapter 5)
- Transfer payments (Chapter 5)

Even with a Shrinking Deficit, Economy Will Continue to Grow

Inventory-to-sales ratios are well below recession-causing levels.

Despite the seemingly endless dithering and prevarication, Washington has truly begun to attack the federal deficit. In the first half of 1987, the cyclically adjusted deficit will average about the same as in calendar 1986 and then will begin receding—reaching a $105-billion rate by the middle of 1988. So after several quarters in neutral, the budget will shift abruptly toward restraint, with the deficit shrinking as much in a year as it had swelled in 2½ years—an amount equaling nearly 2 percent of GNP. This sort of jolt is the stuff of recession, but once again offsetting forces will come into play. The declining deficit will make room for private credit demands to expand without pressing interest rates up. And business spending for capital goods and inventories, which has been weak for quite a while, may be ripe for expansion soon.

Inventory-to-sales ratios are well below recession-causing levels. The ratio of inventories to final sales for all business is nearly 1.5 percent lower than a year ago, and inventory growth is only 0.5 percent a year. According to *Fortune's* quarterly survey of inventory policy, to be sure, business people would like their ratios 1 percent lower than they are now, and slightly more than half the executives would rather risk holding too little inventory than too much. Nevertheless, they expect to add inventory in the year ahead.

Another reason to expect brisker stock building: U.S. production will benefit from faster-growing exports and slower imports. Not many people noticed, but in the fourth quarter of 1986 the trade balance measured in physical volume, not in dollars, improved. *Fortune* expects trade to become a major plus for the economy for at least the next couple of years.

In the next year or so, consumer incomes should rise at a substantial 3.5 percent rate after inflation, aided by a $16-billion tax cut in 1987 and a $35-billion cut in 1988. Meantime, after increasing 4 percent last year, spending should grow only mildly. Thus, the savings rate will rise toward more normal levels.

Source: Todd May, Jr., "The Great Federal Shrink Begins at Last," *FORTUNE*, March 2, 1987, 49. © 1987 Time Inc. All rights reserved. Reprinted by permission. Photo Source: Reuters/Bettmann Newsphotos.

FORECASTS like this appear continually in the business press. Business managers have an insatiable appetite for any information that might give them a glimpse of the future. Such articles can bewilder the casual reader, however. There are so many pieces to the puzzle: government spending, taxes, the deficit, business capital spending, inventories, imports, exports, consumer income and spending, saving. How can they all possibly fit together? How do the actions of millions of individual firms and households, each making decisions independently, interact to produce recessions, recoveries, slowdowns, and booms? This chapter identifies the major pieces of the puzzle and their relationships to one another. In so doing, it lays the foundation for all of the macroeconomic models that follow.

The Circular Flow in a Simple Economy

Circular flow of income and product
The flow of goods and services between households and firms balanced by the flow of payments made in exchange for them.

The model around which this chapter is built is the **circular flow of income and product**—that is, the flow of goods and services between households and firms balanced by the flow of payments made in exchange for them.

To see the circular flow in its simplest form, we will begin with an economy in which there is no government, no financial markets, and no imports or exports. To make things even simpler, imagine that the households in this economy live entirely from hand to mouth, spending all their income on consumer goods as soon as they receive it, and that firms sell all their output directly to consumers as soon as they produce it.

The Basic Circular Flow

Exhibit 6.1 shows the circular flow of income and product for this ultra-simple economy. Real goods and services are shown flowing clockwise. Two sets of markets link households and firms. *Product markets*, which appear at the top of the diagram, are those in which households buy goods and services that firms produce. *Factor markets*, which appear at the bottom, are those in which firms obtain the labor services, capital, and natural resources that they need from households.

The clockwise flows of goods and services through these markets are balanced by counterclockwise flows of payments. Households make payments for the things they buy in product markets. Firms make factor payments—wages, interest payments, rents, royalties, and so on—in exchange for the factor services they buy.

By convention, when firms use labor, capital, or natural resources that they themselves own, they are counted as "buying" those factors from the households that are the ultimate firm owners. All production costs therefore can be viewed

Exhibit 6.1   The Basic Circular Flow

In this simple economy, households spend all their income on consumer goods as soon as they receive it and firms sell all their output to households as soon as they produce it. Goods and services flow clockwise, and the corresponding payments flow counterclockwise.

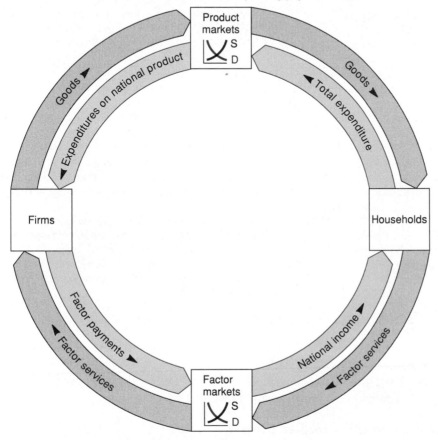

as factor payments. If a firm has something left over after meeting all its costs, it earns a profit. Profits too are counted as flowing directly to the households that own the firms, even though a firm may retain some profit to increase owners' equity rather than paying it out as dividends. For purposes of the circular flow, then, profit is lumped together with payments for labor, capital, and natural resources to make up total factor payments.

Stocks and Flows

We refer to all the amounts shown as arrows in Exhibit 6.1 as **flows** because they are continuously occurring processes. Flows are measured in units per time period—dollars per year, gallons per minute, or tons per month. Measurements of flows are measurements of rates at which things are happening.

It is important to distinguish flows from stocks. **Stocks** are quantities that exist at a given point in time. (The word *stock* in this sense has nothing to do with the common stocks that represent shares of ownership in a corporation.) Stocks

Flow
A process that occurs continuously through time, measured in units per time period.

Stock
A quantity that exists at a given point in time, measured in terms of units only.

White Water Canyon

King's Dominion is a huge amusement park near Richmond, Virginia. The summer weather is hot here, which helps explain why one of the most popular rides in the park is one called White Water Canyon.

In White Water Canyon, riders are seated in a round rubber raft. Once they are buckled in, the raft is swept down a twisting concrete chute through a series of wild rapids. Riders are guaranteed to get soaked to the skin in cool water as they hit waves and shoot under waterfalls. Then they get back in line, hoping to reach the boarding point again before they dry off.

The chute down which the rafts ride looks much like a real river. An electric pump circulates the water from a pond at the bottom of the chute back up to the top. The speed of the ride is controlled by the motor's speed. When the motor runs faster, more water is pumped through the chute and the rafts are carried along at a higher speed. If the speed of the pump is reduced, the rafts slow down until they hit bottom and cease to move at all.

The system is connected to a pipeline that can be used

to add water to replace that lost by splashing and evaporation. However, adding water does not in itself control the speed of the ride. If the pump's speed remains constant, extra water added to the system simply collects in the pond at the bottom of the chute.

This amusement park ride provides a simple illustration of the concepts of stocks and flows. The *stock* of water used in the ride means the number of gallons the system contains at any given time. When the pumps are turned off for the night, the stock of water in the system stays the same; all those gallons just trickle down into the pond at the bottom of the chute. When the pumps are turned back on in the morning, the same stock of water is set in motion again.

The *flow* of water through the ride means the number of gallons per minute passing a given point in the system—say, the point at which riders board the rafts. The faster the pumps run, the faster the flow. When the pumps are turned off, the flow falls to zero even though the stock of water remains constant.

---

are measured in terms of dollars, gallons, tons, and so on at a given point in time. The amusement park ride described in "Perspective 6.1" provides a simple illustration of the relationship between stocks and flows.

Money in the Circular Flow

The fluid that keeps the economy's plumbing working is not water but money. *Money* is what we use as a means of payment for buying goods and services. A formal definition of money will be given in Chapter 12. There we will see that the most commonly used forms of money are coins, paper currency, and bank account balances on which checks can be written. Just as there is a certain stock of water in the White Water Canyon ride on any given day, there is a given stock of money in the economy at any point in time—so many dimes, so many $20 bills, and so on. For example, on March 9, 1987, the U.S. money stock was $732 billion according to the most widely used measure. Unless the government or private banks do something to change the stock of money (such as printing more $20 bills and putting them into circulation), that $732 billion is what the economy has to work with just as the stock of water in the ride is what its operators have to work with (unless they change it by opening the drain or inlet valve).

The economy's money stock, like the water in the ride, doesn't just lie there. To do any useful work, it must be constantly circulated through the plumbing. Economic flows, such as income and expenditures, are measures of the speed with which money is moving through the system. These economic flows are measured in dollars per year as the flow of water in the ride is measured in gallons per minute. National income—in dollars per year—is several times the stock of money because each unit of money is spent several times each year as workers spend their pay at supermarkets, supermarkets spend their revenues to meet their payrolls, and so on. For example, in March 1987 national income was flowing at a rate of about $4 trillion per year even though the stock of money was just $732 billion. That means that each dollar of the money stock was changing hands more than five times each year.

Note that in both the White Water Canyon ride and the economy, stocks and flows are related and changes in one are often associated with changes in the other. Yet stocks and flows can also vary independently:

- In the case of the ride, turning on the inlet valve will increase the stock of water. However, so long as the pumps continue to run at the same speed, the added water will just sit at the bottom and the rate of flow through the chute will not change. On the other hand, the flow can be increased by speeding up the pump even while drain and inlet valves remain closed and the stock of water in the system stays fixed.

- In the case of the economy, adding more money—in the form of $20 bills, bank balances, or whatever—will not speed up the flow of income if the money just sits in people's pockets and bank accounts. On the other hand, the flow of income can be speeded up even if the stock of money remains fixed if people increase the rate at which they pass the money from hand to hand.

The relationship between the stock of money in the economy and the flow of income is one of the crucial keys to understanding macroeconomics. We will return to this relationship repeatedly in later chapters.

National Income and Product

Turning back to Exhibit 6.1, two of the flows deserve special attention. The first is labeled *national income*. **National income** is the total value of all wages, rents, interest payments, and profits earned by households. The second is labeled *expenditures on national product*. **National product** is the total value of all goods and services produced. Expenditures on national product are the dollar flow to firms that balances the flow of the products themselves from firms to product markets. National income is the dollar flow from firms to households that balances the flow of factor services. National income and national product are, by definition, equal in this simple economy.[1] This can be verified in two ways.

First, consider household expenditures as a link between national income and national product. Households are assumed to spend all their income on consumer goods as soon as they receive it, and firms are assumed to sell all their output directly to households. The payments made by buyers must equal the payments received by sellers; thus, viewed from this side of the circular flow, national product must equal national income.

National income
The total income earned by households, including wages, rents, interest payments, and profits.

National product
The total value of all goods and services produced in the economy.

---

[1]As we will see in the next chapter, establishing the equality of national income and product as measured in the official national income accounts requires a bit more detail than is shown here. Among other things, we will have to distinguish between *gross* and *net* national product, which are two ways of measuring this part of the circular flow. However, these details of national income accounting are not critical to the discussion of macroeconomic theory in this and later chapters.

Second, consider factor payments as a link between national income and national product. When firms receive money for the goods and services they sell, they use part of it to pay workers, resource owners, and suppliers of capital. Anything left over is profit. Thus, factor payments, including profits, account for all the money earned by households, and total factor payments equal national income. From this it follows that national income and national product are equal when viewed from this side of the circular flow, too.

Saving and Investment

The circular flow shown in Exhibit 6.1 is only a first step in laying out the linkages between households and firms. The next step is to add a second set of linkages that involve saving, investment, and financial markets.

Chapter 4 introduced the idea of financial markets as links between firms, which on average spend more for new investment than they earn, and households, which on average take in more than they spend. Exhibit 6.2 shows households as lenders that supply the funds flowing into financial markets and firms as borrowers that use those funds. To simplify this and the following circular flow diagrams, the clockwise flows of goods and services are omitted. Also, no distinction is made between direct financing (sales of stocks, bonds, and other financial instruments directly to households) and indirect financing (borrowing from financial intermediaries such as banks, thrift institutions, and insurance companies).

Saving

Saving

The part of household income that is not used to buy goods and services or to pay taxes.

The flow of funds from households to financial markets is labeled "saving" in Exhibit 6.2. **Saving** is the portion of household income that is not used to buy goods and services or to pay taxes. (There are no taxes in this economy yet, but they will soon be added.) The most familiar form of saving is the use of part of a household's income to make deposits in bank accounts or buy stocks, bonds, or other financial instruments rather than to buy goods and services. Economists, however, take a broader view of saving. They also consider households to be saving when they repay debts. Debt repayments are a form of saving because they too are income that is not devoted to consumption or taxes. Like other forms of saving, debt repayment is a source of funds for financial markets. For example, a bank that receives a $100 payment on an auto loan can use that sum to make new loans in the same way that it could use a $100 deposit in a savings account.

Investment

Fixed investment

Purchases by firms of newly produced capital goods, such as production machinery, office equipment, and newly built structures.

Inventory investment

Changes in the stocks of finished products and raw materials that firms keep on hand; figure is positive if such stocks are increasing and negative if they are decreasing.

Investment

The sum of fixed investment and inventory investment.

Businesses use the funds they obtain from financial markets to make two kinds of investments, both of which are noted in the article that opens this chapter. The first is **fixed investment**—the purchase of newly produced capital goods, such as production machinery, office equipment, and newly built structures. The second is **inventory investment**—the accumulation of stocks of raw materials prior to use or of finished products prior to sale. (Inventory investment can be less than zero in periods when firms are reducing their stocks of raw materials and finished products.) In this book, the term **investment** by itself means *total investment*—the sum of fixed investment and inventory investment.

Note that *investment* is defined somewhat more narrowly in economics than in everyday usage. In common terms, it means the purchase of almost any kind

Exhibit 6.2   The Circular Flow with Saving and Investment

When saving and investment are added to the circular flow, there are two paths by which funds can travel on their way from households to product markets. One path is direct, via consumption expenditures. The other is indirect, via saving, financial markets, and investment. The clockwise flows of goods and services have been omitted from this diagram; only flows of funds are shown.

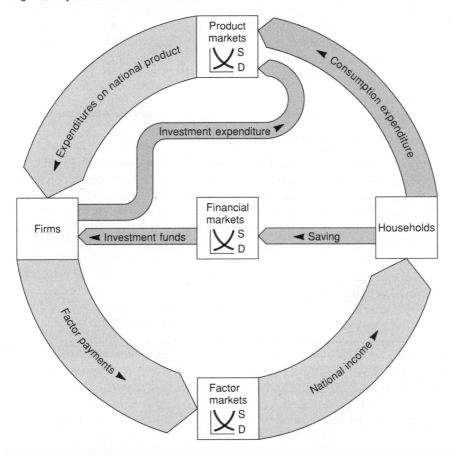

of asset; thus, a person or firm might be said to "invest" in common stocks, real estate, or secondhand oil tankers. However, none of these purchases is an investment in the economic sense because it adds nothing to the economy's total stock of capital goods or total inventories.

Suppose, for example, that Exxon buys a brand-new, custom-built oil tanker. That would be an investment, because it is a part of the flow of goods and services produced by the economy in the year it is built. The tanker goes onto Exxon's balance sheet as an asset, and it is also an addition to the economy's total stock of capital. A few years later, Exxon decides to sell the tanker to Mobil. For carrying oil, a used tanker is just as good as a new one. Yet the purchase is not an investment in the economic sense; it is not part of the economy's output of goods and services in the year it changes hands. Although it shows up on Mobil's balance sheet as a new asset, it passes off Exxon's balance sheet at the same time. Thus, when the used tanker changes hands, there is no change in the economy's total stock of capital. Likewise, purchases of other used capital goods, real estate (other than new structures), mineral deposits, forests, and so on are not investments in the economic sense. They are simply transfers of assets from the balance sheet of one household or firm to that of another.

Purchases of securities also are not investments in the economic sense. When Exxon buys its new tanker, it may finance the purchase by selling bonds to households. Households use part of their saving to buy the bonds, but it is the purchase of the tanker, not the purchase of the bonds, that constitutes the investment. The bondholders may later decide that they would rather have cash, in which case they sell the bonds to other households. But that transaction also is not an investment in the economic sense. No new tanker is being built; instead, households are adjusting their balance sheets by trading one kind of asset (the bonds) for another (money).

Aggregate Supply and Demand

Adding saving and investment to the circular flow raises a new issue. There are now two pathways along which funds flow from households to product markets: a direct path, through consumption expenditures, and an indirect path, through saving and financial markets to investment expenditures. Corresponding to these two paths are two separate sets of decision makers: households, which make consumption decisions, and businesses, which make investment decisions. How can we be sure that when the two types of expenditures are added together they will match the amount of available goods and services? In other words, how can we be certain that national income will still equal national product?

Aggregate supply
The value of all goods and services produced in the economy; a synonym for national product.

Aggregate demand
The value of all planned expenditures.

These questions can be answered using the familiar concepts of supply and demand in a new way. First, we define **aggregate supply** as the value of all goods and services produced in the economy. We already have another term for the same thing: *national product*. Next, we define **aggregate demand** as the value of all the purchases of newly produced goods and services that buyers plan to make. Thus, we can compare aggregate supply and aggregate demand to see whether, for the economy as a whole, buyers' plans mesh with sellers' in the same way that we compare supply and demand in the case of a single market.

Equilibrium in the Circular Flow

To see how aggregate supply can be compared with aggregate demand, imagine an economy in which only three goods are produced: apples, radios, and milling machines. The firms in this economy plan to produce apples at a rate of $30,000 per year, radios at a rate of $30,000 per year, and milling machines at a rate of $40,000 per year. As they carry out their plans, output flows at a rate of $100,000 units per year. This flow, which can be called either national product or aggregate supply, is shown in lines 1 through 4 of Exhibit 6.3.

While producers are busy carrying out their plans, buyers are making their own. Consumers plan to buy apples at a rate of $30,000 per year and radios at a rate of $30,000 per year. The firms that make radios plan to buy milling machines at a rate of $40,000 per year in order to increase their radio-producing capacity. No one plans either to increase or decrease the stocks of finished products held in inventory; thus, planned inventory investment is zero. All of these buying plans are expressed in lines 5 through 11 of Exhibit 6.3. The value of all

Exhibit 6.3   Example of a Simple Economy in Equilibrium

This exhibit shows a simple economy in which aggregate supply is exactly equal to aggregate demand. The plans of buyers and sellers match when they are tested in the marketplace, and no unplanned inventory changes take place. National product and total planned expenditures are equal.

Output Resulting from Producers' Plans

1	Total national product (aggregate supply)			$100,000
2	Apples	$30,000		
3	Radios	30,000		
4	Milling machines	40,000		

Expenditures Resulting from Buyers' Plans

5	Total consumption expenditures		$60,000	
6	Apples	$30,000		
7	Radios	30,000		
8	Total planned investment		40,000	
9	Fixed investment	40,000		
10	Planned inventory investment	0		
11	Total planned expenditure (aggregate demand)			$100,000

planned expenditures (consumption plus fixed investment plus planned inventory investment) is shown in line 11 as aggregate demand.

Comparing line 1 with line 11, we see that in this example buyers' and sellers' plans match perfectly. Aggregate supply and aggregate demand are equal. When the plans of buyers and sellers mesh in this way, we say that the circular flow as a whole is in *equilibrium* just as we say that a market is in equilibrium when its buyers' and sellers' plans mesh.

Disequilibrium

In practice, the plans of buyers and sellers almost never fit together as neatly as they do in Exhibit 6.3. In fact, it would be surprising if they did. After all, buyers and sellers do not always consult each other before production takes place. Each firm bases its production plans on the information available to it. Buyers base their plans on market prices and expectations about the future. Since production plans are often set before buyers' plans are formed, there is no way to be sure they will mesh.

To see what happens when buyers' and sellers' plans do not mesh, look at Exhibit 6.4. Here the situation is the same as in Exhibit 6.3 except that now consumers plan to buy only $25,000 worth of apples and firms only $35,000 worth of investment goods (milling machines). Thus, aggregate demand (line 11) is only $90,000 even though aggregate supply (line 1) is still $100,000.

When buyers' and sellers' plans are tested in the marketplace, there will be some disappointment: All the radios will be sold, but $5,000 worth of apples and $5,000 worth of milling machines will be left over. What will happen to these unsold goods? Once produced, they will not vanish into thin air; instead, they will pile up as inventories in the warehouses of apple farmers and machine tool companies. Those producers did not *plan* to make any inventory investments, but they nevertheless find themselves doing so. The $5,000 of unsold apples and the $5,000 of unsold milling machines are therefore listed in lines 12 through 14 of Exhibit 6.4 as *unplanned* inventory investments. Because buyers' and sellers' plans do not mesh, the circular flow is said to be in *disequilibrium*.

Reactions to Disequilibrium

In Exhibit 6.4, aggregate supply exceeds aggregate demand. Because buyers' and sellers' plans fail to mesh, there is an unplanned buildup of inventories. Firms would not want this inventory buildup to continue. In order to limit or reverse it, they would do one or both of two things. First, they might cut their prices in order to stimulate sales. If they did this, the volume of the circular flow, measured in nominal terms (that is, in terms of dollars' worth of goods and services at current prices), would shrink. Second, they might cut their rate of output. If they did this, the circular flow would shrink in both real terms (that is, in terms of output of goods and services adjusted for changes in prices) and in nominal terms.

At another time, aggregate demand might exceed aggregate supply. Suppose, for example, that instead of the planned expenditures shown in Exhibit 6.4, consumers plan to buy $35,000 worth of apples and firms $45,000 worth of milling machines. When these plans are tested in the marketplace, sales will exceed current output. The result will be unplanned depletion of inventories as

Exhibit 6.4   Example of a Simple Economy in Disequilibrium

In this example, planned purchases of apples and milling machines fall short of the amounts of those goods produced. When plans are tested in the marketplace, producers of apples and milling machines experience an unplanned increase in inventories. Total planned expenditure (aggregate demand) falls short of national product (aggregate supply). However, total realized expenditures, including both planned expenditures and unplanned inventory investment, equal national product.

Output Resulting from Producers' Plans				
1	Total national product (aggregate supply)			$100,000
2	Apples	$30,000		
3	Radios	30,000		
4	Milling machines	40,000		
Expenditures Resulting from Buyers' Plans				
5	Total consumption expenditures		$55,000	
6	Apples	$25,000		
7	Radios	30,000		
8	Total planned investment		35,000	
9	Fixed investment	35,000		
10	Planned inventory investment	0		
11	Total planned expenditure (aggregate demand)			$ 90,000
Other Expenditures				
12	Total unplanned inventory investment			10,000
13	Unsold apples	5,000		
14	Unsold milling machines	5,000		
Summary				
15	Total national product			$100,000
16	Total realized expenditure			100,000
17	Planned	$90,000		
18	Unplanned	10,000		

stocks of apples and milling machines are used to meet the strong demand. Firms will react in a way opposite to their reaction to an unplanned inventory buildup. If they try to stop the inventory depletion by raising prices, the circular flow will grow in nominal terms. If they also increase output, the circular flow will grow in both real and nominal terms.

Equality of National Income and Product

As Exhibits 6.3 and 6.4 show, national product (aggregate supply) equals planned expenditure (aggregate demand) only when the economy is in equilibrium. However, whether or not the economy is in equilibrium, national product always equals **realized expenditure,** that is, the total of planned and unplanned expenditures. This is so because unplanned inventory investment acts as a balancing item. When planned expenditure falls short of aggregate supply, inventories pile up. In that case, adding unplanned inventory investment to planned expenditure makes total realized expenditure equal to aggregate supply. On the other hand, if planned expenditure exceeds aggregate supply, inventories are run down. In that case, adding the negative unplanned inventory investment to planned consumption and investment makes total realized expenditure equal to aggregate supply. In equation form,

Realized expenditure
The sum of all planned and unplanned expenditures.

$$\begin{array}{c}\text{National}\\\text{product}\end{array} = \begin{array}{c}\text{Total}\\\text{planned}\\\text{expenditure}\end{array} + \begin{array}{c}\text{Unplanned}\\\text{inventory}\\\text{investment}\end{array} = \begin{array}{c}\text{Total}\\\text{expenditure}\end{array}$$

Another way of writing the same thing is:

$$\begin{array}{c}\text{Aggregate}\\\text{supply}\end{array} = \begin{array}{c}\text{Aggregate}\\\text{demand}\end{array} + \begin{array}{c}\text{Unplanned}\\\text{inventory}\\\text{investment}\end{array}$$

Having shown that national product equals total realized expenditure in this economy, we can also show that national product equals national income. As in the ultra-simple economy of Exhibit 6.1, the equality of national income and product can be shown in one of two ways.

First, we can use the link that factor payments provide between national income and national product. In Exhibits 6.3 and 6.4, firms are shown as producing $100,000 worth of goods each year, all of which is either sold to investors and consumers or added to inventory. In the course of producing this quantity of goods, firms incur factor costs, which go into the national income stream as wages, interest payments, rents, and so on. Anything left over after all costs are paid is profit for the firms—and this too is counted as going into the national income stream. Total factor payments, including profits, thus account for the entire $100,000 of national product (sales to final users plus inventory change).

Second, the equality of national income and product can be shown using expenditures as a link. In Exhibit 6.3, households plan to spend $60,000 on consumer goods (radios and apples). The other $40,000 leaves the circular flow as saving. Firms plan to invest $40,000 in milling machines; the missing $40,000 is injected back into the economy as investment spending. Total expenditures (consumption plus investment) thus equal national income (saving plus consumption). Also, total expenditures, as shown earlier, equal national product.

In Exhibit 6.4 the plans of households and firms do not mesh so neatly, but total expenditures still provide a link between national income and national product. Households plan to spend just $55,000 and save $45,000; firms plan to invest only $35,000. Saving thus exceeds planned investment by $10,000. However, as we saw before, the $10,000 of goods that firms produce and no one plans to buy do not vanish into thin air but pile up in inventory, where they are counted as unplanned inventory investment. When this is taken into account, total **realized investment** ($35,000 planned plus $10,000 unplanned) equals saving. Again, therefore, national income (saving plus consumption) equals total realized expenditure (consumption plus realized investment) and, as always, total realized expenditure equals national product.

Realized investment
The sum of planned and unplanned investment.

Adding Government to the Circular Flow

The next step in our analysis of the circular flow is to add the public sector. As we saw in Chapter 5, government is linked to the rest of the economy in three ways: through taxes, expenditures, and government borrowing. These three links are added to the circular flow in Exhibit 6.5.

First, consider taxes. For purposes of macroeconomic theory, we need to measure the flow of dollars withdrawn from the household sector by government. Clearly, taxes—including income, payroll, and property taxes—are withdrawals. However, this flow of funds from the household sector is partly offset by a flow of funds returned to them in the form of transfer payments. Therefore, in order to get a proper measure of the net flow of funds from households to government, we must subtract transfer payments from total taxes. The difference between taxes and transfers is called **net taxes** and is indicated in Exhibit 6.5 by the arrow linking households and government.

Net taxes
Taxes paid to government minus transfer payments made by government.

Next, consider the link between government and product markets. We have already accounted for transfers in calculating net taxes. The remainder of government spending consists of purchases of goods and services, including those bought from private firms and the wages and salaries of government employees. For purposes of the circular flow, government employees' wages and salaries can be treated as if they passed through product markets on their way to households.

Finally, consider the link between government and financial markets. As we saw in Chapter 5, governments do not always balance their budgets. Taking federal, state, and local governments together, the public sector tends to spend more than it takes in as taxes. (The federal government almost always runs a deficit. State and local governments often have surpluses, but—at least in recent years—these have not been large enough to offset the federal deficit.) For example, in 1986 the federal government had a budget deficit of $205 billion while state and local governments had a surplus of $61 billion, for a combined deficit of $144 billion.

The government deficit must be financed by borrowing in financial markets. Usually this borrowing takes the form of sales of government bonds and other securities to the public or to financial intermediaries. In Exhibit 6.5, the arrow drawn from financial markets to government represents government borrowing. Over the years, repeated government borrowing adds to the national debt. The *debt* is a stock that corresponds to the annual *deficit*, which is a flow.

In years when the public sector as a whole runs a budget surplus (that is, when net taxes exceed government purchases), the arrow is reversed. Govern-

Exhibit 6.5 The Circular Flow with Government Included

This circular flow diagram shows three links between government and the rest of the economy. The first is net taxes (taxes minus transfer payments), which flow from households to government. The second is government purchases, which flow from government to product markets. If government purchases exceed net taxes (a budget deficit), the government must borrow from financial markets. The deficit case is shown here. If net taxes exceed government purchases, government repayments of past borrowing will exceed new government borrowing, resulting in a net flow of funds from government to financial markets. This case is not shown here.

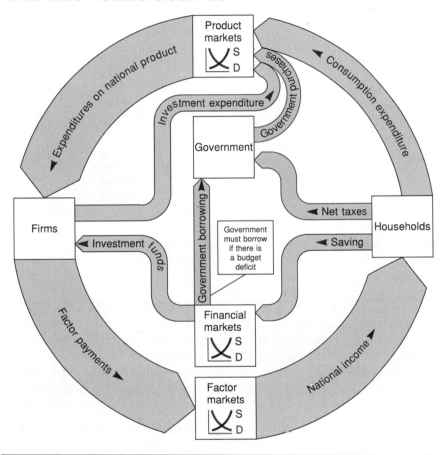

ments pay off old borrowing at a faster rate than new borrowing occurs, thereby creating a net flow of funds into financial markets. In the United States, the combined government sector last showed a budget surplus in 1979.

Equality of National Income and Product

Adding government to the circular flow does not disturb the equality of national income and national product. Exhibit 6.6 shows an economy in equilibrium with the government sector added. Line 1 indicates that national product is $100,000. Lines 2 through 6 show the spending plans of households, firms, and government. Households plan to buy $70,000 worth of consumer goods and services; firms plan to buy $15,000 worth of investment goods; and the government plans

Exhibit 6.6   Example of Circular Flow with Government Included

This exhibit shows the equality of national income and product for an economy with government purchases and taxes included. Note that the total of consumption plus investment plus government purchases equals the total of consumption plus saving plus net taxes. As shown here, the economy is in equilibrium and there is no unplanned inventory investment. However, the equality would hold even if total realized investment included some unplanned inventory investment.

1	National product		$100,000
	Expenditures		
2	Consumption		$70,000
3	Investment		15,000
4	Planned	$15,000	
5	Unplanned	0	
6	Government purchases		15,000
7	Total expenditures		$100,000
8	National income		$100,000
	Uses of National Income		
9	Consumption		$70,000
10	Saving		20,000
11	Net taxes		10,000
12	Total uses		$100,000

to buy $15,000 worth of goods and services. Total planned expenditures come to exactly $100,000, and there are no unplanned inventory changes. When planned expenditures (aggregate demand) just equal national product (aggregate supply), we know that the economy is in equilibrium.

Production of $100,000 worth of goods and services generates a national income, consisting of wages, interest, profits, and so on, of $100,000 (line 8). Lines 9 through 11 show how this national income is used: $70,000 goes for consumption (as we saw before); $20,000 is saved; and $10,000 is taken in in taxes. These three uses account for the entire national income of $100,000.

The relationships shown in Exhibit 6.6 can be summarized in the following equation:

National product = Consumption + Investment + Government purchases
= Consumption + Saving + Net taxes
= National income.

These equations hold even if the economy is not in equilibrium. In that case, investment includes some unplanned inventory investment along with planned investment. But national product, including planned plus unplanned investment, equals national income whether or not the economy is in equilibrium.

Government Influence on the Circular Flow: A Preview

A close look at Exhibit 6.5 suggests that the government is able to regulate the size of the overall circular flow through its control over some of its parts. Much of the discussion in later chapters will be devoted to describing this power and how it is used. For now, we will simply give a preview.

One way in which government can affect the circular flow is through its purchases of goods and services. Starting from a state of equilibrium, a reduction in government purchases would lead to unplanned inventory buildup by the firms that made the products that the government unexpectedly stopped buying. As unwanted inventories piled up, firms would react by cutting output, reducing prices, or some of both. As they did so, the volume of the circular flow would fall in both real and nominal terms. If, on the other hand, the government increased its purchases of goods and services—again starting from equilibrium— there would be unplanned inventory depletion. Firms would react by increasing output, raising prices, or some of both. This would cause the volume of the circular flow to rise in both real and nominal terms. We see, then, that by adding to aggregate demand through increased purchases or reducing aggregate demand through reduced purchases, government can cause the level of national product to rise or fall.

Taxes give the government a second means of controlling the circular flow. If taxes are raised, households will have less after-tax income to spend on consumer goods. This will reduce aggregate demand and cause an unplanned inventory buildup. In response, firms will cut output, prices, or both, thereby reducing the volume of the circular flow. If taxes are cut, the process will work in reverse. With more after-tax income, consumer spending will increase. The additional aggregate demand will cause an unplanned inventory depletion, to which firms will react by raising output, prices, or both. In this case, the volume of the circular flow and national product will rise. Changes in taxes and government purchases, which together are known as *fiscal policy*, will be discussed in Chapter 11.

The government has a third, indirect means of regulating the volume of the circular flow: its influence over the money stock. The Federal Reserve System, an agency of the federal government, can take actions that affect the stock of money in the economy. As we saw earlier in the chapter, increasing the stock of money would not necessarily cause the rate of flow of income and product to increase if the new money lay idle in people's pockets and bank accounts. However, as we will see in coming chapters, the actions through which the Federal Reserve injects new money into the economy have many indirect effects, including effects on interest rates and credit markets. If monetary policy eases the availability of credit and lowers interest rates, firms will be encouraged to step up their rate of investment spending. This, in turn, will cause the circular flow to expand. On the other hand, if monetary policy actions cause the interest rate to rise, firms will be discouraged from making investments and the circular flow will tend to shrink. These matters will be discussed in detail in Chapters 12 through 15.

Adding the Foreign Sector to the Circular Flow

Up to this point, the circular flow model has been developed only for a **closed economy,** that is, one that has no links to the rest of the world. The U.S. economy is not closed to the rest of the world, however; it is an **open economy**— and increasingly so. Goods and services with a value equal to some 20 percent of national product cross its borders in the form of either imports or exports, not to mention hundreds of billions of dollars' worth of international financial transactions that take place each year. This section extends the circular flow model to the case of an open economy by adding a foreign sector to the household, firm, and government sectors already included.

Closed economy
An economy having no links to the rest of the world.

Open economy
An economy linked to the outside world by imports, exports, and financial transactions.

Exhibit 6.7   Circular Flow with Foreign Sector Included

This circular flow diagram shows three links between the domestic economy and the rest of the world. Imports are the first link. Payments for imports are shown as an arrow from households to foreign economies. Exports are the second link. Payments by foreign buyers of exports are shown as an arrow leading to domestic product markets. If too few goods and services are exported to pay for all the imports, the remaining imports must be paid for by borrowing from foreign sources or by selling real or financial assets to foreign buyers. Such transactions, known as *capital inflows,* are shown as a flow into domestic financial markets. Exports might also exceed imports, in which case the arrow would be reversed to show *capital outflows.*

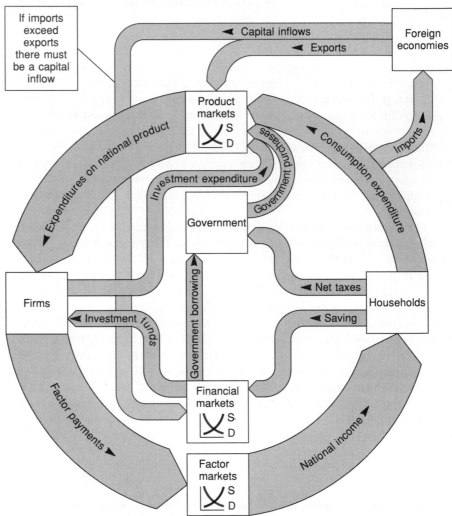

Exhibit 6.7 shows that the foreign sector, like the government, is linked to the rest of the economy in three ways.

Imports of goods and services provide the first link. Recall that all the components of the circular flow represent flows of money payments, not flows of goods. Payments for imports are shown by an arrow leading away from the economy to the rest of the world. Households, firms, and government all buy some imported goods and services. To keep Exhibit 6.7 manageable, however, only imports by consumers, which form part of total consumption expenditure, are shown.

Exports provide the second link between the domestic economy and the rest of the world. Funds received in payment for goods and services sold abroad flow into product markets, where they join funds received from sales of goods and services to domestic households, government, and firms. Receipts from the sale of exports are shown as an arrow leading into product markets. The value of exports minus the value of imports is referred to as **net exports.** If the value of imports exceeds the value of exports, we can say that there are *negative net exports* or, more simply, that there are *net imports.*

The third link between the domestic economy and the rest of the world consists of international financial transactions. These include international borrowing and lending and international purchases and sales of assets. Like imports and exports of goods and services, international financial transactions give rise to flows of dollar payments into or out of the U.S. economy. Suppose, for example, that a Japanese pension fund buys a bond issued by the U.S. government. It pays for the bond with dollars; thus, dollars flow into the U.S. economy just as they do when a Japanese firm buys a U.S.-built computer. Much the same thing happens when a U.S. chemical company borrows $1 million from a London bank. The bank is given a promissory note and in return sends the $1 million to the U.S. firm. In both cases, there is an inflow of dollars from abroad to the U.S. economy as a result of the financial transactions.

Flows of dollars into the economy that result from net purchases of assets by foreign buyers and net borrowing from foreign financial intermediaries are known as **capital inflows.**[2] Strictly speaking, it might be better to call them *financial inflows,* since we are talking about the direction of dollar flows, not flows of physical capital equipment. However, the term *capital inflows* is well established.

Capital inflows have their mirror images. If a U.S. pension fund buys stock in a Swedish paper company or a U.S. bank makes a loan to a Jamaican mining concern, funds flow out of the U.S. economy. Net purchases of foreign assets and net loans to foreign borrowers by U.S. financial intermediaries are known as **capital outflows.**

There is a link between the flows of payments that arise from imports and exports of goods and services and those that arise from financial flows. The logic of this connection can be seen in a highly simplified example. Suppose you are the only person in the United States doing business with France. You want to buy French wine and, at the same time, are willing to sell U.S.-made maple syrup to the French. You place an order for $1,000 worth of wine, but you can find French buyers for only $600 worth of syrup. Does your failure to export as much as you want to import mean that you will have to cancel part of your wine order? No, because there are other ways to settle your accounts with the French: You can either borrow the $400 you need from a French bank or sell a French buyer $400 worth of common stock in your syrup company. To put it another way, you can pay for your imports via either exports or capital inflows in any combination you desire. If the tables were turned and the French wanted to buy syrup worth more than the wine you wanted to import, they would have to

Net exports
Exports minus imports.

Capital inflows
Borrowing from foreign financial intermediaries and funds earned through sales of real or financial assets to foreign buyers.

Capital outflows
Lending to foreign borrowers and funds used to purchase real or financial assets from foreign sellers.

---

[2]By *net* borrowing, we mean new borrowing minus repayments of old loans. Similarly, we say *net* sales of U.S. assets to foreign buyers to allow for the possibility that foreign parties holding previously purchased U.S. assets will resell them to U.S. buyers. For example, suppose Japanese pension fund A buys $100 million of U.S. bonds while Japanese pension fund B sells $10 million in previously purchased U.S. government bonds to a U.S. insurance company. In this case, there is a *net* increase in foreign holdings of U.S. government bonds of $90 million.

borrow from a U.S. financial intermediary or sell assets to a U.S. buyer. In this case, there would be a capital outflow from the U.S. economy.

Chapter 7 will add details, but the principle is clear from this simple example. A country can import more than it exports if it borrows from abroad or sells assets to foreigners; in economic terminology, it can experience net imports if it also experiences a net capital inflow. This is the case shown in Exhibit 6.7, and it corresponds to U.S. experience in the mid-1980s.

By the same token, a country can export more than it imports if it makes loans to foreigners or buys assets from them. Thus, a country with net exports must also experience a capital outflow. In this case, the arrow between the foreign sector and financial markets in Exhibit 6.7 would be reversed and labeled *capital outflow*. This would represent U.S. experience in earlier post–World War II decades.

All of our discussions of open-economy macroeconomics in the chapters to come will be based on the interplay of imports, exports, and capital flows. In reading these sections, it may be helpful to turn back occasionally to Exhibit 6.7.

Equality of National Income and Product with the Foreign Sector

Adding the foreign sector to the circular flow still leaves all of the basic equalities intact, as we will now see. In Exhibit 6.8, the economy is once again shown with a national product of $100,000 (line 1). Lines 2 through 12 list expenditures. Line 2 shows that households plan to spend $70,000 on consumer goods during the year. Of this, they will spend $10,000 on imports, which means that only $60,000 of their total spending will flow into domestic product markets. An adjustment for this fact is shown further down in the table, as we will see in a moment.

Lines 5 through 7 show that firms plan to invest $10,000, and line 8 shows planned government purchases of $15,000. Lines 9 through 11 show the contribution of the foreign sector. Foreign buyers plan to purchase $15,000 of domestically produced goods and services (line 10). These purchases represent a flow of expenditures into domestic product markets. However, $10,000 of this flow is offset by the planned purchases of imported goods by domestic consumers. This item, first shown in line 3, is repeated in line 11 with a negative sign. The net contribution of foreign trade to expenditures on domestic goods and services is thus $15,000 minus $10,000, or $5,000. The difference between exports and imports (net exports) is shown in line 9. Adding total consumption (consumption of domestic goods plus consumption of imports), planned investment, government purchases, and net exports gives total expenditures on domestic goods and services of $100,000 (line 12).

Lines 13 through 16 of Exhibit 6.8 show the uses of national income. Consumption expenditures account for $70,000 (of which $10,000 is consumption of imports). Another $10,000 goes to the government as net taxes. The remaining $20,000 is saving. These uses of funds thus account for the entire $100,000 of national income, which in turn equals total expenditures on domestic goods and national product.

In Exhibit 6.8, the plans of buyers and sellers mesh, putting the circular flow in equilibrium. If they did not, however, national income and product would still be equal. Suppose, for example, that firms planned to invest a little

Exhibit 6.8   National Income and Product in the Complete Circular Flow

This example shows the equality of national income and product for the complete circular flow. Note that in the case shown here, there are net exports of $5,000. The corresponding capital outflow is not shown directly in the table, but it can be computed as follows. First, $20,000 flows into financial markets in the form of saving. Of this, $5,000 is used by government to cover its budget deficit. (Government purchases exceed net taxes by $5,000.) Another $10,000 is borrowed by domestic firms to finance their planned-investment expenditures. The remaining $5,000 of saving is loaned to foreigners or used to buy foreign real and financial assets to enable foreign countries to purchase $15,000 worth of U.S. goods while selling only $10,000 worth of goods to the United States.

1	National product		$100,000
Expenditures on Domestic Goods and Services			
2	Consumption (including imports)		$ 70,000
3	Imports	$10,000	
4	Consumption of domestic goods	60,000	
5	Investment		10,000
6	Planned	10,000	
7	Unplanned	0	
8	Government purchases		15,000
9	Net exports		5,000
10	Exports	15,000	
11	Imports	−10,000	
12	Total expenditures on domestic goods		$100,000
Uses of National Income			
13	Consumption		$ 70,000
14	Saving		20,000
15	Net taxes		10,000
16	Total uses of national income		$100,000

less, or foreign buyers planned to purchase fewer exports, or government planned to spend less on goods and services, or consumers planned to spend more on imports. If any or all of these things happened, total planned expenditures on domestic goods would fall short of national product. Some sellers would be disappointed and find themselves holding inventories of unsold goods. These would be entered in Exhibit 6.8 as unplanned investment, just making up the shortfall in planned expenditures. Total realized expenditures, including planned and unplanned expenditures, would, as always, equal national product and, in turn, national income.

Then again, the combined spending plans of households, firms, government, and foreign buyers might add up to more than national product. If this were the case, producers would find themselves selling goods faster than they were producing them. As a result, their inventories would fall below planned levels. The inventory change would show up as a negative number on the unplanned investment line, just balancing the excess aggregate demand. The basic equality of national income and product would, as always, hold.

As before, these rules can be expressed in the form of a four-part equation as follows:

$$\frac{\text{National}}{\text{product}} = \text{Consumption} + \text{Investment} + \frac{\text{Government}}{\text{purchases}} + \text{Exports} - \text{Imports}$$

$$= \text{Consumption} + \text{Saving} + \text{Net taxes}$$

$$= \text{National income.}$$

Looking Ahead

The circular flow model presented in this chapter gives a good overview of the macroeconomy, but it leaves many questions unanswered. One is how actual measurements can be taken of national product, national income, and the other quantities in the circular flow. We will deal with this matter in Chapter 7.

Other unanswered questions concern the government's control over the volume of the circular flow via spending, taxes, and monetary policy. Just how are these policy tools used, how large are the effects of a given policy tool, and how do the various tools interact? These questions will be answered in Chapters 11 through 15.

Still another set of questions concerns the connections among changes in nominal national product, in real national product, and in the average price level. We have seen that when aggregate demand rises, firms tend to respond by increasing real output, raising prices, or some of both. Under what conditions are they likely to do each? The answer is crucial for the macroeconomic goals of full employment, price stability, and real economic growth. This set of questions will be previewed in Chapter 8 and examined more fully in Chapters 16 through 19.

Summary

1. **How are households and firms linked by incomes and expenditures?** The *circular flow of income and product* is the flow of goods and services between households and firms balanced by the flow of payments made in exchange for them. In the simplest case, households spend all their money on consumer goods produced by firms and firms use all the proceeds of the sales to pay wages, rent, interest, and profits to households. *National product* is the value of all goods and services produced in the economy. *National income* is the total income earned by households, including wages, rents, interest payments, and profits. The two are always equal, because for every dollar that firms receive from the sale of their products, they pay out one dollar in factor payments and profits.

2. **How is income related to money?** In economics, the term *flow* refers to any process that occurs continuously through time and *stock* is the total amount of something that exists at a point in time. The distinction between stocks and flows is useful for understanding the role of money. The *stock* of money consists of the coins, paper currency, and checking account balances used to make payments. As money is spent it moves through the economy, creating various *flows*, such as income, saving, investment, and government purchases.

3. **How can the concepts of supply and demand be applied to the economy as a whole?** *Aggregate supply* is the value of all goods and services produced in the economy; it means the same thing as national product. *Aggregate demand* is the value of all planned expenditures in the economy. The circular flow is said to be in equilibrium when aggregate supply and aggregate demand are equal. In this case, there are no unplanned changes in inventories. If aggregate demand exceeds aggregate supply, there will be unplanned decreases in inventory (negative inventory investment). Firms will tend to react by raising output, raising prices, or some of both. The circular flow will then expand. If aggregate supply exceeds aggregate demand, there will be unplanned increases in inventories. Firms' reactions will cause the circular flow to shrink.

4. **How do the various pieces of the economy— households, firms, government, and financial markets—fit together?** Firms are linked to households through product markets (expenditures on national product) and factor markets (national income). Both

are linked to financial markets, through which household saving flows to firms, which use the funds to make investments. The government sector is connected to the circular flow in three ways. First, households pay *net taxes* (taxes minus transfer payments) to the government. Second, the government buys goods and services in product markets. Third, the government borrows from financial markets to finance a deficit or supplies funds to financial markets when it runs a surplus.

5. **How is the U.S. economy linked to the rest of the world?** The foreign sector, like the government sector, is connected to the circular flow in three ways. First, households pay foreign sellers for imported goods. Second, foreign buyers make payments to domestic firms for exported goods. Third, the foreign sector supplies funds to U.S. financial markets if the United States has negative net exports. The funds thus supplied are called *capital inflows*. Positive net exports by the United States must be offset by *capital outflows* to foreign financial markets.

Terms for Review

- circular flow of income and product
- flow
- stock
- national income
- national product
- saving
- fixed investment
- inventory investment
- investment
- aggregate supply
- aggregate demand
- realized expenditure
- realized investment
- net taxes
- closed economy
- open economy
- net exports
- capital inflows
- capital outflows

Questions for Review

1. Sketch the circular flow of income and product for an economy made up of only households and firms. Show both flows of payments and flows of goods and services. Give examples of payments that flow from households to firms and of payments that flow from firms to households.

2. Give several examples of stocks and related flows other than those used in the chapter.

3. What is the link between aggregate supply and national product? Between aggregate demand and national product? What does it mean to say that the circular flow of income and product is in equilibrium?

4. Sketch a circular flow for an economy in which there are households, firms, financial markets, and government. Show the three connections between the government sector and the rest of the economy.

5. Sketch a circular flow for an economy in which the foreign sector is added. How is the foreign sector linked to households, product markets, and financial markets?

Problems and Topics for Discussion

1. **Examining the lead-off case.** Show the position in the circular flow diagram of as many as possible of the terms in this case.

2. **Stocks and flows.** Turn to the balance sheet for Great Falls Manufacturing Inc. presented in Exhibit 4.3 (p. 89). Are the firm's assets, liabilities, and net worth stocks or flows? Are its receipts from sales and its payments to workers, suppliers, and owners stocks or flows? How are these receipts and payments related to the balance sheet items?

3. **Your personal money stock.** What is the stock of money that you own at this moment? Include coins, paper currency, and the balance in your checking account, if you have one. What was your flow of income in the past month? How would a change in your income affect your stock of money? What else can affect it?

4. **Planned inventory changes.** Not all changes in inventories are unplanned. Why would a firm plan to increase or decrease its inventories? How would you plan your inventories over the course of the year if you were a seller of children's toys? Of air conditioners? How would you plan your inventories of parts if you were an auto parts store in a town with a growing population? In one with a shrinking population?

5. **Disequilibrium with excess aggregate demand.** Rework the table in Exhibit 6.4 for the case of excess aggregate demand. (Let consumption of apples be $35,000, consumption of radios $30,000, and planned investment in milling machines $40,000.) How would producers tend to adjust to these changes? Now assume that radio dealers plan to add $5,000 to their inventories. What does this do to total aggregate demand? Will the dealers be able to carry out their plans?

6. **Financial flows.** The circular flow diagrams in Exhibits 6.5 and 6.7 contain arrows flowing into and out of "financial markets." Using what you learned about

financial intermediaries in Chapter 4, give some examples of these flows. Give examples of direct and indirect financing, the role of financial intermediaries, and the role of primary and secondary financial markets.

7. **Reactions to disequilibrium in the circular flow.** Starting from a state of equilibrium, trace the effects of each of the following through the circular flow. What happens to inventories? How do firms tend to react? What happens to the size of the circular flow as measured in nominal terms?

   a. Business managers suddenly decide to increase investment in order to expand their firms' productive capacity.

   b. The federal government cuts income taxes.

   c. Good crops throughout the world reduce the demand for exports of U.S. farm products.

8. **Real and nominal output changes.** In response to an increase in demand, the nation's hay farmers increase production of hay from 1 billion to 1.2 billion bales per year. At the same time, as the market moves up its supply curve, the price rises from $2 to $2.50 a bale. What happens to the output of hay measured in real terms (in terms of the value of output at unchanged prices)? In nominal terms (in terms of the value of output with respect to the prices at which the output was sold)?

Auto sales declined in the third quarter of 1984.

Case for Discussion
Summer Doldrums

Summer doldrums beset the largest sector of the economy in 1984 as consumers retrenched sharply. After a 6 percent annual rate of increase in real terms during the first 18 months of the recovery from the 1981–1982 recession, personal consumption expenditures fell back in July and August of 1984 to a level barely above the second-quarter average. A 5 percent decline in third-quarter auto sales contributed to the weakness, no doubt partly due to shortages of popular models. But consumers stayed away from lots of other goods.

Business outlays for capital goods also slowed dramatically during the third quarter, judging by monthly data available for shipments of machinery and equipment as well as for business construction. After rising at a 20 percent annual rate in real terms for a year, the pace probably slowed to around 10 percent. But although increases are likely to be smaller in the months ahead, construction contracts and orders for new equipment indicate continued expansion.

The most worrisome signal regarding third-quarter activity is from a sector that speeded up—inventory accumulation. Business replenishing empty shelves and showrooms added a powerful push to the economy right from the start of the recovery. Now a few hints are appearing that they have enough stocks on hand. *Fortune* estimates that the ratio of inventory to final sales increased 2 percent in the third quarter, bringing it above what business wants for the first time since early 1983. To the extent that the third-quarter bulge in inventory was unplanned and unwanted, the effect will be felt quickly. Industrial production, which hardly grew in August, could level off for a few more months.

Questions

1. Circle each word in this news item that you can identify as part of the circular flow as depicted in Exhibit 6.5.

2. Explain why a decrease in consumer spending on automobiles would tend to (a) slow the rate of expansion of the circular flow or (b) cause it to increase.

3. Do you think that the growth of inventories during 1984 represented planned inventory investment, unplanned inventory investment, or some of both? Is there anything in the news item that gives you a clue? Discuss.

4. Compare this news item with the article that opens this chapter, which appeared in the same source two-and-a-half years later. For each period, list the elements of the circular flow that tended to promote growth and those that tended to cause a slowdown or shrinkage of the circular flow.

7 Measuring National Income and Product

After reading this chapter, you will understand . . .

- How gross national product is officially defined and measured.
- How national income differs from gross national product.
- What the major types of international transactions are.
- How changes in the price level are measured.
- What the limitations of official economic statistics are.

Before reading this chapter, make sure you know the meaning of . . .

- Real and nominal values (Chapter 1)
- Government purchases and transfer payments (Chapter 5)
- National income and product (Chapter 6)
- Investment (Chapter 6)

Growth Estimate Trimmed

WASHINGTON, D.C. The Commerce Department trimmed its estimate of the economy's fourth-quarter growth rate to a sluggish 1.3 percent annual rate from the 1.7 percent reported earlier.

The weak fourth-quarter expansion in the real gross national product—the inflation-adjusted value of the nation's output of goods and services—followed growth at a 2.8 percent rate in the third quarter. For all of 1986, the economy grew at a 2.5 percent rate.

Several economists asserted that the new report suggests the economy is posed for a pick-up in growth. The revision occurred largely because the department found that nonfarm inventory investment was lower in the fourth quarter than originally reported.

"The story is the big decline in inventories and what that implies for the first quarter," said David Berson, senior economist at Wharton Econometric Forecasting Associates in Philadelphia, who predicted that businesses will rebuild inventories in the first quarter.

Commerce Department officials said that the drop in inventories came mostly in machinery and electrical goods.

At the same time, growth was buoyed by a greater increase in nonresidential capital spending and a further narrowing of the trade deficit than was estimated earlier. In fact, imports fell from the third quarter total, the first quarterly drop since the first quarter of 1985.

The report showed that inflation remained subdued in the fourth quarter. Prices, as measured by a GNP-based gauge known as the deflator, rose at a 0.7 percent annual rate in the period, rather than the 1 percent rate reported earlier. In the third quarter, the deflator increased at a 3.6 percent pace.

Before adjustment for inflation, fourth-quarter GNP ran at an annual rate of 4.261 trillion, compared with a $4.241 trillion pace in the third quarter.

Source: Rose Gutfeld, "GNP Estimate Cut to 1.3% Rate for 4th Quarter," *The Wall Street Journal*, February 20, 1987, 3. Reprinted by permission of *The Wall Street Journal*, © Dow Jones & Company, Inc. 1987. All Rights Reserved.

Government reports on GNP are big news in the financial press.

GOVERNMENT reports of the latest data for national product and the price level regularly make headlines in the financial press. This typical report drives home the point that the concepts introduced in Chapter 6—national product, national income, investment, price levels, and so on—can be put to work by decision makers in business and government only if they are *measured*—that is, only if numbers are fitted to the various stocks and flows.

The government statisticians whose job it is to make these measurements for the U.S. economy are widely held to be the best such team in the world. Yet, as this chapter will show, they face many problems. There are technical problems of sampling errors and survey methods. There are conceptual problems that arise when real-world institutions do not match the theoretical categories of economic models. Finally, there are problems of timeliness. Because of budgetary and monetary priorities, government decision makers must sometimes work with preliminary data, which, as the above news item shows, are later subject to substantial revision.

In this chapter, we examine the problems of measuring national income, national product, and the price level. We begin with a look at the methods used to measure the economy in nominal terms. Following a short discussion on measuring international linkages, we turn to methods of measuring real income and the price level. Finally, we examine the question of how well the nation's national income accountants are doing their job.

Measuring National Income and Product

We begin with the measurement of national income and product in nominal terms, that is, in terms of the prices at which goods and services are actually sold. However, it is widely recognized that nominal measures do not tell the whole story. If we read that the value of output of the U.S. automobile industry was $45 billion in 1977 and $90 billion in 1987, we know that we must interpret these numbers with care. The doubling of nominal output does not mean that the number of cars produced doubled, because we know that the price of cars went up in the meantime. Suppose that 1977 output was 9 million units at an average price of $5,000 per unit. Was 1987 output 9 million units at $10,000 per unit, 10 million units at $9,000 per unit, or 6 million units at $15,000 per unit? With no information on prices, data on nominal quantities tell only part of the story.

Nonetheless, nominal measurements provide a starting point. Data are collected in nominal form, and only after a set of nominal accounts have been assembled can the process of adjusting for price changes begin.

Gross National Product

Gross national product (GNP)
The dollar value at current market prices of all final goods and services produced annually by a nation's factors of production.

The most comprehensive measure of total production is gross national product. We have mentioned this concept before and will now define it precisely: **Gross national product (GNP)** is the dollar value at current market prices (that is, the nominal value) of all final goods and services produced annually by a nation's factors of production.

Why Final Goods?

The term **final goods and services** is a key part of the definition of gross national product. GNP attempts to measure the sum of the economic contributions of each firm and industry without missing anything or counting anything twice. In order for it to do this, care must be taken to count only goods sold to *final users*—parties that will use them for domestic consumption, government purchases, investment, or export. *Intermediate goods*—those that are purchased for use as inputs in producing other goods or services—are excluded.

Exhibit 7.1 shows why counting both final and intermediate goods would overstate total production. The exhibit traces the process of producing a kitchen table that retails at $100. The final stage of production takes place in the furniture plant, but the manufacturer does not do $100 worth of work. Instead, the manufacturer takes $40 worth of lumber, turns it into a table, and gets $60 in exchange for the labor, capital, and other factors of production used in the process of running the furniture plant. The $40 worth of lumber is an intermediate good; the $60 contribution made by the manufacturer is the **value added** to the product at its final stage. (Of course, in practice other intermediate goods, such as paint and fuel for heating the plant, are used in making the table. It is only to simplify the example that we assume the table is made solely from lumber plus the manufacturer's effort.)

The second section of Exhibit 7.1 shows the next-to-last stage of production: making the lumber. The lumber mill buys $15 worth of logs, saws them into lumber that sells for $40, and gets $25 in exchange for the mill's work. The value added at the sawmill stage is $25.

Going still further back, we come to the stage at which the logs were produced. To produce $15 worth of logs, some forest products company bought $5 worth of fuel, equipment, and so on and kept $10 in exchange for the effort

Final goods and services
Goods and services that are sold to or are ready for sale to parties that will use them for consumption, investment, government purchases, or export.

Value added
The dollar value of an industry's sales less the value of intermediate goods purchased for use in production.

Exhibit 7.1   Value Added and the Use of Final Products in GNP

This table shows why GNP must include only the value of final goods and services if it is to measure total production without double counting. The value of sales at each stage of production can be divided into the value added at that stage and the value of purchased inputs. The selling price of the final product (a $100 table, in this case) equals the sum of the values added at all stages of production.

Final stage—manufacturing:		
Value of one table	$100	
Less value of lumber	−40	
Equals value added in manufacturing	60 ──────→	$ 60
Next to final stage—sawmill:		
Value of lumber	$ 40	
Less value of logs	−15	
Equals value added at sawmill	25 ──────→	25
Second to final stage—timber farming:		
Value of logs	$ 15	
Less value of fuel, equipment, etc.	−5	
Equals value added in timber farming	10 ──────→	10
All previous stages:		
Value added in fuel, equipment, etc.	$ 5 ──────→	5
Total value added		$100

involved in tending the trees and harvesting the logs. That makes an additional $10 of value added.

Clearly, the process of making the table could be traced back indefinitely. The last section of the exhibit sums up the value added at all stages of production prior to timber farming—the fuel and equipment suppliers, their own suppliers, and so on. If production were traced back far enough, every penny could be attributed to the value added somewhere in the chain of production.

Now compare the first and last lines of the exhibit. Lo and behold, the value of the final good—the table—turns out to be a precise measure of the sum of the values added at each stage of production. That is why only final goods are counted in GNP. Adding together the $100 value of the table, the $40 value of the lumber, the $15 value of the timber, and so on would far overstate the true rate of productive activity (the true total value added) in the economy.

The Expenditure Approach to Measuring GNP

In principle, GNP could be measured by adding together the value of each final good or service sold or by adding up the value added at each stage of production, as shown in Exhibit 7.1. To simplify the process, however, national income accountants utilize the equality of national product and total expenditure. It is easier to gather data on the total expenditures of households, investors, governments, and buyers of exports of final goods produced in the domestic economy than it is to stand at factory gates and count goods as they roll off assembly lines. This method of measuring GNP is known as the *expenditure approach*. Exhibit 7.2 shows how it works, using 1986 data for the U.S. economy.

Exhibit 7.2 Nominal Gross National Product by Type of Expenditure, 1986 (Dollars in Billions)

Gross national product is estimated using the expenditure approach. This involves adding together the values of expenditures on newly produced goods and services made by all economic units to get a measure of aggregate economic activity. Net national product is derived from gross national product by excluding the value of expenditures made to replace worn-out or obsolete capital equipment.

Personal consumption expenditure		$2,762.4
Durable goods	$ 388.3	
Nondurable goods	932.7	
Services	1,441.3	
Plus gross private domestic investment		686.4
Fixed investment	675.1	
Change in business inventories	11.4	
Plus government purchases of goods and services		865.3
Federal	367.2	
State and local	498.1	
Plus net exports of goods and services		−105.7
Exports	373.0	
Less imports	−478.7	
Equals gross national product (GNP)		$4,208.5
Less capital consumption allowance		−455.1
Equals net national product (NNP)		$3,753.4

Source: President's Council of Economic Advisers, *Economic Report of the President* (Washington, D.C.: Government Printing Office, 1987), Tables B-1, B-21.

Consumption. The first line of Exhibit 7.2 gives total household consumption of both domestically produced and imported goods and services. The national income accounts divide consumption into three categories: durable goods, nondurable goods, and services. In principle, goods that do not wear out in one year—such as cars, furniture, and appliances—are durable; goods that are used up in less than a year—such as soap, food, and gasoline—are nondurable. In practice, however, these categories are somewhat arbitrary. For example, all clothing is considered nondurable, whether a pair of stockings that may last only a few weeks or a woolen coat that may last ten years. The remaining item—services—includes everything that is not in the form of a physical object when sold, such as haircuts, legal advice, financial services, and education.

Both the goods and the services components of consumption contain some items that bypass the marketplace on their way to consumers. One such item is an estimate of food produced and consumed on farms; another is an estimate of the rental value of owner-occupied homes. However, by no means are all non-market goods and services captured in the national income accounts.

Investment. The item called *gross private domestic investment* is the sum of all purchases of newly produced capital goods (fixed investment) plus changes in business inventories. The fixed-investment component includes both business fixed investment—all new equipment and structures bought by firms—and the value of newly constructed residential housing. In the national income accounts, then, a home-owning household is treated like a small firm. When the house is bought, it is counted as an investment. Then, as we saw earlier, the firm's "product"—the rental value of its shelter services—is considered as part of consumption each year.

Government Purchases. Government's contribution to GNP at the federal, state, and local levels is treated much like consumption. The goods and factor services bought by government are considered as being "used up" as soon as they are purchased. Government purchases are valued at cost in the national income accounts. No attempt is made to measure the value added by government, because most government outputs—primary and secondary education, defense services, and police protection, to name a few—are provided free rather than sold to the public. Transfer payments are not included in the expenditure approach to GNP because they do not represent purchases of newly produced final goods and services.

Net Exports. The last item in the GNP account is *net exports*—exports minus imports. In calculating GNP, imports must be subtracted from exports in order to avoid double counting. Some of the goods bought by consumers, investors, and government and included in their expenditures are not produced in the domestic economy. The figures for consumption, investment, and government purchases therefore overstate the final use of domestically produced goods and services to the extent that some of those goods and services were produced abroad. To correct for the overstatement in earlier lines in Exhibit 7.2, imports are subtracted from exports at the bottom. Total consumption plus total investment plus total government purchases plus exports less imports gives the same sum as would be obtained by adding domestic consumption of domestically produced goods, domestic purchases of domestically produced capital goods, domestic government purchases of domestically produced goods, and total exports.

Gross versus Net National Product

What makes gross national product "gross" is the fact that gross private domestic investment measures total additions to the nation's capital stock without adjusting for losses through wear and tear or obsolescence. Gross private domestic investment minus an allowance for depreciation and obsolescence gives *net private domestic investment*, a measure of the actual net addition to the nation's capital stock each year. Only net investment adds to the capital stock, thus helping to expand the economy's production possibility frontier. The part of gross investment needed to cover depreciation and obsolescence is needed just to keep the frontier from shrinking inward. Although it is hard to measure depreciation and obsolescence accurately, national income accountants use an approximate measure called the *capital consumption allowance*. Gross national product minus the capital consumption allowance is called **net national product (NNP)**.

Net national product (NNP)
Gross national product minus an allowance (called the *capital consumption allowance*) that represents the value of capital equipment used up in the production process.

National Income

In Chapter 6, we looked at the economy in terms of a circular flow of income and product. The official national income accounts cut into the circular flow at two points, one at which they measure GNP by the expenditure approach and the other at which they measure national income by the income approach. As the term implies, the *income approach* measures economic activity by adding together all the different kinds of income earned by households.

In Chapter 6, national income was divided into wages, rents, interest, and profits according to the theoretical classification of factors of production. The version of the income approach used in the national income accounts breaks down total income into a set of categories that is only loosely related to the theoretical breakdown of factor payments. These categories are shown in Exhibit 7.3.

Compensation of employees includes wages and salaries plus certain supplements. The first is employer contributions to social insurance (social security). As the social security tax law is written, employees are legally required to pay only half of the tax; employers must pay the other half. Because both halves contribute to employees' retirement benefits, however, both are counted as part of employee compensation. The *supplements* line of the national income accounts also includes fringe benefits other than social insurance that employers pay for, such as health insurance and private pension plans.

Rental income of persons includes all income in the form of rent and royalties received by property owners. It does not exactly correspond to the theoretical concept of payments for natural resources as a factor of production, and it departs still more from the notion of economic rent introduced in Chapter 5. For example, if a person lives in one apartment of a three-unit building and rents the others for $500 a month each, part of the $1,000 of rental income is really implicit wages for the work of maintaining the building, another part implicit interest on the investment the owner made in buying the building, and so on. *Net interest* includes interest income received by households less consumer interest payments.

Exhibit 7.3   Nominal National Income, 1986 (Dollars in Billions)

National income is measured using the income approach. This involves adding together the values of all forms of income earned by households. Some items of income, such as the portion of corporate profits that goes to pay corporate profits taxes, are counted as "earned" by households even though households never receive the income.

Compensation of employees		$2,498.3
Wages and salaries	$2,073.8	
Supplements	424.5	
Plus rental income of persons		15.6
Plus net interest		294.9
Plus corporate profits		299.7
Dividends	87.8	
Corporate profits taxes	102.8	
Undistributed corporate profits	46.0	
Inventory and capital consumption adjustments	63.1	
Plus proprietors' income		278.9
Equals national income		$3,387.4

Source: President's Council of Economic Advisers, *Economic Report of the President* (Washington, D.C.: Government Printing Office, 1987), Table B-23.

Corporate profits include all income earned by the stockholders of corporations, regardless of whether they actually receive that income. Dividends are the part of corporate income that stockholders actually receive. Another part of corporate profits goes to pay corporate profits taxes. A third part—undistributed corporate profits—is kept by corporations for use in making investments. In measuring national income, corporate profits must be adjusted for changes in inventory values and for capital consumption (depreciation). The national income profit category also does not exactly correspond to the theoretical concept of profit. For example, much of oil companies' "profit" constitutes rent earned for the natural resources they own rather than true economic profit.

The final component of national income, *proprietors' income*, lumps together all forms of income earned by self-employed professionals and owners of unincorporated businesses. No attempt is made to divide this income among labor, capital, and natural resources.

Reconciling the Income and Expenditure Approaches

In the simplified circular flows of Chapter 6, national income and national product are always equal. In the official national income accounts, however, the two sums fit together less neatly. Some adjustments must be made in order to match GNP, measured by the expenditure approach, with national income, measured by the income approach. Exhibit 7.4 shows these adjustments.

First, the capital consumption allowance must be subtracted from gross national product to yield net national product. In a sense, gross national product overstates the volume of the circular flow because it includes investments that are made solely to replace worn-out or obsolete equipment. Such expenditures are counted as costs by the firms that make them and thus do not show up as proprietors' or stockholders' income.

Next, an adjustment must be made for the fact that part of the revenue firms

Exhibit 7.4   National Income Related to
Gross National Product, 1986 (Dollars in Billions)

In economic theory, national income and national product are equal by definition. In the
official accounts, however, some adjustments must be made to get the two to fit because
they are measured in different ways. First, the capital consumption allowance is subtracted
from GNP to get net national product. Then indirect business taxes and the statistical
discrepancy are subtracted from NNP to get national income.

Gross national product	$4,208.5
Less capital consumption allowance	−455.1
Equals net national product	3,753.4
Less indirect business taxes[a]	−360.6
Less statistical discrepancy	−5.4
Equals national income	$3,387.4

[a] Includes minor adjustments for business transfer payments and subsidies
to government enterprises.

Source: President's Council of Economic Advisers, *Economic Report of the President*
(Washington, D.C.: Government Printing Office, 1987), Table B-21.

receive for their products never reaches the suppliers of factor services or the
firm's owners. Instead, it is taken by government in the form of so-called *indirect
business taxes*, which include sales taxes, excise taxes, and business property
taxes. These taxes are treated differently from the corporate profits tax, which is
viewed as being earned by owners and then taken from them by the tax collector.
Indirect taxes are included in the prices at which goods and services are sold;
therefore, they are part of national product but are not counted as earned in
national income.

In principle, subtracting the capital consumption allowance and indirect
business taxes from GNP should yield national income, but in practice there is
a further problem. GNP is measured by the expenditure approach using one set
of data, and national income is measured by the income approach using a different set of data. No matter how carefully the work is done, there will be some
errors and omissions and, therefore, the two sets of figures will not quite fit. The
difference between NNP minus indirect business taxes on the one hand and
national income on the other is called the *statistical discrepancy*. Most of the time
this error is well below 1 percent of GNP.

Personal Income

National income, as we have repeatedly seen, is a measure of income earned by
households regardless of whether those households ever actually get their hands
on it. For some purposes, it is more useful to measure what households actually
receive than what they earn. The total income received by households is called
personal income.

Exhibit 7.5 shows the steps required to go from national to personal income.
First, three items earned but not received by households are subtracted: contributions for social insurance (both employer and employee), corporate profits
taxes, and undistributed corporate profits. Next, transfer payments—payments
received by households but not earned by them—are added. The result is personal income.

Personal income
The total income received by
households, including earned
income and transfer
payments.

Exhibit 7.5   National Income and Personal
Income, 1986 (Dollars in Billions)

National income is a measure of all income earned by households; personal income is a measure of the income that households actually receive. To go from national income to personal income, subtract payroll taxes, corporate profits taxes, and undistributed corporate profits; then add transfer payments. If personal taxes are subtracted from this figure, the result is disposable personal income.

National income	$3,387.4
Less contributions for social insurance	−376.1
Less corporate profits taxes and undistributed profits	−218.5
Plus transfer payments[a]	694.2
Equals personal income	$3,487.0
Less personal taxes	−513.4
Equals disposable personal income	$2,973.7

[a]Includes business and personal transfer payments, plus adjustments for interest payments.

Source: President's Council of Economic Advisers, *Economic Report of the President* (Washington, D.C.: Government Printing Office, 1987), Tables B-22, B-25.

One further income measure is shown at the bottom of Exhibit 7.5: **disposable personal income,** or simply **disposable income.** This is the personal income that is left over after households have paid personal taxes (particularly income taxes) to federal, state, and local governments.

Disposable personal income (disposable income) Personal income less personal taxes (particularly income taxes).

Conclusion

This completes our discussion of the domestic national income accounts. The next section looks at the linkages between the domestic economy and the rest of the world. After that, we will turn to the problem of adjusting nominal income and product measures for changing price levels.

Measuring the Balance of Payments

The item "net exports" in the national income accounts gives a glimpse of the linkage of the domestic economy to the rest of the world. These ties have grown stronger in recent years. In 1960, U.S. exports equaled only 6 percent of GNP and imports less than 5 percent. By 1986, exports had grown to 9 percent of a much larger GNP. Imports grew even more rapidly over this period, reaching 11 percent of GNP. In view of the growing importance of the foreign sector, then, it is worth taking a closer look at the international ties of the U.S. economy.

Any discussion of an economy's balance of international payments is complicated by the fact that thousands of different kinds of international payments are made every day. Payments for goods and services exported and imported come to mind first, but there are many others. Equally important are long- and short-term loans made to finance imports and exports and payments made in international markets in connection with purchases or sales of assets such as securities or real estate. In addition, governments and private individuals make many kinds of transfer payments to residents of other countries, including out-

Exhibit 7.6   Actual U.S. International Accounts
for 1986 (Dollars in Billions)

This table gives details of U.S. international transactions for 1986. As in the simplified
accounts, uses of dollars (flows of funds out of the domestic economy) are shown with a
minus sign and sources of dollars (flows of funds into the domestic economy) with a plus
sign. Because of errors and omissions, there is a large statistical discrepancy. The
discrepancy is believed to result largely from unrecorded capital inflows.

Current Account		
Merchandise balance		−144.3
Exports	$224.4	
Imports	−368.7	
Plus Services, net		18.6
Investment income	20.8	
Other services	−2.2	
Equals Net exports of goods and services		−125.7
Plus Transfers		−15.7
Equals Current account balance		−141.4
Capital Account		
Plus Capital account balance		84.2
Net capital outflows	−94.0	
Net capital inflows	178.2	
Official Reserve Account		
Plus Net change in official reserves		33.3
Change in U.S. official reserve assets	0.3	
Change in foreign official reserve assets	33.0	
Plus Statistical discrepancy		23.9
Equals Total of all accounts plus statistical discrepancy		0

Source: U.S. Department of Commerce, Bureau of Economic Analysis, Press Release BEA
87-28, June 16, 1987.

right gifts, pension payments, and official foreign aid. Finally, the U.S. Federal
Reserve System and foreign central banks engage in many kinds of official transactions. Exhibit 7.6 shows a simplified version of the accounts used to keep track
of these international transactions for the United States.

The Current Account

The first section of the international accounts shown in Exhibit 7.6 contains
what are called **current account** transactions. These include imports and exports of goods and services and international transfer payments. The current
account, in turn, is broken down into several components.

Merchandise Imports and Exports

Imports and exports of merchandise (goods) are the most widely publicized
items in the international accounts. During much of the nineteenth century, the
United States was a net importer of merchandise. From 1894 to 1970, it was a
net exporter. Since 1970, it again has become largely a net importer. Exhibit 7.6
shows a negative **merchandise balance** for 1986. The negative number indicates

Current account
The section of a country's
international accounts that
consists of imports, exports,
and unilateral transfers.

Merchandise balance
The value of a country's
merchandise exports minus
the value of its merchandise
imports.

net merchandise imports. (News reports often refer to the merchandise balance as the *balance of trade*.)

Services
In addition to trade in merchandise, the United States and other countries carry on a very large trade in services. Among these are transportation, tourism, insurance, and other financial services. Net earnings on foreign investment, including interest on financial assets, are also considered an export of services. In 1986, the United States had a positive net balance of trade in services, as shown in Exhibit 7.6. Adding net exports of services to the merchandise balance gives *net exports of goods and services*.

Transfers
The final item on the current account balance consists of net transfer receipts. This typically is a negative item in the U.S. international accounts, because transfers to other countries exceed transfers received from them. This item takes into account both government transfers, such as foreign aid and social security payments to retired workers living abroad, and private transfers, such as private famine relief and church missions.

Current Account Balance
When merchandise trade, net trade in services, and net transfers are combined, the result is the country's **current account balance.** (News accounts that refer to the *balance of payments* usually mean the current account balance.) In 1986, the small surplus on services was more than offset by the large merchandise deficit and the smaller transfer deficit, giving the country a large current account deficit.

Current account balance
The value of a country's exports of goods and services minus the value of its imports of goods and services plus its net transfer receipts from foreign sources.

The Capital Account

Current account transactions are not the only ones that take place among residents of different countries. The international lending and borrowing and international sales and purchases of assets mentioned in Chapter 6 also account for an enormous volume of daily transactions. A U.S. company, for example, might obtain a short-term loan from a London bank to finance the purchase of a shipload of beer for import to the United States. The Brazilian government might get a long-term loan from Citibank of New York to help finance a hydroelectric project. A U.S. millionaire might open an account in a Swiss bank. A Japanese automaker might buy a piece of land in Tennessee on which to build a new plant. All of these transactions are recorded in the **capital account** section of Exhibit 7.6.

As explained in Chapter 6, purchases of U.S. assets by foreigners and borrowing from foreign financial intermediaries by U.S. firms and individuals create flows of funds into the United States called *capital inflows*. Purchases of foreign assets by U.S. residents or loans by U.S. financial intermediaries to foreigners create flows of funds out of the United States called *capital outflows*. The value of net private capital inflows less the value of net private capital outflows is known as the **capital account balance.**

As we saw in Chapter 6, capital inflows and outflows are logically related to the current account surplus or deficit. If the United States runs a current account deficit, its earnings from the sales of exports will not be enough to pay for

Capital account
The section of a country's international accounts that consists of purchases and sales of assets and international borrowing and lending.

Capital account balance
The value of net private capital inflows less the value of net private capital outflows.

all imports. Additional funds for financing imports can be obtained through net capital inflows, that is, through U.S. borrowing from abroad that exceeds U.S. lending to foreigners or sales of U.S. assets to foreigners that exceed purchases of assets abroad. As shown in Exhibit 7.6, this was the case for the United States in 1986, where net capital inflows were $178.2 billion while net capital outflows were just $94 billion, giving a positive capital account balance of $84.2 billion. Likewise, a country with a current account surplus can use its extra import earnings to make net loans to foreign borrowers or net purchases of foreign assets. This would result in a negative capital account balance.

The Official Reserve Account

For completeness, we must add one more type of transaction to the international accounts that was not mentioned in Chapter 6: transactions by the central banks of various countries—the Federal Reserve System in the United States, the Bank of England in the United Kingdom, and so on. In principle, purchases and sales of assets by central banks are much like private capital flows. However, these transactions play a special role in international economic policy. For this reason, central bank transactions are kept in a special section of the international accounts labeled the **official reserve account** in Exhibit 7.6.

Official reserve account
The section of a country's international accounts that consists of changes in central banks' official international reserves.

In 1986, the U.S. government made little change in its holdings of foreign reserve assets. However, in that year foreign central banks acquired some $33 billion in U.S. assets, principally U.S. government securities. This created an inflow of dollars into the U.S. economy exactly as would have occurred had foreign individuals and private firms bought the same quantity of securities.

In principle, the sum of the current account balance, the capital account balance, and the net change in official reserves ought to equal zero. The reason is that the three account components taken together include all the sources and uses of the funds that change hands in international transactions. Every dollar used in international transactions must have a source; thus, when the sources (+) and the uses (−) are added together, the sum should be zero.

In practice, however, government statisticians always miss some items when they tally up imports, exports, and capital flows. As a result, the numbers don't quite add up. In the official accounts, this measurement problem is reflected in an item labeled *statistical discrepancy*, formerly called "errors and omissions." In the actual U.S. international accounts for 1986, shown in Exhibit 7.6, the statistical discrepancy was $24 billion. Much of the discrepancy is believed to reflect unrecorded capital inflows.

Measuring Real Income and the Price Level

Between 1976 and 1986, the U.S. gross national product, measured in nominal terms, rose from $1,782 billion to $4,208 billion. To anyone living through those years, however, it is clear that even though nominal GNP more than doubled, the real output of goods and services did not. Much of the increase in the dollar value of GNP reflected an increase in the prices at which goods and services were sold. To understand what really happened to output in those years, then, we must adjust the growth of nominal GNP to account for inflation.

Real Gross National Product and the Deflator

In order to adjust nominal GNP for the effects of inflation, we need a measure of the change in the average prices of goods and services. The most broadly based measure of price changes for the U.S. economy is the GNP deflator. The appendix to this chapter explains how it is calculated. For now, we will simply define the **GNP deflator** as a weighted average of prices of all the final goods and services that make up GNP.

Choosing a Base Year

When we speak of price changes, the first question that comes to mind is: change beginning from what? We can answer this question by choosing a convenient **base year** as a benchmark against which to measure change. At present, U.S. national income accountants use 1982 as a base year for calculating the GNP deflator. The base year is changed from time to time; for example, before 1986 the base year was 1972.

The base year can be used in one of two ways in stating a weighted average of prices. One way is to let the base year value equal 1.0. A statement of average prices relative to a base year value of 1.0 is called a statement of the **price level;** for example, the 1986 price level, relative to the 1982 base year, was 1.15. The other way is to let the base year value equal 100. A statement of average prices relative to a base year value of 100 is known as a **price index.** Thus, using 1982 as a base year we could say that the 1986 price index was 115. The price index and price level are two different ways of stating the same information. In news reports the index form is most frequently used, whereas in building economic models the price level form is more convenient.

Using the GNP Deflator

Exhibit 7.7 shows nominal GNP, real GNP, and the GNP deflator (stated in price level form) for the United States in each year since 1960. To convert nominal GNP for any year to real GNP stated in constant 1982 dollars, we simply divide nominal GNP by the price level for that year. For convenience, we can refer to the year for which we are making the adjustment as the *current year*. In equation form, then, the rule for adjustment can be stated as follows:

$$\text{Current-year real GNP} = \frac{\text{Current-year nominal GNP}}{\text{Current-year price level}}.$$

As Exhibit 7.7 shows, applying this formula to current years after 1982 yields real GNP values measured in constant dollars of the 1982 base year that are below current-year nominal GNP. Applying it to current years before 1982, when the GNP deflator had values of less than 1.0, gives real-GNP values in 1982 dollars that exceed nominal GNP for those years.

For example, dividing the 1976 nominal GNP of $1,782.8 billion by the 1976 price level of .631 gives a 1976 real GNP of $2,825 billion. (This figure does not quite agree with the one in Exhibit 7.7 because of rounding.) Likewise, dividing the 1986 nominal GNP of $4,208.5 billion by the 1986 price level of 1.145 gives a 1986 real GNP of $3,676 billion. Comparing the 1986 real GNP with the 1976 real GNP shows that real GNP increased about 30 percent over the period. The remainder of the increase in nominal GNP can be attributed to the

GNP deflator
A weighted average of prices of all final goods and services produced in the economy.

Base year
The year chosen as a basis for comparison in calculating a price index or price level.

Price level
A weighted average of the prices of goods and services expressed in relation to a base year value of 1.0.

Price index
A weighted average of the prices of goods and services expressed in relation to a base year value of 100.

Exhibit 7.7   Nominal GNP, Real GNP, and the GNP Deflator, 1960–1986 (Dollars in Billions)

This table shows nominal and real GNP and the GNP deflator for the U.S. economy for the years 1960 to 1986. The base year for the GNP deflator is 1982. To calculate real GNP in constant 1982 dollars for any current year, divide current-year nominal GNP by the GNP deflator. Your answer may differ slightly from the real GNP given in the table because of rounding.

	Nominal GNP	Real GNP	GNP Deflator
1960	515.3	1,665.3	.309
1961	533.8	1,708.7	.312
1962	574.6	1,799.4	.319
1963	606.9	1,873.3	.324
1964	649.8	1,973.3	.329
1965	705.1	2,087.6	.338
1966	772.0	2,208.3	.350
1967	816.4	2,271.4	.359
1968	892.7	2,365.6	.377
1969	963.9	2,423.3	.398
1970	1,015.5	2,416.2	.420
1971	1,102.7	2,484.8	.444
1972	1,212.8	2,608.5	.465
1973	1,359.3	2,744.1	.495
1974	1,472.8	2,729.3	.540
1975	1,598.4	2,695.0	.593
1976	1,782.8	2,826.7	.631
1977	1,990.5	2,958.6	.673
1978	2,249.7	3,115.2	.722
1979	2,508.2	3,192.4	.786
1980	2,732.0	3,187.1	.857
1981	3,052.6	3,248.8	.940
1982	3,166.0	3,166.0	1.000
1983	3,405.7	3,279.1	1.039
1984	3,765.0	3,489.9	1.079
1985	3,998.1	3,585.2	1.115
1986	4,208.5	3,676.5	1.145

Source: President's Council of Economic Advisers, *Economic Report of the President* (Washington, D.C.: Government Printing Office, 1987), Tables B-1, B-2, B-3.

81 percent increase in the price level between 1976 and 1986. (The 1986 price level of 1.145 is approximately 81 percent higher than the 1976 price level of .631.)

The Consumer Price Index

Although the GNP deflator is the most broadly based price index for the U.S. economy, it is not the best-known one. That honor belongs to the consumer price index. Rather than taking into account the prices of all final goods and services produced in the economy, as the GNP deflator does, the **consumer price index (CPI)** considers only the goods and services that make up the market basket purchased by a typical urban household.

Exhibit 7.8 gives values for the CPI (stated in index form) from 1960 to the present. Note that the CPI uses 1967 rather than 1982 as its base year. The appendix to this chapter explains how the CPI is calculated.

The CPI plays a key role in the economy partly because it is widely used to "index" wages, government transfers, and many other payments. **Indexing** a payment means automatically adjusting it on a regular schedule for changes in the price index involved. Take, for example, the indexing of social security payments. From 1983 to 1984, the CPI rose from 298.4 to 311.1, an increase of 4.3 percent. As a result, social security payments were automatically increased

Consumer price index (CPI)
A price index based on the market basket of goods and services purchased by a typical urban household.

Indexing
Adjusting a value or payment automatically in proportion to changes in a specific price index.

Exhibit 7.8 Consumer and Producer Price Indexes, 1960–1986

This table shows two commonly used price indexes that are more narrowly based than the GNP deflator. The first is the consumer price index, which is based on a market basket of goods purchased by a typical urban household. The second is the producer price index for finished goods, which is based on a sample of finished goods traded among business firms.

	CPI	PPI
1960	88.7	93.7
1961	89.6	93.7
1962	90.6	94.0
1963	91.7	93.7
1964	92.9	94.1
1965	94.5	95.7
1966	97.2	98.8
1967	100.0	100.0
1968	104.2	102.8
1969	109.8	106.6
1970	116.3	110.3
1971	121.3	113.7
1972	125.3	117.2
1973	133.1	127.9
1974	147.7	147.5
1975	161.2	163.4
1976	170.5	170.6
1977	181.5	181.7
1978	195.4	195.9
1979	217.4	217.7
1980	246.8	247.0
1981	272.4	269.8
1982	289.1	280.7
1983	298.4	285.2
1984	311.1	291.1
1985	322.2	293.7
1986	328.4	289.6

Source: President's Council of Economic Advisers, *Economic Report of the President* (Washington, D.C.: Government Printing Office, 1987), Tables B-55, B-60.

by the same percentage. Millions of workers whose contracts include *cost-of-living-adjustment (COLA)* clauses also have their wages raised as a result of increases in the CPI.

Producer Price Indexes

Another widely publicized set of price indexes consists of **producer price indexes.** These are price averages for three classes of goods traded among business firms. Exhibit 7.8 shows the producer price index for *finished goods*—investment goods plus other goods ready for final use but not yet sold to consumers. Other producer price indexes cover intermediate goods and crude materials ready for further processing. Because producer price indexes measure prices at early stages in the production process, they are often studied for hints of trends in consumer prices. They are also frequently used to index payments that firms agree to make to one another.

The GNP deflator, CPI, and producer price indexes by no means exhaust the possible ways of measuring changes in the price level. There are many other indexes, including regional price indexes and special-purpose indexes that give higher or lower weights to various items. There is even a "nuisance index" that is a weighted average of the prices of small, frequently purchased items (see "Economics in the News 7.1"). Each of these indexes has the ability to shed light on some aspect of the general question of how prices are changing.

Producer price index (PPI)
A price index based on a sample of goods and services bought by business firms.

Nuisance Index Signals Inflation

Linda Barbanel is still fuming. To get a silk blouse dry-cleaned, the New Yorker recently paid $6, up 33 percent from the $4.50 she paid less than a year ago. "You can buy the blouse in China for what they now want to clean it," she complains.

Although economists are just beginning to worry that inflation is reawakening after a five-year slumber, consumers such as Barbanel say they noticed its early stirrings months ago.

That's because prices of commonly used goods and services that shape consumers' perceptions about inflation—things such as toothpaste, coffee, haircuts and taxi rides—are soaring even though the overall rise in the cost of living continues moderate.

"Consumers have a gnawing suspicion that there is more inflation out there than is captured in official government statistics—and the skepticism is justified," says Irwin Kellner, the chief economist at Manufacturers Hanover Trust Co.

Source: Constance Mitchell, "Prices of Small Items, Services Rise Rapidly, Hint of New Inflation," *The Wall Street Journal*, April 24, 1987, 1.

In a recent survey, the New York bank found that prices of these so-called nuisance items are rising three to four times faster than the government's consumer price index. The bank's nuisance index, which consists of three dozen goods and services commonly purchased during a month's time, rose at an average rate of 15 percent a year in 1985 and 1986.

The government, in a first-quarter report yesterday on the economy, said prices as gauged by a measure known as the deflator rose at a 3.5 percent annual rate in the first quarter of 1987 after increasing at a 0.7 percent pace in the fourth period of 1986.

Meanwhile, the government's closely watched CPI—which gives more weight to expensive items such as houses and cars—rose only 3.8 percent in 1985 and a scant 1.1 percent in 1986.

Some economists contend that the nuisance index may provide a truer picture of how inflation is depleting consumers' pocketbooks. Raymond DeVoe calls it the "piranha" factor. A jump in a hairdresser's or housekeeper's bill "won't devour your budget at once the way an auto-price increase will, but those small bites are sharp and can be just as painful," the economist at Legg Mason Wood Walker Inc. says.

Two Measures of Consumer Price Changes

The Nuisance Index[a]				The Consumer Price Index[b]	
Item	January 1985	January 1987	Percent Change	(Percent Change on Selected Items from February 1985 to February 1987)	
Ground coffee (1 lb.)	$ 1.79	$ 3.19	78.2%		
Toothpaste (5 oz.)	.99	1.39	40.4	New car	7.6%
Taxi (2-mile ride)	3.10	4.25	37.1	Refrigerators	−2.7
Pack of gum	.45	.60	33.3	Rent	11.5
Dry cleaning of a suit	6.00	6.75	12.5	Television	−11.5
Woman's haircut	20.00	25.00	25.0	Furniture	4.5
Shoe shine	1.25	1.50	20.0		

Notes: [a] Based on New York retail prices.
[b] Changes are calculated using unadjusted figures and represent percent changes in the index for urban consumers.

Source: Manufacturers Hanover Trust Company.

How Good Are the National Income Accounts?

This chapter began by stressing the importance of the national income accounts to economics and warning that they are less than perfect. Now that we have surveyed the main components of the nominal and real national income accounts, it is time to try to answer the question of how good those accounts are. We will focus on four possible problem areas: the timeliness of the data, the underground sector of the economy, price index biases, and the nonmaterial aspects of the standard of living.

Timeliness

Government decision makers pay close attention to national income accounting data to get an indication of unfolding economic trends. Unfortunately, however, there is a trade-off between the timeliness and the accuracy of GNP data. A case in point was the "flash" estimate of real GNP that until 1986 was published two weeks before the end of each calendar quarter. The flash estimate was given widespread publicity, but it was not a reliable number; it was subject to revision up or down averaging some 2.5 percentage points. (A 2.5 percentage point revision in the upward direction would mean revising a 4.0 percent growth rate estimate to 6.5 percent; in a downward direction, it would mean revising a 4.0 percent estimate to 1.5 percent.) In 1986, the Department of Commerce stopped trying to calculate such early estimates of GNP growth, but even the preliminary estimates now released 15 and 45 days after the end of the quarter are subject to revisions of about two percentage points. In later chapters, we will see that lags in the availability of accurate data on GNP, inflation, and other economic quantities have major implications for policymakers' ability to fine-tune economic policy to fit events as they unfold.

The Underground Economy

The economic activity measured in the national income accounts constitutes the observed sector of the economy. But a vast amount of production, consumption, and investment is never officially measured. This unobserved sector includes activities ranging from teenage baby-sitting to multi-million-dollar drug and gambling rings to the multi-billion-dollar value of cooking, cleaning, and child care performed in the home. The national income accounts attempt to consider this unobserved sector when they include estimates of the rental value of owner-occupied housing and the value of food produced and consumed on farms. Those items are only the tip of the iceberg, however. The bulk of the unobserved sector is missing from the official accounts. Although no one knows exactly how big this sector is, some parts of it are known to be enormous.

Organized crime alone has been estimated as producing some $150 billion a year in illegal goods and services in the form of drugs, gambling, pornography, and so on. If this estimate is correct, it makes organized crime the second largest industry in the United States after the oil industry. However, organized crime is probably not the largest sector of the so-called underground economy. Unreported income of businesses and self-employed people may add as much as $250 billion. This includes cash income that goes unreported for tax purposes (a plumber fixing leaky faucets for cash on her day off) and barter transactions that involve no cash at all (the plumber gets her teeth straightened in exchange for installing a new bathroom in the orthodontist's home).

But even if the U.S. underground economy amounts to as much as 10 percent of officially measured GNP, that is moderate by world standards. The French underground economy is thought to equal a third of that country's GNP; in Italy, the figure may be 40 percent; and in many Third World countries, the official GNP data bear only the haziest relationship to what is actually going on in the economy.

Price Index Biases

A third problem with the official national income accounts is that of price index biases. The accuracy with which price level changes are measured became a matter of growing concern as inflation increased in the late 1970s and indexing and automatic cost-of-living adjustments became more widespread. If the official price indexes are found to understate inflation, we may want to make a greater effort than usual to restore price stability. On the other hand, if price indexes overstate inflation, contracts providing automatic adjustments for inflation may be too generous.

The problem of price index biases has been closely studied, and the results are far from reassuring. The consumer price index has been criticized for two built-in biases that have caused it to overstate inflation in recent years.

Substitution Bias

The first reason that the consumer price index tends to overstate the true rate of increase in the cost of living is the so-called substitution bias. As the appendix to this chapter explains, the CPI is a weighted average of the prices of goods typically purchased by urban consumers. Because the weights used to calculate the index remain constant, they always reflect patterns of consumption at some point in the past. However, since patterns change over time, the weights typically are not those of the most recent year being observed.

If changes in buying patterns were random, an obsolete set of weights would cause only random errors, not an upward bias, in the CPI. The bias results from the fact that consumer demand is influenced by changes in relative prices. As time passes, consumers tend to buy less of the goods whose prices have risen most and more of those whose prices have lagged behind the average or actually fallen. Today's CPI tends to overstate the increase in the cost of living because it assigns unrealistically large weights to products such as heating oil and gasoline, which have soared in price but are now consumed in relatively smaller amounts than formerly.

Quality Bias

A second source of bias in the consumer price index is the failure to adjust product prices for changes in quality. It would be highly misleading, for example, to say that a 1987 model car costs three times as much as a 1967 one without considering the fact that the 1987 model gets better gas mileage, can go longer between tune-ups, and is much safer than the 1967 model. In terms of dollars per unit of transportation service, the newer model clearly would be less than three times as expensive.

For automobiles and a few other major goods, the Bureau of Labor Statistics does try to make quality adjustments. This effort is haphazard, however, and fails to adjust many items in any way. Robert J. Gordon of Northwestern University, who has studied this problem, cites the case of calculators. As recently as the late 1960s, it cost over $1,000 to buy a desk-size electromechanical calculator that would add, subtract, multiply, and divide. Today $5 will buy a calculator that will add, subtract, multiply, divide, take square roots, remember things, and perhaps even play a Mozart sonata. Yet because of the way the prices of the new electronic calculators were "linked" to those of the old electromechanical ones, the true decrease in price was understated in official price indexes by a factor of at least 10.[1]

Nonmaterial Sources of Welfare

The final problem with gross national product is that it measures only material sources of welfare (which, after all, is all it tries to do). Sometimes per capita GNP is used as an indication of living standards, but when one is comparing living standards over time and across countries, nonmaterial sources of welfare are important too.

One key nonmaterial component of the standard of living is the quality of the environment. This not only varies widely from place to place but has changed greatly over time. Today's problems of acid rain, toxic wastes, and nuclear radiation are "bads" that, in principle, should be subtracted from GNP just as "goods" are added to it. Yet the direction of environmental change over the years has not been entirely for the worse. A dramatic example can be found in Colonial Williamsburg, a restored eighteenth-century town in rural Virginia. This is surely one of the most pleasant towns in the country with its carefully restored houses, hidden telephone wires, and prohibition of onstreet parking during daylight hours. But as the official Williamsburg guidebook notes,

> The paved streets, brick sidewalks, streetlights, and fire hydrants would look strange to 18th century eyes. . . . The whole town would seem tidier than the former inhabitants remembered. . . . They would miss the dozens of saddle and draft horses . . . ; the cows, chickens, sheep, and other livestock in every part of town; the streets and paths mired with mud or deep in dust; and the clouds of flies and mosquitoes in summer. Perhaps most of all they would miss the pungent smells of animal manure, rooting hogs, backyard privies, and unwashed humanity.[2]

A second nonmaterial source of welfare is the state of human health. By broad measures, especially life expectancy, standards of health in the United States appear to be improving. For example, since World War II the life expectancy of a typical 45-year-old American has increased from 72 to 77 years, and a 65-year-old American can now expect to live to 81. This increase clearly improves human welfare even for those people who add nothing to measured GNP after they retire from their jobs.

The list of nonmaterial sources of welfare is endless. How important are satisfying work, friendship, social justice, economic equality, and freedom? Everyone knows of people who have been willing to give up income and wealth in pursuit of these things. Yet they must remain unmeasured.

For all of these reasons, then, GNP cannot be used as a measure of the true level of human welfare and can be used only with the greatest caution even for comparisons over time and place.

---

[1]Robert J. Gordon, *Macroeconomics*, 2d ed. (Boston: Little, Brown, 1981), xii.

[2]*Colonial Williamsburg Official Guidebook* (Williamsburg, Va.: Colonial Williamsburg Foundation, 1979), v.

Summary

1. **How is gross national product officially defined and measured?** Two national product concepts are featured in the official accounts of the United States. *Gross national product* is defined as the dollar value at current market prices of all *final goods and services* produced in a given year. *Net national product* is derived from GNP by subtracting a capital consumption allowance that reflects the value of capital goods worn out during the year. National product is measured by adding together the total of consumption, investment, government purchases, and net exports.

2. **How does national income differ from gross national product?** National income is measured by adding together the total of wages and supplements, rental income of persons, corporate profits, and proprietors' income. Gross national product and national income differ by the amount of the capital consumption allowance, indirect business taxes, and the statistical discrepancy. *Personal income* is the total income that households receive; national income is the total income that they earn. Personal income includes transfer payments, which households receive but do not earn, and excludes contributions to social insurance, corporate profits taxes, and undistributed corporate profits, which households earn, but do not receive. Personal income less personal taxes equals *disposable personal income*.

3. **What are the major types of international transactions?** Many types of transactions appear in the nation's international accounts. Exports less imports of goods constitute the *merchandise balance*. Adding exports less imports of services gives net exports of goods and services. Adding net international transfers (normally a negative number for the United States) gives the most publicized balance-of-payments measure, the *current account balance*. In addition, the international accounts record capital inflows and outflows resulting from private financial transactions and official reserve transactions of the Federal Reserve and foreign central banks.

4. **How are changes in the price level measured?** The *GNP deflator* is the most broadly based measure of the *price level*. It can be viewed as a weighted average of the prices of all final goods and services that go into GNP. The *consumer price index (CPI)* includes only the market basket of goods purchased by a typical household. The *producer price index* is based on goods typically bought and sold by business firms.

5. **What are the limitations of official economic statistics?** The national income statistics of the United States are considered among the best in the world. However, they have some limitations. Potential prob-lem areas include timeliness of data, the unobserved sector of the economy, price index biases, and nonmaterial aspects of the standard of living.

Terms for Review

- gross national product (GNP)
- final goods and services
- value added
- net national product (NNP)
- personal income
- disposable personal income (disposable income)
- current account
- merchandise balance
- current account balance
- capital account
- capital account balance
- official reserve account
- GNP deflator
- base year
- price level
- price index
- consumer price index (CPI)
- indexing
- producer price index (PPI)

Questions for Review

1. What is the difference between *gross* and *net* national product?

2. What three items are subtracted from gross national product to arrive at national income? How does personal income differ from national income? How does disposable personal income differ from personal income?

3. List examples of transactions recorded in the current account, capital account, and official reserve account of the international accounts of the United States.

4. How can the GNP deflator be used to calculate real income for a given current year in terms of the prices of a chosen base year? What are the differences among the GNP deflator, the consumer price index, and the producer price index?

5. What are four potential problem areas concerning the accuracy and completeness of the U.S. national income accounts?

Problems and Topics for Discussion

1. **Examining the lead-off case.** Highlight each term in the news item that opens this chapter and, if possible, locate the corresponding line in the GNP accounts.

What does this article suggest regarding the trade-off between timeliness and accuracy of economic data?

2. **Updating the national income accounts.** Using the *Economic Report of the President* or another suitable data source, update the national income and product accounts in this chapter to the most recent year. Note that in some ways the official accounts are more detailed than those given in the text.

3. **Inventory in the GNP accounts.** A firm sells $10,000 worth of shoes that it has held in inventory for several years. What happens to GNP as a result? Which of its components are affected, and how?

4. **Payroll taxes in the GNP accounts.** The government raises employers' share of the social security payroll tax from 6 to 10 percent of wages. What happens to GNP, national income, and personal income?

5. **International accounts.** Following the pattern of the table given in Exhibit 7.6, show how the international accounts might look for a year in which there was a $50 billion surplus on current account, zero activity in the official reserve account, and zero statistical discrepancy. What would the capital account balance have to be?

6. **The current account deficit.** "A current account deficit is a very healthy thing. If we can get foreigners to give us real goods and services and talk them into taking pieces of paper in return, why should we want anything different?" Do you agree or disagree with this statement? Discuss.

7. **Real and nominal quantities.** In 1967, the base year for the consumer price index, the average earnings of construction workers were $154.95 per week. By 1986, earnings in construction had reached $465.75 per week but the consumer price index had risen to 328. What were construction workers' real earnings in 1986 stated in 1967 dollars?

8. **Changes in prices and qualities.** Try to find a Sears or similar catalog that is at least 10 years old and a recent catalog. Compare the ads for such items as (a) a basic work shirt, (b) a set of top-quality automobile tires, (c) a can of tennis balls, and (d) a stereo or record player. By how much has the price of each item gone up? What changes in quality have occurred? Assuming that you could buy at list price from either the new or the old catalog, which items would you buy from the old one and which from the new?

Case for Discussion
Laid-Off Steelworkers Join the Underground Economy

A closed steel mill in Youngstown, Ohio

HOMESTEAD, PA. A half-dozen men lounge on metal folding chairs outside a storefront on Ann Street, sweating in the muggy afternoon air and talking baseball. A pay phone rings inside, and a young man runs to answer it. Moments later, he speeds off in a long, beat-up sedan.

The man is about to cheat the government. He and the other men drive people around town for a fee, but they don't pay any taxes on the fares they receive. What's more, they don't see why they should.

Most of the men used to work at the sprawling Homestead Works a half block away. Now that the steel mill has closed, their car service allows them to make a living. "It ain't bothering anyone. It ain't stealing," says Earl Jones, who was laid off last December after 36 years at the mill. How much does he make? "Ain't saying," he replies with a smile.

The men are part of a vast underground economy made up of people who work "off the books" for cash. From the tired mill towns of the Midwest to the oil patches dotting the Southwest, the underground thrives. In communities that have suddenly lost a major employer, it helps those who were laid off make ends meet, and it helps keep towns like Homestead alive.

The number of Homestead residents with off-the-books livelihoods began to increase in the early 1980s when USX Corp.'s Homestead Works, which employed about 15,000 at its peak, started to lay off workers in droves. The mill's few remaining workers lost their jobs early in 1986. For most residents here, where only half the people have their high-school diplomas, the mill was all there was.

After they were laid off, many older workers retired and some of the younger ones withdrew their savings and migrated south, chasing dreams of work in more prosperous states. But many others stayed, bound by their unmarketable homes, their families or a strong sense of community. Unable to find legitimate jobs, they have parlayed their handyman skills underground.

One former mill worker says that half the people he knows are working off the books. For the most part, they are intensely proud people who hang the American flag from their neat front porches on holidays and respect the law, believing strongly in right and wrong. They definitely don't like the underground's seamy side—thefts and drugs. But their changed circumstances have altered the way many of them think.

"You tell me. Your kids go to bed crying at night because they're hungry. Is 'off the books' going to bother you?" asks a former steelworker.

Source: Clare Ansberry, "Laid-Off Steelworkers Find That Tax Evasion Helps Make Ends Meet," *The Wall Street Journal,* October 1, 1986, 1. Reprinted by permission of *The Wall Street Journal,* © Dow Jones & Company, Inc. 1986. All Rights Reserved. Photo Source: UPI/Bettmann Newsphotos.

Questions

1. What are the advantages of work "off the books" from the viewpoint of the people involved?

2. How might the failure to measure off-the-books activity affect economic policy decisions?

3. How might off-the-books work affect the statistical discrepancy in the national income accounts?

Suggestions for Further Reading

Porter, Richard D., and Amanda S. Bayer. "A Monetary Perspective on Underground Economic Activity in the United States," *Federal Reserve Bulletin* 70 (March 1984): 178–190.

This article reviews evidence from monetary statistics as they bear on the question of the size and growth of the underground sector of the U.S. economy.

President's Council of Economic Advisers. *Economic Report of the President.* Washington, D.C.: Government Printing Office, published annually.

A readily available source of national income and other useful data.

U.S. Department of Commerce. *Survey of Current Business.* Washington, D.C.: Government Printing Office, published monthly.

The most recent data on national income may be found in this publication.

U.S. Department of Commerce. *The National Income and Product Accounts for the United States, 1929–74.* Washington, D.C.: Government Printing Office, 1976.

Provides historical data on all items in the national accounts.

U.S. General Accounting Office. *A Primer on Gross National Product Concepts and Issues.* Washington, D.C.: U.S. General Accounting Office, 1981.

Details the definitions and methods behind the accounts.

Computation of Price Indexes

This appendix provides further information on the GNP deflator and consumer price index. Knowing these details will make it easier to see the differences between the two indexes and to understand the source of the substitution bias, which affects each one differently.

The GNP Deflator for a Simple Economy

A much simpler economy than that of the United States will serve to illustrate the computation of price indexes. Exhibit 7A.1 shows price and quantity data for two years for an economy in which only three goods are produced: movies, apples, and shirts. The exhibit shows that nominal GNP grew from $400 in 1982 to $1,000 in 1987. But what do these figures indicate? Do they mean that people really had more of the things they wanted in 1987 than in 1982? More precisely, do they mean that people had 2.5 times as much? These questions cannot be easily answered by looking at the exhibit in its present form.

A line-by-line comparison of the two years shows that the figures on nominal product do not tell the whole story. Clearly, prices went up sharply between 1982 and 1987. Movies cost twice what they used to, apples three times as much, and shirts half again as much. Note too that the amounts of goods produced have changed. Twice as many movies and shirts were produced in 1987 as in 1982 but only half as many apples.

If we wish to know how much better off people were in 1987 than in 1982, we need a way to separate the quantity changes that have taken place from the

Exhibit 7A.1 Nominal GNP for a Simple Economy

In this simple economy in which only three goods are produced, nominal national product grew from $400 in 1982 to $1,000 in 1987. Prices also went up during that time, however; thus, people did not really have 2.5 times as many goods in 1987 as they did in 1982.

1982	Quantity	Price	Value
Movies	50	$ 2.00	$ 100
Apples	1,000	.20	200
Shirts	10	10.00	100
1982 nominal GNP			$ 400
1987			
Movies	100	$ 4.00	$ 400
Apples	500	.60	300
Shirts	20	15.00	300
1987 nominal GNP			$1,000

price changes. One way to do this is to ask how much the total value of output would have changed from 1982 to 1987 if prices had not changed. This approach gives the results shown in Exhibit 7A.2. There we see that the 1987 output of 100 movies, 500 apples, and 20 shirts, which had a value of $1,000 in terms of the prices at which the goods were actually sold, would have had a value of only $500 in terms of the prices that prevailed in 1982. The $500 thus is a measure of real GNP for 1987. It is this measure that we should compare to the 1982 GNP of $400 if we want to know what really happened to output between the two years. Instead of having 250 percent as much output in 1987 as in 1982, as indicated by the change in nominal GNP from $400 to $1,000, the people in this simple economy really had only about 125 percent as much, as indicated by the change in real GNP from $400 to $500.

Now we know how to compute real and nominal GNP for 1987 directly from price and quantity data without using a price index to convert nominal values into real values. But although we have not explicitly used a price index, we have created one implicitly. This implicit index, or implicit GNP deflator, is the ratio of current-year nominal GNP to current-year real GNP times 100, as expressed by the following formula:

$$\text{GNP deflator} = \frac{\text{Current-year output valued at current-year prices}}{\text{Current-year output valued at base-year prices}} \times 100.$$

Applying the formula to the data in Exhibits 7A.1 and 7A.2 gives a value of 200 for the deflator.

The Consumer Price Index for a Simple Economy

The consumer price index differs from the GNP deflator in two ways. First, as mentioned in Chapter 7, it takes into account only the prices of goods and services consumed by a typical urban household. Second, it is calculated according to a formula that uses base-year rather than current-year quantities. The first

Exhibit 7A.2   Nominal and Real GNP for a Simple Economy

This table shows how the figures from Exhibit 7A.1 can be adjusted to take changing prices into account. The 1987 quantities are multiplied by 1982 prices to get the value of 1987 GNP that would have existed had prices not changed. The total of 1987 quantities valued at 1982 prices is a measure of real GNP for 1987 stated in constant 1982 dollars. The implicit GNP deflator for 1987, calculated as the ratio of 1987 nominal GNP to 1987 real GNP, has a value of 200.

	1987 Quantity	1987 Price	Value at 1987 Price	1982 Price	Value of 1987 Output at 1982 Price
Movies	100	$ 4.00	$ 400	$ 2.00	$200
Apples	500	.60	300	.20	100
Shirts	20	15.00	300	10.00	200
Totals		1987 nominal GNP =	$1,000	1987 real GNP =	$500

Exhibit 7A.3   A Consumer Price Index for a Simple Economy

The consumer price index can be calculated as the base-year market basket of goods valued at current-year prices divided by the base-year market basket valued at base-year prices multiplied by 100. This table shows how such an index can be calculated for a simple economy. The 1982 output cost $400 at the prices at which it was actually sold. Had it been sold at 1987 prices, it would have cost $950. Thus, the CPI for 1987 is 237.5.

Good	1982 Quantity	1982 Price	Value of 1982 Quantity at 1982 Price	1987 Price	Value of 1982 Quantity at 1987 Price
Movies	50	$ 2.00	$100	$ 4.00	$200
Apples	1,000	.20	200	.60	600
Shirts	10	10.00	100	15.00	150
Totals			$400		$950

$$CPI = \frac{\$950}{\$400} \times 100 = 237.5$$

difference does not matter for this simple economy in which all goods are consumer goods, but the second does, as Exhibit 7A.3 shows.

To calculate the CPI for this economy, instead of asking how much current-year output would have cost at base-year prices, we begin by asking how much base-year output would have cost at current-year prices. We then calculate the index as the ratio of the two different valuations of base-year quantities:

$$\text{Consumer price index} = \frac{\text{Base-year market basket valued at current-year prices}}{\text{Base-year market basket valued at base-year prices}} \times 100.$$

We calculate the CPI using base-year quantities partly because current price data are easier to collect than current output data. This index, therefore, can be announced each month with little delay.

Comparing the CPI and the GNP Deflator

As Exhibit 7A.3 shows, the CPI for 1987 in our simple economy had a value of 237.5, whereas the GNP deflator for 1987 was only 200. Both indexes were calculated using the same data, and both used 1982 as a base year. Which, if either, is the true measure of the change in prices between the two years?

The answer is that neither the CPI nor the GNP deflator is the only correct measure of change in the price level; instead, each answers a different question. The GNP deflator answers the question "How much more did the 1987 output cost at the prices at which it was actually sold than it would have cost had it been sold at 1982 prices?" The CPI, in contrast, answers the question "How much more would the 1982 output have cost had it been sold at 1987 instead of 1982 prices?"

A close look at the data shows why the answers to the two questions differ. In 1982, lots of apples and few shirts were produced compared to 1987. Yet between the two years, the price of apples increased 200 percent while the price of shirts increased only 50 percent. Because the CPI uses base-year quantities, it gives a heavy weight to apples, which showed the greatest relative price increase, and a lower weight to shirts, which showed only a modest price increase. In contrast, the GNP deflator uses current-year quantities, thereby decreasing the importance of apples and increasing that of shirts.

We can now see why the CPI tends to have an upward substitution bias relative to the GNP deflator. However, that does not make the GNP deflator a true measure of change in the cost of living. It could just as easily be said that the GNP deflator has a downward substitution bias relative to the CPI or that each has an opposite bias from some "true" price index. As yet there is no foolproof way to calculate the true cost-of-living index, although some interesting attempts have been made. A discussion of these more complex types of price indexes would take us far beyond the scope of this book. However, the basic types of price indexes covered here are the ones most commonly used for policymaking purposes.

8 Unemployment, Inflation, and the Business Cycle

After reading this chapter, you will understand . . .
- What unemployment means and how it is measured.
- The pattern that the business cycle follows.
- How changes in real output are linked to changes in unemployment.
- How supply and demand curves can be drawn for the macroeconomy.
- How changes in real output are linked over time to changes in the price level.

Before reading this chapter, make sure you know the meaning of . . .
- Transaction costs (Chapter 4)
- Stocks and flows (Chapter 6)
- Aggregate supply and demand (Chapter 6)
- Measurement of the price level (Chapter 7)

Jobless Rate Holds Steady

FEBRUARY 9, 1987. A strong January unemployment report, showing the civilian jobless rate unchanged from December at 6.7 percent of the labor force, suggests the economy continued to pick up steam as the year began.

The Labor Department said that with the 6.7 percent report, the rate remained at its lowest since it was 6.3 percent in March 1980, despite a big increase in the labor force. Using a separate measure that counts the military among the employed, the jobless rate was also steady, at 6.6 percent.

Construction employment managed to rise 142,000 in January 1987.

Non-farm payroll employment rose a sharp 448,000 last month after increasing a revised 225,000 in December. The December gain was previously reported as 269,000.

Many private economists hailed the report as an indication of solid growth. "I think it's an unmistakable sign of an improving economy," said Allen Sinai, chief economist at Shearson Lehman Brothers Inc. "The economy is shifting gears to better growth and better balance."

Construction employment rose 142,000 in January after a rise of 4,000 in December. A negative note came from the mining industry, where employment fell 11,000 after a 2,000-job decline. Overall, employment in goods-producing industries rose 134,000 last month after a 29,000-job increase in December.

The strongest gains, as usual, came in the services sector. Retail trade, affected by smaller-than-usual holiday hiring and firing, posted a rise of 166,000 jobs after an increase of just 1,000 in December. Janet Norwood, commissioner of the Labor Department's Bureau of Labor Statistics, said gains were robust in business and health services, and in finance, insurance, and real estate.

The unemployment rate increased sharply last month for teen-agers and blacks and edged up for Hispanics.

Source: Rose Gutfeld, "Jobless Rate Stayed at 6.7 Percent During January," *The Wall Street Journal*, February 9, 1987, p. 3. Reprinted by permission of *The Wall Street Journal*, © Dow Jones & Company, Inc. 1987. All Rights Reserved. Photo Source: Reuters/Bettmann Newsphotos.

CHANGES in the unemployment rate are big news—and justly so. Together with the rate of inflation and the growth of real output, the unemployment rate is one of the key indicators of the health of the macroeconomy. However, as this news item suggests, there is a complex story behind the one headline-catching unemployment number. In this chapter, we look at that story behind the headlines. We begin with the way in which unemployment is measured. Next, we turn to a discussion of the business cycle, paying special attention to the linkages between changes in unemployment and changes in the growth of real output at which the above news item hints. Finally, we examine how the supply and demand model, applied in a macroeconomic context, can serve as a powerful tool with which to explore these linkages.

Measuring Unemployment

In Chapter 7, we covered the methods of measuring all the major dollar flows within the circular flow of income and product in both nominal and real terms. We now turn to measurement of employment and the unemployment rate. These concepts differ from those discussed in the last chapter in that they concern stocks rather than flows and are not measured in dollar terms.

Classifying People by Labor Status

The official measure of unemployment is based on a breakdown of the U.S. population into a number of groups and subgroups, as shown in Exhibit 8.1. The first box represents all people under 16 years of age plus those in the armed services and those in prisons and other institutions. For statistical purposes, these people are not considered even potential members of the labor force, although some of them do work. Movements into and out of this part of the

Exhibit 8.1 Breakdown of the Population by Employment Status

This exhibit shows how the U.S. population is broken down into groups and subgroups based on employment status. People under 16, in the armed forces, prisons, or other institutions are viewed as not even potential participants in the labor market. Of the noninstitutional adult civilian population, only people who are working or looking for work are considered part of the labor force. The unemployment rate is the ratio of the number of unemployed people to the total labor force.

Total Population

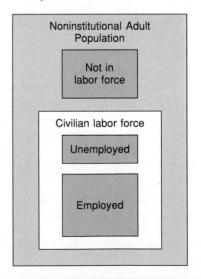

population are a result of noneconomic factors such as aging and institutionalization.

All people who are not in the above group belong to what is called the *noninstitutional adult civilian population*. This group, in turn, is divided into three subgroups, as shown in the second box in Exhibit 8.1. The first subgroup consists of all people who are employed. The Bureau of Labor Statistics counts as **employed** all people who work at least 1 hour a week for pay or at least 15 hours a week as unpaid workers in a family business. People who have jobs from which they are absent because of bad weather, labor disputes, or vacations are also counted as employed.

The second subgroup is made up of the officially unemployed. In order to be considered **unemployed,** a person must be without a job but actively looking for one. There are two exceptions to this rule. One is that people who have found jobs that they expect to start within 30 days are counted as unemployed even if they are not actively looking for work to fill the time remaining until the jobs begin. The other is that people who have been laid off from jobs to which they expect to be recalled need not be actively looking for other work in order to be counted as unemployed.

Taken together, the employed and the unemployed make up the **civilian labor force.** The remaining subgroup in Exhibit 8.1 thus consists of all noninstitutionalized civilians age 16 and over who are not in the civilian labor force—that is, who are neither working nor looking for work. Although these people are not employed, they are not officially counted as unemployed. This division of the population into groups and subgroups is the basis of the official **civilian unemployment rate,** which is simply the percentage of the civilian labor force that is not employed.

Many economists consider it unrealistic to exclude members of the armed services from the labor force. In this era of the volunteer armed forces, they claim, membership in the military is a job like any other. If members of the armed services are added to both the labor force and the ranks of the employed, a different measure of unemployment—sometimes called the *total unemployment rate*—results. Because there is no such thing as an unemployed member of the armed services, the total unemployment rate is about .1 percentage points lower than the civilian rate. Despite the conceptual superiority of the total rate, however, it is the civilian unemployment rate that continues to make headlines. Bowing to common practice, then, when we refer to the unemployment rate without modification, we will mean the civilian rate.

Criticisms of the Unemployment Rate

The Bureau of Labor Statistics, in conjunction with the Bureau of the Census, gets the data needed for calculating unemployment from a monthly sample of about 50,000 randomly selected households. Field agents go to those households and ask a series of questions about the job status of each member. These questions include such things as: Did anyone work last week? Did anyone look for work? How long has the person been looking for work? How did the person go about looking?

Clearly there are many gray areas in the measurement of unemployment. The official unemployment rate can be criticized for both understating and overstating the "true" number of unemployed. One way to better understand these

Employed
A person working at least 1 hour a week for pay or 15 hours a week as an unpaid worker in a family business.

Unemployed
A person who is not employed but is actively looking for work.

Civilian labor force
The sum of the employed and the unemployed; excludes members of the armed forces on active duty.

Civilian unemployment rate
The percentage of the civilian labor force that is unemployed.

gray areas is to compare the official definition of unemployment with two commonsense definitions, namely "not working" and "can't find a job."

"Unemployed" versus "Not Working"

The official definitions of employment and unemployment differ greatly from the simple definitions of "working" and "not working."

On the one hand, there are many people who work but are not officially employed. By far the largest such group consists of people who work full-time at housekeeping and child care. These occupations are counted as employment if they are performed for pay, but the bulk of such work is done without pay. There are also a certain number of children under 16 who work for pay but are not counted as employed. Children under 16 working without pay for a family farm or business also are not counted as employed, although they are counted as employed for doing the same work once they reach their sixteenth birthday.

On the other hand, not everyone who does not work is counted as unemployed. There are, of course, millions of people who are not looking for work and who therefore are not counted in the labor force. There are also those who are absent from their jobs because of illness, bad weather, or labor disputes but are still counted as employed. Finally, there are those who work part-time and are counted as employed but are actively seeking full-time employment. People in this situation are sometimes referred to as *underemployed*.

"Unemployed" versus "Can't Find a Job"

The second commonsense definition of unemployment, "can't find a job," also only loosely fits the official definition.

In some ways, the official definition overstates the number of people who cannot find jobs. As just mentioned, some people who are counted as unemployed actually have jobs to which they expect to be recalled or jobs that they expect to start within 30 days. Other people who are counted as unemployed could easily find a job of some kind but prefer to take their time and find just the kind of job they want. (People who are not the sole income earners in their households, for example, may be able to afford to look longer and be more selective than those in households with no other income.) Still other people register as unemployed in order to meet the requirements of income transfer programs even though they may not be qualified for any available work and only go through the motions of looking for a job. Finally, there is some doubt as to whether the description "can't find a job" fits people who could have stayed on at their last jobs but instead quit to look for better ones.

In other ways, however, the official definition of unemployment understates the number of people who cannot find jobs. The most important group of people who cannot find work but are not counted as unemployed are the so-called **discouraged workers.** These are people who are not looking for work because they believe no suitable jobs are available. The Bureau of Labor Statistics officially counts as a discouraged worker anyone who has looked for work within the last six months but is no longer actively looking. The description "can't find a job" also fits many workers who have part-time jobs but would take full-time jobs if they could find them.

Discouraged worker
A person who would work if a suitable job were available but has given up looking.

The Unemployment Rate versus the Employment Rate

Although the unemployment rate is the most widely publicized measure of the state of the labor market, not all economists think it is the best one. In addition to the problems of definition that we have seen, there is a problem pertaining to the fact that the denominator of the unemployment ratio (size of the labor force) is as readily subject to change as the numerator (number of unemployed). This problem is illustrated by the news item that leads off this chapter, which notes that in January 1987, the unemployment rate held steady even though the economy generated 448,000 new jobs. A closer look at the data given in the news item shows why this occurred. In the month in question, of all those who entered the labor force, about 93.3 percent were successful in finding jobs but about 6.7 percent failed to find jobs even though they began actively looking for them. If the percentage of unsuccessful entrants is the same as the previous unemployment rate, the unemployment rate will not change even though many jobs have been generated.

Because of this property of the unemployment rate, some economists think that the employment rate is a more revealing indicator of the economy's health. The **employment rate** is the percentage of the working-age population that is employed. The denominator of the employment rate—the size of the working-age population—is governed by demographic factors and changes slowly and predictably. Thus, the employment rate is less likely than the unemployment rate to stand still while the economy moves ahead or to give other misleading signals.

Sometimes the employment rate not only gives a better picture of the short-term state of the economy than does the unemployment rate but presents a quite different picture of long-term trends. Measured in terms of the unemployment rate, the U.S. economy has not performed very well over the last two decades. For example, over the decade 1967 to 1976 the unemployment rate averaged 5.3 percent, while over 1977 to 1986 it rose, on average, to 7.4 percent. However, employment figures show that the U.S. economy over this period was a remarkable job-creating machine. In 1967, jobs were available for only 58 percent of the working population; by 1986, that percentage had increased to about 61 percent, an all-time record. In absolute terms, the number of people holding jobs rose from 74 million to 110 million over this period.

The image of the United States as a job-creating machine is further enhanced by some international comparisons. Between 1973 and 1983, while the U.S. economy added some 15 million new jobs, the United Kingdom lost 2 million jobs and West Germany 1 million. Job growth in the United States over this period included manufacturing as well as the service sector, although the latter grew more rapidly. In this decade, the United States added some 343,000 manufacturing jobs while the United Kingdom lost more than 2 million, West Germany 1.2 million, France nearly 500,000, and Japan (surprisingly) 70,000.

Despite this remarkable performance, however, problems remain. After 1980, the U.S. economy began to lose manufacturing jobs, although the total-jobs figure continued to grow. Some critics claim that employment statistics are being swelled by "junk jobs" and that the United States is changing from an economy of steel- and autoworkers into one of hamburger flippers and parking lot attendants; "Perspective 8.1" addresses this issue. A more serious concern is

Employment rate
The percentage of the working-age population that is employed.

PERSPECTIVE 8.1

A "Junk Job" Explosion?

The U.S. economy has a remarkable record of job creation, but even this has its critics. In a study released in late 1986 by the Joint Economic Committee of Congress, economists Barry Bluestone of the University of Massachusetts and Bennett Harrison of MIT voiced their concern over an "alarming trend toward low-pay jobs." In particular, Bluestone and Harrison found that in the 1979 to 1984 period, 58 percent of new jobs were in the category paying less than half of the median wage, or $7,102 a year, stated in constant 1984 dollars, up from the 37.5 percent of the mid-1970s. In the same period, there was a loss of 5.5 percent in jobs paying more than twice the median versus the 11.2 percent gain of the mid-1970s.

These data were cited in support of several programs aimed at protecting high-pay jobs (for example, by blocking imports or restricting factory closings) and reducing low-pay jobs (such as by raising the federal minimum wage to half of the median wage).

But the accompanying table shows that the trend is not so clear if the Bluestone-Harrison data are put in a broader context. When the data are arranged in terms of presidential budget cycles, the job-creating performance of the economy in the Reagan years appears to be better, not worse, than the previous record. (This arrangement of years takes into account the fact that the government, in the first year of each president's term, operates under a budget tailored by the preceding president.)

As Janet Norwood, the nonpartisan commissioner of labor statistics, said, "The findings are extremely sensitive to the particular set of data used and the years chosen for analysis." The Bluestone-Harrison study focused on the worst possible case by including the double-digit inflation of 1979 and 1980 and the back-to-back recessions of 1980 and 1981 to 1982. These episodes were especially tough on high-pay jobs. Since then, high-pay jobs have rebounded.

As economic columnist Robert Samuelson puts it, "Welcome to Economics Propaganda 101. The notion that the U.S. economy is producing mostly low-paying, unskilled jobs . . . is an exercise in statistical mythmaking designed to advance a political agenda."

Source: Based on Joint Economic Committee and Warren T. Brookes, "Low-Pay Jobs: The Big Lie," *The Wall Street Journal*, March 25, 1987, 30. Reprinted by permission of *The Wall Street Journal*, © Dow Jones & Company, Inc. 1987. All Rights Reserved; Robert J. Samuelson, "An Imperfect Job Machine," *Washington Post*, February 18, 1987, F1. The table is taken from the Brookes article.

Net New Jobs
(Thousands)

	Low (Under $7,012)		Middle ($7,012–$28,048)		High ($28,048 and over)	
	Number	Share	Number	Share	Number	Share
Nixon-Ford 1973–1977	2,550	37.5%	3,490	51.3%	758	11.2%
Carter 1977–1981	3,837	41.7	6,277	68.2	−912	−9.9
Reagan 1981–1985	412	6.0	3,180	46.2	3,169	46.1
Bluestone-Harrison 1979–1984	4,687	58.0	3,837	47.5	−442	−5.5

Note: Salaries in 1984 constant dollars.

Source: Joint Economic Committee

the fact that unemployment is concentrated in certain subgroups of the population—workers displaced by plant closings, workers with few skills and little education, and members of some minority groups. As the article that opens this chapter notes, the unemployment rate among minority groups and teenagers sometimes rises even when the rest of the economy is enjoying prosperity. The next section looks at three different types of unemployment, some of which are greater causes of concern than others.

Types of Unemployment

A change in the unemployment rate reflects a change in the flows into and out of the pool of unemployed workers. Given a constant size of labor force, the unemployment rate rises when the rate of flow into the pool of the unemployed exceeds the rate of outflow and falls when the outflow from the pool exceeds the inflow. The difference between the rate of inflow and the rate of outflow determines how long the average person remains unemployed. During the past 20 years, the average duration of unemployment has ranged from a low of 7.8 weeks in 1969 to a high of 20.0 weeks in 1983.

The duration of unemployment varies not only from year to year but from one unemployed worker to another. As Exhibit 8.2 shows, depending on the state of the economy between one-third and three-fifths of all unemployed people are out of work for less than five weeks. At the other end of the scale, 5 to 25 percent of unemployed people are out of work for six months or more. Variations in the duration of unemployment serve as a basis for distinguishing among *frictional, structural,* and *cyclical unemployment.*

Frictional Unemployment

The term **frictional unemployment** refers to the short periods of unemployment needed to match jobs and job seekers within the mainstream of the economy. Much of this short-term unemployment is voluntary. It represents people who have quit old jobs to look for new ones, people who take a week or so to move or go on vacation before starting a newly found job, and people who have entered occupations, such as construction work, in which temporary layoffs are a part of life but earnings are good on a year-round basis. Economists view a certain level of frictional unemployment as necessary for matching workers with jobs in a labor market in which information is incomplete and transaction costs are often high.

Frictional unemployment
The portion of unemployment that is accounted for by short periods of unemployment needed for matching jobs with job seekers within the mainstream of the economy.

Structural Unemployment

The term **structural unemployment** refers to people who spend long periods out of work, often with little prospect of finding adequate jobs. These workers face prolonged joblessness partly because the shifting structure of the economy has made their skills obsolete. The structurally unemployed also includes people with few skills and little work experience. Teenagers and some minority groups are particularly affected by this type of unemployment.

For these people, structural unemployment is not merely a problem of lack of jobs. Certain types of jobs—hospital orderly jobs, fast-food work, and car washing, for example—are almost always available and require few specific skills. But structurally unemployed workers either avoid these kinds of jobs or work at them only for short periods before quitting. Working for brief periods at dead-end jobs tends to build up a pattern of poor work habits and absenteeism that makes many structurally unemployed people unattractive to employers.

Structural unemployment
The portion of unemployment that is accounted for by people who are out of work for long periods because their skills do not match those required for available jobs.

Exhibit 8.2   Duration of Unemployment, 1965–1986

As this chart shows, there is considerable variation in the length of time people are unemployed. Depending on the state of the economy, about a third to three-fifths of all unemployed workers spend less than five weeks out of work. On the other hand, 5 to 25 percent are out of work for six months or more.

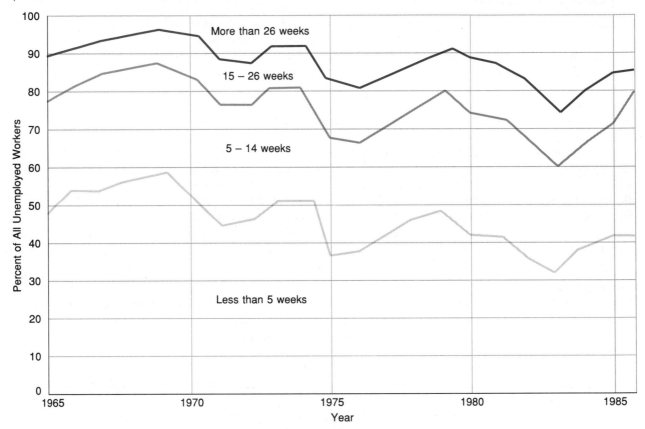

Source: President's Council of Economic Advisers, *Economic Report of the President* (Washington, D.C.: Government Printing Office, 1987), Table B-32.

The Natural Rate of Unemployment

Frictional and structural unemployment are present in good as well as bad years. In a healthy economy, frictional unemployment reflects the process of matching workers to jobs. Structural unemployment may be a sign of shifting composition of industry or of broader social problems, but its causes and cures are more microeconomic than macroeconomic in nature. The sum of frictional and structural unemployment is often referred to as the **natural rate of unemployment.** This term can be thought of as the rate of unemployment that persists during a period of macroeconomic stability—that is, a period of neither accelerating nor decelerating inflation.

Some economists object to using the term "natural" to refer to unemployment that is partly structural, because it seems to imply that the human suffering that structural unemployment brings is acceptable in some normative sense.

Natural rate of unemployment
The sum of frictional and structural unemployment; the rate of unemployment that persists when the economy is experiencing neither accelerating nor decelerating inflation.

They have tried to replace it with a more "neutral" term such as "nonaccelerating-inflation rate of unemployment (NAIRU)." Whatever the merits of the issue, however, the simple term "natural" is the one that has caught on and the one we will use in this course.

Cyclical Unemployment

In practice, unemployment is not always at its "natural" benchmark. As we will see in the next section, over time the economy undergoes cycles of expansion and contraction. As it does so, the unemployment rate changes. As a result of vigorous economic expansion, unemployment may drop below its natural rate. In such a period, the job market may be so strong that even many of the hardcore structurally unemployed find jobs. As a result of business contraction, the unemployment rate rises above its natural rate. At such times, even many workers with strong job attachment and excellent skills may find themselves temporarily laid off.

The difference between the actual unemployment rate at a given time and the natural rate is known as **cyclical unemployment.** When the economy slows down, cyclical unemployment is added to frictional and structural unemployment. At the peak of an expansionary period, cyclical unemployment may be negative. The following section looks more closely at this cyclical behavior of the economy.

Cyclical unemployment
The difference between the actual rate of unemployment at a given point in the business cycle and the natural rate of unemployment.

The Business Cycle

Over the last two centuries, the U.S. economy has grown enormously, but it has not grown at a steady pace. Instead, growth has proceeded in a series of spurts alternating with periods of contraction. Exhibit 8.3 shows 100 years of this pattern, which is known as the **business cycle.**

Business cycle
A pattern of alternating economic growth and contraction.

Phases of the Business Cycle

The actual business cycle pattern shown in Exhibit 8.3 can be compared with that of an idealized business cycle, also shown in the exhibit. The idealized cycle can be divided into four phases. The *peak* of the cycle is the point at which real output reaches a maximum. The period during which real output falls is known as the *contraction* phase. At the end of the contraction, real output reaches a minimum, known as the *trough* of the cycle. After the trough, real output begins to grow again and the economy enters an *expansion* that lasts until a new peak is reached.

The actual business cycles shown in Exhibit 8.3 display a number of small wiggles within the larger cyclical swings. Normally only cycles containing a contraction phase of six months or more are considered important. A contraction lasting six months or more is known as a **recession.**

In the nineteenth and early twentieth centuries, there were a number of cyclical contractions that were, in proportion to the smaller economy of the day, much more severe than any of the post–World War II recessions. These were called *depressions*. The most spectacular of all was the *Great Depression* of the 1930s, which actually consisted of two contractionary periods separated by an incomplete recovery. During this episode, real output fell by a third, the price

Recession
A cyclical contraction usually lasting six months or more.

Exhibit 8.3   Business Cycles in the United States

This historical chart shows 100 years of the pattern of alternating booms and recessions that has been observed in the United States for some two centuries. The inset shows an idealized business cycle with its phases: peak, contraction, trough, and expansion. A contraction lasting six months or more is called a *recession*. (For a chart of U.S. business cycles dating back to 1790, see the front and back endsheets of this text.)

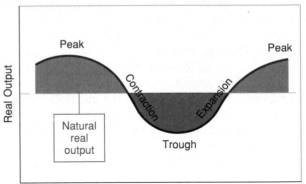

Idealized Business Cycle

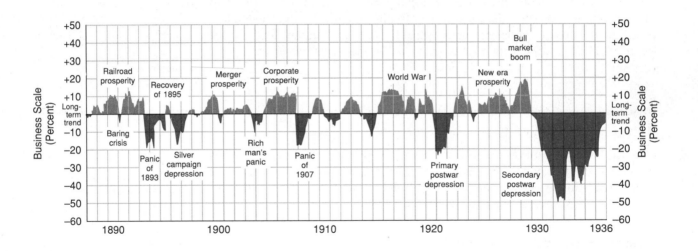

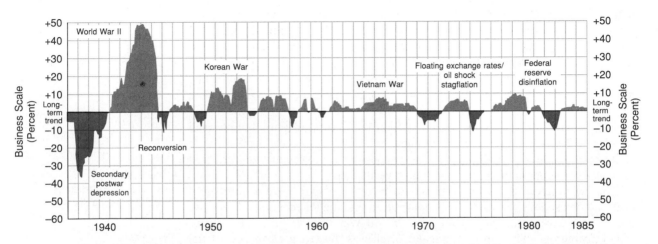

Source: AmeriTrust Corporation. The vertical scale on the chart shows, in percentage terms, how high the level of business activity in a given year rose above the long-term trend or how far it fell below it.

level fell by a quarter, and the unemployment rate climbed to 24 percent of the labor force. Because no succeeding contraction has come close to it in severity, the term "depression" has passed out of use.

Unemployment and Output over the Business Cycle

In Exhibit 8.3, the business cycle is portrayed in terms of real national product, but changes in real output are linked to changes in employment. The trend line around which the idealized business cycle centers represents a state of affairs in which the economy expands at a rate that is consistent with its long-run growth potential. Under such conditions, the economy is said to be at its **natural level of real output** or, alternatively, *natural level of real national product*. The natural real output is the level that is consistent with the natural rate of unemployment.

When an expansion carries real national product above its natural level, unemployment tends to fall below its natural rate. The underlying reason is simple: More workers are needed to produce the added output. Likewise, when contraction takes real output below the natural level, unemployment rises above its natural rate because fewer workers are required.

However, the linkage between changes in real output and unemployment is not a simple one-to-one relationship as the assumption that "more output requires more workers" implies. Instead, according to a widely used rule of thumb, for each 3 percent by which real output rises above its natural level, the unemployment rate tends to fall by one percentage point and for each 3 percent by which real output falls below its natural level, the unemployment rate tends to rise by one percentage point. This rule of thumb is known as **Okun's law.** It is named after Arthur Okun, who was a member of President Kennedy's Council of Economic Advisers at the time he formulated it (see "Who Said It? Who Did It? 8.1").

Suppose, for example, that the natural level of real output is $1 trillion and the natural rate of unemployment is 6.5 percent. In that case, a 6 percent decrease in real output, to $940 billion, would tend to raise the unemployment rate to 8.5 percent. Likewise, a 3 percent increase in real output from its natural level of $1 trillion to $1.03 trillion would push unemployment one percentage point below its natural rate, to 5.5 percent.[1]

Why the 3-to-1 ratio between changes in real output relative to its natural level and changes in the unemployment rate relative to its natural rate? Why doesn't adding 1 percent to real output cut unemployment by a full percentage point? There seem to be two basic reasons.

First, hires and layoffs in labor markets, like exchanges in any other market, involve transaction costs. Firms that hire new workers must bear the costs of advertising for applicants and screening them when they arrive. Also, new workers may not be fully productive until they have gone through a period of on-the-job training. Firms that lay off workers also bear some transaction costs. Some contracts call for severance payments. Some skilled workers may get other jobs after being laid off. Employers that have made many layoffs may be required by law to make higher payments to state and federal unemployment insurance funds. Because of these transaction costs, firms tend to "hoard" labor during

Natural level of real output
The level of real output associated with the natural rate of unemployment.

Okun's law
A rule of thumb according to which each 3 percent by which real output rises above (or falls below) its natural level results in an unemployment rate one percentage point below (or above) the natural rate.

---

[1] We use the phrase "percentage point change" because the unemployment rate itself is already expressed in percentage terms. It would be misleading to say "a 1 percent change in the unemployment rate," which might be taken to mean a drop in the unemployment rate from 6.5 to 6.435 percent (6.435 being 99 percent of 6.5).

Arthur Okun: Policy Economist

Arthur Okun was one of the best known of a generation of "new economists" who dominated economic policymaking during the Kennedy and Johnson administrations of the 1960s. In 1961, the young associate professor left Yale to join the "New Frontier" as a staff economist on the President's Council of Economic Advisers. In 1964, he became a full member of the council, and in 1968 to 1969, he served as its chairman. When Johnson left office, Okun stayed in Washington as a senior fellow of the Brookings Institution, a position that permitted him to combine research wih active public affairs involvement.

Okun's name first became well known in connection with research relating changes in unemployment to changes in real national product. In a paper written for the American Statistical Association in 1962, he tried to answer the question of how much output the economy could pro-

Photo Source: Courtesy of The Brookings Institution.

duce under conditions of full employment. Because of his concern for "the enormous social cost of idle resources," he found this question crucial to economic policy.

During Okun's service on the Council of Economic Advisers, economists' enthusiasm for economic growth was at its height. Okun saw rapid economic growth as essential to avoiding the waste and extravagance of unemployment. "The economy loses ground if it stands still," he wrote. He added:

> Unless the growth of total output keeps pace with our ever-expanding potential, the unemployment rate tends to rise. The nation needs continually to set new records in production and sales. Its economy needs to grow bigger and better than ever before—because its labor force, capital stock, technology, and managerial and organizational resources are always getting bigger and better.

Okun's work at Brookings reflected the change from the optimistic, growth-oriented 1960s to the problem-ridden, inflationary 1970s. Okun contributed to the understanding of chronic inflation and proposed a variety of initiatives for combatting it, including reduction of sales and payroll taxes and provision of tax rewards for wage-price restraints. In 1979, Okun was awarded the Seidman Foundation prize for his impact on public policy.

business downturns by cutting their workers' hours or finding make-work projects for them instead of laying them off. Further, during upturns they may find it cheaper to put workers on overtime, even at time-and-a-half wages, rather than go to the trouble of finding new ones.

But labor hoarding does not fully explain the 3-to-1 ratio of Okun's law. A second explanation for the ratio lies in the way the unemployment rate itself is calculated. The unemployment rate is the ratio of unemployed workers to the civilian labor force. During a business upturn, when firms are creating new jobs at a rapid rate, some previously unemployed workers find jobs. At the same time, however, the improved job market draws into the labor force workers who previously had not even looked for work. Not all the new entrants find work right away; some join the ranks of the unemployed instead. The upshot is that when output expands, the number of employed, the number of unemployed, and the size of the civilian labor force all grow. As a result, a 1 percent increase in the number of jobs tends to be linked with less than a one-percentage-point drop in the unemployment rate.

On a quarter-to-quarter basis, Okun's law does not hold exactly. But for a time horizon of several quarters, this rule of thumb has held up well over the 25 years since it was first set forth. Several studies suggest that today the ratio is close to 2.5 to 1 rather than 3 to 1, but in our numerical examples we will stay with the traditional 3-to-1 ratio.

Real Output and the Price Level in the Aggregate Supply and Demand Model

Okun's law links two of the three key macroeconomic variables—real output and the unemployment rate. In this section, we turn to another relationship: that of real output and the price level.[2] We will examine this relationship with the help of a model based on the concepts of aggregate supply and demand introduced in Chapter 6.

The Aggregate Demand Curve

In Chapter 3, we introduced demand curves for individual markets. For reasons that accord with common sense and everyday experience, these curves have negative slopes—that is, they indicate that, other things being equal, people will tend to buy less of a good as its price rises.

It might seem that we could move directly from these familiar graphs to an **aggregate demand curve**—a graph that shows the relationship between total planned expenditures on all goods and services in real terms and the average price level. However, there is a problem in making the transition from market demand to aggregate demand. The problem concerns the other-things-being-equal assumption. In the case of a market demand curve, one of the things we hold constant as we move along it is the prices of other goods. But when we deal with changes in the average prices of all goods, this assumption no longer holds. A second thing we hold constant in drawing a market demand curve is nominal income. However, the circular flow model suggests that an increase in the average price level of all goods will tend to swell the stream of wages, rents, interest, and profits from which incomes are derived. Because neither other prices nor nominal incomes can be assumed constant as the average price level changes, then, the reasoning used in deriving market demand curves will not work for the aggregate demand curve. Instead, we take a different approach: We look in real terms at each component of aggregate demand—consumption, planned investment, government purchases, and net exports—to see how real planned expenditures change when the price level rises.

Aggregate demand curve
A graph showing the relationship between the price level and the total level of real planned expenditures.

Consumption

We begin with consumers. During a period of inflation, consumers' nominal incomes rise as the price level rises. This shields them, in part, from the effects of inflation. However, consumers are not fully protected because some of the assets they own have fixed nominal values. The money they hold in the form of currency and checking account balances is an important example. As the price level increases, the real purchasing power of nominal money balances falls. For example, one year a $100 checking account balance might be enough to buy a week's worth of groceries; the following year, after prices have gone up 15 percent, $100 will buy enough groceries for only about six days. Because of the falling real value of nominal money balances, then, consumers will tend to buy less in real terms than they would had the price level not risen. Hence, we

---

[2]Chapter 19 addresses a third linkage—that between the unemployment rate and the inflation rate. This relationship is based on an extension of the model introduced here and used through Chapter 18.

conclude that an increase in the price level tends to cause the consumption component of real aggregate demand to decrease.

Investment
Investment also will be affected by an increase in the price level, but for a different reason. For reasons that will be explained more fully in coming chapters, an increase in the price level tends to push interest rates higher. Rising interest rates raise the cost of borrowing and hence discourage firms from undertaking fixed-investment projects. High interest rates also raise the costs of carrying inventories of finished products; thus, firms may react by reducing inventories. Therefore, an increase in the price level, via its effect on interest rates, tends to depress the real planned-investment component of aggregate demand.

Government Purchases
Some government purchase decisions are made in real terms. For example, Congress might decide to authorize the Pentagon to buy 100 jet fighters. If the price per plane goes up, more dollars will be spent to purchase the authorized quantity. However, other government purchase decisions are made in nominal terms. For example, the Virginia highway department may be given a budget of $50 million for road improvements. If the price of asphalt goes up, the department, constrained by its $50 million budget, will be unable to pave as many miles of roads as it had planned. Perhaps it will be able to persuade the legislature to raise its budget next year, but in the meantime the price increase means less spending in real terms.

Generalizing from this example, we conclude that to the extent that some elements of government budgets (federal, state, and local) are set in nominal terms, the government purchases component of aggregate demand may tend to fall in real terms as the price level rises, at least in the short run.

Net Exports
Prices can rise in one country and remain the same in others. Suppose, for example, that the United States experiences higher prices while domestic prices in Japan stay the same. With a given exchange rate between the dollar and the Japanese yen, U.S. goods will become more expensive for Japanese buyers and Japanese goods will become relatively cheaper for U.S. buyers. As U.S. buyers switch from domestic goods to imports and U.S. exports become harder to sell abroad, the real net export component of aggregate demand falls.

A complete analysis of the effects of price level changes on net exports requires taking into account changes in exchange rates and interest rates. These issues will be discussed in Chapter 20.

Shifts in the Aggregate Demand Curve
Our preliminary review of the consumption, investment, government purchases, and net exports components of aggregate demand suggests that all will tend to decrease, in real terms, as the price level increases. This means that the aggregate demand curve will have a negative slope, as in Exhibit 8.4. Other things being equal, a change in the price level will alter real planned expenditure and thus cause a movement up or down along one such curve, for example, AD_1.

As in the case of individual demand curves, a change in market conditions other than the price level will cause the aggregate demand curve to shift to the

Exhibit 8.4   The Aggregate Demand Curve

An aggregate demand curve shows the relationship between the price level and the level of real planned expenditure, other things being equal. A change in economic conditions can cause the aggregate demand curve to shift. For example, a rightward shift, as from AD_1 to AD_2, might be caused by a shift in consumer or business expectations toward greater optimism; an expansionary change in government policy; or expansion of a foreign economy, boosting demand for U.S. exports.

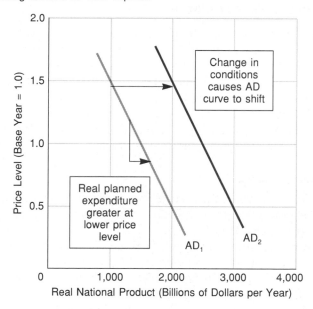

left or to the right. Among the sources of shifts—each of which will be discussed in detail in coming chapters—are the following:

- *Expectations.* If consumers become more optimistic about the future, they may increase their real planned expenditures at any given price level. Similarly, an increase in business optimism about future profit opportunities may increase real planned investment at any given price level. In either case, the aggregate demand curve shifts to the right, such as from AD_1 to AD_2 in Exhibit 8.4. A swing toward pessimistic expectations by consumers or firms will shift the aggregate demand curve to the left.

- *Changes in government policy.* An increase in real government purchases, other things being equal, tends to shift the aggregate demand curve to the right. On the other hand, an increase in taxes, by cutting into consumers' disposable incomes, tends to depress consumption and shift the aggregate demand curve to the left. Finally, as we will see in Chapters 12 through 15, Federal Reserve policies that increase the economy's stock of money tend to shift the aggregate demand curve to the right, while policies that restrict the stock of money tend to shift it to the left.

- *Changes in the world economy.* Events in foreign countries have an impact on aggregate demand in the United States. For example, suppose that real economic growth speeds up in the economy of a major trading partner—say, West Germany. When this happens, German firms and consumers will tend to buy more imported goods, thus boosting the net exports component of U.S. aggregate demand. Also, changes in foreign countries' price levels will affect U.S. net exports by changing the relative prices of imported and exported goods.

The Aggregate Supply Curve

Aggregate supply curve
A graph showing the relationship between the price level and the real output (real national product) supplied by the economy.

We turn now to the supply side of our aggregate model. In Chapter 6, we introduced the term *aggregate supply* as a synonym for the economy's total real output, or real national product. Thus, an **aggregate supply curve** can be understood as showing the quantity of real national product supplied by the economy at various price levels. As with aggregate demand, we cannot move directly from individual market demand curves to the aggregate case because we must rethink the other-things-being-equal assumptions that lie behind it. In the case of aggregate supply, the key lies in what we assume to happen to input prices.

Fully Flexible Input Prices
One possibility is that when the average level of prices of the final goods that go into GNP changes, input prices will change in the same proportion. There are two reasons to expect this to happen.

One reason stems from the impact of changes in output prices on the price of labor inputs, that is, on wages and salaries. Wages and salaries account for about three-quarters of all input costs for a typical firm. When the average price level of outputs of final goods rises, workers' costs of living also increase. If nominal wages and salaries remain the same, real wages will fall; for example, when the price level doubles, a wage of $5 per hour will buy only half the groceries or pay half the rent as formerly. Workers will ask for raises to maintain their standard of living, and firms—which are, after all, getting twice as much as formerly for their outputs—will be able to afford to grant these raises. If some employers try to hold the line against wage increases, they will lose their most skilled and mobile workers to other employers that are willing to protect workers' real earnings from inflation.

The other reason is that many goods serve as both final goods and inputs. Oil, electric power, natural gas, and other forms of energy are examples. If supply and demand raise the prices paid for these products in markets where they are sold as final goods, their prices will also rise in markets where they are sold to firms for use as productive inputs.

Suppose, then, that firms expect the prices of all inputs to rise proportionately whenever the price level for outputs of final goods rises. What will happen to real output as the price level changes? The conclusion must be that the quantity of real national product supplied will remain constant. After all, firms decide how much to produce by balancing the prices they can get for their goods against those they must pay for the inputs they use. If both output and input prices rise, profit margins, in real terms, will be unchanged. There is thus no reason to produce either more or less than before.

We conclude, then, that the assumption of fully flexible input prices implies a vertical aggregate supply curve such as the one shown in part a of Exhibit 8.5. This curve is located at the economy's natural level of real output.

Exhibit 8.5   The Aggregate Supply Curve

The aggregate supply curve shows the relationship between the price level and the level of real output (real national product) supplied by the nation's economy. Its slope depends on what happens to input prices as the price level of the outputs of final goods that go into GNP changes. In the long run, input prices tend to rise and fall in proportion to the change in final goods prices, making the aggregate supply curve vertical, as in part a of the exhibit. In the short run, input prices adjust only gradually to changes in the level of final goods prices. This makes the short-run aggregate supply curve positively sloped, as in part b.

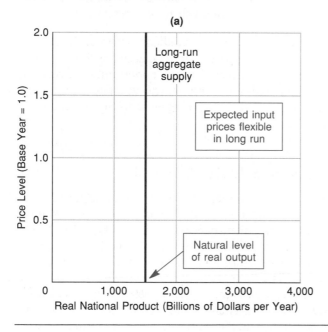

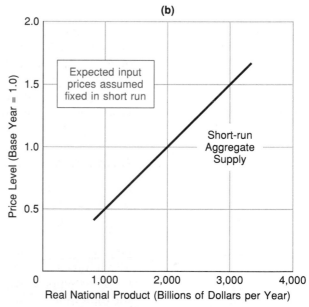

Gradual Adjustment of Input Prices

As a long-run proposition, most economists would agree that input prices tend to move in proportion to output prices. However, there are strong reasons to think that the adjustment of input prices to output prices is not instantaneous. Instead, when rising demand forces output prices higher, firms react as though they expect input prices to adjust only gradually. There are several reasons for the gradual adjustment of input prices.

- *Long-term contracts*. The prices of some inputs are fixed by long-term contract. Union labor contracts are one important example. Some firms may also rent buildings, buy fuel, or hire transportation services under long-term contracts. Even when output prices rise, the prices of these inputs cannot rise until it is time to renegotiate the contracts.

- *Inventories*. Inventories tend to have a cushioning effect on input prices. To illustrate, suppose that a bakery experiences an increase in demand for its bread. At first, it will gladly bake and sell more bread, running down its inventories of flour in the process. If prices have been rising throughout the economy, the bakery may have to pay more for the next batch of flour it orders. This change in input prices will cause it to revise its output plans, but by then a certain amount of time will have passed.

- *Incomplete knowledge.* Firms may mistake economywide changes in demand for local changes that will affect only their own market. For example, the bakery might think that the increased demand for bread is limited to the city it serves. Such a local change in demand would not be expected to have a perceptible effect on the price of flour, which is determined in a nationwide market. Only later will the bakery find out that the increase in demand for its bread is part of a broad increase in aggregate demand—but again some time will have passed by then.

If firms expect input prices to adjust only gradually when an increase in demand causes output prices to rise, expected profit margins will temporarily increase. To take advantage of the increased profit opportunities, firms will expand their real output, at least until input prices catch up. Thus, when firms expect gradual adjustment of input prices, the aggregate supply curve will have a positive slope as in part b of Exhibit 8.5.

Interaction of Aggregate Supply and Demand

Putting the aggregate supply curve together with the aggregate demand curve permits us to see how prices, real national product, and real planned expenditures move over time in response to a disturbance. Consider Exhibit 8.6. In part a, the economy is shown in an initial equilibrium at E_0. There real national product equals real planned expenditure and also the natural real output of $1,500 billion. The price level is 1.0.

Now suppose that something causes the aggregate demand curve to shift to the right from AD_1 to AD_2. For the moment, it does not matter what the cause is—it could be booming export demand, an upturn in consumer confidence, or a major tax cut. Whatever the cause, the increase in aggregate demand puts upward pressure on final output prices throughout the economy. Wages and other input prices do not adjust right away; thus, firms increase output in response to improved profit margins. With both real national product and the price level rising, the economy moves up and to the right along the short-run aggregate supply curve toward the short-run equilibrium point, E_1.

Now we shift our attention to part b of Exhibit 8.6, where a long-run aggregate supply curve has been added. This curve is vertical and located at the natural level of real output. The economy cannot remain at E_1 forever, because the short-run supply curve was based on an assumption of incomplete adjustment of input prices. Given time, though, input prices will gradually adjust to the change in final goods prices that has taken place. Contracts will expire and be renegotiated at higher levels. Raw materials inventories will be depleted and restocked at higher prices. Firms will learn that the changes in demand that boosted output prices in their local markets are affecting input prices throughout the economy. As input prices gradually rise, the economy will move away from E_1 toward the long-run equilibrium point, E_2, where the aggregate demand curve intersects the long-run aggregate supply curve.

Exhibit 8.6   The Economy's Reaction to an
Expansion of Aggregate Demand

The economy's response to a rightward shift of the aggregate demand curve from AD_1 to AD_2 depends on the time horizon. In part a of the exhibit, the economy is assumed to start from an equilibrium at E_1, where real output is at its natural rate. At first, the shift in the aggregate demand curve carries the economy up and to the right along the short-run aggregate supply curve. As this happens, real national product and the price level rise while unemployment falls below its natural rate. After a time, input prices adjust to the new situation and real output returns to its natural level at E_2, where AD_2 intersects the long-run aggregate supply curve. In the new equilibrium at E_2, unemployment returns to its natural rate and the price level has risen from 1.0 to 1.75.

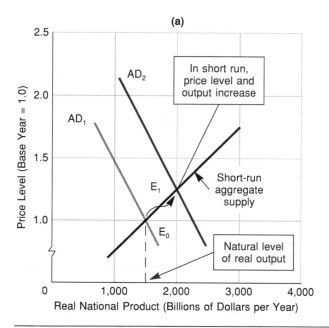

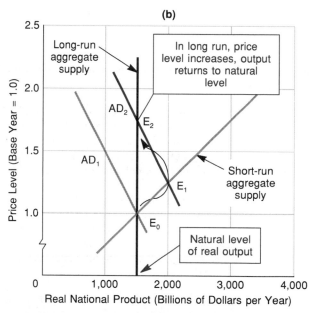

Looking Ahead

This chapter has dealt with three key variables of the macroeconomy: unemployment, the price level, and real output. It has established linkages among them in the form of Okun's law, which links changes in real output to changes in the unemployment rate, and of the aggregate supply and demand model, which links changes in real output to changes in the price level. Together these linkages give us a preliminary outline of the way the key variables behave over the course of the business cycle.

In this chapter, we saw that the expansion phase of the business cycle carries the economy to a peak of real national product above the natural level. We see now that this expansion will also create a drop in the unemployment rate and a rise in the price level. However, the economy cannot come to rest at that peak output. As firms, workers, and households adjust to these changes, real output will fall back toward its natural level.

In later chapters, we will see that a mirror image of these events takes place during a recession. The recession carries the economy to a trough of real national product below the natural level. As it does so, the unemployment rate rises. In some recessions, the price level falls. If inflation has gripped the economy strongly during the preceding expansion, the price level may not fall, but even then the inflation rate will slow down. Just as the economy cannot remain forever at the peak of the cycle, it cannot remain permanently at the trough. Eventually the economy will return to the natural level of real output and—if the historical cyclical pattern persists—pass beyond the natural level to a new peak.

A great many details must be added, some of which have been hinted at in this chapter. We need to better understand the roles of government tax and expenditure policy, money and interest rates, consumers' and firms' expectations, and the interaction of the national and international economies. The model outlined in this chapter provides a framework that we can use in exploring all of these issues.

Summary

1. **What is unemployment, and how is it measured?** People are counted as *employed* if they work at least 1 hour a week for pay or 15 hours a week as an unpaid worker in a family business. They are considered *unemployed* if they are not employed but are actively looking for work. The *civilian labor force* is the sum of the employed and the unemployed. The *civilian unemployment rate* is the percentage of the civilian labor force that is not employed. The *employment rate*, an alternative measure of the state of the labor market, is the percentage of the adult civilian population that is employed.

2. **What pattern does the business cycle follow?** For at least 200 years, the growth of the U.S. economy has proceeded in spurts, sometimes rising above the long-term trend and sometimes falling below it. A typical *business cycle* begins from a peak at which real output reaches a maximum. In the contraction phase, real output falls. A contraction lasting six months or more is called a *recession*. The low point of real output is called the "trough" of the cycle. Following the trough, a phase of expansion carries real output to a new peak.

3. **How are changes in real output linked to changes in unemployment?** The *natural rate of unemployment* is the rate that persists during a period of stability, when the economy is experiencing neither accelerating nor decelerating inflation. The natural rate of unemployment is associated with a corresponding *natural level of real output*. As real output rises above the natural level, the unemployment rate falls. According to *Okun's law*, a 3 percent increase in real output relative to the natural level will be associated, other things

being equal, with a one-percentage-point decrease in the unemployment rate.

4. **How can supply and demand curves for the macroeconomy be drawn?** Although aggregate supply and demand curves look much like the supply and demand curves for individual markets, the reasoning behind them differs. The *aggregate demand curve* has a negative slope because an increase in the price level tends to reduce real planned expenditures on consumption, investment, government purchases, and net exports. The slope of the *aggregate supply curve* depends on the assumption made regarding expected input prices. In the long run, input prices tend to move in proportion to the level of prices of the final goods and services that go into GNP; thus, in the long run, the aggregate supply curve is vertical at the natural level of real output. In the short run, input prices tend to lag behind changes in output prices; hence, in the short run, the aggregate supply curve has a positive slope.

5. **How are changes in real output linked over time to changes in the price level?** In the short run, the economy will respond to an increase in aggregate demand (a rightward shift in the aggregate demand curve) by moving up and to the right along a short-run aggregate supply curve. As this happens, real output and the price level will both rise and the unemployment rate will fall. As firms, workers, and households fully adjust to the changed circumstances, input prices will rise in proportion to the change in output prices. If there is no new disturbance, real output will return to its natural level and unemployment to its natural rate. In the new equilibrium, the price level will be higher than before the shift in aggregate demand.

Terms for Review

- employed
- unemployed
- civilian labor force
- civilian unemployment rate
- discouraged worker
- employment rate
- frictional unemployment
- structural unemployment
- natural rate of unemployment
- cyclical unemployment
- business cycle
- recession
- natural level of real output
- Okun's law
- aggregate demand curve
- aggregate supply curve

Questions for Review

1. Distinguish among frictional, structural, and cyclical unemployment. What is their relationship to the natural rate of unemployment?

2. Sketch a graph of a typical business cycle, listing its four phases. What is a recession? What was the Great Depression?

3. State Okun's law. Why is the ratio of changes in real output to changes in the unemployment rate approximately 3 to 1 rather than 1 to 1?

4. Contrast the "other-things-being-equal" assumptions lying behind market supply and demand curves with those that lie behind the aggregate supply and demand curves.

5. What happens to real output, unemployment, and the price level as the economy reacts to an increase in aggregate demand beginning from the natural level of real output? Distinguish between short-term and long-term effects.

Problems and Topics for Discussion

1. **Examining the lead-off case.** Civilian employment was 61,393,000 in December 1986. Using that figure plus those given in the article that opens this chapter, calculate the following:
   a. The size of the civilian labor force in December 1986.
   b. The number of employed and the number of unemployed.
   c. The approximate number of people in the armed services in January 1987.

2. **Your personal labor force status.** What is your current labor force status? Are you a member of the noninstitutional adult population? Of the labor force? Are you employed? Unemployed? Explain the basis for your answers. When was the last time your labor force status changed? Do you expect it to change soon? Give details.

3. **Voluntary versus involuntary unemployment.** It is sometimes suggested that the government should try to keep involuntary unemployment to a minimum but voluntary unemployment is not a problem. Do you agree? How would you distinguish between voluntary and involuntary unemployment?

4. **Employment hardship.** It has been suggested that the unemployment rate be replaced by an "employment hardship index" that tries to measure the percentage of people who suffer hardship because of their labor force status. What kinds of people who are not now counted as unemployed might fit into the hardship category? What kinds of people who are now counted as unemployed would not suffer hardship? Discuss.

5. **Current state of the labor market.** The Department of Labor announces unemployment data for each month early in the following month. Watch your local newspaper, *The Wall Street Journal*, or business magazines such as *Business Week* for discussions of the most recent unemployment data. What changes have there been? What is happening to the employment rate? Are the employment and unemployment rates moving in the same or opposite directions? Judging from unemployment trends and other data, in which phase of the business cycle does the economy appear to be at the moment?

6. **Shifts in the aggregate demand curve.** Which of the following events would cause a shift in the aggregate demand curve, and in which direction? Discuss each item.
   a. The GNP deflator rises by two percent.
   b. A recession in the Canadian economy reduces Canadian demand for goods made in the United States.
   c. The federal government raises real taxes by $100 billion.
   d. An optimistic forecast of expanding business opportunities in the coming year causes firms to increase the size and number of fixed-investment projects.

7. **The economy in recession.** Draw a pair of graphs similar to those in Exhibit 8.6. Shift the aggregate demand curve to the left instead of to the right. What will happen to real output, unemployment, and the price level in the short run? In the long run? (This and similar scenarios will be investigated in detail in later chapters.)

Discouraged workers return to school.

Case for Discussion

"No Matter Where I'd Go, I'd Be One of the First Laid Off"

After five jobs in seven years, 49-year-old Al Kaczor saw a pattern he didn't like. "I had seen my parents laid off and all the relatives laid off from factories," he says. "No matter where I'd go, I'd be one of the first laid off."

Instead, Kaczor is dropping out of the work force this fall to complete his bachelor's degree. He also will disappear from the unemployment statistics, becoming what economists call a discouraged worker, someone who wants a job but has given up looking. Economists estimate that if discouraged workers were included in unemployment figures, unemployment rates would be much higher than they are now.

For Kaczor, the decision came slowly. In April, he lost his $2,300-a-month job as a safety engineer at InteCom Inc. in a 200-worker cutback. During the next three months, he applied to 50 companies, certain that a job would come along.

"I'd been unemployed once before for eight months. Things came through then," he says. That was in 1981, when his contract as a maintenance engineer at a nuclear power plant expired. Eventually he got a lower-paying job as a technical writer. And jobs worked out before that. A high-school dropout, he found a career in the Air Force. When he left the Air Force 22 years later, in 1978, he worked at two minimum-wage jobs before landing the nuclear plant job.

This time, however, many nearby manufacturing concerns, like InteCom, fell victim to the current electronics slump, and Kaczor didn't get a single interview. "I could find work, I'm sure, although I may have to work at McDonald's," he says. But it hit home that a college degree might be the only way to a more secure job, or at least to help him start his own business.

Source: Karen Blumenthal, "Low Unemployment in Boston and Dallas Isn't a Job Guarantee," *The Wall Street Journal*, August 26, 1985, p. 1. Reprinted by permission of *The Wall Street Journal*, © Dow Jones & Company, Inc. 1985. All Rights Reserved. Photo Source: © 1987 Phyllis Woloshin.

Questions

1. Trace Kaczor's labor market status at the points in his career at which he is (a) in the Air Force; (b) working for InteCom; (c) applying to 50 jobs in 3 months after leaving InteCom; (d) working at a McDonald's (if he did so) while waiting for college to start in the fall; (e) in college, first semester; (f) in college, first year; (g) out of college, looking for a new job but not yet having found one; (h) working in his own business.

2. Discuss Kaczor's position at various times in terms of the concept "can't find a job."

3. Would you classify Kaczor's unemployment spells as frictional, structural, or cyclical? Are there elements of each type of unemployment at various points in the story? Explain.

Suggestions for Further Reading

Galbraith, John Kenneth. *The Great Crash.* Boston: Houghton Mifflin, 1961.

A particularly readable account of the Great Depression and the stock market crash that touched it off.

Kaufman, Bruce E. *The Economics of Labor Markets and Labor Relations.* Hinsdale, Ill.: Dryden Press, 1986.

Chapter 13 of this text deals with the measurement of unemployment and the distinctions among various types of unemployment.

Terkel, Studs. *Hard Times: An Oral History of the Great Depression.* New York: Pantheon Books, 1970.

Contains vivid, firsthand accounts of life during the Great Depression, when the unemployment rate soared to nearly 25 percent of the labor force.

A Basic Model of Macroeconomic Equilibrium

Part Three

9 Classical and Keynesian Theories of Income Determination

After reading this chapter, you will understand . . .

- Why the classical economists thought flexible prices would prevent lasting depressions.
- How planned investment and saving respond to changes in the interest rate.
- Why the theories of John Maynard Keynes were so favorably received by economists of the 1930s.
- Why Keynes thought that small changes in planned expenditures could cause large disturbances in the economy.
- The implications of Keynes's theories for economic policy.

Before reading this chapter, make sure you know the meaning of . . .

- Financial markets and financial intermediaries (Chapter 4)
- Equilibrium in the circular flow (Chapter 6)
- Aggregate supply and demand (Chapter 8)

We Weren't Talking Revolution; We Were Talking Jobs.

Ed Paulsen's family was from South Dakota. He finished high school in 1930, as the country was sliding toward the depths of the Great Depression. He went west to pick apples in Washington State and then worked on road gangs. In 1931, he ended up in San Francisco. These are his words:

I tried to get a job on the docks. I was a big husky athlete, but there just wasn't any work. Already by that time, if you were looking for a job at a Standard Oil service station, you had to have a college degree. It was that kind of market. . . .

Depression-era workers harvesting peanuts in Georgia

I'd get up at five in the morning and head for the waterfront. Outside the Spreckles Sugar Refinery, outside the gates, there would be a thousand men. You know dang well there's only three or four jobs. The guy would come out with two little Pinkerton cops: "I need two guys for the bull gang. Two guys to go into the hole." A thousand men would fight like a pack of Alaskan dogs to get through there. Only four of us would get through. I was too young a punk. . . .

These were fathers, eighty percent of them. They had held jobs and didn't want to kick society to pieces. They just wanted to go to work and they just couldn't understand. There was a mysterious thing. You watched the papers, you listened to rumors, you'd get word somebody's going to build a building.

So the next morning you get up at five o'clock and you dash over there. You got a big tip. There's three thousand men there, carpenters, cement men, guys who knew machinery and everything else. These fellas always had faith that the job was going to mature somehow. More and more men were after fewer and fewer jobs. . . .

We weren't greatly agitated in terms of society. Ours was a bewilderment, not an anger. Not a sense of being particularly put upon. We weren't talking revolution; we were talking jobs.

Source: Excerpts from Studs Terkel, *Hard Times: An Oral History of the Great Depression*, pp. 29–31. Copyright © 1970 Pantheon Books, a Division of Random House, Inc. Reprinted with permission. Photo Source: George W. Ackerman, 1929. Records of the Federal Extension Service.

THE Great Depression of the 1930s, when a thousand men would fight over a day's work as a common laborer, brought many changes to law, politics, and social consciousness. It also created a revolution in economic thought.

Before the Great Depression, economists had stressed the economy's ability to adapt to changing conditions and absorb shocks. Of course, they recognized that business cycles interrupted the nation's prosperity from time to time, but they saw such episodes as temporary and recovery from them as automatic. Then, following the spectacular stock market crash of 1929, the economy slid into a depression from which there seemed no hope of rebounding. Prices fell. Wages fell. Real output fell. Unemployment soared until nearly a quarter of the labor force was out of work. These conditions lasted not months but years. Although the economy hit rock bottom in 1933, it did not return to its 1929 level of real output for a full decade. What went wrong?

The most influential attempt to answer this question proved to be that of the British economist John Maynard Keynes. Keynes denied the adequacy—indeed, the very existence—of the economy's shock-absorbing mechanisms. He saw an expanded role for government in stabilizing the economy and preventing repetition of the 1930s disaster. Although not all details of Keynes's work have withstood the test of time, his general approach has left its mark to this day. A review of Keynes's theory and the context in which it emerged is therefore an essential part of the study of macroeconomics.

The Classical Self-Regulating Economy

A fundamental tenet of pre-Keynesian economics—"classical" economics, to use Keynes's term—was the notion that the economy would gravitate toward a natural level of real output.[1] The natural level was seen as determined by resources, technology, and willingness to work, that is, by the conditions that determine the economy's production possibility frontier. At the peak of the business cycle, the economy might temporarily move a bit beyond the frontier as the result of overtime work and negative cyclical unemployment. Conversely, during a slump it might fall below the natural level, but this too would be temporary. In this section, we look briefly at the mechanisms that, in the classical view, direct the economy toward the natural level of real output.

Price Flexibility

One of the mechanisms that drives the economy toward the natural level of real output is the flexibility of prices and wages. Exhibit 9.1 uses the aggregate supply and demand model to illustrate this.

Initially the economy is in equilibrium at point E_0. There the price level is 1.0, real output is at its natural level, and total planned expenditures, shown by

---

[1]The term "classical economics" has a confusing variety of meanings. Karl Marx used it to refer to his predecessors, Adam Smith and David Ricardo. Later the term was broadened to include Marx and his more orthodox contemporary, John Stuart Mill. The term is used in this sense to distinguish classical economics from the neoclassical tradition founded by Alfred Marshall.
Keynes used the term still more broadly to include Marshall and Marshall's successor at Cambridge, A. C. Pigou. Today the term "classical economics" is generally used in the Keynesian sense in macroeconomic contexts and in the pre-Marshallian sense in microeconomic contexts.

Exhibit 9.1 Recovery from Recession
in the Classical Model

This exhibit illustrates recovery from recession through the classical mechanism of flexible prices. Beginning from equilibrium at E_0, where real output is at its natural level, the aggregate demand curve shifts leftward from AD_1 to AD_2. As it does, prices, output, and employment all decline. The economy moves along the short-run aggregate supply curve, AS, to E_1. Soon, however, competition among unemployed workers and owners of other idle resources begins to push input prices down. As input prices fall, the economy moves back to the long-run aggregate supply curve, which is a vertical line at the natural level of real output. At the new equilibrium, E_2, real output returns to its natural level, unemployment reverts to its natural rate, and only the price level is permanently affected.

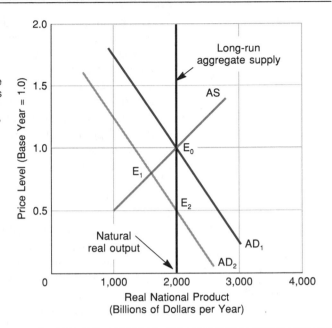

aggregate demand curve AD_1, are sufficient to absorb all of the national product. Now something happens to decrease the planned expenditure that will be undertaken at any given price level. The demand curve shifts leftward to AD_2. At a price level of 1.0, there is insufficient aggregate demand, and inventories accumulate. The classical economists would have referred to this inventory buildup as a "glut" of commodities.

The classical economists were prepared to admit that a glut might temporarily depress output as well as prices. In our modern aggregate supply and demand model, this would be shown as a movement along the short-run aggregate supply curve to E_1. But this situation will not last long. At E_1, some workers who are willing to work will not find jobs; they will compete with those who still have jobs, thus driving down wages. Owners of capital or natural resources temporarily idled by the glut will behave in a similar way. As factor prices drop in response to the drop in demand, prices of final goods will also fall. The economy will move down aggregate demand curve AD_2 to a new equilibrium at E_2. There real output will have returned to its natural level. All factor prices and final goods prices will have declined in proportion to the drop in aggregate demand. Real wages (that is, nominal wages adjusted for the drop in the price level) and real output will be the same as before the disturbance.

The classical economists outlined this mechanism most clearly for the case in which the shift in demand originated with a disturbance in the stock of money. In those days, "money" meant gold and silver. An increase in the stock of gold and silver was thought to cause a rightward shift in the aggregate demand curve and a decrease in gold and silver a leftward shift. In later chapters, we will see that it remains true today that a change in the money stock—now consisting of currency and checking account balances—will shift the aggregate demand curve. However, the classical mechanism of flexible prices would, in principle, work regardless of the source of the shift in demand.

The Classical Theory of Saving and Investment

The classical economists identified a second shock-absorbing mechanism: the tendency for flexible interest rates to adjust planned investment to the level of saving that takes place when the economy is producing at its natural level of national product. This mechanism can most easily be explained in terms of a simple economy with no government or foreign sector, such as the one illustrated in the circular flow diagram in Exhibit 6.2 (page 135).

In such an economy, total real planned expenditures will not add up to real national product unless firms plan to undertake an amount of investment equal to household saving. If firms plan too little investment, aggregate demand will fall short of aggregate supply. Since goods already produced cannot vanish into thin air, they will pile up as unplanned inventory investment. Firms will react by cutting output and prices, and real output will fall below its natural rate.

To keep the economy in equilibrium at the natural level of output, then, the classical economists needed a mechanism that would guarantee that planned investment would automatically absorb whatever portion of national income households decided to save. The mechanism they came up with depended on the interest rate as a link between saving and investment. We will begin by looking at the effect of the interest rate on planned investment, which plays a role not only in classical theory but in Keynesian and post-Keynesian theory as well.

The Opportunity Cost of Investment

Business firms constantly plan to make both fixed and inventory investments. In order to do so, they must somehow acquire the funds needed to finance the investments. Many firms are fortunate enough to have steady flows of profits, some of which can be used for investment before the rest is paid out to owners. Others obtain funds by borrowing, either directly from the public or through financial intermediaries. Still others bring in new partners or stockholders as a means of raising investment funds.

Whatever the source of a firm's investment funds, acquiring new fixed capital or inventories always involves an opportunity cost. The opportunity cost of investment is the interest rate that must be paid for funds that are obtained from outside the firm or that could be earned by investing the firm's own funds elsewhere. There is no free source of funds. A firm that spends its own profits on new office equipment could have earned interest on those funds by depositing them in a bank, buying government securities, or lending them to another firm. A firm that borrows in order to buy its capital goods must pay the interest rate charged by lenders. Finally, a firm that obtains investment funds by drawing in new partners or stockholders must offer those new owners a rate of return on the funds they bring in that is at least equal to what they could have obtained by putting their funds to work elsewhere.[2]

At any given time, dozens or hundreds of investment opportunities may present themselves to a firm. A regional sales office could be built in a distant city. Production equipment could be modernized. Larger supplies of raw materials could be kept on hand to guard against supply disruptions. Somehow the

---

[2]In the real world, the opportunity cost of investment may vary according to the source of funds. The job of the firm's financial managers is to choose carefully among the sources of funds so as to keep the firm's total cost of investment to a minimum. Because this is not a course on managerial finance, however, we will ignore such details; as far as we are concerned, the firm will face the same opportunity cost or interest rate regardless of its source of funds.

firm's managers must decide which projects to undertake and how far to carry each one. In doing so, they must balance the potential benefits, in terms of increased profits, against the opportunity cost of obtaining the investment funds.

Suppose, for example, that a firm decides to improve the insulation in the roof of its warehouse. A consultant estimates that 6 inches of insulation will reduce the firm's fuel costs by $2,000 per year and doubling the added insulation to 12 inches will save another $1,000 per year, bringing the total yearly savings to $3,000. Each six inches of insulation costs $10,000. How much insulation should be used—12 inches, 6 inches, or none?

The correct choice can be made by comparing the return on investment, stated as a percentage of the investment's cost to the opportunity cost of capital, that is, the rate of interest. In this case, the return on investment takes the form of a reduction in fuel costs. The first six inches of insulation brings a reduction of $2,000 per year, or 20 percent of its cost. Installing it thus will be worthwhile so long as the interest rate is less than 20 percent. The second six inches will reduce fuel costs by another $1,000 per year, or 10 percent of its cost. Adding it will be worthwhile only if the interest rate is less than 10 percent. Thus, we see that the firm will install 12 inches of insulation if the interest rate is below 10 percent, 6 inches if it is 10 percent or more but less than 20 percent, and none if it is 20 percent or more.

The Planned-Investment Schedule

As simple as it is, this example illustrates a basic principle: Other things being equal, the lower the opportunity cost of investment, the higher a firm's rate of planned investment. Generalizing from this principle, we can draw a **planned-investment schedule** for a firm and, by extension, for the economy as a whole. Such a schedule shows the amount of planned investment associated with each interest rate.

Part a of Exhibit 9.2 shows the planned-investment schedule for our hypothetical firm based on the example just given. At an interest rate of 20 percent or more, it will not be worthwhile to do any insulating. As soon as the interest rate drops below 20 percent, the first $10,000 of insulation becomes worthwhile. The second six inches of insulation begins to pay for itself when the interest rate falls below 10 percent. Given the 15 percent rate shown in the diagram, investment is cut off at $10,000.

Part b of Exhibit 9.2 shows an investment schedule for the economy as a whole. With tens of thousands of firms and millions of potential investment projects, the stairsteps of the single-firm, single-project investment schedule are smoothed out. As this schedule is drawn, a 15 percent interest rate is associated with $225 billion of real planned-investment spending for the economy as a whole.

Any change in the interest rate, other things being equal, will produce a movement along the planned-investment schedule. In part b of Exhibit 9.2, for example, a decrease in the interest rate to 10 percent will increase planned investment to $250 billion. Likewise, an increase in the interest rate to 20 percent will reduce total planned investment to $200 billion.

Of course, the interest rate is not the only factor that affects investment decisions. Anything else that affects the expected profitability of an investment— forecasts of product demand, expected changes in technology, trends in labor supply—will also cause the amount of investment to change. Increased opti-

Planned-investment schedule
A graph showing the relationship between the total quantity of real planned-investment expenditure and the interest rate.

Exhibit 9.2　Planned-Investment Schedules for a
Hypothetical Firm and the Economy as a Whole

Part a shows planned investment for a hypothetical firm; part b shows a planned-investment
schedule for the economy as a whole. In both cases, the amount of real planned investment
rises as the interest rate falls, other things being equal.

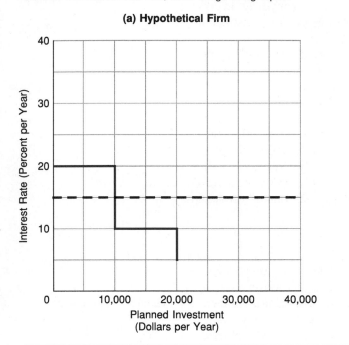

(a) Hypothetical Firm

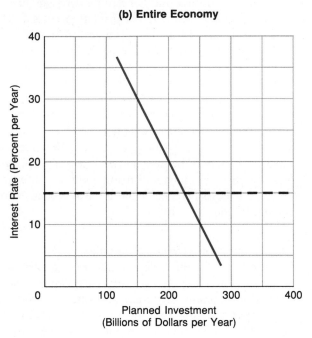

(b) Entire Economy

mism about profit opportunities will thus cause the planned-investment schedule to shift to the right, and increased pessimism will cause it to shift to the left.

Saving and the Interest Rate

The classical economists thought that saving would also be affected by the interest rate. Interest may be paid to a saver by a firm that borrows investment funds
directly from a household, for example, by selling bonds. It may instead be paid
by a financial intermediary like a bank that accepts savings or other deposits and
loans the proceeds to firms seeking investment funds. In either case, interest
payments represent the reward for saving. The greater the reward, thought the
classical economists, the greater the saving that would be forthcoming. This
implies a positively sloped **saving schedule.**

Saving-Investment Equilibrium

Exhibit 9.3 shows how the planned-investment (PI) and saving (SS) schedules
can be combined to establish an equilibrium in which real saving and real
planned investment are equal. Both schedules are drawn as they would appear
when real national product is at its natural level. In part a, the two intersect at an
equilibrium interest rate of 4 percent. At any lower interest rate—say, 2 percent—
the quantity of saving would fall short of planned investment. Investors, competing among one another for the available funds, would bid the interest rate up.

Saving schedule
A graph showing the
relationship between the
total quantity of real saving
and the interest rate.

Exhibit 9.3   The Classical Investment/Saving Stabilization Mechanism

In classical economic theory, the planned-investment schedule, PI, is negatively sloped because the interest rate is the opportunity cost of investment and the saving schedule, SS, is positively sloped because the interest rate is the reward for saving. Part a shows that in this case real saving and investment are equal at the natural level of real output given a 4 percent interest rate. If a change in business expectations shifts the planned-investment schedule leftward, as in part b, the interest rate will fall by enough to maintain the equality of saving and planned investment with real output remaining at the natural level. The decrease in saving as households move down and to the left along their saving schedule is equivalent to an increase in consumption in a simple economy in which the government and foreign sectors are omitted.

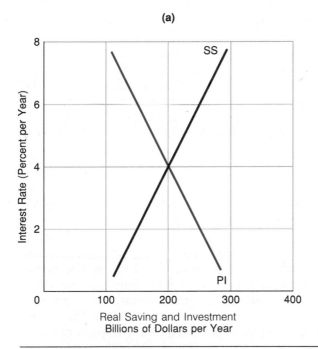

(a)

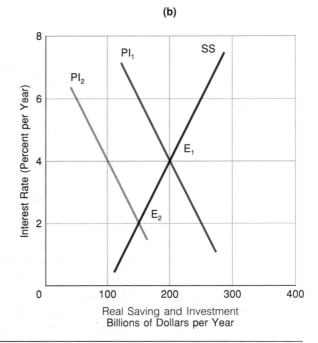

(b)

As the interest rate rose, the quantity of saving would increase and planned investment would decrease as both savers and investors moved along their respective schedules. When the interest rate reached 4 percent, saving and investment would again be equal.

If the interest rate were higher than 4 percent, savers would not find takers for all of their savings. Given the surplus of savings, investors would realize that they could pay a lower rate and still get all the funds they need. As the interest rate fell toward 4 percent, equilibrium would be restored under conditions consistent with production of the natural level of real output.

Response to a Shift in Investment

In the classical view, flexibility of the interest rate would keep aggregate demand equal to aggregate supply at the natural rate of real output despite changing market conditions. This is illustrated in part b of Exhibit 9.3. Initially real output is at its natural level, the interest rate is 4 percent, and saving and investment are equal at $200 billion. Then some change in conditions—say, the end of a railroad-building boom—causes firms to scale back their investment plans. The planned-investment schedule shifts from PI_1 to PI_2. If the interest rate stayed at 4 percent, planned investment would drop by $100 billion. Unless this investment is replaced by some other category of expenditure, inventories will accumulate, the circular flow will begin to contract, and national product will fall in both real and nominal terms.

Before this happens, according to the classical view, the interest rate will begin to fall. By the time it reaches 2 percent, firms will find some projects worthwhile that they previously passed over and planned investment will rise to $150 billion. (This increase in investment in response to the lower interest rate corresponds to a movement downward along PI_2.) At the same time, households, faced with a smaller reward for thrift, will cut back their saving by $50 billion. (The decrease in saving in response to the lower interest rate corresponds to a movement downward along SS.) Because saving is the part of income not consumed, this is the same as saying that households will increase real consumption by $50 billion. When the economy reaches E_2, where SS and PI_2 intersect, equilibrium will be restored. In the new equilibrium, investment will be $50 billion less than it was to begin with, but this will have been offset by the $50 billion increase in consumption. The level of real aggregate demand thus will remain sufficient to absorb all of the natural level of real output.

Say's Law

Say's law

The proposition that aggregate demand will automatically be sufficient to absorb all of the output that firms and workers are willing to produce with given technology and resources.

In short, the classical economists were convinced that there could not be a persistent deficiency of real aggregate demand that would depress real output below its natural level. The view that demand would always be sufficient to absorb all of the output that firms and workers were willing to produce with given technology and resources came to be known as **Say's law,** after the French economist Jean Baptiste Say. Say himself, an early follower of Adam Smith, did not elaborate the flexible-price and flexible-interest-rate mechanisms, but other nineteenth-century economists did. Economic heretics, including Karl Marx, challenged the prevailing doctrine from time to time. Marx was convinced that gluts and general depressions were not only possible but would grow so severe that they would bring down the capitalist system. By and large, however, the classicists' faith in the self-adjusting economy remained intact until the Great Depression of the 1930s.

Keynes's Challenge to the Classicists

The length and severity of the Great Depression cast doubt on the adequacy of the classical self-correcting mechanisms. However, such facts alone are not enough to cause abandonment of an established theory. A new theory is needed for that—one that offers a superior interpretation of the facts. Economists of the 1930s found the theory they were looking for in Keynes's 1936 work, *The General Theory of Employment, Interest, and Money* (see "Who Said It? Who Did It? 9.1"). In this section, we look first at Keynes's critique of classical theory and then at the theory that he himself advanced to replace it.

John Maynard Keynes

John Maynard Keynes was born into economics. His father, John Neville Keynes, was a lecturer in economics and logic at Cambridge University. John Maynard Keynes began his own studies at Cambridge in mathematics and philosophy. However, his abilities so impressed Alfred Marshall that the distinguished teacher urged him to concentrate on economics. In 1908, after Keynes had finished his studies and done a brief stint in the civil service, Marshall offered him a lectureship in economics at Cambridge, which Keynes accepted.

Keynes is best remembered for his 1936 work, *The General Theory of Employment, Interest, and Money,* in which he departed from classical and neoclassical theory. Although this was by no means his first major work, it was the foundation for Keynes's reputation as the outstanding economist of his generation. Its major features are a bold theory based on broad macroeconomic aggregates and a strong argument for activist and interventionist policies.

Photo Source: The Bettmann Archive/BBC Hulton.

Keynes was no "narrow" economist. He was an honored member not only of the British academic upper class but also of Britain's highest financial, political, diplomatic, administrative, and even artistic circles. He had close ties to the colorful "Bloomsbury set" of London's literary world. He was a friend of Virginia Woolf, E. M. Forster, and Lytton Strachey and, in 1925, married the ballerina Lydia Lopokovia. He was a dazzling success at whatever he turned his hand to, from mountain climbing to financial speculation. As a speculator, he made a huge fortune for himself; as bursar of Kings College, he built up an endowment of 30,000 to 380,000 pounds.

In *The General Theory,* Keynes wrote:

The ideas of economists and political philosophers, both when they are right and when they are wrong, are more powerful than is commonly understood. Indeed the world is ruled by little else. Practical men, who believe themselves to be quite exempt from any intellectual influences, are usually the slaves of some defunct economist. Madmen in authority, who hear voices in the air, are distilling their frenzy from some academic scribbler of a few years back. . . . There are not many who are influenced by new theories after they are twenty-five or thirty years of age, so that the ideas which civil servants and politicians and even agitators apply to current events are not likely to be the newest.

Was Keynes issuing a warning here? Whether or not he had any such thing in mind, his words are ironic because he himself has become one of the historical economists whose ideas remain influential even though they are not the most up to date.

Unresponsive Saving and Investment

Keynes had little faith in the ability of interest rate changes to bring saving and investment into equilibrium, as the classical theory maintained they would. In his view, neither the saving schedule nor the planned-investment schedule was sufficiently sensitive to the interest rate.

Keynes believed that the dominant influence on saving is the level of disposable income, with the interest rate playing only a minor role. "There are not many people," he wrote, "who will alter their way of living because the rate of interest has fallen from 5 to 4 percent."[3] Therefore, little can be expected from the saving side to bring saving and investment into line.

---

[3]John Maynard Keynes, *The General Theory of Employment, Interest, and Money* (New York: Harcourt, Brace, and World, 1936), 94.

On the investment side, Keynes acknowledged that, other things being equal, a drop in the interest rate would increase the quantity of planned investment. However, other things did not remain equal for long. Changes in expectations could shift the planned-investment schedule, and, in Keynes's view, expectations were quite volatile. Psychological and speculative impulses were more important than economic calculations in determining whether or not a business would undertake a particular project. As Keynes put it,

> It is characteristic of human nature that a large proportion of our positive activities depend on spontaneous optimism rather than on a mathematical expectation. . . . Most, probably, of our decisions . . . can only be taken as a result of animal spirits—of a spontaneous urge to action rather than inaction, and not as the outcome of a weighted average of quantitative benefits multiplied by quantitative probabilities.[4]

In graphical terms, then, the Keynesian version of the relationship of real saving and investment to the interest rate would look like Exhibit 9.4 rather than Exhibit 9.3. At one moment, the market rate of interest might be such as to bring saving and investment into equality at the natural level of real output. This situation corresponds to point E in Exhibit 9.4, where planned-investment schedule PI_1 intersects the saving schedule, SS. Then a pessimistic turn in the "animal spirits" of entrepreneurs carries the planned-investment schedule leftward to PI_2. The interest rate falls, but saving remains unaffected because the saving schedule is vertical. Further, even if the interest rate dropped to zero, planned investment and saving would not be brought into equality at the natural level of real output because the new planned-investment schedule would never intersect the saving schedule. As a result, aggregate demand would fall short of aggregate supply, inventories would accumulate, the circular flow would begin to contract, and output would fall below its natural level.

As if this were not enough, the power of interest rate changes to bring saving and planned investment into equality at the natural level was further limited, in Keynes's view. As we will discuss in Chapter 14, the interest rate has the function of equilibrating the supply and demand for money as well as the relationship between saving and investment. Keynes stressed the role interest rates play in the money market and thought that the interest rate established in the money market might be too high to bring saving and investment into equality at the natural level of real output. We will return to this element of Keynes's thought at a later point.

Critique of the Flexible-Price Mechanism

Having cast doubt on the effectiveness of the interest rate mechanism, Keynes turned his attention to the issue of price flexibility. Up to a point, Keynes concurred with the classicists regarding the effects of a decrease in aggregate demand. He agreed that a drop in aggregate demand would carry the economy down and to the left along a positively sloped aggregate supply curve, with prices, real output, and employment all falling.[5] However, Keynes sharply disa-

---

[4]Ibid., 161.

[5]For example, at the end of Chapter 20 of *The General Theory*, Keynes notes that "a deflation of effective demand below the level required for full employment [the natural level, in modern terminology] will diminish employment as well as prices" (page 291).

Exhibit 9.4   Keynes's Critique of the Investment/Saving Mechanism

Keynes thought saving to be unresponsive to changes in the interest rate, making the saving schedule, SS, vertical. He also believed that investment is somewhat unresponsive to changes in the interest rate, making the planned-investment schedule very steep. In this exhibit, planned investment and saving are equal at E for planned-investment curve PI_1. However, if the curve shifts leftward to PI_2, as it might during a depression, there will be no interest rate low enough to bring planned investment and saving back into line at the natural level of real output.

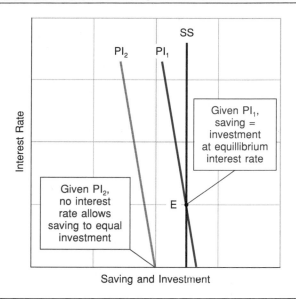

greed with the classical belief that a continued fall in the price level would bring real output back to its natural level. He used two arguments to make his point: rigid wages and the slope of the aggregate demand curve.

Rigid Wages

In Chapter 8, we saw that the short-run aggregate supply curve shows how firms would react to a change in aggregate demand if they expected that input prices would not change, at least for the time being. But we noted that input prices would eventually adjust to the changed conditions. At that point, the original short-run aggregate supply curve would no longer be valid and output would return to its natural level.

Keynes's first criticism of this mechanism was that wages—the most important class of input prices—are not very flexible in the downward direction. To be sure, workers sometimes accept cuts in their nominal wages, and many did so in the 1930s. However, these cuts met widespread resistance in the form of strikes and protests. The resistance was strong enough, Keynes thought, to indicate that as a working approximation, one would do better to assume that wages are completely rigid in a downward direction than to suppose that they are completely flexible. This being the case, the short-run aggregate supply curve would also be a long-run aggregate supply curve. When aggregate demand fell, the economy would move down along the aggregate supply curve to a point below the natural level of real output and stay there.

The Slope of the Aggregate Demand Curve

In making this argument, Keynes was not straying very far from the classical view. In the 1930s, some of the classicists themselves had pointed to wage rigidity as a factor prolonging the depression. They favored active government policies to promote wage cuts as a way of bringing real output back to the natural level.

But at this point, Keynes advanced his second argument: Even if both wages and prices fall flexibly, the aggregate quantity of goods demanded will be affected only slightly, if at all. If nominal wages fall, Keynes argued, the nominal spending power of the working population will fall by the same amount. Even if firms cut prices to match the fall in wages, workers will be able to buy no greater a quantity of goods, in real terms, than before. If firms temporarily step up their output in the hope of selling more at the lower prices, they will be disappointed. The extra goods they produce will pile up unsold in inventory, and they will have to retrench again. "There is, therefore," Keynes wrote, "no ground for the belief that a flexible wage policy is capable of maintaining a state of continuous full employment. . . . The economic system cannot be made self-adjusting along these lines."[6]

In terms of the model we have been using, this argument amounted to saying that the aggregate demand curve was vertical or nearly so. But what about the four factors listed in Chapter 8 that today are thought to give the aggregate demand curve a negative slope?

Two of them—the impact of prices on consumption via changes in the real value of nominal money balances and the impact of prices on the government budget—were not considered by Keynes. The third factor—the favorable impact of falling prices on net exports—was considered as possibly important for Britain but not for the United States. (At that time, the sum of imports and exports came to just 8 percent of U.S. GNP compared with 20 percent today.) The fourth factor—the impact of falling prices on investment via a reduction of interest rates—was admitted as a theoretical possibility. However, because Keynes thought that planned investment was not highly sensitive to interest rates and also that there were monetary limits on how low interest rates could fall, he believed that this effect would be too weak to do the job.

The Keynesian Version of Aggregate Supply and Demand

Although Keynes himself did not use the aggregate supply and demand model, this modern model can be used to contrast his views with the classicists'. This is done in Exhibit 9.5, where part a shows the world according to Keynes and part b represents the classical theory.

In both parts of the exhibit, the story begins at E_0, with real output at its natural level. Now a disturbance takes place—say, a reduction in planned investment that is not offset by an increase in consumption. This shifts the aggregate demand curve leftward to AD_2. In both the Keynesian and classical cases, real output, employment, and the price level decline and the economy moves along the short-run aggregate supply curve to E_1.

At this point, the two theories part ways. If Keynes's rigid wage argument is accepted, the economy simply comes to rest at E_1. Prices fall no further, and the economy remains parked in an underemployment equilibrium until something happens to revive aggregate demand.

For the sake of argument, however, Keynes was willing to consider the case in which wages and prices are perfectly flexible. In this case, the classical economy leaves the original short-run aggregate supply curve and moves to a new equilibrium at E_2, where the demand curve intersects the natural level of real output. As we have seen, the vertical line at the natural level of real output serves as the economy's long-run aggregate supply curve in the classical view. But in

---

[6]Keynes, *General Theory*, 167.

Exhibit 9.5   Adjustment to Falling Aggregate
Demand: Keynesian and Classical Views

This exhibit contrasts the Keynesian and classical views regarding the economy's adjustment to a leftward shift in the aggregate demand curve. In both cases, the leftward shift initially causes a movement down and to the left along the short-run aggregate supply curve from E_0 to E_1. In the classical case (part b), input prices then fall, moving the economy off the initial short-run aggregate supply curve back to the natural level of real output at E_2. Keynes argued that downward rigidity of nominal wages would force the economy to remain at E_1 rather than moving on down the aggregate demand curve. Keynes believed that even if nominal wages and other input prices did fall, the aggregate demand curve would be too steep to restore equilibrium at the natural level of real output. Thus, the economy could remain in a state of depressed output and high unemployment for a prolonged period.

(a) Keynesian Theory

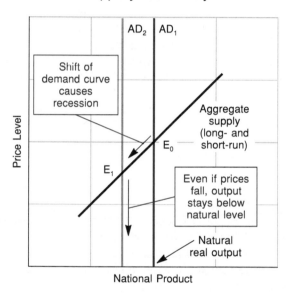

(b) Classical Theory

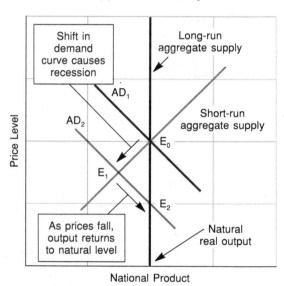

the Keynesian version, even if prices and wages move below the levels reached at E_1, the economy will not return to its natural level of real output because the aggregate demand curve is too steep. Prices and wages simply go into a free fall downward along AD_2 without ever intersecting the natural level of real output.

Given the abysmal performance of the U.S. and other economies at the time Keynes was writing, the Keynesian scenario seemed to fit the facts much more closely than did the sunny classical story of self-adjustment.

The Multiplier Effect

We now have a clear contrast between the classical view of the self-stabilizing economy and the Keynesian version of an economy at the mercy of investors' "animal spirits." In the classical view, a shift in the planned-investment schedule will not disturb aggregate demand for long because a flexible interest rate will quickly bring real saving and real planned investment back into line at the natural level of real output. Even if this defense fails and there is a drop in aggregate demand, flexible prices will return the economy to its natural level of real output. In the Keynesian view, interest rate flexibility will not prevent a drop in planned investment from affecting aggregate demand. Further, wage rigidity and the insensitivity of aggregate demand to changes in the price level will prevent a return to the natural level of real output.

But this is not the whole story. In *The General Theory*, Keynes argued that the economy's stability is even more threatened by shifts in planned investment (or in other components of aggregate demand) than we have yet seen. From what we have said so far, it might seem that a given drop in planned investment—say, $100 million—would shift the aggregate demand curve to the left by just that amount. But Keynes instead maintained that the shift would be a multiple of $100 million—$400 million, $500 million, or even more. This phenomenon is called the **multiplier effect.** Let's see how it comes about.

Multiplier effect
The tendency for a given shift in planned investment (or another component of aggregate demand) to cause a larger shift in total aggregate demand.

Marginal propensity to consume
The proportion of each added dollar of real disposable income that households devote to real consumption.

Marginal Propensity to Consume

The origin of the multiplier effect lies in the relationship between disposable income and consumption. Keynes argued that for each $1 change in real disposable income, households change their real consumption in the same direction by a fraction of a dollar. He called this fraction the **marginal propensity to consume.** For example, suppose that households tend to spend $.75 of every $1 of additional disposable income on consumer goods and save the rest. In this case, the marginal propensity to consume is .75. Given this marginal propensity to consume, a $100 million increase in disposable income for the economy as a whole will cause total consumption expenditure to rise by $75 million. Likewise, a $100 million drop in disposable income will cause consumption to fall by $75 million.

Tracing the Effects of a Drop in Planned Investment

Given a marginal propensity to consume of .75, let's trace the effects of a $100 million drop in planned investment. Specifically, we will assume that this decline takes the form of a slowdown in construction of new factories. This drop in planned investment reduces aggregate demand by $100 million. It is recorded as the "first-round" effect in Exhibit 9.6.

The $100 million reduction in factory construction means that many construction workers, subcontractors, and materials suppliers will face a loss of income of $100 million. According to the assumed marginal propensity to consume, they will then cut their consumption expenditures by $75 million. This $75 million is recorded in Exhibit 9.6 as the "second-round" effect of the slowdown in factory construction.

The repercussions of the slowdown do not end here. The $75 million drop in consumption expenditures by unemployed construction workers means that a lot of grocers, barbers, and so on will find their own real incomes reduced by $75 million. For each dollar of lost income, they too will cut consumption expenditures by $.75. The resulting $56,250,000 cutback in their real consumption is the "third-round" effect of the original cutback in factory construction.

Next, the grocers' and barbers' tailors and bartenders will feel the pinch; then the tailors' and bartenders' accountants and coal dealers will be hit; and so the process will continue round after round, as shown in Exhibit 9.6. Nevertheless, there is a limit to the *total* reduction in planned expenditures, because with each round the reduction gets smaller. If the series given in the exhibit is added up over an infinite number of rounds, the total comes to $400 million, in-

Exhibit 9.6   The Multiplier Effect

Keynes observed that households tend to devote a fraction of each dollar of added real disposable income to consumption and to reduce real consumption by the same amount when disposable income falls. The fraction, assumed to be .75 in this case, is called the *marginal propensity to consume.* This behavior tends to amplify the effect of any change in planned investment. Here real planned investment drops by $100 million in the first round. This causes a loss of $100 million in income for construction workers, who cut back their consumption expenditures by $75 million in the second round. In turn, the people who supplied them with consumer goods lose $75 million in income as a result and cut back their own consumption by $56,250,000. By the time the whole process has run an infinite number of rounds, total planned expenditure (planned investment plus consumption) will have fallen by four times the initial change in planned investment.

Round	Change in Income	Change in Expenditure	
1		$100,000,000	(Planned investment)
2	$100,000,000	75,000,000	(Consumption)
3	75,000,000	56,250,000	(Consumption)
4	56,250,000	42,187,500	(Consumption)
5	42,187,500	31,640,625	(Consumption)
.			
.			
.			
Infinite number of rounds		$400,000,000	(Total planned expenditure)

cluding $100 million of planned investment in the first round and a total of $300 million in consumption in all successive rounds. We can conclude that a $100 million drop in planned expenditures will decrease aggregate demand by $400 million rather than just $100 million.

The ratio of the total change in planned expenditure at the original level of prices to the initial change in planned investment expenditure is known as the **expenditure multiplier.** The size of the multiplier depends on the marginal propensity to consume. A larger marginal propensity to consume will make the cutback in consumption at each round larger and hence raise the multiplier; a smaller marginal propensity to consume will make the cutback at each round smaller and hence lower the multiplier. The value of the expenditure multiplier for any given marginal propensity to consume (mpc) can be calculated using the following formula:

$$\text{Expenditure multiplier} = \frac{1}{1 - \text{mpc}}$$

Thus, a marginal propensity to consume of .75 implies a multiplier of 4; an mpc of .9 a multiplier of 10; an mpc of .5 a multiplier of 2; and so on.

Expenditure multiplier
The ratio of the induced shift in aggregate demand to an initial shift in planned investment (or other expenditure).

Policy Implications of the Keynesian Theory

The multiplier effect, combined with other elements of the Keynesian theory, has strong implications for economic policy. The economy is seen as inherently unstable. A small change in real planned investment (or in other elements of real planned expenditure) will be amplified by the multiplier effect and thus cause a large shift in the aggregate demand curve. Further, when the aggregate demand curve shifts, no reliable automatic mechanism exists for bringing the economy back to its natural level of real output. Once a depression sets in, then, it can go on for years, as in the 1930s.

However, at the same time that the Keynesian theory suggests that the private economy is unstable, it also implies that the government has powerful policy tools with which to remedy the instability. The chief tool of Keynesian policy is the federal budget. Government purchases, like planned investment, are subject to the multiplier effect. Thus, if workers laid off from factory construction can be put to work building highways and dams for the government, not only they but their grocers, barbers, tailors, bartenders, and so on can be kept working. To a lesser extent, tax cuts can be used to boost disposable income and thus give a multiple boost to consumption expenditures. Policies regarding government purchases and net taxes—which, when taken together, are known as *fiscal policy*—are the subject of Chapter 11. Readers interested in a detailed graphical exposition of the Keynesian multiplier model may read Chapter 10 before proceeding to Chapter 11, but this is not strictly necessary.

Looking Ahead

Much of the remainder of the macroeconomics course consists of a closer examination of themes raised in this chapter. One major task will be to examine in greater detail the financial sector of the economy, particularly the role of money and monetary policy. Another will be to scrutinize the behavior of the economy under conditions of inflation. As we move through this material, we will find that some elements of the Keynesian view have withstood the test of time well and are widely accepted today. On the whole, however, modern economists are neither as pessimistic about the stability of the private economy as Keynes was nor as optimistic about the government's ability to remedy problems. As we will see, many elements of the classical vision have been rehabilitated and today's Keynesians state their views more cautiously than their predecessors did.

Summary

1. **Why did the classical economists think that flexible prices would prevent lasting depressions?** In the classical view, a leftward shift in the aggregate demand curve at first would carry the economy down and to the left along a short-run aggregate supply curve. As this happened, the price level, real output, and employment would fall. However, competition among unemployed workers and owners of other idle factors of production would soon depress input prices. As input prices fell, the economy would leave the original aggregate supply curve and move to a new equilibrium in which the aggregate demand curve intersects the natural level of real output. In effect, the long-run aggregate supply curve for the economy was thought to be vertical at the natural level of real output.

2. **How do planned investment and saving respond to changes in the interest rate?** The interest rate is the

opportunity cost of investment. In deciding whether to undertake an investment, a firm must balance the opportunity cost against the investment's expected returns. Other things being equal, the lower the interest rate, the greater the amount of real planned investment that will be undertaken. The classical economists thought that real saving would also be responsive to the interest rate. Because the interest rate is the reward for saving, they believed that a higher interest rate would call forth a larger volume of saving. Taking these two effects together, the classical economists thought that flexibility of the interest rate would maintain equality of saving and planned investment at the natural level of real output.

3. **Why were the theories of John Maynard Keynes so well received in the 1930s?** During the Great Depression, economists lost faith in the classical model of a self-stabilizing economy. Keynes's work offered an

explanation for the economy's failure to maintain equilibrium at the natural level of real output. He put the blame primarily on three factors: a lack of responsiveness of saving and investment to changes in interest rates; a rigidity of nominal wage rates against downward pressure; and a lack of responsiveness of aggregate demand to changes in the price level. Keynes's theory can be represented in terms of a positively sloped long-run aggregate supply curve and a vertical or nearly vertical aggregate demand curve.

4. **Why did Keynes think that small changes in planned expenditures could cause large disturbances to the economy?** Keynes thought that a given disturbance to one category of real planned expenditure—say, planned investment—would cause aggregate demand to change by a multiple of the initial disturbance. The cause of this *multiplier effect* was households' tendency to reduce real consumption by a fraction of each dollar of real disposable income (the *marginal propensity to consume*). Thus, a drop in planned investment would put people out of work; the unemployed workers would reduce their consumption, thus lowering the income of merchants from whom they formerly bought; the merchants and their suppliers would have to cut back on consumption in turn; and so on. The ratio of the change in aggregate demand to the initial change in planned expenditure is called the *expenditure multiplier*. Its value is given by the formula $1/(1 - mpc)$, where mpc is the marginal propensity to consume.

5. **What were the implications of Keynes's theories for economic policy?** Keynes's multiplier theory implied that the economy would contract sharply in response to a relatively small drop in planned investment. His critique of the classical theory implied that the contraction would not easily correct itself. However, the multiplier effect would also apply to changes in government purchases. By increasing government purchases to offset any drop in private planned investment, the government could keep the economy at full employment.

Terms for Review

- planned-investment schedule
- saving schedule
- Say's law
- multiplier effect
- marginal propensity to consume
- expenditure multiplier

Questions for Review

1. According to the classical theory, how do final goods prices, wages, real output, and employment respond

to a drop in aggregate demand in the short run? In the long run?

2. Explain why the interest rate represents the opportunity cost of investment even when a firm is able to finance an investment project from its own profits.

3. Use a planned-investment schedule and a saving schedule to show how a flexible interest rate was thought to keep saving equal to planned investment at the natural level of real output in the classical theory.

4. How did Keynes compare the relative importance of expectations and the interest rate as factors affecting the level of planned investment?

5. Why would workers' resistance to cuts in nominal wages prevent a return to the natural rate of real output following a drop in aggregate demand?

6. Why did Keynes think the aggregate demand curve would be vertical or nearly so?

Problems and Topics for Discussion

1. **Examining the lead-off case.** Why is a decline in real output during a recession or depression accompanied by an increase in the unemployment rate? Why, in Keynes's view, does unemployment sometimes persist for years rather than disappearing as workers compete with one another for available jobs?

2. **Aggregate supply and demand in expansion and contraction.** Compare the classical version of the economy's response to a drop in aggregate demand to the response to an increase in aggregate demand as outlined in Chapter 8. What are the similarities and differences?

3. **The classical investment/saving model.** Use a classical planned-investment schedule and saving schedule to show how the economy would respond to (a) an increase in planned investment caused by a general trend toward optimism in business expectations and (b) a decision by households to increase the proportion of any given income level that they would save at any given interest rate. For each case, show which schedule shifts and explain the responses of firms, households, and financial markets in both words and graphical form.

4. **An investment decision.** Your college football stadium is sold out for 10 games each year. Tickets cost $20 each. The school is thinking of adding a new section to the stands that would hold 1,000 more people. Its construction would cost $1 million. The school can borrow the money at an interest rate of 14 percent. Should it do so? If it keeps adding seats, at some point it will become impossible to fill them all for every game. At what point would it no longer be worthwhile to add more seats?

5. **Say's law.** Say's law is sometimes explained in terms such as the following: "Nobody will supply labor or any other factor of production unless they have a use in mind for the income they will earn by doing so. The use must be to either spend the income on consumption goods or make an investment. Therefore, the act of supplying factors of production guarantees that there will always be enough demand for all the goods supplied. There can never be a general glut of goods, because supply creates its own demand." Do you think this explanation is adequate? How does it compare with the classical investment/saving and flexible-price mechanisms?

6. **The classical model.** Suppose that the classical investment/saving mechanism works quickly and smoothly in the manner shown in Exhibit 9.3. Show that in this case a change in planned investment will not cause a recession even if the Keynesian assumptions about wage rigidity and the slope of the aggregate demand curve hold true.

7. **The multiplier effect.** Rework Exhibit 9.6 for the following cases:

   a. A $100 million reduction in planned investment assuming a marginal propensity to consume of .9

   b. A $100 million increase in government purchases devoted to highway construction

   For part b, tell a "story" to go with your table as is done in the text for the case of a drop in planned investment.

Highway construction fuels the economy.

Case for Discussion
President Struggles with Congress over Highway Bill

MARCH 28, 1987. President Ronald Reagan yesterday vetoed a popular $87.5 billion transportation bill that contained funds for highway construction in every state. Reagan called the bill a "budget buster" and "pork barrel politics." Reagan was especially critical of "demonstration projects" in the bill that demonstrated such things as construction of parking lots in the districts of key members of Congress.

In place of the bill Reagan vetoed, the administration offered an $82 billion alternative that cut most of the demonstration projects.

Democrats in Congress vowed that they would vote to overturn the veto. (A two-thirds majority of both houses of Congress is required to overturn a veto.) They claimed that the bill would create hundreds of thousands of jobs in the construction industry and elsewhere in the economy. The administration's alternative bill could not be passed by Congress in time for the short construction season in Northern states, supporters said.

Supporters of the vetoed measure pointed to the slowdown in economic growth in the fourth quarter of 1986. In that quarter, the economy was estimated to have grown by just 1.1 percent—almost a standstill. The slowdown was attributed in large part to a decline in business fixed investment. Without the highway spending, supporters claimed, the economy might slow further or even slide into a recession.

Photo Source: © 1987 Phyllis Woloshin.

Questions

1. Use aggregate supply and demand curves to show how a reduction in business fixed investment might cause a recession assuming that investment continued to drop in 1987.

2. Speaking from a Keynesian point of view, justify an increase in federal highway construction spending as an offset to declining private investment. Include the multiplier effect in your argument.

3. Speaking from a classical point of view, argue against passage of the highway bill. Explain why the drop in private investment observed in the fourth quarter of 1986 is likely to be only temporary and why any recession—if one occurs—will be short.

Suggestions for Further Reading

Breit, William, and Roger L. Ransom. *The Academic Scribblers,* rev. ed. Hinsdale, Ill.: Dryden Press, 1983.

The title of this book is taken from Keynes's remark that policymakers are the slaves to past economists. Chapter 7 covers Keynes, and Chapters 8 and 9 discuss two of his important followers in the United States.

Hansen, Alvin H. *A Guide to Keynes.* New York: McGraw-Hill, 1953.

This book by an early follower of Keynes is an aid to reading The General Theory.

Keynes, John M. *The General Theory of Employment, Interest, and Money.* New York: Harcourt, Brace, and World, 1936.

Much of this book is hard going even for professional economists, but other passages are quite accessible to the general reader.

10 The Income-Expenditure Model

After reading this chapter, you will understand . . .

- More about the relationship between consumption and disposable income.
- How consumption is affected by various kinds of taxes.
- How the equilibrium level of national income is determined in the income-expenditure model.
- How the income-expenditure model can be used to demonstrate the multiplier effect.
- How the income-expenditure model can be reconciled with the aggregate supply and demand model.

Before reading this chapter, make sure you know the meaning of . . .

- Net worth (Chapter 4)
- Net taxes and transfer payments (Chapter 6)
- Planned versus unplanned investment (Chapter 6)
- Marginal propensity to consume (Chapter 9)
- Multiplier effect (Chapter 9)

If I'm Even Tempted, I'll Walk Right Past

It is late 1982. The economy is near the low point of its most severe recession since World War II. Consumers are deeply pessimistic.

Jack Lenburg could easily afford the things he desperately wants: a car, an apartment, and furniture. The 35-year-old divorced job placement officer earns $24,000 a year and has only $500 of debt.

But he is postponing his spending plans. He worries about the high cost of credit and says he will wait until late next year, when he will have saved enough to pay cash for his purchases.

That means living at his mother's house for the third year in a row. It means scrimping on clothing and entertainment. And it means avoiding impulse purchases the way a reformed addict avoids drugs.

"If I see a store where I might be even tempted to buy something, I'll walk right past," Lenburg says. "If I can show some degree of self-sacrifice, I'll be a happier person."

Source: John Curley, "Penny Pinchers: Fearing Loss of Jobs, Many Consumers Cut Purchases, Save More," *The Wall Street Journal*, November 24, 1982, p. 1. Reprinted by permission of *The Wall Street Journal*, © Dow Jones & Co., Inc. 1982. All Rights Reserved. Photo Source: © 1987 Phyllis Woloshin.

Department stores feel the effects of consumer pessimism during a recession.

THE Jack Lenburgs of the world—consumers—have enormous power over the economy. They control some two-thirds of the spending flows that pour into national product. In this chapter, we will see that Keynes's model of the determination of the level of national income focuses on the factors that determine how much consumers spend and on those that may cause them to change their spending plans. We will see how consumer pessimism can make a bad recession worse and how a return to optimism—as occurred at the beginning of 1983—can fuel a recovery. Chapter 9 introduced some of the basic concepts of the Keynesian income-expenditure model, including the marginal propensity to consume and the multiplier effect. This chapter provides greater detail and presents a graphical version of the model.

In this chapter, we will make a number of simplifying assumptions. At first, we will assume that the price level in the economy is fixed. This is not a true Keynesian assumption—in fact, prices fluctuated dramatically during the period in which Keynes was writing. Keynes recognized this fact and discussed it in his *General Theory*. However, Keynes's followers commonly make the initial presentation of his income-expenditure model in a fixed-price context in order to simplify the analysis.

In addition, we will make three assumptions that eliminate certain differences between the circular flow models of Chapter 6 and the official national income accounts of Chapter 7. First, we will drop the distinction between gross and net national product by assuming the capital consumption allowance to be zero. Second, we will eliminate the difference between net national income, as measured by the income approach, and national product, as measured by the expenditure approach, by assuming that indirect business taxes and the statistical discrepancy are zero. Finally, we will assume undistributed corporate profits to be zero so that disposable personal income equals national income minus net taxes. These assumptions can be expressed in equation form as follows:

$$\frac{\text{Disposable}}{\text{income}} + \frac{\text{Net}}{\text{taxes}} = \frac{\text{National}}{\text{income}} = \frac{\text{National}}{\text{product}}$$

The Consumption Schedule

Consumption schedule (consumption function)
A graph that shows how real consumption expenditure varies as real disposable income changes, other things being equal.

Autonomous consumption
The part of total consumption expenditure that is independent of the level of disposable income; for any given consumption schedule, autonomous consumption equals the level of real consumption associated with zero real disposable income.

Autonomous
In the context of the Keynesian income-expenditure model, refers to an expenditure that is independent of the level of real national income.

As we saw in Chapter 9, Keynes regarded the division of real disposable income between consumption and saving as a key to regulating the circular flow. Starting from the observation that consumers consistently spend part—but not all—of each additional dollar of income, he proposed a relationship between real disposable income and real consumption expenditure that resembled the one shown in Exhibit 10.1. This relationship is known as the **consumption schedule** or **consumption function.**

Autonomous Consumption

The consumption schedule shown in part b of Exhibit 10.1 does not pass through the origin; rather, it intersects the vertical axis somewhere above zero. This indicates that a certain part of consumption expenditure is not associated with any particular level of real disposable income. The component of real consumption equal to the vertical intercept of the consumption schedule is called **autonomous consumption.** In the context of the Keynesian model, the term **autonomous** applies to any expenditure category that does not depend on the income level.

The $100 billion level of autonomous consumption suggests that total consumption expenditure is $100 billion even if total disposable income is zero. In practice, of course, disposable income never falls to zero for the economy as a

Exhibit 10.1 The Consumption Schedule

Parts a and b both present a simple example of the connection between real disposable income and real consumption. The level of autonomous consumption is shown in part b by the height of the intersection of the consumption schedule with the vertical axis. The slope of the consumption schedule equals the marginal propensity to consume.

(a)

Disposable Income (1)	Consumption Expenditure (2)	Change in Income (3)	Change in Consumption (4)	Marginal Propensity to Consume (5)	Average Propensity to Consume (6)
$ 0	$ 100				—
100	175	$100	$75	0.75	1.75
200	250	100	75	0.75	1.25
300	325	100	75	0.75	1.08
400	400	100	75	0.75	1.00
500	475	100	75	0.75	0.95
600	550	100	75	0.75	0.91
700	625	100	75	0.75	0.89
800	700	100	75	0.75	0.88
900	775	100	75	0.75	0.86
1,000	850	100	75	0.75	0.85
1,100	925	100	75	0.75	0.84
1,200	1,000	100	75	0.75	0.83

Note: All amounts are in billions of dollars per year.

(b)

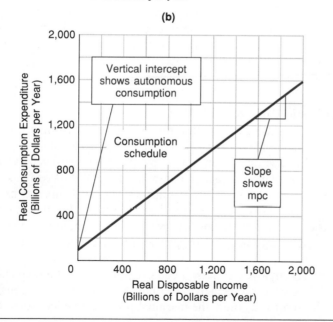

whole. Individual households, however, sometimes have zero income, and when they do, they do not cut consumption to zero. Instead, they draw on past savings or borrow against future income to maintain some minimal consumption level. In this sense, the concept of autonomous consumption is rooted in actual consumer behavior.

Marginal Propensity to Consume

Columns 1 through 4 in part a of Exhibit 10.1 show that whenever disposable income rises, some of the additional income is spent on consumption above and beyond autonomous consumption. As we saw in Chapter 9, the fraction of each added dollar of real disposable income that goes to added consumption is called the *marginal propensity to consume (mpc)*. For example, a $100 billion increase in disposable income—from $500 billion to $600 billion—raises consumption by $75 billion—from $475 billion to $550 billion. Likewise, a $100 billion decrease in disposable income—from $500 billion to $400 billion—causes consumption to fall by $75 billion—from $475 billion to $400 billion. Thus, the value of the marginal propensity to consume in this example is .75 ($75 ÷ $100).

In geometric terms, the marginal propensity to consume equals the slope of the consumption schedule. In part b of Exhibit 10.1, a horizontal movement of $100 billion in disposable income corresponds to a vertical movement of $75 billion in planned consumption. The slope of the consumption schedule, then, is $75 ÷ $100 = .75, the same as the marginal propensity to consume.

Marginal versus Average Propensity to Consume

Average propensity to consume

Total consumption for any income level divided by total disposable income.

It is helpful to contrast the marginal propensity to consume with the average propensity to consume. The **average propensity to consume** for any real income level equals total real consumption divided by real disposable income. It is shown in column 6 of Exhibit 10.1. For income levels below $400 billion, consumption exceeds disposable income such that the average propensity to consume is greater than 1. As disposable income increases, the average propensity to consume falls. However, because total consumption always includes a constant level of autonomous consumption—at least in the short run—the average propensity to consume is always greater than the marginal propensity to consume.[1]

Short Run versus Long Run

In practice, the actual values of both the average and marginal propensities to consume depend on the time horizon. In the United States, consumption spending has tended to rise over long periods by about $.90 for every $1 increase in disposable income, which implies a long-run marginal propensity to consume of about .9. (Since 1970, however, the implied long-run marginal propensity to consume has been higher than the historical average.) Also, the long-run level of autonomous consumption, as implied by historical data, approaches zero. As a result, the average and marginal propensities to consume are equal in the long run.

In the short run (a year or less), people tend to change their consumption by less than $.90 for every $1 change in income. Also, autonomous consumption is positive in the short run; thus, the marginal propensity to consume is less than the average propensity to consume.

---

[1]The relationship between average and marginal propensity to consume can also be expressed in algebraic terms. Let C represent consumption, Y disposable income, a autonomous consumption, and b marginal propensity to consume. The consumption schedule can then be written as $C = a + bY$ and the average propensity to consume as $C/Y = (a + bY)/Y = a/Y + b$. The latter expression clearly shows that the average propensity to consume exceeds the marginal propensity to consume as long as autonomous consumption is greater than zero.

Exhibit 10.2   Consumption Schedules for Various
Marginal Propensities to Consume

The slope of the consumption schedule equals the marginal
propensity to consume. Here consumption schedules are
shown for marginal propensities to consume of .9, .66, and
.5. Autonomous consumption of $100 billion is assumed for
all the curves.

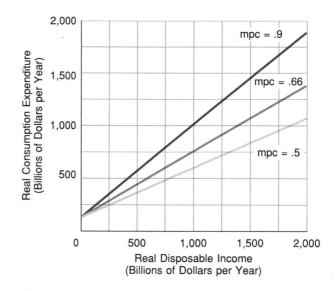

One reason for this is that year-to-year changes in disposable income are not
always permanent. People tend to make smaller changes in their spending in
response to temporary changes in income than they do in response to permanent
ones. For example, a household that is used to a $20,000 annual income would
no doubt cut back somewhat on its spending in a year when its income temporarily dropped to $18,000. However, as long as it expected good times to return, it
would probably reduce its spending by less than it would if it expected the lower
income level to be permanent. Therefore, as long as the drop in income was seen
as temporary, it would be offset to some degree by dipping into past savings or
borrowing.

Even permanent changes in income are not always perceived as permanent
in the short run. Thus, a household that experiences a permanent income increase of $2,000 per year might at first tend to treat part of the added income as
temporary and spend less of it than it otherwise would. Over a longer period, as
it becomes clear that the increase in income is permanent, more of the increase
will likely be consumed.

Because this book focuses mainly on short-run economic stabilization policy, the examples in this chapter use a marginal propensity to consume of .75,
somewhat lower than the observed long-run mpc for the United States. However, there is nothing sacred about the value .75; under different short-run
conditions, a higher or lower value might be appropriate. Exhibit 10.2, for
example, shows what the consumption schedule looks like for marginal propensities to consume of .9, .66, and .5. A $100 billion level of autonomous con-
sumption is assumed for each schedule; thus, they differ only in their slopes.
The higher the marginal propensity to consume, the steeper the consumption
schedule.

Shifts in the Consumption Schedule

The consumption schedules that we have drawn so far show the link between real disposable income and real consumption spending. A movement along the consumption schedule shows how real consumption spending changes along with real disposable income, other things being equal. In this section, we will see what is covered by the other-things-being-equal clause in this case. This will generate a list of factors that can shift the consumption schedule.

Wealth

One factor that is assumed to remain constant as we move along the consumption schedule is real wealth. *Wealth* is another term for a household's net worth—its assets minus its liabilities. Of two households with equal income, we expect the one with greater wealth to spend more freely than the one with less wealth. Thus, anything that happens to increase the total real wealth of all households will cause an upward shift in the consumption schedule. This effect shows up as a change in autonomous consumption; the marginal propensity to consume and, hence, the slope of the consumption schedule remain unchanged.

For example, many people hold some of their wealth in the form of corporate stocks. A rise in the average price of all corporate stocks thus could produce an upward shift in the consumption schedule. Similarly, a drop in total wealth could cause consumption to fall. Some people think that the stock market crash of 1929 caused a downward shift in the consumption schedule that helped trigger the Great Depression (see "Perspective 10.1").

Although the price level is being held constant for the moment, it is worth mentioning that a change in it can affect real wealth via a change in the real purchasing power of nominal money balances. A rise in the price level means that a $20 bill or $100 in a checking account will buy less than before; a fall in the price level means that it will buy more. Thus, a rise in the price level tends to cut real autonomous consumption and shift the consumption schedule downward, and a fall produces an upward shift. In Chapter 8, this effect was listed among the factors that give the aggregate demand curve a negative slope.

Expectations

People's spending decisions depend not only on their current real income and wealth but on their expected future real income and wealth. Any change in their expectations can cause a shift in the consumption schedule. This chapter opened with an example of a person who was holding down his level of spending because he was pessimistic about the state of the economy. When all consumers become pessimistic—as they tend to do during a recession—the consumption schedule can shift downward; when they become more optimistic, it can shift upward again.

Net Taxes

Up to this point, we have graphed the consumption schedule using real disposable income on the horizontal axis. For many purposes, however, it is more useful to substitute real national income. In a world with no taxes or transfer

PERSPECTIVE 10.1

The Stock Market and the Economy

The prosperity of the "Roaring Twenties" was marked by a soaring stock market. Then, on October 28, 1929, the market crashed. The widely watched Dow Jones average of industrial stock prices fell 38 points to close at 261, a 12.8 percent drop, and dove another 31 points the next day. These two days of panic came to be known as the Great Crash. Wall Street saw nothing like them again until the Dow fell 508 points, or 22.6 percent, on October 19, 1987.

The Great Crash of 1929 came to be viewed as the start of the decade-long Great Depression. But was it merely a symbol, or actually a factor helping to cause the downturn? This question, much debated over the years, took on a new relevance in light of the market turmoil of 1987.

Evidence that the 1929 crash was merely symbolic is found in the fact that the peak of the 1920s expansion had been reached in August 1929. From then to October, production fell at an annual rate of 20 percent and personal income at an annual rate of 5 percent. This suggests that the crash only reflected a decline that had already begun. In contrast, the economic news in the July to September quarter of 1987 was dominated by an increased rate of GNP growth and the lowest unemployment rate of the 1980s.

But there are two plausible arguments to the effect that the stock market crash of 1929 helped cause, or at least deepened, the Great Depression. Many economists believe that they apply to the 1980s as well.

One argument notes that a drop in stock prices is a reduction in personal wealth. Since wealth can affect consumption independently of changes in income, a drop in stock prices will tend to shift the consumption function downward. A rule of thumb used by some forecasters in the 1980s links each $1 drop in stock market wealth to a $.05 drop in consumption. That would mean a $50 billion loss of consumption for the trillion-dollar loss of wealth in the bear market of August to October 1987. The numbers in 1929 were smaller, but of comparable significance to the much smaller economy of that time.

A second argument emphasizes the psychological impact of falling stock prices. One needs to consider not only the confidence of consumers but also of business managers who make investment decisions. Both the consumption function and the planned-investment curve are sensitive to changes in expectations. Therefore, a big drop in stock prices can shift these curves via an expectations effect as well as via a wealth effect.

Changes in expectations are easier to capture in words than in numbers. The significance of the 1929 crash to contemporaries was expressed by Fred Allen in his book, *Only Yesterday*: "There was hardly a man or woman in the country whose attitude toward life had not been affected by it [the bull market of the 1920s] in some degree and was not now affected by the sudden and brutal shattering of hope."

When Allen wrote these words in 1931, no one yet knew how long or severe the Great Depression would be. Similarly, in the days following the crash of October 1987, observers could only speculate as to long-term effects. Many foresaw that fundamental changes since 1929, especially a far stronger banking system, would "decouple" the stock market from the economy at large. Others immediately began to issue downward revisions of their GNP forecasts. Now as then, it will take time to show who was right.

Sources: Milton Friedman and Anna J. Schwartz, *A Monetary History of the United States* (Princeton, N.J.: Princeton University Press, 1963), Chapter 7; Peter Temin, *Did Monetary Forces Cause the Great Depression?* (New York: Norton, 1976), Chapter 3. The quote from Allen is as cited in Temin.

payments, making such a change would not affect the consumption schedule at all, because without taxes national income and disposable income would be equal. Once we introduce taxes, however, the level of disposable income on which consumption decisions depend will differ from that of national income. As a result, changes in taxes become another source of shifts in the consumption schedule.[2]

---

[2]We continue to assume that there are no indirect business taxes. Only corporate profits taxes, payroll taxes, and personal taxes, such as personal income taxes and personal property taxes, are taken into account. Thus, it continues to be true that national income minus net taxes equals disposable income.

Autonomous Net Taxes

Autonomous net taxes
Taxes or transfer payments that do not vary with the level of national income.

Taxes and transfer payments that do not vary with national income are called **autonomous net taxes.** Personal property taxes are a major example on the revenue side of the net tax picture. On the transfer side, items ranging from interest on the national debt to government pensions are not directly linked to income changes.

Exhibit 10.3 shows how the consumption schedule is affected by introducing autonomous net taxes of $100 billion into an economy that had no taxes before. The first two columns of part a, which are the same as those in Exhibit 10.1, show national income and the resulting level of consumption that would take place if there were no taxes. The consumption schedule assumes autonomous consumption of $100 million and a marginal propensity to consume of .75. Columns 3 and 4 show that the $100 billion autonomous net tax reduces disposable income to a level $100 billion below that of national income. As column 5 shows, this $100 billion reduction cuts $75 billion from consumption at each income level in accordance with the .75 marginal propensity to consume. The remaining $25 billion of the tax is accounted for by a reduction in saving. As before, consumption is at the autonomous level of $100 billion when disposable income is zero. However, zero disposable income now corresponds to $100 billion of national income, as line 2 of the table shows. At a national income of zero, consumption is $25 billion.

Part b of Exhibit 10.3 shows the effect of the autonomous net tax in graphical terms. Introducing the tax produces a downward shift in the consumption schedule as drawn here with real national income on the horizontal axis. The new schedule is parallel to the old one but is shifted downward by an amount equal to the marginal propensity to consume times the level of autonomous net taxes—in this case, $75 billion. The vertical intercept of the new schedule equals autonomous consumption minus the marginal propensity to consume times the level of autonomous net taxes, or $25 billion in this case.

Income Taxes

Marginal tax rate
The percentage of each added dollar of disposable income that must be paid in taxes.

Autonomous taxes are an important source of revenue for state and local governments and autonomous transfers an important item on the expenditure side of the federal budget. The largest sources of federal revenue, however, are the social security payroll tax and the personal income tax. These income-linked taxes have a somewhat different effect on the consumption schedule, as Exhibit 10.4 shows.

Part a of Exhibit 10.4 assumes a 20 percent **marginal tax rate** on income from all sources and autonomous net taxes of zero. As columns 3 and 4 show, this means that the tax takes $.20 of each added dollar of national income. Disposable income thus increases by $.80 for each added dollar of national income. As columns 4 and 5 show, the marginal propensity to consume of .75 applies to this $.80 of added personal income. All told, then, of each added dollar of real national income, $.20 goes for taxes and $.60 of the remaining $.80 for consumption.

Part b of Exhibit 10.4 shows the effect of introducing the income tax in graphical terms. Instead of a downward shift that leaves the new schedule parallel to the old one, the income tax reduces the slope of the consumption schedule. With no income tax in effect, the slope of the schedule equals the marginal propensity to consume (in this case, .75). With a 20 percent proportional income

Exhibit 10.3   National Income and
Consumption with Autonomous Net Taxes

Autonomous net taxes do not change when the level of real national income changes. This exhibit shows how introducing an autonomous net tax of $100 billion shifts the consumption schedule downward when the schedule is drawn with national income on the horizontal axis. The amount of the shift is equal to the level of autonomous net taxes times the marginal propensity to consume.

(a)

National Income (1)	Consumption with No Tax (2)	Autonomous Net Tax (3)	Disposable Income (4)	Consumption with Tax (5)
$ 0	$ 100	$100	$−100	$ 25
100	175	100	0	100
200	250	100	100	175
300	325	100	200	250
400	400	100	300	325
500	475	100	400	400
600	550	100	500	475
700	625	100	600	550
800	700	100	700	625
900	775	100	800	700
1,000	850	100	900	775
1,100	925	100	1,000	850
1,200	1,000	100	1,100	925

Note: All amounts are in billions of dollars per year.

(b)

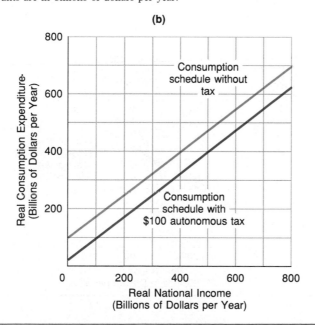

tax in effect, the slope is reduced to .6. The formula for the slope of the consumption schedule with an income tax in effect is:

$$\text{Slope of consumption schedule} = \text{mpc}(1 - t),$$

where t stands for the marginal tax rate.

Exhibit 10.4   The Consumption Schedule with an Income Tax Added

When the consumption schedule is drawn with national income on the horizontal axis, introducing an income tax reduces its slope. This example assumes a marginal propensity to consume of .75 and a marginal tax rate of .20. The slope of the consumption schedule with the income tax in effect equals $mpc(1 - t)$, where t is the marginal tax rate.

(a)

National Income (1)	Consumption with No Tax (2)	20% Income Tax (3)	Disposable Income (4)	Consumption with Tax (5)
$ 0	$ 100	$ 0	$ 0	$100
100	175	20	80	160
200	250	40	160	220
300	325	60	240	280
400	400	80	320	340
500	475	100	400	400
600	550	120	480	460
700	625	140	560	520
800	700	160	640	580
900	775	180	720	640
1,000	850	200	800	700
1,100	925	220	880	760
1,200	1,000	240	960	820

Note: All amounts are in billions of dollars per year.

(b)

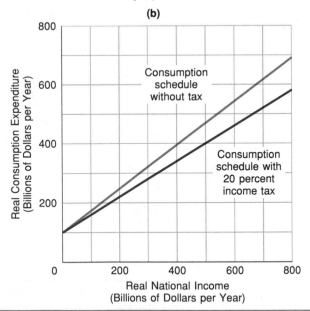

Graphing the Income-Expenditure Model

In Chapter 6, we saw that the circular flow can be in equilibrium only when planned expenditure (aggregate demand) equals national product (aggregate supply). If planned expenditure exceeded national product, buyers' attempts to purchase more than was being produced would lead to unplanned decreases in business inventories. Firms would react to those decreases by increasing their output, thereby causing the level of the circular flow to rise. Except in the present case, where the price level is held constant by assumption, the expansion of the circular flow would also tend to be accompanied by a rise in the price level. Similarly, if planned expenditure fell short of national product, business inventories would build up more rapidly than planned. Firms would react by cutting their output and—except in the present special case—lowering prices.

These principles are central to Keynes's theory of equilibrium national income. In this section, we will use them to develop a graphical model of that theory. Because Keynes saw planned expenditure as a function of income rather than of prices, the model presented here is called the **income-expenditure model.**

Income-expenditure model
The Keynesian model in which the equilibrium level of real national income is determined by treating real planned expenditure and real national product as functions of the level of real national income.

The Planned-Expenditure Schedule

The first step is to construct a **planned-expenditure schedule** for the economy. This is a graph that shows the total real planned purchases of goods and services corresponding to each level of real national income. Note that this curve differs from the aggregate demand curve introduced in Chapter 8 in that it relates the level of real planned expenditure to the level of real national income rather than to the price level. In constructing the planned-expenditure schedule, we will deal with each component of expenditure in turn.

Planned-expenditure schedule
A graph showing the level of total real planned expenditure associated with each level of real national income.

Consumption

We have already discussed the relationship between consumption and national income. The consumption schedule forms the foundation of the planned-expenditure schedule. The vertical intercept of the consumption schedule equals the level of autonomous consumption adjusted, if necessary, for autonomous net taxes. Its slope equals the marginal propensity to consume adjusted, if need be, for the marginal income tax rate. In this initial effort to construct a planned-expenditure schedule, we will assume that there is no income tax and autonomous net taxes are fixed by law at $100 billion as in Exhibit 10.3.

Investment

The second component of planned expenditure is planned investment. As explained in Chapter 6, this includes fixed investment plus planned changes in inventories; unplanned inventory changes are not counted.

As we saw in Chapter 9, the level of real planned investment depends on interest rates and business expectations. In the simple version of the income-expenditure model developed here, neither the interest rate nor expectations will be assumed to vary systematically with the income level. This means that we can treat investment as a type of autonomous expenditure along with autonomous consumption.

Once we know the level of planned investment for a given year, we can add it to planned consumption spending as a second component of planned expenditure, as shown in Exhibit 10.5. The C + I schedule in part b of the exhibit is the sum of the consumption and planned investment shown in columns 2 and 3 of part a.

Exhibit 10.5   The C, I, and G Components
of the Planned-Expenditure Schedule

This exhibit shows the consumption, planned investment, and government purchases
components of the planned expenditure schedule. In the simple case represented here,
consumption is the only element that varies directly with real national income. The slope of
the C + I + G schedule thus equals the marginal propensity to consume of .75.

(a)

National Income (1)	Consumption Expenditure (2)	Planned Investment (3)	Government Purchases (4)	C + I + G (5)
$ 0	$ 25	$125	$150	$ 300
100	100	125	150	375
200	175	125	150	450
300	250	125	150	525
400	325	125	150	600
500	400	125	150	675
600	475	125	150	750
700	550	125	150	825
800	625	125	150	900
900	700	125	150	975
1,000	775	125	150	1,050
1,100	850	125	150	1,125
1,200	925	125	150	1,200
1,300	1,000	125	150	1,275
1,400	1,075	125	150	1,350
1,500	1,150	125	150	1,425
1,600	1,225	125	150	1,500

Note: All amounts are in billions of dollars per year.

(b)

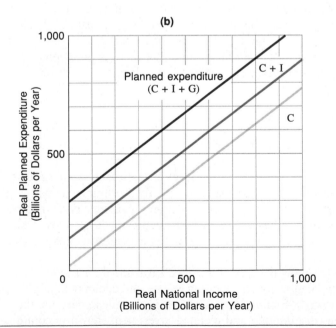

Government Purchases

The third component of planned expenditure is government purchases. Under the federal government's current budget procedures, the President proposes a level of expenditures for each year as part of the administration's budget message. Congress takes the proposed budget into account, together with the views of its own members, in setting a spending limit for the coming year. The congressional budget resolution is supposed to serve as a ceiling on expenditures for the year, including both government purchases and transfer payments. Similar budget procedures are used at the state and local levels. Chapter 11 details federal budget procedures.

In practice, political and economic conditions often disrupt these budget procedures, necessitating adjustments during the course of the year. For our purposes in this chapter, however, we will proceed as if government purchases for each year are fixed by law in real terms. This will allow us to treat government purchases as a category of autonomous expenditure.

Exhibit 10.5 shows how government purchases can be added to consumption and planned investment as a third component of planned expenditure. The C + I + G schedule in part b corresponds to the sum of columns 2 through 4 of part a. Regardless of the national income level, government purchases are assumed to be limited to $150 billion.

The Net Exports Component of Planned Expenditure

The final component of planned expenditure is net exports, that is, exports minus imports. Exports can be considered autonomous from the standpoint of the domestic economy; they are determined by economic conditions in foreign countries. Imports, however, do depend on the level of domestic national income. Since part of the goods households consume are imported, imports increase when consumption expenditures do. In order to calculate total planned expenditure including net exports, these imports, which are already included in the consumption component of planned expenditure, must now be subtracted.

For example, suppose that, as in Exhibit 10.3, the marginal propensity to consume is .75 and autonomous consumption and autonomous net taxes are $100 billion. Suppose too that one-fifth of each added dollar of consumption expenditures is devoted to imported goods. That means that for each $1 increase in disposable income, imports will rise by $.15. In economic terminology, there is a **marginal propensity to import** of .15.

Part a of Exhibit 10.6 shows how imports, exports, and net exports are related to national income. Consider imports first. As in the example of Exhibit 10.3, consumption is $25 billion when national income is zero. One-fifth of this is spent on imported consumer goods; thus, imports are $5 billion when national income is zero. For each added $100 billion of national income, imports increase by $15 billion in accordance with the marginal propensity to import of .15. Thus, the slope of the import schedule is .15.

Next, consider exports. These depend on the income level and the marginal propensity to import in foreign countries. In this case, we assume that foreign buyers purchase $185 billion of exports. This quantity does not depend on the level of domestic national income; hence, the export schedule in part a of Exhibit 10.6 is a horizontal line. Subtracting imports from exports gives the net export schedule. Like the import schedule, this has a slope equal to the marginal pro-

Marginal propensity to import
The percentage of each added dollar of real disposable income that is devoted to consumption of imported goods and services.

Exhibit 10.6   Adding Net Exports to the
Planned-Expenditure Schedule

Part a shows how imports, exports, and net exports behave
as real national income changes. Real national income in
the domestic economy does not affect exports; hence,
exports are represented by a horizontal line at an assumed
level of $185 billion. When national income is zero,
consumption is $25 billion; thus, imports are $5 billion. With
a marginal propensity to import of .15, imports increase by
$15 billion for each $100 billion increase in real national
income. The net export line shows exports minus imports.
Net exports are equal to zero at $1,200 billion. Part b of the
exhibit shows how net exports can be added to
consumption, government purchases, and planned
investment to give the complete planned-expenditure
schedule.

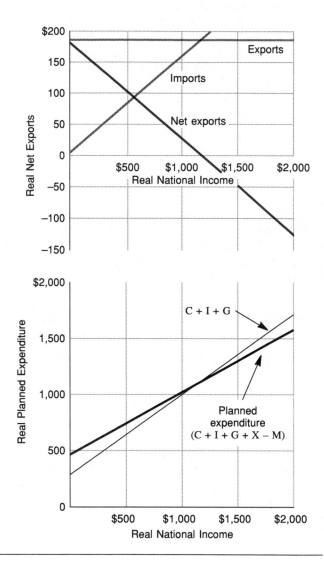

pensity to import. When national income is zero, net exports equal $180 billion
($185 billion of exports minus $5 billion of imports). Net exports remain positive
up to a national income of $1,200 billion; are zero at $1,200 billion; and negative
at national income levels above $1,200 billion.

    Part b of Exhibit 10.6 adds the net export schedule to consumption, planned
investment, and government purchases to give the complete planned-expenditure schedule. The autonomous component of this schedule (shown by its vertical intercept at $480 billion) is the sum of autonomous consumption adjusted for
autonomous net taxes ($25 billion), planned investment ($125 billion), government purchases ($150 billion), and net exports ($180 billion). The slope of the
schedule (in this case, .6) equals the marginal propensity to consume minus the
marginal propensity to import.

In the example under consideration, there is assumed to be no income tax. If there were, calculation of the slope of the planned-expenditure schedule would have to take this into effect as well. Using mpc for the marginal propensity to consume, mpm for the marginal propensity to import, and t for the marginal tax rate, the formula for the slope of the planned-expenditure schedule becomes $(mpc - mpm)(1 - t)$.

In this treatment, net exports depend only on national income in the domestic economy. In practice, they also depend on national income in foreign countries, which determines the level of exports, and also on the exchange rate of the dollar relative to foreign currencies, which affects both imports and exports. We will explore these aspects of the foreign sector in later chapters.

Determining the Equilibrium Level of National Income

The planned-expenditure schedule shows how aggregate demand varies as national income changes with the price level held constant. In order to find the equilibrium level of national income, all we need to do now is find the income level at which aggregate demand—that is, planned expenditure—equals aggregate supply—that is, national product. Exhibit 10.7 shows how this is done. The example is simplified by assuming a closed economy, that is, zero net exports.

The Income-Product Line

The first step is to add a line showing the relationship of national income to national product. Under our simplifying assumptions, national income and product are equal. Using the horizontal axis to represent real national income and the vertical to represent real national product, then, the relationship between the two can be shown as a straight line with a slope of 1 passing through the origin. We will refer to this line as the **income-product line.** It is simply a graphical representation of the equality of national income and product. In Chapter 6, we saw that this is a fundamental property of the circular flow.

Planned Expenditure and National Product

When the income-product and planned-expenditure lines are drawn on the same diagram, as they are in Exhibit 10.7, it is a simple matter to find the income level for which real planned expenditure and real national product are equal. This equality occurs at the intersection of the two lines—$1,200 billion in Exhibit 10.7. Because "planned expenditure" is but another term for "aggregate demand" and "national product" a substitute for "aggregate supply," this intersection point is an equilibrium for the circular flow.

The circular flow can be in equilibrium at no other level of national income. If national income is lower than the equilibrium level—say, $1,000 billion— planned expenditure (aggregate demand) will exceed national product (aggregate supply). There will be an unplanned drop in inventories equal to the vertical distance between the planned-expenditure schedule and the income-product line. In trying to restore inventories to their planned levels firms will increase output, thus causing national income to rise. As income rises planned expenditure increases, but only by a fraction of the amount by which national product does. The gap thus narrows until equilibrium is restored.

If, on the other hand, national income is higher than the equilibrium level— say, $1,500 billion—planned expenditure will fall short of output. The unsold goods will become unplanned inventory investment equal to the gap between the

Income-product line
A graph showing the level of real planned expenditure (aggregate demand) associated with each level of real national income.

Exhibit 10.7   Using the Income-Expenditure Model to Find the Equilibrium Level of Real National Income

The income-expenditure model is formed by the planned-expenditure schedule and the income-product line. This exhibit shows a simple way to determine the equilibrium level of real national income given the underlying conditions that determine the position of the planned-expenditure schedule. Any national income higher than the equilibrium level will cause unplanned inventory buildup and downward pressure on real output. Any level of national income below equilibrium will cause unplanned inventory depletion and upward pressure on real output. The example is simplified by assuming a closed economy, so that net exports are zero at all levels of real national income.

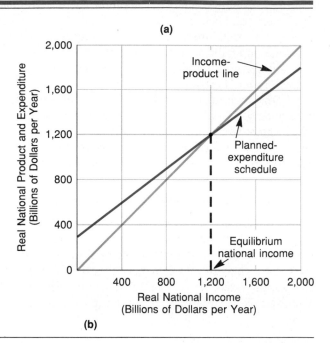

(a)

(b)

Real National Income (1)	Real Planned Expenditure (2)	Real National Product (3)	Unplanned Inventory Change (4)	Tendency of Change in National Income (5)
$ 0	$ 300	$ 0	−$300	Increase
100	375	100	−275	Increase
200	450	200	−250	Increase
300	525	300	−225	Increase
400	600	400	−200	Increase
500	675	500	−175	Increase
600	750	600	−150	Increase
700	825	700	−125	Increase
800	900	800	−100	Increase
900	975	900	−75	Increase
1,000	1,050	1,000	−50	Increase
1,100	1,125	1,100	−25	Increase
1,200	1,200	1,200	0	No change
1,300	1,275	1,300	25	Decrease
1,400	1,350	1,400	50	Decrease
1,500	1,425	1,500	75	Decrease
1,600	1,500	1,600	100	Decrease

Note: All amounts are in billions of dollars per year.

planned-expenditure and income-product lines at the $1,500 billion income level. Firms will react to the unplanned inventory buildup by cutting production. Their actions will cause real national income and product, measured in nominal terms, to fall to the equilibrium level.

In Exhibit 10.7, the same story is told twice—graphically in part a and numerically in part b. Both approaches confirm that $1,200 billion is the only possible equilibrium level for national income given the underlying assumptions on which the planned-expenditure schedule is based.

The Multiplier Effect

The level of real planned expenditure for the economy depends on many factors. First and foremost, planned spending varies as real national income changes. In the graphs used in this chapter, these are shown as movements upward or downward along the planned-expenditure schedule. Other factors that affect planned expenditure—changes in expectations, consumer wealth, interest rates, taxes, government purchases, or foreign markets—cause upward or downward shifts in the planned-expenditure schedule. In the preceding section, we saw how under given conditions the level of real national income tends to move upward or downward along the planned-expenditure schedule to the point of equilibrium. Now we turn to the effects of shifts in the planned-expenditure schedule on the equilibrium level of national income.

Exhibit 10.8 shows the effects of a $100 billion annual increase in planned expenditure at each possible national income level. For the moment, it does not matter whether the shift begins in the household, investment, or government sector; the effect in any case is to shift the planned-expenditure schedule upward by $100 billion from PE_1 to PE_2.

What happens to the equilibrium level of real national income when the planned-expenditure schedule shifts upward by $100 billion? The immediate effect is that planned expenditure exceeds national product. As a result, inventories start to fall at a rate of $100 billion per year. Firms react to this unplanned inventory depletion by increasing output. (In a model with flexible prices, they would tend to increase both real output and prices.) As a result, the circular flow expands. National income continues to rise until the gap between planned expenditure and national product—that is, between aggregate demand and aggregate supply—disappears. This occurs at an income level of $1,600 billion.

We see, then, that a $100 billion upward shift in the planned-expenditure schedule has caused a $400 billion increase in equilibrium real national income. This ability of a given vertical shift in planned expenditure to cause a greater

---

Exhibit 10.8   Multiplier Effect in the Income-Expenditure Model

A given vertical shift in the planned-expenditure schedule produces a greater increase in the equilibrium level of real national income. This is known as the *multiplier effect*. Here a $100 billion upward shift in the planned-expenditure schedule causes a $400 billion increase in equilibrium real national income. The ratio of the change in equilibrium income to the initial shift in demand, which is the expenditure multiplier, has a value of 4 in this example. In this simplified example, the marginal tax rate and the marginal propensity to import are assumed to be zero.

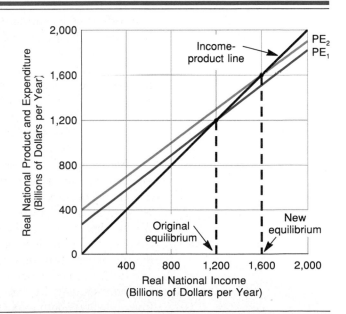

increase in the equilibrium level of national income is the multiplier effect. At this point, it may be helpful to compare the graphical demonstration of the multiplier effect in Exhibit 10.8 with the numerical example given in Exhibit 9.6 (page 221).

Modifications to the Multiplier Formula

In Chapter 9, the formula given for the expenditure multiplier was $1/(1 - \text{mpc})$. However, we have since added some details to the model that necessitate modifying the formula. The general principle is that anything that affects the slope of the planned-expenditure schedule will affect the multiplier. In fact, a general form for the multiplier is:

$$\text{Expenditure multiplier} = \frac{1}{1 - \text{Slope of planned-expenditure schedule}}.$$

The Effect of an Income Tax in a Closed Economy

Earlier in this chapter, we saw that the addition of an income tax changes the slope of the consumption schedule from mpc to $\text{mpc}(1 - t)$, where t is the marginal tax rate. The formula for the multiplier in a closed economy with a proportional income tax imposed at a marginal tax rate of t is thus

$$\text{Expenditure multiplier with income tax added} = \frac{1}{1 - \text{mpc}(1 - t)}.$$

This formula shows that the imposition of an income tax reduces the multiplier's value. For example, a closed economy with a marginal propensity to consume of .8 will have an expenditure multiplier of 5 if there is no income tax. With an income tax at a 25 percent marginal rate, the denominator of the multiplier formula will be .4, and the multiplier will thus fall to 2.5. In general, the higher the marginal tax rate, the smaller the effect of a disturbance to planned expenditure on the equilibrium level of real national income.

The Effect of Net Exports

Inclusion of the foreign sector also changes the slope of the planned-expenditure schedule and, therefore, the multiplier. In an open-economy model that includes both an income tax and a marginal propensity to import, the slope of the planned-expenditure schedule is $(\text{mpc} - \text{mpm})(1 - t)$. The formula for the expenditure multiplier then becomes

$$\text{Expenditure multiplier} = \frac{1}{(\text{mpc} - \text{mpm})(1 - t)}.$$

For example, suppose that the marginal propensity to consume is .9, the marginal propensity to import is .15, and the marginal tax rate is .33. With no income tax or imports, the multiplier for an economy with an mpc of .9 will be 10. Adding imports will reduce the slope of the planned-expenditure curve to .75 and, hence, reduce the multiplier to 4. Adding a marginal tax rate of .33 will further reduce the slope of the planned-expenditure schedule to .5, thus reducing the expenditure multiplier to 2.

In Chapter 9, we noted that in his *General Theory* Keynes emphasized the economy's sensitivity to even small changes in planned investment. Since that time, however, both imports and income taxes have become much more important in relation to the economy's size. By reducing the multiplier, the increased importance of imports and income taxes is thought to have enhanced the economy's stability, lessening the chances of a cyclical contraction on the scale of the Great Depression.

Relationship of the Income Determination Models

We now have two models for determining the equilibrium level of real national income and product: the aggregate supply and demand model, which treats real planned expenditure and national product as functions of the price level, and the income-expenditure model, which treats them as functions of the level of real national income. This section briefly outlines how these two models can be reconciled; a fully rigorous reconciliation is a subject for a more advanced course.

In this section, we drop our assumption of a fixed price level.

The Two Models in the Short Run

Exhibit 10.9 looks at the relationship between the two models in the short run. Initially the economy is in equilibrium with real national product at its natural level and the price level at 1.0. This equilibrium is shown as E_1 in the aggregate supply and demand model of part a and as e_1 in the income-expenditure model of part b. Now suppose that something happens to increase autonomous expenditure by $500 billion; for present purposes, it does not matter whether the increase comes from autonomous consumption, planned investment, government purchases, or net exports. The increase in autonomous expenditure shifts the planned-expenditure schedule upward. This causes unplanned depletion of inventories, and the economy begins to expand.

Short-Run Equilibrium with Flexible Prices

If there were no change in the price level, a $500 billion increase in autonomous expenditure would move the planned-expenditure schedule to PE_2 and real output would find a new equilibrium at $3,000 billion.[3] In part b, this equilibrium would occur at e_2. In part a, a $1,000 billion increase in national product with no price change would put the economy at E_2.

However, we are no longer dealing with a fixed-price economy. In a world of flexible prices, an increase in aggregate demand causes the price level to increase as well as the level of real output. This is shown in part a of Exhibit 10.9 as a movement up and to the right along the economy's short-run aggregate supply curve, AS. As soon as the economy begins to move up along the aggregate supply curve, things start to happen in the income-expenditure model of part b. As discussed in Chapter 8, the rising price level reduces real consumption via its effect on the real value of nominal money balances; it affects planned investment via an increase in the interest rate; it may lower government pur-

---

[3]In Chapter 15, we will see that expansion of the economy even without a change in the price level can cause the interest rate to rise, thus depressing planned investment. Here we assume, in effect, that the initial change in autonomous expenditure is strong enough to increase autonomous expenditure by $500 and thus to shift the planned-expenditure curve upward by that amount even after this interest rate effect is taken into account.

Exhibit 10.9   Reconciling the Income-Expenditure
and Aggregate Supply and Demand Models

Both the income-expenditure and aggregate supply and
demand models determine the equilibrium level of real
national income and product. This exhibit shows how they
can be reconciled when the effect of a change in the price
level on planned expenditure is taken into account. The
economy begins at E_1 in part a and e_1 in part b.
Autonomous expenditure then increases by $500 billion. The
aggregate demand curve shifts from AD_1 to AD_2. With no
price change, the economy would end up at E_2 and e_2.
However, the price level increases as the economy moves
up along the aggregate supply curve to E_3. This causes the
planned-expenditure schedule to halt its upward movement
at PE_3. Thus, the short-run equilibrium as shown in the
income-expenditure model is e_3, which occurs at the same
level of national product shown by E_3 in part a.

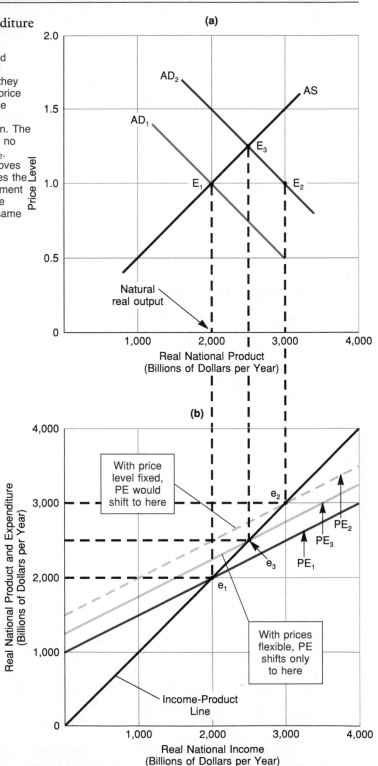

chases if government budgets are set partly in nominal terms; and it affects net exports by changing the relative prices of foreign and domestic goods. These effects partially offset those of the original increase in autonomous expenditure. Instead of moving all the way to PE_2, the rise in the price level limits the shift of the planned-expenditure schedule to PE_3.

Because the planned-expenditure schedule shifts only to PE_3, equilibrium real output rises only to $2,500 billion rather than to $3,000 billion as it would if prices remained fixed. The new short-run equilibrium in the income-expenditure model is e_3. This corresponds to point E_3 in the aggregate supply and demand model—a point on the aggregate supply curve above and to the right of the initial equilibrium, E_1.

Effect on the Aggregate Demand Curve

Let's now look at what we have learned about the aggregate demand curve in the course of the movement to the new equilibrium. The initial equilibrium, E_1, lies on aggregate demand curve AD_1 at the point at which it intersects the aggregate supply curve, AS. What about points E_2 and E_3? E_2 shows what would have happened to the equilibrium level of aggregate demand had the price level remained at 1.0. E_3 shows what happens to it when the economy instead moves up along the aggregate supply curve. The two points both lie on a new aggregate demand curve, AD_2. The various points along that curve show the level of aggregate demand at different possible price levels given the shift in autonomous expenditure that moved the economy away from its old equilibrium.

Our example thus confirms two points about the aggregate demand curve that were made in Chapters 8 and 9. First, we see that the negative slope of the aggregate demand curve arises from the effects of a change in the price level on real planned expenditure. These are the same forces that limit the shift in the planned-expenditure schedule to PE_3. Second, we see that an increase in autonomous expenditure, whether in the form of a change in autonomous consumption, planned investment, government purchases, or net exports, causes a horizontal shift in the aggregate demand curve. This shift (the distance between E_1 and E_2 in part a of Exhibit 10.9) equals the expenditure multiplier times the increase in autonomous expenditure.[4] However, the actual increase in equilibrium aggregate demand is less than the horizontal shift in the aggregate demand curve. The reason is that the price level increases as the economy moves up and to the right along its short-run aggregate supply curve.

The Two Models in the Long Run

So far our reconciliation of the income-expenditure model with the aggregate supply and demand model has dealt only with short-run effects. The effect of long-run adjustments in the two models is demonstrated in Exhibit 10.10. This exhibit begins where Exhibit 10.9 left off—with the economy in short-run equilibrium at E_3 in part a and at e_3 in part b. The schedule PE_2 and the corresponding points e_2 and E_2 have been deleted to simplify the diagrams.

As we have seen in previous chapters, the economy can remain in short-run equilibrium at E_3 only so long as firms expect input prices to remain constant. Of course, this will not be forever. In the long run, input prices will adjust and

---

[4]The qualification regarding the interest rate that was given in footnote 3 applies here as well.

Exhibit 10.10   Long-Run Effects of
Expansion in the Two Models

This exhibit picks up where Exhibit 10.9 left off. The short-run equilibrium following an increase in autonomous expenditure is E_3 in part a and e_3 in part b. Over time, as input prices adjust, the economy leaves the original short-run aggregate supply curve and moves to E_4 on the long-run aggregate supply curve. As it does, prices rise further and the planned-expenditure schedule in part b shifts all the way back down to its original position at PE_1. The final equilibrium in part b is e_4, which is identical to the initial equilibrium, e_1. Thus, we see that in a fully flexible-price model, an increase in real autonomous expenditure has no permanent effect on the equilibrium level of real national income and product.

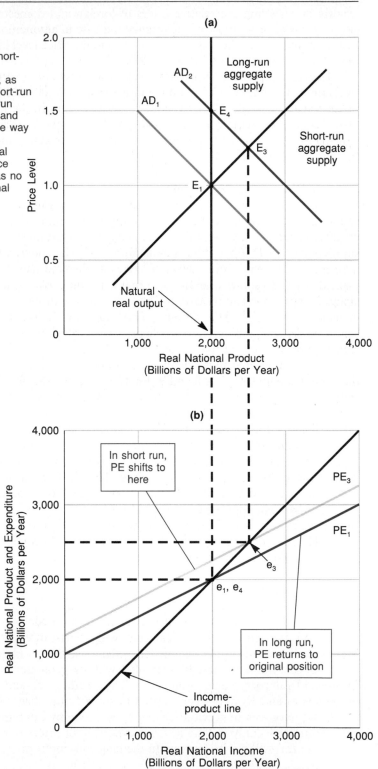

the economy will leave its original short-run aggregate supply curve. As input prices adjust completely to the new situation, the economy will eventually reach a long-run equilibrium at E_4 in part a of Exhibit 10.10. That is the point at which aggregate demand curve AD_2 intersects the long-run aggregate supply curve, which is a vertical line at the natural level of real output.

The move from E_3 to E_4 involves a further increase in the price level. As prices rise beyond the level of 1.25 reached at E_3, real planned expenditure falls. This happens because the real value of money continues to fall, the interest rate continues to rise, the government budget is further strained, and net exports continue to taper off. Looking at these events in terms of the income-expenditure model (part b of Exhibit 10.10), the planned-expenditure schedule shifts downward again; it drops below PE_3 and does not stop until it is all the way back to PE_1. At that point, the depressing effects on planned expenditure of the rising price level fully offset the initial increase in autonomous expenditure. The long-run equilibrium in the income-expenditure model is thus e_4, which is exactly the same as the initial equilibrium, e_1. This result is a modern restatement of the classical proposition that in a flexible-price world, a change in autonomous planned expenditure has no lasting effect on the equilibrium level of real national income and product. The only lasting effect is on the price level. We will return to the implications of this proposition at several points in later chapters.

Looking Ahead

Although this chapter has introduced no new conclusions, it has revealed some of the inner workings of the aggregate supply and demand model. In particular, it has shown how the slope of and shifts in the aggregate demand curve can be interpreted in terms of the Keynesian income-expenditure model.

Chapter 11 applies the two models to the topic of fiscal policy—that is, to changes in government purchases and net taxes. Fiscal policy was considered by Keynes and his followers as providing the government with a powerful tool for stabilizing the economy, although, as we will see, that belief has been somewhat shaken in recent years.

Following that, we will be ready to move ahead with the next stage of model building, in which money, financial markets, and interest rates are incorporated. Those additions will enable us to understand the evolution of macroeconomics in the decades since Keynes.

Summary

1. **How is consumption related to disposable income?** The relationship between real consumption and real disposable income can be represented in the form of a graph known as the *consumption function*. The vertical intercept of the consumption function, which represents the part of consumption expenditure not associated with a particular income level, is known as *autonomous consumption*. The slope of the consumption function equals the marginal propensity to consume. Changes in real wealth or expectations can shift the consumption function.

2. **How is consumption affected by various forms of taxes?** The basic form of the consumption function relates real consumption expenditure to real disposable income. The consumption function can be redrawn with national rather than disposable income on the horizontal axis provided an appropriate adjustment for the effect of taxes is made. An *autonomous net tax* shifts the consumption function downward by an amount equal to the tax times the marginal propensity to consume. Such a tax does not change the slope of the consumption function. An income tax does change

the slope. With an income tax, the slope of the consumption function is mpc$(1 - t)$, where t is the *marginal tax rate*.

3. **How is the equilibrium level of national income determined in the income-expenditure model?** The income-expenditure model consists of the *planned-expenditure schedule* and the *income-product line*. The point at which they intersect shows the level of real national income corresponding to equilibrium in the circular flow, that is, the level of national income at which planned expenditure (aggregate demand) equals national product (aggregate supply). At any higher level of national income, there will be unplanned inventory accumulation, shown by the vertical gap between the two schedules. At any lower level of national income, there will be unplanned inventory depletion.

4. **How can the income-expenditure model be used to demonstrate the multiplier effect?** Any shift in the position of the planned-expenditure schedule will change the income level at which it intersects the income-expenditure line. The greater the slope of the planned-expenditure schedule, the greater the change in equilibrium national income that will result from a given change in autonomous expenditure. This is the multiplier effect.

5. **How can the income-expenditure model be reconciled with the aggregate supply and demand model?** The income-expenditure model relates real planned expenditure to the level of real national income, whereas the aggregate supply and demand model relates real planned expenditure to the price level. The two can be reconciled if the effects of price level changes on planned expenditure are taken into account. In general, an increase in the price level causes the planned-expenditure schedule to shift downward and a decrease causes it to shift upward. An increase in autonomous planned expenditure shifts the aggregate demand curve to the right by an amount that depends on the size of the expenditure multiplier. In the short run, there is an increase in both real output and the price level as the economy moves up and to the right along the aggregate supply curve. In the long run, a change in autonomous planned expenditure has no lasting effect on the equilibrium level of real national income, because the price level changes by enough to bring real national product back to its natural level.

Terms for Review

- consumption schedule (consumption function)
- autonomous consumption
- autonomous

- average propensity to consume
- autonomous net taxes
- marginal tax rate
- income-expenditure model
- planned-expenditure schedule
- marginal propensity to import
- income-product line

Questions for Review

1. What assumptions are needed to establish the condition that disposable income plus net taxes equals national product and the condition that gross and net national product are equal?

2. What factors determine the slope and intercept of the consumption function?

3. How is the consumption function affected by (a) an increase in real wealth, (b) an increase in the price level while the nominal quantity of money balances remains constant, and (c) a shift in expectations?

4. When the consumption function is graphed with national income on the horizontal axis, how are its slope and intercept affected by autonomous taxes? By income taxes?

5. What is the relationship between the planned-expenditure schedule and the consumption function? Between the planned-expenditure schedule and the aggregate demand curve?

6. Why does the income-product line always pass through the origin and have a slope of 1?

7. How is the value of the expenditure multiplier related to the slope of the planned-expenditure schedule?

8. How is the aggregate demand curve affected by an increase in autonomous expenditure? By a decrease in autonomous expenditure?

Problems and Topics for Discussion

1. **Examining the lead-off case.** Use the income-expenditure model to show what happens to the equilibrium level of real national income when a large proportion of consumers develop the kind of pessimistic attitude exemplified by Jack Lenburg. Show too what happens when the Jack Lenburgs of the economy become optimistic again and begin buying the cars, apartments, and furniture they want. In each case, assume that the change in mood is not initially caused by a change in disposable income. Once the mood change is established, however, will it cause a change in total disposable income? Why or why not?

2. **Permanent and transitory changes in income.** Suppose you won $1,000 in a lottery. How much would you spend, and how much would you save? (Remem-

ber that debt repayment counts as saving.) Would you save more or less of this $1,000 windfall than of the first $1,000 of a pay increase that you expected to be permanent? Would it surprise you to learn that some surveys have found that the marginal propensity to consume from windfall income is smaller than that from permanent income changes? Explain.

3. **Graphing the consumption schedule.** On a sheet of graph paper, draw consumption schedules for the following values of autonomous consumption (a) and the marginal propensity to consume (mpc): a = 1,000, mpc = .5; a = 1,200, mpc = .6; a = 500, mpc = .9.

4. **Taxes and the consumption schedule.** On a sheet of graph paper, draw a consumption schedule assuming no taxes at all, autonomous consumption of $100 billion, and a marginal propensity to consume of .8. Label the horizontal axis "real national income." Now modify this schedule for the following tax assumptions:
    a.   Autonomous net taxes of $50 billion
    b.   An income tax with a marginal tax rate of 25 percent

c.   Both of the above taxes at the same time

Bonus question: Calculate the value of the expenditure multiplier for each of the above cases.

5. **Effects of a decrease in autonomous expenditure.** Rework Exhibit 10.8 for a $100 billion decrease in autonomous planned expenditure. Explain step by step what will happen on the way to the new equilibrium.

6. **Income-expenditure model with special Keynesian assumptions.** In his *General Theory*, Keynes argued that a change in the price level would have little or no effect on real planned expenditure. Rework Exhibit 10.9 using these Keynesian assumptions. Your aggregate supply and demand diagram should resemble part a of Exhibit 9.5 (page 219).

7. **Effects of a decrease in autonomous expenditure with flexible prices.** Rework Exhibits 10.9 and 10.10 for a $250 billion decrease in autonomous planned expenditure. Explain what happens at each step in the transition to a new short-run and long-run equilibrium.

Case for Discussion
Investment Marches On

JUNE 1984. Capital spending is where the beef is. It leaped last quarter at a 14 percent annual rate, about equal to 1983's exceptionally rapid pace. Now it's slowing—but not much. Expect confident business managers to spend at a 9 percent rate for the rest of the year before reining in again.

One reason is that manufacturing capacity utilization, which powerfully shapes the need for new plant and equipment, has grown faster than in previous recoveries. Over the last few years, business has not been adding much new capacity. By year-end the capacity utilization rate should approach 84 percent, the average for the late 1970s. Since business spending on plant and equipment usually accelerates when utilization reaches that area, the pressure to expand facilities should keep growing.

Capital spending is where the beef is.

Source: "Investment Marches On," *Fortune,* June 11, 1984, 27. Photo Source: Arthur Rothstein, *The American West in the Thirties* (New York: Dover Publications, Inc., 1981), p. 7.

Questions

1. How does an increase in capital spending by businesses affect the economy? Explain in terms of the circular flow model discussed in Chapter 6, the aggregate supply and demand model discussed in Chapters 8 and 9, and the income-expenditure model of this chapter. Compare and contrast the three approaches.

2. At the end of the second quarter of 1984, total capital spending in the U.S. economy was about $400 billion. Assuming that the planned-expenditure

schedule has a slope of .75, how much will the equilibrium level of nominal national income increase as a result of a 9 percent increase in capital spending assuming a constant price level, as at the beginning of this chapter? How will the effects differ if a flexible price level is assumed?

3. In this chapter, we have assumed that the level of planned investment is not affected by the level of national income. However, this article suggests that growth of the economy pushes up the capacity utilization rate, which in turn triggers investment. How would the assumption that investment increases when national income does affect the slope of the planned-expenditure schedule? Would this assumption affect the value of the multiplier? Why or why not?

11 Fiscal Policy

After reading this chapter, you will understand . . .

- How fiscal policy—changes in government purchases and net taxes—can be used to fight recession and inflation.
- How government receipts and expenditures are affected by changing economic conditions.
- How the federal budgetary system works and what its limitations are.
- The priorities that have guided federal tax and spending decisions in the 1980s.
- How the deficit is measured and why it has grown.
- Whether large federal deficits are a threat to economic stability.

Before reading this chapter, make sure you know the meaning of . . .

- Government purchases and transfer payments (Chapter 5)
- Net taxes (Chapter 6)
- Indexing (Chapter 7)
- Multiplier effect (Chapter 9)

Getting Control of the Budget Monster

"We must get control of the budget monster, get control of our economy and, I assure you, get control of our lives and destinies." So said Ronald Reagan in March 1981, shortly after he was inaugurated President of the United States. But Reagan did not manage to gain control over the budget. By the 1984 election, the federal deficit was approaching $200 billion and economic policy had become a major election issue.

Reagan's 1984 opponent, Walter Mondale, stated his position on the budget issue early in the campaign. Reagan had cut taxes too far and spent too much, especially on the military. Mondale pledged that if elected he would raise taxes, restrain the growth of military spending, and restore some of Reagan's cuts in social programs.

Candidate Reagan remained coy about his economic policy plans for a second term. Would he raise taxes? No. Would he cut spending? Of course—but at the same time military spending and social security, the largest budget items, were placed off limits for cuts.

In the end, Reagan won reelection easily. His second term continued the main budgetary trends of the first. Personal taxes were cut again in 1986 as part of a general tax reform package, although these cuts were offset by increases in business taxes. Social security and other middle-class entitlements remained untouchable. Domestic spending was squeezed, but not enough to make much of a dent in the deficit, which remained deep in 12-digit territory. Between the 1981 inauguration and 1986, the national debt had doubled. As the presidential campaign for the 1988 election got underway, the budget monster was still on the loose. If anyone was to slay it, it would not be Ronald Reagan.

Photo Source: UPI/Bettmann Newsphotos

Republican Presidential Candidate Ronald Reagan in 1980.

Fiscal policy
Policy concerning
government purchases,
taxes, and transfer
payments.

THE growth of the budget deficit has brought **fiscal policy**—policy concerning government purchases, taxes, and transfer payments—to the forefront of national debate. In this chapter, we use the models developed earlier to explore the economics of fiscal policy and the "budget monster." Our main focus will be the short-run effects of changes in government purchases and net taxes. For our purposes in this chapter, we will temporarily set aside the issue of the economy's long-run adjustment to policy changes.

The Theory of Fiscal Policy

Economists of all schools agree that fiscal policy has important effects on the economy. In the policy debates of the past half-century, however, the view of fiscal policy as a constructive tool for furthering the goals of full employment, price stability, and growth has been most closely associated with Keynes and his followers. It is fitting, then, to begin our discussion of fiscal policy where Chapter 9 left off—with the use of fiscal policy as a tool for combating economic contractions.

Using Government Purchases to Combat a Contraction

Exhibit 11.1 begins from a situation described in Chapter 9. The economy has fallen into recession at point E_1, where the aggregate supply curve, AS, meets aggregate demand curve AD_1. There real national product is $500 billion below its natural level of $2,000 billion and unemployment is thus above its natural rate. In the classical view of things, input prices would gradually adjust to this level of demand in the long run. Real output would eventually return to its

Exhibit 11.1 Using Fiscal Policy to Combat an Economic Contraction

In this figure, the economy has fallen into recession at E_1. In order to reach the natural level of real output at E_2, the aggregate demand curve must be shifted to the right by $1,000 billion, from AD_1 to AD_2. This can be done by increasing real government purchases and taking advantage of the multiplier effect. Given an expenditure multiplier of 4, a $250 billion increase in government purchases will bring about the required $1,000 billion shift in the aggregate demand curve. However, because the price level rises, equilibrium real national product does not increase by the full $1,000 billion by which the aggregate demand curve shifts. The same shift can be accomplished with a cut in net taxes, but the multiplier effect of a tax cut will be smaller than that of an increase in government purchases.

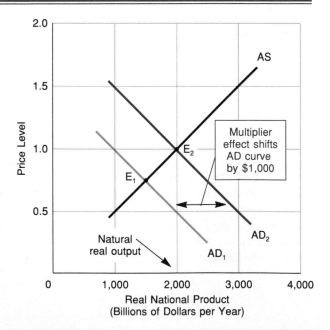

natural level as the economy slid down and to the right along AD_1. But, as Keynes once said, "in the long run, we are all dead."

The President and Congress do not want to wait for the long run—they want to do something about the recession now, before the next election. The problem is deficient aggregate demand. Given the position of the aggregate supply curve, the aggregate demand curve needs to be shifted from AD_1 to AD_2 in order to bring real output back to its natural level at E_2. How can this be done?

Identifying the Spending Gap

Although real national product is only $500 billion below its natural level, the horizontal gap between AD_1 and AD_2 is $1,000 billion, as shown by the arrow in Exhibit 11.1. That means that the equilibrium level of planned expenditure at any given price level falls short of what is needed by $1,000 billion. If policymakers can find a way to fill that gap, they can shift the aggregate demand curve to the position AD_2 and bring national product to the natural level.

In principle, any increase in autonomous expenditure can serve to fill the gap. Exports might pick up; business managers might become more optimistic and increase planned investment; a rise in consumer confidence might spur autonomous consumption. But although these things might happen, they also might not occur. Instead of waiting and hoping, policymakers turn to the element of autonomous planned expenditure most directly under their control: government purchases. There is always a backlog of federal spending projects that members of Congress would gladly see undertaken. A new postal sorting station here, a stretch of interstate highway there, new vehicles for park rangers somewhere else—it is easy to list the things that the government might buy. But just how much spending for new government purchases is needed?

Using the Multiplier Effect

Moving the aggregate demand curve to the right by $1,000 billion does not require increasing government purchases by that amount. The reason, as explained in Chapter 9, is that each dollar of new government purchases is amplified by the multiplier effect. Spending $1 on a federal highway project boosts the income of construction workers, who then spend more on, say, groceries, clothing, and cars. Their spending raises the incomes of grocers, textile workers, and autoworkers, who in turn consume more. As the multiplier effect cascades through the economy, each $1 of new government purchases stimulates more than $1 of total planned expenditure.

Let us assume, as we did in Chapter 9, that the marginal propensity to consume is .75. Using the formula for the expenditure multiplier, $1/(1 - mpc)$, the value of the expenditure multiplier comes out to be 4. In that case, $1 of government purchases will raise the equilibrium level of planned expenditure at a given price level by $4. This takes into account both the actual government purchases and the induced increases in consumption expenditure. Given an expenditure multiplier of $4, then, it will take $250 of additional government purchases to shift the aggregate demand curve to the right by $1,000.[1]

---

[1]This is an approximation. It assumes both that there are no income taxes and that net exports and net investment are unaffected by a change in real national product at a given price level. In a more elaborate model that allowed for these factors, the general principles discussed in this section would still hold. However, in that model, each $1 in additional government purchases would shift the aggregate demand curve to the right by more than $1 but less than the $4 predicted by the simple expenditure multiplier calculated using a marginal propensity to consume of .75.

Changing Prices and Aggregate Demand

As the aggregate demand curve shifts from AD_1 to AD_2, the economy moves up and to the right along the aggregate supply curve. As it does, the increase in prices affects planned expenditure in ways that partially offset the multiplier effect of the original increase in government purchases. Chapter 8 offered four reasons why a change in the price level will affect real planned expenditure, all of which are at work in the present situation:

1. Real consumption is restrained by the fact that the real value of nominal money balances falls as the price level rises.

2. Real planned investment is damped by the higher interest rates associated with a higher price level.

3. The parts of government budgets that are set in nominal terms will command fewer real goods and services as the price level rises.

4. Real net exports will fall because domestic prices will rise relative to prices abroad.

These effects of a change in the price level on aggregate demand are built into the slope of the aggregate demand curve. They do not cause the aggregate demand curve to shift away from its new position at AD_2. Instead, they make the economy end up at a point on AD_2 at which the equilibrium level of real planned expenditure increases by less than the full $1,000 billion horizontal shift in the aggregate demand curve. In Exhibit 11.1, the new equilibrium is at point E_2. There planned expenditure is $2,000 billion; this is only $500 billion greater than the $1,500 billion of real planned expenditure at E_1 despite the fact that the aggregate demand curve has shifted by $1,000 billion.

In short, because a rise in the price level tends to lower every type of planned expenditure, the equilibrium level of real national product rises by less than the expenditure multiplier times the change in government purchases.

Using a Change in Taxes or Transfer Payments to Combat a Contraction

Government purchases are only one side of the fiscal policy equation. The other side consists of net taxes. As explained in Chapter 6, the term *net taxes* means taxes collected by government minus transfer payments made by government to individuals. A tax cut or an increase in transfer payments operates on the economy via its effect on consumption.

Let's return to point E_1 in Exhibit 11.1 and see how a change in net taxes can be used to combat the contraction. As before, the problem is to shift the planned-expenditure schedule to the right by $1,000 billion. Suppose that to help stimulate the economy, Congress votes a $100 billion increase in social security benefits while leaving taxes unchanged. This is a $100 billion cut in net taxes. How does it affect aggregate demand?

In the first instance, the action raises the disposable incomes of social security recipients by $100 billion. In response—once again assuming a marginal propensity to consume of .75—they raise their consumption by $75 billion. As in the earlier case, the increase in consumer spending on groceries, cars, and the like boosts the incomes of grocers, autoworkers, and others by $75 billion; those people, in turn, increase consumption expenditures by $56,250,000,000; and so on.

In short, a cut in net taxes touches off a multiplier process similar to that resulting from an increase in government purchases. This is true whether the reduction in net taxes takes the form of a cut in taxes paid to government or an increase in transfer payments made by government.

Multiplier Effects of a Change in Net Taxes

The multiplier effects of a change in net taxes are shown in Exhibit 11.2, which compares the effects of the net tax cut to those of a $100 billion increase in government purchases. The difference between the two lies in the first round of the process. A $100 billion increase in government purchases is itself a $100 billion *direct* addition to aggregate demand. The multiplier chain goes on from there with additional *induced* increases in consumption expenditures that total $300 billion. Thus, the total change in planned expenditure is $400 billion. However, a $100 billion tax cut or increase in transfer payments is not in itself a direct addition to aggregate demand, because it does not represent a government decision to buy any newly produced goods and services. Therefore, the only effect of the cut in net taxes is the induced increases in consumption expenditures. These total just $300 billion.

Generalizing from this example, we see that a change in net taxes has a multiplier effect that is smaller than that of an equal change in planned expenditure. The ratio of an induced shift in aggregate demand to a given change in real net taxes is known as the **net tax multiplier.** Mathematically, the value of the net tax multiplier is given by the formula

Net tax multiplier
The ratio of an induced shift in aggregate demand to a given change in net taxes.

$$\text{Net tax multiplier} = \text{Expenditure multiplier} - 1.$$

Substituting $1/(1 - \text{mpc})$ for the expenditure multiplier and simplifying, we can also write this as follows:

$$\text{Net tax multiplier} = \frac{\text{mpc}}{1 - \text{mpc}}.$$

Exhibit 11.2   The Net Tax Multiplier

This exhibit compares the multiplier effects of a $100 billion cut in net taxes with those of an equal increase in government purchases. Both result in $300 billion of induced consumption expenditure over an infinite number of rounds. However, the increase in government purchases itself adds $100 billion to aggregate demand; thus, the total effect, combining direct and induced planned expenditure, is greater for the increase in government purchases. In general, the net tax multiplier equals the expenditure multiplier minus 1.

	Change in Income	Change in Expenditure for a		
		Increase in Government Purchases	Cut in Net Taxes	
1		$100,000,000		(Direct)
2	$100,000,000	75,000,000	$ 75,000,000	(Induced)
3	75,000,000	56,250,000	56,250,000	(Induced)
4	56,250,000	42,187,500	42,187,500	(Induced)
5	42,187,500	31,640,625	31,640,625	(Induced)
.				
.				
.				
All rounds		$400,000,000	$300,000,000	(Total)

Do Tax Changes Really Affect Aggregate Demand?

The net tax multiplier correctly predicts the effect of tax changes on equilibrium aggregate demand only if people treat a dollar of added disposable income received through a tax cut in the same way as that received from any other source: dividing it between saving and consumption according to the marginal propensity to consume. However, recent U.S. experience suggests that in practice, saving is more strongly affected by tax changes and consumption less strongly affected than by other changes in disposable income.

The accompanying chart shows personal saving and personal tax payments as a percentage of personal income since 1960. Tax cuts, such as the tax rebate of 1975, appear to produce an offsetting jump in saving; as a result, they add little to consumption. Likewise, tax increases, such as the tax surcharge of 1968 and the one-time increase in tax payments in April 1987, produce a jump in tax payments but an offsetting drop in saving. This implies a smaller net tax multiplier than the usual formula gives. If a tax change is fully offset by a change in saving, it will have no multiplier effect at all.

Economists differ in the reasons they give for the seeming ineffectiveness of tax cuts. One far-reaching hypothesis has been put forth by Robert J. Barro of Harvard University. Barro points out that today's tax cut has implications for tomorrow's fiscal policy. If the government cuts taxes today and does not cut spending, it will have to increase its borrowing in order to cover the resulting deficit. In the future, then, taxes will have to be raised to repay this borrowing or at least to pay interest on it. If households think ahead, Barro says, they will react to a tax cut today by increasing their saving. Income from assets they buy

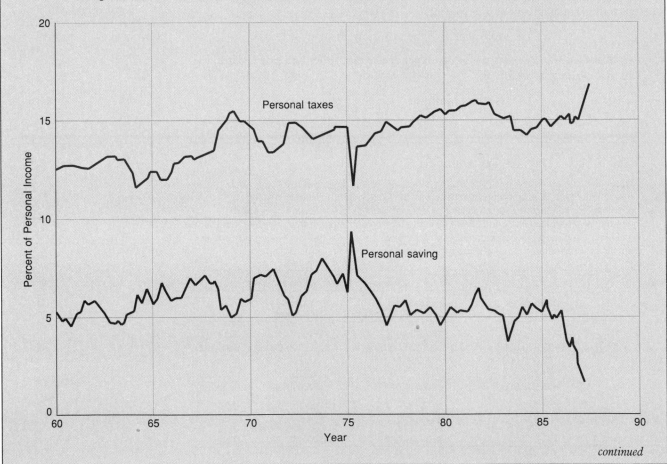

continued

PERSPECTIVE 11.1

continued

with the added savings will allow them to afford the higher future taxes needed to cover today's government borrowing. In order to protect themselves fully against the higher future taxes, they must save 100 percent of today's tax cut.

Other economists doubt that consumers are so far-sighted as to adjust their saving to offset the future effects of today's tax cuts in full. They see a simpler explanation for the apparent ineffectiveness of tax cuts, namely consumers' tendency to save a higher percentage of temporary changes in income than of permanent changes. Some recent tax changes have been explicitly labeled as temporary,

such as the income tax surcharge of 1968 and the tax rebate of 1975. There was also a temporary bulge in tax revenues in the second quarter of 1987. This reflected heavy realization of capital gains in late 1986 in anticipation of higher capital gains tax rates scheduled to go into effect in 1987. As the chart shows, these tax changes were almost fully offset by changes in saving, at least in the short run. Even tax changes that are said to be permanent may at first be treated as if they were temporary. Only after enough time has passed for consumers to adjust to the tax changes will these changes affect consumption in proportion to the full marginal propensity to consume.

Applying the Net Tax Multiplier

We can now return to Exhibit 11.1 and see how much of a cut in real net taxes is needed to bring the economy out of its recession. The required shift in the aggregate demand curve is $1,000 billion. Using the formula just given, a marginal propensity to consume of .75 gives a net tax multiplier of 3. Thus, $333 billion in tax cuts or transfer payment increases are needed to shift the aggregate demand curve to the right by $1,000 billion. In response to this shift, real output rises by $500 billion, taking into account the effects of a rising price level on the various components of real planned expenditure.

Qualifications

This analysis suggests that on a dollar-for-dollar basis, changes in net taxes are only slightly less effective than changes in government purchases in influencing the level of aggregate demand. Note, however, that the analysis makes a number of simplifying assumptions. The most important of these is the idea that households will spend the same fraction of an additional dollar received through tax cuts as they will of an additional dollar in earned income. As "Perspective 11.1" indicates, there is some evidence to suggest that this may not be the case. If not, the usefulness of tax changes as a fiscal policy tool may be less than our simple model suggests.

Fiscal Policy and Inflation

In previous sections, we have seen how fiscal policy can be used to speed up recovery from a contraction caused by, say, a drop in planned investment. Keynesian economics, born of the Great Depression, has tended to stress this role of fiscal policy. However, fiscal policy can also play a part in fighting inflation or, for that matter, causing inflation if used irresponsibly.

Counteracting Projected Inflation

Consider the situation shown in Exhibit 11.3. The economy has been in equilibrium for some time at E_2, where real output is at its natural level. As the federal budget for the coming year is being prepared, forecasters warn of a danger of

Exhibit 11.3   Fiscal Policy and Inflation

Initially the economy is at E_1. Forecasts show that if no policy changes are made, increases in real private planned expenditure will shift the aggregate demand curve from AD_1 to AD_2, causing the price level to rise. To prevent the price increase, government purchases can be cut or net taxes increased in order to offset the projected change in private planned expenditure, thus keeping the aggregate demand curve at AD_1.

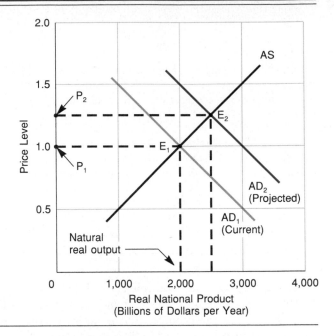

inflation. The threat stems from a projected growth in the private components of aggregate demand—a surge in export demand, a consumer spending boom, or an increase in planned investment. If something is not done, say the forecasters, the aggregate demand curve for the coming year will shift rightward to AD_2. That will drive the economy up and to the right along the aggregate supply curve to E_2.

The result will be an increase in the price level from P_1 to P_2. Moreover, upward pressure on the price level may persist beyond the following year. A rise in final goods prices in the coming year can cause a rise in wages and other input prices in successive years. As a result, the short-term rise in the price level shown in Exhibit 11.3 may touch off a lasting inflationary spiral. For reasons to be discussed in later chapters, such an inflationary spiral, once established, is hard to bring under control.

Restrictive fiscal policy is one means of warding off the inflation threat. The federal budget for the coming year can be written to include a combination of cuts in government purchases and increases in net taxes that will offset the projected increases in private aggregate demand. Suppose that the marginal propensity to consume is .75 as in our earlier examples. For each $100 by which aggregate demand is projected to shift beyond the level needed to reach the natural level of real output, government purchases can be cut by $25 or net taxes increased by $33. The right combination of cuts in government purchases, cuts in transfer payments, and increases in taxes will hold the aggregate demand curve in the desired position at AD_1.

Expansionary Fiscal Policy as a Source of Inflation

In the preceding example, federal policymakers have played the "good guys," crafting a sensible budget with which to restrain inflation. That is the role we would hope for them to play. However, the same diagram could be used to tell a different story.

In this scenario, the economy is peacefully in equilibrium at E_1 and forecasters expect it to stay there. However, there is an election coming up. Members of Congress would like to please the voters by boosting federal benefits, cutting taxes, and initiating public works projects. The president, who is also up for reelection, is happy to cooperate. At the end of August of the election year, Congress votes a grossly expansionary budget for the coming year. The president signs it in a televised ceremony with smiling congressional leaders looking on. Voters are pleased, and everyone is reelected.

The next year the new budget goes into effect, shifting the aggregate demand curve rightward to AD_2. Prices start to creep up and threaten to gallop before long. The hangover from the election year party sets in, leaving the country with some hard choices of how to set things aright.

Automatic Fiscal Policy

The type of fiscal policy discussed so far—that is, changes in the laws setting government purchases, taxes, and transfer payments made for the purpose of affecting aggregate demand—is known as **discretionary fiscal policy.** In practice, however, the levels of government purchases and net taxes can change even if no discretionary changes are made in the laws governing them. The reason is that many tax and spending laws are written in such a way that the levels of fiscal policy variables change automatically as economic conditions vary. Such changes in government purchases or net taxes, which are known as **automatic fiscal policy,** are most closely associated with changes in real output, the price level, and interest rates. In some cases, the changes are real; in others, they are only nominal.

Discretionary fiscal policy
Changes in the laws setting government purchases and net taxes.

Automatic fiscal policy
Changes in government purchases or net taxes caused by changes in economic conditions given unchanged tax and spending laws.

Changes in Real Output

The level of real output is important because it affects both tax receipts and outlays. An increase in real output increases real revenues from all major tax sources, including income taxes, social security payroll taxes, corporate profits taxes, and sales taxes. At the same time, an increase in real output cuts real government outlays for transfer payments. This occurs largely because increases in real output are associated with decreases in the unemployment rate. Taking both effects together, an increase in real national product tends to reduce the federal budget deficit in both real and nominal terms.

Changes in the Inflation Rate

An increase in the inflation rate affects both sides of the federal budget. With real output held fixed, an increase in inflation tends to increase federal tax receipts in nominal terms. Where tax rates are not indexed—that is, not adjusted automatically to reflect inflation—inflation can also cause real tax receipts to rise. This used to be the case with the federal income tax. However, income taxes are now indexed so that inflation does not push taxpayers into higher tax brackets. At the same time, an increase in the inflation rate tends to increase nominal expenditures. This is partly because most major transfer programs are now indexed so that they can be adjusted for changes in the cost of living and partly because inflation raises the prices of the goods and services that government buys. However, as pointed out before, some elements of government expenditures are fixed in nominal terms. This means that the increase in nominal expenditures will tend to be less than proportional to the increase in the price level, so that real expenditures will fall.

Estimating the Impact of Economic Growth, Interest Rates, and Inflation on the 1988 Federal Budget Deficit

Every January, the president sends a proposed budget to Congress that serves as the basis for spending and tax decisions for the coming year. When the president's budget message arrives, it is the job of the Congressional Budget Office (CBO) to review the assumptions on which it is based and call the attention of Congress to any possible trouble spots. In particular, the CBO looks at the economic and other technical assumptions that were used by the Office of Management and Budget (OMB), which prepares the president's message. If the OMB's assumptions are too optimistic, the CBO must warn Congress that it will be harder to make ends meet than the president's message indicates.

This was the case with the budget for fiscal year 1988, submitted to Congress by President Reagan in January 1987. The president's budget message forecasted a $108 billion deficit if all recommended program changes were adopted. The CBO reported to Congress, however, that even with adoption of all the president's programs, the deficit would be closer to $134 billion. Why the difference?

One source of the discrepancy was a more optimistic administration forecast for economic growth. The OMB projected a 3.7 percent real growth rate for 1988, which

would bring the unemployment rate down to 6.3 percent. According to the CBO, 2.9 percent real growth would be more realistic, lowering the unemployment rate to only 6.5 percent. This adjustment alone added $20 billion to the deficit estimate.

A second source of the difference concerned interest rates. The OMB projected a 5.6 percent rate for 3-month Treasury bills and a 6.6 percent rate for 10-year government bonds, while the CBO projected interest rates of 5.7 and 7.2 percent, respectively. This added another $3 billion to the deficit estimate.

A third adjustment partially offset the first two. The administration had forecasted a 3.6 percent increase in the consumer price index, while the CBO thought 4.4 percent was more realistic. If the CBO's estimate of inflation were correct, the deficit would be $8 billion below the administration's forecast for that reason alone.

The net effect of the various economic assumptions used by the OMB, then, was to increase the OMB's deficit estimate by $15 billion. That included a forecast of $9.7 billion lower revenues and $5.3 billion higher outlays. In addition, the CBO disagreed on technical grounds with the administration's projections for medicare and medicaid outlays and certain other items. These technical adjustments added another $11 billion to the estimated budget deficit.

As Senator Everett Dirksen once said, "A million here, a million there—pretty soon it adds up to real money."

Source: Congress of the United States, Congressional Budget Office, *An Analysis of the President's Budgetary Proposals for Fiscal Year 1988* (Washington, D.C.: Government Printing Office, 1987).

If all elements of the budget were indexed, an increase in the price level would have no effect on the real deficit. In practice, the budget is not perfectly indexed, so that nominal taxes rise more both absolutely and in percentage terms than nominal expenditures. Thus, an increase in the price level, other things being equal, reduces the deficit in nominal terms and causes a proportionately greater reduction in the real deficit.

Changes in Interest Rates

An increase in interest rates raises the nominal cost of financing the national debt. This is only slightly offset by increases in nominal government interest income. Therefore, on balance, an increase in interest rates shifts the budget toward deficit both in nominal and real terms.

"Applying Economic Ideas 11.1" illustrates the effects of different forecasts for real output, inflation, and interest rates on the federal government's projected 1988 budget.

Automatic Stabilization

We have seen that when the economy expands real output rises, the price level rises, and unemployment falls. Each of these effects tends to move the government budget toward surplus in real terms, that is, either to increase receipts, depress outlays, or both. Whichever side of the budget we look at, then, automatic fiscal policy operates so as to restrain aggregate demand during an expansion. By the same token, when the economy slows down, the growth rate of real output drops and unemployment rises. The inflation rate slows even if the contraction is not severe enough to cause the price level actually to fall. Thus, during a contraction the federal budget swings toward deficit.

Because automatic fiscal policy operates to offset changes in other elements of planned expenditure, budget components such as income taxes and unemployment benefits are known as **automatic stabilizers.** These mechanisms serve to moderate the economy's response to changes in consumption, private planned investment, and net exports.

Automatic stabilizers
Those elements of automatic fiscal policy that move the federal budget toward deficit during a contraction and toward surplus during an expansion.

Fiscal Policy in the Income-Expenditure Model[2]

The income-expenditure model developed in Chapter 10 provides an alternate way of looking at the effects of fiscal policy. This income-expenditure model has the advantage of focusing more directly on the multiplier effect. However, it can be misleading if not used cautiously, because it tends to lose sight of the effects of changes in the price level.

Fiscal Stimulus

Part a of Exhibit 11.4 uses the fixed-price version of the income-expenditure model to show how fiscal stimulus can be used to avoid a recession. In this case, we suppose that policymakers wish to keep the economy at its natural level of real output of $2,000 billion. However, as they prepare a budget for the coming year, their forecasters say that given current tax and spending laws, planned expenditure will be insufficient and the planned-expenditure schedule will slip to PE_1, putting equilibrium national income at only $1,000 billion.

In order to keep income at the natural level, the planned-expenditure schedule must be at PE_2 rather than PE_1. If nothing is done, the shortfall of autonomous expenditure will cause a recession. The autonomous-expenditure shortfall is shown by the vertical gap between the two planned-expenditure curves. As the exhibit is drawn, the shortfall is $250 billion.

To avoid the recession, tax and spending laws must be changed so as to plug the gap. A $250 billion increase in government purchases would be one way to do this. Another would be to stimulate autonomous consumption through a cut in autonomous net taxes. However, it must be kept in mind that a $250 billion cut in autonomous net taxes will not be enough to fill the gap. The reason is that households will spend only $.75 of each $1 of added disposable income that the tax cut (or increase in transfers) provides. A $250 billion upward shift of the planned-expenditure curve will thus require a $333 billion cut in autonomous net taxes.

Note that the $1,000 billion gap between the projected level of national income and the natural level equals the expenditure multiplier times the shortfall

---

[2]If Chapter 10 was omitted, omit this section also and turn to p. 268.

Exhibit 11.4   Fiscal Policy in the Income-Expenditure Model

This exhibit illustrates fiscal policy in terms of the fixed-price income-expenditure model introduced in Chapter 10. In part a, forecasters project an equilibrium real national income for the coming year that is $1,000 billion below the natural level. The low equilibrium value for national income is caused by a $250 billion shortfall of autonomous planned expenditure. A $250 billion increase in government purchases or a $333 billion cut in autonomous net taxes will restore autonomous expenditures to the desired level, shifting the planned-expenditure curve from PE_1 to PE_2. In part b, the situation is reversed. A projected excess of autonomous expenditure will put the planned-expenditure curve at PE_3 unless something is done. The prescription for this situation is a $250 billion cut in government purchases or a $333 billion increase in autonomous net taxes.

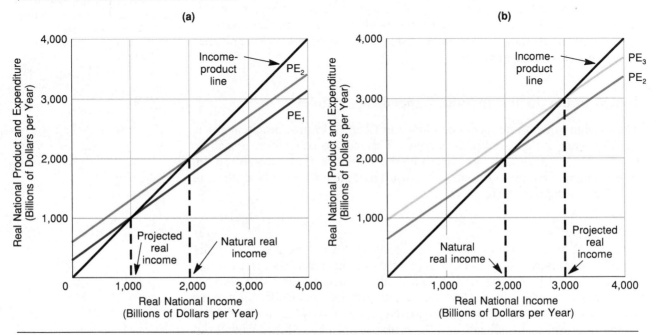

of autonomous expenditure. It also equals the required cut in autonomous net taxes times the net tax multiplier.

Fiscal Restraint

Part b of Exhibit 11.4 shows how fiscal restraint can be used to stem an excess of aggregate demand that would cause real output to rise above its natural level—an occurrence that would cause inflation in a flexible-price world. In this case, we suppose that forecasts for the coming year show that with current tax and spending laws, the planned-expenditure curve will be at PE_3. This will cause equilibrium national income to rise to $3,000 billion, which is $1,000 billion above the natural level. Unless something is done, there will be an overheating of the economy.

The overshoot of real national income is produced by a projected excess of autonomous expenditure, shown by the vertical gap between PE_2 and PE_3 in part b of Exhibit 11.4. Fiscal policy can be used to close this gap as in the case of recession, but the direction of the policy change must be reversed: Either government purchases must be cut by $250 billion, autonomous net taxes increased by $333 billion, or some combination of the two.

A Change in the Income Tax Rate

The preceding examples looked at the effects of changes in government purchases and autonomous net taxes. The income-expenditure model can also be used to show the effects of a change in the marginal tax rate.

In Exhibit 11.5, the natural level of real income is again assumed to be $2,000 billion. Forecasts show that if no changes are made in tax or spending laws in the coming year, the planned-expenditure schedule will be at PE_1, which is based on a marginal propensity to consume of .75 and a 33 percent marginal tax rate. As we saw in Chapter 10, the slope of the planned-expenditure schedule under these conditions is mpc $(1 - t)$ or, in this case, .5; this means that the expenditure multiplier is 2. Total autonomous expenditure is $800 billion, as seen from the vertical intercept of the planned-expenditure schedule. The projected level of national income ($1,600 billion) equals total autonomous expenditure ($800 billion) times the expenditure multiplier (2).

The equilibrium level of national income can be increased to $2,000 billion without changing the level of autonomous expenditure if the planned-expenditure schedule is shifted to PE_2. This can be done by cutting the marginal tax rate from .33 to .20. The slope of the planned-expenditure schedule will then increase from .5 to .6. The expenditure multiplier for the new schedule will be 2.5. Applying that multiplier to the same $800 billion of autonomous expenditure will yield the required $2,000 billion equilibrium level of national income.

A Word of Caution

Exhibits 11.3 and 11.4 are based on the fixed-price version of the income-expenditure model. Thus, they exaggerate the impact of a given change in government purchases, taxes, or transfer payments on the equilibrium level of real national income. In a flexible-price world, as we saw in Chapter 10, price changes would cause additional shifts in the planned-expenditure schedule that

---

Exhibit 11.5   Using a Change in the Marginal Tax Rate to Boost Planned Expenditure

This exhibit shows how a change in the marginal tax rate of an income or payroll tax can be used to boost planned expenditure. Initially forecasts show a projected equilibrium real national income of $1,600 billion, $400 billion short of the natural level. This projection assumes $800 billion in autonomous planned expenditures, a marginal propensity to consume of .75, and a marginal tax rate of .33; the slope of planned-expenditure schedule PE_1 is, consequently, .5. By cutting the marginal tax rate to .20 with no change in autonomous planned expenditure, the slope of the planned-expenditure schedule is increased to .6. This puts the planned-expenditure schedule at PE_2, which restores equilibrium real national income to its natural level.

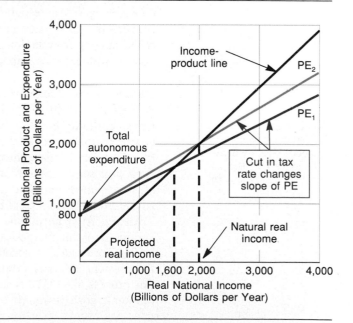

would offset some of the impact of the fiscal policies considered here even in the short run and could very well offset them completely in the long run. Hence, when the price level is subject to change—as it is in the real U.S. economy—the aggregate supply and demand model gives a better picture of the effects of fiscal policy than does the fixed-price income-expenditure model.

U.S. Fiscal Policy in the 1980s

The discussion of fiscal policy in the preceding section is couched in terms of what ought to be done to stabilize the economy at its natural level of real output. Our discussion would be incomplete, however, without at least a brief look at the important question of how federal officials actually go about making tax and spending decisions.

The actual decision-making process for fiscal policy often has little to do—and sometimes nothing at all to do—with the theory we have just discussed. The large federal budget deficits that have made headlines throughout the 1980s have not been the product of systematic decisions to apply fiscal stimulus. Rather, they are better understood as the residual outcome of a certain set of spending decisions and another of tax decisions, neither of which have focused consistently on macroeconomic goals.

We will begin our survey of U.S. fiscal policy in the 1980s with a discussion of the budget-making process and its limitations. We will then turn to budget priorities. Finally, we will examine the federal deficit and the national debt that have resulted from recent tax and spending decisions.

The Federal Budgetary System

Economists view fiscal policy as the management of aggregate demand through changes in taxes, transfers, and government purchases. However, the federal budgetary process is more complex than this definition suggests. For one thing, no single agency is responsible for fiscal policy; budgetary authority is divided between the president and Congress. Also, budgetary policy must serve many goals, ranging from national security and social equity to simple political ambition, as well as price stability, full employment, and economic growth.

Outline of the Budgetary System

Fiscal year
The federal government's budgetary year, which starts on October 1 of the preceding calendar year.

A brief look at the federal budgetary process will give an idea of where the formal authority for fiscal policy lies. The U.S. government operates on a **fiscal year** that runs from October through September; for example, fiscal 1989 runs from October 1, 1988, through September 30, 1989. About 18 months before a fiscal year starts, the executive branch begins preparing the budget. The Office of Management and Budget (OMB) takes the lead in this process. It receives advice from the Council of Economic Advisers (CEA) and the Department of the Treasury. After an outline of the budget has been drawn up, it is sent to the various departments and agencies. Within the executive branch, a period of bargaining ensues in which the Pentagon argues for more arms spending, the Department of Transportation for more highway spending, and so on. During this process, the OMB is supposed to act as a restraining force and keep macroeconomic goals in mind.

By January—nine months before the fiscal year starts—the president must submit the budget to Congress. After that, Congress assumes the lead in the budgetary process. Its committees and subcommittees look at the president's proposals for the programs and agencies under their jurisdiction. The Congressional Budget Office (CBO) maintains a staff of professionals who advise the committees on economic matters; somewhat as the OMB and CEA advise the president. In May, the House and Senate are expected to pass a first budget resolution that sets forth overall spending targets and revenue goals.

Bargaining among committees, between the House and Senate, and between Congress and the executive branch continues throughout the summer. Committees prepare specific spending and tax laws during this period; these are supposed to be guided by the May resolution. Finally, in September, Congress is supposed to pass a second budget resolution that sets binding limits on spending and taxes for the fiscal year beginning October 1. Any bills passed earlier that do not fit within these guidelines are expected to be changed accordingly.

Limitations of the Budgetary Process

In practice, many things can—and do—go wrong with this process.

The first and most basic problem is that macroeconomic goals—full employment, price stability, and economic growth—in practice carry little weight in the budgetary process. The actual tax and spending decisions are made in dozens of subcommittees, where they are dominated by interest group pressures, vote trading, and the desire of each member of Congress to help the folks at home.

A second problem is that Congress has proven unwilling to follow its own rules. The required budget resolutions often do not get passed on time; if passed, they are not treated as binding. Often the fiscal year starts without a budget. Then agencies must operate on the basis of "continuing resolutions," meaning that they can go on doing whatever they were doing the year before. In 1986, Congress failed to pass a single one of the appropriations bills that are supposed to set spending for various government areas. In a last-minute rush, Congress passed a massive continuing resolution that rolled all spending decisions for the entire year into a single vote. In some years even the continuing resolutions have not been passed on time, and federal workers have had to be sent home until there were funds to pay them.

Finally, there is the problem of so-called "uncontrollable" costs. These include **entitlements,** which are transfer programs governed by long-term laws that are not subject to annual budget review. Examples include social security, military retirement pay, and medicare. Another major expense that is uncontrollable—for a different reason—is interest on the national debt. Given the debt's size, its interest costs are determined by market interest rates that, in turn, are influenced by many factors beyond the control of fiscal policy. Today well over half of the federal budget is in the "uncontrollable" category. Of course, Congress could control most of these costs by passing new laws to replace the current ones, but doing so is not part of the normal budgetary process.

Entitlements
Transfer payments governed by long-term laws that are not subject to annual budget review.

"The basic fact is," writes Herbert Stein, a former chairman of the Council of Economic Advisers, "that we have no long-run budget policy—no policy for the size of deficits and for the rate of growth of the public debt over a period of years." Each year the president and Congress make short-term budgetary decisions that are wholly inconsistent with their declared long-run goals, hoping "that something will happen or be done before the long-run arises, but not yet."[3]

The Gramm-Rudman-Hollings Experiment

In 1985, Congress made a heroic attempt to reform the budgetary system. The focus of its effort was on reducing the federal deficit as a symbol of concern for the macroeconomic impact of the federal budget. The result was the Gramm-Rudman-Hollings law, passed in December 1985. In that year (that is, fiscal year 1986), the federal budget deficit was a record $221 billion. The law established a declining set of deficit targets, beginning with $144 billion for fiscal 1987, $108 billion for fiscal 1988, and so on until the deficit would be eliminated in 1991. An exception was written into the law allowing the deficit ceiling to be waived in the event of a recession.

The feature that was supposed to give Gramm-Rudman-Hollings some real teeth was a provision for making mandatory spending cuts if Congress and the administration failed to come up with a budget that would come within $10 billion of the law's targets. Suppose, for example, that Congress passed and the president signed laws that would result in a $158 billion deficit for fiscal 1988 despite a set deficit limit of $108 billion. In that case, spending would automatically have to be cut by $50 billion. However, programs comprising over half the budget were shielded from the Gramm-Rudman-Hollings ax. The protected programs included social security, medicare, the major antipoverty programs, and interest on the national debt. Each of the remaining budget areas—national defense and unprotected domestic programs—were to bear about half of any automatic reductions. The bill's sponsors hoped that the mandatory cuts would not be necessary and that instead the threat of such cuts would force Congress to make rational decisions on budget priorities.

The original Gramm-Rudman-Hollings experiment was at best a mixed success. The Supreme Court found its key provision—the mandatory budget cuts—to be unconstitutional. Both President Reagan and Congress resolved to adhere voluntarily to the Gramm-Rudman-Hollings schedule for deficit reductions and they agreed to work together on a new version of the law. Plans fitting the original targets were submitted for fiscal 1987 and 1988. However, the actual deficit for fiscal 1987 failed to fall within the $144 billion target despite a substantial one-time boost to tax receipts stemming from the implementation of tax reform. Even so, the 1987 deficit—and, according to projections, the 1988 deficit as well—were substantially below the record deficit of 1986. How much higher they would have been without the Gramm-Rudman-Hollings law and whether a new version of the law will work no one can say for sure.

Budgetary Priorities in the 1980s

Many people both inside and outside government castigate Congress and the White House for an inability to set priorities. In one sense, the failure to adhere to an orderly budgetary process and the tendency to lump everything into "continuing resolutions" bear this out. But in another sense, it can be said that priorities have been set—that is, those implicit in the decisions that actually have been made. Let's see what these priorities were.

---

[3]Herbert Stein, "After the Ball," *AEI Economist* (December 1984): 2.

Exhibit 11.6 Federal Revenues, Outlays, and Deficit as a Percentage of GNP

This exhibit shows federal revenues, outlays, and deficits as a percentage of GNP for the period 1962 to 1986. Column 1 shows that despite the cuts in personal income tax rates that resulted from the 1981 tax law, federal revenues took about the same share of GNP in the 1980s as in earlier years. Federal outlays, on the other hand, have grown to record levels, as shown in Column 2. The conclusion is that the increase in the federal deficit, shown in column 3, stems from spending increases rather than tax cuts.

Period	Revenues (1)	Outlays (2)	Deficit (3)
1962–1965	17.9%	18.6%	0.8%
1966–1970	18.8	19.7	0.9
1971–1975	18.1	20.0	1.9
1976–1980	18.5	21.4	2.8
1981–1985	18.9	23.6	4.7
1986	18.5	23.8	5.3

Source: Jonathan Rauch, "The Fiscal Ice Age," *National Journal*, January 10, 1987, 63.

Taxes and Spending

Exhibit 11.6 gives data on federal taxes and total federal outlays (government purchases of goods and services plus transfer payments) from the 1960s to the 1980s. Column 1 shows that cutting the overall tax burden, as opposed to cutting tax rates for selected taxpayers, was not taken seriously as a priority. The share of federal taxes in GNP held roughly steady from the mid-1960s through the 1980s. Cutting government spending was an even lower priority. Column 2 shows that outlays rose to an unprecedented share of GNP in the 1980s. Thus, despite the Reagan administration's pledge to cut taxes, hold the line on spending, and balance the budget, the story told by the numbers is a rise in the deficit caused not by tax cuts but by spending increases.

Priorities among Programs

Exhibit 11.7 shows what happened to the composition of federal spending by type of program. Column 1 shows that with respect to national defense, announced priorities were carried out. The share of GNP going to defense did rise significantly from 1981 to 1986. However, some qualifications are in order.

First, the base from which the 1980s defense buildup began was a low point for the post–World War II years—so low, in fact, that the Democratic Carter administration, in its last budget, had already shifted spending toward defense. The 1980s thus can be viewed as the continuation of a trend that began at the end of the 1970s. Second, although Exhibit 11.7 does not show it, there *were* indications that 1986 would turn out to be the peak of the defense buildup. The bipartisan consensus that propelled the buildup in the early 1980s was weakened, if not broken, toward the middle of the decade.

If the numbers are allowed to speak for themselves, another spending priority has been entitlements, as shown in column 2 of Exhibit 11.7. The Reagan administration and Congress, in deed if not always in word, agreed that entitlements were untouchable. A balanced budget, slowdown of government growth, and cutting the tax burden all ranked behind entitlements in terms of priorities.

Exhibit 11.7   Composition of the Federal Budget as a Percentage of GNP

This exhibit shows the changing composition of the federal budget from 1962 to 1986. Figures give each category of expenditure as a percentage of GNP. The 1980s have seen defense spending rise toward the average level for earlier years, starting from the unusually low base of the late 1970s. Entitlements continued the unbroken upward trend of earlier years, with a slight drop in 1986. High interest rates and a growing national debt meant that interest on the national debt consumed an increasing share of GNP. Discretionary nondefense spending was the big loser, falling from 5.5 percent of GNP (25 percent of all federal outlays) in the late 1970s to 4.1 percent of GNP (17 percent of all federal outlays) in 1986. However, cuts in this category were just enough to offset the increase in interest costs.

Period	Defense (1)	Entitlements (2)	Interest (3)	Discretionary Nondefense (4)	Total (5)
1962–1965	8.8%	5.5%	1.3%	4.4%	18.6%
1966–1970	8.7	6.1	1.4	4.8	19.7
1971–1975	6.3	8.8	1.4	4.8	20.0
1976–1980	5.0	10.3	1.7	5.5	21.4
1981–1985	6.0	11.3	2.8	4.8	23.6
1986	6.6	11.0	3.3	4.1	23.8

Source: Jonathan Rauch, "The Fiscal Ice Age," *National Journal*, January 10, 1987, 63. Details do not round to totals because offsetting receipts have been omitted.

This can be seen, for example, in the Gramm-Rudman-Hollings bill, which exempted most entitlements, but not defense, from automatic budget cuts.

Within the entitlements budget, the fastest-growing segment consisted of programs for the elderly. The share of the entitlement budget going to social security and medicare began to increase during the 1970s. By 1980 it had reached 54 percent of the entitlement budget, and by 1986 59 percent.

Column 3 of Exhibit 11.7 shows the increasing share of GNP taken by interest on the national debt. This reflects partly higher interest rates and partly growth of the debt itself. Once the debt is incurred, there is no way to control this category of spending. However, debt grew so rapidly because balancing the budget has ranked lower on the list of priorities than entitlements and defense.

Finally, column 4 of the exhibit shows the big budgetary loser in the 1980s—discretionary nondefense spending. This includes everything from student aid to the federal judiciary to national parks. If the Reagan administration's budget-cutting intentions had any impact, it was here. But all discretionary nondefense programs combined add up to only a small fraction of the total budget. The cuts in this category—from 25 percent of the total budget in the late 1970s to just 17 percent by 1986—were not enough to offset the rise in interest payments on the debt.

Consumption versus Investment

In the eyes of many observers, there is another priority hidden in the federal budgets of the 1980s: that of consumption over investment. One way to think of this is in terms of the circular flow of income and product. Setting aside the foreign sector for a moment, as in Exhibit 6.5 (page 141), there is one flow of saving into financial markets, namely net private domestic savings. This must finance two outflows: private investment and the combined budget deficit of federal, state, and local governments. What is used for one purpose cannot be used for another. In the 1960s, net private domestic saving was 8.1 percent of GNP. The combined government deficit took .3 percent, leaving 7.8 percent potentially available for private investment. In the 1970s, saving held steady at 8.1 percent of GNP but the deficit grew to .9 percent, leaving 7.2 percent for private investment. In the 1980s, saving fell to 6.2 percent of GNP while the combined government deficit grew to 2.6 percent, leaving just 3.9 percent for private investment.

Taking the foreign sector into account gives domestic private investment a little more breathing room than these figures suggest. In the 1960s and 1970s, part of U.S. domestic savings went to making investments abroad. In the 1980s, borrowing from foreign sources has allowed U.S. private investment to stay one GNP percentage point or more higher than it otherwise would be. Thus, the actual drop in net private domestic investment has been from 6.9 percent of GNP in the 1970s to 4.6 percent in the 1980s—still a major shift.

There are other indications of priority being given to consumption over investment. These include reductions in federal civilian research and development spending and support for education; a shift in federal capital spending away from civilian infrastructure projects, such as highways and sewers, toward defense goods, such as aircraft carriers; and, with the 1986 tax reform, a shift from taxes on households toward taxes on business.

On balance, then, fiscal priorities in the 1980s can be characterized as follows:

- A priority for holding the line on the overall tax burden but not for actually cutting it; low priorities for restricting total spending and the federal deficit.

- A high priority for increasing defense spending; a slightly lower priority for increasing entitlements; a moderate priority for reducing discretionary nondefense spending.

- A priority for consumption at the expense of investment.

The Debate over the Deficit and the National Debt

Federal budget deficits are not new to the 1980s. What distinguishes the deficits of the 1980s is their size. Between 1950 and 1980, the cumulative deficit was $388 billion, slightly offset by a cumulative $17 billion surplus. In the 1980s, as much has been added to the cumulative deficit every 2 years as in the previous 30, and there have been no offsetting federal surpluses. In this section, we look at some economic principles that will shed some light on the origins of the deficit and its effects.

Structural versus Cyclical Deficit

The first distinction to be made concerns the origins of the federal deficit. In part, the deficit is a result of discretionary policy decisions. However, policymakers do not determine precise levels of government receipts and expenditures. Instead, they pass general laws setting tax rates, benefit formulas for transfer payments, and goals for purchases of goods and services. Given these laws, the actual levels of receipts and expenditures are strongly affected by the stage of the business cycle. As we saw earlier in the chapter, the budget shifts toward deficit when the economy contracts, as tax collections fall and transfer payments rise. During expansions, the budget shifts toward surplus.

One way to sort out the effects of discretionary policy changes from those of the business cycle is to calculate what the federal surplus or deficit would be at the natural rate of unemployment. An unemployment rate of 6 percent, which is thought to be close to the natural rate, is commonly used as a benchmark.

Structural deficit
The budget surplus or deficit that the federal government would incur given current tax and spending laws and a 6 percent unemployment rate.

Cyclical deficit
The difference between the actual federal deficit and the structural deficit.

The budget surplus or deficit that the federal government would run given the 6 percent benchmark unemployment rate is called the **structural deficit.** Changes in the structural deficit are interpreted as representing discretionary fiscal policy. The difference between the actual and structural deficits is called the **cyclical deficit.** When unemployment rises above the 6 percent benchmark level, the cyclical deficit becomes positive because the actual deficit exceeds the structural deficit. When unemployment falls below the benchmark, the actual deficit is less than the structural deficit. At such times, the cyclical deficit is negative. Changes in the cyclical deficit reflect changes in taxes and spending that occur automatically as real output, unemployment, and inflation change over the course of the business cycle.

Exhibit 11.8 shows actual and structural federal budget deficits for the U.S. economy in relation to GNP in recent years. The cyclical deficit appears on the chart as the difference between the two. Note the continued growth of the structural deficit even after the actual deficit was stabilized, as a percentage of GNP, after 1982. From 1982 to 1986, growth of the structural deficit was offset by a drop in the cyclical deficit as the unemployment rate declined toward 6 percent.

The Deficit as a Policy Issue

As far back as the 1930s, when Keynesian theories of discretionary fiscal policy were first gaining popularity, fiscal conservatives became worried about the asymmetry of fiscal policy. They warned that if the government allows larger and more frequent deficits than surpluses, it will run up an endlessly growing national debt that could lead to financial ruin. They also raised some important questions: Can the government go on spending beyond its means forever? Should the government be required to balance its budget each year, financing all programs on a pay-as-you-go basis, in order to avoid bankruptcy? Even if debts are paid on time, does financing today's spending programs with borrowed money create distortions in the economy and place an unfair burden on future generations?

Almost half a century after Keynes, these questions are still being asked. They have been given new prominence by the growing size of the deficit. In addition, the size of the national debt—the accumulated result of past deficits—has begun to grow as a percentage of GNP after reaching a post–World War II low in 1974 (see Exhibit 11.9).

Many economists—and noneconomists as well—regard the current size of the federal deficit relative to GNP with foreboding. We will look at their reasons for worrying shortly. But before turning to the worries, we should look briefly at the thinking of a minority of economists who believe that the concern over the current level of the federal deficit has been overblown.

Exhibit 11.8   Cyclical and Structural Federal Deficits, 1970–1986

This chart breaks down the actual federal deficit stated as a percentage of GNP into cyclical and structural components. The structural component is the estimated deficit that would be produced given current tax and spending laws and a 6 percent unemployment rate. The cyclical component is the difference between the actual deficit and the structural component. Note the increase in the structural deficit after 1981. This growth is attributable to increased defense and entitlements spending.

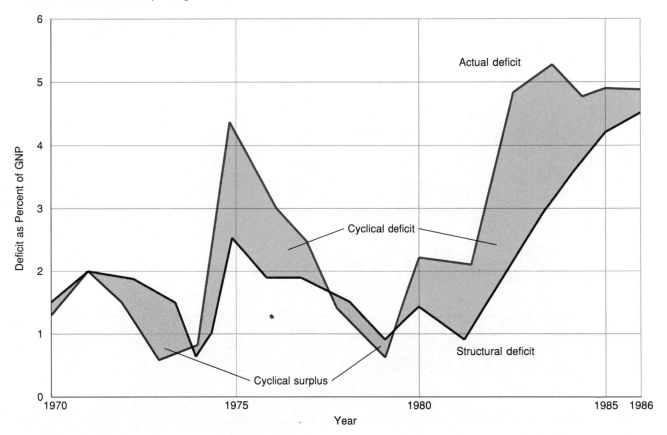

Source: Department of Commerce, Bureau of Economic Analysis. The actual deficit is given on a calendar year national income accounts basis. The structural deficit is the Department of Commerce's cyclically adjusted deficit as it would be if GNP followed a trend reflecting 6 percent unemployment.

Reasons Not to Worry about the Deficit

Economists who argue that the federal deficit is nothing to worry about begin by making a series of numerical adjustments. These adjustments, they say, show that the federal deficit is not really as large as it seems, either in absolute terms or by comparison with past years. We will look at four of these adjustments here.

Adjusting for the State and Local Surplus

The first adjustment is based on the notion that it is not the federal deficit that matters but the combined deficit or surplus of federal, state, and local govern-

Exhibit 11.9 Federal Debt Held by Private Investors as a
Percentage of Gross National Product, 1940–1986

As this chart shows, the federal debt reached a record high of 108 percent of GNP at the
end of World War II. From that time through 1974, the debt grew less rapidly than GNP.
Since 1974, this trend has been reversed. The debt is now growing in relation to GNP.

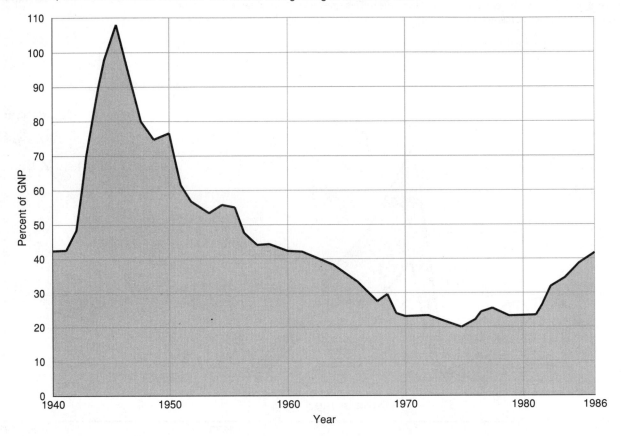

Source: Office of Management and Budget. Data exclude the portion of the federal debt held by
federal agencies and the Federal Reserve.

ments. While the federal government has been running record-breaking deficits,
state and local governments have been running unprecedented surpluses. Thus,
the consolidated government deficit was a smaller percentage of GNP in 1986
than it was in 1975.

Adjusting for the Cyclical Component
In assessing the impact of fiscal policy on the economy, the federal deficit should
also be adjusted to remove its cyclical component. The reason is that the cyclical
component reflects the state of the economy rather than discretionary policy
decisions. For example, in 1983, when the unemployment rate averaged 9.6
percent, this adjustment would have taken some $88 billion off the deficit. By
1986, however, when the unemployment rate had dropped below 7 percent, this
adjustment became much less important.

Adjusting for Capital Expenditures

Households and private firms routinely make a distinction between borrowing for purposes of capital investment and borrowing to cover current expenses. Suppose, for example, that you borrow $1,000 to take a vacation. You enjoy the vacation, but you acquire nothing tangible to offset the burden of paying off the loan in the months ahead. On the other hand, suppose you borrow $60,000 to buy a townhouse. Doing so allows you to move out of your rented apartment. In this case, you acquire a tangible asset to offset the debt, and your saving in rent offsets your monthly mortgage payments.

The federal government makes no such distinction between capital and current expenses in figuring its surplus or deficit, but many economists think that it should. After all, suppose that the government builds a new office building to replace rented office space. The funds borrowed to finance the construction will be no burden on taxpayers, because interest payments on the borrowing will be offset by reduced rent payments. Federal government net capital spending is hard to calculate precisely, but estimates suggest that the adjustment for the mid-1980s should be on the order of $20 billion per year.[4]

Adjusting for Inflation

A final adjustment is needed to take the effects of inflation into account. Each year inflation erodes the real value of federal debt held by the public. In order to maintain the real value of federal securities they hold, private investors must reinvest a portion of the federal interest payments they receive. For example, in 1983 the nominal value of federal debt in the hands of private investors was about $1 trillion and the inflation rate was about 4 percent. Thus, private investors would be willing to absorb $40 billion in new nominal debt just to keep the real value of the total debt constant. This part of the deficit, it is argued, puts no burden on the rest of the economy. Some economists claim that the deficit should be adjusted for the expected inflation rate rather than for the actual rate. In recent years the expected rate has been higher than the actual rate, which would make for a larger adjustment.

Exhibit 11.10 summarizes these four adjustments to the federal deficit for 1983 and 1986. When allowances are made for state and local surpluses, the cyclical component of the deficit, capital spending by government, and inflation, the 1983 deficit of $179 billion, considered shocking at the time, actually turns into a $13 billion surplus. Adjustments to the 1986 deficit are less dramatic but still substantial.

The Deficit and Private Saving

Some economists offer another, rather different reason not to worry about the deficit. This is based on Robert Barro's argument, mentioned in "Perspective 11.1," that changes in taxes tend to be fully offset by changes in private saving. If true, this means that the burden the federal budget puts on the rest of the economy depends only on the level of government purchases, not on how they

---

[4]Robert Eisner has estimated federal net investment at $20 billion for 1982. See "Which Budget Deficit?" *American Economic Review* 74 (May 1984): 138–143. Using a different methodology, Michael J. Boskin, Marc S. Robinson, and John M. Roberts have estimated federal net investment at $23 billion for 1983 and $19 billion for 1984. See "New Estimates of Federal Government Tangible Capital and Net Investment" (Working Paper No. 1774, National Bureau of Economic Research, December 1985).

Exhibit 11.10   Adjustments to the Federal Deficit,
1983 and 1986 (Billions of Dollars)

In nominal terms, the federal deficit rose to record levels in both 1983 and 1986. Many
people found these numbers alarming, but some economists think they overstate the
deficit's impact on the economy. To assess the true impact, they say, the deficit should be
adjusted to take into account state and local government surpluses, the cyclical component
of the federal deficit, capital spending by the federal government, and the effects of inflation.
As this exhibit shows, these adjustments turn the $179 billion federal deficit for 1983 into a
$13 billion surplus. They reduce the 1986 deficit to $76 billion. The data are for calendar
years on a national income accounts basis.

	1983	1986
Actual federal deficit	$179	$205
Less:		
State and local surplus	44	61
Cyclical component of federal deficit	88	15
Capital spending by federal government	20	20
Inflation adjustment	40	33
Equals: Adjusted deficit	−$13	76

are financed. In Barro's world, the public would respond to a tax cut by increasing saving by just the amount needed to buy the extra securities the Treasury
would have to sell in order to finance the added deficit. Likewise, a tax increase
made to reduce the deficit would decrease saving by the same amount, thus
leaving no additional resources with which to finance private investment.

To be sure, most economists doubt that changes in taxes are fully offset by
changes in saving. But even if there is only a partial adjustment of saving, the
burden of the deficit will be eased and the case for raising taxes to cut the deficit
weakened.

Reasons to Worry about the Deficit

Despite the arguments just given, many economists—probably a majority of
them—still consider current and projected federal deficits a problem. Let's look
at some of their concerns.

Effects on Investment

Earlier in the chapter, we saw that when the Treasury borrows to finance a
deficit, it adds to the total demand for the limited funds made available by
private domestic saving, thus pushing up interest rates. Private borrowers are
then "crowded out" of financial markets. The reduction in private investment is
a burden on the economy that slows economic growth and reduces the living
standards of future generations. Thus, the drop in the share of net private investment in GNP from 6.9 percent in the 1970s to 4.6 percent in the 1980s is seen as
one of the most harmful effects of deficits.

Borrowing from Abroad

In defense of deficits, it is sometimes said that the national debt is something
"we owe to ourselves." By this it is meant that taxes collected for repaying the
debt come out of the pockets of some U.S. citizens but go back into the pockets

of others, leaving the country as a whole no poorer. However, it is widely argued, federal budget deficits push up interest rates in the United States relative to those in the rest of the world. Attracted by the high rates, foreign buyers purchase many of the securities that the Treasury sells to finance the deficit. In addition, since high interest rates on government securities push up the rates on competing private securities, many private U.S. securities also move into foreign hands. In future years, repaying the part of public and private debt owed to foreign investors will place a real burden on the U.S. economy. The argument that we owe it to ourselves does not apply in this case.

The Enlarged Structural Deficit

It is widely acknowledged that the cyclical component of the federal deficit is less of a problem than the structural component. What worries many economists is the way the structural component has grown in the 1980s as the cyclical component has fallen. In 1982, at the trough of the last recession, the cyclical deficit came to $85 billion out of a total deficit of $146 billion. By 1986, the cyclical component had fallen to about $15 billion and by mid-1987, to zero. Had the structural component remained constant, the actual deficit would have fallen to $76 billion, four-fifths of which would have been offset by the state and local government surplus. But instead of shrinking, the actual deficit ballooned to $205 billion as the structural deficit rose to almost $190 billion.

In short, the increase in tax receipts that came from the 1982 to 1986 expansion of the mid-1980s was used not to reduce the deficit but to finance an increase in government expenditures. A recession in the late 1980s could easily raise the cyclical deficit to $100 billion. In that event, the total deficit could approach or even surpass $300 billion. Yet tax increases or spending cuts would be problematic, because their multiplier effects would deepen the recession.

The Danger of an Exploding Deficit

The growth of the structural deficit calls attention to another worry: the growth of the part of the deficit associated with interest payments on the debt. As mentioned earlier, this part of the deficit has already doubled as a percentage of the budget since 1974. Some economists think that interest payments are poised for "explosive" growth.

In the explosive-growth scenario, the amount of borrowing needed just to make interest payments on the debt is so great that the debt grows faster than national income even if the rest of the budget remains in balance. As the government borrows more and more each year to make interest payments, it adds to the demand for loanable funds in credit markets. This pushes interest rates higher, making it necessary to borrow even more to make the interest payments. Eventually the deficit "explodes" and threatens to swallow the entire national income.[5]

As the point of explosive growth approaches, the government is left with only one way out. It begins to "monetize" the deficit, which in effect means that it finances the deficit by creating new money rather than by borrowing. But

[5]The issue of the exploding deficit was raised in Thomas J. Sargent and Neil Wallace, "Some Unpleasant Monetarist Arithmetic," *Federal Reserve Bank of Minneapolis Quarterly Review* (Fall 1981): 1–17. Michael R. Darby refines the argument by showing that the deficit will explode if the real rate of interest (that is, the nominal market rate minus the inflation rate), adjusted for the average tax rate on federal interest payments, exceeds the long-term rate of growth of real GNP. See "Some Pleasant Monetarist Arithmetic," *Federal Reserve Bank of Minneapolis Quarterly Review* (Spring 1984).

financing deficits with newly created money is the classic formula for inflation—too much money chasing too few goods. Thus, monetization of the deficit converts an explosive deficit into explosive inflation.

Is this scenario too far-fetched to be a real threat? Not at all. Creating new money to cover the government deficit is the source of the runaway inflation, at rates of hundreds or even thousands of percent per year, that devastated such countries as Bolivia, Argentina, Brazil, and Israel in the early 1980s. In the next four chapters, we will look at the mechanisms used to create and control money in the U.S. economy. In Chapter 16, we will return to the topic of runaway inflation.

Today inflation is not running out of control in the United States; in fact, it has slowed dramatically from the double-digit rates of a few years ago. Nonetheless, many economists think that the large federal deficits of the mid-1980s are a time bomb just waiting to explode. Perhaps President Reagan was right after all—maybe we *do* need to get control of the budget monster.

Summary

1. **How can fiscal policy be used to fight recession and inflation?** *Fiscal policy* means policy related to government purchases and net taxes. If a fall in private planned expenditure threatens to send the economy into a recession, an increase in government purchases or a cut in net taxes can be used to shift the aggregate demand curve to the right, restoring the economy to its natural level of real output. (In terms of the income-expenditure model, such expansionary fiscal policy will shift the planned-expenditure schedule upward.) If an excess of private planned expenditure threatens the economy with inflation, a cut in government purchases or an increase in net taxes can shift the aggregate demand curve to the left, restoring stability. (In terms of the income-expenditure model, restrictive fiscal policy will shift the planned-expenditure schedule downward.)

2. **How are government receipts and expenditures affected by changing economic conditions?** Some changes in government receipts and expenditures reflect *discretionary* changes in the laws that govern fiscal policy. However, changes in the levels of these items can also result *automatically* from changes in economic conditions, including real output, unemployment, and the price level. In general, economic expansion tends to raise receipts and restrain expenditures, thus moving the budget toward surplus. Contraction tends to lower receipts and raise expenditures, thus moving the budget toward deficit. These automatic changes in receipts and expenditures damp the economy's response to shifts in private planned expenditure and, hence, are known as *automatic stabilizers*.

3. **How does the federal budgetary system work, and what are its limitations?** Fiscal policy authority in the United States is divided between the President and Congress. Each year the President submits a budget plan, which Congress modifies and enacts into law by the start of the *fiscal year* on October 1. In practice, macroeconomic goals play a role secondary to political considerations in setting budget priorities. Also, in recent years Congress has found it difficult to follow its own budgetary rules and to pass required legislation in a timely manner.

4. **What priorities have guided federal tax and spending decisions in the 1980s?** If budget numbers are allowed to speak for themselves, they tell a different story than does the rhetoric of tax cuts and spending restrictions that has dominated the political scene in the 1980s. In practice, taxes have not been cut but have held steady as a share of GNP. The large deficits of the 1980s have been caused not by tax cuts but by increased spending. Defense and *entitlements* have accounted for the greatest spending increases. Cuts in discretionary nondefense programs—which now comprise less than a fifth of the budget—have not been enough to offset the growth in interest payments on the national debt. A final implicit fiscal priority has been to favor consumption at the expense of saving and investment.

5. **How is the federal deficit measured, and why has it grown?** The federal deficit can be divided into a cyclical and a structural component. The *structural deficit* is the estimated level of the deficit given current tax and

spending laws and a benchmark unemployment rate of 6 percent. The *cyclical deficit* is the difference between the actual and structural deficits. The cyclical deficit tends to increase in a recession and decrease in an expansion. If unemployment drops below 6 percent at the peak of an expansion, the cyclical deficit can be negative. During the expansion that followed the 1981 to 1982 recession, the cyclical component of the deficit has declined while the structural component has grown dramatically.

6. **Are large federal deficits a threat to economic stability?** The degree of threat posed by federal deficits is a matter of dispute. Some economists argue that if the federal deficit is adjusted for the state and local surplus, capital expenditures, the cyclical component of the deficit, and the effects of inflation, it looks somewhat less threatening than supposed. Others claim that the deficit crowds out private investment. They are also concerned about borrowing from abroad to finance the deficit and the possibility that explosive growth of the deficit could ultimately cause severe inflation.

Terms for Review

- fiscal policy
- net tax multiplier
- discretionary fiscal policy
- automatic fiscal policy
- automatic stabilizers
- fiscal year
- entitlements
- structural deficit
- cyclical deficit

Questions for Review

1. How does each of the following affect the aggregate demand curve: (a) an increase in government purchases; (b) an increase in taxes; and (c) an increase in transfer payments? (In the income-expenditure model, how does each of these affect the planned-expenditure schedule?)

2. Why is the net tax multiplier less than the government purchases multiplier?

3. How could fiscal policy cause price increases?

4. Why does the government budget tend to move toward surplus during an expansion and toward deficit during a contraction?

5. What are the responsibilities of the president and Congress in preparing the federal budget? What agencies provide economic advice to each?

6. In what respects has the federal budgetary process encountered difficulties in recent years? What was the intent of the Gramm-Rudman-Hollings experiment? Did it succeed?

7. What have been the budgetary priorities in the 1980s as revealed in actual tax and spending figures?

8. How have the actual, cyclical, and structural federal budget deficits behaved in the 1980s?

9. List four adjustments to the federal budget deficit that appear to reduce its impact.

10. Why do many economists think that the high budget deficits of the 1980s are a threat to economic stability?

Problems and Topics for Discussion

1. **Examining the lead-off case.** On balance, has "controlling the budget monster" been a high priority during the Reagan administration? If not, which priorities have outranked it? In your opinion, should balancing the budget have been given a higher priority?

2. **Unemployment and fiscal policy.** At point E_1 in Exhibit 11.1, real output is $1,500 billion compared with a natural level of real output of $2,000 billion. Apply Okun's law to estimate the unemployment rate at E_1 assuming a natural unemployment rate of 6 percent.

3. **Applying the multipliers.** Suppose that real output is at its natural level in the current year but forecasts show that if no action is taken, the aggregate demand curve will shift to the left by $500 billion in the coming year. Assuming an expenditure multiplier of 2.5, what change in real government purchases will be needed to keep real output at the natural level? If a change in real net taxes is used instead, what change will be required?

4. **Impact of government purchases financed by increased taxes.** Assume that real output is currently at its natural level. For the coming year, Congress passes a budget that includes $100 million in added government purchases to be paid for by a $100 million increase in taxes. What will be the effect on the aggregate demand curve? On the equilibrium level of real output? Does your answer depend on the value of the expenditure multiplier? Why or why not?

5. **Tax increases versus spending cuts.** As the federal budget deficit rose toward the $200 billion mark in the mid-1980s, a majority of policymakers agreed that efforts should be made to reduce it. However, there was much disagreement as to whether this should be done by raising taxes or by cutting government spending. Outline a debate between a person who favors a tax increase and another who favors a spending cut. What

normative and positive economic arguments might each use?

6. **A balanced budget amendment.** From time to time, it has been proposed that a law or constitutional amendment be passed that will force the federal government to balance its budget every year. Do you think it would be possible to keep the actual budget deficit at zero each year, or should such an amendment aim only to keep the structural deficit at zero? Discuss.

Governor James R. Thompson

Case for Discussion
Fiscal Policy at the State Level

In February 1982, when the U.S. economy was deep in recession, the Chicago Tribune *published the following item discussing the tax and spending problems of the Illinois state government:*

Warning that state revenues are lagging behind expectations, Governor James R. Thompson announced Tuesday that he has halted most new state construction work for the next six months.

Referring to "disturbing news on the economic front" the governor also announced that:

- He is reworking his proposed state budget to include additional spending cuts.

- He has ordered state agencies under his control to cut $30 million from their budgets.

- He repeated his call for a new state liquor tax to raise an additional $50 million a year.

To save an estimated $20 million in interest payments, the amount of money to be raised by State of Illinois bond issues during the next five months will be cut almost in half, from $380 million to $200 million.

"Interest rates are too high," the governor told a press conference in the Westin Hotel here.

Later, in a speech to the Illinois Board of Higher Education, Thompson said that in January state income tax revenues were $10 million lower than projected while sales tax revenues were $25 million less than projected.

"Right now, we don't know if it's an aberration or a trend. I suspect it's a trend," Thompson said.

He warned that if the revenue shortfalls continue for a full year, the loss in state revenue could total $420 million.

Thompson also had other bad news for the educators.

Speaking of the financial problems facing the state, he said, "There will be some pain for higher education and for elementary and secondary education."

He described the upcoming budget as "the tightest of the six budgets I have presented to the General Assembly."

Source: Casey Banas, "In State, Thompson Freezes New Building for Six Months," *Chicago Tribune*, February 3, 1982, sec. 1, pp. 1, 8. Copyrighted 1982, Chicago Tribune Company. All Rights Reserved. Used with permission. Photo Source: Courtesy of the state of Illinois.

Questions

1. Do Governor Thompson's policy actions count as fiscal policy even though they take place at the state level? Assuming an expenditure multiplier of 2.5 for the economy as a whole, what would his $30 million in spending cuts do to the U.S. aggregate demand curve? To equilibrium real national income?

2. Why do you think income tax revenues were $10 million and sales tax revenues $25 million lower than had been projected?

3. Suppose all state governors follow Thompson's lead and try to cut spending and raise taxes when state budget deficits rise during a recession. Will this make it easier or harder for the economy to recover from a recession? What would happen if the federal government followed policies similar to Thompson's when the economy entered a recession?

Suggestions for Further Reading

Aaron, Henry J., et al. *Economic Choices 1987*. Washington, D.C.: Brookings Institution, 1986.

A comprehensive discussion of fiscal policy and the federal budgetary process.

Fink, Richard H., and Jack C. High. *A Nation in Debt*. Frederick, Md.: University Publications of America, 1987.

This collection of essays gives a thorough and balanced treatment of all aspects of the problem of the federal budget deficit.

President's Council of Economic Advisers. *Economic Report of the President*. Washington, D.C.: Government Printing Office, annually.

Discusses current fiscal policy issues each year. The 1982 issue contains a discussion of adjustments to the deficit. Use the table of contents to find the relevant sections.

Rauch, Jonathan. "The Fiscal Ice Age," *National Journal*, January 10, 1987, 58–64, and "The Politics of Joy," *National Journal*, January 17, 1987, 125–130.

This pair of articles discusses fiscal priorities in the 1980s and the state of health of the federal budget process.

Rivlin, Alice M. "Economics and the Political Process," *American Economic Review*, March 1987, 1–10.

Reflections on ways to improve the federal budget process by a former director of the Congressional Budget Office.

U.S. House of Representatives, Committee on the Budget. *Economic Stabilization Policies: The Historical Record, 1962–1976*. Washington, D.C.: Government Printing Office, 1978.

Contains studies of the effectiveness of fiscal policy, with comments by leading economists.

Monetary Economics

Part Four

12 Money and the Banking System

After reading this chapter, you will understand . . .

- What money is and what it does.
- How the stock of money in the economy is measured.
- The structure of the U.S. banking system.
- How the safety and stability of the banking system are maintained.

Before reading this chapter, make sure you know the meaning of . . .

- Balance sheet (Chapter 4)
- Financial intermediaries (Chapter 4)
- The role of money in the circular flow (Chapter 6)

Money to Smoke

BUCHAREST, ROMANIA. It isn't true that Romania, a hard-core Communist country, doesn't operate on the market principle. It does. Call it the farmers' market principle, but this is how it works:

As dawn breaks, a crowing rooster on sale at the downtown market signals the opening of an intense round of barter trading. Apples will get you peppers. Cauliflower will get you beets. Turnips will get you garlic. And Kent cigarettes will get you everything.

"Pssst. Mister. With the Kents," whispers a young farmer rushing from behind his fruit and vegetable stand to pursue someone who has just flashed a pack of Kents. Never mind the line of customers at the stand. They can wait; they have only lei, the official Romanian currency. The other guy has Kents.

"You want apples?" asks the farmer. He pulls out a bag hidden at the bottom of the pile. These aren't the yellow apples for the regular customers— the ones with lei. These are red apples for the man with the Kents.

Under the farmers' market principle, the fruit and vegetable farmer perhaps will trade away his Kents to get his tractor fixed. The mechanic will use the Kents to get a rare and relatively good cut of meat at the butcher shop. The butcher will pass on the Kents to get a table at a packed restaurant. The maitre d' will use the Kents to pay his doctor. The doctor will flash the Kents at the farmers' market to get some attention. And some farmer will come running after.

"In Romania, Kents are the ultimate affirmation of the market theory," says a Western diplomat here. "You've heard of the gold standard. Well, this is the Kent standard. Everyone in this country wants Kents." And only Kents. Winston, Marlboro, Pall Mall won't do.

Kents, it seems, can get every question answered, except one: Why Kents?

"Why Kents? Why gold?" replies an American historian in Bucharest. "Limited supply, universal acceptance. That's it."

Certainly, the supply is severely limited. The Kents, which are made in the United States, are sold only in the hard-currency shops, such as at the big hotels or at the airport. Other sources are diplomats and foreign travelers. But there never seem to be enough to go around—and certainly not enough to smoke with regularity. For the truly odd part of the Kent phenomenon is that so few people seem to smoke them.

"Kents are for nonsmokers," says a Romanian journalist, chain-smoking a pack of domestic cigarettes. A Western diplomat, whose office contains a large box of Kent cartons, says: "Sometimes you'll get a pack of Kents with the wrapping coming off and the box all beat up. But they've never been opened. Not a single cigarette has been smoked."

In Romania, smoking a Kent would be like lighting up with a $100 bill.

Source: Roger Thurow, "In Romania, Smoking a Kent Cigarette Is Like Burning Money," *The Wall Street Journal*, January 3, 1986, p. 1. Reprinted by permission of *The Wall Street Journal*, © Dow Jones & Company, Inc. 1986. All Rights Reserved. Photo Source: Copyright © 1987 B. E. White. All rights reserved.

As we saw in Chapter 6, money is the fluid that moves in the circular flow of income and product. Money can take many forms: cigarettes in Romania; giant stones on the Pacific island of Yap; coins, paper currency, and checking deposits in the United States.

Although we have mentioned money often, in this and the following three chapters we give it center stage. We will begin with a formal definition of money and a brief discussion of the complicated matter of measuring how much of it exists in the economy. Next, we will explore the banking system. In Chapter 13, we will look at the ways in which the Federal Reserve, a government agency, controls the stock of money. In Chapter 14, we will turn to a discussion of the demand for money and how that demand interacts with supply in financial markets.

Finally, in Chapter 15 we will come to the central question: Why does money matter? We will see that changes in the money stock can have a strong impact on the decisions of households, firms, and government units. This fact makes monetary policy a powerful weapon in the fight for price stability, full employment, and economic growth.

With this introduction, let's begin our study of monetary economics.

Money: What It Is and What It Does

Money
An asset that serves as a means of payment, a store of purchasing power, and a unit of account.

Money is best defined in terms of what it does: It serves as a means of payment, a store of purchasing power, and a unit of account. Money serves these functions regardless of its name or form—U.S. dollars, Japanese yen, or Kent cigarettes.

The Functions of Money

As a means of payment, money reduces transaction costs. Using money avoids the complexities of barter. This can be seen in the example of the Romanian farmers' market. There apples will get you peppers, cauliflower will get you beets, and turnips will get you garlic. But what if you want garlic and have only potatoes? What you need is a universal means of exchange—one that all sellers will accept because they know that the others they deal with will also accept it;

one that is in limited supply so that you know the market won't be flooded with it tomorrow, driving down its exchange value; and one that is easily recognized and hard to counterfeit. Why not Kent cigarettes? In Romania, these have the same attributes of acceptability, limited supply, and difficulty in counterfeiting that dollars have in the United States. Anything having these properties could work as a means of payment.

As a store of purchasing power, money makes it possible to arrange economic activities in a convenient manner over time. Income-producing activities and spending decisions need not occur simultaneously. Instead, we can accept payment in money for our productive efforts and keep the money handy until we decide how to spend it. The U.S. dollar is a fairly good store of purchasing power, although, as we saw in Chapter 7, its purchasing power has been hurt by inflation in recent decades. Cigarettes in Romania work reasonably well too, provided you can resist the temptation to smoke them.

Finally, as a unit of account, money makes it possible to measure and record economic stocks and flows. A household's needs for food, shelter, and clothing can be expressed in dollar terms in planning a household budget. The nation's output of movies, apples, and airplanes can be added together in dollar terms to provide a basis for planning economic policy. Without money as a unit of account, private and public economic planning would be virtually impossible.

However, a single kind of money does not always serve all three functions. On the island of Yap, a type of money in the form of huge stone wheels serves as a store of value and a unit of account even though the stones are too heavy to carry around as a means of paying for ordinary purchases. To buy groceries, the Yapese use ordinary coins and paper currency. On the other hand, in countries battered by inflation at hundreds of percent per year, the money that circulates as a means of exchange makes a poor unit of account because its purchasing power changes from day to day. In such countries, another unit of account must be used, such as gold or U.S. dollars. A monetary system works best when one type of money serves as a means of payment, a store of value, and a unit of account, as dollars do in the United States.

Money as a Liquid Asset

Any asset that a household, firm, or government unit owns is a store of purchasing power in that it can be sold and the proceeds used to buy something else. Money, however, has two important traits that no other asset has, or at least not to the same extent. One is that money itself can be used as a means of payment without first having to be exchanged for something else. A house, bond, or blast furnace may have great value, but it can rarely be traded without first being exchanged for an equivalent amount of money. The other trait is that because money serves as a unit of account it can, by definition, neither gain nor lose in nominal value. A house, bond, or blast furnace may be worth more or fewer dollars next year than this year, but the nominal value of a dollar is always a dollar—no more and no less.

An asset that can be used directly as a means of payment or readily converted to one and that is protected against gain or loss in nominal value is said to have **liquidity**. No other asset is as liquid as money. In fact, a comparison of the definition of money (an asset that can be used as a means of payment and serves as a unit of account) and the definition of liquidity suggests that any perfectly liquid asset is, by definition, a form of money.

Liquidity
An asset's ability to be used directly as a means of payment, or readily converted to one, and remain fixed in nominal value.

Measuring the Stock of Money

For purposes of economic analysis and policy, we need to know not only what money is but how it can be measured. In all modern economies, the stock of money is controlled by government. As we will see, if government fails to supply enough money, real output and employment will decrease, at least temporarily. Indeed, some economists believe that the Great Depression was caused, or certainly greatly worsened, by such a failure. On the other hand, flooding the economy with too much money tends to be inflationary.

Although the post–World War II U.S. economy has been free of major depressions and extreme inflation rates, in recent decades the record has not been as good as we would like. If the economy is to perform well in the future, sound monetary policy will be needed. Also, because the money stock cannot be controlled if it cannot be measured, the problem of measurement is just as important now as ever.

Currency and Transaction Deposits

Currency
Coins and paper money.

Transaction deposit
A deposit from which funds can be freely withdrawn by check in order to make payment to a third party.

The money stock traditionally has been defined as consisting of two highly liquid types of assets—currency and transaction deposits. **Currency** is coins and paper money. **Transaction deposits**—also known as *checking accounts*—are deposits from which money can be freely withdrawn by check, without advance notice, for the purpose of making payments to third parties. (*Third parties*, in this sense, are parties other than the depositor or the institution that houses the account.)

In the United States, currency consists of the familiar Federal Reserve notes, which are issued in denominations of $1, $2, $5, $10, $50, and $100 and of coins minted by the Treasury. Coins and paper money were once backed by precious metals. Until 1934, the U.S. government issued both gold coins and paper currency that could be exchanged for gold on demand. Silver coins and silver-backed paper money survived until the mid-1960s. Today coins and paper money are simply tokens whose value is based on the public's faith in their usefulness as means of payment for goods and services. In that regard, the use of dollars in the United States is no different from the use of cigarettes in the Romanian farmers' market.

Exhibit 12.1 shows that the currency in circulation in the United States as of June 1987 totaled almost $200 billion. A small quantity of traveler's checks is included in this total.

Commercial banks
Financial intermediaries that provide a broad range of banking services, including accepting demand deposits and making commercial loans.

Thrift institutions (thrifts)
A group of financial intermediaries that operate much like commercial banks, including savings and loan associations, savings banks, and credit unions.

Transaction deposits are available in a number of forms from both **commercial banks** and **thrift institutions (thrifts).** One major type of transaction deposit is the *demand deposit*. By law, demand deposits cannot pay interest, but banks do provide their demand-deposit customers various services below cost. Until the mid-1970s, demand deposits were the only kind of transaction deposits available in the United States and were offered only by commercial banks. They have since been joined by interest-bearing checkable deposits, especially NOW accounts. These deposits are available at commercial banks, savings and loan associations, and savings banks. Credit unions offer a similar type of transaction deposit known as a *share draft account*. (We will look in more detail at the distinctions among banks and the various thrift institutions later in the chapter.)

As Exhibit 12.1 shows, in mid-1987 demand deposits made up somewhat more than half of total transaction deposits and all other checkable deposits somewhat less than half.

Exhibit 12.1   Components of the U.S. Money Stock, June 1987 (Billions of Dollars)

This table breaks down the U.S. money supply into its components as of June 1987. It gives two of the most commonly used money supply measures. M1 is the total of currency and transaction deposits; M2 includes M1 plus other highly liquid assets.

Currency[a]		$ 197.9
Plus transactions deposits		548.8
Demand deposits	$297.5	
Other checkable deposits	251.3	
Equals M1		749.3
Plus money market deposit accounts[b]		553.5
Plus money market mutual fund shares[b]		211.3
Plus savings deposits		415.0
Plus small-denomination time deposits		851.1
Plus overnight repurchase agreements[b]		53.0
Plus selected other liquid assets[b]		11.7
Equals M2		$2,842.8

[a] Includes traveler's checks.

[b] Not seasonally adjusted. Components do not add to total because of incomplete seasonal adjustment.

Source: Federal Reserve H-6 Statistical Release, July 16, 1987.

Currency plus all forms of transaction deposits totaled nearly $750 billion as of June 1987. The sum of currency and transaction deposits, known as **M1,** is a widely used measure of the nation's money stock.

Some readers may find it odd that "plastic money"—credit cards—does not appear in Exhibit 12.1 along with transaction deposits. After all, from a consumer point of view, paying for a purchase with a credit card is a close substitute for paying by cash or check. "Perspective 12.1" discusses the nature of credit cards and explains why they do not figure in the measurement of the nation's money stock.

M1
A measure of the money supply that includes currency and transaction deposits.

The Broadly Defined Money Supply

M1 gained popularity as a measure of the money stock because almost all transactions are made with either currency or transaction deposits. However, if one chooses instead to focus on the function of money as a store of value, there are a number of other assets that, although less perfectly liquid than the components of M1, are liquid enough to serve as close substitutes.

Take shares in money market mutual funds, for example. A *money market mutual fund* is a financial intermediary that sells shares to the public. The proceeds of these sales are used to buy short-term, fixed-interest securities, such as Treasury bills. Almost all the interest earned on securities bought by the fund is passed along to shareholders. The fund charges only a small fee for its services. Shareholders can redeem their shares in a number of ways—by writing checks on the fund (usually with a minimum amount of $500 per check), by telephone transfer, or by transfer to another fund. Because the proceeds from sales of shares are invested in very safe assets, a money market mutual fund is able to promise its shareholders a fixed nominal value of $1 per share, although the

PERSPECTIVE 12.1

"Plastic Money"

What about "plastic money"—the MasterCards, Visa cards, and other bank cards that so many people carry these days? Where do they fit into the "Ms"?

Credit cards, the most common form of plastic money, are not really a form of money at all. What sets credit cards apart from currency, bank deposits, and other forms of money is the fact that they are not a store of value. Instead, they are documents that make it easy for their holders to obtain a loan.

When you go into a store, present your credit card, and walk out with a can of tennis balls, you have not yet paid for your purchase. What you have done is borrow from the bank that issued the card. At the same time, you have instructed the bank to turn over the proceeds of the loan to the store. Later the bank will send money to the

store (either in the form of a check or by crediting the amount to the store's bank account). This will pay for the tennis balls. Still later, you will send money to the bank to pay off the balance on your credit card account.

A less common form of plastic money—but one that is spreading—is the *debit card*. A debit card looks just like a credit card, but it doesn't work the same way. When you present your debit card to a merchant, you instruct your bank to transfer money directly from your bank account to the store's account. If the store is linked to the bank by a special computer hookup, the transfer may be made instantly. If you have no money in your account, you can't use your debit card. Whether you write a check or present your debit card when making a purchase, the balance in your transaction account is part of M1.

Savings deposit
A deposit at a bank or thrift institution from which funds can be withdrawn at any time without payment of a penalty.

Time deposit
A deposit at a bank or thrift institution from which funds can be withdrawn without payment of a penalty only at the end of an agreed-upon period.

Repurchase agreement (RP)
A short-term liquid asset that consists of an agreement by a firm or person to buy securities from a financial institution for resale at an agreed-upon price at a later date (often the next business day).

interest paid on the shares varies with market rates. Except for the restriction on the size of checks, then, money market mutual fund balances are almost as liquid as ordinary transaction accounts. Money market fund shares grew rapidly in the late 1970s and early 1980s, when market interest rates rose but rates paid by banks and thrifts were limited by federal regulations.

In late 1982, as part of the process of deregulating interest rates paid by banks and thrifts, these institutions were allowed to compete with money market mutual funds by offering so-called *money market deposit accounts (MMDAs)*. These accounts are allowed to have only limited checking privileges, but they do give higher interest rates than the transaction accounts included in M1. MMDAs therefore are fairly liquid. Their volume grew very rapidly after their introduction; by 1987, as Exhibit 12.1 shows, MMDAs had reached a total of more than $550 billion.

Banks and thrifts also offer the public a number of other accounts that serve as reasonably liquid stores of purchasing power. **Savings deposits** are a familiar example. Although checks cannot be written on these deposits, they are fully protected against loss in nominal value, and they can be redeemed at any time. Banks and thrifts also offer **time deposits.** In the case of small-denomination time deposits (up to $100,000), funds must be left on deposit for a fixed period, ranging from less than a month to many years, in order to earn the full interest rate, and they normally cannot be transferred to another person before maturity. This feature makes them less liquid than savings deposits or MMDAs, but in return they usually pay a higher interest rate. They too are protected against loss of nominal value. Interest rate regulations on savings and time deposits were phased out during the early 1980s, the last restrictions being lifted in April 1986.

One other liquid asset that deserves mention is the **repurchase agreement (RP),** which is an arrangement in which firms (and occasionally consumers) buy securities from a financial institution subject to an agreement to sell them back—

often the next business day—at a slightly higher price. The difference between the buying and selling prices amounts to an interest payment for the institution's use of the funds. Repurchase agreements are popular because they allow firms to put large sums of cash to work earning interest for short periods. In part, they are popular because business firms are not allowed to use interest-bearing transaction deposits such as NOW accounts. As Exhibit 12.1 shows, overnight repurchase agreements totaled $53 billion as of mid-1987.

    Money market mutual fund shares, MMDAs, savings deposits, small time deposits, and overnight repurchase agreements, along with small amounts of other liquid assets, are added to M1 to get a measure of the money supply known as **M2.** As Exhibit 12.1 shows, M2 amounted to $2,843 billion in June 1987.

M2
A measure of the money supply that includes M1 plus money market mutual fund shares, savings deposits, small time deposits, overnight repurchase agreements, and certain other liquid assets.

Which "M" Is Best?

Exhibit 12.1 shows two different measures of the money stock—M1 and M2. However, there are other, still broader measures, such as M3, which includes items such as large-denomination time deposits ($100,000 and up) and repurchase agreements with longer terms, and one called L, which includes short-term Treasury securities, among other assets. Although M1 and M2 are the most frequently used measures, they and all other measures of the money stock are really arbitrary cutoff points along a range of financial assets of varying degrees of liquidity, from currency at one end to long-term securities at the other. No hard and fast answer can be given to the question of which M is "best" without also asking, "Best for what?"

    As we have mentioned, the purpose of M1 is to measure the money stock available for use as a means of payment. However, it does not do this perfectly. On the one hand, some consumers use interest-bearing transaction accounts, such as NOW accounts, primarily as a store of purchasing power. This savings motive is reflected in the fact that some of these accounts have a low *turnover rate,* that is, a low ratio of the volume of transactions made per year to the average balance. On the other hand, as we have seen, money market mutual funds and MMDAs have limited checking features that allow them to serve as means of payment. These assets are not included in M1 partly because they have even lower turnover rates, but they are still used for some transactions. Thus, M1 is far from perfect as a measure of means-of-payment money.

    Similar problems plague M2, which conceptually is intended to measure the stock of money as a short-term, highly liquid store of purchasing power. For this reason, M2 includes items such as savings and small time deposits that have fixed nominal values despite their low turnover rates. But the cutoff line between M2 and M3—for example, the $100,000 cutoff for time deposits—is essentially arbitrary.

    There have been experiments to devise still other measures of the money stock. One such approach is to compute a weighted average of currency, transaction deposits, savings deposits, and so on with the weights related to the assets' turnover rates. These new measures of the money stock show some promise, but they are by no means problem free.

    For purposes of macroeconomic modeling and policy, the best money stock measure would be the one having the most stable and predictable relationship to other significant variables, such as real and nominal GNP and the price level. For many years economists were confident that M1, whatever its imperfections, was the best available measure in this regard. In the 1980s, however, there has been a loss of confidence in M1, for reasons that we will explore in later chapters. For the present, it is sufficient to note that economists in business and government, like pilots in a complex airplane cockpit, find it necessary to watch several dials at the same time, each of which has the potential to yield useful information.

The Banking System

In Chapter 4, we introduced *financial intermediaries*. These are institutions that gather funds from households and other savers and pass them along to borrowers, by either making loans or buying bonds or other securities. There are many kinds of financial intermediaries, including pension funds, life insurance companies, and mutual funds. But the financial intermediaries of special interest to students of monetary economics are a group known as **depository institutions,** which comprise commercial banks and thrifts. They are so called because deposits made by households, firms, and government units are their principal source of funds. Other intermediaries raise funds by selling securities, insurance policies, annuities, and so on, but these do not accept deposits.[1]

Depository institutions
Financial intermediaries, including commercial banks and thrift institutions, that accept deposits from the public.

Depository institutions are of interest because, as Exhibit 12.1 shows, more than 80 percent of the nation's money stock, broadly defined, consists of their liabilities: transaction deposits, MMDAs, savings deposits, small time deposits, and RPs. In this section, we will look at the U.S. system of depository institutions and the federal agencies that regulate it.

Types of Depository Institutions

There are four principal types of depository institutions in the United States. They differ from one another in the types of loans and deposits in which they specialize, although there is an increasing degree of overlap in their operations.

The largest group of depository institutions is *commercial banks*. These usually include the word "bank" in their business names. One of their specialties is making commercial loans—that is, loans to businesses, frequently short term, used to finance their operations. They also make consumer loans and home mortgage loans. Until the 1970s, commercial banks were the only institutions that could offer checkable transaction accounts, and they still hold the bulk of demand and other checkable deposits. They also raise funds by offering savings and time deposits, RPs, and other financial instruments. Large commercial banks provide many services to business customers, such as wire transfers and international banking facilities.

Savings and loan associations specialize in home mortgage lending, although they also make consumer loans and a limited number of commercial loans. Household savings and time deposits traditionally have been their main source of funds, but today they also offer fully checkable deposits in the form of NOW accounts, as well as MMDAs with their limited checking privileges. While they

---

[1]Money market mutual funds, which compete with banks and thrifts for household savings, make every effort to make their operations as convenient as their competitors'. They provide statements, checkbooks, deposit slips, and so on that closely resemble those used by banks and thrifts. Technically, however, their liabilities are shares in the fund's portfolio of assets, not deposits. Therefore, money market mutual funds are not considered depository institutions.

may not use the word "bank" in their names, some savings and loan associations shape their operations to resemble those of commercial banks as closely as regulations permit. Many savings and loans are "mutuals," that is, owned by their depositors and with no common stock outstanding.

Savings banks are a type of depository institution that emerged in the nineteenth century to serve the needs of workers and small savers. Some still have names such as "Dime Savings Bank" that reflect these origins. They originally were organized as benevolent institutions with mutual ownership, but this characteristic of their operations has faded. They offer the same range of deposits as do savings and loan associations but tend to offer more diversified types of loans.

Credit unions are small financial intermediaries organized as cooperative enterprises by employee groups, union members, or certain other groups with common work or community ties. They specialize in small consumer loans, although a few also make mortgage loans. They offer both transaction and savings deposits.

Since the mid-1970s, the traditional distinctions among these four types of institution have eroded. Today, from the viewpoint of both the consumer and macroeconomics, there is no real difference between a transaction deposit in a commercial bank and one in a thrift institution. For these reasons (and also because the phrase "depository institution" is somewhat of a tongue twister), we will use the terms "bank" and "banking system" to refer to all depository institutions except where there is a particular reason to single out one type.

The Banking Balance Sheet

We have seen that banks play a dual role in the economy—as financial intermediaries and as suppliers of means of payment. A good way to understand the connection between these roles is to look at a balance sheet. Exhibit 12.2 shows a total balance sheet for U.S. commercial banks. Balance sheet items for thrift institutions would differ in size, but the concepts involved would be the same.

Assets

On the assets side of the balance sheet, the first line lists the non-interest-bearing deposits that banks maintain with the Federal Reserve System (which we will look at in more detail shortly). The next line, vault cash, consists of currency that banks keep in their own vaults. Deposits at the Federal Reserve plus vault cash constitute a bank's **reserves.** In the past, the reason banks held reserves of cash or deposits that could be quickly converted into cash was that at any moment some depositors might want to withdraw their funds. They could do this by either writing a check to someone who would deposit it in another bank or walking up to the teller's window and asking for currency. Today the minimum level of reserves is not left to the judgment of banks; rather, minimum reserve levels are set by federal regulation. As we will see shortly, these regulations make the Federal Reserve's power to control the level of reserves in the banking system a major tool of monetary policy. Other cash assets, shown in line 3 of the balance sheet and sometimes known as *secondary reserves*, provide banks with liquidity for meeting unexpected needs.

The next two items on the assets side of the balance sheet show the banks' main income-earning assets. The largest item is loans made to businesses and consumers. In addition, commercial banks hold a substantial quantity of securities, including securities issued by federal, state, and local governments. The

Reserves
Cash in bank vaults and non-interest-bearing deposits of banks with the Federal Reserve System.

Exhibit 12.2   Total Balance Sheet for U.S. Commercial
Banks, July 1, 1987 (Billions of Dollars)

This table shows the total balance sheet for U.S. commercial banks as of July 1, 1987.
Assets of banks include non-interest-bearing reserves and interest-bearing loans and
securities. Liabilities include deposits of all kinds and other borrowings. Net worth equals
assets minus liabilities. The balance sheets of thrift institutions would show the same basic
categories but would differ in details.

Assets		Liabilities and Net Worth	
Reserve deposits with		Transaction deposits	$ 644.7
Federal Reserve banks	$ 30.8	MMDAs and savings deposits	539.6
Cash in vaults	23.3	Time deposits	807.2
Other cash assets	187.9	Borrowings	434.0
Loans	1,183.0	Miscellaneous liabilities	191.4
Securities	510.7	Total liabilities	$2,616.7
Miscellaneous assets	204.1	Net worth	171.1
		Total liabilities and	
Total assets	$2,787.8	net worth	$2,787.8

Source: Federal Reserve H8(510) Statistical Release, July 27, 1987.

final item on this side includes some smaller income-earning items plus the value
of the banks' buildings and equipment.

Liabilities

The first three items on the liabilities side of the banks' balance sheet are various
kinds of deposits. They are liabilities because they represent funds to which
depositors hold legal claim.

Funds that banks have borrowed also appear as liabilities. A small portion of
these are borrowed from the Federal Reserve and the rest from private sources.
Because the banks' total liabilities are less than their assets, they have a positive
net worth. This sum represents the claim of the banks' owners against the banks'
assets.

The Federal Reserve System

We have already mentioned the Federal Reserve System, or the *Fed*, as it is
known in financial circles. The Fed is the central banking system of the United
States. It operates a check-clearing system, runs a system for wire funds transfers, and provides other banking services to private banks and thrifts as well as
the federal government. It is one of the chief regulators and supervisors of the
banking system. Its responsibility for monetary policy makes it a major partner
in overall macroeconomic policymaking together with Congress and the executive branch of the federal government.

The Fed was established in 1913 as an independent agency of the federal
government and thus not under the direction of the executive branch. It is
subordinate to Congress, but Congress does not intervene in its day-to-day decision making. The reason for making the Fed independent was to prevent the
Department of the Treasury from using monetary policy for political purposes.

In practice, however, the Fed's monetary actions are coordinated with the Treasury's fiscal actions. The chairman of the Fed's Board of Governors is in frequent contact with the secretary of the Treasury, the chairman of the President's Council of Economic Advisers, and the director of the Office of Management and Budget. By law, the Fed also makes a formal report to Congress twice a year on its monetary policy objectives. It also explains how these objectives are related to economic conditions and the economic goals set by the administration and Congress.

Federal Reserve Banks

The structure of the Federal Reserve System is shown in Exhibit 12.3. At the heart of the system are the 12 Federal Reserve banks. These district banks have 25 branches. The district boundaries and the banks' locations are shown in part b of the exhibit.

Each Federal Reserve bank is a separate unit chartered by the federal government. Its stockholders are commercial banks that are members of the Federal Reserve System. Although Federal Reserve banks issue stock to their members, they are not typical private firms in that they are neither operated for profit nor ultimately controlled by their stockholders. The Federal Reserve banks earn income from their holdings of federal securities and, since 1981, from charges for services they provide to banks and thrift institutions. Each year the Reserve banks return all their income, minus operating costs, to the Treasury.

Each bank is managed by a nine-member board. Six of those members are selected by the member banks and the other three appointed by the Fed's Board of Governors. Each board sets the policies of its own bank under supervision of the Board of Governors. The Board of Governors also approves appointments of each Reserve bank's top officers.

The Federal Reserve banks perform a number of key functions in the banking system; these include clearing checks, handling reserve deposits, and making loans to depository institutions. They also issue paper currency in the form of Federal Reserve notes and supply Treasury coins. Finally, they provide banking services for the Treasury.

Board of Governors

The highest policymaking body of the Federal Reserve System is its Board of Governors. The Board, which supervises the 12 Federal Reserve banks, has seven members who are appointed by the President and confirmed by the Senate. Each governor serves a single 14-year term, with one term expiring every other year. The President appoints one of the Board members to serve as chairperson for a four-year term.

The Board of Governors has the power to approve changes in the interest rate on loans to banks and thrifts made by the Reserve banks. It also sets, within limits determined by law, the minimum level of reserves that banks and thrifts are required to hold relative to certain deposits. The Board supervises and regulates many types of banking institutions, including state-chartered member banks, bank holding companies, and U.S. offices of foreign banks. It also approves bank mergers and implements consumer credit regulations.

Federal Open Market Committee

Authority over purchases and sales of government securities held by the Fed—its most important monetary policy tool—rests with the Federal Open Market Committee. The FOMC is made up of the seven members of the Board of

Exhibit 12.3   Structure of the Federal Reserve System

Part a of this exhibit shows the structure of the Federal Reserve System. The highest policymaking body of the Fed is the Board of Governors. The map in part b gives the locations of the 12 Federal Reserve banks.

(a)

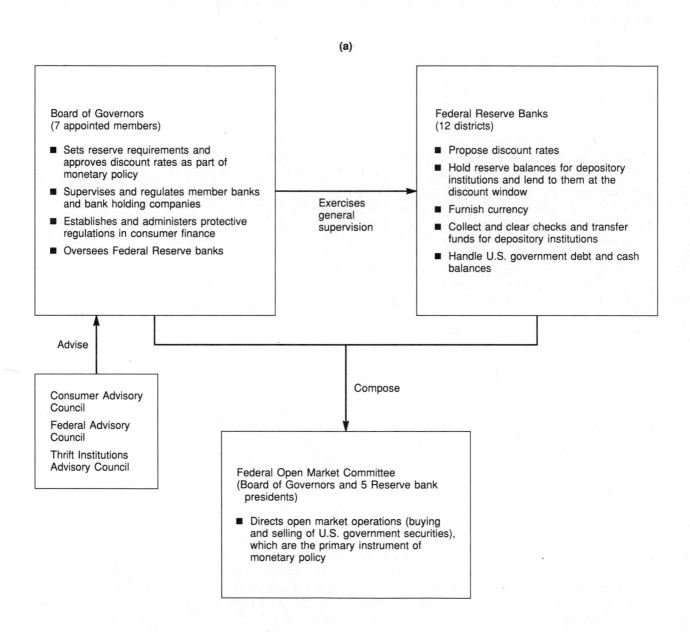

Source: Board of Governors, Federal Reserve System, *The Federal Reserve System: Purposes and Functions*, 7th ed. (Washington, D.C.: Federal Reserve System, 1984), 5, 8.

(b)

Boundaries of Federal Reserve districts
Boundaries of Federal Reserve branch territories
Board of Governors of the Federal Reserve System
Federal Reserve bank cities
Federal Reserve branch cities
Federal Reserve bank facility

Governors plus five district bank presidents. The president of the Federal Reserve Bank of New York is a permanent member; the remaining four seats rotate among the other eleven district banks. The committee meets about eight times a year, and also confers by telephone, to set a general strategy for monetary policy. Committee decisions regarding changes in the Fed's holdings of securities are carried out through the open market trading desk of the Federal Reserve Bank of New York.

Member and Nonmember Banks

About 5,700 of the country's approximately 15,000 commercial banks, including most large banks, are members of the Federal Reserve System. National banks—those that are chartered by the federal government—are required to be members; state-chartered banks may or may not be members. Until 1980, member banks enjoyed certain privileges and free services from the Fed, but in return they were subject to generally stricter regulation than nonmember banks, especially with regard to the minimum reserve levels they could hold. The reserve requirements were felt to be burdensome, and as a result many banks were leaving the Federal Reserve System. This made it more difficult to conduct monetary policy.

In 1980, hoping to improve the Fed's ability to conduct monetary policy, Congress passed the Depository Institutions Deregulation and Monetary Control Act. This act did away with many of the distinctions between member and nonmember banks and between commercial banks and thrift institutions. As a result, since 1980 member banks, nonmember commercial banks, savings and loans, savings banks, and credit unions have all been subject to more uniform reserve requirements. In return, thrift institutions have won the right to compete more directly with commercial banks in making certain types of loans and offering transaction accounts. Nonmember institutions have achieved access to such Fed services as check clearing, wire transfers, and loans on the same terms as member banks. (In 1982, small depository institutions were exempted from reserve requirements.) As a result of the Monetary Control Act, the distinction between banks and thrift institutions has become less important.

The Fed's Balance Sheet

Exhibit 12.4 shows a balance sheet for the Federal Reserve System. Government securities are by far its largest asset. As we will see shortly, these security holdings play a key role in the Fed's control of the money stock. Loans to member banks are small in comparison to other assets, but they are listed separately because they are important for policy purposes. Normally these loans are made on a short-term basis to depository institutions to enable them to meet their reserve requirements. However, in special circumstances longer-term loans are made to banks and thrifts experiencing financial difficulties. Other assets include those denominated in foreign currencies; these are important in carrying out the Fed's functions in the international monetary system.

Federal Reserve notes, which account for almost all of the nation's stock of currency, are the Fed's largest liability. These are followed by the reserves deposited with the Fed by banks and thrifts. Other liabilities include deposits of the Treasury and of foreign central banks. Since the Fed's assets exceed its liabilities, it has a positive net worth.

Exhibit 12.4 Consolidated Balance Sheet of the
Federal Reserve Banks, July 1, 1987 (Billions of Dollars)

The Federal Reserve banks have liabilities to the general public in the form of Federal
Reserve notes and to banks and thrifts in the form of reserve deposits. The Fed's main
assets are government securities. Loans to banks with which to meet reserve requirements
are small, but they are a key aspect of banking and monetary policy.

Assets		Liabilities and Net Worth	
Securities	$209.6	Federal reserve notes	$198.8
Loans to banks and thrifts	0.8	Reserves on deposit	35.3
Other assets	48.1	Other liabilities and net worth	24.4
Total	$258.5	Total	$258.5

Source: Federal Reserve H4.1 Statistical Release, July 2, 1987.

Risks of Banking

Banks earn a profit only by lending or investing most of their deposits at an
interest rate higher than the rate they pay to depositors, after setting aside a
fraction of their deposits, as required by the Fed, in the form of non-interest-
bearing reserves. Banks have been doing business in much the same way for
hundreds of years, but it entails some well-known risks.

One is the risk of loan losses. What happens if a bank makes a loan to a
customer who is unable to repay it? When a loan goes bad, the loss is absorbed
by the bank's net worth. (In balance sheet terms, writing off the bad loan is a
reduction in assets. Liabilities—that is, deposits and borrowing—do not
change. Thus, net worth, which equals assets minus liabilities, must fall.) If loan
losses are too great, however, the bank's net worth may be used up. At that
point, the bank will no longer have enough assets to pay off its depositors and
other creditors. A bank whose liabilities exceed its assets is said to be *insolvent*
and usually must cease doing business.

A second risk that banks face is *illiquidity*, that is, an insufficient amount of
liquid assets to meet withdrawals. When a depositor withdraws funds from a
bank, the bank pays by drawing down the reserves it holds on deposit with the
Fed, supplemented, perhaps, by drawing down other liquid assets that it holds
for this purpose. Under normal conditions, new deposits approximately offset
withdrawals. There is no need for the bank to draw on its less liquid assets, such
as loans and long-term securities, in order to meet withdrawals. If there is an
unexpected wave of withdrawals, however, the bank may use up all of its liquid
assets. It will then have to convert some of its less liquid assets into cash. This
may not be easy, especially if the wave of withdrawals takes place when business
conditions are unfavorable, requiring the bank to sell the assets at less than face
value. Sales of assets at less than face value, like loan losses, erode the bank's net
worth and can make it insolvent.

Whether the bank's troubles begin with loan losses or illiquidity, there is a
danger that they may trigger a run on the bank. A *run* is a situation in which
depositors begin to withdraw their funds from a bank because they fear it may
become insolvent even though it is not yet so. Fearing that the bank may be able

to pay only the first in line, depositors compete for first place. Thus, their fears become self-fulfilling, and the bank fails.

In the worst possible case, the whole banking system, rather than just one bank, could get into trouble. If many banks faced loan losses or runs at the same time, they could not help one another out through temporary loans of reserves. If large banks failed, smaller banks, which keep deposits in the large ones or make other loans to them, might be brought down too. If many banks simultaneously tried to meet deposit outflows by selling their holdings of securities, the market price of the securities might fall, adding to their losses. A general bank *panic,* in which the stability of the whole system would be threatened, could ensue.

Ensuring the Safety and Soundness of the Banking System

During the nineteenth century, a number of bank panics were touched off by recessions. Both state and federal governments experimented with policies designed to ensure the safety and soundness of the banking system. Out of these efforts has evolved a system that is based on three basic tools: bank supervision and regulation; loans to troubled banks; and deposit insurance.

Supervision and Regulation
Bank inspections were the first tool devised to ensure the banking system's safety and soundness. These inspections, conducted by state or federal officials, were intended to check that banks did not make unduly risky loans; valued their assets honestly; and maintained an adequate level of net worth. Honest bookkeeping, prudent lending, and adequate net worth, it was hoped, would allow banks to survive business downturns without becoming insolvent. Today a variety of federal and state agencies, including the Federal Reserve and the Comptroller of the Currency, a part of the Treasury, share the responsibility for supervision and regulation. Today bank inspections are conducted as part of the enforcement process for a whole battery of banking regulations designed to ensure the safety and soundness of the system. Among the most important of these are *capital requirements,* under which net worth must be kept at or above a minimum fraction of all assets.

Loans to Troubled Banks
Despite inspections, banking panics continued to occur. In 1907, an especially severe panic took place. This led to the establishment of the Federal Reserve System in 1913. Among other duties, the Fed was given the power to aid the banking system in times of trouble by acting as a lender of last resort. This function remains important today. For example, when the stock market experienced a record 22.6 percent loss on October 19, 1987, the Fed quickly announced that it stood ready to loan extra funds to any banks needing additional cash because of customers' stock market losses.

Deposit Insurance
But even with these powers, the Fed failed to prevent a major bank panic in 1933, during the Great Depression. At that time, business conditions were so bad that even loans that had appeared prudent when made during the 1920s were not paid off. Even the Fed's powers to lend reserves to troubled banks were insufficient to maintain public confidence in the banking system. Panicky depos-

itors converted hundreds of millions of dollars of deposits to currency, and bank failures became widespread.

In response to the collapse of the banking system, Congress established the Federal Deposit Insurance Corporation (FDIC) in 1934. Today the FDIC insures all deposits up to $100,000 per customer per bank and even more in special cases. The idea of deposit insurance is to short-circuit runs on banks. If deposits are insured, depositors need not run to the bank to withdraw their funds; even if the bank fails, the government will pay them their money. Also, if runs can be avoided, the problems of one or a few banks will not touch off a panic that threatens the whole system. Banks bear the cost of deposit insurance through a small premium that the FDIC charges for its services.

The Banking System in the 1980s: Problems and Prospects

Since 1933, there have been no widespread bank panics in the United States. However, individual banks, including some large ones, have failed—in fact, more banks have failed in the mid-1980s than at any time since the 1930s.

Several factors have combined to cause bank failures. Many of the failures have been caused by loans that went bad. In the 1970s, when oil prices seemed headed ever higher, banks loaned vast sums to energy-related industries. When oil prices fell in the 1980s, many of these loans could not be repaid. Banks made many loans to farmers based on the then rising value of farmland. When the prices of crops and farmland turned down in the 1980s, some of them went sour. Finally, in the 1970s banks made large loans to Third World countries, partly to help them pay for oil imports, but not all of them have been paid on time. "Perspective 12.2" describes the problems of Continental Illinois, the largest bank to get in trouble in recent years. Its problems and the measures taken to rescue it illustrate the tools used to ensure safety and soundness of the banking system.

Not all banking problems have been caused by bad loans. The mid-1980s also saw the collapse of the savings and loan systems of Ohio and Maryland. These systems were governed by state rather than federal regulations and deposit insurance. When some large institutions became insolvent because of fraudulent management practices, the small reserves of the state insurance funds ran out, and full-scale runs brought down even honestly managed institutions within these state systems.

The problems of the banking system in the mid-1980s have caused economists to wonder whether some of the government's efforts to ensure the banking system's soundness are adequate. One criticism has been that deposit insurance and even the Fed's function as a lender of last resort have encouraged banks to take undue risks. The government's safety net has, in effect, put banks in a position in which the government bears the risks of a spate of bad loans while banks reap the profits if enough risky loans by luck are repaid. To counter this problem, the FDIC has been considering reforms in its deposit insurance system. The goal would be to make banks bear the costs of risk taking by charging higher insurance premiums to those that take the most risks. Higher capital requirements for banks that take greater risks are also under consideration.

In addition, the Federal Savings and Loan Insurance Corporation (FSLIC), an agency that insures deposits in savings and loan associations, has been lenient with many institutions that have become insolvent. Institutions that are in fact insolvent but still allowed to continue operations are sometimes called *zombies*.

Continental Illinois Rattles Some Windows

The stability of the U.S. banking system is maintained by means of supervision and regulation, inspections, deposit insurance, and loans to troubled banks. For over 50 years, these precautions have prevented banking panics. However, there have been sóme close calls. The collapse of Continental Illinois Bank & Trust Company of Chicago in 1984 did not bring down the banking system, but it certainly rattled some windows.

In the late 1970s, Continental soared to a leadership position among midwestern banks. Parts of its growth strategy were risky, however. It made many loans in the energy field, including $1 billion that it took over from Penn Square Bank of Oklahoma City. To obtain the funds it needed to make these loans, Continental relied heavily on short-term borrowing from other banks and large, 30-day certificates of deposit—"hot money," in banking jargon. At least one Continental officer saw danger signs and

wrote a warning memo to her superiors, but the memo went unheeded. Although the Comptroller of the Currency inspected Continental on a regular basis, it failed to see how serious its problems were getting to be.

Penn Square Bank was closed by regulators in July 1982. When energy prices began to slip, most of the $1 billion in loans that Continental had taken over from the smaller bank turned out to be bad. Other loans to troubled companies such as Chrysler, International Harvester, and Braniff looked questionable. Seeing these problems, "hot money" owners began to pull their funds out of Continental.

By the spring of 1984, a run on Continental had begun. In May, the bank had to borrow $3.5 billion from the Fed to replace overnight funds it had lost. But this was not enough. To try to stem the outflow of deposits from Continental, the FDIC agreed to guarantee not just the first $100,000 of each depositor's money but all of it. Nevertheless, the run continued.

Federal regulators tried hard to find a sound bank that could take over Continental—a common way of rescuing failing banks. But Continental was just too big for anyone to buy. By July, all hope of a private sector rescue was dashed. Regulators faced a stark choice: Let Continental collapse, or take it over themselves.

Letting the bank fail seemed too risky. It was estimated that more than 100 other banks had placed enough funds in Continental to put them at risk if Continental failed. Thus, on a rainy Thursday at the end of July, the FDIC in effect nationalized Continental Illinois at a cost of $4.5 billion. This kept the bank's doors open and prevented a chain reaction. However, in all but a technical sense, Continental had become the biggest bank failure in U.S. history.

The zombie count among savings and loan associations rose sharply in the mid-1980s. In part, legislation passed by Congress mandated accounting standards that artificially buoyed the net worth of these institutions. More important, the FSLIC simply did not have a sufficient insurance fund to pay off depositors if all insolvent savings and loan associations were closed. In 1986 and 1987, Congress acted to increase the funds available to the FSLIC, but these actions were not sufficient to solve all of the problems.

At the same time, pressures have been building to relax certain regulatory restrictions on depository institutions. One trend has been a gradual erosion of the traditional prohibition on interstate branch banking. Many economists think that allowing banks to branch across state lines will make them less vulnerable to business downturns that focus on a single area, such as the problems of farming and the oil industry. Another trend has been to allow banks to enter lines of business, such as insurance and security underwriting, from which they traditionally have been excluded. Still another area of change has been the growing involvement of nonfinancial firms, such as Sears, Roebuck, in financial services and ownership of banking-type facilities.

It is certain that the banking system will continue to change in the years ahead. Despite some close calls, the safety and soundness of the system have so far been maintained.

Summary

1. **What is money, and what does it do?** *Money* is an asset that serves as a means of payment, a store of purchasing power, and a unit of account. The use of money reduces transaction costs in comparison with the alternative of barter. To serve as money, an asset must be generally accepted and limited in supply. Because money can be used as a means of payment and has a fixed nominal value, it is said to be *liquid*.

2. **How is the stock of money in the economy measured?** One approach to measuring the stock of money focuses on its use as a means of payment. This measure includes *currency* (coins and paper money) plus *transaction deposits* (deposits on which checks can be freely written). This measure of the money stock is known as *M1*. A broader measure, *M2*, also includes a number of assets that serve as a liquid store of purchasing power but are used for making transactions only to a limited extent, if at all. These include money market mutual fund shares, money market deposit accounts at banks and thrifts, *savings deposits*, small-denomination *time deposits*, overnight *repurchase agreements*, and certain other liquid assets.

3. **What is the structure of the U.S. banking system?** The U.S. banking system consists of four types of *depository institution*. The most important are *commercial banks*, which specialize in commercial loans and transaction deposits. In addition, there are three types of *thrift institution:* savings and loan associations, savings banks, and credit unions. These can also offer transaction deposits but make only a relatively limited number of commercial loans. The Federal Reserve System is the nation's central bank. It provides services to depository institutions, holds their required *reserves*, and, together with other federal agencies, regulates the banking system.

4. **How are the safety and stability of the banking system maintained?** Banks fail if they become insolvent, that is, if their assets fall below the level of their liabili-

ties. This may happen because of loan losses or because deposit withdrawals have exhausted liquid assets. The government has three principal tools for ensuring the safety and soundness of the banking system: supervision and regulation; loans to banks and thrifts facing liquidity problems; and deposit insurance.

Terms for Review

- money
- liquidity
- currency
- transaction deposits
- commercial banks
- thrift institutions (thrifts)
- M1
- savings deposits
- time deposits
- repurchase agreements
- M2
- depository institutions
- reserves

Questions for Review

1. What properties make an asset suitable for use as money? What are some examples of assets that serve as money in the U.S. economy today? In other economies, past or present?

2. List some assets that you own, ranging from the most to the least liquid.

3. What assets serve most frequently as means of payment? List some assets that serve as a liquid store of purchasing power but only to a limited extent, if at all, as a means of payment.

4. What characteristics distinguish commercial banks, savings and loan associations, savings banks, and

credit unions from one another? What distinguishes them from other financial intermediaries?

5. What is the role of the Federal Reserve System? The Federal Reserve banks? The Board of Governors of the Federal Reserve? The Federal Open Market Committee?

6. What are the policy tools used to ensure the safety and soundness of the U.S. banking system?

Problems and Topics for Discussion

1. **Examining the lead-off case.** What characteristics of Kent cigarettes makes it possible for them to serve as money in the Romanian economy? Would apples serve just as well? Domestic cigarettes? Discuss.

2. **The functions of money.** Money serves three functions: as a means of payment, a store of purchasing power, and a unit of account. How does inflation undermine each of these functions?

3. **Barter in the modern economy.** For most purposes, money lowers the cost of making transactions relative to barter—the direct exchange of one good or service for another. However, barter has not disappeared, even in an advanced economy such as the United States'. Can you give an example of the use of barter in the U.S. economy today? Why is barter used instead of money in this case?

4. **Plastic money.** Do you use any credit cards? Does their use reduce the amount of money you need? Of which forms of money do you need less because you have a credit card?

5. **The banking balance sheet.** Go to a commercial bank or thrift institution in your area and ask for a copy of a summary balance sheet (these are readily available at most banks). How does this balance sheet compare to that of all commercial banks as given in Exhibit 12.2? (*Bonus question:* Obtain and compare the balance sheets of a bank and a thrift.)

6. **Current monetary data.** Every Thursday, the Federal Reserve reports certain key data on money and the banking system. These are published in the Friday edition of *The Wall Street Journal* and other major financial newspapers. Find the Federal Reserve report from *The Wall Street Journal* for the most recent Friday, and use it to answer the following questions:

   a. What items are included in M2 that are not included in M1? What was the total of such items in the most recent month for which data are reported? M3 is a money supply measure that includes large-denomination certificates of deposit and long-term repurchase agreements. What is the total of these items? Which of these money measures grew most quickly in the most recent month for which data are reported?

   b. The tables report key assets and liabilities of the 10 leading New York banks. Demand and other transaction deposits at these banks account for about what percentage of M1?

7. **Recent bank failures.** Look in *The Wall Street Journal* or other business publication for news of a recent bank failure. Why did the bank fail? How did federal authorities respond to the failure?

French soldiers were paid in makeshift money.

Case for Discussion
Makeshift Money in the French Colonial Period

The following letter was written by de Meulle, Governor of the French Province of Quebec, in September 1685:

My Lord—

I have found myself this year in great straits with regard to the subsistence of the soldiers. You did not provide for funds, My Lord, until January last. I have, notwithstanding, kept them in provisions until September, which makes eight full months. I have drawn from my own funds and from those of my friends, all I have been able to get, but at last finding them without means to render me further assistance, and not knowing to what saint to pay my vows, money being extremely scarce, having distributed considerable sums on every side for the pay of the soldiers, it occurred to me to issue, instead of money, notes on [playing] cards, which I have had cut in quarters. I send you My Lord, the three kinds, one is for four francs, another for forty sols, and the third for fifteen sols, because with these three kinds, I was able to make their exact pay for one month. I have issued an ordinance by which I have obliged all the inhabitants to receive this money in payments, and to give it circulation, at the same time pledging myself, in my own name, to redeem the said notes. No person has refused them, and so good has been the effect that by this means the troops have lived as usual. There were some merchants who, privately, had offered me money at the local rate on condition that I would repay them in money at the rate in France, to which I could not consent as the King would have lost a third; that is, for ten thousand ecus he would have paid forty thousand livres; thus personally, by my credit and by my management, I have saved His Majesty thirteen thousand livres.

[Signed] de Meulle

Quebec, 24th September, 1685

Source: From *Canadian Currency, Exchange and Finance During the French Period*, vol. 1, ed. Adam Shortt (New York: Burt Franklin, Research Source Works Series no. 235, 1968). Photo Source: *Historic Costume in Pictures* by Braun & Schneider (New York: Dover Publications, Inc., 1975), plate # 53.

Questions

1. What indication do you find in the letter that the playing card notes issued by the governor served as a means of payment? Why were they accepted as such?

2. What indicates in the letter that the notes served as a store of value? What made them acceptable as such?

3. Did the invention of playing card money change the unit of account in the local economy?

Suggestions for Further Reading

Board of Governors, Federal Reserve System. *The Federal Reserve System: Purposes and Functions*, 7th ed. Washington, D.C.: Federal Reserve System, 1984.

This useful booklet provides many details on topics covered in this and the following chapters. A copy can be obtained free from Publications Services, Division of Support Services, Board of Governors of the Federal Reserve System, Washington, DC 20551.

Campbell, Colin, Rosemary Campbell, and Edwin G. Dolan. *Money, Banking, and Monetary Policy.* Hinsdale, Ill.: Dryden Press, 1988.

Chapters 1 through 10 parallel the discussion in this chapter, but in much greater detail.

Federal Reserve Bank of New York. *The Story of Money; The Story of Checks and Electronic Payments; The Story of Consumer Credit; The Story of Banks; The Story of Inflation.*

These comic-book-style publications of the Federal Reserve Bank of New York look almost silly, but they pack in a lot of information that textbooks leave out. They are available from the bank's Public Information Department, 33 Liberty Street, New York, NY 10045.

Federal Reserve Bulletin, monthly.

Each issue contains the most recent monetary data, which can be used to update the exhibits in this chapter.

13 Central Banking and Money Creation

After reading this chapter, you will understand . . .

- How banks create money.
- Why the size of the money stock is limited by the quantity of bank reserves.
- The instruments available to the Fed for controlling the money stock.
- How well the money stock can be controlled.
- The activities that the Fed undertakes in the international sphere.

Before reading this chapter, make sure you know the meaning of . . .

- M1, M2 (Chapter 12)
- Balance sheets of banks and the Fed (Chapter 12)
- Bank reserves (Chapter 12)

"I Think It's Had It!"

Rachel Fleming is peacefully driving home from work one afternoon when her car begins to sputter and lose power. A glance in the rear view mirror shows her ten-year-old Fiat trailing a cloud of blue smoke. There is a Shell station on the next corner. She manages to chug in just as the car dies. A mechanic lifts the hood. The engine compartment is smeared with black crankcase oil. Whiffs of smoke rise from a hot manifold. The mechanic shakes his head. "Looks bad. A broken piston, maybe, I don't know. I think it's had it!"

The banking system takes some of the hassle out of buying a car.

Saturday finds Fleming, driving a car borrowed from a friend, doing the rounds of the auto dealers. She's not looking for a luxury vehicle—just some basic transportation that, with luck, will give her another ten years of service. What to buy? They aren't selling Fiats in the United States anymore. She looks at Hondas, Mazdas, Subarus. Nice cars—but the prices! She checks the Ford and Chevy dealers next. Finally, she settles on a new Corsica from Brown Brothers Chevrolet. Still more than she wanted to pay, but it seems to her the best buy for what it has to offer. She turns down the dealer's offer of cut-rate financing, taking a cash discount instead. She thinks she can get a loan at a good interest rate from her own bank. She'll come back on Tuesday to pick up the car.

The Monday lunch hour finds her at the North County National Bank, filling out a loan application. It is a small bank at which she has done business for several years, and the loan officer assures her that the loan can be approved in 24 hours. Before leaving the bank, she transfers $2,000 from her savings account to her checking account. The next morning at work, she gets a call from the bank: The $8,000 she asked to borrow has been credited to her checking account balance. Together with her savings, that will give her what she needs for the car, including taxes, tags, and a few extras. That evening she picks up the car, paying for it with a check written on her North County account.

By Friday, she has decided that she likes the car so much that she will take a

weekend drive to the beach. On the way out of town, she stops by the automatic teller machine at her bank and withdraws $100 in cash. Then she picks up a friend, and it's off for the weekend.
Photo Source: © 1987 Phyllis Woloshin.

GETTING an auto loan, writing checks, transferring money between accounts, getting cash from an automatic teller machine—these are things that people do without much thought. Yet, as this chapter will show, understanding the effects of these transactions is critical to understanding how the banking system works and how the stock of money is determined.

In this chapter, we draw on our knowledge of the structure of the banking system as outlined in Chapter 12. We begin by examining how banks create money in a simplified system. Then we discuss the tools that the Federal Reserve uses to control the money stock.

Creation of Money by Banks

As we saw in Chapter 12, the bulk of the U.S. money supply consists of the liabilities of banks and thrift institutions. In this section, we will see how these institutions create money on the basis of reserves supplied by the Federal Reserve System.

A Simplified Banking System

As we have done in building models of other parts of the economy, we begin with a simplified situation; details will be added later. Initially we will deal with the following simplified banking system:

1. The system consists of ten completely identical banks.
2. The banks' only assets are reserve deposits at the Fed and loans; vault cash is zero.
3. The banks' only liabilities are demand deposits; net worth is zero.
4. Demand deposits are the only form of money in the banking system.
5. The system is regulated by a simplified Federal Reserve System that has the power to set uniform reserve requirements on all deposits.
6. The Fed's only assets are government securities, and its only liabilities are the reserve deposits of member banks. Banks do not borrow reserves from the Fed in this system.

Simplified as it is, this ten-bank system can show us a great deal about the mechanics of money creation in the U.S. banking system.

Reserves: Required and Excess

Required reserves
The minimum reserves that the Fed requires depository institutions to hold.

Required-reserve ratio
Required reserves stated as a percentage of the deposits to which reserve requirements apply.

The Federal Reserve System sets a minimum percentage of deposits that each bank or thrift must hold in the form of reserve deposits with the Fed or vault cash. These are called **required reserves.** The ratio of required reserves to these deposits is the **required-reserve ratio.** If the bank holds more than the minimum required reserves, the balance is known as **excess reserves.** In equation form, the relationships among required reserves, excess reserves, deposits, and the required-reserve ratio can be stated as follows:

$$\text{Required reserves} = \text{Deposits} \times \text{Required-reserve ratio}$$

and

$$\text{Excess reserves} = \text{Total reserves} - \text{Required reserves}.$$

For our simplified banking system, we will assume a required-reserve ratio of 10 percent on all deposits. This is somewhat above the average required-reserve ratio for transaction deposits in the U.S. banking system, which stood at 7.7 percent as of June 1987.

Balance Sheet Equilibrium

As profit-seeking firms, banks want to earn all the interest they can; thus, they normally use up almost all excess reserves by making loans or buying securities. In recent years, U.S. banks' excess reserves have tended to be less than 2 percent of total reserves. For the most part, these small excess reserves are held as a precaution against unexpected reserve outflows. If a bank falls below its required-reserve level, it must make up the difference. There are several ways it can do this: It can "run off" loans, that is, stop making new loans to replace those being repaid; it can sell assets; or it can borrow, either from the Fed or from another bank. Legally, a bank can hold more than the required level of reserves, but there is a strong incentive not to do so because reserves earn no interest.

Ignoring the small amount of excess reserves that banks desire to hold, the situation in which required reserves equal total reserves can be thought of as a state of equilibrium. Although excess reserves may briefly depart from their equilibrium level, in our simplified banking system we will assume that banks soon bring them back to zero.

Mechanics of Money Creation

Now we are ready to examine the mechanics of money creation in our simplified banking system. As the following example will show, money creation is governed by the required-reserve ratio, the amount of reserves supplied, and banks' efforts to maximize their profits.

Initial Balance Sheets

Assume that each bank in the system starts out with a balance sheet that looks like this:

Initial Balance Sheet of a Representative Bank

Assets			Liabilities	
Reserves		$ 10,000	Demand deposits	$100,000
Required	$10,000			
Excess	0			
Loans		90,000		
Total assets		$100,000	Total liabilities	$100,000

Assume that the initial balance sheet for the simplified Federal Reserve System looks like this:

Assets		Liabilities	
U.S. government securities	$100,000	Reserve deposits	$100,000

The Fed's liabilities consist of $10,000 in reserve deposits by each of its ten member banks.

Injecting New Reserves

Now we will look at the effects of an injection of new reserves into the banking system. Each member bank receives new reserves every time a customer deposits funds that were withdrawn from another bank. However, this does not increase the reserves in the banking system as a whole. In order for total reserves to be increased, new reserves must come from outside the system. The chief source of new reserves is the Fed.

Suppose the Fed decides to increase the amount of reserves available to the banking system by $10,000. It usually does this by adding to its holdings of government securities by buying them from a securities dealer. Such an action is called an **open market operation** (in this case, an open market purchase) because the Fed, acting through the New York Federal Reserve Bank, goes to the securities market and bids against other buyers to purchase the securities. Thus, the Fed buys $10,000 in securities from a dealer and pays for them through a wire transfer to the dealer's bank, which we will call Albany National Bank. The *wire transfer* is an electronic instruction made through the Fed's computer network that credits Albany National Bank's reserve account at the Fed with $10,000 and simultaneously directs the bank to credit the same amount to the dealer's demand deposit account.

At that point, the Fed's initial goal of injecting $10,000 of new reserves into the system has been achieved. The balance sheets of the Fed and Albany National Bank now look like the following (in this and subsequent balance sheets, changes from the previous balance sheet are shown in parentheses):

Open market operation
A purchase (sale) by the Fed of government securities from (to) the public.

The Fed

Assets		Liabilities	
U.S. government securities	$110,000 (+10,000)	Reserve deposits	$110,000 (+10,000)

Albany National Bank

Assets			Liabilities	
Reserves		$ 20,000 (+10,000)	Demand deposits	$110,000 (+10,000)
Required	$11,000 (+1,000)			
Excess	9,000 (+9,000)			
Loans		90,000		
Total assets		$110,000 (+10,000)	Total liabilities	$110,000 (+10,000)

Loaning Out the Excess Reserves

Note how the $10,000 in new reserves at Albany National Bank is divided between required and excess reserves. Deposits have gone up by $10,000, meaning that the bank must hold $1,000 more in required reserves. The other $9,000 in new reserves need not be held against deposits and thus is listed as excess reserves. Albany National Bank is no longer in equilibrium; it can increase its profits by loaning out the excess reserves.

Of course, in order to make a loan the bank must find a borrower. Suppose that on the morning on which Albany gets its new reserves, James Anderson walks in and applies for a $9,000 auto loan. The loan is granted and the $9,000 credited to Anderson's checking account balance. (If Anderson had no checking account at Albany, he could instead ask the bank to pay him the proceeds of the loan in the form of a check or even currency. In that case, some of the intermediate steps in the following process would differ but the end result would be the same.) At the moment at which the loan is completed—but before Anderson pays for the car—Albany National Bank's balance sheet looks like this:

Albany National Bank

Assets			Liabilities	
Reserves		$ 20,000	Demand deposits	$119,000
Required	$11,900			
	(+900)			
Excess	8,100			
	(−900)			
Loans		99,000		
		(+9,000)		
Total assets		$119,000	Total liabilities	$119,000
		(+9,000)		(+9,000)

Checking Away the Loan Proceeds

In crediting Anderson's account with $9,000, Albany National Bank has created a new $9,000 asset (the loan) matched by a new $9,000 liability (the deposit). Because of the new deposit, its required reserves have risen by $900. At this point, Albany still has $8,100 in excess reserves. Why, then, does it not use those reserves to make yet another loan?

The reason the bank cannot safely make new loans greater than the original amount added to its excess reserves is that it knows Anderson will not leave the $9,000 sitting in his account; instead, he will write a check to pay for his new car. Let's see what happens when he does so.

We will call the dealer who sells the car Joyce Barnard and assume that she keeps her checking account at Bethel National Bank. When Barnard deposits Anderson's Albany National Bank check in her Bethel account, Bethel sends it to the Fed for clearance. *Clearing the check* simply means that the Fed credits $9,000 to Bethel's reserve account and subtracts $9,000 from Albany's reserve account. The Fed then puts the check itself in the mail so that Albany can forward it to Anderson for his records. When all these transactions have taken place, the two banks' balance sheets look like this:

Albany National Bank

Assets			Liabilities	
Reserves		$ 11,000	Demand deposits	$110,000
		(−9,000)		(−9,000)
Required	$11,000			
	(−900)			
Excess	0			
	(−8,100)			
Loans		99,000		
Total assets		$110,000	Total liabilities	$110,000
		(−9,000)		(−9,000)

Bethel National Bank

Assets			Liabilities	
Reserves		$ 19,000	Demand deposits	$109,000
		(+9,000)		(+9,000)
Required	$10,900			
	(+900)			
Excess	8,100			
	(+8,100)			
Loans		90,000		
Total assets		$109,000	Total liabilities	$109,000
		(+9,000)		(+9,000)

A careful look at these balance sheets reveals two important things. First, we clearly see why Albany National Bank could not safely loan out more than its initial $9,000 of excess reserves. It knew that the $9,000 deposit it created by writing the loan to Anderson would not stay on its books for long. As soon as the check cleared, $9,000 of deposits and reserves would be lost (unless the car dealer also kept an account at Albany). The $9,000 loss in deposits lowered its required reserves by only $900 (10 percent of the change in deposits); thus, it needed the $8,100 of excess reserves in order to make up the difference.

Second, we see that Albany's loss is Bethel's gain. Albany lost $9,000 in reserves ($900 required and $8,100 excess) when the check was written and cleared, and Bethel gained exactly the same amounts. The check-clearing process thus has left the banking system's total reserves unchanged.

Keeping the Expansion Going with Another Loan

The clearing of Anderson's check put Albany National Bank back in equilibrium, with $10,000 more in total assets and $10,000 more in liabilities than it started with. But now Bethel is out of equilibrium, with $8,100 in excess reserves. The logical thing for Bethel to do is to make a loan of its own using its excess reserves. (We now know that the proceeds of this loan will be checked away quickly, so we will skip the intermediate balance sheet.) After Bethel's borrower has written a check for $8,100, which is deposited in, say, Cooperstown National Bank, Bethel's and Cooperstown's balance sheets looks like this:

Bethel National Bank

Assets			Liabilities	
Reserves		$ 10,900	Demand deposits	$109,000
		(−8,100)		
Required	$10,900			
	(unchanged)			
Excess	0			
	(−8,100)			
Loans		98,100		
		(+8,100)		
Total assets		$109,000	Total liabilities	$109,000

Cooperstown National Bank

Assets			Liabilities	
Reserves		$ 18,100	Demand deposits	$108,100
		(+8,100)		(+8,100)
Required	$10,810			
	(+810)			
Excess	7,290			
	(+7,290)			
Loans		90,000		
Total assets		$108,100	Total liabilities	$108,100
		(+8,100)		(+8,100)

Further Rounds in the Expansion of Deposits

We need not go through all the rounds of the expansion process in detail, since a clear pattern has emerged. The initial open market purchase of securities by the Fed injected $10,000 of new reserves into the system. The first bank to receive the funds kept $1,000 (10 percent) as required reserves and loaned out the remaining $9,000. When the loan proceeds were checked away, they became $9,000 in new deposits and reserves for a second bank, which kept $900 (10 percent) and loaned out the remaining $8,100. The next bank, in turn, would be able to loan out $7,290, the next one $6,561, and so on round after round. The loans create new deposits at each round; therefore, the money supply, made up entirely of deposits, expands by $10,000 + $9,000 + $8,100 + $7,290 + $6,561 and so on. In the end, the whole process creates $100,000 in new deposits.

To summarize the process of deposit expansion, let's compare the beginning and final balance sheets for the ten-bank system as a whole. Initially the balance sheet looked like this:

Initial Balance Sheet for the Ten-Bank System

Assets			Liabilities	
Reserves		$ 100,000	Demand deposits	$1,000,000
Required	$100,000			
Excess	0			
Loans		900,000		
Total assets		$1,000,000	Total liabilities	$1,000,000

After the injection of $10,000 in new reserves, the combined balance sheet for the ten banks looks like this:

Final Balance Sheet for the Ten-Bank System

Assets			Liabilities	
Reserves		$ 110,000 (+10,000)	Demand deposits	$1,100,000 (+100,000)
Required	$110,000 (+10,000)			
Excess	0			
Loans		990,000 (+90,000)		
Total assets		$1,100,000 (+100,000)	Total liabilities	$1,100,000 (+100,000)

We see, then, that the expansion of deposits continues until excess reserves have disappeared. By the time the new reserves have become fully absorbed, total demand deposits will have expanded by $100,000. On the assets side of the balance sheet, this $100,000 of new liabilities will be offset by $10,000 in new required reserves and $90,000 in new loans.

Contraction of the Money Supply

When the Fed withdraws reserves from the banking system, the whole process works in reverse. For example, assume that all the banks are back in the position from which they started in the last example and that the Fed decides to withdraw, say, $1,000 in reserves. It can do this by making an open market sale of $1,000 of securities from its portfolio. Now suppose that the securities are bought by a dealer who pays for them with a check drawn on Denver National Bank. When the Fed gets the dealer's check, it clears it by deducting $1,000 from Denver's reserve account. At that point, Denver's balance sheet looks like this:

Denver National Bank

Assets			Liabilities	
Reserves		$ 9,000 (−1,000)	Demand deposits	$99,000 (−1,000)
Required	$9,900 (−100)			
Excess	−900 (−900)			
Loans		90,000		
Total assets		$99,000 (−1,000)	Total liabilities	$99,000 (−1,000)

The loss of $1,000 in deposits when the dealer wrote his check reduced required reserves by only $100, whereas Denver's total reserves fell by $1,000 when the Fed cleared the check. This leaves the bank with negative excess reserves—that is, a $900 reserve deficiency—that it must attempt to correct. In this simplified banking system, Denver must make up the deficiency by reducing its loans. It therefore leaves the next $900 it receives in loan payments in its reserve account. (We assume that if the bank did not have the reserve deficiency, it would make new loans as old ones were paid off, keeping its total loan holdings steady.) In the real world, a bank with a reserve deficiency has a number of other options. One is to sell other assets, such as government securities. Another is to borrow from a bank that has excess reserves. Still another is to borrow from the Fed itself. We will return to these options later.

When Denver National Bank reduces its loan holdings to make up its reserve deficiency, it drains reserves from some other bank in the system. For example, suppose that Maria Espinosa writes a check on Englewood National Bank to pay off $900 that she borrowed from Denver. At the moment when the transaction is complete and the check cleared, the balance sheets of the Denver and Englewood banks will look like this:

Denver National Bank

Assets		Liabilities	
Reserves	$ 9,900	Demand deposits	$99,000
	(+900)		
Required	$9,900		
	(unchanged)		
Excess	0		
	(+900)		
Loans	89,100		
	(−900)		
Total assets	$99,000	Total liabilities	$99,000

Englewood National Bank

Assets		Liabilities	
Reserves	$ 9,100	Demand deposits	$99,100
	(−900)		(−900)
Required	$9,910		
	(−90)		
Excess	−810		
	(−810)		
Loans	90,000		
Total assets	$99,100	Total liabilities	$99,100
	(−900)		(−900)

At this point, then, Denver has made up its reserve deficiency, but $810 of it has been passed along to Englewood. Now it is Englewood's turn to reduce its loan holdings. By using an $810 loan repayment received from some other bank, Englewood will build up its reserves by the required amount, but a $729 deficiency will appear somewhere else. The contraction process will continue until deposits in the banking system as a whole have been reduced by $10,000—ten times the loss of reserves that resulted from the Fed's open market security sale.

The Money Multiplier for the Simplified Banking System

As these examples have shown, the total amount of demand deposits that the banking system can hold depends on the total amount of reserves supplied by the Fed and on the required-reserve ratio. In equation form, with rr standing for the required-reserve ratio, the relationship is as follows:

$$\text{Total demand deposits} = \frac{1}{rr} \times \text{Total reserves}.$$

Thus, when total reserves were $100,000, the total money stock (consisting entirely of demand deposits in our example) was $1 million. When the Fed injected $10,000 of new reserves, bringing total reserves to $110,000, the money stock rose by $100,000 to $1.1 million. When the Fed withdrew $1,000 of reserves through an open market sale, reducing total reserves to $99,000, the money stock fell by $10,000 to $990,000.

Money multiplier
The ratio of the equilibrium money stock to the banking system's total reserves.

The term 1/rr in the above equation is called the **money multiplier** and is the ratio of the equilibrium money stock to total reserves. In our simplified banking system, where the required-reserve ratio was 10 percent, the value of the money multiplier was 10. Each injection or withdrawal of reserves by the Fed thus increases or decreases the money stock by ten times the change in reserves.

The Tools of Monetary Policy

In Chapter 12, we discussed the Fed's role in providing services to the banking system and in ensuring the system's safety and stability. Our discussion of money creation here shows that the Fed has another power, namely the power to control the money stock. Now that we know how money is created, we can examine the policy tools that give the Fed this power.

Open Market Operations

The preceding section illustrated the most important of the policy tools that the Fed uses to control the money stock: open market operations. If the Fed wants to expand the money stock, it instructs the open market trading desk at the Federal Reserve Bank of New York to buy government securities. This is known as an *open market purchase*. Sometimes an outright purchase is made, but more frequently the Fed buys the securities subject to a repurchase agreement. In such an arrangement, the dealer selling the securities to the Fed agrees to buy them back at a later date. Whichever form the purchase takes, the Fed pays for the securities by a wire transfer that adds funds to the reserves of the seller's bank. Since these are newly created reserves and not just a transfer of reserves from one bank to another, they add to the banking system's total reserves. Further, each dollar of reserves added to the banking system permits the volume of transaction deposits to expand by several dollars. The amount of the expansion—the number of dollars added to the money stock per dollar of added reserves—is determined by the money multiplier. In the real world, however, the factors determining the value of the money multiplier are more complex than in the simplified system discussed in the preceding section.

If the Fed wants to decrease the money stock, it reverses this process: It instructs the trading desk to carry out an open market sale of securities, either outright or subject to a repurchase agreement. If a dealer buys securities from the Fed and pays for them with a check or wire transfer drawn on a commercial bank, reserves will be drained from the banking system. The money supply will contract by an amount equal to the money multiplier times the size of the open market sale.

However, although open market operations are the most frequently used tool for controlling the money stock, they are not the only one. Once we remove some of the simplifying assumptions used so far in this chapter, we can see how these other tools work.

The Discount Rate

In our simplified banking system, banks can acquire new reserves only by attracting additional deposits. In practice, however, banks and thrifts that want additional reserves to either meet the Fed's requirements or expand their loans have another option: to borrow reserves.

One possibility is to borrow the reserves from another bank. The market in which banks make short-term loans of reserves among one another is known as the **federal funds market.** The interest rate charged on such loans is called the **federal funds rate.** This market, in which the usual loan term is 24 hours, has an activity of billions of dollars per day.

Banks can also borrow reserves from the Fed through the so-called **discount window.** (This facility is a department of the district Reserve banks and not, of course, an actual window.) Banks borrow from the Fed in two kinds of situations. Most often they borrow for short periods to adjust their reserves when unexpected withdrawals have left them with less than the required amount of reserves. Such borrowing is subject to administrative constraints. Banks are discouraged from borrowing too often or too much, and the more frequently an institution borrows at the discount window, the greater the administrative pressure to reduce borrowing. In cases where banks want to expand their reserves simply because they see profitable loan opportunities, they are encouraged to seek other sources of funds, such as new deposits.

In addition to short-term loans from the discount window, the Fed sometimes makes longer-term loans under special conditions. Sometimes, for example, loans are made to small banks to help them meet seasonal needs. Also, loans are sometimes made to troubled banks to give them time to get their affairs in order. The Fed's huge loan to Continental Illinois Bank & Trust in the spring of 1984 (see "Perspective 12.2," page 304) is a case in point.

The interest rate that the Fed charges on loans made through the discount window—known as the **discount rate**—is a second policy tool for controlling the money supply. If the Fed wants to encourage more discount window borrowing, it lowers the discount rate. As the discount rate falls relative to the federal funds rate, the explicit cost of discount borrowing falls relative to the cost of borrowing from other banks and the volume of discount borrowing expands. However, banks do not abandon the federal funds market altogether even when the discount rate is below the federal funds rate. Instead, as discount borrowing expands, the implicit cost of the administrative pressures that the Fed uses to discourage too much discount borrowing at some point becomes great enough to offset the interest rate advantage of the discount window.

If the Fed wants to reduce borrowing from the discount window, it raises the discount rate. As the discount rate rises relative to the federal funds rate, the discount window becomes less attractive as a source of funds.

Funds that banks borrow from one another through the federal funds mar-

Federal funds market
A market in which banks lend reserves to one another for periods as short as 24 hours.

Federal funds rate
The interest rate banks charge for overnight loans of reserves to one another.

Discount window
The department through which the Federal Reserve lends reserves to banks.

Discount rate
The interest rate the Fed charges on loans of reserves to banks.

ket have no effect on total bank reserves; this type of borrowing just moves reserves around from one bank to another. However, funds borrowed through the discount window are net additions to reserves. They form a basis for multiple expansion of deposits as do reserves injected through open market purchases. Because this form of borrowing affects the volume of reserves, then, changes in the discount rate give the Fed its second tool for controlling the money stock. Raising the discount rate cuts borrowed reserves and hence tends to lower the money stock; lowering it boosts borrowed reserves, which tends to allow the money stock to increase.

Changes in Required-Reserve Ratios

Changes in required-reserve ratios are a third policy tool that the Fed has used to control the money supply. Earlier in the chapter, we showed that the total volume of demand deposits in a simplified banking system is determined by the formula

$$\text{Total demand deposits} = \frac{1}{rr} \times \text{Total reserves},$$

where rr stands for the required-reserve ratio. A similar but somewhat more complex formula applies to the relationship between all transaction deposits and required-reserve ratios in the actual U.S. banking system. Thus, any reduction in required-reserve ratios will increase the money supply that a given quantity of reserves can support and an increase in the ratios will decrease the money supply for a given quantity of reserves.

Although changes in required-reserve ratios were never used for day-to-day control over the money supply in the past, the Fed sometimes changed the ratios when it wanted to make a strong move toward expansion or contraction of the money supply. For example, during the severe recession of 1974 to 1975, the Fed lowered reserve requirements three times.

The Monetary Control Act of 1980 broadened the coverage of the Fed's required-reserve ratios. Before the act was passed, the Fed could set such ratios only for member commercial banks. Now it can set reserve requirements on transaction deposits at all but the smallest depository institutions. By law the Fed can adjust the required-reserve ratio within a range of 8 to 14 percent for institutions with transaction deposits over a certain amount as well as impose supplemental reserve requirements on transaction deposits under some conditions. It can also impose a required-reserve ratio of no more than 3 percent on nonpersonal time deposits and certain other liabilities at institutions above a minimum size.

In practice, however, technicalities connected with the phased implementation of reserve requirements under the Monetary Control Act have dissuaded the Fed from changing the ratios as a policy tool, at least for the time being. Thus, this tool, although legally still available, has been shelved during the 1980s. Whether it will be used in the future is not known at this time.

Defensive versus Dynamic Open Market Operations

In a simplified banking system such as that in our example, the Fed's control over the money stock is direct and complete. In the real world, things are far less simple. Both the quantity of reserves and the money multiplier can change for reasons that are not directly under the Fed's control. When such changes occur, the Fed must undertake *defensive* open market operations in order to maintain the money stock at a desired level. These operations are in contrast to *dynamic* open market operations aimed at causing a change in the money stock.

A decline in either reserves or the money multiplier will tend to cause the money stock to drop. This effect can be prevented with a defensive open market purchase. Similarly, the effects of an increase in either reserves or the money multiplier, which tend to cause the money stock to rise, can be offset with a defensive open market sale. Let's look at some situations that may result in a need for defensive open market operations.

Shifts among Deposits

In our simplified banking system, the money multiplier equals 1 divided by the required-reserve ratio. In the real world, however, the money multiplier can vary from month to month even if no changes are made in required-reserve ratios. Exhibit 13.1 shows changes in the money multiplier in recent years, measured in this case as the ratio of M1 to total reserves.

One source of variation in the money multiplier is the fact that required-reserve ratios vary across types of deposits and banks. For example, transaction deposits at large banks are subject to a 12 percent required-reserve ratio and large certificates of deposit to a 3 percent ratio. If a depositor uses $100,000 held in a transaction account to buy a large certificate of deposit, $3,000 must be kept on reserve against the certificate, which does not count as part of M1. Thus, of the $12,000 of reserves previously held against the transaction deposit, only $9,000 is now available to support creation of M1. The banking system's total reserves do not drop, but the amount of transaction deposits that they can support does; hence, the money multiplier decreases. Similarly, the money multiplier falls when funds move from transaction deposits in very small banks, which are not required to hold reserves, to larger banks, which must hold reserves at the full 12 percent rate. Moving funds from large banks to small ones, on the other hand, causes the money multiplier to rise.

Changes in Currency Holdings

In the simplified economy discussed in the first section of this chapter, demand deposits were the only form of money. In reality, currency accounts for more than one-quarter of M1. Changes in the way the public divides its holdings of M1 between currency and transaction deposits are another source of variation in the money multiplier as well as in total reserves.

To illustrate, consider what happens when you deposit $100 in your checking account that you had previously held in the form of currency. At the moment you make your deposit, there is no effect on the total stock of M1; you have simply exchanged $100 in currency for a $100 addition to your checking account balance. What has become of the currency you deposited? Once in the bank's hands it no longer counts as part of M1, since that measure of the money stock includes only transaction deposits plus currency outside of banks. However, the currency does count as reserves for the bank, because vault cash, as well as deposits with the Fed, are part of reserves. Thus, the act of depositing $100 in currency increases the banking system's total reserves by $100. The bank must hold $10 of this as required reserves (if we continue to assume a 10 percent required-reserve ratio) but can use the remaining $90 to loan out or to purchase

Exhibit 13.1   Variations in the Money Multiplier

As this chart shows, the money multiplier—measured here as the ratio of M1 to total reserves—is subject to variations from month to month. Some of these variations can be predicted. The Fed can neutralize the effects of predictable variations in the money multiplier by making offsetting changes in the level of total reserves. However, unpredicted changes in the multiplier will cause the money stock to depart from its desired level.

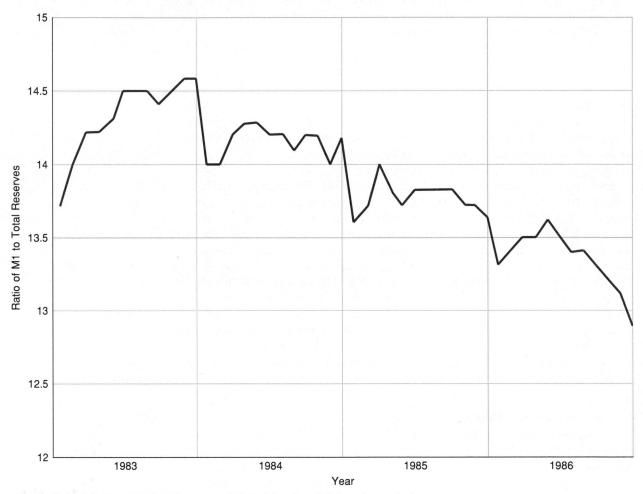

Source: Federal Reserve Board of Governors. Adjusted for phased changes in required reserve ratios mandated by the Monetary Control Act.

securities. The loan would set off a multiple expansion of deposits just as if the bank had acquired $100 in new reserves through an open market purchase.

How much new money will be created as a result of the expansion of deposits? If all of the money created at each step of the expansion process were held as demand deposits, the $100 in new reserves would allow $1,000 in new transaction deposits to be created. However, now that we have incorporated currency into the monetary system, we must consider the possibility that people will want to hold some of the newly created money as currency. Any money that leaks out of the expansion process to be held as currency rather than being redeposited in banks will reduce the total amount of new money created.

In summary, in an economy with currency, a deposit of currency will increase total bank reserves, allowing a multiple expansion of deposits. However, the quantity of new money created will be less than that predicted by the simple money multiplier (1/rr) partly because the initial deposit will reduce the currency component of M1 and partly because some of the money will leak back out of the banking system in the form of currency. The greater the proportion of money held in the form of currency, the smaller the money multiplier's actual value.

Withdrawing money from your checking account in the form of currency causes a reversal of the process: The banking system will lose reserves, setting off a multiple contraction of deposits.

Currency holdings follow a fairly predictable pattern over the course of a year, peaking during the Christmas shopping season and growing somewhat less during summer holidays. Such seasonal variations are routinely accommodated by adding or withdrawing reserves via defensive open market operations. These defensive operations prevent any undesired effect on total reserves and deposits.

Other Factors Affecting the Money Multiplier and Reserves

Certain other factors can affect the value of the money multiplier or the quantity of reserves. For example, in our simplified banking system it was assumed that banks wanted to keep the level of excess reserves at zero. In practice, banks purposely hold small quantities of excess reserves in connection with check-clearing operations as a precaution against unexpected reserve outflows. Funds held voluntarily as excess reserves do not contribute to the multiple expansion of deposits. Hence, the higher the desired level of excess reserves, the lower the money multiplier. In addition, total reserves, and hence the money stock, can be affected by receipts and expenditures of the U.S. Treasury and by international financial transactions, as discussed in the final section of this chapter.

Today the Fed routinely uses defensive open market operations to keep reserves and the money stock at their desired levels in the face of changing economic conditions. This was not always the case, however. "Perspective 13.1" tells the story of monetary policy during the Great Depression, when the Fed failed to use open market operations to offset currency drains and accumulation of excess reserves. Its failure in this regard is considered to have made the Depression longer and more severe than it need have been.

The Federal Reserve in the International Economy

Earlier in the chapter, we saw that the Fed is an active trader in markets for U.S. securities. Its sales and purchases in this market are its principal means for controlling the stock of dollars. However, the Fed is also an active participant in the **foreign exchange markets,** in which the dollar is exchanged for Japanese yen, West German marks, British pounds, and the currencies of nearly every other country. As the U.S. economy has become increasingly open to international influences, the Fed's activities in the foreign exchange markets have made the financial headlines at least as much as its domestic open market operations

Foreign exchange market
A market in which the currency of one country is traded for that of another.

Monetary Policy during the Great Depression

Although economists have debated the causes of the Great Depression for nearly 60 years, they still do not completely understand why what began as a fairly ordinary business contraction in the summer of 1929 led to a four-year downward spiral in which real output fell by a third and unemployment rose to a quarter of the labor force. But it is widely believed that a collapse of the banking system and a precipitous decline in the money stock, as shown in the accompanying chart, played a major role.

The question is: Why did the money stock fall? In their book *A Monetary History of the United States*, Milton Friedman and Anna J. Schwartz examine the decline in detail. In the initial phase of the contraction, which lasted from August 1929 to October 1930, the money supply fell because reserve borrowing at the Fed's discount window declined. The Fed could have kept total reserves from declining either by lowering the discount rate enough to keep it in line with falling short-term market rates or through open market purchases of securities. However, it did neither. The discount rate was lowered, but not as quickly as market rates fell, and little use was made of open market operations. Nevertheless, the decline in the money stock was modest during this period.

Then, in October 1930, the character of the contraction changed dramatically. A crop of bank failures, particularly in farm states such as Missouri, Indiana, Illinois, Iowa, Arkansas, and North Carolina, spread fear among depositors nationwide. As there was no federal deposit insurance in those days, a bank failure could completely wipe out a depositor's savings. All over the country bank runs began as people tried to convert their deposits into currency. The runs brought down hundreds of banks; 256 banks failed in November and 352 in December. Many of these were small, rural banks, but the December crop included the giant Bank of the United States in New York. Although this was in fact an ordinary commercial bank, its official-sounding name made its failure a tremendous blow to confidence in the system.

The bank runs show up clearly in the accompanying chart in the form of a sharp decline in the ratio of deposits to currency. The rush to convert deposits into currency continued through a second banking crisis in 1931 and a final one in 1933. To cope with the last, newly elected President Franklin Roosevelt declared a banking holiday, closing all banks in the country for more than a week while matters were sorted out.

The conversions of deposits into currency drained reserves from the banking system and accelerated the decline in the money stock. Matters were worsened by banks' reactions to the crisis. Knowing that a run of depositors was an ever present danger, banks that had not yet failed increased their liquidity by building up excess reserves. This precaution caused a decrease in the ratio of deposits to total reserves, as shown in the chart. Banks' reluctance to lend out their excess reserves also lowered the overall money multiplier. In a period in which reserves were already falling, the decline in the money multiplier made the money stock fall even more rapidly.

What did the Fed do? It could have used open market operations to pump new reserves into the system, replacing those lost to currency and offsetting the declining deposit-to-reserve ratio. But the Fed did not act vigorously enough. It allowed some increase in what Friedman and Schwartz call "high-powered money," meaning the total of reserves plus currency. However, the increase in high-powered money was not nearly enough to offset the decline in reserves and in the money multiplier and, hence, in the money stock itself.

Friedman and Schwartz sum up their analysis of the period as follows:

> Prevention or moderation of the decline in the stock of money . . . would have reduced the contraction's severity and almost as certainly its duration. The contraction might still have been relatively severe. But it is hardly conceivable that money income could have declined by over one-half and prices by over one-third in the course of four years if there had been no decline in the stock of money.

Source: Milton Friedman and Anna Jacobson Schwartz, *A Monetary History of the United States*, 1867–1960, Chapter 7. Copyright © 1963 by NBER. Published by Princeton University Press. Graph reprinted with permission of Princeton University Press.

have. This section takes a preliminary look at the mechanics of the Fed's activities in the foreign exchange market and these activities' relationship to domestic

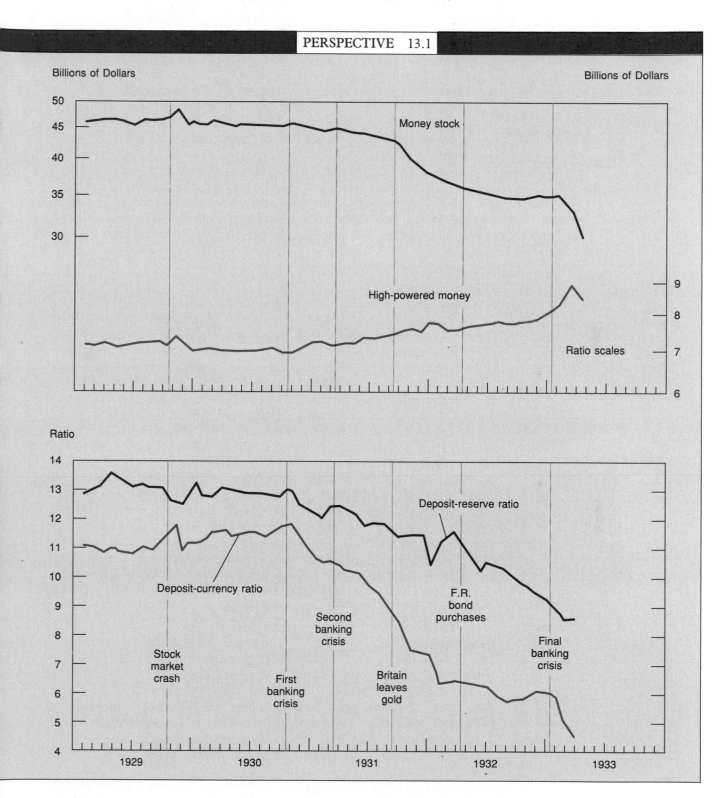

monetary policy. Succeeding chapters add details relating exchange rates to the
balance of payments, interest rates, inflation, and economic growth.

The Structure of Foreign Exchange Markets

As a traveler you may have had occasion to exchange U.S. dollars for Canadian dollars, Mexican pesos, or the currency of some other country. This trading in paper currencies is a small corner of the largest set of markets in the world—the foreign exchange markets, in which hundreds of billions of dollars are traded each day. Such trading reflects the fact that virtually every international transaction in goods, services, or financial assets is preceded by the exchange of one currency for another.

Suppose, for example, that a U.S. department store chain wants to buy a shipload of Japanese video recorders and to pay for it in dollars. However, in order to meet its payroll, pay its suppliers, and so on the Japanese firm needs yen, not dollars. The solution: The U.S. importer goes to the foreign exchange market and uses its dollars to buy the yen that the Japanese firm wants as payment.

Market Institutions

Obviously, large exchange market transactions are not carried out with paper currency; like large domestic transactions, they are conducted with transaction deposits in commercial banks as the means of payment. The central players in the foreign exchange markets are large banks in the world's money centers—London, Zurich, Tokyo—known as *trading banks*. Unlike the typical small-town savings and loan, these banks have branches all over the world and accept deposits denominated in many different currencies. U.S. banks act as trading banks through their foreign branches even though banks are not allowed to accept deposits denominated in foreign currencies in their U.S. offices. Outside the United States, foreign banks and foreign branches of U.S. banks can accept deposits both in dollars and in foreign currencies.

Thus, if a Macy's department store in New York needs to buy yen, it can ask Chase Manhattan Bank to debit its dollar-denominated account and credit a deposit of equal value to an account in Tokyo denominated in yen that it can use to pay a Japanese supplier. Similarly, if a Japanese pension fund wants to buy U.S. Treasury bills, it can exchange a deposit denominated in yen at a Japanese or U.S. trading bank for a deposit denominated in dollars and then use those dollars to buy the T-bills. The trading banks make a profit on these transactions by charging an *asked* price for the currency they sell that is slightly higher than the *bid* price they pay for the currency they buy.

Exchange Rates

What determines the number of yen that a customer gets in exchange for its dollars? Why, on a given day, 150 yen per dollar rather than 125 or 200? The answer is supply and demand. Foreign firms that want to buy U.S. goods or assets demand dollars in exchange for their own currencies. U.S. firms that want to buy foreign goods or assets supply dollars in exchange for foreign currencies. The interaction of supply and demand in the foreign exchange markets determines the daily price of currencies in much the same way that it does the price of wheat, IBM common stock, or any other competitively traded item. (Chapter 20 explores the determinants of supply and demand in the foreign exchange markets in detail.)

The prices of one currency in terms of another are published daily in finan-

Exhibit 13.2   Foreign Exchange Rates

In foreign exchange markets, the dollar is traded for the currencies of other countries. Exchange rates vary from day to day according to supply and demand conditions. This exhibit shows the foreign exchange quotations from *The Wall Street Journal* for April 21, 1987. Exchange rates are quoted in terms of both U.S. dollars per unit of the foreign currency (such as $.1657 per French franc) and units of the foreign currency per dollar (6.03 francs per dollar). For some major currencies, forward rates are given. *Forward exchange contracts* are agreements to buy or sell a currency at a future date at a price that is agreed on today.

FOREIGN EXCHANGE

Tuesday, April 21, 1987

The New York foreign exchange selling rates below apply to trading among banks in amounts of $1 million and more, as quoted at 3 p.m. Eastern time by Bankers Trust Co. Retail transactions provide fewer units of foreign currency per dollar.

Country	U.S. $ equiv.		Currency per U.S. $	
	Tues.	Mon.	Tues.	Mon.
Argentina (Austral) ...	.6502	.6502	1.538	1.5380
Australia (Dollar)	.7083	.7120	1.4118	1.4045
Austria (Schilling)	.07843	.0783	12.75	12.77
Belgium (Franc)				
Commercial rate	.02662	.0266	37.56	37.53
Financial rate	.02653	.0265	37.70	37.74
Brazil (Cruzado)	.04188	.04193	23.88	23.85
Britain (Pound)	1.6360	1.6315	.6112	.6129
30-Day Forward	1.6318	1.6273	.6128	.6145
90-Day Forward	1.6253	1.6200	.6153	.6173
180-Day Forward	1.6170	1.6115	.6184	.6205
Canada (Dollar)	.7553	.7590	1.3241	1.3175
30-Day Forward	.7547	.7586	1.3250	1.3182
90-Day Forward	.7534	.7575	1.3273	1.3201
180-Day Forward	.7508	.7552	1.3319	1.3241
Chile (Official rate) ...	.004744	.004744	210.80	210.80
China (Yuan)	.2693	.2693	3.7128	3.7128
Colombia (Peso)	.004329	.004329	231.00	231.00
Denmark (Krone)	.1467	.1465	6.8150	6.8280
Ecuador (Sucre)				
Official rate	.006264	.006264	159.65	159.65
Floating rate	.006826	.006826	146.50	146.50
Finland (Markka)	.2273	.2278	4.4000	4.3900
France (Franc)	.1657	.1657	6.0340	6.0345
30-Day Forward	.1655	.1655	6.0405	6.0425
90-Day Forward	.1653	.1651	6.0510	6.0565
180-Day Forward	.1648	.1645	6.0685	6.0800
Greece (Drachma)	.007505	.0075	133.25	133.59
Hong Kong (Dollar) ...	.1282	.1282	7.7980	7.8010
India (Rupee)	.07819	.07792	12.79	12.93
Indonesia (Rupiah)	.0006083	.0006083	1644.00	1644.00
Ireland (Punt)	1.4755	1.4745	.6777	.6782
Israel (Shekel)	.6234	.6711	1.604	1.49

Country	U.S. $ equiv.		Currency per U.S. $	
Italy (Lira)	.0007734	.000773	1293.00	1293.50
Japan (Yen)	.007030	.00702	142.25	142.40
30-Day Forward	.007049	.00704	141.86	142.05
90-Day Forward	.007084	.00707	141.17	141.37
180-Day Forward	.007140	.00713	140.05	140.30
Jordan (Dinar)	2.9674	2.9674	.3370	.3370
Kuwait (Dinar)	3.6590	3.6590	.2733	.2733
Lebanon (Pound)	.008666	.008666	115.40	115.40
Malaysia (Ringgit)	.4042	.4029	2.4740	2.4820
Malta (Lira)	2.8777	2.8777	.3475	.3475
Mexico (Peso)				
Floating rate	.0008598	.000862	1163.00	1160.00
Netherland(Guilder) ...	.4886	.4888	2.0466	2.0460
New Zealand (Dollar) ..	.5740	.5775	1.7422	1.7316
Norway (Krone)	.1487	.1477	6.7260	6.7725
Pakistan (Rupee)	.05780	.0584	17.30	17.12
Peru (Inti)	.06716	.06716	14.89	14.89
Philippines (Peso)	.04878	.04878	20.50	20.50
Portugal (Escudo)	.007156	.007133	139.75	140.20
Saudi Arabia (Riyal) ..	.2667	.2666	3.7498	3.751
Singapore (Dollar)	.4687	.4684	2.1335	2.1350
South Africa (Rand)				
Commercial rate	.4990	.5000	2.0040	2.0000
Financial rate	.3213	z	3.1123	z
South Korea (Won)	.001184	.001184	844.30	844.30
Spain (Peseta)	.007872	.00786	127.03	127.20
Sweden (Krona)	.1587	.1588	6.3000	6.2975
Switzerland (Franc) ..	.6702	.6693	1.4920	1.4940
30-Day Forward	.6742	.6712	1.4832	1.4898
90-Day Forward	.6757	.6747	1.4799	1.4821
180-Day Forward	.6813	.6802	1.4677	1.4702
Taiwan (Dollar)	.02981	.02959	33.55	33.80
Thailand (Baht)	.03887	.03887	25.73	25.73
Turkey (Lira)	.001271	.001271	786.50	786.50
United Arab(Dirham) .	.2723	.2723	3.673	3.673
Uruguay (New Peso)				
Financial	.004953	.004953	201.90	201.90
Venezuela (Bolivar)				
Official rate	.1333	.1333	7.50	7.50
Floating rate	.04230	.04230	23.64	23.64
W. Germany (Mark) ..	.5513	.5513	1.8140	1.8140
30-Day Forward	.5527	.5525	1.8093	1.8099
90-Day Forward	.5554	.5553	1.8004	1.8008
180-Day Forward	.5601	.5593	1.7855	1.7879

– – –

Source: *The Wall Street Journal*, April 22, 1987, 40.

cial newspapers. Exhibit 13.2 shows the foreign exchange rate quotations from *The Wall Street Journal* for a typical day. Each currency is quoted in two equivalent ways, for example, yen per dollar and dollar per yen. Most currencies are quoted on a *spot* basis, that is, for immediate delivery. Some of the major currencies are also traded on a *forward* basis, meaning an exchange of currencies at an agreed-upon future date at a price that is set today.

Intervention in the Foreign Exchange Markets

Exchange rates are not empty numbers; they have major impacts on the economy. For example, if the dollar rises in price relative to the yen, as it did during the first half of the 1980s, more yen can be bought for a dollar. Japanese goods thus become inexpensive for U.S. consumers. Imports from Japan increase, and U.S. firms competing with imports face possibly devastating competition. When the dollar falls in value relative to the yen, as it did after February 1985, more dollars must be spent to import a given quantity of Japanese goods. The price that U.S. consumers pay for imports rises, and U.S. firms face less competition than before. Similarly, U.S. exporters benefit from a low value of the dollar but find it hard to sell their products when the value of the dollar is high.

Because exchange rates affect imports and exports so strongly, their level is a matter of concern for policymakers. Consequently, from time to time central banks in the United States and other countries intervene in foreign exchange markets in an attempt to offset market pressures that tend to raise or lower the exchange values of their currencies. In the United States, foreign currency operations are directed by the Federal Open Market Committee in close cooperation with the Treasury, which has overall responsibility for the management of international financial policy. They are carried out by the Fed through its foreign trading desk in New York.

Mechanics of Intervention

The mechanics of intervention in the foreign exchange markets are similar to those for open market operations. Suppose, for example, that the Treasury wants to resist downward pressure on the dollar relative to the yen, as it did in early 1987. In order to support the price of the dollar relative to the yen, it must raise both the quantity of dollars demanded and the quantity of yen supplied.

The Fed is able to do this because on the assets side of its balance sheet it holds foreign securities along with its holdings of U.S. government securities; these include yen-denominated securities issued by the Japanese government. The Fed first sells these securities to a securities dealer in Tokyo and receives payment in the form of a yen-denominated transaction deposit at the Bank of Japan, that country's central bank. The Bank of Japan acts as the Fed's agent in this transaction. The Fed then uses that deposit to buy dollars from a U.S. trading bank; more precisely, it sells the yen-denominated deposit to a Tokyo branch of one of the New York trading banks. The bank pays for the yen deposit by drawing on the reserves it has on deposit with the Fed in the United States. In this way, the Fed has increased the quantity of yen supplied and at the same time increased the quantity of dollars demanded, thus nudging up the dollar's value relative to the yen.

If at another time the Fed wants to counter upward pressure on the dollar's value, it must reverse these transactions. In that case, it buys a yen-denominated deposit from the New York trading bank and pays for it with a wire transfer crediting the appropriate number of dollars to the bank's reserve account at the Fed. The Fed then uses the yen deposit to buy Japanese government securities for its portfolio. This set of trades tends to nudge down the dollar's value in the foreign exchange markets.

Effects on the Domestic Money Stock

As the preceding description of exchange market intervention makes clear, these transactions affect the U.S. banking system's reserves at the same time they influence the dollar's exchange value. When the Fed buys foreign currencies to push down the value of the dollar, it increases the U.S. banking system's reserves in exactly the same way that it does when it buys securities on the open market. When it sells foreign currencies to support the value of the dollar, bank reserves are depleted exactly as they are when the Fed conducts an open market sale of securities. Thus, the Fed's actions in the exchange markets closely affect its domestic monetary policy, and vice versa.

To offset the effects of its foreign exchange activities on domestic bank reserves, the Fed routinely engages in a special type of defensive open market operation known as **sterilization.** To sterilize a sale of foreign currencies, which tends to decrease U.S. bank reserves, the Fed simultaneously makes an equal open market purchase of U.S. government securities. The open market purchase restores total reserves to their previous value. To sterilize a purchase of foreign currencies, which tends to increase bank reserves, the Fed carries out an offsetting domestic open market sale.

Stated in these terms, sterilization sounds simple: One set of transactions offsets the other. However, in practice, sterilization fails to achieve a complete separation of domestic monetary policy from exchange rate policy. Sterilization or no, the two remain linked through interest rates, changes in expected inflation rates, fluctuations in the GNP growth rate, and so on. For these reasons, one rarely reads a newspaper article related to domestic monetary policy that does not also discuss effects on the international value of the dollar or a story on the value of the dollar that does not end by discussing the money stock and interest rates. Our discussion of exchange market intervention here is just the starting point for the story of the interaction between domestic and international monetary policy; more details will be added in the following chapters.

Sterilization
The Fed's use of open market operations to offset the effects of exchange market intervention on domestic reserves and the money stock.

Summary

1. **How do banks create money?** Banks can make loans whenever their *reserves* exceed the minimum *required reserves* set by the Fed. When a bank makes a loan, it credits the proceeds to the borrower's transaction account. When the borrower spends this newly created money, the recipient deposits it in another bank, which in turn can use its excess reserves to make another loan. In this manner, each dollar of new reserves that the banking system receives becomes the basis for a multiple expansion of deposits.

2. **Why is the size of the money stock limited by the quantity of bank reserves?** Although banks can create money, they can do so only to the extent that they have *excess reserves*. This means that the total quantity

of deposits that the banking system can create is limited by the total quantity of reserves available and the *required-reserve ratio*. In a simplified banking system, the number of dollars of deposits that can be created for each dollar of reserves equals 1/rr, where rr is the required-reserve ratio. The ratio 1/rr is the *money multiplier* for the simplified banking system. The formula for the money multiplier in the actual U.S. banking system is more complex, but required-reserve ratios still play a central role in it.

3. **What instruments are available to the Fed for controlling the money stock?** *Open market operations*, in which the Fed affects the banking system's reserves through purchases or sales of government securities,

are the Fed's principal instrument of monetary control. An open market purchase injects reserves and allows the money stock to expand; an open market sale drains reserves and causes the money stock to contract. Changes in the *discount rate* charged by the Fed for loans of reserves to banks and thrifts are a second instrument. An increase in the discount rate reduces the quantity of reserves borrowed and hence tends to cause the money stock to contract. Lowering the discount rate encourages borrowing of reserves and thus tends to allow the money stock to expand. Changes in required-reserve ratios are a third instrument, but this mechanism has not been used in recent years. A decrease in the required-reserve ratio allows the money stock to expand; an increase in the ratio causes the money stock to contract.

4. **How well can the money stock be controlled?** The Fed is able to control the money stock reasonably closely through use of open market operations and changes in the discount rate. However, its control is not perfect; unpredicted variations in the money multiplier or in total reserves can cause unexpected changes in the money stock. Sources of variations in reserves or the money multiplier include movements of funds from one type of bank or account to another; changes in excess reserves held by banks; changes in public holdings of currency; operations of the U.S. Treasury; and certain international transactions. To the extent that these events can be predicted, as in the case of seasonal variations in currency demand, they can be offset with open market operations.

5. **What activities does the Fed undertake in the international sphere?** Each day, billions of dollars are traded for currencies of other countries in the *foreign exchange market*. Because the exchange rate of the dollar relative to other currencies affects U.S. importers and exporters, the Fed sometimes intervenes in foreign exchange markets to counteract upward or downward pressure on the dollar's value relative to other currencies. It can lower the exchange value of the dollar by selling dollars and buying foreign currencies and raise it by buying dollars and selling foreign currencies. Intervention in the foreign exchange markets tends to affect the U.S. banking system's reserves and, hence, the domestic money stock. These effects on the domestic money stock can be avoided if the Fed offsets the reserve impact of its interventions by using domestic open market operations—a practice known as *sterilization*. However, sterilization does not completely break the linkage between domestic and international monetary developments.

Terms for Review

- required reserves
- required-reserve ratio
- excess reserves
- open market operation
- money multiplier
- federal funds market
- federal funds rate
- discount window
- discount rate
- foreign exchange market
- sterilization

Questions for Review

1. Why cannot a bank safely make loans in amounts greater than its excess reserves?

2. What does the Fed buy or sell in an open market operation? If the Fed wants to increase bank reserves, should it conduct an open market sale or an open market purchase?

3. If a withdrawal leaves a bank with reserves that are below the required level, what can the bank do to correct the situation?

4. What are the Fed's three main instruments for controlling the money stock? Which does it use most frequently? Least frequently?

5. What is the federal funds market? Why does the level of the discount rate relative to the federal funds rate affect the level of bank reserves?

6. How does a deposit of currency in a bank affect bank reserves and the money stock? A withdrawal of currency?

7. What actions does the Fed take when it wants to intervene in foreign exchange markets to raise the dollar's exchange value relative to, say, the British pound? What actions does it take when it wants to lower the dollar's value? Why do these actions affect the domestic money stock unless offset through sterilization?

Problems and Topics for Discussion

1. **Examining the lead-off case.** Review the story with which this chapter opens. Under what conditions is Rachel Fleming's bank able to give her a loan? How is her bank's balance sheet affected when she writes a check to pay for her car? How is the car dealer's bank's balance sheet affected when the check is deposited there? How is the balance sheet of Fleming's bank affected when she shifts $2,000 from her savings to her checking account? (No reserves are required

against personal savings accounts; assume a 10 percent reserve requirement for the checking account.) Does this shift affect the total quantity of M1 supplied by the banking system? Why or why not? How is the balance sheet of Fleming's bank affected when she withdraws $100 in cash? (The money stored in automatic teller machines counts as reserves until it is withdrawn.) How is the money stock affected by this withdrawal? *Bonus question:* How is Fleming's choice between a Honda and a Chevrolet affected by the exchange rate of the dollar relative to the yen?

2. **Multiple expansion of deposits.** Rework the deposit expansion examples in this chapter on the basis of the following assumptions:
    a. An injection of $5,000 in reserves via an open market purchase
    b. An injection of $20,000 in reserves with a 20 rather than 10 percent required-reserve ratio
    c. Withdrawal of $500 in reserves via an open market sale

3. **Currency and the money stock.** Use a balance sheet approach to trace the effects of a $1,000 withdrawal of currency from a bank. Assume that reserves are held half in the form of vault cash and half in the form of reserves on deposit with the Fed. Also assume that after the initial currency withdrawal there are no further changes in currency holdings by the public.

4. **The federal funds rate and the discount rate.** The *Federal Reserve Bulletin*, published monthly by the Fed, gives the values of the discount and federal funds rates and data for total and borrowed reserves. What has happened to the difference between these rates recently? Has the discount rate been changed? What has happened to the volume of borrowed reserves? Have they moved in the direction you would expect given the behavior of interest rates?

5. **Foreign exchange markets.** In *The Wall Street Journal* or the financial pages of another newspaper, find the most recent foreign exchange quotations. How has the value of the dollar changed relative to other major currencies compared with the data given in Exhibit 13.2?

Case for Discussion

Dollar Rises on Persian Gulf Worries

JULY 30, 1987. The dollar firmed in foreign exchange trading as dealers cited concern about a possible U.S.-Iranian showdown in the Persian Gulf.

The dollar was also supported by anticipation of next month's planned Treasury auction of bills and notes. The sale is expected to attract substantial interest from Japanese investors, and they may need to buy additional dollars to participate.

A rumor that a second ship hit a mine in the Persian Gulf prompted speculative buying of the dollar in early U.S. trading, dealers said, but the report was never confirmed. The dollar would be expected to benefit from any heightening of tensions in the Middle East as international investors seek what they consider the relative safety of U.S. securities.

Anticipation of the Treasury Department's announcement late in the day tentatively rescheduling its postponed bill and note auctions for next Thursday gave additional buoyancy to the dollar. Japanese investors have recently stepped up their buying of U.S. debt, a trend that is expected to continue.

Source: Charles W. Stevens, "Dollar Gets Boost from New Worry over Persian Gulf," *The Wall Street Journal,* July 30, 1987, 29.

Questions

1. In order to buy U.S. securities, Japanese and other investors must first buy dollars. How is this done, and why does it tend to push up the dollar's exchange rate relative to foreign currencies?

2. If the Fed and the Treasury want to resist the upward pressure on the dollar relative to the yen and other currencies, what steps could they take? Outline the procedures involved.

3. If the Fed intervenes to resist upward pressure on the dollar's value, how will the domestic money stock be affected? What can the Fed do to prevent an effect on the domestic money stock?

14 The Supply of and Demand for Money

After reading this chapter, you will understand . . .

- How classical economists viewed the demand for money.
- How income and interest rates affect money demand according to current theory.
- How money demand has behaved in the U.S. economy in recent years.
- How supply and demand determine interest rates in the money market.
- What targets the Fed has used as guides to its open market operations.

Before reading this chapter, make sure you know the meaning of . . .

- Bonds (Chapter 4)
- Primary and secondary securities markets (Chapter 4)
- Stocks and flows (Chapter 6)
- Liquidity (Chapter 12)

"Snugging Up" Monetary Policy

Paul A. Volcker

Federal Reserve Chairman Paul A. Volcker, in an unusual disclosure, said yesterday the central bank has tightened monetary policy. Volcker stressed that while the Fed had begun to follow a "less accommodative policy," the actual degree of tightening was very small, what market analysts call a "snugging up." He used similar words, adding, "Our actions have been quite limited in a technical sense."

As usual, the Fed chairman refused to speculate on the future course of interest rates, including whether the Federal Reserve Board may raise its $5\frac{1}{2}$ percent discount rate—the rate the Fed charges when it makes loans to financial institutions.

But the Fed chairman specifically said long-term interest rates have gone up "without any action" by the Fed to cause them to do so. And he also said that recent increases in the federal funds rate have also been caused by factors in addition to the Fed tightening.

The federal funds rate, which heavily influences other short-term interest rates, hovered between 6 percent and 6.2 percent early in April. This week, it has gone as high as 7 percent, and many analysts believed the Fed was responsible.

Source: John M. Berry, "Volcker Reveals Fed Tightened Credit," *The Washington Post*, May 1, 1987, p. F1. Reprinted with permission. Photo Source: Courtesy of Federal Reserve Board.

W E now know what money is, how it is measured, and how it is controlled by the Fed, but this story adds an important new element to the picture: the effects of monetary policy on interest rates. In this chapter, we will use the tools of supply and demand to analyze this link between monetary policy and interest rates. This will set the stage for Chapter 15, in which we will take up the broader relationships among monetary policy and inflation, unemployment, and economic growth.

The Demand for Money

We begin with the demand for money. In talking about demand for most goods and services, such as watches, radios, or movies, we deal in terms of *flows*—so many watches sold per year, so many radios sold per month, so many movies viewed per week. The case of money differs, however. Here we are concerned with the demand for a *stock*. The amount of money demanded is the stock of money that people want to possess at a given point in time under particular conditions. Let us see what determines this quantity.

Classical Theory of Money Demand

Equation of exchange
An equation that shows the relationships among the money stock (M), the velocity of money (V), the price level (P), and the level of real income (y); written as
MV = Py.

Velocity
The ratio of nominal national income to the money stock; a measure of the average number of times each dollar of the money stock is used each year for income-producing purposes.

The classical economists viewed money demand in terms of the **equation of exchange.** This formula can be written in the form

$$MV = Py,$$

where M stands for the quantity of money, V for the **velocity** of money (that is, the average number of times each dollar of the money stock is spent each year for income-producing purposes), P for the price level, and y for real national income. This equation must always hold given the way the term *velocity* is defined. Suppose, for example, that real national income is $1 trillion in constant dollars and the price level is 2. Nominal national income thus will be $2 \times \$1$ trillion = $2 trillion per year. If each dollar is spent for income-producing purposes an average of five times a year, a money stock of $400 billion will be required in order to sustain the $2-trillion-per-year nominal national income. Sustaining that income with a smaller money stock will require each dollar to be used more than five times a year. If the money supply is larger, the same level of nominal national income can be sustained with a velocity of less than 5. Thus, the money stock times the velocity of money must always equal nominal income (real income times the price level).

The equation of exchange is not a theory in itself; it simply shows the arithmetical relationships among money, velocity, real income, and the price level. An early step toward a theory of the demand for money was to assume that velocity is determined independently of monetary policy by such institutional factors as how often workers are paid and how quickly banks process transactions. This assumption meant that velocity could be treated as a constant or at least as varying around a constant equilibrium value that would be attained in the long run. With equilibrium velocity held constant, the amount of money required for sustaining any given level of nominal national income could be found by dividing nominal national income by that value of velocity. In equation form, using MD to stand for money demand, P for nominal income, and V for equilibrium velocity, this theory of money demand could be written as

$$MD = Py/V.$$

Keynes on the Demand for Money

When John Maynard Keynes began work on his *General Theory of Employment, Interest, and Money*, he was not content with the simple view that the demand for money is proportionate to nominal income because equilibrium velocity is constant. Instead, he developed a more complex theory based on three motives for holding money.

Keynesian Motives for Holding Money

Keynes called the need to hold money as a means of payment the *transactions motive*. Besides holding money for day-to-day purchases, people may also hold some extra money for dealing with unexpected events, which Keynes called the *precautionary motive*. He believed that both the transactions and precautionary motives were roughly proportional to nominal income as in the equation of exchange.

Keynes also believed that people had a third and somewhat different motive for holding money: They may want to hold part of their wealth in the form of money if they think that other forms of wealth are temporarily too risky. Suppose, for example, that investors believe there is a high probability that the price of other assets—bonds, stocks, and real estate—will fall in the near future. Thus, they may prefer to hold much of their wealth in the form of money, which has a fixed nominal value and, after the prices of other assets have fallen, use their money to buy those assets at bargain prices. Keynes called this the *speculative motive* for holding money.

Interest Rates, Bond Prices, and the Speculative Motive

Whereas Keynes saw the level of nominal national income as the primary determinant of the money demand for transactions and precautionary purposes, he saw interest rates as the key determinant of demand for speculative money balances. His reasoning is most easily explained in terms of an economy in which money and bonds are the principal alternative assets between which people choose. The speculative demand for money then depends on interest rates because of the way interest rates are linked to bond prices.

As we saw in Chapter 4, bonds are a form of IOU issued by corporations and government units, typically in $1,000 denominations. The issuer promises to pay the bondholder a certain sum per year—say, $100—for a specified number of years, such as 30. At the end of that period, the bond matures and its $1,000 face value is repaid. The payments made during the bond's life are determined by the interest rate prevailing at the time the bond is issued. Suppose, for example, that the prevailing interest rate is 10 percent per year when the bond is issued. In that case, each $1,000 bond will pay the purchaser $100 per year. (Actually, in most cases there would be two semiannual payments of $50.)

The annual payment is agreed to at the time the bond is issued and is known as the bond's *coupon rate*. (The term comes from a former requirement that bond owners turn in paper coupons attached to bond certificates in order to claim their interest payments. Today computers keep track of who gets the interest payments.) The coupon rate remains fixed for the bond's life and is expressed as a percentage of its face value. Thus, a bond that pays $100 per year is said to have a 10 percent coupon rate.

Although a bond is issued for a long term, the original buyer need not hold it until maturity. Instead, as we saw in Chapter 4, bonds can be bought and sold at any time in secondary markets. The price that a bond will bring in the secondary market depends on both its coupon rate and the market rate of interest prevailing at the time it is sold.

Suppose, for example, that a bond carries a 10 percent coupon rate but a year later the prevailing market interest rate has fallen to 8 percent for assets of comparable maturity and risk. Sellers of newly issued bonds thus will be offering only an 8 percent coupon. Now put yourself in the position of a buyer who has the choice between a bond that will pay $1,000 at maturity and $100 per year in the meantime and one that will pay $1,000 at maturity and $80 per year. Clearly you will pay more for the first bond—in fact, you will be willing to pay up to $1,250 for a bond paying $100 per year if the alternative is to pay $1,000 for a newly issued bond paying $80 annually. At those prices, the two bonds' *yields*— that is, their annual interest payment expressed as a percentage of their purchase price rather than as a percentage of their face value—will be equal. (The $80 payment is 8 percent of $1,000; the $100 is 8 percent of $1,250.) Generalizing from this reasoning gives us two important principles regarding bond prices:

1. When market interest rates fall, issuers reduce the *coupon rate* promised on newly issued bonds. The prices of previously issued bonds then rise by enough to make their *yields* equal to those of the newly issued bonds.

2. When market interest rates rise, firms increase the *coupon rate* promised on newly issued bonds. The prices of previously issued bonds then fall by enough to make their *yields* equal to those of newly issued bonds.

In short, when interest rates go up bond prices fall, and when interest rates go down bond prices rise.

Keynes used this linkage between interest rates and bond prices to explain the relationship between interest rates and the speculative demand for money. Suppose there is some "normal" level toward which people expect interest rates to tend over time. If the present interest rate is below the normal level, people will expect it to rise in the future. An expected rise in the interest rate means an expected fall in bond prices. Thus, in Keynes's view, when interest rates are low, people will be cautious about holding bonds to avoid a possible capital loss. Instead, they will choose to hold speculative money balances. Similarly, high interest rates will mean a likelihood that rates will fall and bond prices rise in the future. In this case, people will be eager to hold bonds in the hope of realizing future capital gains and will spend their speculative money balances to buy them.

In sum, then, Keynes thought that the demand for money depends on both the level of nominal national income and interest rates. As national income rises, other things being equal, the demand for money will increase because of the transactions and precautionary motives. But given the level of national income, the speculative motive will tend to make the quantity of money demanded increase as interest rates fall and decrease as they rise.

Portfolio Balance Theory of Money Demand

Today most economists accept the notion that the demand for money responds to changes in both national income and interest rates. However, Keynes's three-way classification of motives for holding money is widely viewed as too rigid and his concept of the link between interest and money demand as too narrow. Today the demand for money is often explained in terms of the importance of liquidity to holders of a balanced portfolio of assets. (Economists use the word **portfolio**—meaning a case for carrying papers—as a shorthand term for all of a person's or firm's assets, including money, bonds, real estate, and others.)

Recall that an asset is said to be liquid if it can be used directly as a means of exchange or readily converted to one and has a fixed nominal value. There are thus two potential advantages to holding a liquid asset such as money in place of

Portfolio
A person's or firm's
collection of assets.

less liquid ones such as stocks, bonds, or real estate. The first advantage is that liquidity reduces transaction costs. No one wants to have to make a trip to a bank or a broker each week in order to exchange stocks or bonds for money with which to buy groceries. The second advantage is that one can avoid the risk of loss of nominal value that is associated with less liquid assets.

Opportunity Cost of Liquidity

The advantage of liquidity is offset by a major disadvantage: More liquid assets tend to pay less interest. Currency and demand deposits pay no interest at all. NOW accounts and other interest-bearing transaction deposits included in M1 pay some interest, but not as much as less liquid assets. Some of the assets included in M2, such as money market mutual funds and overnight repurchase agreements, pay higher interest than transaction deposits and are almost as liquid. But even these assets tend to pay a smaller return than some others, such as stocks or long-term bonds, when yields are averaged over a long period.

Thus, loss of the interest available on other assets is the opportunity cost of holding non-interest-bearing money to be weighed against liquidity value. For interest-bearing forms of money such as NOW accounts, the opportunity cost is the difference between the interest rate paid on a representative nonmonetary asset (say, a short-term government security) and the interest rate earned on the interest-bearing form of money.

Experience has shown that interest rates on interest-bearing forms of money, such as NOW accounts, tend to move over a much narrower range than do those on nonmonetary assets, such as short-term securities. As a result, an increase in interest rates on nonmonetary assets increases the opportunity cost of holding both non-interest-bearing and interest-bearing forms of money.

A Money Demand Schedule

In the portfolio balance theory of money demand, the amount of money that people want to hold depends on both nominal national income and interest rates on nonmonetary assets. Other things being equal, an increase in nominal national income increases the demand for money. This is because with higher incomes people will make more or larger transactions and will need more money in order to do so conveniently. At the same time, other things being equal, an increase in the interest rate will decrease the amount of money demanded. The reason is that an increase in the interest rate raises the opportunity cost of holding money.

The relationship of the amount of money demanded to the interest rate and level of nominal national income for a simple economy is shown in Exhibit 14.1. The entries in part a give the amount of money demanded when the interest rate is as shown in the first column and the level of nominal national income is as shown in the remaining columns. For example, when the interest rate is 10 percent per year and the level of nominal national income is $600 billion, the amount of money demanded is $72 billion.

Part b of Exhibit 14.1 presents the money demand schedule in graphic form. At any given income level, the relationship between the amount of money demanded and the interest rate takes the form of a negatively sloped curve that looks much like any other demand curve. For example, the curve labeled MD_1 shows how money demand varies as the interest rate changes when nominal national income is $600 billion. This curve is based on the data for $600 billion

Exhibit 14.1   A Money Demand Schedule for a Simple Economy

This exhibit shows how the amount of money demanded varies in a simple economy as the interest rate on a representative nonmonetary asset and the level of nominal national income vary. The entries in part a show the amount of money demanded at the interest rate corresponding to each row and the nominal national income corresponding to each column. Each column can be graphed to get a money demand curve for a given level of nominal national income. MD_1 corresponds to the fourth column ($600 billion) and MD_2 to the last column ($1,200 billion).

(a)

Interest Rate (Percent)	Nominal National Income (Billions of Dollars)					
	$200	$400	$600	$800	$1,000	$1,200
2	$120	$240	$360	$480	$600	$720
4	60	120	180	240	300	360
6	40	80	120	160	200	240
8	30	60	90	120	150	180
10	24	48	72	96	120	144
12	20	40	60	80	100	120
14	17	34	51	68	85	102
16	15	30	45	60	75	90

(b)

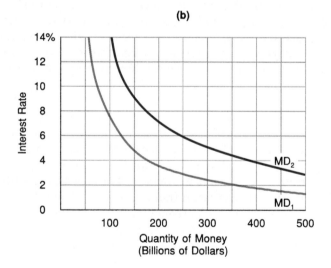

in part a. A change in the income level will produce a shift in the money demand curve. For example, if income increases to $1,200 billion, the money demand curve will shift to the position labeled MD_2. The data given in the last column of part a show that when income doubles, the amount of money demanded at any given interest rate doubles as well.

Money and Interest Rates in the U.S. Economy

Having looked at the theory of money demand, we will now examine the behavior of money demand in the U.S. economy in recent years. In so doing, we will focus on the effects of interest rates on money demand. The money demand curve in Exhibit 14.1 incorporates nominal income as well as interest rates as a variable. In this section, we will eliminate the effects of changes in nominal national income by employing an income-adjusted money demand curve of the type drawn in Exhibit 14.2. The horizontal axis in this diagram shows the ratio of money to nominal national income. (The ratio of money to national income is the reciprocal of velocity, which is the ratio of national income to money.) A change in nominal national income (equivalent to moving across a row in part a of Exhibit 14.1) does not cause this income-adjusted money demand curve to shift. Any observed shifts in the relationship between interest rates and income-adjusted money demand must be due to causes other than changes in nominal income.

Exhibit 14.3 shows actual data for M1 and the interest rate on three-month Treasury bills for the U.S. economy from 1961 to 1986. If the money demand curve had held still while the economy moved up and down along it, the points in the figure would all have fallen along a curve shaped like the one in Exhibit 14.2. This is not what happened, however. How can we best interpret the pattern that the data follow?

The 1960s and 1970s

The 1960s and 1970s show a consistent saw-toothed pattern. The quantity of M1 demanded per dollar of GNP decreased during each upswing of the interest rate, as would be expected. However, the leftward movement of the annual data points continued in years when the interest rate fell. This pattern can best be explained by a leftward drift of the income-adjusted money demand curve during this period.

What caused the drift? The most likely candidates are financial innovations induced by the rising cost of holding non-interest-bearing demand deposits, which were the dominant form of transaction deposit at the time. (NOW accounts did not become available nationwide until 1981, and then only for households.) The innovations concerned the cash management practices of firms and households. For firms, these included increased use of repurchase agreements to earn overnight interest on idle cash balances and the establishment of "sweep accounts" from which idle demand deposits were automatically withdrawn at the end of the day. The spreading use of computers in financial planning and

Exhibit 14.2   An Income-Adjusted Money Demand Curve

The money demand curve is sometimes drawn in an income-adjusted form as shown here. The horizontal axis in this graph shows the quantity of money demanded per dollar of nominal national income. A change in nominal national income will not cause this curve to shift, but changes in businesses' payments practices or in banking regulations, such as the introduction of new types of accounts or the removal of interest ceilings on existing types of accounts, may produce shifts.

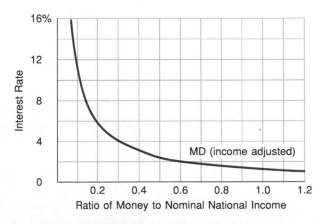

Exhibit 14.3   Money Demand in the U.S. Economy, 1961–1986

This exhibit shows the link between income-adjusted money demand (M1 divided by nominal national income) and the interest rate (the rate on three-month Treasury bills) from 1961 to 1986. Had the money demand curve remained unchanged during this period, all the points would have fallen along a smooth curve. Instead, however, the saw-toothed pattern of money and interest rates during the 1960s and 1970s suggests that the money demand curve drifted to the left. This appears to have happened as a result of financial innovations and regulatory changes. In the 1980s, the leftward shift of the curve appears to have slowed or stopped. The data for 1985 and 1986 indicate a possible increasing responsiveness of M1 demand to changes in interest rates.

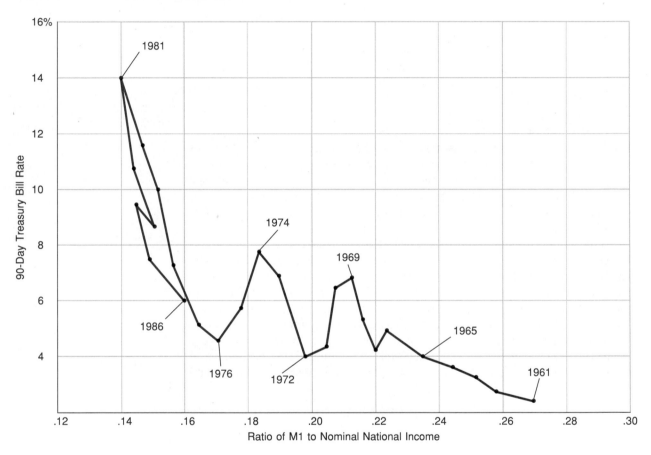

transaction processing helped matters along by allowing firms to predict their cash needs more accurately than in the past. Especially in the late 1970s, consumers got into the act with massive purchases of money market mutual fund shares, which had a degree of checkability and paid attractive market interest rates.

All of these innovations meant that firms and households could support a given volume of transactions on the basis of smaller M1 balances than before. Of course, rising interest rates, which increased the opportunity costs of holding non-interest-bearing money, spurred on the innovations. However, once the new regulations and cash management techniques were in place, they were not abandoned when interest rates fell. The result was the saw-toothed pattern that Exhibit 14.3 shows for the 1960s and 1970s.

The 1980s

The 1980s show a change of pattern—a change that may, in fact, have begun as early as 1977 depending on how the chart is interpreted. Most of the points after 1977 come much closer to a pattern explainable by a stable demand curve. In this period, for the first time the economy moves down and to the right as interest rates fall. This period requires a different interpretation.

One contributing factor may have been a slowdown in the pace of financial innovation as the spread of new cash management practices through the economy began to run its course. But the explanation also lies partly in regulatory changes that came after 1980. Following the Monetary Control Act of 1980, the removal of interest rate restrictions accelerated, ending with complete decontrol of deposit interest rates by 1986 except for the continued prohibition of interest payments on demand deposits. During this period, market interest rates on securities fell but returns offered on the new forms of interest-bearing transaction deposits remained relatively stable. This combination of factors greatly reduced the opportunity cost of holding interest-bearing transaction deposits. As a result, households increased their holdings of NOW accounts and related deposits. By 1986, these had become a much larger component of M1 than in the past. In addition, there was also some increase in the ratio of non-interest-bearing money, that is, currency and demand deposits, to income during this period. This quite possibly reflected the growing share of non-interest-bearing money held by businesses, whose demand tends to be more sensitive to changes in interest rates than household demand.

The behavior of the M1-to-GNP ratio during 1985 and 1986 attracted particular attention. At that time, the economy moved strongly to the right on our chart, actually reaching its previous path for the first time in the 25-year period. A likely interpretation is that deregulation has made the money demand curve less steep so that the quantity of M1 demanded has become much more responsive to changes in the interest rate than previously.[1]

As we will see later, this increased responsiveness of money demand to interest rates—if it holds up in the later 1980s—could have important implications for the conduct of monetary policy.

Supply, Demand, and Interest Rates in the Money Market

We are now ready to put the demand for money together with the money supply. The result is a graph like that shown in Exhibit 14.4. The horizontal axis shows the money stock, measured in dollars; the vertical axis shows the interest rate as

---

[1]The reason for this lies partly in the fact that market interest rates move much more freely than rates on NOW accounts. This, in turn, indicates that a given percentage change in market rates means a larger percentage change in the opportunity cost of holding NOW accounts. For example, suppose that initially the market rate paid by, say, 3-month Treasury bills is 12 percent and the NOW account rate is 6 percent. The opportunity cost of holding NOW accounts is then 6 percent. Now suppose that the market rate falls by a third to 8 percent while the NOW account rate falls only to 5 percent. This means that the opportunity cost of holding NOW accounts falls to 3 percent. Thus, a one-third decline in the market rate cuts the opportunity cost of holding NOW accounts in half.

a percentage per year. The interest rate is the "price" of holding money—or, as explained earlier, the opportunity cost of holding part of a portfolio of assets in the form of non-interest-bearing money rather than of a representative nonmonetary interest-bearing asset.

The money demand curve in Exhibit 14.4 shows the amount of money that people want to hold at each given interest rate. An increase in nominal national income will shift the money demand curve to the right and a decrease will shift it to the left. Other factors, such as changes in payments practices, can also cause the demand curve to shift, as we have seen.

As discussed in Chapter 13, the money supply is under the control of the Federal Reserve. The exact shape of the money supply curve depends on how the Fed chooses to use its tools of monetary control. The supply curve in Exhibit 14.4 assumes that the Fed sets a target for the money stock ($180 billion, in this case) and uses open market operations to adjust reserves so as to hold the money stock on target regardless of what happens to the interest rate. This assumption results in a vertical money supply curve. The final section of this chapter discusses other possible money supply curves.

We will refer to the supply and demand situation shown in Exhibit 14.4 as the "money market," but it should be understood that this is not a market in the usual sense. We typically think of a market as a place where people buy and sell things, that is, exchange things for money; in this sense, they do not "buy" and

Exhibit 14.4   Equilibrium in the Money Market

The money demand curve shown here is based on the data given in Exhibit 14.1 assuming a nominal national income of $1,200 billion. The money supply curve assumes that the Fed sets a money supply target of $180 billion and adjusts total reserves to maintain this quantity of money regardless of what happens to interest rates. Under these conditions, the equilibrium interest rate is 8 percent.

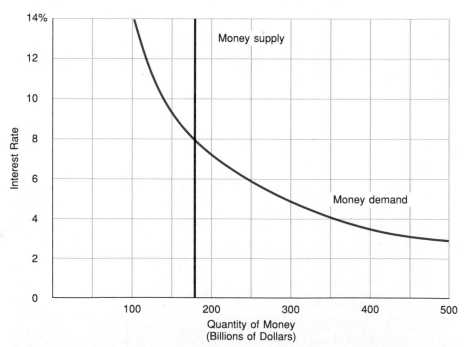

"sell" money. Also, the vertical axis in this market does not show the price of money relative to the price of something else; rather, it shows the opportunity cost of holding money as measured by the interest rate. Despite these unusual features, however, supply and demand interact in the so-called money market to produce an equilibrium much as they do in the more familiar kinds of markets.

Equilibrium in the Money Market

The supply and demand curves in Exhibit 14.4 intersect at an interest rate of 8 percent. At that rate, the amount of money supplied by the banking system (which is determined, in turn, by the amount of reserves the Fed supplies to the banking system) just equals the amount that people want to hold in their portfolios. There is neither upward nor downward pressure on interest rates.

No other interest rate would permit such an equilibrium. Suppose, for example, that the interest rate were just 4 percent. With such a low opportunity cost of money, people would want to hold more of it. Any individual person or firm can add money to a portfolio by selling something else—stocks, bonds, Treasury bills, or real goods. If many people try to sell, say, bonds for money at the same time, the price of bonds will tend to fall. As explained earlier in the chapter, a fall in the price of bonds means an increase in the bonds' yield. If people were trying to sell other kinds of assets to get money, yields on those assets would rise too. In time, the whole family of interest rates would rise to the level corresponding to 8 percent on the vertical axis of Exhibit 14.4. The money market would then be back in equilibrium.

Note that as Exhibit 14.4 is drawn, a rising interest rate brings the market back into equilibrium by reducing the amount of money demanded rather than by increasing the amount of money supplied. As long as the Fed provides no more reserves to the banking system, banks cannot supply any more money. Even though any one person can add money to his or her portfolio by selling some other asset, this will not affect the amount of money in the banking system as a whole; it will merely move reserves from the buyer's bank to the seller's.

The same story can be told in reverse for the case in which the interest rate is higher than its equilibrium value. In that event, people will want to hold less money. They will try to get rid of money by buying other assets. This will drive up the price of those assets and force interest rates down. But as long as the Fed keeps the banking system's total reserves constant, such buying and selling will only move money from one bank to another; it will not change the money stock as a whole.

The process of reaching an equilibrium in the money market is closely connected to the process of reaching an equilibrium in other financial markets. In those markets, as explained in Chapters 4 and 6, funds flow from savers to borrowers in the form of loans and in exchange for securities. Purchases of newly issued securities by savers and of existing securities by people who want to adjust their portfolios of assets by exchanging money for securities take place at the same prices. Thus, the family of interest rates that estabilishes an equilibrium in the financial markets also creates equilibrium in the money market.

Effects of a Change in the Money Supply

Our description of the money market is useful for a number of purposes. Let's begin by using it to analyze the effects of shifts in the money supply curve.

Exhibit 14.5 shows the money market in equilibrium at E_1 with a money

Exhibit 14.5   Effects of an Increase in the Money Supply

The money stock starts out at $180 billion, putting the money supply curve in the position MS_1. An open market purchase by the Fed injects new reserves into the banking system. Banks' efforts to put the new reserves to work by buying securities and making loans drive the interest rate down as the money supply expands. At the new equilibrium, E_2, the interest rate has fallen by enough to make people willing to hold the larger quantity of money.

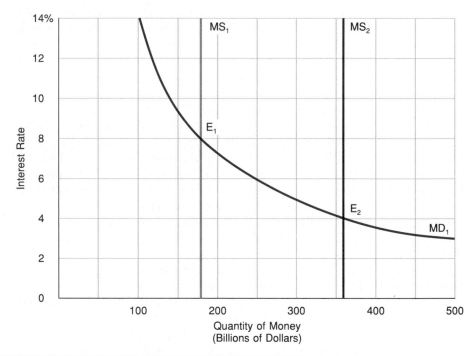

supply of $180 billion and an interest rate of 8 percent. Starting from this point, the Fed decides to increase the money supply to $360 billion. Assuming a money multiplier of 10, it can do this by injecting $18 billion of new reserves into the banking system by means of open market purchases.

The immediate impact of the open market operation is to boost banks' excess reserves. In order to restore their balance sheets to equilibrium, banks set out to convert the excess reserves into earning assets. In part, this means buying securities. The increased demand for securities pushes up their price and forces the interest rate down. The banks also convert their excess reserves into earning assets by making new loans. Competition among banks in making loans also tends to push down interest rates.

As banks work off their excess reserves, the money supply expands, as explained in Chapter 13. In Exhibit 14.5, this is shown as a shift in the money supply curve from MS_1 to MS_2. At E_1, people were content to hold the old quantity of money, $180 billion, in their portfolios. Now falling interest rates reduce the opportunity cost of holding money and make people willing to absorb the increased quantity that banks supply. Thus, as the injection of reserves shifts the money supply curve to the right, falling interest rates cause people to move downward and to the right along their money demand curve. In time a new equilibrium is reached at E_2, where the money stock is greater and the interest rate lower than before.

If the Fed withdraws reserves from the banking system through an open market sale, the same process operates in reverse. Banks find themselves with less than the required quantity of reserves. They respond by selling securities or reducing their volume of loans—actions that tend to raise the interest rate. As the money supply curve shifts to the left, rising interest rates make people content to hold only the reduced quantity of money in their portfolios. A new equilibrium in which the money supply is smaller and the interest rate higher than before is reached.

Interest Rates and the Value of the Dollar

Chapter 13 showed how the Federal Reserve can affect the international value of the dollar through intervention in the foreign exchange market. When the Fed buys dollar-denominated deposits from trading banks, paying for them with foreign currency from its own reserves, it reduces the supply of dollars in the foreign exchange markets. This tends to raise the exchange rate for the dollar, expressed in units of foreign currency. When the Fed buys deposits denominated in foreign currencies, paying for them with newly created dollar reserves, the supply of dollars is increased and the exchange value of the dollar tends to fall.

However, exchange market intervention is only one channel by which the Fed's operations affect the dollar's exchange value. Interest rates constitute an equally important medium. To understand how interest rates affect the value of the dollar, we must recall the distinction made in Chapter 7 between international transactions made on *current account* and those made on *capital account*. Current account transactions involve imports and exports of goods and services. Capital account transactions involve international purchases and sales of assets and international borrowing and lending.

Suppose, then, that restrictive monetary policy on the Fed's part pushes up U.S. interest rates. To keep things simple, assume that interest rates stay the same in the rest of the world. What will occur in the foreign exchange markets? While little will happen immediately to current account transactions, capital account transactions are highly sensitive to interest rates.

Put yourself in the position of manager of a Japanese pension fund. You want to buy securities that will earn the highest available return. The rise in U.S. interest rates means that you will want to buy more U.S. securities than otherwise. You use some of the yen in your fund to buy dollars and then use the dollars to buy U.S. Treasury bills. Your action in buying dollars pushes up their exchange value.

Alternatively, put yourself in the position of a Brazilian industrialist looking for a bank from which to borrow. Before the interest rate went up, you might have borrowed from the Bank of America. You then would have taken the dollars you borrowed and sold them to buy Brazilian cruzados. This would have increased the supply of dollars, pushing the exchange rate down. But now that the U.S. interest rate has gone up, you will borrow from a British or Japanese bank instead. Your decision not to borrow in the U.S. will tend to raise the exchange rate.

Chapter 20 develops a more detailed model of exchange rate determination, but these examples make the general principles clear: An increase in U.S. interest rates encourages capital inflows and discourages capital outflows, thereby raising the dollar's value in foreign exchange markets. Similarly, a reduction in U.S. interest rates discourages capital inflows and encourages capital outflows, thereby lowering the dollar's international value. It follows, then, that domestic monetary policy moves by the Fed, as well as direct intervention in foreign exchange markets, affect the dollar's value.

The practical result of this is that the Fed cannot conduct its monetary policy solely with domestic objectives in mind. Its domestic open market operations and changes in the discount rate will always have international repercussions. During times of turmoil in international markets, such as in 1987, the international implications of monetary policy may strongly influence the conduct of policy. As "Economics in the News 14.1" illustrates, it is now rare to encounter a news report of monetary policy that does not have something to say about the dollar's foreign exchange value.

Effects of an Increase in Income

In discussing the effects of a change in money supply, we have assumed that the level of nominal national income stayed constant. Let's reverse that assumption and see what happens to the money market when nominal national income changes while the money supply curve stays put.

ECONOMICS IN THE NEWS 14.1

Monetary Policy and Support of the Dollar

Domestic monetary policy cannot be carried out in isolation from exchange rate policy. Intervention in foreign exchange markets to influence currency rates can affect the domestic money stock via its effect on reserves; at the same time, domestic monetary policy can affect the exchange rate via its effects on interest rates and capital flows. The excerpts from the news item with which this chapter opens provide a case in point; they emphasize domestic aspects of the monetary policy actions under discussion. Here are additional excerpts from the same news item that discuss international aspects of these policy actions:

In discussing the recent "snugging up" of monetary policy, Federal Reserve Chairman Paul A. Volcker said that the central bank has tightened monetary policy to support the value of the dollar.

The Fed action to make cash less readily available to the banking system normally would mean higher interest rates.

As U.S. interest rates go up and those abroad go down, foreign investors are more likely to put their money in the United States. To do so requires that they buy dollars, which helps boost the dollar's value relative to the currency they sell. A major factor in the dollar's decline [in 1986 and early 1987] has been a reluctance of foreign investors to continue to provide the capital needed to finance the large U.S. trade deficit.

Volcker called upon the Japanese and West German central banks to take "complementary" actions to support the dollar and to stimulate their economies by reducing their interest rates. Japanese Prime Minister Yasuhiro Nakasone, visiting here, told President Reagan yesterday that the Bank of Japan would do so.

Volcker told the House banking subcommittee that the tightening was in line with the basic policy he had outlined earlier in April in congressional testimony. At that time he warned that it might be necessary for the Fed to tighten the money supply if the dollar continued to fall. That warning was directed primarily at the Japanese and West Germans, whose export markets in the United States would shrink if the dollar kept falling or if economic growth slowed in this country. Far better for those countries to lower interest rates and stimulate their economies, he argued earlier in April, than for the U.S. to have to defend its currency by increasing rates in this country.

Source: John M. Berry, "Volcker Reveals Fed Tightened Credit," *Washington Post*, May 1, 1987, F1.

Exhibit 14.6 sets the stage. It shows the market in equilibrium at E_1 with an interest rate of 4 percent and a money supply of $180 billion. Nominal national income is assumed to be $600 billion, which puts the money demand curve in the position MD_1.

Now assume that nominal national income rises to a level of $1,200 billion. As we saw earlier in the chapter, an increase in nominal national income, other things being equal, shifts the money demand curve to the right. The new position of the money demand curve is MD_2.

At the new, higher income level, people will be making a greater volume of transactions than before. Other things being equal, they will want more money with which to carry out the extra transactions—but the money stock is limited to $180 billion by Federal Reserve policy. Because banks are not supplying more money to support the higher income, people will try to get the extra money by selling other assets. This will not increase the money stock as a whole, but it will drive up interest rates. The higher interest rates will make people willing to get along with the limited money stock available despite their higher incomes. Thus, the economy will move to a new equilibrium at E_2. There nominal national income and the interest rate are higher than before and the money stock has not changed.

If nominal national income falls, the same process will occur in reverse. With lower incomes, people will require less money. They will buy other assets to replace money in their portfolios. This will tend to push interest rates down. When interest rates fall enough to make people content to hold the existing money stock even at a lower level of nominal national income, the money market will be back in equilibrium. The interest rate will be lower than before; nominal national income will be lower; and the money stock will be unchanged.

The Money Market, Interest Rates, and the Aggregate Demand Curve

In the preceding section, we saw that an increase in nominal national income tends to raise the equilibrium interest rate because it shifts the money demand curve to the right. This is true regardless of the form of the increase in nominal national income.

One possibility is an increase in real income with no change in the price level. In this case, people will want to hold a greater quantity of money in order to make the transactions connected with the production and sale of a larger volume of real output. The money supply curve will shift to the right, as shown in Exhibit 14.6, and the interest rate will rise.

On the other hand, the increase in nominal income may take the form of a higher price level with no change in the real income level. In that case, the physical volume of transactions will not change, but more money will be needed to carry out the transactions than before because goods and services will then have higher prices. Thus, an increase in the price level is also capable of shifting the money demand curve to the right and driving up the equilibrium interest rate.

In practice, changes in nominal national income usually reflect some combination of changes in the price level and changes in real income. However, separating the two effects is useful because it helps us understand the nature of the economy's aggregate demand curve. In Chapter 8, a list of the reasons for the negative slope of the aggregate demand curve included an assertion to the effect

Exhibit 14.6   Effects of an Increase in Nominal National Income

A nominal national income of $600 billion puts the money demand curve at MD₁. The
equilibrium interest rate is 4 percent given this income and the money supply of $180 billion.
If an increase in nominal income to $1,200 billion shifts the money demand curve to MD₂,
there will be an excess demand for money at the initial interest rate. People will try to
increase the quantity of money in their portfolios by selling other assets. In the process, the
prices of those assets will be bid down and interest rates will rise.

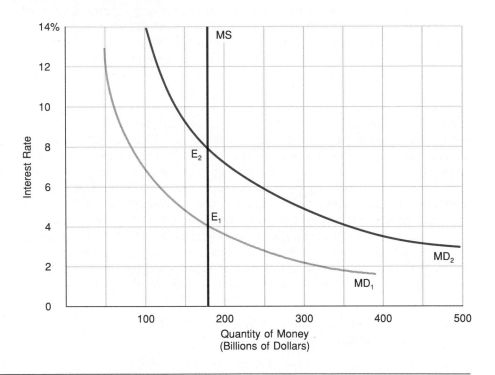

that, other things being equal, a rise in the price level tends to increase the
interest rate, thus depressing the level of planned investment expenditure. We
now see why this is so. A higher price level pushes up the interest rate because it
shifts the money demand curve. A given money stock can be considered one of
the "other-things-being-equal" conditions that lies behind the economy's aggregate demand curve.

Operating Targets, Interest Rates,
and the Money Supply

The examples given in the previous section used a vertical money supply curve,
indicating that the Fed set a target value for the money stock and undertook
open market operations as necessary to keep it at this value. The key variable
used by the Fed to guide its open market operations—in this case, a fixed value

for the money stock—is known as the Fed's **operating target.** As we will see in this section, other operating targets are possible, and the choice of target will affect the money supply curve.

As we look at the various operating targets that the Fed might use—or has used at one time or another—we will find that the role played by interest rates in guiding the Fed's operations is a matter of controversy. Some economists believe that the Fed's job is to keep the money supply under control; once it has done so, it should let interest rates go wherever the market sends them. Other economists, along with many businesspeople, think that part of the Fed's job should be to prevent sharp ups and downs in interest rates. Large swings in interest rates, they say, can disrupt business planning, thus hurting employment and productivity.

Operating target
The financial variable—the money stock, the federal funds rate, or whatever—for which the Fed sets a short-term target and uses as a day-to-day guide to the conduct of open market operations.

Three Operating Targets

Exhibit 14.7 shows three possible operating targets, each represented by a different money supply curve. Part a shows a money stock target as assumed in the preceding section. Here the Fed selects a target for the money stock and adjusts the level of bank reserves to maintain the money stock at that level regardless of what happens to interest rates. This procedure results in the vertical money supply curve MS_1. With the money demand curve in the position MD_1, a money supply of $180 billion would, as shown, result in an equilibrium interest rate of 8 percent for a representative short-term security.

The second operating target, shown in part b of the exhibit, focuses on the interest rate. In this case, the Fed begins by deciding what the interest rate should be. It then uses open market operations to adjust the money supply to bring the equilibrium interest rate to the target level. This strategy is represented by a horizontal money supply curve. If the interest rate target is 8 percent, the money supply curve will be in the position MS_2. Given the money demand curve MD_1, the Fed would have to allow the money stock to settle at $180 billion in order to hit the 8 percent target. If the money demand curve were to shift to the right or left, the Fed would use open market purchases or sales to adjust the money stock along the path MS_2.

The third possibility is represented by MS_3 in part c of the exhibit. In this case, the Fed targets neither the money supply nor the interest rate. Instead, it allows the money supply to expand whenever the interest rate rises, but not by enough to completely offset the rise in the interest rate.

Responses to Changes in Money Demand

The economy's money demand curve, as we have seen, is subject to occasional shifts. Changes in nominal income are one major source of such shifts. Institutional changes, such as the introduction of new types of transaction deposits, are another. Short-term shifts that are hard to predict or explain also take place. Exhibit 14.7 can be used to show how the money market responds to shifts in money demand under various operating targets.

The first case—that of a money stock target—has already been discussed. When the money demand curve shifts from MD_1 to MD_2, there is an excess demand for money at the initial interest rate of 8 percent. People try to obtain more money by selling other assets. This pushes down the price of those assets

Exhibit 14.7   Operating Targets and the Money Supply Curve

The slope of the money supply curve depends on the Fed's operating target. The Fed can set a target for the money supply and stick to it regardless of what happens to interest rates. In this case, the money supply curve will be vertical as shown by MS_1 in part a. Instead, the Fed can set a target for the interest rate and use open market operations to stabilize it (at least in the short run) regardless of what happens to the money stock. In this instance, the money supply curve is horizontal as shown by MS_2 in part b. Finally, the Fed can allow the money supply to expand as the interest rate rises. This results in an upward-sloping money supply curve as shown by MS_3 in part c. A given shift in money demand, such as from M_1 to M_2, will have different effects on the money stock and interest rate depending on the shape of the money supply curve.

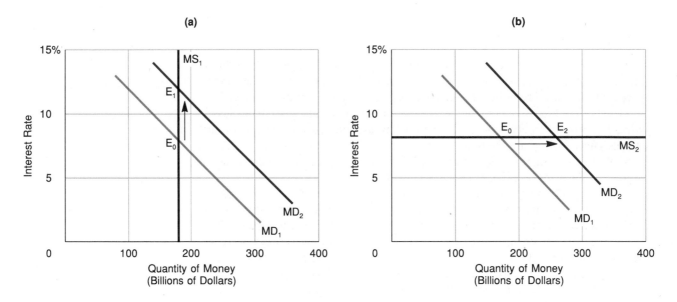

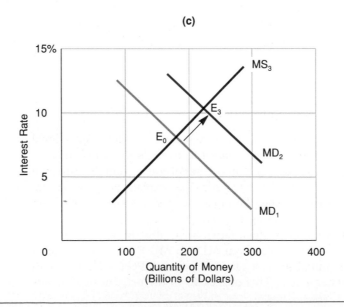

and pushes up interest rates, but as long as the Fed does not supply more reserves to the banking system, the money supply as a whole cannot increase. A new equilibrium is reached at E_1 with an interest rate of 12 percent.

Next, consider the effects of a shift in the money demand curve when the Fed is following an interest rate target as in part b of Exhibit 14.7. This target produces money supply curve MS_2. Again assume that the money demand curve shifts from MD_1 to MD_2. As before, the initial effect is an excess demand for money, which puts upward pressure on interest rates. Now, however, the Fed's reaction is different. Suppose the manager of the Fed's open market desk in New York has been instructed to keep an eye on interest rates. We assume that of all market interest rates, the manager has been instructed to watch most closely the federal funds rate—the rate that banks charge one another for overnight loans of reserves—which is the first to respond to changes in money supply and demand.

As soon as the excess demand for money starts to push up the federal funds rate, the open market desk begins buying securities. As explained in Chapter 13, this increases the banking system's total reserves. The increase in reserves relieves the upward pressure on interest rates. Also, as banks expand deposits on the basis of the new reserves, the money stock grows. The result of this whole process is a movement rightward along the money supply curve MS_2 to a new equilibrium at E_2. In the new equilibrium, the money supply has increased to $260 billion and the interest rate is unchanged at 8 percent.

Finally, consider the third possibility, represented by money supply curve MS_3 in part c of the exhibit. Here, as in part b, the Fed reacts to an upward movement in the federal funds rate by injecting new reserves into the banking system. Now, however, it makes only a limited volume of open market purchases. Enough reserves are supplied to let the money supply expand somewhat, but the amount supplied is not enough to keep the interest rate from rising. The result is a new equilibrium at E_3. The interest rate rises less than with a money stock target but more than with an interest rate target; the money stock expands more than with a money stock target but less than with an interest rate target.

Evolution of the Fed's Operating Strategy

Over the years, the Fed's strategy for the conduct of its operations has changed. At one time or another it has included elements of each of the three approaches just described.

Interest Rate Targeting and Its Problems
During World War II, the Fed set strict interest rate targets. These were very low by today's standards: $2\frac{1}{2}$ percent on government bonds with maturities longer than 10 years, $\frac{7}{8}$ percent on 1-year government securities, and just $\frac{3}{8}$ percent on 90-day Treasury bills. The purpose of these low ceilings was to reduce the interest cost to the Treasury of financing the huge federal budget deficit caused by the war. Also, because the interest rate ceilings would stabilize bond prices, they would prevent wartime speculation in government bonds.

The interest rate ceilings were kept in force for several years after the war. They were abandoned in 1951, but interest rates remained the chief focus of the Fed's policy. While interest rates were allowed to rise and fall to some extent, the Fed still tended to respond to increases in money demand by supplying new reserves.

As inflation began to accelerate in the late 1960s and early 1970s, economists became critical of the Fed's emphasis on stabilizing interest rates. The problem as they saw it was that targeting interest rates gave monetary policy either an inflationary bias or a deflationary bias, depending on underlying macroeconomic conditions. For example, they feared that if interest rates were pegged at too low a level, monetary policy would serve as part of a feedback process that worked like this:

- Expansion of nominal national income increases money demand, putting upward pressure on interest rates.

- The Fed responds by increasing bank reserves.

- Increased reserves lead to an expansion of the money stock and to more borrowing and spending by firms and households.

- More borrowing and spending add to aggregate demand; prices and real output rise as the economy moves up along its aggregate supply curve.

- The increase in prices and real output means that nominal national income rises, resulting in a further increase in money demand.

Where does the process stop if the Fed responds to each increase in money demand with actions that create conditions for a further increase? According to the critics, as long as the Fed keeps supplying new money to feed the growth of nominal income, there is nothing to halt the process short of runaway inflation.

Under other circumstances, the opposite could occur. Suppose the interest rate is pegged too high and the economy begins to contract. As it does, there will be a tendency for interest rates to fall below the Fed's target level. If the Fed reacts by cutting back on bank reserves to support interest rates, the result will be a deepening contraction.

The Mid-1970s

By the mid-1970s, the Fed was heeding its critics. It continued to use a federal funds rate target as its guide for day-to-day open market operations, but it also set longer-term targets for the growth rates of M1 and M2. Those targets were set at a level that the Fed believed would keep inflation in check. If the money supply grew faster than the targets over a period of weeks or months, and if inflation seemed to be speeding up, the Fed took this as a sign that its federal funds rate target was too low. To slow the growth rate of the money supply, it would set a new, higher federal funds rate target for guiding its day-to-day operations.

Unfortunately, this strategy did not work very well. It appears that the Fed's reactions to faster than intended money growth in a context of rising inflation were too little too late. Inflation and interest rates continued to drift upward. By 1979, both the inflation rate and short-term interest rates were in the teens, and there was an outcry for something to be done.

1979 to 1982

In October 1979, the Fed announced a dramatic shift in its monetary control strategy: It would stop using the federal funds rate as a guide for day-to-day policy and instead focus on bank reserves. At each meeting of the Federal Open Market Committee, a target would be set for *nonborrowed* reserves of the banking system. By "nonborrowed reserves" it meant all bank reserves except those that the Fed loans to banks through its discount window. By maintaining tight control over nonborrowed reserves, the Fed would restrain excess money supply growth and inflation.

This strategy did not amount to strict targeting of the money stock. Total reserves and the total money stock could still fluctuate to the extent that banks' borrowings from the discount window varied. Thus, the nonborrowed-reserves strategy produced a positively sloped money supply curve. Banks could respond to increased demand for money by borrowing more reserves from the Fed. But because the Fed does not allow unlimited or continual borrowing from its discount window, increased money demand still put upward pressure on interest rates.

The Fed stuck to this strategy for three turbulent years—from October 1979 to October 1982. The results were dramatic. On the plus side, the chain reaction from money growth to inflation to more money growth and more inflation was broken. On the negative side, however, interest rates as well as real output went on a roller coaster ride. (The behavior of interest rates and the money stock during this period is discussed in "Applying Economic Ideas 14.1.") As expected when the money supply curve has a positive slope, in periods when money demand strengthened, the money stock was pulled above its target level and interest rates rose. When the demand for money moderated, the money stock fell below its target range and interest rates declined.

The Current Period

In late 1982, the Fed changed its strategy again. It was pleased with the progress in fighting inflation that had been made, but it was concerned about possible adverse effects of continuing its policy. For one thing, experience had shown that the policy of nonborrowed-reserves targeting could produce huge swings in interest rates in periods of unstable money demand. The Fed wanted to avoid another extreme peak of interest rates. It felt that another such episode would severely damage a depressed U.S. economy as well as the economies of Third World countries that owed billions of dollars to U.S. banks. In addition, the Fed was unsure of the impact of certain changes in banking regulations that were underway. These included the relaxing of interest rate ceilings on certain kinds of deposits and the introduction of super-NOW accounts and MMDAs scheduled around the beginning of 1983.

Also during this period, the Fed had increasing doubts about the wisdom of continuing to focus so closely on M1. The growth of highly liquid assets that are not included in M1 and the growth of savings-type balances in the NOW component of M1 were viewed as a sign that the links between M1 and broader economic activity might be less predictable than in the past. Finally, in 1987 the Fed even stopped announcing a policy target for M1.

By late 1982, the Fed had decided that its monetary policy should not be guided by hard-and-fast rules for the time being; instead, it should take a broad range of factors—interest rates, growth of broader measures of money and credit, growth of real national income, and price level changes—into account in guiding open market operations and changes in the discount rate. As a practical matter, since that time it has guided day-to-day operations with a borrowed-reserves operating target rather than a nonborrowed-reserves target. This change has removed the automatic feedback from a surge in money demand and the money stock to higher borrowed reserves to a higher federal funds rate. Instead, the Fed reacts to a tendency for borrowed reserves to increase by using

Interest Rates and the Money Stock, 1979–1982

During the period from October 1979 to October 1982, the Fed used nonborrowed reserves as its operating target. Given the level of nonborrowed reserves, total reserves were allowed to vary as banks increased or decreased the quantity of reserves they borrowed from the discount window. The result was an upward-sloping money supply curve. Two recessions plus changes in banking institutions caused the demand for money to be unstable during this period.

Under these conditions, increases in money demand tended to pull M1 above its target level and increase interest rates, as shown in the accompanying chart. (Interest rates are represented here by the federal funds rate.) In periods of weak money demand, M1 tended to fall below its target level and interest rates to fall. In contrast, if the money demand curve had held steady while the money supply curve shifted, M1 would have fallen below the target level in periods of high rather than low interest rates.

Several factors contributed to the instability of money demand during this period, including back-to-back recessions in 1980 and 1981 through 1982, changes in banking regulation, and a reversal of the inflationary spiral of the 1970s.

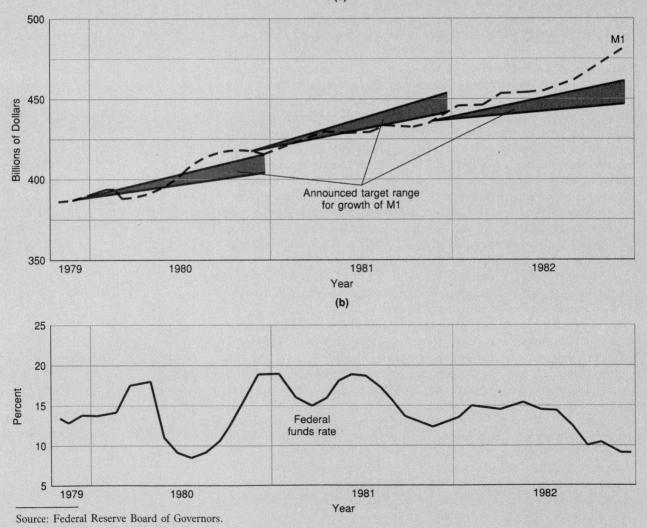

Source: Federal Reserve Board of Governors.

open market purchases to supply the desired reserves through nonborrowed channels. To be sure, the target level of borrowed reserves frequently has been adjusted during this period, as has the discount rate, in response to economic developments. Nonetheless, unless there is a deliberate decision to make such a change, there is a constraint on the movement of the federal funds rate.

In view of the occasional deliberate changes in the borrowed-reserves target and the discount rate taken in response to variations in money growth and other variables, it is difficult to present the Fed's current policy in graphic form. It is safe to say, though, that current policy lies somewhere between the extremes of strict money supply targeting and strict interest rate targeting. The Fed often seems willing to allow shifts in money demand to affect both interest rates and the money stock. In this sense, the Fed appears to be operating along an upward-sloping money supply curve. It is clear, however, that the curve is much flatter than during the October 1979 to October 1982 period and more subject to discretionary shifts.

Looking Ahead

This chapter has filled out our picture of the banking system and the money market by showing how the Fed's actions affect interest rates. In addition, it has described the evolution of the Fed's monetary policies. The next chapter develops linkages between monetary policy and the rest of the economy and explores the interaction between monetary and fiscal policy.

Summary

1. **How did the classical economists view the demand for money?** The classical economists viewed the demand for money in terms of the *equation of exchange*. Using M for the quantity of money, V for the velocity of money, P for the price level, and y for real national income, the equation of exchange can be written as $MV = Py$. The term *velocity* means the average number of times each year that each dollar of the money stock is used for income-producing purposes.

2. **How do income and interest rates affect money demand according to current theory?** According to the modern theory of money demand, people hold part of their assets in the form of money in order to gain the benefits of liquidity. Since most forms of money pay no interest or a lower interest rate than less liquid assets, the interest rate can be thought of as the opportunity cost of holding non-interest-bearing money. Other things being equal, a decrease in the interest rate or an increase in nominal national income tends to increase the demand for money. The demand for money can be represented by a downward-sloping curve on a graph in which the horizontal axis measures the quantity of money and the vertical axis measures the interest rate. An increase in nominal national income shifts the money demand curve to the right, and a decrease shifts it to the left.

3. **How has money demand behaved in the U.S. economy in recent years?** The income-adjusted money demand curve for the U.S. economy shifted gradually to the left during the 1960s and 1970s. This happened because financial innovations, spurred by a higher opportunity cost of money, caused firms and households to find ways of reducing the quantity of money they needed to support a given volume of transactions. In the 1980s, the shift appears to have stopped. There is some evidence that the quantity of M1 demanded has become more responsive than before to interest rate changes.

4. **How do supply and demand determine interest rates in the money market?** The money market can be represented by a vertical money supply curve and a downward-sloping money demand curve. If the quantity of money is increased while nominal national income remains constant, the market will move to a new equilibrium in which the interest rate is lower than before. The lower interest rate is needed to persuade people to hold a greater quantity of money. If nominal national income rises while the quantity of money remains constant, there will be an excess demand for money. This will cause people to try to adjust their *portfolios*, selling other assets in order to obtain money. In so doing, they will push up interest rates

and move the money market to a new equilibrium. A decrease in nominal national income will cause an excess supply of money, leading to a fall in interest rates.

5. **What targets has the Fed used as guides for its open market operations?** The slope of the money supply curve is determined by the Fed's *operating target*. If the Fed chooses a money stock target, the money supply curve will be vertical. If it sets an interest rate target, the money supply curve will be horizontal. In cases in which the interest rate is allowed to vary but an increase in the interest rate resulting from an increase in money demand is partly offset by a rise in the money stock, the money supply curve is upward sloping. During and after World War II, the Fed set targets for interest rates on government securities. Later interest rates were allowed to move somewhat, but they remained the focal point of the Fed's policies. During the 1970s, the Fed began to place more emphasis on the money supply. From 1979 through 1982, it pursued a strategy of targeting nonborrowed reserves. This resulted in a much steeper—though not vertical—money supply curve. Since 1982, monetary policy has depended more on the judgment of FOMC members and less on any formal rules.

Terms for Review

· equation of exchange
· velocity
· portfolio
· operating target

Questions for Review

1. If the quantity of money is $100 billion and nominal national income is $500 billion, what is the velocity? If the money stock and real national income remain constant while velocity increases to 10, what will happen to the price level?

2. According to the portfolio balance theory, how does a change in the interest rate affect the demand for money? How does a change in nominal national income affect the demand for money?

3. Are the effects of an increase in nominal national income more properly shown by a movement along or a shift in the money demand curve? In which way are the effects of a change in the interest rate best shown?

4. Are the effects of an open market purchase by the Federal Reserve best shown by a rightward shift in a vertical money supply curve, a leftward shift in the curve, or a movement along it? How does the interest rate change in response to an open market purchase, other things being equal?

5. With no change in the money supply, are the effects of an increase in nominal national income best shown by a rightward shift in, a leftward shift in, or a movement along the money demand curve? What happens to interest rates as a result of an increase in nominal national income?

6. What is the shape of the money supply curve when the Fed pursues a money stock operating target? An interest rate target? What conditions result in a positively sloped money supply curve?

7. If the demand for money increases, what happens to the amount of money supplied and the interest rate assuming that the Fed follows a money stock target? An interest rate target? A nonborrowed-reserves target?

8. How has the Fed's monetary control strategy changed over time? How can the evolution of its strategy be represented in terms of the money supply curve?

Problems and Topics for Discussion

1. **Examining the lead-off case.** Turn back to the case with which this chapter opens. Assume an upward-sloping money supply curve. Use a money market diagram to show how a "snugging" or "tightening" of policy can be represented by an upward shift of such a money supply curve assuming no change in the demand curve. Suppose that the supply curve does not shift or shifts only very slightly. What circumstances can then cause interest rates to rise "with no action" by the Fed as reported in the story?

2. **Velocity.** Using the *Economic Report of the President,* the *Federal Reserve Bulletin,* or another source, find the most recent values for the money stock (both M1 and M2), the price level (use the GNP deflator), and real national income. Use the equation of exchange to determine the velocities of M1 and M2. Which velocity is greater?

3. **Money demand and the price level.** Some economists draw a different type of money demand curve than the one used in this book. They begin with a diagram that shows the quantity of money demanded on the horizontal axis and the price level on the vertical axis. Sketch these axes on a sheet of graph paper. Number the vertical axis from 0 to 10 and the horizontal axis from 0 to $500 billion. Assume a constant real national income of $200 billion and a constant nominal interest rate of 4 percent. Using part a of Exhibit 14.1 as a guide, draw a curve showing how the quantity of money demanded varies as the price level changes. (Remember that nominal national income equals real national income times the price level.)

How does this version of the money demand curve shift if the interest rate rises from 4 to 6 percent?

4. **Updating Exhibit 14.3.** Find the most recent available data on nominal national income and M1. Plot them on the chart in Exhibit 14.3. Do the data indicate a renewed leftward drift in the money demand curve or movement along a fairly stable demand curve? Discuss.

5. **Effects of a decrease in the money supply.** Rework the example given in Exhibit 14.5 for the case of a decrease in the money supply from $180 billion to $120 billion.

6. **Effects of a decrease in nominal national income.** Rework the example given in Exhibit 14.6 for the case of a decrease in nominal national income from $600 billion to $400 billion. (Use part a of Exhibit 14.1 to draw the demand curve for a nominal national income of $400 billion.)

7. **Money supply and demand, 1979 to 1982.** The chart in "Applying Economic Ideas 14.1" (page 356) shows the relationship between interest rates and the money stock from 1979 to 1982. In that period, the interest rate tended to rise whenever the money stock was moving above its target growth range and to fall when it was moving below it. Use a supply and demand diagram to explain why this pattern is best explained by a stable, upward-sloping money supply curve and a shifting demand curve. What would the relationship between money and interest rates have been had the money demand curve remained fixed while the money supply curve shifted? Illustrate this case by sketching the pattern of interest rates and money supply over time using a pair of diagrams similar to the chart.

Case for Discussion

Interest Rates Up as Money Stock Soars

Bond prices tumbled when interest rates rose.

NEW YORK. Bond prices slumped yesterday amid speculation that the Federal Reserve System is tightening its credit hold in an attempt to stem the recent sharp growth of the money supply.

Fears about Fed policy intensified after the central bank reported that the basic money supply, known as M1, soared $4.7 billion in the week ended January 21. The rise was nearly twice as much as most analysts had expected and left the money measure far above the Fed's target.

Prices of some actively traded U.S. government long-term bonds tumbled about ⅝ point, or about $6.25 for each $1,000 face amount. Interest rates on short-term Treasury bills rose sharply.

Some analysts pointed to a recent climb in the interest rate on federal funds as an indication that the Fed has become less generous in its monetary policy. The funds rate, which is the fee banks charge on loans of reserves to one another, rose to 9 percent at one point yesterday. In the week ended Wednesday, the rate averaged 8.45 percent, up from 8.19 percent the previous week.

"It looks like the Fed may be in the process of tightening its credit policy," said Rudolf Thunberg, an economist at Ried, Thunberg, & Co., a New Canaan, Connecticut, investment advisory firm.

Source: E. Foldessy and T. Herman, "Surging Money Supply Sparks Fears of Tighter Credit, Cutting Bond Prices," *The Wall Street Journal*, February 1, 1985, p. 31. Reprinted by permission of *The Wall Street Journal*, © Dow Jones & Company, Inc. 1985. All Rights Reserved.

Questions

1. Explain why prices of bonds "tumbled" while interest rates "rose sharply." Why did bond prices and interest rates not move in the same direction?

2. In the period just prior to this story, both M1 and interest rates increased. Would this combination of circumstances best be represented by a vertical, positively sloped, or horizontal money supply curve assuming that the

curve, whatever its shape, did not shift during the period in question but the money demand curve did?

3. A "tightening" of monetary policy usually refers to a shift in the money supply curve rather than a movement along it. Given your choice of slope for the money supply curve in question 2, illustrate the type of tightening to which this article refers. Why would such a tightening of policy raise the interest rate? Assuming that the money demand curve remains fixed while policy is tightened, what will happen to the money stock?

Suggestions for Further Reading

Bryant, Ralph C. *Controlling Money: The Federal Reserve and Its Critics*. Washington, D.C.: The Brookings Institution, 1983.

This book discusses alternative operating targets and other issues raised in this chapter.

Campbell, Colin D., Rosemary G. Campbell, and Edwin G. Dolan. *Money, Banking, and Monetary Policy*. Hinsdale, Ill.: Dryden Press, 1988.

Chapters 15 through 17 cover the subject of this chapter in greater detail.

Darby, Michael R., William Poole, David E. Lindsey, Milton Friedman, and Michael J. Bazdarich. "Recent Behavior of the Velocity of Money." *Contemporary Policy Issues* (January 1987): 1–33.

A roundtable discussion among noted experts that focuses on the behavior of money demand during the period 1985 to 1986.

15 An Integrated View of Monetary and Fiscal Policy

After reading this chapter, you will understand . . .

- How changes in the money stock affect real output, the price level, and unemployment.
- What is meant by the *neutrality* of money.
- How fiscal policy affects interest rates and planned investment.
- The role that Keynes understood money to have played during the Great Depression.
- How the *monetarists* have influenced economic thought.

Before reading this chapter, make sure you know the meaning of . . .

- Natural real output (Chapter 8)
- Keynesian and classical theories of depression (Chapter 9)
- Multiplier effect (Chapter 9)
- Money market (Chapter 14)

Balancing the Risks

Two opposing types of risk are inherent in the conduct of monetary policy. One risk is that monetary policy might be too expansionary and that excess monetary growth will ultimately generate higher inflation and the subsequent need to disinflate. The second risk is that inadequate monetary growth might constrain the growth of real economic activity. While the balancing of these two types of risk is never easy, the task has been made more difficult in recent years. . . .

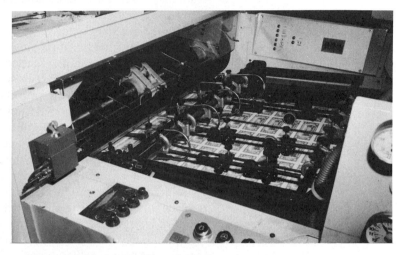

Excess monetary growth may generate higher inflation.

In 1986, monetary policy was influenced by a wide range of economic and financial market developments. In the first four months of 1986 . . . the Federal Reserve Board reduced the discount rate twice in order to realign it with lower market rates. Monetary growth was relatively modest early in the year as M1 expanded along the upper bound of its target range and the broader aggregates were within or below their prescribed ranges. . . .

By the summer of 1986, the broader monetary aggregates were also growing more rapidly and M2 reached the upper bound of its target range in August. The Federal Open Market Committee appeared to become more concerned about the inflationary potential for money growth, a concern that had been apparently discounted earlier in the year. . . .

By historical standards, M1 growth in 1986 was high. It substantially exceeded the Federal Reserve's own target range, as well as most analysts' a priori views of appropriate money growth. . . .

Analysts agree that at some point monetary growth must be reduced if the ultimate goal of price stability is to be achieved. The difficult policy issue is one of timing. . . .

From the outset, the Administration has emphasized the importance of promoting sustainable real economic growth within an environment of long-run price stability. With a continuation of lower than expected economic growth, moderate inflation, and serious stress in some sectors of the economy, the dangers of a monetary restriction of economic activity are real and important. Given the economic dislocation associated with the rise of inflation in the 1970s and its

363

reduction in 1981–1982, the Nation also cannot afford to ignore the dangers of allowing a reacceleration of inflation and the inevitable economic cost of disinflation.

Source: President's Council of Economic Advisers, *Economic Report of the President* (Washington, D.C.: Government Printing Office, 1987), 53–56. Photo Source: Courtesy of Bureau of Engraving and Printing.

IN the last three chapters, we looked at the monetary sector of the economy in isolation. We saw how the banking system operates, how the Fed controls the money stock, and how monetary policy affects interest rates. In this chapter, we return to the broader themes of inflation, real output, and employment and see how these are shaped by developments in the monetary sector. In this chapter, we will combine what we have learned about the monetary sector of the economy with what we previously learned about fiscal policy and the determination of real output, employment, and the price level.

The passages quoted above from the 1987 *Economic Report of the President* emphasize the Fed's monetary policy as a key to the health of the macroeconomy. The Fed's job is not an easy one; it must steer between the risks of policy that is too restrictive, preventing the growth of real output needed to provide jobs for a growing labor force, and a policy that is too expansive, incurring the risk of inflation. By combining the money market model of Chapter 14 with the aggregate supply and demand model developed earlier, we will gain a better understanding of these risks.

In addition, by combining these two models we will better understand how fiscal and monetary policy interact. We will see that the risks of excessive or inadequate stimulus apply just as much to the one type of policy as to the other.

Money and Aggregate Demand

In earlier chapters, we saw that a change in any of the components of aggregate demand affects prices, real output, and employment. An increase in aggregate demand pushes the economy up along the aggregate supply curve in the short run; as this happens, prices and real output rise while the unemployment rate falls. A decrease in aggregate demand has an opposite effect: In the short run, prices and real output fall while the unemployment rate rises. In Chapter 11, we saw that fiscal policy is capable of affecting output, prices, and employment via its effect on aggregate demand. We will begin this chapter by showing that monetary policy also acts on the economy by way of its effects on aggregate demand.

Short-Run Effects of Monetary Policy

Transmission mechanism
The set of channels through which monetary policy affects real output and the price level.

The set of channels through which money affects the economy is known as the **transmission mechanism.** In this section, we will focus on the most important aspect of the transmission mechanism, which runs from money to interest rates to the planned-investment component of aggregate demand. Exhibit 15.1 shows how this transmission mechanism works when the economy is exposed to a one-time change in the money stock.

Exhibit 15.1 Short-Run Effects of Expansionary Monetary Policy

A one-time increase in the money stock shifts the money supply curve from MS_1 to MS_2. The interest rate begins to fall. Real planned investment begins to increase as the economy moves down and to the right along the planned-investment schedule. The increase in planned investment shifts the aggregate demand curve from AD_1 to AD_2, raising real output and the price level. The resulting rise in nominal national income shifts the money demand curve to the right from MD_1 to MD_2. This shift is enough to limit the drop in the interest rate but not sufficient to prevent it altogether. In the new short-run equilibrium, the interest rate is lower and real investment, real output, and the price level are all higher than they were initially.

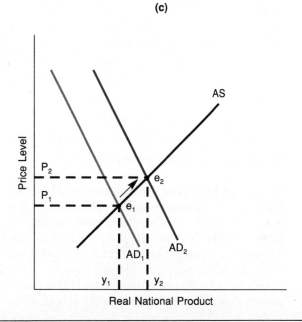

Initially the money market is in equilibrium at E_1 in part a of the exhibit. The money supply curve is in the position MS_1, and the money demand curve is at MD_1; thus, the equilibrium interest rate is R_1. According to the planned-investment schedule in part b, interest rate R_1 will result in a level of real planned investment indicated by I_1. This level of planned investment is built into aggregate demand curve AD_1 in part c along with given conditions regarding consumption, government purchases, and net exports. The initial equilibrium point in part c is thus e_1, at the intersection of AD_1 and the aggregate supply curve, AS. Equilibrium real output is y_1, and the price level is P_1.

Effects of Expansionary Monetary Policy

Now we assume that the Fed raises its target value for the money stock. This is shown in part a of Exhibit 15.1 as a rightward shift of the money supply curve to the position MS_2. The shift is accomplished by an injection of new reserves into the banking system via open market purchases.

As banks receive their new reserves, they use them to make loans and buy securities, causing the interest rate to drop. The falling interest rate lowers the opportunity cost of investment; thus, firms move down and to the right along the planned-investment schedule shown in part b. The increase in real planned investment, in turn, causes the aggregate demand curve to shift to the right as shown in part c. In response to the boost in demand, real output and the price level both increase and the economy moves up and to the right along its short-run aggregate supply curve.

As the economy expands, the increase in prices and real output causes nominal national income to rise. Bringing the story full circle back to the money market, the rise in nominal national income causes the money demand curve to shift to the right from MD_1 to MD_2. This limits the fall in the interest rate, but the curve does not shift enough to prevent the interest rate from falling somewhat. The money market comes into equilibrium at E_2, where the new money supply and demand curves intersect. At the new equilibrium interest rate, R_2, planned investment is I_2. This level of planned investment, together with the same underlying conditions as before regarding consumption, government purchases, and net exports, puts the aggregate demand curve in the position AD_2. The new short-run equilibrium for the economy is thus e_2 in part c, where real national product is y_2 and the price level is P_2.

To summarize, expansionary monetary policy has the following effects in the short run:

1. A reduction in the interest rate
2. An increase in the level of real output
3. An increase in the price level

Short-Run Effects of Contractionary Monetary Policy

Exhibit 15.1 can also be used to illustrate the short-run effects of contractionary policy. Starting at E_2 in the money market, the Fed lowers its money stock target, shifting the money supply curve to the left. All the arrows are now reversed. A rising interest rate cuts planned investment. Falling planned investment shifts the aggregate demand curve to the left, causing prices and real output to fall. This, in turn, means that nominal income declines, causing the money demand curve to shift to the left as well, but not by enough to prevent some increase in the interest rate. In the new short-run equilibrium, the money market returns to E_1 and the economy as a whole returns to e_1.

To summarize, contractionary monetary policy has the following effects in the short run:

1. An increase in the interest rate
2. A decrease in the level of real output
3. A decrease in the price level

Long-Run Effects and the Neutrality of Money

In Chapter 8, it was emphasized that the positively sloped aggregate supply curve is a short-run phenomenon. Movements along it are based on firms' assumption that input prices will not change. However, a change in the prices of the final goods that go into national product will inevitably affect the level of input prices. As input prices adjust to changes in the prices of final goods, the economy moves off its initial short-run aggregate supply curve and returns to the natural level of real output.

Long-Run Effects of Expansionary Monetary Policy

The economy will undergo such a long-run process of adjustment when the money stock changes and then remains at its new level. This process of long-run adjustment is shown in Exhibit 15.2; part b of that exhibit is just like part b of Exhibit 8.6 (page 199).

Part a of Exhibit 15.2 is added to show what goes on in the money market as the economy fully adjusts to a once-and-for-all expansion of the money supply. Beginning from E_1, the Fed uses open market purchases to shift the money supply curve to MS_2. As before, this causes the interest rate to fall and planned investment (not shown here) to increase. The aggregate demand curve shifts rightward from AD_1 to AD_2, and the economy moves to a new short-run equilibrium at e_2 in part b. The increase in nominal national income as the economy moves from e_1 to e_2 causes the money demand curve to shift from MD_1 to MD_2. This is where we left off in Exhibit 15.1. Now let's see what happens next.

As the economy moves from e_1 to e_2, the level of final goods prices increases. After a time, this causes input prices to increase as well. As we saw in Chapter 8, this happens partly because some goods serve as both inputs and final goods. Another reason is that the rise in the price level raises the cost of living, which puts upward pressure on wage rates. Once input prices start to rise, the assumption underlying the initial short-run aggregate supply curve no longer holds. The price level rises above the level—P_2—that it reached at e_2. The economy moves off the short-run aggregate supply curve, AS, and follows aggregate demand curve AD_2 up and to the left until it returns to the natural level of real output at e_3. At that point, both final goods prices and input prices have adjusted upward in proportion to the initial increase in the money stock. For example, if the money stock increases by 10 percent, both final goods prices and input prices will also increase by 10 percent.

In the money market, the continued price increase shifts the money demand curve further to the right. This causes the interest rate to rise again as the money market moves straight up along MS_2 toward E_3. Real planned investment, which had increased while interest rates were falling, decreases again as interest

Exhibit 15.2   The Neutrality of Money

A one-time increase in the money stock will not cause real output to remain indefinitely above its natural level as at e_2 in part b of this exhibit. The economy will move along aggregate demand curve AD_2 until it reaches a new long-run equilibrium at e_3. As it does so, nominal national income will continue to rise, shifting the money demand curve further to the right. The new long-run equilibrium in the money market (shown as E_3 in part a) will take place at the same interest rate as the original equilibrium. Thus, in the long run, a one-time increase in the money stock will affect only the price level and leave real output and the interest rate unchanged. This result is known as the *neutrality of money*.

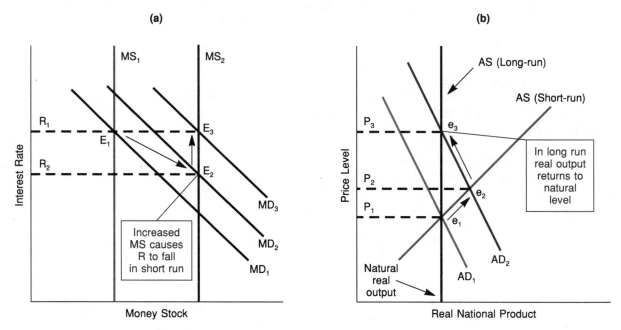

rates rise. By the time the interest rate returns to R_1, real planned investment is back to where it started.

Note that while the movement of the money market from E_1 to E_2 corresponds to a shift in the aggregate demand curve from AD_1 to AD_2, the movement from E_2 to E_3 corresponds to a movement along the new aggregate demand curve, AD_2, from e_2 to e_3. Nominal national income increases as the economy moves upward along the aggregate demand curve—which is why the money demand curve continues to shift to the right. The increase in nominal national income between e_2 and e_3 takes place because the increase in the price level more than offsets the decrease in real output.[1]

Neutrality of Money

The preceding analysis shows that a one-time increase in the money stock has the following long-run effects:

---

[1] For the benefit of readers who have already studied microeconomics, this statement can be reworded in terms of the concept of *elasticity:* Nominal national income rises as the economy moves from e_2 to e_3 because the aggregate demand curve is *inelastic*.

1. An increase in the equilibrium levels of both final goods and input prices in proportion to the change in the money stock

2. No change in the equilibrium level of real output

3. No change in the equilibrium interest rate

This set of conclusions is often referred to as the **neutrality of money** doctrine. Money is neutral in the sense that one-time changes in its level do not affect the long-run equilibrium values of *real* variables such as real output, real planned investment, or employment. In the long run, a one-time change in the money stock affects only price levels.

The neutrality of money doctrine has a long history in economics. It was stated clearly by Adam Smith's friend David Hume (see "Who Said It? Who Did It? 15.1"). It can also be stated in terms of the equation of exchange. In Chapter 14, the equation of exchange was written as $MV = Py$, where M stands for the money stock, V for velocity, P for the price level, and y for the level of real output. By rearranging terms, this can be written in the form

$$P = MV/y.$$

Neutrality of money
The proposition that in the long run a one-time change in the money stock affects only the price level and not real output, employment, interest rates, or planned investment.

WHO SAID IT? WHO DID IT? 15.1

David Hume on the Neutrality of Money

David Hume was an early member of the classical school of economics as well as a noted historian and philosopher. Born in 1711, he was a colleague of Adam Smith at Edinburgh University. He much admired Smith's *Wealth of Nations*, published in 1776, the year Hume died. While today Smith's contributions to economics overshadow Hume's, many of Hume's writings are regarded as insightful for his time.

Source: David Hume, "Of Money," in his *Writings on Economics*, ed. Eugene Rotwein (Madison, Wis: University of Wisconsin Press, 1955). Quotations from Hume are taken from Thomas M. Humphrey, "The Early History of the Phillips Curve," *Economic Review* (September-October 1985). Photo Source: The Bettmann Archive, Inc.

Eighteenth-century economists widely agreed that an increase in the money stock—chiefly gold and silver coins at the time—would raise the price level. Price increases having this origin had been observed, for example, when the Spanish began bringing gold back to Europe from the New World. A less settled question was whether an increase in the money stock would also "stimulate industry," that is, cause real output to increase. Today we would say that the issue concerned whether or not money is "neutral."

On that subject, Hume says that although an increase in the price of goods is a "necessary consequence" of an increase in the stock of gold and silver, "it follows not immediately." The change in the money stock does not affect all markets at once: "At first, no alteration is perceived; by degrees the price rises, first of one commodity, then of another; till the whole at last reaches a just proportion with the new quantity of [money]." Agreeing with modern theory that the stimulus to real output during this phase is only temporary, Hume continues: "In my opinion, it is only in this interval or intermediate situation, between the acquisition of money and the rise of prices, that the increasing quantity of gold and silver is favorable to industry." In Hume's view, there is no long-run effect on real output. In the long run, unlike in the short run, money is neutral. A one-time change in the quantity of money has a lasting proportional effect on the price level, but on nothing else.

In Chapter 14, we saw that the ratio of money to nominal income depends on the interest rate in the modern theory of money demand, which means that velocity, the ratio of nominal income to money, also depends on the interest rate. Since the long-run equilibrium value of the interest rate is not affected by a one-time change in the money stock, velocity too will remain unaffected by such a change. Thus, the above equation tells us that if y is held constant at its natural level and V unchanged, a one-time change in the money stock will produce a proportional change in the price level. For example, in Exhibit 15.2 a doubling of the money stock from MS_1 to MS_2 has the long-run effect of doubling the price level from P_1 to P_3.

Effects of Lasting Changes in Money Growth

Up to this point, we have considered only the effects of one-time changes in the money stock. In practice, changes in the money stock typically do not occur in sudden spurts; rather, the money stock grows gradually as the economy grows. A change in monetary policy is usually reflected in a lasting change in the growth rate of the money stock rather than a sudden, once-and-for-all jump in the stock itself.

Much of our discussion of the effects of one-time changes requires only minor translation to fit the case of a lasting change in money growth. For example, a lasting increase in the rate of money growth tends to increase the level of real output in the short run, but in the long run it is neutral with respect to real output. The long-run effect of an increase in money growth is a rise in the inflation rate for both final goods and input prices, with real output returning to its natural level. However, the effects of lasting changes in money growth on interest rates require some additional explanation. In order to understand these effects, we must introduce a distinction that we have not yet had occasion to mention—that between *real* and *nominal interest rates*.

Nominal interest rate
The interest rate measured in the usual way, in terms of current dollars of interest paid per current dollar of principal.

Real interest rate
The nominal interest rate minus the inflation rate.

In earlier chapters, we saw that the term *nominal* is used to refer to quantities stated in the ordinary way—in terms of current dollars—while the term *real* is used to denote quantities that are adjusted for inflation. In the case of interest rates, the distinction is as follows. The **nominal interest rate** means the interest rate stated in the usual way: in terms of current dollars of interest paid per dollar of principal. The **real interest rate** means the nominal interest rate minus the inflation rate. Letting R be the nominal interest rate, r the real interest rate, and $\dot{P}$ the inflation rate, we can write

$$r = R - \dot{P}.$$

For example, if the nominal interest rate is 10 percent and the inflation rate 7 percent, the real interest rate is 3 percent.

Taking this distinction into account, we must modify our earlier statements about the effects of expansionary monetary policy and the neutrality of money as they apply to interest rates. The most important new conclusion is that a lasting increase in the growth rate of the money stock will tend to raise the *nominal* interest rate rather than lower it. The reasoning behind this conclusion is as follows.

First, although there is no practical limit to the rate at which monetary policy can cause nominal national income to expand, there is a limit to how rapidly real national income can grow. This limit is established by the trends in technology, capital accumulation, and the labor force that determine the growth rate of natural real output over time. Over the post–World War II period, the trend rate of growth of real GNP in the United States has been in the neighborhood of 3 percent per year. In the long run, then, if expansionary monetary policy forces the growth rate of nominal GNP above 3 percent, the excess growth must take the form of inflation.

The next step in this reasoning concerns the reaction of asset holders to inflation. In deciding how to balance their portfolios, potential buyers of fixed-interest securities, especially long-term bonds, will look closely at the real rate of interest they expect to earn—that is, at the nominal interest rate minus the expected inflation rate. For any given nominal interest rate, an increase in the expected inflation rate will drive the expected real interest rate down, making bonds less attractive. Investors will try to reduce their holdings of bonds, thereby driving down bond prices and driving up their nominal yields. For the same reason, potential buyers of newly issued long-term bonds will demand an "inflation premium" in the form of a higher nominal coupon rate in exchange for buying the new bonds at face value. Much the same thing will happen in financial markets other than the bond market. Thus, an increase in the expected rate of inflation will push up the whole family of nominal interest rates.

What happens to real interest rates as a result of a lasting increase in the rate of money growth is less clear. In the short run real interest rates are likely to fall, but whether or not they do depends partly on how quickly assetholders adjust their expectations of inflation following the shift in monetary policy. Many economists think that in the long run there will be no change in the real interest rate. The rates of inflation and nominal interest will both increase in step with the increase in the rate of money growth, leaving the real interest rate where it started.

For example, suppose that initially the rate of money growth is 3 percent, just matching the growth rate of natural real output. There is no inflation, and the real and nominal interest rates are equal at 5 percent. Money growth then increases by seven percentage points to 10 percent, bringing on a steady 7-percent-per-year inflation. The inflation pushes up the nominal interest rate by seven percentage points—from 5 to 12 percent—but the real rate remains at 5 percent.

The proposition that a lasting change in the rate of money growth will, in the long run, not only leave real output unchanged but also leave the real interest rate unchanged is sometimes known as the "superneutrality of money."

Money and Fiscal Policy

In Chapter 11, we looked at the effects of fiscal policy in terms of the aggregate supply and demand model. An increase in government purchases or a cut in net taxes was shown to shift the aggregate demand curve to the right, thus raising real output and the price level in the short run and lowering unemployment, and a decrease in government purchases or an increase in net taxes was shown to have opposite short-run effects. In this section, we return to the topic of fiscal policy to see effects that reach beyond prices and real output to interest rates and investment.

The Crowding-Out Effect

Exhibit 15.3 gives the expanded analysis of the effects of fiscal policy. Initially the economy is in equilibrium at point e_1 in part c. Real output is at its natural level, y_1; the price level is at P_1 and stable. The money market, shown in part a, is in equilibrium at E_1 with an interest rate of R_1; since the price level is stable, the real and nominal interest rates are equal. This interest rate results in planned investment I_1, as shown in part b. Such a planned-investment level is one of the elements that determines the position of aggregate demand curve AD_1 together with given conditions governing consumption, government purchases, and net exports.

Now the government undertakes expansionary fiscal policy in the form of, say, an increase in government purchases. (A cut in taxes or an increase in transfer payments would have essentially the same effects.) As shown in Chapter 11, the result is a rightward shift of the aggregate demand curve. The economy begins to expand. The price level and real output both increase as the economy moves up and to the right along the short-run aggregate supply curve.

Now consider the effects on the money market, shown in part a of Exhibit 15.3. Because both prices and real output are increasing, nominal national income must also be rising. The money demand curve thus shifts to the right. With the money supply curve unchanged, the real and nominal interest rates rise. As they do, firms move up and to the left along the planned-investment schedule shown in part b. The level of real planned investment begins to fall.

Crowding-out effect

The tendency of expansionary fiscal policy to raise the interest rate and thereby cause a decrease in the planned-investment level.

This tendency for an increase in government purchases to cause a decrease in private planned investment is known as the **crowding-out effect.** The crowding out of real investment spending limits the expansion of real output. In Exhibit 15.3, the economy reaches a new short-run equilibrium at e_2 in part c, where real output is at y_2 and the price level at P_2. This point corresponds to point E_2 in the money market diagram of part a.

Chapter 11 discussed the effects of fiscal policy in terms of the multiplier effect. Now we see that because of crowding out, a given increase in government purchases shifts the aggregate demand curve by less than the expenditure multiplier itself implies. Suppose, for example, that the expenditure multiplier is 4 and the change in government purchases is $100 billion. Multiplying these two numbers would lead one to expect a $400 billion shift. But in practice, the shift is less because the expansionary effect of the increase in government purchases is partially offset by a decrease in private planned investment.[2] What is more, the price increases caused by the aggregate demand shift push interest rates up and further reduce planned investment.

---

[2] In Chapter 11 we assumed, as a working approximation, that the change in government purchases times the expenditure multiplier would equal the horizontal shift in the aggregate demand curve. Now we can see why this was only an approximation: There would be some crowding out even if the economy moved horizontally to the right on the aggregate supply and demand diagram with the price level unchanged. Even with no price level change, there would be some increase in nominal national income as a result of the increase in real national product. That alone would be enough to shift the money demand curve to the right, although not as far as the shift to MD_2 shown in Exhibit 15.3. Thus, the interest rate rate would rise somewhat, and there would be some crowding out of private investment. This fixed-price portion of the crowding-out effect keeps the aggregate demand curve from shifting to the right by the full amount of the change in government purchases times the multiplier. However, the amount of the shift can still be thought of as equal to the change in autonomous expenditure times the expenditure multiplier provided that the change in autonomous expenditure is interpreted as the increase in government purchases minus the change in planned investment resulting from the fixed-price component of crowding out.

Exhibit 15.3   The Crowding-Out Effect

Expansionary fiscal policy shifts the aggregate demand curve to the right from AD_1 to AD_2 as shown in part c. The resulting increase in nominal income shifts the money demand curve to the right from MD_1 to MD_2 as shown in part a. As the real and nominal interest rates rise, planned investment will decrease and the economy will move to the left along the planned-investment schedule shown in part b. The tendency of expansionary fiscal policy to reduce private planned investment is known as the *crowding-out effect.*

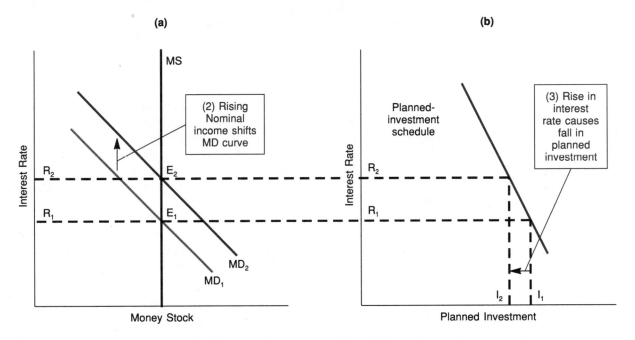

(a)

(2) Rising Nominal income shifts MD curve

(b)

Planned-investment schedule

(3) Rise in interest rate causes fall in planned investment

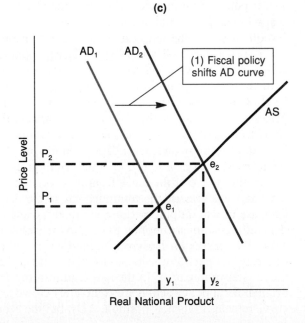

(c)

(1) Fiscal policy shifts AD curve

Crowding Out Extended

The version of the crowding-out effect discussed in the preceding section concerns the tendency of an increase in government purchases to reduce private planned investment. This idea can be extended in several ways.

First, it can be extended to all types of fiscal policy. As Chapter 11 showed, expansionary fiscal policy can also take the form of a cut in taxes or an increase in transfer payments. Because these types of expansionary policy also cause nominal national income to rise, they increase money demand, push up interest rates, and cut into real planned investment.

Second, the concept can be extended to incorporate components of aggregate demand other than planned investment. Chapter 8 showed that all components of aggregate demand are potentially subject to crowding out when expansionary fiscal policy (or any other factor) raises the price level. Consumption may fall because an increase in the price level reduces the real purchasing power of given nominal money balances. Net exports may fall because a higher price level makes domestic goods more costly for foreign buyers while making foreign goods relatively less expensive for domestic buyers. Further, an increase in federal government purchases may, by raising the price level, crowd out some state and local government expenditures (and even some federal expenditures on programs that have not been increased) to the extent that some portions of government budgets are set by law in nominal terms.

Finally, it should be noted that all forms of the crowding-out effect are reversible. A decrease in government purchases or an increase in net taxes causes nominal national income to fall. This shifts money demand to the left and causes interest rates to fall. Real planned investment increases, partly offsetting the contractionary effect of the assumed fiscal policy. The tendency of contractionary fiscal policy to increase planned investment might thus be called "crowding in."

The Long Run and Nonneutrality of Fiscal Policy

Fiscal policy is no more capable than monetary policy of permanently raising real national product above its natural level. Exhibit 15.4 picks up where 15.3 left off; it shows the long-run effects of expansionary fiscal policy.

Expansionary policy has shifted the aggregate demand curve in part c from AD_1 to AD_2, moving the economy to a short-run equilibrium at e_2. Compared with the initial equilibrium, e_1, real output is above the natural level and the level of final goods prices has increased. Over time, as the rise in final goods prices begins to affect the level of input prices, the economy leaves its initial short-run aggregate supply curve. Prices continue to rise, but real output falls back toward the natural level. The economy moves up along the aggregate demand curve to a new long-run equilibrium at e_3.

In the course of the move from e_2 to e_3, nominal income continues to rise. This happens because the continued rise in the price level more than offsets the decrease in real output. Because nominal income continues to rise, the money demand curve must continue to shift to the right, as shown in part a of Exhibit 15.4. This causes further crowding out of private planned investment as rising interest rates push firms up and to the left along the planned-investment schedule, as shown in part b. In the new equilibrium, the expansionary effects of the original fiscal policy action are completely crowded out. The aggregate demand curve remains in its new position, AD_2, but the economy's movement up and to

Exhibit 15.4   Crowding Out in the Long Run

Point e_2 in part c of this exhibit is only a short-run equilibrium. As the economy moves to a new long-run equilibrium at e_3, nominal national income continues to rise. The money demand curve shifts further to the right from MD_2 to MD_3 as shown in part a. As it does, the economy moves further to the left along the planned-investment schedule as shown in part b. Thus, the crowding-out effect intensifies in the long run as real output returns to its natural level.

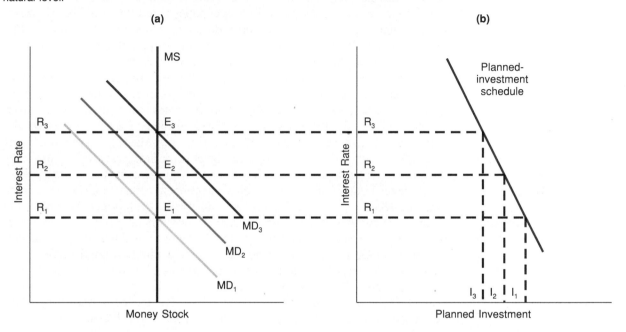

(a)   **(b)**

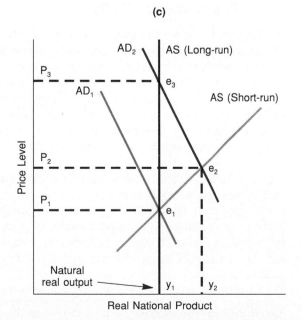

(c)

the left along this curve has brought real national product all the way back to its natural level.

In one respect, the long-run effects of fiscal policy are similar to those of monetary policy: In both cases, there is a higher price level in the new long-run equilibrium but no permanent change in real output. However, there is one important difference. Monetary policy is said to be "neutral" because a one-time increase in the money stock (and perhaps even a lasting change in money growth) has no long-run effects on any real variables—real output, planned investment, or real interest rates. But fiscal policy is not "neutral" in this sense. Even though expansionary fiscal policy does not change the long-run equilibrium level of real output, it does change the long-run equilibrium values of the real and nominal interest rates and real planned investment.

Compare Exhibit 15.4 with Exhibit 15.2 in this regard. In Exhibit 15.2, expansionary monetary policy moves the money market to a long-run equilibrium at E_3, where the real and nominal interest rates are at the same level from which they started. But in Exhibit 15.4, expansionary fiscal policy moves the money market to a long-run equilibrium at E_3, where the real and nominal rates are higher. Consequently, the long-run level of private planned investment is lowered by expansionary fiscal policy but not by expansionary monetary policy.

Chapter 11 mentioned the crowding-out effect in connection with the debate over the federal budget deficit. As we saw there, the budget deficits of the Reagan era resulted partly from increased government purchases and partly from increased transfer payments while tax revenues remained roughly constant as a share of GNP. Increases in both government purchases and transfer payments raise interest rates, thus tending to crowd out private investment. As a result, say the critics, future generations will be left with a smaller stock of capital—buildings, equipment, scientific achievements, and so on—than would be the case had the federal budget been balanced in the 1980s.

Fiscal Policy and the Dollar

In Chapter 14, we saw that monetary policy affects the foreign exchange value of the dollar via its effects on interest rates. Monetary contraction, which raises interest rates in the short run, tends to encourage capital inflows and discourage outflows, thus boosting the dollar's value. Monetary expansion, which lowers interest rates in the short run, tends to discourage capital inflows and encourage outflows, thus depressing the dollar's value. Now we see that fiscal policy also affects interest rates. This being the case, we would expect fiscal policy also to have international implications—and so it does.

Interest Rates, Capital Flows, and Crowding Out

One of the international implications concerns the crowding-out effect. In a closed economy, an increase in government purchases financed by borrowing will reduce the long-run equilibrium value of planned investment almost dollar for dollar.[3] In an open economy, however, investment will be less severely affected. The reason is that the rise in interest rates will encourage net capital

---

[3] We say "almost" because there may be some increase in saving. This could be induced by the rise in interest rates, as in the classical investment-saving mechanism described in Chapter 9. Also, to the extent that an increase in the price level cut the equilibrium value of consumption via a reduction in the real value of nominal money balances, the equilibrium level of saving would increase. In practice, however, both of these effects probably would be small.

inflows (that is, encourage inflows and discourage outflows), as explained in Chapter 14. The net capital inflows are added to domestic saving to increase the pool of funds available for financing domestic planned investment and the government budget deficit. In equation form,

$$\begin{matrix} \text{Net capital} \\ \text{inflow} \end{matrix} + \begin{matrix} \text{Domestic} \\ \text{saving} \end{matrix} = \begin{matrix} \text{Domestic} \\ \text{investment} \end{matrix} + \begin{matrix} \text{Government} \\ \text{deficit} \end{matrix}$$

Part a of Exhibit 15.5 shows this relationship in terms of the circular flow. The diagram highlights net capital inflows and domestic saving, which are flows of funds into financial markets, and domestic investment and the government deficit, which are flows out of financial markets. The total inflows and outflows balance.

Part b of Exhibit 15.5 gives data for the key variables for the 1960s, the 1970s, and the 1980s through 1985. Over this period the combined federal, state, and local government budget deficit increased by 2.3 percent of GNP, from 0.3 to 2.6 percent. During the same period, domestic saving fell by 1.9 percent of GNP, from 8.1 to 6.2 percent. In a closed economy, domestic investment would have had to fall by 4.2 percent of GNP, that is, by the sum of the increase in the deficit and the decrease in private saving. As it happened, however, domestic investment fell by only 2.5 percent of GNP. This was possible because there was a 1.7 percentage point swing from a net capital outflow of .7 percent of GNP in the 1960s to a net capital inflow of 1 percent of GNP in the 1980s.

Budget Deficit and Current Account Deficit

Another international implication of fiscal policy concerns the relationship between the federal budget deficit and the current account balance of payments deficit. As explained in Chapter 7, the current account is the mirror image of the capital account. In the 1960s, a net capital outflow from the United States was possible because the country ran a current account surplus. The earnings from selling more abroad than was purchased were reinvested overseas. In the 1980 to 1985 period, the situation was reversed: There was a current account deficit— that is, the United States purchased more abroad than it sold. The portion of the bill for imports that was not paid for by exporting goods and services was covered by capital inflows, that is, by net sales of assets to foreign buyers or by net borrowing from abroad.

Why did the United States turn from a net exporter into a net importer during those years? Some accounts have blamed the failure on a drop in the quality of U.S. goods, a lag in productivity on the part of U.S. workers, increasingly unfair trade practices on the part of trading partners, or some combination of these. Perhaps those factors did play some role, but many economists have assigned them a minor one. Instead, they attribute the growth of the balance of payments deficit to the rise in the dollar's value in the early 1980s. From 1980 to 1985, the value of the dollar increased more than 60 percent relative to a weighted average of U.S. trading partners' currencies. With the dollar so high, U.S. goods were priced out of many world markets. At the same time, imports became very cheap because the dollar was worth so much in terms of foreign currencies.

Why did the dollar rise? One widely advanced hypothesis focuses on the tendency of an increase in the federal budget deficit to raise interest rates. With U.S. interest rates high relative to those abroad, capital inflows ballooned, driv-

Exhibit 15.5 The Budget Deficit and International Capital Flows

Part a of this exhibit shows two flows of funds into financial markets: domestic saving and international capital flows. These are balanced by two flows of funds out of capital markets: private investment and the government budget deficit. Part b shows data on these four flows for the U.S. economy. As can be seen, the budget deficit has increased in the 1980s over those of the 1960s and 1970s while domestic saving has decreased. The result has been a reduction in private investment. However, this decrease would be even greater were it not for the growth of the net capital inflow from abroad.

(a)

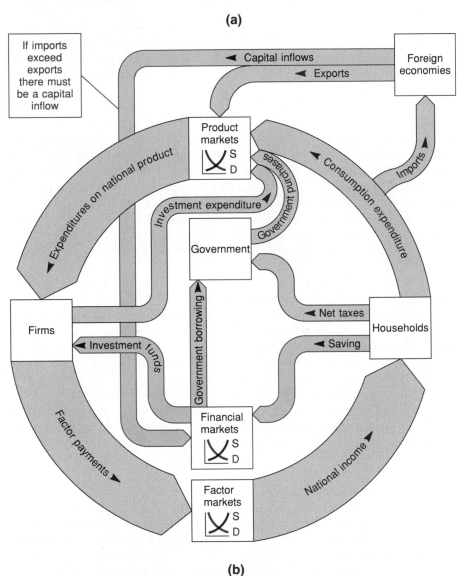

(b)

	Percent of GNP			
	Net Capital Inflow (+) or Outflow (−)	Domestic Saving	Government Deficit	Domestic Investment
1960–1969	−0.7	8.1	0.3	7.1
1970–1979	−0.3	8.1	0.9	6.9
1980–1985	1.0	6.2	2.6	4.6

Source: Adapted from Jonathan Rauch, "The Politics of Joy," *National Journal,* January 17, 1987, 125.

ing up the dollar's exchange value. According to this hypothesis, then, U.S. exporters were more the victim of the budget deficit than of a lack of competitiveness based on weaknesses of labor or management.[4]

The relationship of fiscal policy to imports, exports, and capital flows remains one of the most controversial aspects of the debate over the federal budget deficit. The budget priorities of the 1980s—increased outlays for entitlements and defense with no increase in the share of GNP going to taxes—were described in Chapter 11. Critics charge that the resulting fiscal policy has left the nation burdened with debts owed to foreign lenders and has cost export industries market share in an increasingly competitive world economy as well as starving domestic firms of investment capital via the crowding-out effect.

The Keynesian-Monetarist Debate over the Role of Money

This chapter has presented a view of money's role in the economy that is now widely accepted. This was not always so, however; in particular, John Maynard Keynes and his followers saw a much smaller role for money in the economy, especially under depression conditions. In Chapter 9, we looked briefly at the debate between Keynes and his predecessors, the classical economists, concerning the economy's ability to rebound from a contraction. In this section, we will return to that debate in light of what we have learned about the monetary sector. We will then introduce the *monetarists*, a school of economists who have been strongly influential during the post–World War II period.

The Keynesian View of Money in the Depression

The model presented earlier in this chapter emphasizes a transmission mechanism for monetary policy that runs from money to interest rates to investment. Keynes recognized the existence of this mechanism in his *General Theory*. However, he thought that it was relatively weak, at least under conditions of depression.

The Liquidity Trap
Keynes's reasoning was briefly outlined in Chapter 9. First, Keynes thought that investment is rather insensitive to changes in interest rates—in other words, that the planned-investment schedule is very steep. He also believed that in a depression interest rates might reach a floor below which they could drop no further. Low interest rates mean high bond prices. At some point, Keynes reasoned, speculators would become almost unanimously fearful of future declines in bond prices; they would stop buying bonds and hold money instead. When bond prices stopped rising, interest rates would stop falling. This amounted to saying that the money demand curve would become nearly horizontal at low interest rates. Such behavior was called a "liquidity trap" because people's inclination to accumulate liquid assets (money) would keep interest rates from falling, thus trapping the economy in a state of low planned investment.

---

[4]For evidence in support of this hypothesis, see Martin Feldstein, "The Budget Deficit and the Dollar" (Working Paper No. 1898, National Bureau of Economic Research, April 1986).

The set of circumstances that Keynes hypothesized is represented in part a of Exhibit 15.6. There the money demand curve is shown as having a horizontal "tail" at a low interest rate and the planned-investment schedule as nearly vertical. The weakness of the transmission mechanism under these circumstances has two implications for policy.

First, it means that a fall in the price level will have little effect on aggregate demand. A drop in the price level with real national income constant means a drop in nominal national income. As shown in part b of the exhibit, such a drop in nominal national income will shift the money demand curve leftward from MD_1 to MD_2. However, because of the curve's shape, the interest rate will be barely affected. Given the steep planned-investment schedule, there will be only a very small increase in planned investment, if any. If a drop in the price level does not affect planned investment, the aggregate demand curve will be vertical, or nearly so, as was shown in Exhibit 9.5 (page 219). This means that the economy has no built-in ability to recover from a depression.

Second, a weak transmission mechanism means that expansionary monetary policy will do little or nothing to help recovery. The reason is shown in part c of Exhibit 15.6. A shift in the money supply curve from MS_1 to MS_2 has almost no effect on the interest rate. Speculators are willing to hold all the newly created money at the rate already in effect rather than to buy bonds, which would drive down the interest rate. To the extent that there is some small decline in the interest rate, the effect on planned investment is, in any event, negligible.

We see, then, that a weak transmission mechanism means both that the economy has no power to recover from a depression of its own accord and that expansionary monetary policy will not aid recovery. The conclusion is that only expansionary fiscal policy can save the economy from lasting depression.

The Monetarist Response

After World War II, many of the early Keynesians forecast a new depression and economic stagnation. They thought that private investment would dry up with the end of wartime government spending. They were wrong: The postwar recovery of the United States and Western Europe was rapid. Central banks in most of the major economies pursued easy monetary policies during those years, and inflation was more widespread than depression. The countries that were able to control inflation did so only by using standard policies of monetary restraint. Economists began to take renewed interest in the role of money in the economy.

During the 1950s and 1960s, there was a reaction against the tendency of Depression-era Keynesians to downplay the role of money. The response came most prominently from a group of economists led by Milton Friedman (see "Who Said It? Who Did It? 15.2"). Friedman's research led him to think that movements in the money supply had a much greater effect on economic events even under Depression conditions than the early Keynesians had been willing to admit. Because of the emphasis Friedman and his followers gave to monetary policy, their school of thought came to be known as **monetarism.**

Monetarism
A school of economics emphasizing the importance of changes in the money stock as determinants of changes in real output and the price level.

Reinterpretation of the Great Depression

Friedman's research led to a reinterpretation of the Great Depression. In *A Monetary History of the United States*, Friedman and Anna J. Schwartz pointed to the 25 percent decrease in the narrowly defined money supply that the Fed had allowed between 1929 and 1933 (see "Perspective 13.1," pages 324–325). The 1930s gave no evidence that expansionary monetary policy was ineffective,

Exhibit 15.6   The Keynesian View of Money in the Depression

Keynes and his early followers thought that the monetary sector played an insignificant role in the economy under depression conditions. There were two reasons for this, as shown in part a of this exhibit. One reason was that they thought the money demand curve becomes nearly horizontal at low interest rates. The other is that they believed the planned-investment schedule is nearly vertical. Part b shows that given the shapes of these curves, a fall in the price level will shift the money demand curve to the left but have little or no effect on interest rates or planned investment. This was one of Keynes's reasons for thinking that the economy's aggregate demand curve would be nearly vertical. As a result, the economy could not recover from a depression by itself. In addition, part c shows that under the Keynesian assumptions expansionary monetary policy has little effect on interest rates or planned investment. This means that such a policy would do little to lift the economy out of a depression. That left expansionary fiscal policy as the only reliable route to recovery in the Keynesian view.

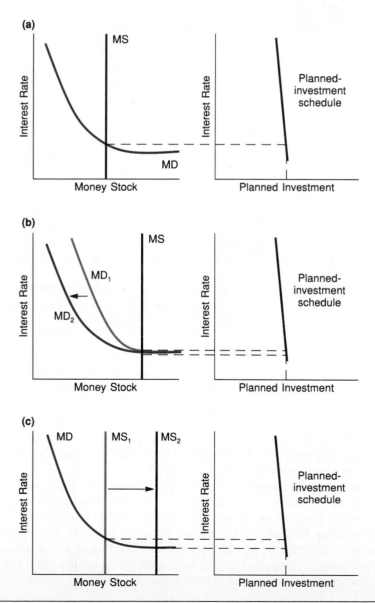

WHO SAID IT? WHO DID IT? 15.2

Milton Friedman and Monetarism

In October 1976, Milton Friedman received the Nobel Memorial Prize in economics, becoming the sixth American to win or share that honor. Few people were surprised. The main puzzle was that he had had to wait in line so long. Perhaps it was because Friedman has built his career outside the economics establishment, by challenging almost every major doctrine of that profession.

Friedman was born in New York in 1912, the son of hard-working immigrant garment workers. He attended Rutgers University, where he came under the influence of Arthur Burns, then a young assistant professor. From Burns, Friedman learned the importance of empirical work in economics. Statistical testing of all theory and policy prescriptions became a key feature of Friedman's later work. From Rutgers, Friedman went to the University of Chicago for an M.A. and then east again to Columbia University, where he got his Ph.D. in 1946. He returned to

Chicago to teach, where he and his colleagues of the "Chicago school" of economics posed a major challenge to the economists of the "eastern establishment."

If one could single out a recurrent theme throughout Friedman's work, it would be his belief that the market economy works—and works best when left alone. This can be seen in his best-known work, *A Monetary History of the United States*. Written with Anna Schwartz, this book attacks two major tenets of Keynesian economics: (1) that the market economy is unstable without the guiding hand of government and (2) that monetary policy was tried and found useless as a cure for the Great Depression. Friedman and Schwartz found both beliefs to be far from the truth. "The Great Depression," Friedman later wrote, "far from being a sign of the inherent instability of the private enterprise system, is a testament to how much harm can be done by mistakes on the part of a few men when they wield vast power over the monetary system of the country."

Friedman strongly favors a hands-off policy by government in almost every area. In his view, the problem is not that government is evil by nature but that so many policies end up having the opposite of their intended effects: "The social reformers who seek through politics to do nothing but serve the public interest invariably end up serving some private interest that was no part of their intention to serve. They are led by an invisible hand to serve a private interest." Transport regulation, public education, agricultural subsidies, and housing programs are among the many policy areas in which Friedman believes the government has done more harm than good and a free competitive market would do better.

Today Friedman continues to take on new challenges. He promotes his ideas before congressional committees, in professional journals, in the press, and in face-to-face debates with his colleagues. Economics has never had a more respected heretic.

said the monetarists, because such a policy was not tried. On the contrary, the fact that the Fed permitted the money stock to collapse emerged as a major cause of the Depression's severity.

The economics profession was slow to convert to monetarism. In fact, in some ways the 1960s were the heyday of Keynesian policy. Many leading Keynesians left their university posts to join the Council of Economic Advisers under Presidents Kennedy and Johnson. Even so, however, the monetarists' ideas proved influential in persuading the Keynesians to give greater attention to money and monetary policy. A central issue in the debate of the 1950s and 1960s was the nature of the transmission mechanism for monetary policy.

Monetarist View of the Transmission Mechanism

In the Keynesian theory, the transmission mechanism through which monetary policy affects the rest of the economy is narrow and indirect. As we have told the story, it begins when an increase in the money supply causes households and firms to readjust their portfolios of assets. In the process of adjusting to the larger money stock, they drive up the prices of bonds and other securities and force down nominal interest rates. This, in turn, is supposed to encourage planned investment, which, finally, stimulates aggregate demand.

Monetarists challenged the Keynesian view that this transmission mechanism is weak. Their statistical studies dispelled the notions that the economy had experienced a "liquidity trap" in the 1930s and investment was unresponsive to interest rates. They claimed there was simply no evidence to support the shapes of the money demand curves and planned-investment schedules shown in Exhibit 15.6. In addition, monetarists, as well as many other economists, came to see the interest rate–investment linkage as only one aspect of a more complex transmission mechanism for monetary policy.

The Keynesian version of the transmission mechanism begins when people adjust their portfolios in response to an increase in the money stock. Keynesians tend to stress the trade-off between money and fixed-interest securities such as bonds. In the real world, the choices are much broader. Besides bonds and money, people own common stocks, real estate, commodities, consumer durables, and even stocks of consumer nondurables. In the monetarist view, an excess supply of money is likely to affect the implicit and explicit returns on a wide variety of assets, both financial and nonfinancial. It is likely, therefore, to spill over into spending on goods as well as securities. As it does, aggregate demand is thought to be stimulated in many ways. An increase in stock prices can spawn new investment by making it less costly for corporations to issue new shares. Increases in the demand for real estate can stimulate new construction. Increases in prices of commodities—wheat, gold, rubber, and so on—can stimulate production of those goods. Even consumption spending can respond directly to a change in the money supply.

In the monetarist view, then, the effect of an injection of money spreads through the whole economy. People become content to hold the newly issued money as a result not just of a change in interest rates but of a broader change in the composition of their portfolios.

Looking Ahead

The monetarists' broader view of the transmission mechanism played a key role in rehabilitating the classical view of a downward-sloping aggregate demand curve that shifts in response to changes in monetary policy. It is this form of the aggregate supply and demand model—not the Depression-era Keynesian form with a vertical aggregate demand curve—that is now widely accepted as standard. However, although the monetarist view of the importance of money as a determinant of aggregate demand is now shared to a substantial degree by most economists, their views have by no means come to dominate the economics profession in all respects. Chapter 18 will show that other aspects of the Keynesian-monetarist debate are still very much alive.

In order to understand these ongoing aspects of the debate, however, we must leave the depression scenario that preoccupied economists of a generation ago. The next two chapters will use aggregate supply and demand analysis to strengthen our understanding of inflation and economic growth—the issues on which macroeconomics has focused in the 1970s and 1980s.

Summary

1. **How do changes in the money stock affect real output, the price level, and unemployment?** An increase in the money stock initially lowers interest rates. The resulting increase in planned investment shifts the aggregate demand curve to the right. As the economy moves up and to the right along the aggregate supply curve, in the short run real output increases, the price level increases, and the unemployment rate falls. A decrease in the money stock has the opposite effects in the short run: Interest rates rise, planned investment falls, and the aggregate demand curve shifts to the left. As a result, real output and the price level fall and the unemployment rate increases.

2. **What is meant by the neutrality of money?** A one-time increase in the money stock can cause real output to rise above its natural level in the short run but cannot hold it there in the long run. As input prices rise, the economy returns to the natural level of real output at a higher price level than initially. In the new equilibrium, the prices of both final goods and inputs will have changed in proportion to the increase in the money stock but the values of all real variables—interest rates, planned investment, real output, and employment—will be unaffected. This proposition is known as the *neutrality of money*. Lasting changes in money growth, as opposed to one-time changes in the money stock, are also neutral with regard to real output and may be neutral with respect to real interest rates. However, lasting changes in the rate of money growth will have a lasting effect on the inflation rate and, hence, affect nominal interest rates.

3. **How does fiscal policy affect interest rates and planned investment?** Expansionary fiscal policy shifts the aggregate demand curve to the right. Real output and the price level rise in the short run, as does nominal national income. The increase in nominal national income shifts the money demand curve to the right, causing both *real* and *nominal* interest rates to increase. This rise in interest rates *crowds out* some real planned investment. As the economy returns to a long-run equilibrium at the natural rate of real output, a further rise in the price level causes nominal national income to rise still higher, putting additional upward pressure on interest rates. Thus, there is a further depressing effect on real investment, and the crowding-out effect intensifies in the long run.

4. **What role did Keynes understand money to have played during the Great Depression?** Keynes and his early followers saw money as playing a relatively minor role during the Great Depression. They thought that under depression conditions, a shift in the money supply or demand curves would have little effect on the interest rate and that any interest rate change that did occur would have little impact on planned investment. These views implied both that the economy would be unable to recover on its own from a depression and that expansionary monetary policy would be of little help. In the Keynesian view, only expansionary fiscal policy could do the job.

5. **How have monetarists influenced economic thought?** After World War II, *monetarists*, led by Milton Friedman, argued that monetary policy was an important determinant of aggregate demand even under depression conditions and all the more so in normal times. They saw the Fed's failure to prevent a contraction of the money stock as a major factor in the Depression's length and severity. Although not all economists were converted to monetarism, the monetarists' work has helped all economists understand the role that monetary policy plays in determining the price level, real output, and employment.

Terms for Review

- transmission mechanism
- neutrality of money
- nominal interest rate
- real interest rate
- crowding-out effect
- monetarism

Questions for Review

1. In the short run, what happens to interest rates, real planned investment, real output, the unemployment rate, and the price level as a result of an increase in the money stock? A decrease in the money stock?

2. Why does a one-time increase in the money stock have no long-run effect on interest rates whereas an increased fiscal stimulus does? How do the effects of a lasting increase in the rate of money growth differ from those of a one-time increase in the money stock?

3. Can the crowding-out effect extend to expenditures other than planned investment? Explain.

4. Why did Keynes and his early followers think that money played a relatively small role in the Great Depression?

5. Why do monetarists think the Depression would have been less severe had the Fed prevented the money stock from falling as it did from 1929 to 1933?

Problems and Topics for Discussion

1. **Examining the lead-off case.** Using government data sources such as the *Economic Report of the President* or current news sources, determine whether there has been a recession or an acceleration of inflation since the end of 1986. Have subsequent events tended to indicate that monetary policy in 1986 was too expansionary, not expansionary enough, or just about right?

2. **Long-run effects of contractionary monetary policy.** Use a set of diagrams similar to Exhibits 15.1 and 15.2 to trace the long-run effects of a one-time contraction of the money stock beginning from equilibrium at the natural rate of real output.

3. **Effects of a tax increase.** Use a set of diagrams similar to Exhibit 15.4 to trace the effects of a contractionary fiscal policy, such as a tax increase. What happens to real output, unemployment, the price level, interest rates, and planned investment in the long and short runs?

4. **Crowding out and the money supply curve.** Use a set of diagrams similar to Exhibit 15.3 to investigate how the crowding-out effect is influenced by the shape of the money supply curve. First use a positively sloped and then a horizontal money supply curve. Discuss the policy implications of your results.

5. **Monetary policy and the value of the dollar.** Using current news sources, such as *The Wall Street Journal*, determine whether the exchange rate for the dollar is now rising, falling, or steady. Do any of the news stories you found on the subject of exchange rates mention the role of U.S. monetary or fiscal policy? If so, discuss that role.

Case for Discussion
Reaganomics, RIP

As the Congressional Budget Office observes in its latest *Economic and Budget Outlook*, published in January [1987], a verdict on Reaganomics boils down to the question of justice between generations. Our fiscal policy since 1981 has allowed people living today to enjoy higher consumption at the expense of those who will be living tomorrow. It is not clear whether President Reagan actually meant to throw this party or whether things simply got out of hand. . . .

Critics charge that thanks to Reaganomics, people today enjoy higher consumption at the expense of future generations.

Will the party soon have to end? Actually, we may go on for a while. As long as other nations are willing to add dollar-denominated American IOUs to their portfolios, we can continue to live happily beyond our means. . . .

An alternative would be to go back to square one and to balance the government's books. During 1980–1986, net private savings—roughly, the amount of investable funds available after replacement of worn-out capital—has averaged 6.2 percent of GNP (down from 8.1 percent in 1970–1979). Savings by state and local governments brought the total available savings pool to 7.5 percent of GNP. The federal deficit alone drained 4.1 percent of GNP from the pool—that is, more than half of it—leaving only 3.4 percent of GNP for net private capital formation beyond the replacement of worn-out capital. We did, as noted, supplement that meager pool by tapping the savings of foreigners through borrowing and the sale of real assets. If that is to cease, we must either bring the federal budget closer into balance or start saving a lot more—that is, start consuming less—as individuals.

Source: Uwe Reinhardt, "Reaganomics, RIP," *The New Republic*, April 20, 1987, 24–27. Photo Source: © 1987 Phyllis Woloshin.

Questions

1. Leaving aside the issue of borrowing from foreigners, explain, in terms of what you learned in this chapter and in Chapter 11, how the policies of the Reagan administration might be said to have enhanced the consumption of those alive today at the expense of those living tomorrow.

2. A counterargument to the position taken by Reinhardt goes like this: "If net taxes were raised or government purchases cut to balance the budget, the economy would be thrown into a recession. That would certainly cut the consumption of those living today, but it is not clear that it would benefit those living tomorrow." Discuss. Is there a way the budget could be balanced without causing a recession? What does this argument assume about monetary policy?

3. Reinhardt thinks that people today are consuming too much and not investing enough. How does one decide what is proper distribution of income and consumption between generations? Should we consume less today so that tomorrow's generations can consume more even though they will probably have higher incomes than we will? Do you think your own parents should save more and consume less now so that you can consume more in the future when you inherit from them? Discuss.

4. Why did the large Reagan budget deficits cause U.S. borrowing from foreigners to increase? Given that the government decides to borrow to finance its expenditures, is it worse to borrow from foreigners than from U.S. citizens? Would we be better off today if we had the same deficit but no capital inflow from abroad? Would future generations be better off? Discuss.

Suggestions for Further Reading

Campbell, Colin D., Rosemary G. Campbell, and Edwin G. Dolan. *Money, Banking, and Monetary Policy.* Hinsdale, Ill.: Dryden Press, 1988.

Readers familiar with the income-expenditure model will find an application of it to the interaction of monetary and fiscal policy in Chapter 20 of this book.

Friedman, Milton, and Walter J. Heller. *Monetary vs. Fiscal Policy.* New York: Norton, 1969.

This book gives an overview of the debate between monetarists and Keynesians as conducted in the 1960s.

Tobin, James. "The Monetarist Counter-Revolution Today." *Economic Journal* 91 (March 1981): 29–42.

An appraisal of monetarism by a leading Keynesian thinker. The article by David Laidler in the same issue is also of interest.

Price Stability, Employment, and Economic Growth

Part Five

16 Inflation in the Aggregate Supply and Demand Model

After reading this chapter, you will understand . . .

- What are the sources of shifts in aggregate supply curves.
- What are the characteristics of inflation that arises from excessive growth in aggregate demand.
- How inflation can arise from shifts in aggregate supply curves.
- What contributions the new classical economists have made.
- What types of policy can be used to combat inflation.

Before reading this chapter, make sure you know the meaning of . . .

- Price level (Chapter 7)
- Base year (Chapter 7)
- Indexing (Chapter 7)

The Great Inflation of the 1970s

If the 1930s were the decade of the Great Depression, the 1970s perhaps should be called the "Great Inflation." Like the Great Depression, the Great Inflation brought lasting changes to economic thought and policy. What went on in this turbulent decade?

The seeds of the Great Inflation were sown in the late 1960s. Under President Lyndon Johnson, federal outlays for the Vietnam War rose steadily. But because the war was unpopular at home, Johnson was reluctant to raise taxes. Many economists see the resulting fiscal stimulus as a key factor in the inflation that followed. In 1968, the inflation rate rose to 4.2 percent per year; in 1969, it reached 5.4 percent.[1] In comparison with what was to come, 5.4 percent inflation was moderate—but it was more than three times the 1.7 percent average rate for the 1958 to 1967 decade.

In August 1971, President Richard Nixon announced a 90-day freeze on all prices and wages.

In 1970 and early 1971, the inflation rate continued to creep upward. Then, in August 1971, President Richard Nixon announced a dramatic new economic program. The centerpiece was a 90-day freeze on all prices and wages. This attempt to control prices administratively worked for a time. The inflation rate fell in late 1971 and during 1972. Prices and wages were subject to some degree of control under three presidents for the rest of the decade.

However, in 1973, when the power of wage and price controls to restrain inflation was already waning, the world received a major inflationary shock. In the aftermath of the Yom Kippur war with Israel, the Arab members of the Organization of Petroleum Exporting Countries (OPEC) doubled the price of oil—a major U.S. import and a key component of the consumer price index. Inflation was underway again, with the added complication of retail price controls on gasoline, which led to long waiting lines at gas stations.

In 1974, the inflation rate reached 11 percent and the United States discov-

---

[1] All figures for inflation given here are year-to-year percentage changes in the consumer price index.

ered an unpleasant new fact. In the past, inflation had been thought to have a silver lining in the form of low unemployment. Now the nation learned that it could suffer from both high unemployment and high inflation at the same time. In the 1974 to 1975 recession, the unemployment rate rose to nearly 9 percent while the inflation rate fell only slightly. A new concept was born: the "misery index," which is the sum of the rates of inflation and unemployment. The misery index hit a value of 18 during the 1974 to 1975 recession and, throughout the subsequent recovery, never fell below 13. This was miserable indeed compared with the under-6 values to which people had grown accustomed in the 1960s.

Theoretically, the Fed could have curbed inflation by restraining growth of the money stock. However, just as it had failed to prevent a drop in the money stock from 1929 to 1933, thereby worsening the Great Depression, during the 1970s the Fed failed to prevent rapid growth of the money stock, thus adding fuel to the Great Inflation.

Finally, in October 1979, the Fed put on the brakes and the economy went through the windshield. In 1980, as the economy entered a recession, both inflation and unemployment rose. The misery index soared to an all-time high of 20. On top of this, OPEC chose 1979 to 1980 to more than double the world oil price for the second time.

Inflation receded during the 1980s, and the misery index returned to single digits. But it will be a long time before Americans can again read about inflation abroad and think complacently that "it can never happen here."

Photo Source: UPI/Bettmann Newsphotos.

AT several points in this course, we have examined the Great Depression and the economic theories to which it gave rise. We have seen how Keynesian economics arose in reaction to classical views that seemed to deny the possibility of a depression such as that experienced in the 1930s and how monetarism emerged to counter the views of Keynes and some of his early followers. In this and the next four chapters, we will look at some aspects of economic theory that are an outgrowth of the "Great Inflation" of the 1970s.

This chapter fills out the basic aggregate supply and demand model and applies it to situations of inflation. Chapter 17 introduces economic growth into the model. Chapter 18 examines the current state of the debate between Keynesians and monetarists over the proper strategy for economic policy. Chapter 19 adds an optional dynamic model of inflation and unemployment. Chapter 20 presents a model of the international economy that takes inflation into account.

Price Expectations, Inflation, and the Aggregate Supply Curve

As Chapter 8 stressed, the short-run aggregate supply curve shows firms' reactions to an increase in demand assuming no change in the expected level of input prices. We saw several reasons why firms might reasonably expect input prices not to respond to a change of demand in the short run: the costs of changing prices and the existence of long-term contracts; the cushioning effects of inventories; and incomplete information on whether changes in demand are economywide or only local. In this section, we elaborate on the role of expectations by allowing for shifts in the short-run aggregate supply curve.

Input Prices and Final Goods Prices

When the economy is in long-run equilibrium at its natural level of real output, markets for individual goods, services, and factors of production are also in equilibrium. In that situation, the prices of final goods and services that firms sell and the prices of the inputs they use have certain consistent relationships with one another. Final goods prices must be at levels that will permit firms to recover the costs of inputs used to produce them. Also, workers' wages and salaries must be sufficiently high relative to the costs of consumer goods to make it worthwhile for them to acquire the skills their jobs demand and to show up for work each day.

If we choose a base year for measuring the price level in which the economy is in long-run equilibrium, we can assign a value of 1.0 to both the level of final goods prices and the level of input prices in that year. Assume that year 0 is such a year. The economy's position in year 0 is represented by point E_0 in Exhibit 16.1. This point is at the intersection of aggregate demand curve AD_0 with the line N, which represents the natural level of real output. In earlier chapters, we saw that this line can be interpreted as the economy's long-run aggregate supply curve.

Now assume that in year 1 something happens to shift the aggregate demand curve to AD_1. This can result from, say, an increase in the money stock. As we have seen several times, the economy will respond by moving up and to the right along aggregate supply curve AS_0. This curve shows how firms react to the increase in demand when they expect the level of input prices to remain at its initial level of 1.0. Thus, *the expected level of input prices that firms use in formulating their plans is marked by the intersection of the short-run aggregate supply curve with the natural level of real output.*

Now consider the situation in which the economy has reached E_1. At that point, the level of final goods prices has risen to 1.25 and real output has climbed above its natural level. However, for the moment the expected level of input prices remains at 1.0. This situation, as we know, cannot last. Before long, the increase in the level of final goods prices will begin to affect input prices, including both wages and the prices of intermediate goods. As soon as that happens, firms will have to revise their expectations regarding input prices, and aggregate supply curve AS will no longer be valid.

A Shift in the Aggregate Supply Curve

When we arrived at this point in earlier chapters, we simply said that the economy moves off its initial aggregate supply curve and shifts up and to the left along aggregate demand curve AD_1—which is exactly what happens. Now, however, we wish to point out that as this happens, the short-run aggregate supply curve itself shifts upward. In fact, *anything that changes the expected level of input prices will cause a shift in the short-run aggregate supply curve.*

At E_1 in Exhibit 16.1, for example, the level of final goods prices has risen to 1.25. Now suppose that in year 2 firms expect the level of input prices to catch

Exhibit 16.1   Shifts in the Aggregate Supply Curve

The short-run aggregate supply curve shows the path along which the economy moves in response to a shift in aggregate demand when input prices are expected to remain constant in the short run. The level of input prices that firms expect to prevail in the short run is shown by the height of the aggregate supply curve at its intersection with line N, which represents the natural level of real output. Any change in the expected level of input prices will cause the aggregate supply curve to shift. For example, suppose that the economy moves from E_0 to E_1 in year 1 and final goods prices rise from 1.0 to 1.25. If in year 2 firms expect input prices to rise to a level consistent with the new level of final goods prices, the aggregate supply curve will shift to AS_1. The curve will continue to shift upward until a new long-run equilibrium is eventually reached at E_3.

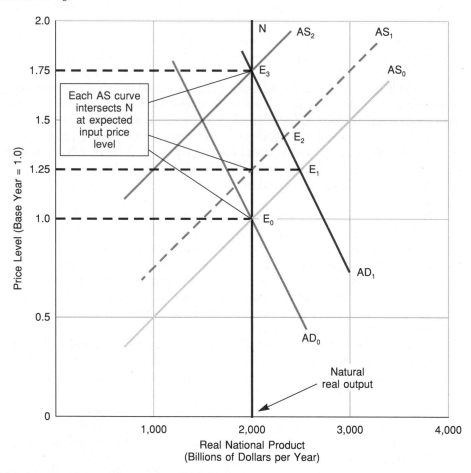

up to this change that has taken place in final goods prices. An increase in the expected level of input prices to 1.25 will shift the aggregate supply curve upward to AS_1, where it intersects the natural level of real output line, N, at 1.25.

Assuming that aggregate demand remains unchanged after its initial shift, the economy will now move to E_2, where AS_1 intersects AD_1. However, even E_2 is not a point of long-run equilibrium. There final goods prices have again risen above the expected level of input prices, thus necessitating a further adjustment.

Without showing all the intermediate steps, we will simply say that the aggregate supply curve must continue to shift upward until an equilibrium is reached at which the expected level of input prices is once again consistent with the level of final goods prices. Such a point occurs at E_3, where real output has returned to its natural level. At E_3, the level of final goods prices is 1.75. When expected input prices catch up to that level, the short-run aggregate supply curve will be at AS_2. At this point, no further revision of expectations or plans will be necessary, because the expected level of input prices will once again be consistent with the level of output prices that actually prevails. This situation is possible only when real output is at its natural level.

Demand-Pull Inflation

In the preceding example, the economy has undergone what is known as **demand-pull inflation,** meaning an increase in the price level caused by an increase in aggregate demand relative to the economy's natural level of real output. In the case shown in Exhibit 16.1, there is a one-time shift in the aggregate demand curve and a corresponding one-time rise in the price level from 1.0 at the initial equilibrium, E_0, to 1.75 at the new long-run equilibrium, E_3.

However, such a one-time expansionary policy action is not the only possibility. Instead, lasting expansionary fiscal or monetary policy may allow aggregate demand to keep growing. In this case, as the aggregate supply curve is driven upward by firms' expectations of higher and higher input prices, the aggregate demand curve keeps apace. Real output does not fall back toward its natural level; rather, it is kept above that level by ongoing demand-pull inflation.

This possibility is illustrated in Exhibit 16.2. There rising aggregate demand and rising inflationary expectations keep up with each other. The aggregate demand and supply curves both shift upward at the same rate, and the economy follows a path from E_1 to E_2 to E_3 and so on, as the arrow shows.

The scenario shown in Exhibit 16.2 has major implications for economic policy. It says that in the short run, starting from a state of long-run equilibrium, an expansionary fiscal or monetary policy is initially effective in stimulating real economic growth and lower unemployment. The initial cost of such a policy is a small amount of inflation. However, according to this interpretation, the initial gains in real output can be sustained only at the cost of ongoing demand-pull inflation.

Once the initial benefits of the expansion have been enjoyed, policymakers will face a dilemma. One choice is to stop the stimulus. If they do this, inflation will cease but output will fall back to its natural level and unemployment will rise to its natural rate. The other alternative is to continue the expansionary fiscal or monetary policy. In that case, according to the above theory, real output can be held above its natural level for some time and unemployment kept below its natural rate. Choosing this path, however, will mean year after year of inflation.[2]

Demand-pull inflation
An increase in the price level caused by an increase of aggregate demand relative to natural real output.

---

[2] As Exhibit 16.2 is drawn, the inflation rate remains steady from year to year as the economy moves up along the path from E_1 to E_2 to E_3. In Chapter 18, which will discuss more elaborate theories of the inflation process, we will show that under one alternative theory of how price expectations are formed, the policy implications of demand-pull inflation are even more discouraging than suggested here. We will see that a steady inflation rate is not enough to keep real output above its natural level for a prolonged period; instead, this requires a steadily accelerating inflation rate.

Exhibit 16.2   Demand-Pull Inflation

Demand-pull inflation begins when a rightward shift in the aggregate demand curve pulls the economy up and to the right along the aggregate supply curve, such as from E_0 to E_1 in this exhibit. Subsequently the aggregate supply curve will begin to shift upward as increases in final goods prices filter through to cause expected increases in wages and other input prices. If expansionary policy continues to shift the aggregate demand curve upward, as shown here, real output can be kept above its natural level for a sustained period. However, the cost of maintaining this high level of real output is inflation.

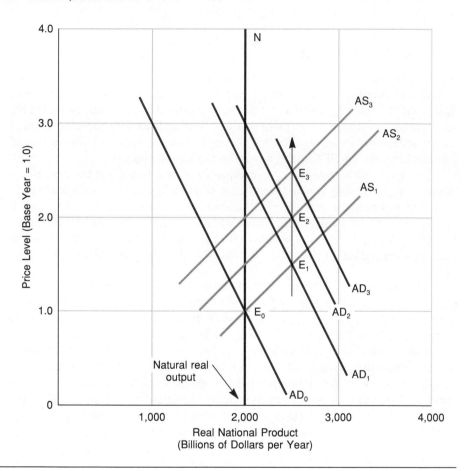

Cost-Push Inflation

Cost-push inflation
Inflation that is caused by an upward shift in the aggregate supply curve while the aggregate demand curve remains fixed or shifts upward more slowly.

Demand-pull inflation occurs when the aggregate demand curve shifts upward while the aggregate supply curve remains fixed or shifts upward at an equal rate. However, inflation is also possible when the aggregate supply curve shifts upward while the aggregate demand curve stays in place or shifts upward more slowly. This type of inflation is known as **cost-push inflation,** because upward shifts in the aggregate supply curve are linked with increases in firms' costs of production.

Supply Shocks

Exhibit 16.3 illustrates one scenario for cost-push inflation. There the economy begins in long-run equilibrium at E_0. The price level is 1.0, and real output is at its natural level of $2,000 billion. At this point, something happens to raise both input prices for all or most firms and workers' costs of living. The sudden increases in the cost of imported oil that hit the U.S. economy in 1974 and 1979 to 1980 are examples of such an event; a major crop failure or natural disaster would be another. Such an upward push on the price level from an outside source is known as a **supply shock.**

Supply shock
An event, such as an increase in the price of imported oil, a crop failure, or a natural disaster, that raises input prices for all or most firms and pushes up workers' costs of living.

Exhibit 16.3   Effects of a Supply Shock

A supply shock is said to occur when an event external to the workings of the domestic economy—say, an increase in the price of imports or bad weather—raises the expected level of input prices. In this exhibit, a supply shock shifts the aggregate supply curve upward from AS_0 to AS_1 while the aggregate demand curve initially stays at AD_0. The result is a cost-push inflation. The price level rises, real output falls, and the unemployment rate rises. If aggregate demand remains unchanged, the economy will eventually return to E_0. Alternatively, expansionary policy can be used to shift the aggregate demand curve to AD_1. This will move the economy to E_2 and hasten the recovery of real output, but it will worsen the inflationary consequences of the supply shock.

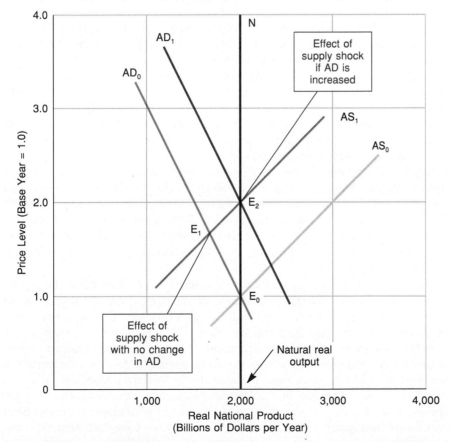

The effect of a supply shock is to raise the level of input prices above the level that firms had expected. As firms see what has happened and adjust their expectations accordingly, the aggregate supply curve shifts upward from AS_0 to AS_1 as shown in Exhibit 16.3. With the higher expected level of input prices but no matching increase in demand, firms must revise their plans. They find it is no longer profitable to produce as much as before. As they cut back their output, each industry moves up and to the left along its industry demand curve. As this happens, the economy as a whole moves upward and to the left along aggregate demand curve AD_0 to E_1. At E_1, real output is below its natural level and unemployment is above its natural rate; thus, this is not a position of long-run equilibrium.

What happens next depends on what happens to the aggregate demand curve. If there are no policy changes, the aggregate demand curve will stay at AD_0. In this case, the excess capacity of firms and excess unemployment will tend to put downward pressure on wages and prices. Some unemployed workers will accept jobs at lower wages than they had hoped for. Firms will find that although energy prices remain high, the average level of input prices is not as high as they initially expected; this will give them a little room to cut their prices in order to boost sales. As the expected level of input prices falls, the aggregate supply curve will begin to shift downward from AS_1. In time, the economy will move back down along AD_0 from E_1 all the way to E_0. The price level will fall back to where it was before oil prices rose, and output will return to its natural level.

This path to recovery from a supply shock is likely to be quite slow, however. In order to follow it, the average price level of both inputs and final goods must fall while energy prices, the assumed source of the supply shock, remain high. For this to happen, there must be a major adjustment in relative prices. Real wages and the prices of goods and services other than energy must fall more than the average in order to bring the average down. This is likely to be a painful process for everyone—and until it is completed, unemployment will remain above its natural rate and output below its natural level.

There is, however, another way to recover from a supply shock—through expansion of aggregate demand. If expansionary monetary or fiscal policy is used to shift the aggregate demand curve from AD_0 to AD_1, the economy can move to an equilibrium at E_2. Output will then be restored to its natural level. In fact, if the expansion of aggregate demand follows the supply shock quickly enough, the economy may be able to avoid any major loss in real output. Instead of moving first to E_1, it will move straight up along the natural level of real output from E_0 to E_2.

Recovery from a supply shock through expansion of demand is likely to be faster than recovery through adjustment of relative prices. Also, the cost of recovery in terms of lost real output will probably be lower. But the cost in terms of increases in the price level will be greater. If policymakers respond to the supply shock by raising aggregate demand, the price level will end up permanently higher, whereas if they keep the lid on aggregate demand, the impact of the supply shock on the average price level will be only temporary.

There is no consensus on the best way to react to supply shocks. The response depends partly on the extent of one's dislike for inflation on the one hand and for unemployment on the other. Some economists have suggested that temporary supply shocks, such as crop failures or natural disasters, should not be fought by raising aggregate demand. They reason that the aggregate supply curve will soon shift back down as the damage is repaired. However, they suggest, a long-lasting supply shock such as the oil price increases of the 1970s might best be at least partially accommodated by raising aggregate demand. It may be worth suffering the resulting permanent increase in the price level in order to avoid a prolonged transition period of low real output and high unemployment.

Inflationary Expectations as a Source of Cost-Push Inflation

Supply shocks are not the only source of cost-push inflation. Cost-push inflation can also be caused by rising inflationary expectations fueled by past experiences of demand-pull inflation. To get this result, we must modify our assumptions regarding how firms form their expectations about the level of input prices. Up to this point, we have assumed that firms expect input prices in the current year to be at a level consistent with that of final goods prices in the previous year. However, this assumption is unrealistic in an economy that has experienced inflation for several years in a row. Under conditions of ongoing inflation, it is more likely that firms will expect the level of input prices to increase this year by a percentage equal to last year's inflation rate. Put another way, it is likely that when firms have seen inflation in the past, they will expect more inflation in the future and make their plans accordingly.

Exhibit 16.4 shows what happens when inflationary expectations become established in the economy. We begin from a situation of ongoing demand-pull inflation similar to that shown in Exhibit 16.2. An expansionary fiscal or monetary policy has held output above its natural level for some time. The economy is moving upward along the arrow through E_1 and E_2. After several years of inflation, firms and workers expect more inflation in the future and have adjusted their plans to cope with it as best they can. Their plans are reflected in a series of upward-shifting aggregate real supply curves that keep pace with the upward-shifting aggregate real demand curve.

What happens now if the government decides to stop inflation by halting the growth of aggregate demand? (We are talking not about reducing the level of aggregate demand but only stopping its growth.) In terms of Exhibit 16.4, the effect will be to stop the upward shift of the aggregate demand curve, leaving it in the position AD_2.

Halting the growth of aggregate demand, however, will not stop inflation in its tracks. So far we have assumed that firms and workers have grown used to inflation and expect it to continue. Workers expect their costs of living to rise and have made contracts with their employers giving them offsetting wage increases each year. Firms expect their input prices to rise and have become used to passing the increases along to their customers. As long as firms expect their input prices to rise and set their prices and output plans on that basis, the aggregate real supply curve will continue to drift upward.

Inflationary Recession

With the aggregate supply curve moving upward while the aggregate demand curve stays put, real output starts to fall and unemployment begins to rise. Meanwhile, the price level keeps going up. In Exhibit 16.4, the economy will soon reach E_3, where real output and unemployment have returned to their natural levels. This is not the end of the story, however. Because firms and workers experienced continued inflation as the economy moved from E_2 to E_3,

Exhibit 16.4   Inflationary Recession

An inflationary recession occurs when aggregate demand slows or stops growing following a period of sustained inflation. In this exhibit, the aggregate demand curve stops shifting after the economy reaches E_2. Firms expect the level of input prices to continue to rise; thus, the aggregate supply curve moves on up to AS_3 in the next year and to AS_4 in the year after that. As it does, the economy enters a recession during which the price level continues to rise. Under certain circumstances, the inflation rate may actually increase as real output falls.

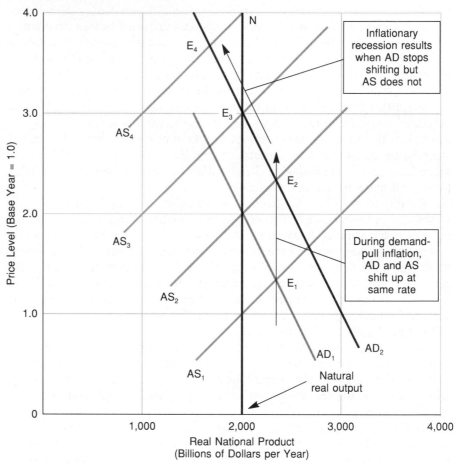

Inflationary recession
An episode in which real output falls below its natural level and unemployment rises above its natural rate while rapid inflation continues.

they are not likely to expect inflation to stop now. As long as they expect prices to keep on rising, firms and workers will continue to make their plans on this basis and the aggregate supply curve will keep on drifting upward, as shown by AS_4 in Exhibit 16.4.

As the economy moves along the aggregate real demand curve toward E_4, the economy enters an **inflationary recession.** This is an episode in which inflation, rising unemployment, and falling real output all occur at the same time.[3]

---

[3] This situation is sometimes called *stagflation*, but the term is not apt. The term *stagflation*—a combination of "stagnation" and "inflation"—was coined in the 1970s to describe a situation of slow or zero growth in real output, high inflation, and unemployment in excess of its natural rate. The term *inflationary recession* is more suitable for periods that combine high inflation rates with actual drops in real output. The 1974 to 1975 and 1980 recessions were inflationary recessions in this sense.

What can be done to bring the economy out of an inflationary recession? A "cold turkey" approach would be to sit tight and keep the lid on aggregate demand. Rising unemployment, declining sales, and an unplanned inventory buildup would, in time, cause firms and workers to revise their expectations about inflation. Prices of raw materials would begin to fall. Workers would accept lower wages. The aggregate supply curve would begin to shift downward. Slowly the economy would slip back down along the the aggregate demand curve toward an equilibrium at E_3. But the experience would be a painful one.

A more moderate approach would be to slow the growth of aggregate demand gradually rather than stopping it cold. With luck, this could bring the economy to a "soft landing" at the natural level of real output. It might take longer to slow inflation this way, but with luck a severe inflationary recession could be avoided.

In practice, though, there is a danger that policymakers will overreact to an inflationary recession. Instead of easing the growth of demand gradually and bringing the economy to a soft landing, they may step on the accelerator with a burst of expansionary fiscal and monetary policy. Such a "reflation" policy might restore economic growth, but only at the expense of ongoing price increases.

The truth is that no one knows a quick, painless way to stop inflation once it has become part of public expectations. As we will see, many economists think the best preventative is to keep inflation from getting started in the first place. This is a theme to which we will return in the last section of this chapter and in Chapter 19, which presents a more complete analysis of inflationary recession. Before discussing policies for stopping inflation, however, we must take a closer look at how expectations are formed.

Rational Expectations and the New Classical Economics

The theory presented in this chapter is built on the idea of an upward-sloping short-run aggregate supply curve along which the economy initially moves when aggregate demand rises or falls. We have explained the upward slope of the short-run aggregate supply curve by saying that when demand rises firms do not—at least at first—expect the prices of their inputs to rise. As a result, each firm behaves as though the increase in aggregate demand were affecting its industry alone. Firms move up along their respective industry supply curves, and real output rises along with the price level.

Is it reasonable for firms to behave this way? Is this in fact how they do behave? These questions are a matter of debate in economics today. The debate hinges on how people form their expectations.

The Adaptive-Expectations Hypothesis

The simplest view of expectations is that people expect the future to be like the past and adapt their plans accordingly. The theory presented so far in this chapter is based on this view, which has come to be known as the **adaptive-expectations hypothesis.** Earlier in the chapter, we assumed that firms expect the level of input prices this year to be consistent with the level of final goods prices last year. In our discussion of inflationary recession, we modified the hypothesis by assuming that firms expect this year's inflation rate for input prices to be the

Adaptive-expectations hypothesis
The hypothesis that people form their expectations about future economic events mainly on the basis of past economic events.

same as last year's inflation rate for final goods prices. More complex economic models often assume that expectations are based on a weighted average of inflation rates over several prior years. But all these assumptions are variations on the theme that people form their expectations of the future primarily on the basis of past experience.

There is a good deal of common sense to this view. If it simply meant that people learn from experience and adjust their plans on that basis, it would be hard to disagree with it. Further, the U.S. economy's experience in the 1970s seems to bear out this hypothesis, at least in general terms. When inflation first began to get serious in the early 1970s, people were caught off guard; they didn't know how to react. As inflation continued, however, people began to expect more of it. They changed their plans and ways of doing business. When inflation slowed in the early 1980s, they did not go right back to the old ways of doing things; their memory of high inflation rates influenced their plans for a time even after inflation slowed.

The adaptive-expectations hypothesis is also attractive because it produces the kind of aggregate supply curve that we want—one that slopes upward in the short run and shifts upward in the long run. Adaptive expectations thus provide a basis for a plausible theory of recession and inflation. Even so, however, many economists are unhappy with this hypothesis.

The Rational-Expectations Hypothesis

The main challange to the adaptive-expectations hypothesis has come from a group of economists who see past experience as only one of a number of factors that affect people's expectations. In forming their expectations about the future, they say, rational people should look forward as well as backward. In particular, they should examine what government policymakers are saying and are likely to do and take into account the probable effects of current and future policy on future economic events. This view, promoted by economists such as Robert Lucas, Thomas Sargent, and Robert Barro, has come to be known as the **rational-expectations hypothesis.**

Rational-expectations hypothesis
The hypothesis that people form their expectations about future economic events on the basis of not only past events but also their expectations about economic policies and their likely effects.

Suppose, for example, that the economy has experienced an inflation rate of 10 percent for the last year or two and that political pressure on policymakers to do something about it has built up. The president responds with a hard-hitting television speech claiming that the government is going to whip inflation now. What do people expect will happen?

The adaptive-expectations hypothesis assumes that people will expect inflation to continue in the future just as it has in the past, regardless of the president's new program. The rational-expectations hypothesis takes a different view: It assumes that people are not simple-minded; they will listen to the president and then try to find out what policies are being undertaken to back up the president's statements.

First suppose they conclude that the president has no influence on Congress and will be unable to control government spending. They also think that the Fed shows little concern about inflation and is continuing to pump up the money supply at a rapid rate. In this case, it is unlikely that they will expect inflation to slow. Firms therefore will base their plans on the expectation of continued inflation. Unions will negotiate contracts protecting their members against future inflation. Households will take inflation into account when buying houses or cars. It would be irrational for people not to act this way.

On the other hand, say backers of the rational-expectations hypothesis, people might listen to the president's speech and conclude that it will be followed up with strong action. Suppose that congressional leaders applaud the president's statements and promise to restrain government spending. Also suppose that the Fed joins the anti-inflation campaign by slowing the growth of money. In this case, according to the rational-expectations theory, firms, workers, and households will modify their plans to prepare for a slowdown in inflation.

Policy Implications of Rational Expectations

The rational-expectations hypothesis has strong implications for economic policy. It suggests that the effects of policy moves that the public anticipates will be quite different from the effects of those that are unexpected. Look at Exhibit 16.5, for example. This exhibit, which greatly resembles Exhibit 16.1, deals with the effects of an increase in aggregate demand. Under the adaptive-expectations hypothesis, firms will initially respond to the shift in the aggregate demand curve by moving upward from E_0 along AS_0 to E_1. As this happens, the price level will rise. As firms adapt their plans to the higher price level, the aggregate supply curve will shift upward, and in time the economy will move to a long-run equilibrium at E_2. Meanwhile, however, the economy will have gained something in return for the experience of inflation. From the time of the initial increase in demand until the economy finally reaches E_2, real output will have been above its natural level and unemployment below its natural rate.

Supporters of the rational-expectations hypothesis say that this sequence of events will take place only if the cause of the increase in aggregate demand is unexpected—say, an unforeseen surge in consumer spending or investment. But if the increase in demand is caused by a shift in fiscal or monetary policy that firms and households expected, the outcome will differ. This might be the case, for example, if the Fed announced an increase in its target for the money stock for the coming year or Congress passed a budget with a larger deficit and higher spending than the year before.

An expected change in policy, according to the rational-expectations hypothesis, will affect firms' plans for dealing with the increase in demand. They will know that an expansionary policy will soon cause a rise in prices, including the prices of their inputs. Workers will expect the cost of living to increase and will demand higher wages. If firms learn about the policy in advance and expect it to raise input prices, they will no longer react as though their respective industries were the only ones affected by the increase in demand. They will know that the whole economy will be affected and modify their plans accordingly. As a result, the aggregate supply curve will shift upward to AS_1 the moment the policy goes into effect. Instead of moving from E_0 to E_1, the economy will move directly from E_0 to E_2. The expansionary policy will have little or no effect on real output; instead, it will only push prices up—and very soon.

In sum, say supporters of the rational-expectations hypothesis, the economy will follow an upward-sloping aggregate supply curve only when shifts in aggregate demand come as a surprise. If they are expected, the upward-sloping aggregate supply curve will not apply; instead, the shift in demand will affect only prices while real output and unemployment will remain at their natural levels. In effect, under the rational-expectations hypothesis the economy's aggregate supply curve in the case of anticipated policy changes is a vertical line that coincides with the natural level of real output in the short run as well as in the long run.

Exhibit 16.5   Effects of a Policy Change: The New Classical View

In the standard view, an expansionary policy causing the aggregate demand curve to shift from AD_0 to AD_1 will cause the economy to move from E_0 to E_1 in the short run. Later the aggregate supply curve will shift up to AS_1 and the economy will reach a long-run equilibrium at E_2 after traveling the path shown by the curved arrow. In the new classical view, an expansionary policy change that is fully anticipated by firms and households will cause the aggregate supply curve to shift up immediately to AS_1. The economy will move straight up along line N to E_2. There will be no intermediate period during which real output rises above its natural level.

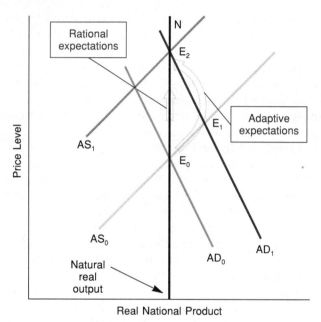

Thus, expected changes in macroeconomic policy will not have even transitory effects on real output or employment.

The same mechanism would work during a contraction of aggregate demand, provided the causes of the contraction were fully expected. In that case, the economy would move straight downward to a new equilibrium at the natural level of real output. There would be no adverse effect on real output or employment.

This scenario can be recognized as the opposite extreme from the position taken by Keynes in his *General Theory* that the economy would never return to the natural level of real output on its own following a contraction of demand. If the rational-expectations hypothesis holds, so does the classical result of an economy that stabilizes itself at the natural level of real output. However—at least when changes in aggregate demand are fully anticipated—the speed of the stabilization process is even more rapid than the classicists would have thought. Similarly, the rational-expectations hypothesis not only vindicates the neutrality of money but makes it a short-run as well as long-run proposition, at least when changes in the money stock are fully anticipated. Because of these similarities with the classical economists' views, proponents of the rational-expectations hypothesis are often referred to as the school of **new classical economics.**

Doubts about Rational Expectations

The new classical economics has had a big impact on macroeconomic thinking in a fairly short time. However, many other economists doubt the rational-expectations hypothesis, or at least its policy implications. Some think it asks too much of firms, workers, and consumers. Do people really pay that much attention to what fiscal and monetary policymakers are doing? Do they understand what policy shifts imply for prices, interest rates, and so on? Can "ordinary" people form rational expectations about the future course of the economy when even professional forecasters so often disagree?

Supporters of the rational-expectations hypothesis claim that they do not require every farmer and shopkeeper to have a Ph.D. in economics. They just say that people do not ignore what they read in the papers and see on the TV news. Such information has an impact on their economic decisions—a greater one than the adaptive-expectations hypothesis acknowledges. Also, many key economic decision makers—big corporations, stock market traders, banks, union leaders, and so on—indeed act on the basis of professional economic advice.

A more telling criticism focuses on the policy implications of the new classical economics rather than on the way in which expectations themselves are formed. The critics point out that in practice, shifts in economic policy seem to affect more than just the price level. On the average, according to one estimate, a one-percentage-point change in the growth rate of aggregate nominal demand has a first-year effect on prices of only .44 percent; the remaining .56 percent takes the form of a movement in real output.[4] In part, this estimate may reflect the result of averaging episodes of expected demand shifts with episodes of unexpected ones. But economists who are not hard-line new classicists think there are reasons why even expected shifts in demand have major effects on real output and unemployment, at least in the short run. We have mentioned a number of these reasons before, but it is worth reviewing them here.

First, these economists point out that prices do not respond to every change in demand because it is often costly to adjust prices. Indeed there are some markets, such as the commodity exchanges on which grain and metals are traded, in which prices respond to demand minute by minute. But in other markets, price responses are more sluggish. For example, it tends to be more costly to change prices in markets for goods that have many styles and sizes, such as clothing and auto parts; catalogs and price tags for such goods are changed only every now and then. In other markets, sellers are reluctant to change prices too often for fear of offending steady customers. In still other markets—unionized labor markets being a case in point—prices are subject to long-term contracts and are rarely changed before the contracts expire.

A second reason for gradual price changes is that inventories slow the rate at which demand shifts are transmitted from one sector of the economy to another. Any increase in aggregate demand tends to be felt first by sellers of final goods.

New classical economics
A school of economics stressing the role of rational expectations in shaping the economy's response to policy changes.

---

[4] Robert J. Gordon, "Output Fluctuations and Gradual Price Adjustment," *Journal of Economic Literature* 19 (June 1981): 493–530.

It is transmitted to producers of intermediate goods only with a lag as inventories are depleted and restocking orders placed.

Finally, there is the fact that firms get information about demand for their own products more quickly than they do information about changes in aggregate demand for the economy as a whole. When a shoe store sees its sales rise and its inventories drop, it does not know at first whether this is an isolated piece of good luck or whether demand is booming throughout the economy. If the firm thinks the demand increase is a local phenomenon, it is less likely to expect the increase to push up its input prices. It initially responds simply by ordering more shoes from its suppliers. Only when the price increases of other firms have passed through to affect input prices does the firm revise its pricing plans.

This kind of reasoning leads to a middle ground between the rational-expectations and adaptive-expectations hypotheses. In this view, the rational-expectations hypothesis is seen as correct in stressing that people take available information into account when they make their economic plans. It is agreed that the new classicists are right in saying that the response to expected policy changes may not be the same as for unexpected ones. But even so, there are many frictions and imperfections in the economy that keep people from responding immediately to every bit of news that comes their way. In practice, then, an economy with rational expectations but also with many frictions and imperfections does not work much differently than one in which expectations are formed adaptively. In both cases, the economy will follow an upward-sloping aggregate supply curve in the short run.

Strategies for Ending Inflation

In the first section of this chapter, we looked at the mechanisms that get inflation started; these include both demand-pull and cost-push elements. Now we turn to strategies for ending inflation once it has gotten under way.

Conventional Policies

All economists agree that inflation can be slowed by conventional demand management via fiscal and monetary policy. The costs of doing so are likely to be high, however. As we explained in the first section of this chapter, inflation can gain momentum as expectations of more inflation push the aggregate real supply curve increasingly higher. Stopping inflation by slowing the growth of demand will then cause an inflationary recession. The momentum of inflation will be broken, but only at the cost of a period of high unemployment and low real output.

Just how great is the cost of stopping inflation by demand management policy alone? In a 1978 paper, Arthur Okun examined six studies of this cost.[5] These studies found that reducing the inflation rate by just one percentage point would, on average, require real output to drop 10 percent below its natural level for a full year. Such a decline in real output would mean an unemployment rate

---

[5] Arthur Okun, "Efficient Disinflationary Policies," *American Economic Review* 68 (May 1978): 348–352.

of more than 9 percent compared with a natural unemployment rate that is probably near 6 percent today.

The cost of stopping the double-digit inflation rate of the late 1970s was not quite as great as Okun's estimate suggests, but it was not small. Inflation had reached an annual rate of about 13 percent in late 1979. At that time, the unemployment rate was 6.3 percent—close to its natural rate. Restrictive monetary policy then slowed the growth of aggregate demand. The economy went through back-to-back recessions in 1980 and 1981 to 1982, with only a brief recovery in between. Unemployment rose to 10.6 percent by the end of 1982. Real output hardly grew at all; thus, by the end of 1982 it was at least 10 percent below its natural level. The reward for this pain was a drop in the inflation rate to a little under 4 percent by 1983—a welcome reduction, but nevertheless a rate that would have been seen as far too high only a few years earlier.

It is little wonder, then, that economists have looked for a less costly strategy for stopping inflation. Let's look at some ideas.

Wage and Price Controls

Wage and price controls are any of a group of policies that range from mild guidelines to mandatory wage and price ceilings. The United States has tried using such controls a number of times, and they have been used even more widely abroad. Let's see how these policies work and why they are controversial.

The Case for Controls

The case for wage and price controls is strongest when they are used as a temporary measure to fight an inflationary recession. When policymakers apply the brakes after a period of rapid inflation, firms and workers do not expect inflation to stop right away. Their inflationary expectations push the aggregate supply curve upward, causing cost-push inflation, as shown in Exhibit 16.4. In effect, the expectation of more inflation becomes a self-fulfilling prophecy. The result is an inflationary recession.

Now suppose that just as the growth of aggregate demand is slowed the government imposes a program of strict wage and price controls. It does this with great fanfare and a show of firm resolve to lick inflation once and for all. It is hoped that workers and firms will believe that the controls are really going to stop inflation, for if they do they will lower their inflationary expectations much sooner than they would if they had to learn from experience.

This reduction in expected inflation—if it happens—will remove the cost-push element from the inflationary recession. Knowing that they need not push for higher wages in order to beat inflation, workers will accept controls. Knowing that their input prices will not be rising, firms will keep the prices of their output in line. A larger part of the reduction in the growth of nominal GNP will take the form of a slowdown in price increases than would otherwise be the case. The drop in real output and the rise in unemployment will be smaller than otherwise. As a result, the transition to price stability will be quicker and less painful than it would be without controls.

Problems with Controls

So much for theory. The problem is that wage and price controls often are used as a substitute for demand management policy rather than as a supplement to it.

The government either tries to use wage and price controls to fight inflation without simultaneously slowing the growth of aggregate demand or leaves controls in force after the transition is over and a new boom is underway. In either case, wage and price controls will either be ineffective or lead to shortages, rationing, and black markets.

The U.S. Experience

There have been several experiments with wage and price controls in the United States. One took place during World War II. The high level of wartime government spending made it hard to control aggregate demand. Strict price controls were used to suppress inflation. The results were predictable: Rationing was introduced for gasoline, tires, sugar, and many other goods, and widespread black markets emerged.

Another experiment with wage and price controls took place from 1971 to 1974 during the Nixon administration. This episode is described in "Applying Economic Ideas 16.1." As indicated there, the Nixon controls were a mixed success at best. They were first introduced when inflation already was falling and may have helped to speed the decline somewhat. But they were left in place after prices began to rise again in mid-1972. At that point, they proved useless or worse.

Despite the dubious success of Nixon's controls, President Carter continued to experiment with controls throughout his four years in office. Carter's guidelines, as he called them, were voluntary, but they were backed by the threat to withhold government contracts to firms that refused to follow them. Because aggregate demand continued to grow strongly, the controls did nothing to prevent the inflation rate from doubling during Carter's term in office. One of President Reagan's first acts upon taking office in 1981 was to end the last vestiges of the Carter controls.

Because of their failure in the 1970s, controls have temporarily fallen out of favor. They conceivably could be revived, however, if rapid inflation returns to the United States. Controls allow politicians to take a "get-tough" stance against big business and big labor, which the public often sees as the villains of inflation—and in the political sphere, appearances are sometimes more important than results.

Indexing

Indexing is sometimes suggested as a means of dealing with inflation. As explained in Chapter 7, indexing means making wages, taxes, debts, interest rates, and a host of other things inflation-proof by adjusting nominal payments in response to price level changes.

Indexing is sometimes used just to make it easier to live with inflation. It has been used this way in countries such as Brazil and Israel during their years of experience with double- and even triple-digit inflation. However, some economists, including Milton Friedman, have suggested that indexing can contribute to controlling inflation as well as easing its pain.

The argument is that indexing can help squeeze the cost-push elements out of inflationary recessions. During a period of inflation, all long-term contracts—union wage contracts, contracts for industrial supplies, loan contracts, and so on—must provide for protection against price increases. If they do this simply by setting higher nominal wage rates, prices, and interest rates, these contracts

Nixon's Wage and Price Controls

On August 15, 1971, President Nixon announced a dramatic new economic policy. The part of the program that drew the most attention was a strict 90-day freeze on all wages and prices. The freeze later became known as Phase I of what proved to be a long-drawn-out experiment with wage and price controls. Phase I was followed by Phase II, in which firms could raise their prices to cover higher costs but not to increase their profit margins. Wage increases were limited to 5.5 percent except under special conditions.

Phases I and II of the Nixon controls came when controls could be expected to work best. As the accompanying chart shows, inflation was already slowing down. Phase I caused the inflation rate to fall more quickly. Some of this gain was lost in a price bulge when the strict controls of Phase I were lifted, but after that inflation continued to fall through mid-1972.

According to a study by Alan S. Blinder and William J. Newton, the combined effect of Phases I and II was to hold the price level 1.22 percent below the level it would have reached in the absence of controls. This modest but measurable reduction in inflation was achieved at the cost of only a few shortages, mainly in lumber. No widespread disruptions of the economy were felt.

Believing that Phases I and II had done their job, Nixon began to put controls back on the shelf. In January 1973, Phase II was replaced by Phase III. This phase imposed slightly looser standards and stressed self-enforcement by firms and unions. By the time Phase III came into effect, a strong recovery of aggregate demand was under way and the inflation rate had turned upward. According to Blinder and Newton, during Phase III prices rose slightly faster than they would have had controls never

[a]Annual rate of change from level of consumer price index 12 months previously.
Source: Alan S. Blinder and William J. Newton, "The 1971–1974 Controls Program and the Price Level: An Econometric Postmortem" (Working Paper No. 279, National Bureau of Economic Research, September 1978). The chart is based on data from President's Council of Economic Advisers, *Economic Report of the President* (Washington, D.C.: Government Printing Office, various issues).

been imposed. This indicates that there was a small "catch-up" effect during that phase.

As the inflation rate increased, political pressure to "get tough" mounted. Nixon responded in August 1973 with a renewed freeze on wages and prices that came to be called "Phase III½". During this phase, inflation was temporarily slowed, but this time, with demand booming, there were serious shortages. Firms began to hoard raw materials for fear of more shortages.

These distortions were judged to be too high a price to pay for keeping the inflation rate down. The freeze was soon dropped in favor of Phase IV, which was a phaseout. In April 1974, Congress let the controls for most products expire. According to Blinder and Newton, catch-up inflation then began in earnest. By August 1974, prices had reached the level they would have attained had controls never been in force. Even after that, however, catch-up inflation persisted for many months. By 1975, the price level was about 1 percent higher than it would have been had controls never been tried.

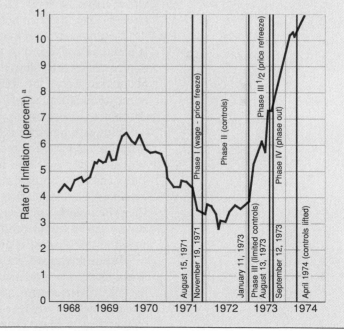

will continue to push up costs even after inflation has slowed elsewhere in the economy. However, if wages, prices, and interest rates in long-term contracts are tied to the inflation rate, they will slow down in step with the general price level. Thus, if indexing is widespread, inflation may respond more quickly to a slowdown in the growth of aggregate demand.

However, indexing can make matters worse instead of better when inflation is caused by a supply shock rather than by excess demand. As explained in the first section of this chapter, adjustment to a supply shock—say, an increase in the price of imported oil—requires a change in relative prices. The price of oil has to rise more rapidly than the inflation rate while other prices rise more slowly. Indexing tends to lock all prices and wages to the average, making the adjustment of relative prices more difficult. The highly indexed Israeli economy is often cited as a case in point. The oil shocks of the 1970s touched off an inflationary spiral in Israel that approached a rate of 1,000 percent per year by the mid-1980s. In the U.S. economy, where indexing is much less widespread, the oil price shocks added only a few percentage points to the inflation rate.

Changing the Policy Regime

At best, indexing and controls only ease the task of taming inflation. When inflation really gets out of control, something more basic is needed. Monetarists and, even more so, the new classicists like to say that what is needed is a change in *policy regime*. By this they mean a change in the basic rules underlying the conduct of economic policy.

Thomas Sargent, a leading member of the new classical school, has developed this line of thought in detail.[6] In Sargent's view, the policy regime of the post–World War II U.S. economy has been one of stop and go, with an inflationary bias. In other words, the government has alternately fought unemployment (with expansionary policies) and inflation (with contractionary policies). On average, however, the expansionary periods have been longer-lived and stronger than the contractionary ones.

Sargent points out that Okun's high estimate of the cost of stopping inflation is based on the record of this policy regime. It should be no surprise, he says, that prices respond slowly to a contractionary policy in such a regime. After all, people know that the contractionary policy will not last long. They therefore resist price and wage cuts in order to position themselves for the inflation that they know will return.

But, says Sargent, think what would happen if, during a period of rapid inflation, there were a credible change in policy regime. What if the government convinced everyone that it would never again—no matter what—allow aggregate demand to outpace natural real output? Believing this, firms and workers would expect the inflation rate to fall to zero. Their changed expectations would alter their short-run response to a contractionary policy. The aggregate real supply curve would promptly stop drifting upward. As it came to rest, the economy could make a quick, painless transition to price stability.

Hyperinflation
Very rapid inflation.

While this sounds too good to be true, Sargent claims there is evidence that it can work. The evidence comes from cases in which **hyperinflation** has been brought under control, such as that of Germany in the 1920s.[7] In late 1923, inflation in Germany reached a rate of 35,000 percent per month. Yet at the end of that year, a sharp change in fiscal and monetary policy, accompanied by a pledge to make the German mark convertible to dollars (which at that time were convertible to gold) stopped inflation cold.

---

[6]Thomas J. Sargent, "The Ends of Four Big Inflations" (Working Paper No. 158, Federal Reserve Bank of Minneapolis, May 1981).

[7]Ibid.

ECONOMICS IN THE NEWS 16.1

Curbing Hyperinflation in Bolivia

Bolivian President Victor Paz Estenssoro

JANUARY 1984. The scene is a large bank in La Paz, Bolivia. A courier stumbles in, struggling under the weight of a huge bag of money he is carrying on his back. He announces that the sack contains 32 million pesos, and the teller slaps on a notation to that effect. The courier pitches the bag into a corner.

"We don't bother counting the money any more," explains Max Loew Stahl, a loan officer standing nearby. "We take the client's word for what's in the bag." Pointing to the courier's load, he says, "That's a small deposit."

At that moment, the 32 million pesos—enough bills to stuff a mail sack—are worth only $500.

Outside the bank, prices are rising by the day, the hour, or the customer. Julia Blanco Sirba, a vendor on the capital city's main street, sells a bar of chocolate for 35,000 pesos. Five minutes later, the next bar goes for 50,000 pesos. The two-inch stack of money needed to buy it far outweighs the chocolate.

In the month in which the above scenes took place, the inflation rate in Bolivia was 116,000 percent per year. Tons of paper money were printed to keep the country of 5.9 million inhabitants going. Planeloads of money arrived twice a week from printers in West Germany and Britain. Purchases of money cost Bolivia more than $20 million in 1983, making it the third-largest import, after wheat and mining equipment.

In the midst of this hyperinflation, a new president, Victor Paz Estenssoro, took charge. His answer to the crisis: a radical change in policy regime. Within a month, he announced a harsh back-to-the-market approach to the economy. The government lifted controls on prices, interest rates, imports, and exports. It freed the official exchange rate. To cut the cost of government, it froze public sector wages and set about dismantling some big state-owned enterprises. It gave companies the right to fire workers. To increase government revenues, it raised the price of gasoline, a state monopoly, tenfold to market levels, and it pushed through Congress an overhaul of the tax system. The airlift of money was curtailed.

Within two months, inflation fell to zero and then averaged 20 percent over the next six months. But there were major costs. The crunch on government jobs came just as forces beyond the government's control were punishing Bolivia's main export industries. World prices of tin and natural gas crashed. At the same time, under pressure from the United States, a major campaign was undertaken against cocaine production, the source of half the country's foreign exchange earnings. However, the stability measures did allow a reopening of Bolivia's line of credit with the world bank.

Said Javier Lopo Gamarra, the president of the National Chamber of Industries, "It isn't easy to erase a period of hyperinflation with a few months of stability. The economy is very fragile." But, he added, the program "has to have positive results because the alternative is chaos."

Source: Sonia L. Nazario, "When Inflation Rate Is 116,000 Percent, Prices Change by the Hour," *The Wall Street Journal,* February 7, 1985, 1; Eric Morgenthaler, "Bolivia Quickly Halts Hyperinflation, but It Does So at Heavy Cost," *The Wall Street Journal,* August 13, 1986, 1. Photo Source: Reuters/Bettmann Newsphotos.

In recent years, several countries that have experienced hyperinflation have attempted similar changes in policy regime, with mixed success; the experience of one country—Bolivia—is discussed in "Economics in the News 16.1." While these recent cases do not support the notion that there are ways to end inflation costlessly, they do indicate that a change in policy regime can be a significant element in a disinflation program.

Summary

1. **What are the sources of shifts in the aggregate supply curve?** The aggregate supply curve shows the path along which firms move, in the short run, in response to a shift in the aggregate demand curve. The level of input prices that firms expect is assumed to be constant along a given aggregate supply curve and is marked by the height of that curve at the natural level of real output. Any change in the expected level of input prices will result in a shift in the aggregate supply curve.

2. **What are the characteristics of inflation that arises from excessive growth in aggregate demand?** Inflation caused by an increase in aggregate demand is known as *demand-pull inflation*. In the short run, an increase in aggregate demand will move the economy up and to the right along its short-run aggregate supply curve. As increases in final goods prices come to be reflected in expected input prices, the aggregate supply curve shifts upward. If continued expansionary policy shifts the aggregate demand curve upward at the same rate, the economy can be held above its natural level of real output for an extended period, but at a substantial cost in terms of inflation.

3. **How can inflation arise from a shift in the aggregate supply curve?** If the aggregate supply curve shifts upward while the aggregate demand curve stays in place or shifts upward more slowly, the economy will experience *cost-push inflation*. Real output will fall, and the economy will enter an *inflationary recession*. One source of cost-push inflation is the momentum of inflationary expectations generated by previous demand-pull inflation. Another possible source is a *supply shock*, such as an increase in import prices.

4. **What contributions have the new classical economists made?** Under the *adaptive-expectations hypothesis*, people form their expectations about the future primarily on the basis of their experience in the recent past. But according to the *new classical economists*, households and firms form expectations rationally, taking into account probable impacts of present and future economic policies as well as past experiences. It is an implication of this *rational-expectations hypothesis* that changes in monetary or fiscal policy that are fully anticipated by firms and households will have no effect on real output or employment even in the short run. Critics of this view, however, think that various frictions and lags in the economy will cause policy changes to affect output and employment even when they are anticipated.

5. **What types of policies can be used to combat inflation?** Conventional methods of stopping inflation by restricting the growth of aggregate demand are able to

stop inflation only at the cost of an inflationary recession. Several unconventional policies for reducing the cost of stopping inflation have been suggested. These include indexing, wage and price controls, and an abrupt change of policy regime.

Terms for Review

-   demand-pull inflation
-   cost-push inflation
-   supply shock
-   inflationary recession
-   adaptive-expectations hypothesis
-   rational-expectations hypothesis
-   new classical economics
-   hyperinflation

Questions for Review

1. What are some of the reasons why firms might expect input prices to remain constant in the short run when demand for their output increases?

2. How can the expected level of input prices be determined given an aggregate supply curve and the natural level of real output?

3. How is demand-pull inflation distinguished from cost-push inflation?

4. What are two possible sources of cost-push inflation?

5. Under what circumstances is it possible for the price level and the unemployment rate to rise at the same time?

6. How does the rational-expectations hypothesis differ from the adaptive-expectations hypothesis?

7. Why do new classical economists think that anticipated changes in economic policy have less effect on real output than unexpected ones?

8. Under what circumstances are wage and price controls likely to be effective in slowing inflation? When are they likely to be ineffective?

9. Why is indexing likely to be beneficial as an aid to slowing demand-pull inflation but harmful when the economy is trying to adjust to a supply shock?

10. What is meant by a "change in policy regime"? How can such a change reduce the cost of slowing inflation?

Problems and Topics for Discussion

1. **Examining the lead-off case.** Given the information provided about the "Great Inflation" in the opening case for this chapter, would you describe the nature of

that inflation as demand-pull, cost-push, or a mixture of the two? Discuss.

2. **Expected input prices.** Three aggregate supply curves are shown in Exhibit 16.2. What is the expected level of input prices associated with each?

3. **Favorable supply shocks.** Supply shocks are not always bad. Use aggregate supply and demand curves to explain the short-run and long-run effects of a favorable supply shock, such as a decline in world oil prices.

4. **Price expectations and real output.** Use the aggregate supply and demand model to show that real output can be above its natural level only when the current level of final goods prices is above the level corresponding to expected input prices. Show too that real output can be below its natural level only when the current level of final goods prices is below that corresponding to expected input prices.

5. **Publicity and policy changes.** Assume that the economy has been going through a long period of demand-pull inflation. The government decides to try to stop the inflation by means of restrictive monetary and fiscal policies. Should it make the required policy changes with as little fanfare as possible, or should it publicize them widely? Will it make any difference? Why or why not?

6. **Forecasting inflation.** What do you expect the inflation rate to be next year? Do you know what it was last year? Last month? On what sources do you rely for information about past and present inflation and for forming your expectations about the future? Do you think this course will affect your ability to forecast future inflation? Discuss.

Case for Discussion

U.S. Macroeconomic Experience in the 1960s

Compared to the 1970s and 1980s, the 1960s seem to have been a golden age for the U.S. economy. Inflation and unemployment rates were low by today's standards (although not everyone was happy with them at the time), and the economy enjoyed its most continuous cyclical expansion ever (106 months). Nonetheless, it is also possible to see the roots of the inflationary 1970s in the long expansion of the 1960s.

The following table gives data for real output (billions of dollars) and the price level (GNP deflator, 1972 = 1.0) for the U.S. economy for the years 1961 through 1969. Plot these data points on a graph (label the vertical axis from 0.5 to 1.0 and the horizontal axis from $500 billion to $1,500 billion), and connect them with line segments.

Year	Real GNP	Price Level
1961	756	0.69
1962	800	0.71
1963	833	0.72
1964	876	0.73
1965	929	0.74
1966	985	0.77
1967	1011	0.79
1968	1058	0.83
1969	1088	0.87

Questions

1. Do you think the points you have plotted are best viewed as a series of points lying along a single upward-sloping aggregate supply curve or as the intersections of a series of upward-shifting aggregate supply curves with an aggregate demand curve that is also shifting upward? Why?

2. Do you think these years were a period of demand-pull inflation or one of cost-push inflation? Why?

3. During the period for which data are given, the unemployment rate fell from 6.7 percent of the labor force to 3.5 percent. At that time, the natural rate of unemployment was about 5 percent. Natural real output can be assumed to have grown during the period because of investment, productivity gains, growth of the labor force, and other factors. Do you think that the actual level of real output grew more quickly or slowly than the natural level? On what do you base your conclusion?

Suggestions for Further Reading

Barro, Robert J. *Macroeconomics*. New York: Wiley, 1984.

An intermediate-level macroeconomics text written by one of the leading new classicists.

Gordon, Robert J. *Macroeconomics*, 3d ed. Boston: Little, Brown, 1984.

Chapters 6 through 9 of this intermediate text parallel the discussion in this chapter.

McCallum, Bennett T. "The Significance of Rational Expectations Theory." *Challenge* (January/February 1980): 37–43.

A nontechnical discussion of rational-expectations theory.

17 Economic Growth and Productivity

After reading this chapter, you will understand . . .

- How the economy can grow while maintaining price stability.
- How insufficient growth of aggregate demand can cause a *growth recession*.
- How expansion of aggregate demand beyond the rate of growth of natural real output can cause inflation.
- What may have caused the slowdown in productivity growth in the U.S. economy beginning in the 1970s.
- What are the traditional Keynesian recommendations for promoting growth of real output.
- What policies are recommended by the *supply-side* school of economics.

Before reading this chapter, make sure you know the meaning of . . .

- Cyclical and structural budget deficit (Chapter 11)
- Crowding-out effect (Chapter 15)
- Demand-pull and cost-push inflation (Chapter 16)

"I Want to Be Prepared When It Gets Here"

YPSILANTI, MICHIGAN. Lavester Frye works at an assembly table eight hours a day building automobile horns, setting a metal plate on a metal dish with one hand, adding a tiny ring with the other.

In the 22 years he has worked at the Ford Motor Company, it never really has mattered that he didn't finish high school. He always has had jobs like this one, jobs that depend more on his hands than his mind.

But Frye has been told that his job soon will become more complicated. To improve productivity, the company is phasing in an intricate statistical system of quality control.

Assembly line workers must adjust to advances in technology designed to increase productivity.

The news made Frye feel nervous and unprepared, and when he looked at the charts he would be expected to keep under the new system, he was even more troubled by what he saw: decimal points. "A long time ago at school, I had decimals, but it faded out of my mind," he says.

On this factory floor, amidst the assembly lines, the huge hulking furnaces and the din of metal on metal, the ability to put a decimal point in the proper place suddenly has become a ticket to a job.

Les Walker came to work at the plant four decades ago as a 17-year-old high school dropout. "If you could read or write a little bit, you could get a job," he said of the booming postwar period when he was hired. "Now there's so much change. . . ."

Walker inspects the valves on shock absorbers that will be built into Ford bumpers. Soon, "statistical process control," which is designed to pinpoint and correct defects in manufacturing, will be introduced to his section of the plant. He'll need to use math skills he hasn't needed before and never learned in school: fractions, division, averaging, and decimals.

When Frye and Walker complete their afternoon shift at 3, they and several others gather in a converted office off the factory floor, hunching over high school books around a cafeteria table. They have volunteered for free courses, arranged under a 1982 United Auto Workers–Ford agreement, to prepare for the high school equivalency test. They also have taken instruction in computers and basic reading and math.

These workers, most of whom could retire in a few years, would not lose their jobs if they failed to learn statistical process control. But they know job promotions depend on their ability to adapt, and many of them believe that they will be better, more productive workers if they learn the new systems. They don't want to be left behind.

"I want to be prepared when it gets here," one of them says of the new technology.

Source: Barbara Vobejda, "The New Cutting Edge in Factories: Education," *The Washington Post*, April 14, 1987, A1. © 1987 *The Washington Post*, reprinted with permission. Photo Source: Courtesy of Ford Motor Company.

FRYE and Walker are at the forefront of a massive effort to improve the productivity of U.S. industry. In an increasingly competitive world economy, enhanced productivity—more output per worker—is the main source of increases in living standards. Ford Motor Company's efforts are typical in that some of the increased productivity comes from new equipment but a lot of it results from people finding better ways to work together to get things done. The example is being duplicated, with variations, in thousands of plants around the country.

In this chapter, we will look at the issue of productivity using the same aggregate supply and demand tools that we applied in Chapter 16. We will begin by discussing the policies required for long-run economic growth without inflation. Next we will look at the record of productivity growth in the U.S. economy and likely future trends. Finally, we will discuss policies for promoting economic growth—both traditional Keynesian policies and the newer policies known as *supply-side economics*.

Economic Growth with Price Stability

As we saw in earlier chapters, real output can, in the short run, rise above its natural level in response to an increase in aggregate demand. It can also fall below its natural level during a recession. Long-run growth, on the other hand, deals not with these short-run ups and downs relative to the natural level of real output but with growth in natural real output itself.

Growth in the natural level of real output has, for the most part, come from increases in the size of the labor force and in output per worker. Output per worker, in turn, has depended on a number of considerations. One of these is the amount of capital and natural resources available per worker. Improvements in technology have been another source of productivity gains; the use of robot welding machines on an auto assembly line would be an example. Finally, human factors such as education, motivation, organization, and quality of management affect productivity; the introduction of statistical process control at Ford Motor Company is a case in point.

Edward F. Denison of the Brookings Institution has estimated the importance of various sources of economic growth in the United States. In the period 1948 to 1973, real output grew at a healthy rate of 3.6 percent per year. Of this, increases in the size and quality of the labor force accounted for about 1 percent and increases in the capital stock for about .6 percent. The remaining 2 percent annual growth reflected increases in output per unit of input, including improvements in technology, organization, and quality of management.[1]

Effects of Economic Growth

Exhibit 17.1 shows the effects of economic growth in terms of aggregate supply and demand. The economy starts out in equilibrium at E_0 with a natural real output of N_0. Over time the labor force grows, capital investments are made, and productivity increases. The result is a rightward shift in natural real output to N_1.

As natural real output grows, the economy need not move upward along its short-run aggregate supply curve as it does when aggregate demand shifts with natural output constant. Instead, the short-run aggregate supply curve shifts to the right along with natural real output. Its intersection with the new natural level of real output, N_1, is at the same price level—1.0—as formerly. The reason for this shift is that the factors causing the growth of real output—more workers, more capital, better technology, improved management, and so on—make it possible for output to grow with no increase in input costs per unit of output and, hence, with no increase in final goods prices.

In Exhibit 17.1, the economy at first is able to produce $1,500 billion of goods and services at a price level of 1.0. The shift in natural real output means that it now can produce $2,500 billion of goods and services at the same price level. As we will see shortly, movements of real output above or below the new natural level would be linked with changes in the price level. These would be shown as movements upward or downward along the new aggregate supply curve, AS_1. However, a movement of the economy from one natural level of real output to another does not require a change in the price level.

Finally, Exhibit 17.1 shows the aggregate demand curve also shifting to the right by the same amount as natural real output. With such an increase in demand, firms will be able to sell all the output produced at the new natural level without cutting their prices. If the demand curve does shift as shown, the economy will move smoothly from E_0 to E_1. At these points, as well as all points in between, the economy will remain in long-run equilibrium. Prices will be stable; input prices will remain at the level expected by business managers; real output will keep up with its rising natural level; and unemployment will be steady at its natural rate.

Managing the Growth of Demand

Exhibit 17.1 shows the ideal condition of steady economic growth with no inflation or excessive unemployment. However, the economy does not always run smoothly; a number of things can go wrong. Fiscal and monetary policy may not

---

[1] Edward F. Denison, *Accounting for Slower Economic Growth* (Washington, D.C.: The Brookings Institution, 1979), Table 8-1.

Exhibit 17.1   Growth with Stable Prices

Over time, growth of the labor force and of output per worker causes natural real output to rise. As natural real output shifts from N_0 to N_1, the aggregate supply curve also shifts to the right. If aggregate demand is allowed to grow at the same rate, the economy will move smoothly from its initial equilibrium at E_0 to a new equilibrium at E_1. Prices will be stable, and unemployment will remain at its natural rate.

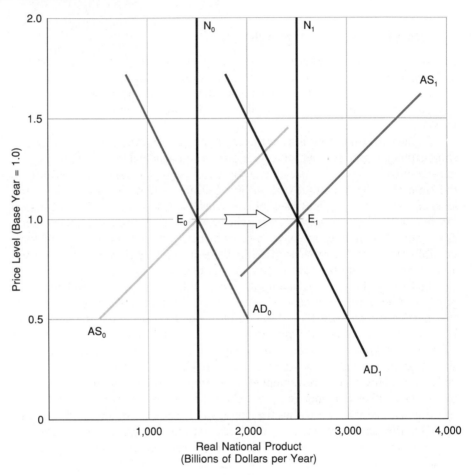

be managed so as to offset swings in aggregate demand originating in consumption, investment, or net exports. Alternatively, fiscal and monetary policy may be mismanaged in a way that disturbs the smooth growth of the economy. In this section, we will look at what happens when demand grows too rapidly or too slowly.

Growth Recession

Exhibit 17.2 shows what happens when aggregate demand fails to keep up with natural real output. As before, the economy starts from an equilibrium at E_0. Natural real output then rises from $1,500 billion to $2,500 billion, as shown by the shift from N_0 to N_1. The aggregate supply curve also shifts rightward, to the position AS_1. This time, however, tight monetary and fiscal policy keep the lid on aggregate demand. With the aggregate demand curve stuck at AD_0, the

Exhibit 17.2   A Growth Recession

In the case shown here, natural real output grows while aggregate demand remains fixed. Thus, as natural real output and the aggregate supply curve shift to the right, the aggregate demand curve remains still. The economy moves downward and to the right along the aggregate demand curve and at the same time moves downward and to the left along the new aggregate supply curve as it shifts to the right. The economy ends up at E_1, where unemployment is higher than its natural rate even though real output has grown. This is called a *growth recession*.

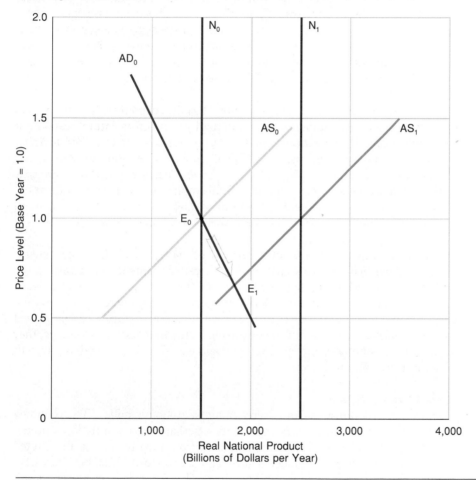

economy cannot reach the intersection of the new aggregate supply curve with N_1.

What will happen? At E_0, the economy is in long-run equilibrium. This means that firms are producing at their normal capacity and not fully using their standby capacity. The unemployment rate is about 6 percent. This is about normal given the number of people who change jobs each year and the time it takes new workers to find their first jobs. The spending plans of households, firms, and government add up to just enough to keep inventories from either increasing or decreasing relative to planned levels.

The economy cannot stand still in this position, however. New equipment, new technology, and improved skills of workers and managers increase output per worker. Although the natural level of real output increases, macroeconomic policy is holding the aggregate demand curve steady.

The initial result is unplanned inventory buildup. Firms' managers are disappointed; they are producing more at the same average cost as before, but they cannot sell all their output. To keep stocks of unsold goods from building up, firms cut their prices, hoping to boost sales. At the same time, they cut back their production plans. They increase output somewhat, but not by as much as they otherwise would given the growth in capacity and productivity.

In terms of Exhibit 17.2, growth of productivity and the labor force have shifted natural real output from N_0 to N_1 and the short-run aggregate supply curve from AS_0 to AS_1. But at the same time that the aggregate supply curve is shifting to the right, firms' price and output cuts are moving them downward and to the left along the curve. Throughout this process, aggregate demand is assumed to be unchanged at AD_0. The economy thus moves to E_1, where AD_0 intersects AS_1.

Now look at what happens to employment as the economy moves from E_0 to E_1. Firms have increased their output, but not by as much as natural real output has grown. Given the new investment that has been made and other productivity gains, the economy could produce \$2,500 billion in real output; but at E_1, output is only a little over \$1,800 billion. Some firms may need a few new workers, while others may lay off a few. Total employment may rise a little or fall a little. Nevertheless, the feeble growth in real output means that not enough jobs will be created to absorb all the new workers entering the labor force. Thus, the unemployment rate will rise.

Growth recession
A situation in which real output grows, but not quickly enough to keep unemployment from rising.

A situation in which real output grows, but not by enough to keep unemployment from rising above its natural rate, is called a **growth recession.** In the U.S. economy, real output has to grow by about 3 percent per year, or close to it, just to keep the unemployment rate from rising. If growth is too slow, the unemployment rate tends to rise. Because real output is growing, employed workers' real incomes continue to rise during a growth recession. However, they do not rise by as much as they would if demand were keeping up with the growth of natural real output.[2]

Growth with Inflation
A growth recession results from overly cautious economic policy. The economy has the capacity to grow, but policymakers—perhaps fearing inflation—do not give it the room it needs. This has happened from time to time in the United States, but more often policymakers have made the opposite mistake: They have pushed the economy beyond the ability of natural real output to grow. The result has been growth with inflation.

The situation of growth with inflation is very much like that of demand-pull inflation discussed in Chapter 16. The difference, as Exhibit 17.3 shows, is that natural real output shifts to the right. As it does so, the short-run aggregate

---

[2] Exhibit 17.2 is an extreme case in that aggregate demand does not grow at all and the price level actually falls. A milder form of growth recession can occur when aggregate demand does grow, but not as rapidly as natural real output. In still other cases, a growth recession can be combined with cost-push inflation. For example, expected inflation, based on past experience, may push the aggregate supply curve upward at the same time that productivity growth is raising natural real output. When that happens, the economy can go through a period in which real output grows, but too slowly to hold unemployment at its natural rate, and the price level rises at the same time. This situation might appropriately be called "stagflation." (See also footnote 3 of Chapter 16, page 399.)

Exhibit 17.3   Growth with Inflation

In this example, aggregate demand is allowed to grow more rapidly than natural real output. As the economy grows, it also experiences demand-pull inflation. As the economy moves from E_0 to E_1, the unemployment rate falls and there is only mild inflation. In later years, the inflation rate must increase just to keep unemployment from rising again. As a result, the inflation/unemployment trade-off worsens.

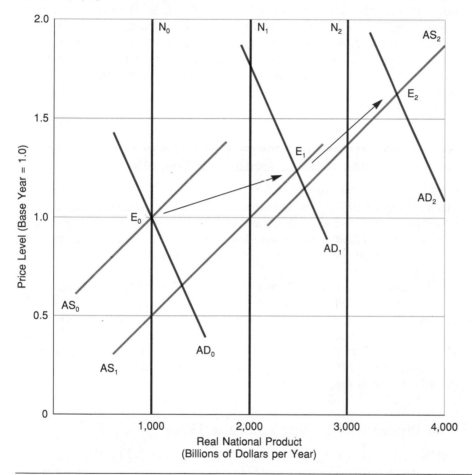

supply curve shifts with it. But while natural real output grows from \$1,000 billion to \$2,000 billion, an expansionary policy boosts the level of aggregate demand even more forcefully. The new aggregate demand curve, AD_1, intersects the new aggregate supply curve at E_1. The actual level of real output grows by more than its natural level. As it does so, firms begin using their standby capacity and unemployment falls below its natural rate.

In moving from E_0 to E_1, the economy experiences demand-pull inflation. This inflation will affect the expectations of both firms and workers. In the following period, an increase in the expected level of input prices will push the aggregate supply curve upward at the same time that growth in natural real output carries it further to the right. This will put it in the position AS_2. To keep real output above its natural level, the aggregate demand curve will have to shift to a position such as AD_2. In moving from E_1 to E_3, output will stay exactly the same distance above its natural level, keeping unemployment from falling further, and prices will rise by more than they did during the move from E_0 to E_1.

The policy implications of growth with inflation can be summarized as follows. In the short run, pushing the growth of aggregate demand to a faster rate than the growth of natural real output can speed the growth of real output and cut unemployment. The price of doing so is a moderate amount of demand-pull inflation. After this initial gain, however, the trade-off between output and inflation becomes less favorable as firms and workers come to expect inflation. Then aggregate demand must grow faster and faster just to keep real output from falling back to its natural level and unemployment from rising back to its natural rate. The growth rate of real output slows, and the inflation rate speeds up.

Recent Trends in U.S. Economic Growth

Up to this point, we have treated the growth rate of natural real output as a given. Until the 1970s, this seemed like a reasonable assumption for the U.S. economy; indeed, fiscal and monetary policy did not prevent a number of recessions during this period. There were also some years of low unemployment and rising inflation. But on the average, real output increased by 3.6 percent per year from 1948 to 1973.

Then problems developed. In the period 1974 to 1981, the average growth rate of real output fell to 1.8 percent. More troubling still was the fact that this happened despite an increase in the growth rate of the labor force and total hours worked. Growth of output per worker-hour slowed from a trend of 2.2 percent per year to .6 percent per year. In this section, we look at the productivity slowdown of the 1970s. Then we examine policies designed to promote the growth of natural real output.

The Productivity Slowdown of the 1970s

Exhibit 17.4 charts the productivity slowdown of the 1970s. The 2.2 percent trend shown for 1955 to 1973 represents only a slight reduction from the 2.75 percent trend of the 50-year period beginning in 1920. Then the trend dropped to about .6 percent in the period 1974 to 1981 and appears to have recovered only partially—to about 1.25 percent—through the mid-1980s.

What went wrong? Over the last 10 years, economists have spent a lot of time trying to answer this question. The blame has been placed on many different factors. The following are among those most often cited.

Changes in the Labor Force
Many accounts of the productivity slowdown point to the entry of millions of women and young people into the labor force during the 1970s. These new workers were, on the whole, skilled and motivated, but they tended to have less experience than those who already held jobs. At the same time, by their sheer number they pulled down the ratio of capital to labor.

Exhibit 17.4   The Productivity Slowdown of the 1970s

During the 1970s, the rate of productivity growth slowed. Among the hypothesized causes were changes in the composition of the labor force, supply shocks, inflation, a slowdown in research and development, and increased regulation. However, productivity growth has recovered somewhat in the 1980s in part due to the reversal of several of these adverse factors.

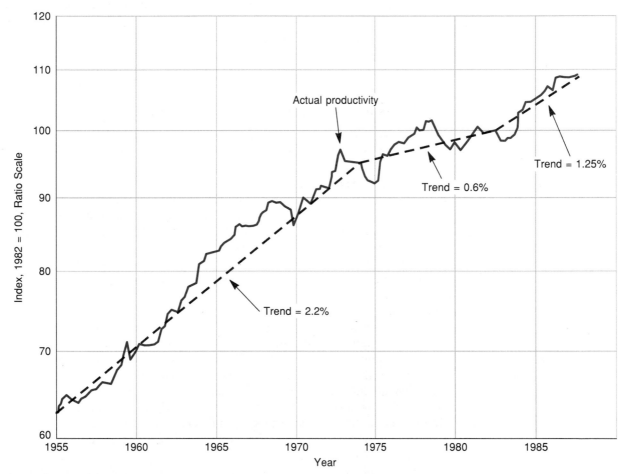

Source: Bureau of Labor Statistics.

However, Denison found that the shift in the age and gender mix of the labor force could explain only a small part of the productivity slowdown. For one thing, that mix was already shifting against productivity before 1973. In addition, it was more than offset after 1973 by improvements in education.

Supply Shocks

Chapter 16 explained how supply shocks, such as the oil price increases of 1974 and 1979 to 1980, can push real output below its natural level. Some economists believe that the oil price shocks of the 1970s also reduced natural real output.

The assumed reason was that higher oil prices rendered much of the economy's capital stock obsolete. Many older trucks, planes, furnaces, generators, and so on had to be retired or placed on standby because high oil prices made them too costly to operate. The effect was almost the same as if the equipment had been destroyed by fire or flood.

Inflation

Many economists have noted that the productivity slowdown of the 1970s occurred at the same time as the speedup of inflation. In part, the productivity decline can be seen as a factor contributing to the inflation; for a given growth rate of aggregate demand, any slowdown in the growth of aggregate supply will cause prices to rise more rapidly. But some economists think that cause and effect worked both ways. Inflation disrupted business planning and labor-management relations. Inflation also distorted the impact of taxes on business and investment income. This not only reduced total investment but tended to channel investment toward uses that did little to enhance productivity, such as housing and tax shelters, and away from more productive projects.

Research and Development

A number of economists have noted that research and development (R&D) spending lagged during the 1970s. It fell from a high of 3 percent of GNP in the mid-1960s to a low of 2.2 percent in 1977. This may have slowed the development of new cost-cutting ideas. However, other economists have pointed out that much of the slowdown was in military R&D, which would not significantly affect the growth of productivity in the rest of the economy.

Regulation

The 1970s saw an upsurge in government regulation of business. Regulations dealing with health, safety, the environment, and discrimination in hiring and promotion are just a few examples. Firms had to spend vast sums in order to comply with these regulations. Although the regulations produced some welcome benefits, such as cleaner air and safer highways, they did not contribute to the growth of real output. As a result, they pulled down productivity growth. Denison's data suggest that regulation and related factors cut about .2 percent from real growth in the period 1973 to 1981. The effect is hard to measure, however; it might have been greater.

Despite all the studies on these possible causes, the full reasons for the productivity slowdown remain hazy.

Performance and Prospects in the 1980s

In the early 1980s, a rapid cyclical recovery of productivity from a recessionary low made it look as if the slowdown of the 1970s was behind us. But as Exhibit 17.4 shows, the pace of productivity growth that was experienced in the early years of the recovery was not sustained. Although the rate of productivity gains for the 1984 to 1987 period appears to be an improvement over the trend for the 1970s, it does not seem to have returned to the 2.2 percent per year trend of the 1950s and 1960s.

The improved growth of productivity after 1984 can be traced, at least in part, to the fact that some of the likely causes of the 1970s slowdown are now operating in reverse. First, the age and gender makeup of the labor force is changing in favor of higher productivity as the new workers of the 1970s gain experience. Second, oil price shocks turned from a negative to a positive factor in the early 1980s as world oil prices fell; even if they were to rise again to their previous peak levels, the economy is now equipped to use energy much more efficiently than in the past. Third, inflation has slowed, enabling managers to focus on improving production rather than simply fighting for financial survival. Finally, the regulatory picture has changed. Most health and environmental regulations remain in place, but more efficient ways of meeting their goals are being found. Meanwhile, regulatory reform and increased competition have benefited such industries as transportation, communications, and financial services.

Moreover, labor-management relations are changing in ways that tend to raise productivity. The story of Ford's Ypsilanti plant is being repeated in thousands of other companies. Although technology helps, U.S. managers have begun to realize that people are the real key to productivity. If given responsibility and challenges, they can do more than has been asked of them in the past. The new attitude has affected unions as well as management. Cooperating with management in efforts to raise productivity is less often seen as a sellout; instead, it is considered a way of creating jobs and raising living standards by making employers more competitive in the world economy.

These favorable trends have had the most dramatic effect on the productivity of goods-producing industries, as Exhibit 17.5 shows. If attention is limited to the much-discussed durable-goods manufacturing sector, the improvement

Exhibit 17.5   Productivity Growth:
Goods versus Services

The productivity slowdown of the 1970s affected both goods-producing and service industries. In the 1980s, productivity growth in goods-producing industries has recovered but that in service industries has disappeared, dragging down overall productivity growth. The reasons for the productivity slowdown in service industries are poorly understood, partly because service industry productivity is hard to measure accurately.

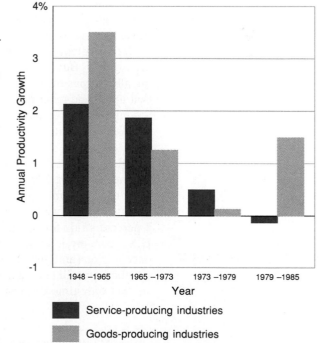

Source: American Productivity Center; Allan Murray, "The Service Sector's Productivity Problem," *The Wall Street Journal,* February 9, 1987, 1. Reprinted by permission of *The Wall Street Journal,* © Dow Jones & Company, Inc. 1987. All Rights Reserved.

appears even more dramatic. Durable-goods manufacturers achieved a 4.7 percent rate of productivity growth in the first half of the 1980s. The automobile industry alone managed a 44 percent increase in output with only an 11 percent increase in employment from 1980 to 1985. In 1986, auto industry output increased another 5.5 percent while labor-hours worked fell by 3.2 percent.

However, durable-goods manufacturing is no longer the heart of the U.S. economy. Service industries, ranging from retailing to high-tech business services, account for about two-thirds of the economy. As Exhibit 17.5 shows, productivity growth in the service sector has been negative in the 1980s. Thus, it appears that one productivity puzzle has been replaced by another—that of lagging service productivity.

Some economists point to a slowdown in net domestic investment as a possible explanation of productivity trends in the 1980s. On the surface, this drop in net U.S. private investment—from 7.1 percent of GNP in the 1960s to 4.6 percent in the 1980s—would appear damaging to productivity growth. But a closer look at where net investment has gone reveals an oddity: Although the quantity of basic industrial capital per production worker essentially has stagnated in the 1980s, these sectors have shown vigorous productivity growth. At the same time, the quantity of high-tech capital, especially computers, per service worker has soared, yet productivity in the service sectors has stood still.

Little is really known about the reasons for the productivity lag in service sectors. Some economists think the explanation is partly a measurement problem. Government data chart every corner of the manufacturing industry, distinguishing between, for example, the tufted fabric industry and the woven fabric industry. At the same time, they lump an enormous number of nonmanufacturing businesses—ranging from window washing to consulting—into the amorphous category "business services." Quality improvements are also hard to chart in service industries. It is relatively easy to determine that automobile tires or flashlight batteries last longer than in the past and to adjust productivity data accordingly. But how does one measure the fact that improved computer modeling allows consultants to produce more accurate sales forecasts than formerly, or that automatic teller machines allow depositors to make withdrawals from bank accounts at more convenient hours, or that stereo TV broadcasts bring more lifelike sound into viewers' homes?

Robert S. Gay and Stephen S. Roach of Morgan Stanley's economics department look back to the beginning of the twentieth century for a comparison.[3] Beginning about 1905, radical technological changes, especially the development of the assembly line, swept U.S. manufacturing. Yet the economy's overall productivity showed no gain until the mid-1920s. Then productivity hit a nearly 3 percent stride for the next 50 years. Could it be, Gay and Roach ask, that the U.S. economy is undergoing a similar period of transition in the 1980s? That once workers and managers have adjusted to the huge influx of high-tech capital, productivity will enter a new, sustained upswing? This is a provocative hypothesis that only time can test.

---

[3] Robert S. Gay and Stephen S. Roach, "The Productivity Puzzle: Perils and Hopes," *Morgan Stanley Economic Perspectives*, April 10, 1986.

Policies for Promoting Economic Growth

Throughout this course, we have listed growth of real output as one of the fundamental goals of macroeconomic policy. The idea that economic growth is good commands wide agreement among economists. Although voices of dissent can be identified both in the past and in our own time (see "Who Said It? Who Did It? 17.1"), Keynesian economists, monetarists, new classicists, and particularly the so-called supply-siders (to be discussed shortly) see growth as impor-

---

WHO SAID IT? WHO DID IT? 17.1

John Stuart Mill on the Stationary State

Economic growth was a major concern of the classical economists of the nineteenth century. Then, as now, most of the leading economists were inclined to deem growth a good thing. However, some of them feared that the pressure of population on limited natural resources would sooner or later bring growth to a halt. Economists' portrayal of the "stationary state" toward which society was moving as one of poverty and overpopulation caused one critic to dub economics the "dismal science."

John Stuart Mill, whose work marked a high point of classical economics, thought otherwise. Mill was one of the most remarkable figures of the nineteenth century. Eldest son of the prominent economist James Mill, John Stuart Mill began studying Greek at age 3, was tutoring the younger members of his family in Latin at age 8, and first read Smith's *Wealth of Nations* at age 13. His *Principles of Political Economy*, published in 1848, stood as the standard text on the subject until Alfred Marshall transformed "political economy" into "economics" at the end of the century.

Mill agreed with earlier classical economists that the economy would sooner or later reach a stationary state, but he did not view the prospect as entirely gloomy:

I cannot . . . regard the stationary state of capital and wealth with the unaffected aversion so generally manifested towards it by political economists of the old school. I am inclined to believe that it would be, on the whole, a very considerable improvement on our present condition. I confess I am not charmed with the ideal of life held out by those who think that the normal state of human beings is that of struggling to get on; that the trampling, crushing, elbowing, and treading on each other's heels, which form the existing type of social life, are the most desirable lot of human kind, or anything but the disagreeable symptoms of one of the phases of our industrial progress. . . .

If the earth must lose that great portion of its pleasantries which it owes to things that the unlimited increase of wealth and population would extricate from it, for the mere purpose of enabling it to support a larger, but not a better or happier population, I sincerely hope, for the sake of posterity, that they will be content to be stationary long before necessity compels them to.

Today Mill's sentiments have been echoed among writers concerned with problems of population, pollution, and resource depletion. E. F. Schumacher's *Small is Beautiful* expressed this line of thought;[a] so did another best-selling book of the 1970s, *The Limits to Growth*, which advocated a policy of stabilizing both world population and the world capital stock by the end of the twentieth century.[b] Its proposals, set forth in the form of computer charts rather than the elegant prose of a John Stuart Mill, were roundly denounced by "orthodox" economists. However, the wide audience that the book attracted indicates that growth is still not universally accepted as good.

---

[a]E. F. Schumacher, *Small is Beautiful* (New York: Harper & Row, 1973).
[b]Donnella H. Meadows, Dennis L. Meadows, Jorgen Randers, and William W. Behrens III, *The Limits to Growth* (New York: Signet, 1972).
Photo Source: The Bettmann Archive, Inc.

tant both to improvements in material welfare and to maintenance of national security. Accordingly, a variety of policies designed to promote growth have been advanced.

For one thing, as we saw in the first section of this chapter, policymakers must allow a growth rate of aggregate demand that will at least roughly match that of natural real output. If demand is permitted to grow too rapidly, higher inflation rates will return—and rapid inflation, as we have seen, was one of the villains of the productivity slowdown of the 1970s. On the other hand, if demand grows too slowly, the economy may slip into a growth recession or worse. We will return to the topic of matching growth of demand with growth of natural real output in Chapter 18.

We now turn to policies that are intended to promote the growth of natural real output itself. First we will look at traditional Keynesian policies. Then we will return to the so-called supply-side economics that came into fashion during the early 1980s.

Keynesian Growth Policies

Today's economists are not the first to be concerned with promoting economic growth. Growth was a top priority of the Keynesian economists who served under Presidents Kennedy and Johnson in the 1960s. We will begin by looking at their ideas, many of which are still very much alive.

Fine-Tuning for Growth

In part, the Keynesian economists believed that their job was to help fine-tune the economy so as to avoid recessions. They noted that during a recession investment tends to fall more than in proportion to output. A recession thus represents a pause in the growth of the economy's capital stock. Even after the economy recovers from the recession, it is left with less capital per worker than it would have had the recession not occurred. As we will see in Chapter 18, many economists today are skeptical of Keynesian fine-tuning techniques. However, almost all would agree that smooth growth is better than bumpy growth.

Shifting the Policy Mix

Keynesian economics suggests that the mix of fiscal and monetary policies is important to long-run economic growth. This follows from the theory presented in Chapter 15. There we showed that there is more than one way to achieve a given degree of stimulus to aggregate demand. A policy objective can be reached through an expansionary fiscal policy combined with a tight monetary policy or via a tight fiscal policy and an expansionary monetary policy. But the two policy mixes have different effects on interest rates. An easy monetary/tight fiscal policy mix, in the Keynesian theory, leads to lower real and nominal interest rates than a tight monetary/easy fiscal policy mix.

Because the easy monetary/tight fiscal policy mix yields lower interest rates, it also results in more real investment. With lower interest rates, firms move further down and to the right along their planned-investment schedules. While low interest rates encourage investment, tax and spending policies are used to keep the consumption and government spending portions of aggregate demand from growing too quickly.

Keynesian economists of the 1960s saw no problem with federal budget deficits as a means of pulling the economy out of a recession. But they firmly believed that the deficit should disappear as the economy approaches its natural level of real output. The existence of a high budget deficit when the economy is operating near capacity would, as explained in Chapter 15, crowd out private investment. In so doing, it would, over time, tend to crowd out economic growth.

These ideas from the policy debates of the 1960s are still alive today. The Reagan administration came to office as deeply committed to economic growth as were the Democratic administrations of the 1960s. But in the Keynesian view, it is pursuing the wrong policy mix. The Reagan program used tight monetary policy to fight inflation in the early 1980s, although monetary policy—at least as conventionally measured by the growth of M1—was later relaxed. Meanwhile, fiscal policy was set on a course that would produce a large budget deficit even with the economy operating at its natural level. In his unsuccessful bid for the presidency in 1984, Walter Mondale, relying on the traditional Keynesian formula, made a shift in policy mix through higher taxes and easier monetary policy a major campaign theme.

Supply-Side Economics

A spirited defense of the Reagan administration's policy mix is offered by economists of the so-called supply-side school. **Supply-side economics** focuses on efforts to raise the growth of natural real output, particularly through the incentive effects of cuts in marginal tax rates. Supply-siders criticize Keynesians for looking only at the effects of tax policy on aggregate demand and ignoring its effects on saving, investment, and work effort.

Supply-side economics
A school of economics that focuses on efforts to increase the growth of natural real output, especially through the incentive of tax cuts.

The Supply-Side Tax Cut Program

The supply-side view strongly influenced fiscal policy during the first years of the Reagan administration. The case for that policy ran something like this. During the 1970s, productivity stagnated. A major reason for the slowdown, in the supply-siders' view, was the U.S. tax system, which was biased against saving, investment, and work effort. Inflation worsened the problem. Taxes on interest and capital gains pushed the inflation-adjusted after-tax rate of return on an added dollar of investment below zero in many cases. Depreciation allowances based on historical costs of business equipment rather than on costs adjusted for inflation drained companies of funds needed to replace worn-out equipment. While taxes discouraged investment in productive plant and equipment, tax loopholes encouraged wasteful investment in tax shelters ranging from luxury condominiums to racehorse breeding partnerships. And it was not just corporations and the wealthy who were hit by high taxes. Inflation, the progressive income tax, and the rising social security payroll tax combined to push ordinary wage earners into ever higher tax brackets. Marginal tax rates of 30 or even 40 percent on the incomes of clerks and factory workers discouraged them from improving their skills, working overtime, or even showing up regularly at their jobs.

The centerpiece of the supply-side program was to be a carefully designed set of cuts in marginal tax rates. First, these would improve work incentives by lowering the tax paid on each added dollar of earned income. Second, they would remove the bias against saving and investment by reforming capital gains taxes and depreciation allowances. Finally, they would index the tax system so that tax rates would not be pushed back up again if inflation returned.

The tax cuts passed by Congress in 1981 included many of the items on the supply-siders' wish list: lower personal tax rates, saving and investment incentives, and a reduction in capital gains taxes. (Some supply-siders were also calling for large cuts in government spending, but Congress was less willing to go along with that part of the program.) The 1986 tax law included further cuts in personal income tax rates and broadened the tax base by eliminating many loopholes, to the supply-siders' satisfaction. However, the law also contained many provisions that displeased them. High on their list of problems were increases in capital gains taxation and reduction of business investment incentives.

Tax Cuts and Deficits

Keynesians warned that the 1981 tax cuts would push up deficits. The deficits, in turn, would raise interest rates. High interest rates would crowd out investment, thereby canceling out the incentive effects of the supply-side tax cuts. But supply-side economists had an answer to this argument.

In the supply-siders' view, cuts in marginal tax rates would not have the kind of crowding-out effects their critics were predicting. For one thing, the supply-siders believed that tax cuts would boost saving. As we saw in Chapter 15, this would in itself tend to mitigate the crowding-out effect. In addition, the supply-siders said that their critics failed to take the incentive effects of tax cuts into account. The supply-siders counted on incentive effects to work in two ways. First, they designed cuts in business taxes in a way that would boost the after-tax return on investment. This would cause a rightward shift in the economy's planned-investment schedule that would cause investment to increase rather than be crowded out. Second, they believed that the incentive effects of cuts in marginal tax rates for individuals would prevent total tax revenues from falling. This last point deserves fuller explanation.

In order to forecast the effects of a tax cut on total revenue, one must predict what will happen to the *tax base*. For an income tax, the tax base means total reported income; for a sales tax, it means total sales; and so on. If the tax base is assumed to stay the same when tax rates are changed, tax revenue will be proportional to the tax rate. This is shown by the straight line in Exhibit 17.6. A revenue forecast that assumes no change in the tax base is often referred to as a *static forecast*.

If the tax base does not remain constant, a static forecast of revenues will be wrong. Supply-siders stress that the tax base tends to shrink as the tax rate rises. This happens because people have a greater incentive than before to avoid the activity that is being taxed or refrain from reporting it. In the case of an income tax, this may mean reducing work in favor of leisure or shifting work to the underground economy. In the case of taxes on investment income, it may mean investing less and consuming more or investing only in tax-sheltered projects. In the case of capital gains taxes, it may mean holding assets for longer periods before selling them. If the tax base shrinks as the tax rate rises, the revenue generated by the tax will fall short of the static forecast. This is shown by the curved line in Exhibit 17.6. Such a graph is sometimes known as a **Laffer curve,** after Arthur Laffer, a strong advocate of supply-side tax cuts.

The Laffer curve lies below the straight line of the static forecast at all points. This indicates that the static forecast will always overestimate the revenue gain from a tax increase and the revenue loss from a tax cut. Also, the Laffer

Laffer curve
A graph that shows the connection between the marginal rate at which a tax is imposed and the revenues raised by the tax.

Exhibit 17.6   Tax Rates and Revenues

The horizontal axis of this graph shows the marginal rate at which a tax is assessed; the vertical axis shows the amount of revenue the tax raises. A static estimate of the effect of the tax rate on revenue raised assumes that the tax base (total reported income for an income tax) remains fixed as the rate changes. In this case, tax revenue will be proportional to the tax rate, as shown by the straight line. In practice, however, higher tax rates have an adverse effect on incentives to earn and report income. As a result, revenue at any given tax rate tends to be lower than the static estimate. The Laffer curve takes these effects into account. It shows that beyond some point, increases in the marginal tax rate will actually reduce tax revenue. The point at which the Laffer curve reaches a peak need not be exactly a 50 percent marginal tax rate as it is here.

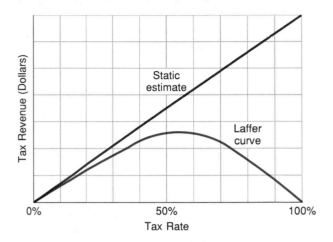

curve reaches a peak at a tax rate of less than 100 percent and then begins to turn downward. Beyond a certain point, then, the gain in tax revenue from a higher tax rate is more than offset by shrinkage in the tax base. In the extreme case of a 100 percent income tax, no one would have an incentive to earn or report income; thus, tax revenue would drop to zero.

Using their own assumptions about the incentive effects of tax cuts, the supply-siders projected large gains in the tax base and small, if any, revenue losses. In some cases, they said, the lower tax rates would raise more rather than less revenue (see "Applying Economic Ideas 17.1"). Thus, there was no reason to fear an ever growing federal deficit.

Other Aspects of the Supply-Side Program

Tax cuts were the most publicized part of the supply-side program, but there was more to it. Other measures were also planned to boost the growth rate of natural real output. Regulatory reform in transportation, communications, and financial services was intended to spur competition and productivity. Environmental regulations that were viewed as burdensome were to be eased. The welfare system was to be reformed in ways that would increase work incentives for the poor. In short, wherever the productivity slowdown of the 1970s could be blamed on public policies, those policies were to be changed.

Meanwhile, the Fed was urged to support the expected speedup of the growth of natural real output. Like everyone else, supply-siders did not want to let aggregate demand outrun the growth of real output. However, they expected natural real output to grow by as much as 5 percent per year over an extended period, in contrast to more conventional estimates of 3 percent or so even with productivity gains. Expecting more real growth, the supply-siders urged the Fed to adopt a somewhat easier monetary policy than the restrictive anti-inflationary stance of the early 1980s. For reasons having more to do with falling inflation and nominal interest rates than with the supply-side agenda, the Fed did permit more rapid money growth after mid-1982, as we have seen.

APPLYING ECONOMIC IDEAS 17.1

Revenue Response to Three Major Tax Cuts

Is it really possible for tax revenues to rise when tax rates are cut, as the Laffer curve indicates? Evidence from three major tax cuts during this century suggests that it is, at least in the highest-income groups, which are subject to the highest marginal tax rates to begin with. In the case of lower-income groups, for which marginal tax rates are inherently lower, a tax cut reduces revenue. These results are consistent with a Laffer curve such as that shown in Exhibit 17.6, which slopes upward at low marginal rates, reaches a peak, and then slopes downward at higher rates.

The data in the accompanying chart show the percentage change in tax revenues by income group for three tax cuts. The first, which was phased in from 1922 to 1925, lowered marginal tax rates from a range of 4 to 73 percent

Sources: John Mueller, "Lessons of the Tax Cuts of Yesteryear," *The Wall Street Journal*, March 5, 1981, 24, and "Soaking the Rich through Tax Cuts," *The Wall Street Journal*, March 21, 1985, 30; Lawrence B. Lindsey, "Individual Taxpayer Response to Tax Cuts 1982–1984 with Implications for the Revenue Maximizing Tax Rate" (Working Paper No. 2069, National Bureau of Economic Research, December 1986).

to one of 1.5 to 25 percent. The second, which took effect in 1964, cut marginal rates from a range of 20 to 90 percent to one of 14 to 70 percent. The third set of data refer to the effects of the first two years of the 1981 tax cuts. (The results of the 1986 tax rate reductions were unavailable at the time of this writing.)

These data support a surprising conclusion about the effect of across-the-board tax cuts: Even when the biggest cuts in marginal rates go to the highest income groups, the effect of the overall cuts is to *increase* the share of the total tax burden borne by upper-income taxpayers and to *decrease* that borne by lower-income groups. They also suggest that there must be a revenue-maximizing tax rate somewhere between the rates of 50 to 70 percent paid by the highest-income groups before 1981 and those paid by lower-income groups. Lawrence B. Lindsey of Harvard has estimated the revenue-maximizing federal income tax rate as no higher than 35 percent. The rate reductions of the 1986 tax reform law, which are just being phased in as this is written, appear to be consistent with Lindsey's estimate of the revenue-maximizing rate.

Did Supply-Side Policy Work?

The tax cuts proposed by the supply-siders began to take effect in the depths of the 1982 recession. Then, from the end of 1982 through 1984, the U.S. economy experienced its most vigorous recovery in the post–World War II period. The unemployment rate fell from a high of 10.7 percent to less than 7.5 percent. Real output grew by 3.7 percent in 1983 and by 6.7 percent in 1984, while productivity increased rapidly. Investment, bolstered by capital inflows, recovered from the low point reached in 1982. Inflation, which had fallen to a rate of about 4 percent per year during the 1982 recession, remained low. Not surprisingly, the supply-side team was ready and willing to take its share of the credit for the solid performance of the U.S. economy during those years.

However, not everyone became a convert to supply-side economics. As the pace of recovery slowed, the initial cyclical rebound of productivity growth slackened, as we saw earlier. Critics pointed out that despite the economy's rapid growth, the federal budget deficit remained very high. Although there were signs that the Laffer curve was working to raise revenues in some high tax brackets, total revenues failed to keep up with government spending. In addition, as we saw in Chapter 11, the structural budget deficit grew even more rapidly than the actual deficit.

The hoped-for gains in saving and investment simply did not materialize. Taking the period 1980 to 1985 as a whole, net private domestic saving as a share of GNP fell by almost 2 percentage points compared to the 1970s and net private

continued

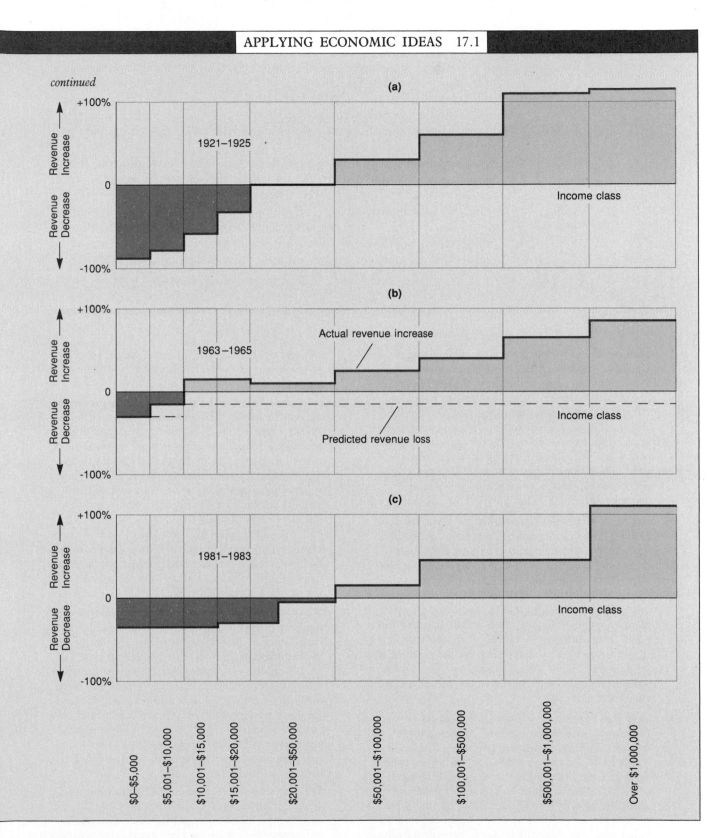

U.S. investment by 2.5 percentage points. Only increasing reliance on foreign sources of saving prevented a total collapse of investment.

In fairness to the supply-siders, it should be said that not all aspects of their program were enacted. The tax reform of 1986 fit the supply-side agenda much less closely than did that of 1981. The overall spending cuts that were supposed to go with the tax cuts were never made. Also, regulatory reform, welfare reform, and other aspects of the supply-side program were carried out only partially.

In sum, the issues raised by the supply-siders—the need to promote growth through incentives for investment and saving and to free the economy from regulatory shackles—persist today. There will be no return to the one-sided emphasis on the demand side of macroeconomic policy that characterized Keynesian economics from the Great Depression through the 1960s. But the policy influence of the supply-side school, more narrowly defined in terms of the policies and personalities prominent in the early Reagan years, has faded.

Summary

1. **How can the economy grow while maintaining price stability?** Over time, natural real output grows mainly as a result of increases in the size of the labor force and in output per worker. As natural real output shifts to the right, the short-run aggregate supply curve shifts with it. If aggregate demand is allowed to grow at the same rate as natural real output, the aggregate demand curve will shift along with the others. Under these conditions output will grow smoothly, the price level will be stable, and unemployment will remain at its natural rate.

2. **How can insufficient growth of aggregate demand cause a growth recession?** If aggregate demand does not keep up with the growth of natural real output, firms will be unable to sell all the output they are able to produce at an unchanged price level. Unplanned inventory buildup will put downward pressure on prices and cause the actual level of real output to grow more slowly than the natural level. The economy will move downward and to the left along the aggregate supply curve at the same time that the curve is shifting to the right. This is called a *growth recession*. During such a recession, real output grows but the rate of unemployment rises.

3. **How can expansion of aggregate demand beyond the growth rate of natural real output cause inflation?** If aggregate demand grows faster than natural real output, demand-pull inflation will result. In the short run, pushing the growth of aggregate demand to a rate faster than the growth of natural real output will speed the growth of real output and cut unemployment at the cost of only moderate inflation. After the initial gain, however, the trade-off between inflation and unemployment will worsen. The inflation rate will have to speed up just to keep the unemployment rate from rising.

4. **What may have caused the slowdown in productivity growth in the U.S. economy beginning in the 1970s?** During the 1970s, the rate of productivity growth fell from about 2.2 percent per year to about .6 percent. Explanations for this decline include changes in the age and gender composition of the labor force, supply shocks caused by oil price increases, inflation, a slowdown in research and development spending, and an increase in regulation. No one of these factors seems to fully explain the slowdown. Some of them have been operating in reverse during the 1980s. Although there has been a pickup in the rate of productivity growth in manufacturing, the service sector is not yet showing a healthy rate.

5. **What are the traditional Keynesian recommendations for promoting growth of real output?** Keynesian economists have long been concerned with promoting economic growth. Part of their program calls for fine-tuning the economy so as to avoid recession and inflation. They also call for a mix of macroeconomic policies that will include a balanced budget as the economy approaches the natural level of real output and a monetary policy that will permit relatively low interest rates. Keynesians have criticized the Reagan administration's policy mix for including too much fiscal stimulus.

6. **What policies are recommended by the supply-side school of economics?** *Supply-side economics* focuses on efforts to increase the growth of natural real output, especially through the incentive provided by cuts

in marginal tax rates. The Reagan administration's tax cuts were inspired in part by supply-side economics. According to this theory, well-designed cuts in marginal tax rates will result in little or no revenue loss for the government. If the incentive effect of the tax rate cuts speeds the growth rate of natural real output, monetary policy can be eased without the danger of inflation.

Terms for Review

- growth recession
- supply-side economics
- Laffer curve

Questions for Review

1. If natural real output is growing, what must happen to aggregate demand in order for prices to remain stable?

2. Under what conditions can the unemployment rate rise and the price level fall while real output is growing?

3. What are the short-run effects on inflation and unemployment if aggregate demand grows faster than natural real output? What are the long-run effects?

4. What factors contributed to the slowdown of productivity growth in the United States in the 1970s?

5. What are the main elements of the Keynesian strategy for promoting economic growth?

6. What are the main elements of the supply-side strategy for promoting economic growth?

Problems and Topics for Discussion

1. **Examining the lead-off case.** Use aggregate supply and demand curves to illustrate what happens to the economy as a result of a general improvement in the education of the labor force. In what ways does such an improvement affect real output, the price level, and economic growth? What policies regarding aggregate demand would be appropriate in response to a general improvement in the educational level of the labor force?

2. **Recent growth experience.** Using the *Economic Report of the President* or another source, find data on real GNP, the price level, and the unemployment rate for the period 1985 to 1987 and for later years, if possible. Assume that the natural rate of unemployment is 6.5 percent. Sketch a series of aggregate real supply and demand curves (including vertical lines to show the approximate level of natural real output), and discuss the movement of the economy.

3. **Stagflation.** Footnote 2 (page 420) describes what could be called a "stagflation." Draw a set of aggregate supply and demand curves to illustrate this situation.

4. **Growth with inflation.** Exhibit 17.3 illustrates growth with inflation. What would happen to the economy if, starting from the situation represented by point E_2, policymakers were to stop the growth of aggregate nominal demand while natural real output continued to grow? Use aggregate supply and demand curves to illustrate your answer.

Case for Discussion
Three Percenters versus Supply-Siders

Following are excerpts from an editorial that appeared in The Wall Street Journal *in November 1984:*

A debate—which ultimately will influence every issue of public policy in the second Reagan administration—has been clearly drawn between the "Three Percenters" and the supply-siders.

The former are those who insist the economy must be held to a 3 percent growth rate or else inflation will accelerate. The latter argue that growth can and must be at a higher rate for several years and that monetary and fiscal policies should be aimed at achieving that growth.

Three percent growth is a level barely sufficient to accommodate new entrants into the work force and a subdued pace of technological advance. It is clearly not sufficient to lower the unemployment rate below its 7 percent-plus level. It isn't enough to reduce the federal budget deficits. And it isn't enough for the economy to absorb imports from the developing world at a level that will enable these countries to service their debts to American banks.

Policymakers consider the impact of their actions on economic growth.

Where did this 3 percent idea come from? The 1981 Report of President Carter's Council of Economic Advisers originated the idea that long-term potential economic growth had slowed from nearly 4 percent a year in 1960–1973 to 3.4 percent in 1973–1983. That "sustainable pace" was mainly the sum of rapid 2.5 percent labor force growth and a pathetic 0.9 percent annual productivity increase.

We dispute this idea and observe that in the first six quarters of this recovery the sum of labor-force and productivity growth was 5.1 percent, which means potential was growing almost as fast as real GNP—even as the Three Percenters were worried about "running out of capacity."

A faster growth path is attainable. Five percent for a decade is not unrealistic. But even the more conservative 3.4 percent track cannot be reached if the Three Percenters dominate policy making and are able to force the economy to that pace by restrictive monetary and fiscal policies.

Source: Jude Wanniski, "Grip of the Three Percenters," *The Wall Street Journal*, November 8, 1984. Reprinted by permission of *The Wall Street Journal*, © Dow Jones & Company, Inc. 1984. All Rights Reserved. Photo Source: Louise Krafft/Time Magazine.

Questions

1. Suppose the supply-siders were right and potential real output (another term for natural real output) had grown at 5 percent per year but the "Three Percenters" held the annual growth of aggregate nominal demand to 3 percent. Explain what would have happened, and illustrate with a diagram.

2. Suppose the supply-siders were wrong and potential real output grew by only 3 percent per year. However, they persuaded fiscal and monetary policymakers to allow aggregate demand to grow by 5 percent per year. Explain what will happen, and illustrate with a diagram.

3. Suppose you are a policymaker and are unsure how rapidly natural real output is growing. Which risk would you rather take—that of letting aggregate nominal demand grow too quickly or that of letting it grow too slowly? Why?

4. Despite real GNP growth of less than 3 percent per year from the end of 1984 to mid-1987, the unemployment rate fell from over 7 percent to under 6 percent. What would Okun's law suggest about the growth of natural real output over this period?

Suggestions for Further Reading

Fink, Richard H., ed. *Supply Side Economics: A Critical Appraisal*. Frederick, Md.: University Publications of America, 1983.

This volume contains papers on all aspects of supply-side economics by authors with a wide range of views.

Gordon, Robert J. *Macroeconomics*, 3d ed. Boston: Little, Brown, 1984.

Chapter 18 discusses economic growth and the productivity slowdown.

Reich, Robert B. *The Next American Frontier*. New York: Times Books, 1983.

A liberal lawyer at Harvard's Kennedy School of Government makes a case for promoting economic growth and suggests ways of doing so.

Reinhardt, Uve. "Reaganomics, RIP." *New Republic*, April 20, 1987, 24–27.

A very negative appraisal of the "supply-side experiment."

18 Strategies for Economic Stabilization

After reading this chapter, you will understand . . .

- Why Keynesian economists favor active use of fiscal and monetary policy to stabilize the economy.
- What are the implications of lags and forecasting errors for the conduct of discretionary policy.
- Why politics may interfere with the conduct of stabilization policy.
- What kinds of rules have been proposed for the conduct of monetary policy.
- What kinds of rules have been proposed for the conduct of fiscal policy.

Before reading this chapter, make sure you know the meaning of . . .

- Business cycle (Chapter 8)
- Budget process (Chapter 11)
- Cyclical and structural deficits (Chapter 11)
- Velocity and money demand (Chapter 14)
- Real and nominal interest rates (Chapter 15)

It Is Now within Our Capabilities . . .

Written during the presidency of Lyndon B. Johnson, the 1966 report of the President's Council of Economic Advisers describes the "new economics."

Two decades of economic analysis and policy experience have shaped the development of a revised economic policy. By some, current policy has been labeled the "new economics." . . .

An industrial economy is vulnerable to cumulative upward and downward movements in activity, so evident in our long-term record. . . . In the future as in the past, policies to avert recession cannot wait until imbalances develop and the signs of a downturn are clear. The fact that economic activity is rising cannot be an assurance of continued growth if the expansion is too slow to match the growth of productive capacity. Nor can a strong level of investment be relied on to sustain expansion if it threatens an excessive growth of productive capacity. Recognizing these tasks, government must apply its fiscal and monetary policies continuously to sustain and support a balanced expansion, sometimes by moderating the strength of an excessive investment boom, sometimes by adding to the strength of lagging final demand. The best defense against recession is a policy to sustain continued expansion. . . .

The ability of economists to diagnose and forecast on the basis of current facts and to evaluate the impact of alternative policy measures is a key determinant of what policy can do to maintain stable balanced growth. Our economic knowledge has made great advances in the past generation, but many important questions remain, answers to which should be and can be improved through further research. . . .

But while much remains to be learned about our economy, it would be a disservice to understate the power of economic analysis, and to underrate the substantial contribution of the profession to the successful course of our economy in the postwar period. . . .

While important problems remain, we are nonetheless at an historic point of accomplishment and promise. Twenty years of experience have demonstrated our ability to avoid ruinous inflations and severe depressions. It is now within our capabilities to set more ambitious goals. We strive to avoid recurrent recessions, to keep unemployment far below rates of the past decade, to maintain price stability at full employment, to move toward the Great Society, and, indeed, to make full prosperity the normal state of the American economy. It is a tribute to our success . . . that we now have not only the economic understanding but also the will and determination to use economic policy as an effective tool for progress.

Source: President's Council of Economic Advisers, *Economic Report of the President* (Washington, D.C.: Government Printing Office, 1966), 180–186. Photo Source: Courtesy of the Library of Congress.

T HESE words are from the 1966 report of the President's Council of Economic Advisers. The report was signed by three of the most distinguished professionals ever to sit on that body: Gardner Ackley, its chairman, Otto Eckstein, and Arthur Okun. The 1960s marked the high-water mark of post–World War II Keynesianism—what was then called the "new economics." In this chapter, we examine the approach to economic policy outlined in these passages in light of the U.S. economic experience of the 1970s and 1980s. We also discuss the different approach to policy recommended by the monetarists and new classical economists.

The Debate over Policy Activism

Chapter 8 called attention to the fact that the economy does not grow steadily year after year but tends to go through a business cycle. Growth is halted from time to time by recessions. When the economy recovers from a recession, it often overshoots its natural level of output. The resulting boom periods are followed by new recessions. This pattern has been observed for more than a century (see Exhibit 8.4, page 195).

Nobody really likes the business cycle. It is disruptive and wasteful in both dollar and human terms. Almost all economists agree that the right policy could moderate the swings in the business cycle. But behind this general agreement lies one of the major debates in economics today: Just what kind of policy is right for dealing with the business cycle?

Keynesians, Monetarists, and New Classicists

On the one hand, there are the heirs to the Keynesian tradition. These are *policy activists* who see the business cycle as a flaw in the capitalist system that the government must try to correct. They perceive the source of the problem as unpredicted ups and downs in consumer confidence, investment plans, the foreign trade balance, and the demand for money and credit. These cause shifts in aggregate demand that are amplified by the multiplier effect.

To moderate the business cycle, government should actively use monetary and fiscal policy to offset disturbances arising in the private sector. Whether the business cycle is on an upward or downward swing, government should lean against the wind in order to shorten recessions and restrain booms.

On the other hand, there are the monetarists, joined today by many economists of the new classical school and others who do not identify closely with any one school of thought. They tend to see mistakes in government policy behind all but the mildest swings of the business cycle. To be sure, they say, there are unpredicted ups and downs in the spending plans of households and firms. But the private economy has built-in stabilizers that prevent serious depressions, prolonged unemployment, and persistent inflation. The really bad episodes—the Great Depression, the double-digit inflation of the 1970s—can be traced to policy errors. In this view, things got out of hand in these cases because attempts to fine-tune the economy only made things worse.

Over the years, the issue of policy activism versus policy rules has come to dominate the long-standing debate among Keynesians and monetarists, now joined by new classicists. The issues of the power of fiscal and monetary policy and the nature of the transmission mechanism discussed in Chapter 15 have taken a back seat; in fact, the gap between Keynesians and monetarists on these issues has narrowed greatly. However, Keynesians tend to argue that fiscal and monetary policies should both be used actively, whereas monetarists and new classicists claim that both should be guided by stable, long-term *policy rules*.

The Case for Policy Activism

The case for policy activism rests on three assumptions that are clearly set forth in the passages quoted at the beginning of the chapter. Although they might be expressed somewhat more cautiously today than they were in 1966, these assumptions are still widely shared.

First, modern Keynesians share the view that the private economy is inherently unstable: "An industrial economy is vulnerable to cumulative upward and downward movements in activity, so evident in our long-term record." Because of rigidities and unresponsiveness, the economy's powers of self-stabilization are weak. Put in terms of our model, modern Keynesians would say that although there is always a theoretical long-term equilibrium where aggregate supply and demand curves cross at the natural level of output, the economy cannot be counted on to move smoothly or rapidly to that point following a disturbance.

Second, proponents of policy activism are confident in economists' ability to forecast the future course of the economy and the effects of policy within an at least workable margin of error: "The ability of economists to diagnose and forecast on the basis of current facts and to evaluate the impact of alternative policy measures is a key determinant of what policy can do. . . . It would be a disservice to understate the power of economic analysis." Further, policy activists are certain that answers to remaining questions can be found through ongoing research.

Third, they are confident that those who wield political authority in the White House and on Capitol Hill will heed the technical advice given to them by economists: "It is a tribute to our success . . . that we now have not only the economic understanding but also the will and determination to use economic policy as an effective tool for progress."

Given these assumptions, the policymaker's job involves continuous application of policy to keep the economy on a course of balanced expansion. As an analogy, think of yourself as the captain of an ocean liner. You are steering your ship through waters in which treacherous winds and currents threaten to push it off course at every moment. Your tools for controlling the ship are the engine telegraph, which regulates the ship's engine speed, and the wheel, which controls the ship's rudder.

You can predict the effects of any movement of the controls. For example, calling for full speed ahead will cause the ship to reach its maximum speed of 30 knots; turning the wheel to the right will swing the rudder and cause the ship to turn; and so on. Your ship is not a sports car—it takes a long (but predictable) time to stop or turn it. Because of the time it takes the controls to act, you must look and plan ahead. Fortunately, you have satellite reports that warn you of changes in wind speed and radar to tell you the course and location of other ships in your area. You are ultimately responsible for the ship, but you would not think of disputing the technical judgments of your navigator, engineer, and harbor pilot.

So it is in the policy activists' world if you are the president or the chairman of the Federal Reserve Board. You have at your command levers and wheels labeled "taxes," "government spending," and "money supply." You have computerized models of the economy that, combined with the judgments of professional forecasters, predict what will happen to real output, employment, the price level, and interest rates when you pull any of these levers or turn the wheels. Your staff economists give you frequent updates warning you of trends in investment, money demand, and other factors that you may have to offset with policy actions. You agree with other policymakers and congressional leaders that prices should be kept stable, unemployment at its natural rate, and real output growing in step with increases in its natural level. Also, you are willing to draw on the technical judgments of your economic advisers.

To be sure, there is more uncertainty in running the economy than in steering an ocean liner. Even the most ardent policy activists admit that the appropriate policy stance is not always clear and that mistakes will be made. These will cause the economy to drift off course now and then; the business cycle will be moderated but not eliminated. Even so, policy activists believe that the best way to stay on course is to adjust the controls quickly at the first sign of impending trouble.

Are Policymakers' Tools Adequate?

Monetarists and new classicists find fault with all of the activists' assumptions. They have more faith in the economy's powers of self-stabilization and see policy errors as the most serious source of instability. They do not think the tools and forecasts available to policymakers are good enough to do the job, even with the best of intentions. They also doubt the ability of the U.S. political system to focus on consistent long-run economic goals. Let's look at the case against policy activism, beginning with the second of these issues: whether policymakers have adequate tools for the job.

The activists assume that the government has a set of tools that can directly affect aggregate demand and indirectly influence real output, employment, and the price level. Their critics wonder how adequate these tools really are. Monetarists agree that monetary and fiscal policy affect aggregate demand, but they argue that changes in aggregate demand have only short-term effects on real output and employment. In the long run, they say, the economy always returns to the natural level of real output and the natural unemployment rate. On this point the new classicists are even more skeptical than the monetarists: They doubt the ability of anticipated changes in monetary and fiscal policy to affect real output and employment even in the short run.

Then there is the related problem of predictability. Unless the effects of monetary and fiscal policies can be predicted, policy activists will not know how hard to pull their levers and twist their dials. They depend partly on large-scale computer models to predict the effects of any given policy. These models, although very elaborate, have the same basic structure as those used in this course. They will make accurate predictions only if the correct values are used for the marginal propensity to consume, the expenditure multipliers, the crowding-out effect, the money multiplier, and so on. However, different computer models give widely varying values for these constants. How can policy activists fine-tune the economy, ask the critics, if they cannot be sure about how much of a policy change is needed to produce a desired effect?

Policy activists consult the same computer models to forecast where the economy is headed in order to decide what corrections are needed. As "Perspective 18.1" shows, the record of forecasting in the past couple of decades has been mixed at best. During tranquil periods, the forecasting models have not done badly. However, they missed crucial turning points in 1973 to 1975, 1979 to 1980, and 1981 to 1982. The average of the various forecasts is often significantly far from the mark, and the forecasts typically encompass a wide range of policy outcomes as well.

The Problem of Lags

In addition to challenging the assumptions on which the case for fine-tuning is based, the critics make much of the problem of delays, or *lags*, in the policymaking process. Two kinds of lags deserve attention. The delay between the time when a policy change is needed and the time when a decision is made is called the **inside lag.** The delay between the time when a decision is made and the time when it has its main effect on the economy is known as the **outside lag.**

Lags in Monetary Policy

For monetary policy, the inside lag is fairly short. Financial information is available most rapidly and monetary data within one to a few weeks. Data on inflation and unemployment are available to the Federal Reserve within a month. Data on changes in real output are available in estimated form within three months. Once the Fed has data on changes in the economy, it can quickly decide to make whatever policy changes are needed. The Federal Open Market Committee—the chief monetary policymaking body of the Federal Reserve System—meets at least eight times a year. If discretionary action is needed between meetings, the committee holds telephone conferences.

The outside lag for monetary policy is a good deal longer than the inside lag, and it also varies. Monetarist studies indicate that slowing the rate of money stock growth in the post–World War II period has slowed the rate of growth of real output only some 3 to 12 months later and has lowered the inflation rate only with an even longer lag. An increase in the rate of money stock growth appears to behave with a similar lag.

Inside lag
The delay between the time a policy change is needed and the time a decision is made.

Outside lag
The delay between the time a policy decision is made and the time the policy change affects the economy.

PERSPECTIVE 18.1

The Accuracy of Economic Forecasts

Economic forecasts—predictions of GNP, inflation, unemployment, and interest rates for the months or years ahead—are regular items of business news, and for good reason. Knowledge of future demand conditions, prices, and credit market conditions is of great value to decision makers in business and government. The thirst for knowledge about the future is a multi-million-dollar business for such forecasting firms as Data Resources Incorporated and Chase Econometrics Associates. Government agencies, including the Federal Reserve System, the Office of Management and Budget, and the Congressional Budget Office, also have large budgets for forecasting.

But despite all the money spent, the track record of economic forecasting leaves much to be desired. A study by two economists at the Federal Reserve Bank of Boston pinpoints some forecasts that were especially bad:

- In 1973 to 1975, forecasters missed the surge in inflation and unemployment rates. They underesti-

Source: Stephen K. McNees and John Ries, "The Track Record of Macroeconomic Forecasts," *New England Economic Review* (November-December 1983): 5–18.

mated inflation by three to four percentage points and unemployment by more than two percentage points. At the same time, they underestimated the severity of the recession.

- In 1978 to 1979, they again failed to forecast a surge in inflation.

- In 1981, they underestimated the speed of the recovery from the short recession of the previous year. Just as they adjusted their forecasts to show strong growth, the economy fell back into recession. This left the GNP forecasts of five of the leading forecasters as much as four percentage points too high—the worst errors of any recent period.

In the forecasters' defense, the Federal Reserve Bank study points out that the forecasters did fairly well in the tranquil periods of 1970 to 1972 and 1975 to 1978. But that is not always good enough for decision makers in business and government. What they want is the ability to foresee turning points and unusual changes in the behavior of the economy. This the forecasters seem unable to deliver.

Lags in Fiscal Policy

Overall lags for fiscal policy seem longer but harder to measure. The long inside lag for fiscal policy is a result of the budget process, in which the administration must first decide on the need for a policy action and then submit a proposal to Congress (see Chapter 11). Consider some examples:

- President Kennedy's advisers began urging him to ask for a tax cut soon after he took office early in 1961, but a proposal was not submitted to Congress until 1962. Congress did not pass the tax cut until 1964, some three years after the need for it had become clear.

- In the late 1960s, during the Vietnam War, President Johnson resisted his economists' advice to raise taxes for almost two years. In that case, Congress acted quickly on the call for a tax surcharge once it was submitted.

- During the 1974 to 1975 recession, President Ford called for tax cuts, including a one-time tax rebate. Congress again acted swiftly. Even so, however, the rebate was not paid out until the month in which unemployment hit its peak. The rebate thus came in time to help speed the recovery but not in time to shorten the recession.

- Congress also acted fairly promptly (within nine months) on President Reagan's call for tax cuts in 1981. However, the cuts were phased in over three years. Only the first phase of the tax cuts came while the economy was still in recession; the rest went into effect after the recovery was already under way.

On the basis of these examples, the inside lag for fiscal policy appears to range from about six months to more than three years. Also, there is a fairly long outside lag for fiscal policy. This is the length of time it takes the multiplier effect to work itself out once a change has been made in taxes or government spending. Some effect on aggregate demand is felt very quickly, but various computer models differ widely in their estimates of how long it takes for the bulk of the effect to be felt. Some models show the peak effect coming only six months after policy action has been taken. Others indicate that the peak effect is not felt for two years. All the models agree that a fiscal policy action continues to affect the economy to some degree as long as three years later.

The total lag for fiscal policy is the sum of the inside and outside lags. At best, the total lag is no less than a year. This allows the President only six months to make a proposal and Congress to act on it and six more months for the multiplier effect to be carried out. However, a total lag of several years is quite possible.

Interaction of Lags and Forecasting Errors
Lags mean that policymakers cannot wait until a problem develops before taking action. If they do, the measures they take to boost the economy during a recession will not take effect until the recovery is already under way. The result may be the turning of a normal recovery into an inflationary boom. Actions intended to restrain the inflation might take effect only after the economy is already plunging into the next recession.

To avoid this problem, policymakers must act on the basis of forecasts. If they know that a recession will begin in a year or two, they can take action now. If they know when inflation will begin to develop, they can adjust money growth or taxes in time to prevent it. But what if the forecasts are faulty, as they often are to at least some degree? A policy of stimulus or restraint based on a faulty forecast is as likely to make things worse as it is to make them better.

Political Problems of Policy Activism

Many activists would agree that lags and forecasting errors are good reasons to proceed with caution. However, they claim that following their advice, even if not perfect, is better than doing nothing and letting the business cycle run its course. At this point, their critics bring up the third assumption on which the case for policy activism is based. The problem, they say, is that even when economists are able to offer valid advice, policymakers may not follow it. They see two main reasons for this.

First, policymakers must respond to the political signals reaching them through the apparatus of democratic politics and not just to the technical advice of their staffs. When things go wrong with the economy, there is great political pressure to "do something." For example, as the economy slides into a recession, there is pressure to create jobs. However, the political pressure reaches a peak not at the time when the recession is forecast or when it first begins; instead, it peaks around the time the recession reaches its trough, which is after the time for action has passed. A spending program or tax cut that is undertaken at the trough of a recession, when unemployment is at its highest, will not create jobs when they are needed most. Instead, it will add to inflationary pressures six months to two years later, after a recovery is already under way.

Second, there is the tendency of politics to stress the short run. This is a problem because the short-run effects of economic policies often differ from their long-run effects. Take, for example, the effects of an expansionary fiscal or monetary policy. If an expansionary policy is applied when real output is at its natural rate, the short-run effects will be an increase in real output and a reduction in unemployment as the economy moves upward along its aggregate supply curve. Only moderate inflation will result at first. However, the long-run effects of a sustained expansionary policy are less positive. To keep real output high and unemployment low, policymakers must be willing to accept ongoing inflation, probably at an ever increasing rate. Reversing the expansionary policy in order to get rid of the inflation is likely to cause an inflationary recession.

In the U.S. political system, the next congressional or presidential election is never more than two years away—not a long time when compared to the lags in macroeconomic policy. As a result, critics of policy activism say, fiscal policymakers who will soon be running for reelection are under pressure to produce short-term results. They will want it to look as though they are doing something to help the economy as the election approaches. If the policy has negative long-term effects . . . well, those will not be felt until after the election.

The critics do not see the problem as one of bad intentions on the part of politicians. Instead, they perceive it as the result of intelligent, well-intentioned people's reaction to the pressures of the system in which they operate. In their view, the case for fiscal fine-tuning, already weakened by lags and forecasting errors, should be thrown out of court because of these political problems.

The Fed and the Time-Inconsistency Problem

What about Federal Reserve officials? New-classicist critics believe that monetary policymakers, despite their 14-year terms, also face a problem of inconsistency between their long-term and short-term goals.

To understand this so-called time-inconsistency problem, suppose that the Fed announces a long-term intention to keep the money stock from growing more quickly than needed in order to keep aggregate demand growing at the same rate as natural real output. If carried out, this policy will eliminate inflation in the long run. If firms and workers believe the Fed's announcement, they will base their plans on the expectation of zero inflation, and the economy will avoid cost-push pressures having their origins in inflationary expectations. The economy will tend toward the natural level of real output with price stability.

Once this happy state of affairs is established, however, the Fed will face a temptation: Why not speed up money growth for a time, causing the aggregate demand curve to shift rightward more rapidly than natural real output? If this is done at a time when people still expect long-term price stability, there will be only a little inflation and a relatively big gain in real output. Then, before expectations have fully adjusted to the faster money growth, the Fed could issue another reassuring policy announcement claiming that its goal is still consistent with long-term price stability.

The trouble with this policy, say the critics, is that the temptation to depart from announced long-term goals to achieve desirable short-term results will cause both the expected and actual inflation rates to drift upward over time. New classicists think that under the assumption of rational expectations, the public would see through the policymakers' temptation from the beginning and, as a result, expect higher inflation all along. In this case, the surprise element in more expansionary policy would be lost. Indeed, monetary policy would have to become more expansionary, meeting the public's expectation of more rapid inflation, simply to avoid a drop in real output as the aggregate supply curve shifted upward. The long-term result—persistent inflation with unemployment no lower than the natural rate—would not be optimal even though each short-term departure from the long-term goals was made with the best intentions given the circumstances.

Implications for Stability

The combination of lags, forecasting errors, and political problems leads critics of activism finally to challenge the first of the activists' assumptions—that the economy is inherently unstable. They look at the same historical record of instability and see not an inherent vulnerability to cyclical disturbances but a record of policy errors that have transformed mild cyclical disturbances into serious ones. Exhibit "A" is the Great Depression. As we have seen, monetarists especially see policy errors—above all, the Fed's failure to resist the collapse of the money stock—as a key cause of the Depression. Exhibit "B" is the Great Inflation of the 1970s. In the critics' interpretation of events, the attempts of the "new economists" to "set more ambitious goals" and "keep unemployment far below" rates of the 1950s and 1960s did not usher in an era of stable growth; instead, the economy was subjected to erratic swings of policy. Not only did this raise the inflation rate; it also made the damage from various supply shocks, especially the oil price increases, worse than it need have been.

While they admit that mistakes have been made, believers in discretionary policy point to the relatively placid 1950s and 1960s as evidence of reasonably successful stabilization policy. They also cite the early to mid-1980s as an example of successful disinflationary monetary policy despite the transitional costs in terms of unemployment. Even in the case of the turbulent 1970s, at least some of them would say that actions that turned out to be inflationary accurately reflected public sentiment that it was better to take the pain of oil price shocks in the form of higher prices than in the form of higher unemployment rates.

Who is right? There is reason to believe that the question cannot be answered simply by looking back at the record. The problem is that the question of whether activist policies worked better or worse than the alternatives requires assessing how the alternative nonactivist policies would have done. And it is inherently difficult to assess how the alternative policies would have worked on the basis of historical data that were generated entirely under an activist regime.

The Search for Policy Rules

The difficulty of proving their case against activism has not kept the critics from developing alternatives of their own. These alternatives propose that activist policy be replaced by some form of long-term policy rule. In view of lags and forecasting errors, they say, it is better to follow rules that are correct on the average than to follow an activist policy that is just as likely to do harm as good.

They claim that as an added benefit, strict policy rules will prevent decision makers from bowing to short-run political temptations regardless of the long-term effects.

However, the argument that policy rules are safer than activists' fine-tuning is only part of the case. To complete it, critics of policy activism need to spell out in detail the rules they wish policymakers to follow and to give an indication of their effects. The fact that the rules have never been tried means that proof is hard to come by; thus, arguments in their support must be based on theory and inferential evidence. Under these circumstances, it is not surprising that there is not full agreement even among those who favor policy rules in principle. In the following sections, we will look first at some proposed rules for monetary policy and then briefly at some proposed fiscal policy rules.

Rules for Monetary Policy

A Monetary Growth Rule

The original monetarist proposal for a policy rule was to have the Fed peg the growth of the money stock to a preannounced constant rate. If the money stock rose above that rate, the Fed would slow it down with open market sales of securities; if it grew too slowly, the Fed would speed it up with open market purchases.

According to the original version of this rule, the growth rate of the money stock would be set at 3 percent per year—about equal to the long-run average growth rate of natural real output in the first 25 years after World War II. Thus, as growth of natural real output shifts the economy's aggregate supply curve to the right, the monetarist rule is supposed to let the aggregate demand curve shift just enough to keep up on the average. Such a policy would permit steady growth of real output without inflation.

The money growth rule avoids problems of lags and forecasts. The Fed receives data on changes in the money supply within a week or two and can adjust open market operations within a few hours. However, it has a potential flaw: Stabilizing money supply growth will stabilize the overall economy only if velocity is constant. (Recall that *velocity* is the ratio of nominal national income to the quantity of money.) If velocity rises, aggregate demand will grow at a rate greater than 3 percent even if money is held to its 3 percent target. Assuming constant growth of natural real output, a sustained rise in velocity will cause inflation. Likewise, if velocity falls, aggregate demand will grow by less than 3 percent even with the money supply on target. This could result in a recession or at least a growth recession.

How stable has velocity been? Exhibit 18.1 shows the behavior of velocity since 1950. From the early 1950s to 1982, M1 velocity rose at an annual rate of about 3 percent per year. In the mid-1980s, the trend was broken and M1 velocity dropped sharply. Throughout the period, the rate of change of velocity has varied from year to year and quarter to quarter. By comparison, M2 velocity does not exhibit the strong upward trend, but it does show proportionately greater year-to-year variations.

The behavior of velocity has led some economists to reject the monetarist proposal. Given the pattern of M1 velocity, they say, a 3 percent growth rate for M1 would not have prevented inflation during the 1960s and 1970s. If M2 rather than M1 had been subject to a 3 percent target, there might have been less

Exhibit 18.1 The Income Velocity of Money in the United States

As this chart shows, the income velocity of M1 rose along a trend of about 3 percent per year from the early 1950s to the early 1980s, with some quarter-to-quarter variations. In the mid-1980s, the trend was broken by a pronounced decline in M1 velocity. M2 velocity (not shown) lacked the strong upward trend of M1 velocity but demonstrated greater quarter-to-quarter and year-to-year variations, and also declined in the early 1980s.

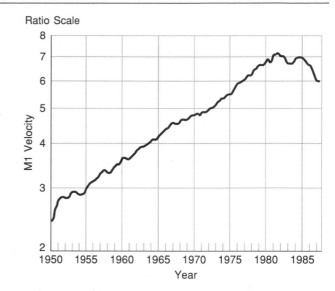

Source: Federal Reserve Board of Governors.

cumulative inflation, but there would have been larger swings in aggregate demand from year to year. Further, adherence to a steady rate of money growth during the drop in both M1 and M2 velocity in the 1980s would have precluded recovery from the 1982 recession.

Milton Friedman and other monetarists respond that the behavior of velocity is largely the result of rising inflation during the 1960s and 1970s and disinflation in the 1980s. Their reasoning is as follows. Rising inflation pushes nominal interest rates higher as lenders demand and borrowers accept an "inflation premium" tacked onto the customary real interest rate. As the nominal interest rate rises, the quantity of money demanded per dollar of GNP falls, as we saw in Chapter 14. Since money demanded per dollar of GNP is the reciprocal of velocity, velocity increases when the nominal interest rate rises and decreases when it falls.

The monetarists say that had the Fed maintained a stable rate of money growth throughout the post–World War II period, the extremes of inflation of the 1970s would have been avoided. To be sure, there still would have been disturbances caused by shocks to aggregate demand and supply and possibly others resulting from institutional changes in the financial system. But there would have been no buildup of inflation to the double-digit levels that pushed short-term nominal interest rates near 20 percent at times during the early 1980s. Nor would it have been necessary to endure the wrenching process of disinflation in the early 1980s, which abruptly lowered nominal interest rates and velocity. In short, say the monetarists, the apparent instability of velocity is not inherent in the structure of the economy; rather, it is largely an artifact of past policy mistakes.

A Nominal National Income Rule

By no means does everyone accept the monetarist argument that variations in velocity are not a serious problem. Thinking that such variation will persist even if discretionary policy is replaced by a policy rule, a number of economists, including some former monetarists, have concluded that the Fed should use nominal national income instead of the money stock as a policy target. The Fed should aim for a constant 3 percent growth of nominal GNP, in the process automatically offsetting variations in velocity with fluctuations in money growth. They claim that this would do a better job of holding the economy to a course of inflation-free growth. Given a fixed growth path for nominal GNP, consider what would happen if, for example, inflation accelerated. Real output would be squeezed, unemployment would rise above its natural rate, and inflation would start to decelerate. When price stability returned, real output would once again resume growing in step with the 3 percent trend of nominal GNP.

However, a nominal national income target has its own problems. One is that data on national income do not become available as quickly as data on the money supply. A second is that a variety of factors other than monetary policy—fiscal policy, for one—also affect nominal national income. A third is that the Fed can control nominal national income only indirectly, by adjusting the money supply. But changes in the money supply act on aggregate nominal demand only with a lag. Therefore, in order to stabilize the growth of nominal national income, the Fed would have to rely on forecasts of velocity. As with discretionary policy, this would raise the problem of possible destabilization due to actions that aim at stabilizing the growth of nominal GNP but take effect only after the conditions that necessitated them have passed. In short, the problems of lags and forecasting errors creep in through the window after having been thrown out through the door.

There is yet another problem: A fixed growth rate for nominal GNP will not work well unless natural real output grows at the same fixed rate. During a productivity slowdown such as that of the 1970s, a nominal national income rule would produce inflation. During a period of faster than expected productivity growth, such a rule could lead to a growth recession.

A Price Level Rule

These problems have led some other economists to propose yet another rule for monetary policy—one that sets its sights on a stable price level. Under such a rule, the Fed would drain reserves from the banking system if the price level rose and inject new reserves into the system if it fell. This rule would keep aggregate demand synchronized with natural real output even if the growth rate of natural real output varied from year to year.

Unfortunately, a price level rule raises the same problems of lags and forecasting errors as does a nominal national income rule. Also, a price level rule works poorly when a supply shock shifts the aggregate supply curve upward. To keep the price level from rising in the face of a supply shock, the Fed would have to reduce the money supply, shifting the aggregate demand curve to the left. This would cause a substantial loss of real output and a sharp rise in unemployment. But as we pointed out in Chapter 16, many economists think it is better to respond to a supply shock with some increase in aggregate demand, at least if the shock is likely to be long lasting. This would allow the price level to rise, but a supply shock would hurt the economy in some way no matter what was done. In this case, the pain of a little inflation probably would be less severe than that of a major recession.

The Fed's Position

To date, the Fed has adopted none of the proposed policy rules. The Fed agrees that a stable monetary policy is needed. As required by law, it announces target ranges for various measures of money and credit growth each year, although these targets are not binding. It also announces projections of nominal and real GNP, the GNP deflator, and the unemployment rate that FOMC members think would be consistent with the projected path of monetary policy. The Fed concurs that lags and forecasting errors make fine-tuning a dangerous game. But it also insists that there is no one policy rule that works well for all conditions. An inflexible money growth rule would not let the Fed respond to unexpected changes in velocity as in the mid-1980s. Attaining a nominal income rule would be beyond the Fed's power, and would risk instability over time. Further, the price level rule would not let the Fed respond flexibly enough to supply shocks, such as the oil price rises of 1974 and 1979 to 1980. For these reasons, the Fed emphasizes the need for judgment and discretion in conducting monetary policy. It reserves the right to depart from its announced guidelines for money growth when necessary, as specified by law.

Rules for Fiscal Policy

Fiscal policy rules raise a different set of issues than do monetary policy rules. One reason is that, as we have noted, there is no single set of policymakers in charge of fiscal policy. Instead, policies regarding taxes, government spending, and the deficit are the outcome of a political process in which not only Congress and the executive branch of the federal government but also state governments and state legislatures are involved. In the process by which these various bodies set fiscal policy, macroeconomic goals are often overshadowed by issues of social policy, defense policy, and vote trading. Even when tax cuts or job programs focus on macroeconomic issues, political factors such as elections are likely to affect their timing.

Another difference between fiscal and monetary policy is that fiscal policy deals with more types of policy actions. Discussions of monetary policy come down to decisions about how large open market operations should be or at what level the discount rate should be set. In the case of fiscal policy, it is not enough just to determine overall targets for taxes, transfers, and government purchases. Instead, decisions must be made regarding the thousands of expenditure programs and countless provisions of federal tax law, their relationship to state and local government fiscal policies, and so on. Any changes will have microeconomic and political impacts quite apart from their effects on aggregate demand.

Given these complexities, most proposed policy rules do not call for active use of fiscal policy as a tool of economic stabilization. Instead, they have the more modest aim of making fiscal policy less likely to be a source of instability. The greatest need, in many economists' view, is that of setting up a firm link between spending and taxes, that is, a set of rules regarding the federal deficit.

An Annually Balanced Budget

The most drastic proposal for a fiscal rule—possibly in the form of a constitutional amendment—would require the federal government to balance its budget each year. Any revenue shortfall would have to be made up right away by either raising taxes or cutting spending.

Proposals for an annually balanced federal budget score high in public opinion polls. Many people think that the government should be forced to live within its means just as they themselves are. But an annually balanced budget is not favored by many economists. The principal reason is that, as explained in Chapter 11, tax revenues tend to fall during a recession while transfer payments tend to rise. To maintain an annually balanced budget, then, taxes would have to be raised or spending cut during a recession. But these actions would cut aggregate demand just when output was already declining, tending to worsen the recession. Thus, an annually balanced budget might well make the economy not more but less stable than it is now.

A Cyclically Balanced Budget

To overcome this problem, some economists suggest that the budget should be balanced only over the business cycle. During recessions, a cyclical deficit would be permitted. When the economy was well into the expansion phase, the budget would be required to show a cyclical surplus. At all times the structural deficit would be held at zero.

A cyclically balanced budget would strengthen the economy's automatic stabilizers. However, it is not clear how the proposal could be put into practice. It does not lend itself to a simple constitutional amendment. In making spending decisions, the president and Congress would have to be guided by technical assessments of the economy's natural level of real output—a controversial matter. Also, policymakers would have to rely on technical forecasts of the levels of tax receipts and spending if the economy were at the natural level. Who would be punished and how if the forecasts or technical assessments turned out to be wrong? Answers to these questions are far from obvious.

Lessons of the Gramm-Rudman-Hollings Experiment

Congress struggled with these issues in 1985 when it formulated the Gramm-Rudman-Hollings law. The result was an elaborate system of triggers and automatic adjustment rules. The basic aim of the law, as Chapter 11 explained, was to force across-the-board cuts in federal expenditures (with important politically protected exceptions) sufficient to meet a scheduled set of reductions in the federal deficit. The size of the required cuts was to be determined by averaging forecasts of the Office of Management and Budget (OMB), an executive branch agency, and the Congressional Budget Office (CBO), part of the legislative branch.

The Gramm-Rudman-Hollings law contained two safety valves for dealing with the problem of recessions. If both the OMB and the CBO forecast a recession, the House and Senate would be required to vote on a joint resolution temporarily discarding the deficit limits. Also, if actual real growth fell below 1 percent for two successive quarters, such a vote would be triggered. However, even these safety valves left open the possibility that automatic spending cuts could be required during a period when growth had slowed to just over 1 percent per year. In such a situation, the cuts might turn a mild growth recession into something more serious.

The danger that a balanced budget rule would prove destabilizing would be reduced if the Fed were able to offset automatic fiscal restraint with discretionary monetary expansion. If both fiscal and monetary policy were "tied to the mast" by rules, however, there would be more cause for concern.

The Supreme Court found the rules of the original Gramm-Rudman-Hollings law unconstitutional. Revised rules passed by Congress in 1987 have not been tested at this writing. Some have taken the Gramm-Rudman-Hollings experience as evidence that the job can be done properly only by constitutional amendment. But others have drawn the opposite conclusion: The required rules for automatic cuts, compromises on forecasting technicalities, and safety valves are too complex to embody in a constitutional amendment.

The State of the Debate

What can we conclude from the current state of the debate over policy activism versus policy rules? Over the years, the two sides have come closer together on many points. For example, both agree that stopping inflation is not easy; it is better to have a strategy that will keep inflation from getting out of hand in the first place. Policy activists recognize that forecasting errors and lags are serious problems. Those who favor policy rules admit that there may be no one rule that works perfectly all the time. What differences remain?

Technical Differences

The technical differences that remain revolve around how best to deal with lags and forecasting errors and whether any policy rule would be adequate under all of the various circumstances that the economy encounters. On these issues, some economists see a middle ground: If activists are unwilling to see human policymakers replaced with rigid rules, why not at least develop a somewhat more flexible set of rules to guide policymakers' actions? To return to the ocean liner example, this approach would not put the ship on automatic pilot, but neither would it leave the course entirely up to the captain's moods. Instead, the captain would be required to announce the chosen course in advance and react to unforeseen events according to the guidelines contained in a seamanship manual.

The Fed has already moved in this direction in that it now announces target growth ranges for money and credit for the coming year. The next step, say supporters of this middle ground, would be to announce a set of rules for adjusting money growth within those ranges and adapting the ranges themselves when macroeconomic conditions develop differently than expected. For example, the target growth range for money might be adjusted upward or downward each quarter according to whether nominal national income is running above or below some target value or velocity is moving above or below its predicted trend.

The rules need not work perfectly. The important thing is that firms, workers, stock market traders, and everyone else would know the rules. In that case, the rules would become a stable framework for expectations. They would build in some room for policy activism but would reduce the scope for discretionary changes in policy compared with the present situation. They would, in effect, discourage policymakers from turning the ship's rudder violently from one side to the other and at the same time allow them to react flexibly to supply shocks, changes in financial institutions, and other unforeseen events.

Policy activists have their doubts about even this middle ground. They believe that in a complex real world, no set of rules fixed in advance could cover all possible contingencies. Thus, any reasonable policy regime needs to allow some scope for human judgment even if that sometimes means throwing the "seamanship manual" overboard.

Political Differences

Aside from these technical matters, the various schools of thought also differ on political issues. Monetarists and new classicists simply do not trust policymakers to use their power in a responsible manner. "Money is too important to be left to central bankers" is how Milton Friedman has put it. It is no help that policymakers are, for the most part, honest and well intentioned. The system forces them to stress the short run at the expense of the long run, to mask their true intentions from the public, and to change courses frequently. This being the case, macroeconomic policy will inevitably have an inflationary bias. In the monetarist view, even an imperfect set of rules would be better than leaving economic policy to the politicians.

Policy activists are less pessimistic. They think that just as economists have learned more about the inflation process from the experience of the 1970s, policymakers have learned to take a longer-term view of things. This also goes for the voting public—the ultimate policymakers in a democracy. In the case that leads off this chapter, we saw that the "new economists" of 20 years ago dared to assert that they had attained "not only the economic understanding but also the will and determination to use economic policy as an effective tool for progress." The hope of someday reaching this state of affairs has not died.

Summary

1. **Why have Keynesian economists favored the active use of fiscal and monetary policy to stabilize the economy?** Economists have long disagreed over the best strategy for economic stabilization. Keynesians have favored the active use of fiscal and monetary policies to fine-tune the economy, keeping it on a path of steady growth without inflation. The case for policy activism rests on three propositions: (1) that the private economy is inherently unstable; (2) that the future course of the economy and the effects of policy actions can be predicted well enough to guide policy decisions; and (3) that policymakers will follow economists' technical advice.

2. **What are the implications of lags and forecasting errors for the conduct of discretionary policy?** Monetarists and other opponents of policy activism draw attention to lags in the policy process. The *inside lag* is the delay between the time a policy change is needed and the time a decision is made. The *outside lag* is the delay between the time a decision is made and the time it affects the economy. Lags in fiscal and monetary policy range from as short as three months to several years. Because of lags, policymakers must act on the basis of forecasts. However, if the forecasts turn out to be seriously in error, their decisions may make things worse rather than better by the time they take effect.

3. **Why may politics interfere with the conduct of stabilization policy?** Even when economists offer valid technical advice, policymakers may not follow it. One reason for this is that there is great political pressure to "do something" when things go wrong with the economy. However, because of policy lags, it may be too late to do anything useful by the time this pressure reaches its peak. Also, some types of policy have favorable effects in the short run but unfavorable ones in the long run. Politicians facing reelection may place undue stress on the short-run effects. Monetary authorities too may be tempted to seek short-term benefits by departing from announced long-term policy goals. Critics of policy activism see these political factors as a major problem.

4. **What kinds of rules have been proposed for the conduct of monetary policy?** A number of rules have been proposed for conducting monetary policy. One is to let the money supply grow at a steady rate equal to the long-term rate of growth of natural real output. A second is to let nominal national income grow at a steady rate equal to the long-term growth rate of natural real output. A third is to use a stable price level as a policy target. None of these policy rules work perfectly all the time.

5. **What kinds of rules have been proposed for the conduct of fiscal policy?** The most often proposed rule for conducting fiscal policy is to require the federal government to balance its budget. An annually balanced budget would require the government to raise taxes or cut spending during a recession. However, this might lead to less rather than more stability. Many economists favor a budget that would be balanced on a structural basis but allow cyclical deficits and surpluses over the course of the business cycle.

Terms for Review

- inside lag
- outside lag

Questions for Review

1. What is the main cause of the business cycle according to economists who favor a strategy of policy activism? According to those who favor policy rules?

2. What three propositions underlie the case for policy activism?

3. What are the sources of the inside and outside lags for monetary policy? For fiscal policy?

4. According to critics of policy activism, what features of the U.S. political system interfere with attempts to stabilize the economy?

5. Describe three possible rules for the conduct of monetary policy.

6. Which is more likely to contribute to economic stability—a federal budget that is balanced every year or one that is balanced, on the average, over the course of the business cycle? Why?

Problems and Topics for Discussion

1. **Examining the lead-off case.** Review the events of the "Great Inflation" of the 1970s as described in the lead-off case in Chapter 16. Compare the actual events of the 1970s with the hopes expressed by the President's economic advisers in 1966 as given at the beginning of this chapter. Why did economic policy fail to achieve the objective of balanced growth with price stability?

2. **A game.** Here is a game that will give you a feeling for the effects of policy lags and forecasting errors. In your classroom or another large room, arrange a dozen chairs to form a "slalom course." The course should consist of pairs of chairs placed about three feet apart to form "gates." The gates should be laid out to form a path of S-shaped turns. The goal is to walk through the gates without bumping into them or wandering off the path. When your slalom course is set up, form teams of three and compete to see who can finish the course the fastest. Whoever hits a gate is disqualified.

   a. For practice, select one team member—A—to walk through the course. Note the time it takes to complete it.
   b. Next, blindfold team member A. Team member B watches and tells A when to turn to the right or left.
   c. With A still blindfolded, B watches A and writes directions to turn left or right on a memo pad. The directions are passed to team member C, who reads them aloud within A's hearing. C must sit facing away from the course so that he or she cannot see B's progress.
   d. Conditions are the same as in part c except that

now B also sits facing away from the course. B is allowed to view the course only by looking over his or her shoulder using a hand-held mirror. B thus must check on A's progress using the mirror and then write instructions for C, who reads them to A.

   What does this game teach you about strategies for steering the economy through the "gates" of the business cycle? Discuss.

3. **A money growth rule.** Draw an aggregate supply and demand diagram to illustrate the use of a policy rule calling for a fixed rate of money growth equal to the growth rate of natural real output. Show what will happen to real output and the price level when velocity rises or falls unexpectedly while the rate of growth of natural real output stays the same.

4. **Nominal national income rule.** Draw an aggregate supply and demand diagram to illustrate the use of a monetary policy rule calling for a fixed rate of growth of nominal national income equal to the expected growth rate of natural real output. Show what will happen to real output and the price level if the growth of natural real output unexpectedly slows down or speeds up.

5. **Policy rules and supply shocks.** Use an aggregate supply and demand diagram to compare the effects of a supply shock when the Fed (a) follows a rule calling for a fixed price level; (b) follows a rule calling for a fixed level of nominal national income; and (c) accommodates the supply shock in order to keep real output equal to its natural level. What are the advantages and disadvantages of each policy?

6. **Project stockpiles and the fiscal policy lag.** Policy activists have long been aware that the process of getting the approval of Congress adds a long and uncertain period to the inside lag for fiscal policy. As a solution to this problem, it has often been proposed that the federal government "stockpile" a number of projects, such as highway improvements, bridges, post office buildings, and so on. All planning and design work for the projects would be completed and the projects kept "on the shelf" until needed. When the economy entered a recession, the president could order that the projects be started. Work on them could begin in a matter of weeks.

   Do you think this strategy would reduce the inside lag for fiscal policy? What problems of lags and forecasting would remain? How would the proposal affect the political problems of fine-tuning?

Students' expectations affect their course of action.

Case for Discussion
The Professor's Dilemma

A professor at a certain university always tells his class at the start of the semester that grades will be based on a final exam. The purpose of the exam is to give students an incentive to study hard and learn all they can about economics. One semester, as exam time approaches, the professor thinks to himself, "My students have studied hard and learned everything they should. My job is done. Why go to the trouble of giving the exam?" He gives everyone an A and cancels the exam.

The next semester, he again announces that he will grade on the basis of the exam and again cancels it at the last minute. But by the end of the third semester, he notices something amiss. Even though he announced a final exam at the start of the semester, no one has studied at all. They didn't believe him. Now he thinks to himself, "Too bad. But what is the point of giving the exam now? They don't know a thing. It would just be a lot of work for me to grade the things." Again he cancels the exam.

One day during vacation, there is a knock on our professor-hero's office door. There stands the head of his department. "What are you going to do about this?" she demands. "Your students aren't learning a thing anymore!"

"I know it's a problem," he replies, "but I don't know what to do. If I announce the exam and everyone believes me, then at the end of the semester the optimal strategy is not to give the exam. But if I announce the exam and no one believes me, then at the end of the semester it is still the optimal strategy to cancel the exam. You can't really blame me for what has happened. After all, every semester I'm doing what is best under the circumstances I'm faced with."

The department head walks out without saying a word. The next morning, there is a big notice on the department bulletin board for both faculty and students to see: BY ORDER OF THE DEPARTMENT HEAD, ALL PROFESSORS MUST GIVE FINAL EXAMS OR THEY WILL BE FIRED. Our friend reads this notice and breathes a sigh of relief. Now he can start giving exams again and be certain that his students will study for them.

Source: Based on a suggestion by Gary Gorton. Photo Source: © 1987 Phyllis Woloshin.

Questions

1. Suppose the Fed has announced a low target for the growth of the money stock. Everyone believes the Fed will stick to it. How does the Fed's situation compare to that of the professor who has reached the end of the semester and must decide whether to give the exam? What will happen if the Fed decides to exceed its money growth target one time only? What will happen to expectations of inflation if the public comes to suspect that the Fed will habitually exceed its target? If the Fed then surprises people by sticking to its initial, low target after all, what will happen to real output?

2. Why would a policymaker ever prefer to be bound by a rule rather than be left free to make discretionary changes in policy? What light does the story of the professor's dilemma shed on the problem of time-inconsistency?

Suggestions for Further Reading

Darby, Michael R., et al. "Recent Behavior of the Velocity of Money." *Contemporary Policy Issues* (January 1987): 1–33.

A panel discussion devoted to the implications of changes in money velocity for the conduct of monetary policy. Milton Friedman, in contributing to the panel, restates the case for a money growth rule. David Lindsey argues for presumptive monetary targets but ones that are subject to change if warranted by unexpected developments.

Gordon, Robert J. *Macroeconomics*, 3d ed. Boston: Little, Brown, 1984.

Chapter 12 covers the debate over fine-tuning versus policy rules.

Mayer, Thomas. "Replacing the FOMC by a PC." *Contemporary Policy Issues* (April 1987): 31–43.

A nontechnical discussion of monetary policy rules. Contains many useful references.

President's Council of Economic Advisers. *Economic Report of the President*. Washington, D.C.: Government Printing Office, 1985, 1986, and 1987.

The 1985 edition of the report leans toward the monetarist position in its discussion of economic policy for the late 1980s; those for 1986 and 1987 are somewhat less monetarist.

Sheffrin, Steven M. "Fiscal Policy Tied to the Mast." *Contemporary Policy Issues* (April 1987): 44–56.

A good discussion of the lessons of the Gramm-Rudman-Hollings experiment.

19 The Accelerationist Model of Inflation[1]

After reading this chapter, you will understand . . .

- How inflation and unemployment are related.
- How accelerating inflation affects the economy.
- How the rates of inflation and unemployment can both rise during an inflationary recession.
- Why the U.S. economy followed a pattern of alternating inflation and recession from the 1950s to the early 1980s.
- How the behavior of the U.S. economy in the 1980s differed from that during earlier post–World War II years.

Before reading this chapter, make sure you know the meaning of . . .

- Okun's law (Chapter 8)
- Adaptive and rational expectations (Chapter 16)
- Supply shocks (Chapter 16)
- Inflationary recession (Chapter 16)
- Supply-side economics (Chapter 17)
- Monetary policy targets (Chapter 18)

---

[1]In an abbreviated course, this chapter may be omitted without loss of continuity.

Breaking the Pattern

In 1981, when I first assumed the duties of the Presidency, our Nation was suffering from declining productivity and the highest inflation of the postwar period—the legacy of years of government overspending, overtaxing, and overregulation.

We bent all of our efforts to correct these problems, not by unsustainable short-run measures, but by measures that would increase long-term growth without renewed inflation. We removed unnecessary regulations, cut taxes, and slowed the growth of Federal spending, freeing the private sector to develop markets, create jobs, and increase productivity. With conviction in our principles,

President Ronald Reagan

with patience and hard work, we restored the economy to a condition of healthy growth without substantial inflation.

Although employment is now rising, business opportunities are expanding, and interest rates and inflation are under control, we cannot relax our economic vigilance. A return to the policies of excessive government spending and control that led to the economic "malaise" of the late seventies would quickly draw us back into that same disastrous pattern of inflation and recession. Now is the time to recommit ourselves to the policies that broke that awful pattern: policies of reduced Federal spending, lower tax rates, and less regulation to free the creative energy of our people and lead us to an even better economic future through strong and sustained economic growth.

Source: Ronald Reagan, *Economic Report of the President* (Washington, D.C.: Government Printing Office, 1985), 3. Photo Source: AP/Wide World Photos.

BRAVE words, these words in Ronald Reagan's economic report to Congress, delivered a few days after the start of his second term. They may yet be confounded by events, as was his 1981 pledge to "slay the budget monster." But as we will see in this chapter, the years of the Reagan administration did in many respects see a break in the "awful pattern" of accelerating inflation and recession that marked the earlier post–World War II period. In this chapter, we examine both the pattern of accelerating inflation and recession that prevailed from the 1960s to the early 1980s and the break in that pattern that occurred in the mid-1980s. Although this chapter makes no attempt to forecast the future, it does discuss the conditions under which stability could be maintained.

The Accelerationist Model of Inflation

Inflation has entered our discussion at many points in this book, but we have not yet developed a theory of the inflation rate. In Chapter 16, we used the aggregate supply and demand model to see how the economy moves from one price level to another. However, a true theory of inflation must show not only how the price level changes but *how quickly* it does so. After all, no one would think twice these days about a doubling of the price level that took 25 years to occur, as was the case in the United States from 1948 to 1973. But a doubling of the price level in eight years, as took place from 1974 to 1982, is another matter.

Accelerationist model of inflation
A theory according to which changes in the inflation rate affect unemployment and real output.

The model of inflation presented in this chapter is based on the idea that the economy behaves differently in periods in which the inflation rate is accelerating or slowing down than it does in periods when it is holding steady. Because of the model's emphasis on changes in the inflation rate, it is known as the **accelerationist model of inflation.** In this section, we look at the foundations on which this model is constructed.

The Phillips Curve

Phillips curve
A graph showing the relationship between the inflation rate and the unemployment rate, other things being equal.

Chapter 16 indicated that expansion of aggregate demand could be used to hold real output above its natural level and unemployment below its natural rate only at the cost of inflation. This association between low unemployment and demand-pull inflation can be represented in the form of a graph called a **Phillips curve.** The curve is named after the British economist A. W. H. Phillips, who first described it in a 1958 paper[2] (see "Who Said It? Who Did It? 19.1").

The Phillips Curve as a Policy Menu
A sample Phillips curve is drawn in Exhibit 19.1. During the 1960s, when the Phillips curve first attracted economists' attention, it was viewed as a menu of policy choices. Liberal Keynesians sometimes argued that we should choose a point such as L on the Phillips curve; this point would "buy" full employment and prosperity at the price of a modest inflation rate. Conservatives expressed horror at the thought of any degree of inflation and argued for a point such as C, which would achieve price stability at the expense of some jobs.

[2]A. W. H. Phillips, "The Relationship between Unemployment and the Rate of Change of Money Wage Rates in the United Kingdom, 1861–1957," *Economica*, new series, 25 (November 1958): 283–299.

A. W. H. Phillips and the Phillips Curve

A. W. H. Phillips was an economist whose reputation was based largely on a single paper on the right topic published at the right time. In the late 1950s, the connection between inflation and unemployment ranked as a major unsolved problem of macroeconomic theory. The curves that Phillips drew in his famous article in *Economica* suggested a simple, stable relationship between inflation and unemployment. Phillips' paper did not present a theory for explaining the relationship, but his curves became the peg on which all future discussion of the problem was hung. Every subsequent article on inflation and unemployment discussed the shape of the Phillips curve, the point on the Phillips curve that best served as a policy target, how the Phillips curve could be shifted, and so on. Today the term is so familiar that Phillips' name enjoys a sort of immortality even though his own interpretation of the curve has fallen into disfavor.

Phillips was born in New Zealand, but he made London his base for most of his academic career. He taught at the London School of Economics during the 1950s and 1960s, moving to Australian National University in 1967. Phillips' training in electrical engineering seems to have influenced his approach to economic problems, which has been described as "scientistic." In the mid-1950s, he was suggesting the use of an "electric analog machine or simulator" as an aid to the study of economic dynamics. This idea seems to have foreshadowed the widespread use of electronic computers in modern economic research.

However, the problem with viewing the Phillips curve as a policy menu was that the courses it offered kept changing while the meal was in progress. As the 1960s unfolded, economists began to notice that inflation-unemployment points for recent years did not fit the curves they had plotted using data from the 1950s. It became common to speak of an upward drift of the Phillips curve; a given level of inflation would "buy" less and less of a reduction in unemployment.

Exhibit 19.1 The Phillips Curve as a Policy Menu

When A. W. H. Phillips first drew attention to the inverse relationship between inflation and unemployment, his "Phillips curve" was treated as a policy menu. Liberals argued that a point such as L should be chosen; this would "buy" a permanent reduction in unemployment at the cost of a little inflation. Conservatives seemed to favor a point such as C, which would offer stable prices at the cost of more joblessness.

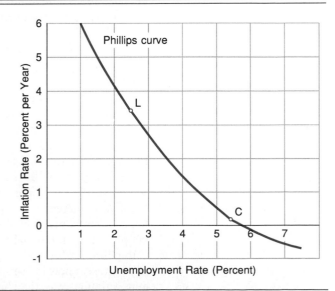

The menu was getting less appealing as time went by. Still, had the upward drift of the Phillips curve been caused by factors outside their control, policy-makers still could have chosen their preferred point from a new, higher Phillips curve. With the advent of the 1970s, however, economists' perception of the Phillips curve started to change. It began to appear that shifts in the Phillips curve were caused by the very policies that had sought to move the economy along it.

The Phillips Curve and the Natural Rate of Unemployment

The distinction between the long-run and short-run effects of aggregate demand on prices, output, and unemployment provides the key to this new view of the Phillips curve. As Chapter 16 showed, a once-and-for-all rise in the level of aggregate demand leads to only a temporary reduction in unemployment. The reason is that the levels of wages and other input prices expected by firms and workers adjust to changes in the level of final goods prices, thereby pushing up the aggregate supply curve. Thus, real output can rise above its natural level only as long as the short-run aggregate supply curve does not completely catch up with the shifting aggregate demand curve.

In Chapter 8, we defined the natural rate of unemployment as the rate that prevailed when the economy was experiencing neither accelerating nor decelerating inflation. We can also say that the natural rate of unemployment is the rate that prevails when the expected inflation rate equals the actual inflation rate. This can happen with real output at its natural level and the expected and actual inflation rates both equal to zero. However, unemployment can also be at its natural rate when the economy is in a moving equilibrium with a constant inflation rate to which everyone has become accustomed.

This modern view of the Phillips curve is illustrated in Exhibit 19.2. Two short-run Phillips curves are shown, each corresponding to a different expected inflation rate. If no inflation is expected, the Phillips curve takes the position Ph_1. The intersection of this Phillips curve with the horizontal axis indicates the natural rate of unemployment, here taken to be 6 percent. If the actual inflation rate unexpectedly goes up to 2 percent per year, the economy will initially move upward and to the left along this Phillips curve from point A to point B. This will correspond to a movement upward and to the right along the economy's aggregate supply curve; real output and the price level will rise as inflation gets under way and the unemployment rate falls.

If the inflation rate remains at 2 percent per year, people will, sooner or later, adjust their expectations accordingly. In terms of the diagrams of Chapter 16, the aggregate supply curve will catch up with the aggregate demand curve, and both will move upward from that point at the same 2 percent rate. As this happens, real output will return to its natural level and unemployment to its natural rate. In Exhibit 19.2, this is shown as an upward shift of the short-run Phillips curve to Ph_2. As a result, the economy moves to point C.

From point C, the economy can move upward or downward along the new short-run Phillips curve depending on what happens to the actual inflation rate. If inflation increases to 4 percent while people expect it to remain at 2 percent, the economy initially will move to point D. If inflation slows to 1 percent while people expect it to remain at 2 percent, the economy at first will move from point C to point E. However, these movements along the short-run Phillips curve will not represent new long-run equilibrium points. As soon as people get used to the new inflation rate, the short-run Phillips curve will shift again.

Exhibit 19.2   Short-Run and
Long-Run Phillips Curves

In the modern view, there is an inverse relationship between
unemployment and inflation only in the short run.
Unexpected inflation lowers the unemployment rate, but only
until people's expectations adjust to the new inflation rate.
Any change in the expected inflation rate shifts the short-run
Phillips curve. The long-run Phillips curve is a vertical line
drawn at the natural rate of unemployment. The long- and
short-run curves intersect at the expected inflation rate for
which the short-run curve is drawn.

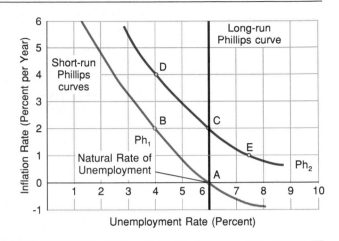

The Long-Run Phillips Curve

A final implication of the new view of the Phillips curve is that it must be vertical
in the long run. This follows from the notions that unemployment attains its
natural rate whenever the actual and expected inflation rates are equal and that
any given steady rate of inflation will be expected to continue. Such a long-run
Phillips curve is shown in Exhibit 19.2 as a vertical line drawn at the natural rate
of unemployment. Each short-run Phillips curve intersects the long-run Phillips
curve at the expected inflation rate for which the short-run curve is drawn.
Thus, unemployment will be at its natural rate only when the actual and expected inflation rates are equal.

Other Elements of the Accelerationist Model

The Phillips curve is one key element of the accelerationist model of inflation.
Our version of the model has two other elements that we have encountered
before: Okun's law and an aggregate nominal demand target.

Okun's Law

In Chapter 8, we stated Okun's law in terms of the connection between the level
of real output and the level of unemployment. Here it is more useful to restate
that law in terms of rates of change in real output and unemployment: The
unemployment rate will remain unchanged in any year in which actual real
output grows at the same rate as natural real output. For each three percentage
points by which growth of real output exceeds that of natural output in a given
year, the unemployment rate tends to fall by about one percentage point. For
each three percentage points by which the growth rate of real output lags behind
the growth of its natural level, the unemployment rate tends to rise by one
percentage point.

An Aggregate Nominal Demand Target

In Chapter 18, we discussed a variety of possible targets for use in guiding
macroeconomic policy—a money stock target, a price level target, and a nominal national income target. In discussing the accelerationist model, it is conve-

nient to assume that policymakers adopt a form of nominal national income target. In particular, we will assume that each year policymakers try to maintain a target growth rate of aggregate demand measured in nominal terms through adjustments in monetary or fiscal policy as needed. Rather than adhering to a fixed target of 3 percent growth of aggregate nominal demand, we will allow discretionary changes in the aggregate nominal demand target from year to year. Also, we will ignore technical difficulties that might prevent policymakers from hitting their target exactly.

A given target growth rate of aggregate nominal demand, nominal national income, and nominal output can be achieved through any combination of growth of real output and inflation that adds up to the target rate. For example, suppose the target growth rate of nominal output is 10 percent per year. This target can be achieved with a 3 percent growth rate of real output and a 7 percent inflation rate, zero growth of real output and 10 percent inflation, 12 percent inflation and a 2 percent drop in real output, and so on.

An aggregate nominal demand target is not, strictly speaking, a required component of the accelerationist model; the model can be made to work for any policy target. But because the sum of the rate of real output growth and the inflation rate is a constant under an aggregate nominal demand target, the arithmetic of the model is greatly simplified.

Other Assumptions

We will incorporate two other simplifying assumptions into our version of the accelerationist model.

First, we will assume that the growth rate of natural real GNP is zero. Since the early 1970s, the growth rate of real output in the United States has indeed slowed down, although not to zero. However, this assumption is not a reference to the productivity slowdown of the 1970s; it is merely an effort to simplify the application of Okun's law. That law relates changes in unemployment to the difference between the rates of growth of actual and natural real GNP. With the growth rate of natural real GNP assumed to be zero, a simplified form of Okun's law can be written as follows:

$$\Delta U = -\frac{\dot{y}}{3},$$

in which ΔU stands for the percentage point change in the unemployment rate over a year's time and $\dot{y}$ stands for the growth rate of real output over the same period. The minus sign indicates that an *increase* in the growth rate of real output is associated with a *decrease* in the unemployment rate, and vice versa.

Second, we will make a simple assumption about inflationary expectations: The expected inflation rate in any year equals the actual inflation rate in the previous year. This will be recognized as a form of the adaptive-expectations hypothesis discussed in Chapter 16. Later in this chapter, we will relax this assumption in order to consider other hypotheses concerning the formation of expectations.

The Effects of Accelerating Inflation

With these assumptions in hand, we may begin discussing the model by examining the effects of accelerating inflation. Because our simplifying assumptions do not fit the U.S. economy exactly, we will base our discussion on a hypothetical country. Like the United States, this country is a democracy dominated by two political parties, which we will call the Blues and the Grays. As we will see, electoral politics play a key role in our story.

Expansionary Policy from a Standing Start

We begin our analysis in year 0 with the economy in a "standing-start" position. This means that both the actual and expected inflation rates are zero; the growth rate of actual real GNP equals the growth rate of natural real GNP, which in this case is also zero; and unemployment is at its natural rate, here assumed to be 6 percent. In year 0, an election is held. The Blues base their campaign on a promise to "get the country moving." They convince the voters that a 6 percent unemployment rate is too high and that a little economic growth would be a good thing. Upon taking over the machinery of government in year 1, they reset the dials of fiscal and monetary policy so as to raise the growth rate of aggregate nominal demand from zero to, say, 8 percent per year. What happens next?

Exhibit 19.3 shows how the economy will react to this dose of expansionary policy in year 1. It shows a vertical long-run Phillips curve drawn at the natural rate of unemployment and a negatively sloped short-run Phillips curve labeled Ph_1. In year 0, the economy is at point A. As the expansionary policy takes hold in year 1, a familiar chain of events unfolds. Increased aggregate demand causes inventories to fall throughout the economy. Some firms react by raising their output, others by raising their prices, and still others by doing some of both. In terms of the diagrams in Chapter 16, at this point the economy is moving upward and to the right along its short-run aggregate supply curve.

Effects on the Labor Market

Soon the effects of the expansionary policy will be felt by the labor market. Firms that are stepping up their output will be recruiting new workers. Some will offer higher wages, knowing that improved demand conditions will allow them to pass along at least part of the higher labor costs to their customers. Job seekers will find both the quantity and the quality of job opportunities better than before. Acting without full knowledge of current and future economic

Exhibit 19.3   Effects of an Expansionary Policy from a Standing Start

This exhibit shows the effects of an increase in the growth rate of nominal GNP to 8 percent from a standing start. As the economy moves from A to B, the unemployment rate drops by two percentage points. Following Okun's law, this means a 6 percent rate of growth of real output. The remaining 2 percent of the 8 percent growth in nominal GNP is accounted for by a 2 percent inflation rate. The 8 percent growth rate of nominal output is more than enough to reach point B' but not enough to reach point B". No inflation-unemployment combination other than B is possible under these conditions.

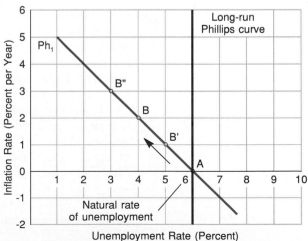

trends, each job seeker will be likely to view the improved labor market conditions as mere good luck. The newly offered jobs will be quickly snapped up. The average length of unemployment spells will fall, and the unemployment rate will drop with it.

Moving Up the Phillips Curve

At this point, the economy is moving up and to the left along the Phillips curve, with the unemployment rate falling and the inflation rate rising. How far it will climb in year 1 can be determined by combining two of the elements of the model described earlier. First, the economy must move to a point at which the inflation rate plus the growth rate of real output equals the 8 percent growth rate of nominal GNP. Second, according to Okun's law, the rate of increase of real output must be equal to three times the drop in the unemployment rate. (This is the simplified form of Okun's law, using zero growth of natural real output.) Putting the two together, we conclude that the economy will move to a point on the Phillips curve at which the inflation rate plus three times the drop in the unemployment rate equals the rate of increase of nominal GNP. This occurs at point B in Exhibit 19.3, where the inflation rate is 2 percent and the two-percentage-point drop in the unemployment rate (from 6 to 4 percent) produces a 6 percent increase in real output for a total of 8 percent.

No other point on the Phillips curve satisfies the required condition. Consider point B', for example. There the inflation rate is 1 percent and the unemployment rate has fallen by 1 percent, giving a 3 percent real growth rate. The 1 percent inflation plus the 3 percent real growth sum to only 4 percent—far short of the assumed 8 percent growth rate of nominal GNP. Now consider point B". There the inflation rate is 3 percent and unemployment has fallen by three percentage points, giving a 9 percent real growth rate. Adding the inflation rate to the real growth rate tells us that point B" could be reached only if nominal GNP grew at 12 percent rather than at the assumed 8 percent rate.

In short, once the growth rate of nominal output, the initial unemployment rate, the slope of the short-run Phillips curve, and the expected inflation rate are given, only one combination of inflation and unemployment rate is possible.

Effects of Repeated Expansionary Policy

The Blues have every reason to be proud of the economic record of their first year in office. From the stagnation of the standing-start position, a little dose of expansionary demand management in year 1 has cut unemployment by a third and boosted the growth rate of real output to 6 percent at the cost of only a 2 percent inflation rate. These results are so encouraging that the Blues repeat the same policy and maintain the 8 percent growth rate of nominal GNP in year 2. Exhibit 19.4 shows what happens.

The most noticeable difference between Exhibit 19.4 and Exhibit 19.3 is the shift in the short-run Phillips curve to the position Ph_2. The Phillips curve shifts because firms and workers, after experiencing 2 percent inflation in year 1, expect a 2 percent inflation in year 2 and firms expect a similar increase in input prices. In terms of the type of diagram used in Chapter 16, this is represented by an upward shift in the aggregate supply curve. In terms of the present diagram, it means an upward shift of the short-run Phillips curve to a point at which it intersects the long-run Phillips curve at the new expected inflation rate of 2 percent.

Exhibit 19.4   Effects of a Second Year
of Expansionary Policy

If an 8 percent growth rate of nominal GNP is maintained for
a second year, the trade-off between inflation and
unemployment will become less favorable. As a result of the
2 percent inflation experienced in year 1, the short-run
Phillips curve for year 2 shifts to the position Ph₂. The
economy moves from B to C. The one-percentage-point drop
in unemployment causes a 3 percent rate of increase in real
output. The remaining 5 percent of nominal-GNP growth is
accounted for by inflation.

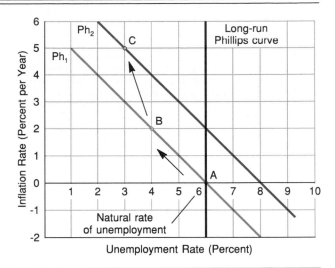

Having concluded that in year 2 the economy will move to some point on the
new Phillips curve, Ph₂, we next must determine to which point it will move.
The same reasoning can be used as before: In year 2, the economy must move to
a point at which the inflation rate plus the rate of increase in real output equals
the rate of growth of nominal GNP.

As before, the growth rate of real output can be calculated using Okun's
law, but now the starting point is the 4 percent unemployment rate reached in
year 1 rather than the 6 percent natural rate. Real output will grow in year 2 only
to the extent that the unemployment rate falls further. If it stays at 4 percent, no
real growth will occur. A little trial and error clearly shows, then, that the
economy must end year 2 at point C. There a further one-percentage-point drop
in the unemployment rate—from 4 to 3 percent—will yield a 3 percent rate of
growth of real output. That plus a 5 percent inflation rate equals the assumed 8
percent growth rate of nominal GNP.

Effects of Continued Acceleration

The Blues' record clearly is not quite as good in year 2 as in year 1. The growth
rate of real output has slowed to 3 percent, and the inflation rate has risen to 5
percent. On the plus side, though, unemployment has dropped to just 3 percent.
All in all, the campaign promise to get things moving has been kept. Now let's
suppose that the growth rate of nominal GNP is held at 8 percent for a third
year.

As Exhibit 19.5 shows, in year 3 the economy will be operating on a new
short-run Phillips curve, Ph₃. This curve's upward shift reflects firms' and
workers' expectation that the inflation rate in year 3 will be the same 5 percent
that was actually experienced in year 2. (Thus, Ph₃ intersects the long-run Phillips curve at a 5 percent inflation rate.) To find the point on Ph₃ at which the
inflation rate plus the growth rate of real output equals 8 percent, we must now
move straight up from point C to point D. There is no room for any further
decrease in unemployment or any growth in real output. The entire 8 percent
growth rate of nominal GNP is absorbed in an 8 percent inflation rate.

Exhibit 19.5   Effects of Continued Expansionary Policy

A third year of 8 percent growth of nominal GNP results in no further reduction in unemployment. The short-run Phillips curve shifts to Ph₃, and 8 percent inflation is required merely to keep unemployment from rising (point D). To keep unemployment at 3 percent for a fourth year, the growth rate of nominal GNP must increase to 11 percent (point E).

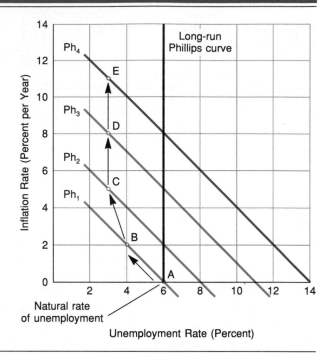

This result leaves the Blues little to brag about except a continued low unemployment rate. Clinging to this one remaining achievement, the Blue policymakers decide that in year 4 they will maintain the 3 percent unemployment rate at all costs. Turning again to Exhibit 19.5, we can easily see what is needed. In year 4, the short-run Phillips curve will shift upward to Ph₄ as a result of the inflationary expectations brought on by the 8 percent inflation rate experienced in year 3. To keep unemployment at 3 percent in year 4, then, the economy must move straight up from point D on Ph₃ to point E on Ph₄. Since point E corresponds to an 11 percent inflation rate and zero real growth, keeping the growth rate of nominal GNP at 8 percent, as in previous years, will not be enough. Instead, an even more expansionary monetary and fiscal policy will have to be used to raise the growth rate of nominal GNP to 11 percent per year. The cost of maintaining the low unemployment rate is, therefore, accelerating inflation.

Some Generalizations

Let's leave the world of the Blues and Grays for a moment and draw some generalizations from our example. The first is that starting from the natural unemployment rate and zero inflation, expansionary policy initially produces falling unemployment and rapid real growth with only moderate inflation. The second is that as people begin to adjust their expectations to the inflationary effects of the expansionary policy, the trade-off between inflation and unemployment becomes increasingly unfavorable. The third is that the unemployment rate can be kept below the natural rate for a prolonged period only at the cost of a constantly accelerating inflation rate, which keeps the actual inflation rate always above the expected rate.

The last conclusion lies at the heart of the accelerationist theory of inflation—indeed, it is the conclusion that gives the theory its name. The early treatment of

Acceleration in the Kennedy-Johnson Era

John Kennedy came to the presidency in 1960 with the stated intent of getting the country moving again after two recessions in the late Eisenhower years. Lyndon Johnson, his successor, was equally determined to pursue an expansionary policy. Economists are still debating the relative impact of the Kennedy tax cut, heavy defense spending, and accelerating monetary growth. But there is no doubt that this combination of policies was as expansionary as anyone could have wished. The result was a sustained period of growth and low unemployment.

The accompanying diagram shows the unemployment-inflation record for the economy during the Kennedy-Johnson era. The pattern is just what the accelerationist theory would lead us to expect. At first, the expansionary policy produced major gains in employment with little additional inflation. But starting in 1964, the year of the tax cut, each successive drop in unemployment was accompanied by a bigger jump in prices. By the end of Johnson's term in office, inflation was rising higher and higher each year just to keep unemployment from growing.

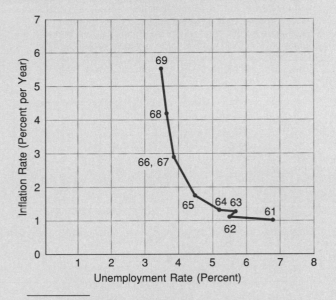

Source: President's Council of Economic Advisers, *Economic Report of the President* (Washington, D.C.: Government Printing Office, 1987), Tables B-35 and B-58. Civilian unemployment rate and changes in annual average CPI.

the Phillips curve as a policy menu suggested that a low unemployment rate could be bought at the cost of a steady, moderate inflation rate. What led to the demise of this view more than anything else was the U.S. macroeconomic experience in the 1960s, as discussed in "Applying Economic Ideas 19.1."

Inflationary Recession and the Stop-Go Cycle

Given our assumption of adaptive expectations, there is no limit to the number of years that unemployment can be held below its natural rate by accelerating inflation. In practice, though, political pressure builds up to a point where something must be done about inflation. Let's suppose that this happens in the land of the Blues and the Grays. In year 4, another election is held. The Blues have a record of 11 percent inflation and stagnant real output. They point proudly to the low unemployment rate they have achieved, but the Grays' promise to do something about inflation wins the day. True to their pledge, once in office the Grays put on the monetary and fiscal brakes.

Effects of Deceleration

Let's assume that the growth rate of nominal GNP is cut from 11 percent in year 4 to just 6 percent in year 5. Exhibit 19.6 shows what happens as a result. First, in year 5 the Phillips curve is still shifting upward as people adjust to the infla-

Exhibit 19.6   An Inflationary Recession

If the growth rate of nominal GNP is cut back from 11 percent in year 4 to, say, 6 percent in year 5, the result will be an inflationary recession. The Phillips curve continues to shift upward from Ph₄ to Ph₅, catching up with the actual inflation rate in year 4. Unemployment rises by two percentage points, resulting in a −6 percent rate of real output growth. With such a large negative real growth rate, the inflation rate must increase to 12 percent in order to account for the entire 6 percent nominal growth rate.

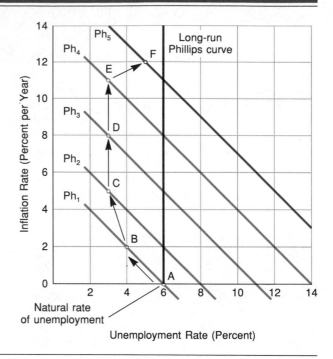

tionary experience of year 4. In year 5, then, the economy must end up somewhere on short-run Phillips curve Ph₅, which intersects the long-run Phillips curve at an 11 percent inflation rate. To keep unemployment from rising, inflation would have to accelerate to 14 percent in year 5, but this is impossible given the Grays' restrictive demand management policy. Unemployment therefore rises. Each one-percentage-point increase in the unemployment rate will, according to Okun's law, produce a negative 3 percent growth (that is, a 3 percent decline) in real output. As real output falls and unemployment rises, the economy will move toward a point at which the inflation rate plus the rate of real growth (which is now negative) equals the assumed 6 percent growth rate of nominal GNP. This happens at point F on Ph₅. There the economy experiences a 6 percent drop in real output as a result of the two-percentage-point rise in unemployment and a 12 percent inflation rate. The sum of 12 percent inflation and negative 6 percent real growth is the required 6 percent growth rate of nominal output.

We already have a name for the events of year 5: *inflationary recession.* Every possible bad thing is happening at once. Real output is falling; unemployment is rising; and inflation, instead of slowing down, is still being carried upward by inflationary expectations. Economists used to think that such a combination of events was impossible. President Eisenhower's chief economic adviser supposedly promised to eat his hat if accelerating inflation and rising unemployment ever struck in the same year. Luckily for him, hats had gone out of style by the 1970s!

To insure that we clearly understand the mechanics of inflationary recession, we can relate the events of Exhibit 19.6 to the graphic framework used in Chapter 16. There an inflationary recession was shown to occur when inflationary expectations push the aggregate supply curve up while the aggregate demand curve remains fixed or (as in this case) rises less rapidly. The aggregate supply curve shifts upward as firms become worried about rising input prices and raise the prices of their outputs. But with aggregate nominal demand rising only slowly, there is not enough real purchasing power to absorb a constant level of real output at a higher price level. Inventories pile up, and firms react by cutting back their output. The economy moves upward and to the left along its aggregate demand curve.

The events of the inflationary recession can also be viewed in terms of what happens in the labor market. Because workers are expecting ever higher prices, they will be reluctant to take jobs that do not pay proportionately higher nominal wages. However, the new demand management policy means that labor demand is no longer increasing as rapidly as before. Workers find it harder and harder to find the jobs they want. Since they lack complete information, they attribute their problems to bad luck. They go on looking for work, stretching out the average duration of unemployment. The unemployment rate therefore rises.

Turning the Corner

Although the events of year 5 win no praise for the Grays, let's suppose that they remain committed to their policies. In year 6, they decide to cut the inflation rate back to 10 percent regardless of the cost in terms of jobs and output. What target should they set for nominal GNP growth in order to achieve this goal?

As Exhibit 19.7 shows, in year 6 policymakers are still fighting against the momentum of inflationary expectations, which are pushing the short-run Phillips curve upward. Under our assumption of adaptive expectations, because the actual inflation rate in year 5 was 12 percent, people will expect 12 percent inflation to continue in year 6. That will put the Phillips curve in the position

Exhibit 19.7   Turning the Corner on Inflation

In order to cut the inflation rate to 10 percent in year 6, the growth rate of nominal GNP must be slowed further. Because the actual inflation rate in year 5 was 12 percent, the Phillips curve will shift upward again in year 6 to Ph_6. In order for the economy to reach point G on Ph_6, where the inflation rate is 10 percent, unemployment must rise by three percentage points; that, in turn, will produce a −9 percent rate of real growth. Thus, if inflation is to be limited to 10 percent in year 6, nominal GNP can be allowed to increase by only 1 percent.

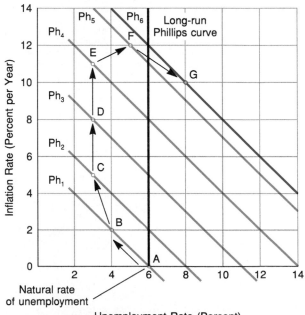

Ph_6. In the short run, then, policymakers must pick some point along that curve. The point on Ph_6 that meets the 10 percent inflation goal is point G.

To get to point G, the unemployment rate must rise by three percentage points, from 5 percent at F to 8 percent at G. According to Okun's law, a three-percentage-point rise in the unemployment rate (with no growth in natural GNP) will produce a 9 percent drop in real output. As always, the rate of change of real output plus the inflation rate must equal the rate of growth of nominal GNP. Inflation of 10 percent plus real growth of negative 9 percent gives 1 percent as the required target for nominal-income growth in year 6. Thus, the Grays must press even harder on the fiscal and monetary brakes in year 6 than in year 5.

After year 6, things get a bit easier because the momentum of inflationary expectations has finally been broken. As Exhibit 19.8 shows, the short-run Phillips curve begins to drift slowly downward. For year 7, the expected inflation rate drops to the 10 percent rate experienced in year 6, putting the Phillips curve at Ph_7. Inflation can be cut by two more percentage points if the economy moves straight down from point G to point H. (Such a move calls for an 8 percent growth rate for nominal GNP—a moderate easing of demand management policy.) In year 8, another two percentage points can be trimmed if the economy moves to point I, and so on.

In short, the Grays' deflationary policy is the mirror image of the policy of accelerating inflation pursued by the Blues. The Blues used accelerating inflation to hold the unemployment rate below its natural level. At first the trade-off between unemployment and inflation was very favorable, but it became less so over time as expectations were adjusted. The Grays, on the other hand, have held the unemployment rate above its natural level in order to bring inflation down. At first the trade-off between unemployment and inflation was terrible,

Exhibit 19.8   Continued Deceleration

In a mirror image of the initial acceleration, inflation can be slowed steadily each year by holding unemployment above its natural rate. Each year the short-run Phillips curve shifts downward as the expected inflation rate falls. In principle, the deceleration could be continued until a "soft landing" is reached back at point A.

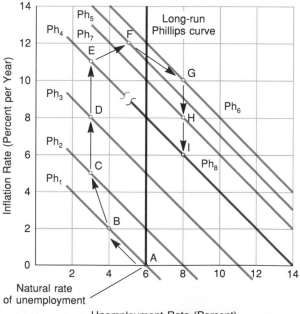

Exhibit 19.9 Reflation

If the growth rate of nominal GNP is again increased after a period of deceleration, the result will be falling unemployment with a minimal increase in inflation. For example, increasing the nominal growth rate from 6 percent in year 8 to 16 percent in year 9 will move the economy from point I to point J. The initial expansion will capitalize on the continued downward drift of the Phillips curve from Ph_8 to Ph_9.

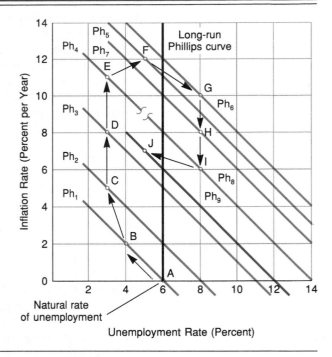

but over time it became more favorable as expectations were adjusted. Thus, the accelerationist theory of inflation works both ways: Unemployment below the natural rate is linked with a rising inflation rate, and unemployment above the natural rate is linked with a falling inflation rate.

Reflation

After year 8, the Grays' game plan calls for three more years of continued high unemployment and falling inflation. Then the economy can be coaxed to a "soft landing" back at point A, with zero inflation and unemployment back at its natural level. However, year 8 is an election year. What kind of record do the Grays have? In year 4, they took over an economy with 11 percent inflation. By year 8, they had cut that figure almost in half to 6 percent. But the reduced inflation rate has been won only at the cost of a major recession. The unemployment rate is five percentage points higher than it was four years before, and real output is a full 15 percent lower. By this time, voters are likely to remember the Blue era more as one of prosperity than as one of excessive inflation.

Further, the Grays' program offers the Blues a tempting opportunity: If the Blues win, for the first year after the election they can pursue an expansionary policy while still taking advantage of the downward momentum of inflationary expectations. Exhibit 19.9 shows how such a **reflation** program could work.

By year 8, the economy will have reached point I, with 6 percent inflation and 8 percent unemployment. In year 9, the short-run Phillips curve will shift to the position Ph_9, reflecting the previous year's inflation. Now consider what will happen if at this point the Blues have been elected and push the growth of nominal GNP upward from 6 percent per year in year 8 to, say, 16 percent. Because firms will still be expecting input price increases to remain moderate,

Reflation
An episode in which policy becomes more expansionary while the expected inflation rate is still falling.

they will react to the renewed burst of demand almost entirely by increasing their real output. Prices will be pushed up only a little more rapidly than in the previous year. Because workers are expecting a relatively moderate rate of increase in the cost of living, they will snap up the newly created job opportunities with little increase in nominal wages. As a result, the economy will move almost horizontally to the left from point I to point J. Real output will grow by 9 percent and unemployment will fall by three percentage points at the cost of only one additional percentage point of inflation.

The Stop-Go Cycle

Compared with the prospect of continued belt tightening under a reelected Gray government, the Blues' promise of prosperity has won them the election. However, the reflation trick works for only one year. After that, the inflationary price that must be paid for keeping unemployment below its natural rate will rise each year. The economy will enter a new upswing until political pressure to do something about inflation leads to another policy reversal.

Alternating periods of expansionary and contractionary demand management policy produce what can be called a *stop-go policy cycle*. If the political system is, on the average, more sensitive to the evils of unemployment than it is to those of inflation, an inflationary bias will be added to the stop-go cycle, with each upswing lasting longer than each downswing. Without pursuing the matter in detail, we can say that the result is an upward spiral of the economy as shown in Exhibit 19.10.

Of course, the assumptions that produce the stop-go policy cycle in the world of the Blues and Grays are highly restrictive. The actual U.S. economy is far more complex, as is the accompanying political system. But even so, as "Applying Economic Ideas 19.2" shows, the path followed by the U.S. economy from 1954 through 1980 is very similar to the spiral pattern of Exhibit 19.10.

Exhibit 19.10   The Stop-Go Cycle
with an Inflationary Bias

The so-called stop-go cycle means alternating acceleration, inflationary recession, deceleration, and reflation as political pressure builds up to do something first about inflation and then about unemployment. If the pressure to reduce unemployment is on the average stronger than the pressure to control inflation, the stop-go cycle will become an upward spiral, as shown in this exhibit.

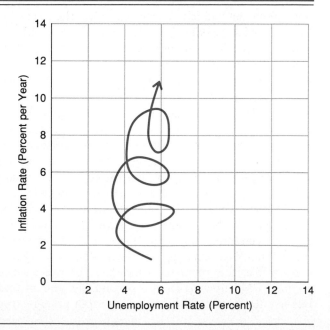

APPLYING ECONOMIC IDEAS 19.2

The U.S. Experience with Unemployment and Inflation, 1954–1980

The accompanying chart presents data on inflation and unemployment in the U.S. economy from 1954 to 1980. We have already discussed one part of this record—the Kennedy-Johnson expansion. Now we will explore some other features.

The overall impression one gets from the figure is of a series of clockwise loops. The lengths and strengths of successive expansions and contractions are irregular, but it takes little imagination to see an upward spiral in them.

Although the inflation rate has drifted upward over the years, it has not done so over every single cycle. Consider the period following the recession of 1957. The recovery from this recession was very weak. The vertical line between the points for 1959 and 1960, which forms the upward portion of the next loop, is shorter and further to the right than most. This weak recovery seems to have happened because President Eisenhower had been frightened by the inflation of 1956 and 1957 and did not want to repeat the experience. Restrictive policies cut the recovery off before the previous peak of inflation was reached.

During the 1970s, in contrast, the loops in the stop-go cycle resumed their upward drift and became more elongated. The acceleration of inflation from the 1972 rate to the high 1974 rate was especially abrupt and was followed by the sharp recession of 1974 to 1975. Beginning from 1976 and continuing throughout the Carter administration, inflation took off again, reaching a 30-year high in 1980.

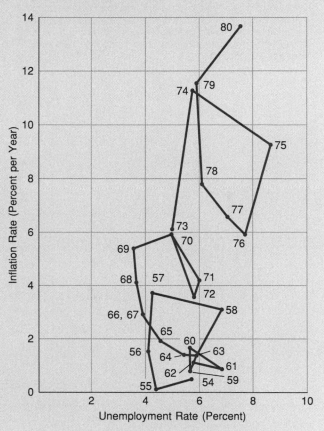

The U.S. Experience Since 1980

This chapter began with a quotation from President Reagan's 1985 economic report to Congress, in which Reagan stressed the need to break the "disastrous pattern of inflation and recession" of the post–World War II period. We have looked in some detail at this stop-go pattern and its causes. What are the chances that it really has been broken? As this is written, the question is a subject of heated debate. Let's take a look at this argument.

The Slowdown of Inflation

Exhibit 19.11 adds the record for the years 1981 through 1986 to the inflation-unemployment chart. These years include the back-to-back recessions of 1980 and 1981 to 1982 and the strong recovery of 1983 to 1984. On the surface, they indicate a break with the past pattern in several respects:

Exhibit 19.11   Deceleration of
Inflation, 1980–1986

Between 1980 and 1983, the economy experienced back-to-
back recessions. Unemployment reached a post–World War
II high, and inflation fell by about 10 percentage points. In
1983, for the first time in 30 years, the low point reached by
inflation dropped below that of the previous cycle. Although
the inflation rate increased slightly in 1984, the second year
of recovery, it turned downward again in 1985 and hit a 22-
year low in 1986.

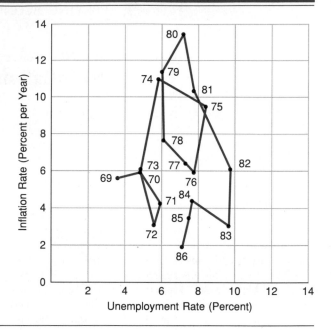

- In each of five previous inflation-recession cycles, the low point of inflation (1955, 1959, 1961, 1972, and 1976) was higher than the low point
  of the previous cycle. In contrast, the inflation rate reached in 1986 was
  the lowest in 22 years.

- The deceleration phase of the cycle was longer than it had been in any
  previous case.

- Although the inflation rate edged up a bit in 1984, the second year of
  the recovery, it fell again in 1985 and 1986 despite continued improvement in the unemployment rate.

What do these differences mean? Not surprisingly, explanations differ.

Claiming Credit

Supporters of the Reagan administration claim that the stop-go cycle has finally been broken and that their policies, aided by the Fed, deserve the credit.
They like to compare the record for the period from 1980 to 1983 with earlier
estimates of the cost of stopping inflation. For example, they cite Arthur
Okun's 1978 estimate that an unemployment rate three percentage points
above the natural rate would trim only one percentage point a year from the
inflation rate.

Exhibit 19.12 presents Okun's estimate in graphic form. Between 1980
(point A) and 1983 (point B), the inflation rate fell by 10 percentage points. In
this period, the unemployment rate averaged 9 percent—2.5 to 3 percentage
points above its natural level. In contrast, Okun's estimate implies that six years
of unemployment averaging 5 percentage points above the natural rate—that is,
11 to 11.5 percent—would be needed to get from point A to point B. This
implied path is shown as a broken line in Exhibit 19.12.

What aspects of policy deserve the credit for this seemingly remarkable
achievement? Administration supporters usually cite two factors.

Exhibit 19.12   Was the Cost of the 1980–1983 Deceleration Less than Expected?

Backers of the Reagan administration's policies were quick to claim that the cost of the 10-percentage-point drop in the inflation rate was less than had been predicted. They cite estimates from the 1970s implying that six years of unemployment rates of 11 percent or more would be needed to slow inflation to that extent. The pessimistic estimate is represented by the broken line from A to B; the actual path of the economy is shown by the solid line. Reagan supporters say that the economy's good performance was a result of supply-side policies and the credibility of the administration's anti-inflation campaign. However, skeptics attribute much of the slowdown to favorable supply shocks. They claim that the economy's performance during this period is consistent with earlier predictions when falling oil prices and the rising international value of the dollar are taken into account.

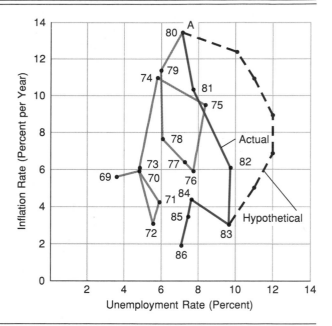

The first factor is the *credibility* of the administration's and Fed's anti-inflation campaign. To understand the role of credibility, we must replace our adaptive-expectations assumption with a rational-expectations hypothesis. Under previous administrations, the argument goes, people could rationally expect each recession to be followed by renewed inflation—after all, that is what had always happened in the past. Their expectations of renewed inflation limited the downward shift of the short-run Phillips curve even during periods in which the actual inflation rate was falling. Okun's pessimistic estimate of the cost of stopping inflation makes good sense under such conditions.

In contrast, the team of Ronald Reagan in the White House and Paul Volcker at the Fed convinced people that the government was serious about fighting inflation. With everyone expecting the inflation rate to fall, the short-run Phillips curve shifted downward more rapidly than adaptive expectations alone would have predicted. Hence, the cost of slowing inflation from 1980 to 1983 was lower than had been estimated.

Supply-side economists who support the Reagan administration cite a second factor in the slowdown of inflation. They point out that for any given rate of growth of nominal GNP, the higher the rate of growth of real output, the lower the inflation rate. There are two sources of growth of real output: cyclical growth that, according to Okun's law, is linked with changes in unemployment and long-run growth of natural real output. The second factor is not captured in our simplified accelerationist model, which assumes no growth in natural real output. However, say the supply-siders, faster growth of natural real output during the early part of the recovery from the 1981 to 1982 recession helped the anti-inflation effort. They credit the improved growth to supply-side tax cuts and other policies.

In sum, supporters of the Reagan administration claim that there has been a change of policy regime. If the newly credible policy is continued, they say, the stop-go cycle will not be renewed.

The Skeptics

Not everyone buys the argument that the early 1980s represent a complete break with the past. The skeptics include not only political opponents of the Reagan administration but many economists who claim that the recent progress in the battle against inflation isn't all that remarkable. Let's look at their arguments.

First, say the skeptics, any analysis of inflation during the 1980s must take into account the role played by supply shocks. Two major supply shocks were at work during this period, one involving oil prices and the other the international value of the dollar.

The first supply shock involved energy prices. In one year—from 1979 to 1980—the producer price index for energy products rose by a stunning 40 percent. This pushed costs and prices up in every sector of the economy. Then energy prices not only stopped rising—they started to fall. From 1982 to 1986, producer prices for energy dropped by 24 percent. This downward supply shock depressed costs and prices in other sectors of the economy.

The second supply shock concerned the international value of the dollar. In 1980, the dollar was at a low point; it would buy only 4.2 French francs, 1.8 West German marks, or 227 Japanese yen. By early 1985, the dollar had rebounded to historic highs—equal to more than 10 francs, over 3 marks, and more than 250 yen. A low value for the dollar, as was the case in 1980, makes imports expensive. High prices for imported finished goods and raw materials push up prices directly. A low value for the dollar also shields domestic firms from import competition and gives them more room to raise their own prices. In contrast, a high value for the dollar makes imports cheap—and low-priced imports mean stiff competition for domestic firms, which find it hard to raise their own prices.

Describing the rise of the dollar and the fall in oil prices as supply shocks is in one sense misleading. The term "shock" seems to imply something that affects the economy from the outside, independently of any policy actions taken. This is not entirely true of the favorable supply-side developments under discussion here. Both the rise in the international value of the dollar and the fall in oil prices were intensified by the strength of the 1982 to 1984 recovery and the high level of real interest rates in the United States. Nonetheless, in evaluating the claims made by supply-side economists for the success of the Reagan policies, it seems fair to treat these developments as though they were true supply shocks. Although they were related to U.S. economic policies, they were not brought on specifically by supply-side elements of those policies, that is, by either the credibility effect or the incentive effect of tax cuts.

Whether we choose to call these events supply shocks or something else, the changes in world oil prices and the international value of the dollar accounted for a large part of the slowdown in the inflation rate. High oil prices and a depressed dollar pushed the inflation rate to a peak of 13 percent in 1980. Without these developments, that year's rate probably would have been no higher than 10 percent. Also, falling oil prices and a soaring dollar pushed inflation down in 1983 and 1984. Without these factors, the inflation rate very likely would have been 5 percent or so in those years.

In short, favorable developments in the world economy not connected with supply-side elements of Reagan administration policy appear to account for about half of the 10-percentage-point drop in the inflation rate in the early 1980s. Most of the remaining five percentage points can be explained by high unemployment. Even under Okun's assumptions, unemployment during the 1981 to

1983 period was high enough to cut 3.5 percentage points from the inflation rate. That leaves the Reagan administration with only a 1.5-percentage-point gain to attribute to credibility and the supply-side effects of tax cuts.

Moreover, some economists now claim that Okun's estimate was too pessimistic in the first place. The studies that Okun examined in 1978 assumed that the Phillips curve becomes flatter as the economy moves further to the right along it. Such a shape for the Phillips curve would reduce the impact of high unemployment rates on inflation. However, experience since that time suggests that the short-run Phillips curve has a fairly constant slope, as in the diagrams of this chapter. If the effects of high unemployment on inflation are recalculated assuming a straight-line Phillips curve, the entire slowdown in inflation from 1980 to 1983 can be accounted for by unemployment and supply shocks without appealing to either the credibility effect or the incentive effect of tax cuts.

The further decline in inflation on balance from 1983 to 1986 reflected an unemployment rate that, though falling, remained above the estimated natural rate of 6 percent or so. In addition, oil prices fell again in 1986, with the spot price hitting a low of $8 per barrel at one point. The result was an inflation rate lower than it otherwise would have been.

Looking Ahead

It is too soon to be sure whether the stop-go cycle has been broken and, if so, who deserves the credit. Events of the next few years may settle the issue, however. What should we watch for as the economic scene unfolds?

One possibility is that inflation will be renewed. In late 1986 and in 1987, the favorable developments in oil prices and the exchange rate were reversed once again. Oil prices rose from their low point to hover around $20 a barrel, and the dollar resumed its descent from its 1985 peak. Higher inflation in 1987 than in 1986 was the result. If combined with overly expansionary policy actions, the adverse supply-side developments of 1986 and early 1987 could become entrenched in the form of inflationary expectations. If unemployment then fell below the natural rate, inflation could accelerate.

Alternatively, the threat of a recession could not be ruled out. Some observers were disappointed that a falling dollar cut only a little from the trade deficit. Others feared a collapse in consumer or investor confidence as a result of some such event as the stock market collapse of October, 1987. Efforts to restore investor confidence by cutting the federal budget deficit could backfire, especially if other components of aggregate demand were also falling.

However, more favorable developments are also possible. Cautious monetary and fiscal policy and a renewal of productivity gains may be able to contain inflation without an increase in unemployment. Moderate inflation rates could become firmly rooted in expectations. This process would be aided by stabilization of the dollar's exchange rate. The economy may manage a "soft landing" at a moderate inflation rate and an unemployment rate in the area of 6 percent. While it would be unrealistic to expect the business cycle to disappear entirely, the wild spiral of the 1960s and 1970s might be replaced with a more gentle circling around a point of long-run equilibrium.

More will be known by the time you read this than was known at the time of this writing. Play the role of macroeconomist yourself. Read and watch the story of the economy as it unfolds.

Summary

1. **How are inflation and unemployment related?** The short-run relationship between inflation and unemployment is shown by the *Phillips curve*. This is a downward-sloping curve that shows that for a given expected inflation rate, lower actual inflation rates tend to be linked with higher unemployment rates. An increase in the expected inflation rate tends to shift the Phillips curve upward. Unemployment will be at its natural rate only when the actual inflation rate equals the expected inflation rate. The Phillips curve forms the basis for the *accelerationist theory of inflation*.

2. **How does accelerating inflation affect the economy?** If an expansionary policy is pursued from a standing start, it at first cuts unemployment below its natural rate with only a moderate increase in inflation. As time goes by, however, the trade-off between inflation and unemployment becomes less and less favorable. Inflation must accelerate to a faster rate each year just to keep unemployment from rising back toward its natural rate.

3. **How can the rates of inflation and unemployment both rise during an inflationary recession?** Slowing the growth of aggregate nominal demand after a period of accelerating inflation will cause an inflationary recession. Until the momentum of inflationary expectations is broken, the inflation and unemployment rates may both rise while real output falls. After the expected inflation rate begins to fall, the actual rate can continue to decelerate as long as unemployment remains above its natural rate. The deceleration may continue until the economy reaches a "soft landing" at zero inflation and the natural unemployment rate, or it may be interrupted by a renewal of expansionary policy, or *reflation*.

4. **Why did the U.S. economy follow a pattern of alternating inflation and recession from the 1950s to the early 1980s?** Alternating expansionary and contractionary demand management policies creates a stop-go policy cycle. On the inflation-unemployment chart, the economy moves in clockwise loops around the vertical long-run Phillips curve. If the political system is, on the average, more sensitive to the problem of unemployment than it is to that of inflation, the loops may become an upward spiral. U.S. experience from the 1950s through the 1970s fits such a pattern.

5. **How did the behavior of the U.S. economy in the 1980s differ from that of earlier post–World War II years?** From 1980 to 1983, the economy went through severe back-to-back recessions during which the inflation rate dropped about 10 percentage points. Backers of the Reagan administration's policies claim that this represents a complete break with the earlier stop-go policy cycle. Other economists attribute much of the slowdown to favorable supply shocks combined with traditional monetary restraint. They take a wait-and-see attitude on the question of whether the stop-go cycle really has been broken.

Terms for Review

- accelerationist model of inflation
- Phillips curve
- reflation

Questions for Review

1. Under what conditions will the economy move up or down along a Phillips curve? Under what conditions will the Phillips curve shift?

2. What are three elements on which the accelerationist theory of inflation is based?

3. Use an inflation-unemployment chart to trace the economy's response to accelerating inflation over a period of years according to the accelerationist model. Has this pattern ever been observed in the U.S. economy?

4. Use an inflation-unemployment chart to trace an inflationary recession. Why is it possible for both the inflation rate and the unemployment rate to rise in the same year?

5. Under what conditions will the stop-go policy cycle turn into an upward spiral?

6. What explanations have been given for the rapid slowdown of inflation in the United States between 1980 and 1983?

Problems and Topics for Discussion

1. **Examining the lead-off case.** Using the latest *Economic Report of the President* or another source, find the rates of inflation (year-to-year change in the CPI) and unemployment for 1987 and later years, if available. Add them to Exhibit 19.11. Does it continue to appear that the "awful pattern" of the stop-go cycle was broken by the Reagan administration's policies?

2. **Calculating required nominal GNP growth.** Turn to Exhibit 19.3. What growth rate of nominal GNP would be needed to reach point B′? Point B″?

3. **Setting policy targets.** Turn to Exhibit 19.4. If the Blues want only to keep the unemployment rate at 4

percent in year 2, what target rate of growth for nominal GNP should they set? What target should they set if they want to keep the inflation rate at 2 percent?

4. **Effects of slowing nominal GNP growth.** Turn to Exhibit 19.5. If the rate of growth of nominal GNP slows to 7 percent in year 4 instead of accelerating to 11 percent, what will happen to unemployment? To inflation? To real output?

5. **Effects of a rapid halt in inflation.** Turn to Exhibit 19.6. What rate of growth of nominal GNP would be needed to keep the inflation rate at 11 percent in year

5? What would happen to the unemployment rate in that case?

6. **Aiming for a soft landing.** Turn to Exhibit 19.8. Suppose the Grays decided to aim for a "soft landing" at a 6 percent inflation rate and 6 percent unemployment instead of zero inflation and 6 percent unemployment. Beginning from point I, what policy for nominal GNP would they need in order to do this? Could they keep the economy at 6 percent inflation and 6 percent unemployment indefinitely? If so, what policy would be required?

Case for Discussion
A Very Good Year

From President Richard Nixon's economic report for 1972:

As predicted, 1972 was a very good year for the American economy.

From the end of 1971 to the end of 1972, total output rose by about $7\frac{1}{2}$ percent. This is one of the largest 1-year increases in the past 25 years. This growth took place in a largely peacetime economy; it was not achieved by a war-fed, inflationary boom. In fact, real defense spending declined 5 percent during the year. More important is the fact that the big increase in production of the year just ended was accompanied by a reduced rate of inflation. Consumer prices increased a little more than 3 percent from 1971 to 1972—a far cry from the runaway inflation rate of 6 percent that confronted us in 1969.

A year ago, looking ahead to 1972, I said that the great problem was to get the unemployment rate down from the 6-percent level where it was in 1971. During 1972 the rate was reduced to a little over 5 percent. We should get this down further, and expect to do so, but what was accomplished was gratifying. . . .

The general prediction is that 1973 will be another very good year for the American economy. I believe that it *can* be a great year. It can be a year in which we reduce unemployment and inflation further and enter into a sustained period of strong growth, full employment, and price stability. But 1973 will be a great year only if we manage our fiscal affairs prudently and do not exceed the increases in Federal expenditures that I have proposed. This is the practical lesson of the experience from 1965 to 1968, when loose fiscal policy turned a healthy expansion into a feverish boom followed by a recession. I am determined to live by this lesson. And I urgently appeal to the Congress to join me in doing so.

Source: President's Council of Economic Advisers, *Economic Report of the President* (Washington, D.C.: Government Printing Office, 1973), 3–7.

Questions

1. These passages from Nixon's 1973 economic report discuss the course of the economy from 1965 to 1972. Is the story given consistent with the accelerationist model of inflation?

2. Assuming a natural rate of unemployment of about 5.5 to 6.0 percent for the early 1970s, do you think it was realistic to predict further declines in both

the unemployment rate and the inflation rate in 1973? Explain your answer in terms of the accelerationist model.

3. In retrospect, do you think that 1972 possibly was *too* good a year? What policies could have been used to bring the economy to a "soft landing" more gradually?

4. As expressed in this report, Nixon's only worry about the coming year concerned government spending. In fact, federal defense spending fell, in real terms, another 9 percent in 1973, and nondefense purchases of goods and services edged downward slightly. Thus, runaway government spending would not appear to account for the renewal of inflation in 1973. The first oil-related supply shock did not occur until the very end of the year. What else might have accounted for the renewal of inflation in 1973?

Suggestions for Further Reading

Friedman, Milton. "The Role of Monetary Policy," *American Economic Review* 58 (May 1968): 1–17.

Friedman's presidential address to the American Economics Association is thought to be the first statement of the accelerationist theory discussed in this chapter.

Gordon, Robert J. *Macroeconomics*, 3d ed. Boston: Little, Brown, 1984.

Chapter 8 of this book provides a more advanced treatment of the accelerationist theory.

Phelps, Edmund S. *Inflation Policy and Unemployment Theory*. New York: Norton, 1972.

A readable statement of the accelerationist theory by one of its pioneers. The theory is sometimes known as the Friedman-Phelps theory of inflation.

20 Foreign Exchange Markets and International Monetary Policy

After reading this chapter, you will understand . . .

- How supply and demand curves can be used to represent foreign exchange market activity arising from current account transactions.
- How the supply and demand framework can be extended to incorporate the capital account.
- How changes in rates of real economic growth affect exchange rates.
- How changes in real interest rates affect exchange rates.
- What actions governments take to influence exchange rates.
- How the international monetary system has evolved since World War II.

Before reading this chapter, make sure you know the meaning of . . .

- Balance of payments accounts (Chapter 7)
- Intervention in foreign exchange markets (Chapter 13)
- Sterilization (Chapter 13)

World Trade on a Seesaw

Phil Mattison, Jr., vice-president of a family-owned machine-tool factory in Rockford, Illinois, sees early but convincing signs that the U.S. trade problem is beginning to ease.

In late March or April 1986, after a hiatus of about two years, orders from West Germany and Switzerland began trickling into his company, Mattison Machine Works. In June the company landed contracts from Europe for $1.2 million of new equipment. And more recently, it has begun receiving inquiries about new orders from Japan.

Unemployment has become a hot issue in Japan.

Mattison is so encouraged by the foreign demand that this week he is sending company representatives on a sales trip to Europe. And pressure from foreign competition here in the U.S. market has begun to ease somewhat as well. "There's been some definite improvement in the trade picture," he says.

Both the revival of business from Europe and Japan and reduced foreign competition at home are "flat-out the result" of the recent depreciation of the dollar, Mattison says. The greenback has fallen 36 percent against a basket of major currencies over the past 20 months and even more sharply against the West German mark and the Japanese yen. The dollar's high value between 1981 and 1985, combined with sluggish economic growth abroad, "pulled the hell out of our European market," Mattison recalls. Several years ago, "overseas business went from very good to zero" in a matter of months.

Meanwhile Japan is on the other end of the foreign trade seesaw. Social harmony is highly valued there, but it wasn't much in evidence recently when the largest employer in Innoshima pulled the plug on that island city of 37,500. An official of Hitachi Zosen Corporation came before the city council and said the big shipbuilder was in trouble. Soon it would have to eliminate 1,000 of its 1,200 jobs.

485

Unemployment is becoming a hot issue in Japan for the first time in many years. Nearly every day, there is some disturbing announcement about loss of wages or jobs. Shipbuilders are closing down yards. Steelmakers are experimenting with "rotational" layoffs. Japan's remaining coal mines are closing. The weaker automakers are shunting workers into obscure affiliates or turning them into car dealers.

It's more than just an unemployment problem. It's a social problem, a perceived threat to Japan's "lifetime employment" system.

The steep appreciation of the Japanese yen—which forces companies either to raise their export prices and risk losing sales or to hold the line on prices and probably lose revenue anyway in terms of yen—has greatly accelerated the decline of these industries since the fall of 1985. All this could leave whole communities high and dry.

Sources: Art Pine, "U.S. Trade Problems Begin to Ease, Spurred by the Dollar's Decline," *The Wall Street Journal*, October 31, 1986, 1; Bernard Wysocki, Jr., "Japanese are Suffering Unemployment Rise in a Shifting Economy," *The Wall Street Journal*, November 6, 1986, 1. Reprinted by permission of *The Wall Street Journal*, © Dow Jones & Company, Inc. 1986. All Rights Reserved.

THE effects of the foreign trade seesaw always seem to be in the news. In the early 1980s, with the dollar soaring, U.S. exporters were suffering while the Japanese were riding high. Then, after the dollar began to fall in March 1985, their roles reversed, as these news items from late 1986 relate. The future course of exchange rates cannot be predicted, but one thing is certain: When exchange rates undergo wide swings, as they have in the 1980s, they touch lives in towns and cities around the globe.

At several points in this course, we have raised the topics of imports, exports, capital flows, and exchange rates.[1] In this chapter, we tie those topics together and add new detail. The principal tools we will use for doing this are our old friends supply and demand, this time applied to the foreign exchange markets.

Foreign Exchange Markets

As we have seen in earlier chapters, transactions in international trade differ from payments within a country in that countries have their own national currencies. Because of this, every international transaction involves a visit to the foreign exchange markets, where one country's currency can be exchanged for another's. Chapter 13 discussed the operation of the foreign exchange markets in general terms. This section will show how supply and demand operate in foreign exchange markets to determine the relative values of different currencies—the number of French francs, West German marks, Japanese yen, and so on that can be bought for a dollar.

---

[1] Sections on international topics, identified by the globe symbol, appear in Chapters 6, 7, 10, 13, 14, and 15. This chapter builds on those earlier sections. It may be useful to review them before proceeding.

Exchange Markets: Current Account Only

To keep things simple, we will begin with a world in which international transactions are limited to imports and exports of goods and services and transfer payments on current account. There are no net capital flows, since exchanges of bank deposits and currency in payment for a country's imports and net transfers are just balanced by payments for its exports.

Assuming these conditions, suppose that a West German clothing importer wants to buy a shipment of Levis. The importer has West German marks in a Frankfurt bank account, but the U.S. manufacturer wants to be paid in dollars, which it can use to pay workers and buy supplies in the United States. The importer's bank sells the necessary number of marks on the foreign exchange market and receives dollars in return. The dollars are then sent to the manufacturer to pay for the Levis.

Meanwhile, thousands of other people in the United States and Germany are also buying and selling dollars and marks for their own purposes. Total activity in the foreign exchange market, like that in any other market, can be viewed in terms of supply and demand curves such as those shown in Exhibit 20.1. This figure shows the supply of and demand for dollars, with the price (the exchange rate) in terms of marks per dollar. It could also have been drawn to show the supply of and demand for marks, with the price in dollars per mark. The ratios of dollars to marks and marks to dollars are two ways of expressing the same thing; there is just one exchange rate.

The Demand Curve for Dollars

Look first at the demand curve for dollars in Exhibit 20.1. If we focus on current account transactions, the shape and position of the demand curve will depend on how German demand for U.S. goods and services fluctuates as the exchange rate varies, other things being equal. Suppose, for example, that Levis sell for $20 a pair in the United States. At an exchange rate of 3 marks per dollar, German

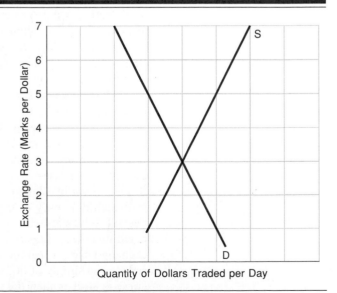

Exhibit 20.1 Supply of and Demand for Dollars on Current Account

This exhibit shows the supply and demand curves for dollars in the foreign exchange market in which dollars are exchanged for West German marks. Only current account transactions—exports, imports, and transfer payments—are assumed to take place. The slope and position of the demand curve reflect the German demand for U.S. exports; the slope and position of the supply curve indicate U.S. demand for German imports. In the case shown here, U.S. demand for German imports is assumed to be elastic; thus, the supply curve has a positive slope.

consumers will have to pay 60 marks per pair. They may buy a total of, say, 1,000 pairs a day, thereby creating a demand for $20,000 per day in the foreign exchange market. If the exchange rate falls to 2.5 marks per dollar while the U.S. price remains unchanged, German consumers will be able to buy Levis more cheaply—for 50 marks a pair ($20 a pair × 2.5 marks per dollar). At the lower price, German consumers are likely to buy a larger quantity—say, 1,250 pairs a day. The demand for dollars created by these sales will thus increase to $25,000 per day.

The Supply Curve for Dollars

In a world limited to current account transactions, dollars are supplied to the foreign exchange market by U.S. citizens who want to buy West German goods. The supply curve for dollars in Exhibit 20.1 slopes upward, showing that more dollars will be supplied to the foreign exchange market as the price of dollars in terms of marks rises. This will be the case whenever U.S. demand for German goods is *elastic*—that is, whenever a 1 percent change in the U.S. price of German goods causes a greater than 1 percent change in the quantity demanded.

An example will show why the slope of the dollar supply curve depends on the elasticity of U.S. demand for German goods. Suppose that a certain model of the German BMW automobile has a price of 60,000 marks. At an exchange rate of 3 marks per dollar, the car will sell for $20,000 in the United States (ignoring shipping costs and other charges). If 500 BMWs a day are sold at that price, U.S. buyers will have to supply $10 million per day to this foreign exchange market in order to get the 30 million marks needed to pay the German manufacturer. Suppose that the exchange rate rises to 4 marks per dollar, enabling U.S. buyers to get the car for just $15,000 (a 25 percent decrease in the dollar price). Since we are assuming an elastic demand for BMWs, the number of BMWs imported will rise more than in proportion to the decrease in the dollar price— say, by 50 percent, to 750 a day. In order to obtain 750 cars at 60,000 marks per car and an exchange rate of 4 marks per dollar, U.S. buyers will have to supply $11.25 million per day to the foreign exchange market (750 cars per day × 60,000 marks per car × .25 dollars per mark). The number of dollars supplied to the market will have increased in response to a rise in the price of the dollar in terms of marks, as shown in Exhibit 20.1.

In Exhibit 20.1, the supply of and demand for dollars are equal at an exchange rate of 3 marks per dollar. The value of imports is equal to the value of exports and the current account is in balance, assuming zero net transfers.

If U.S. demand for foreign goods is inelastic rather than elastic, the supply curve for dollars on the foreign exchange market will have a negative slope. An inelastic demand means that a 1 percent change in the U.S. price of German goods will cause a less than 1 percent change in the quantity demanded. The BMW example can easily be changed to illustrate this. Suppose that when the exchange rate rises from 3 to 4 marks per dollar (bringing the U.S. price of BMWs down by 25 percent—from $20,000 to $15,000), only 50 more cars are sold each day (only a 10 percent increase). In order to get the German marks needed to buy 550 cars at 60,000 marks per car at an exchange rate of 4 marks per dollar, U.S. buyers need supply only $8.25 million per day to the foreign exchange market. An increase in the price of dollars in terms of marks will thus reduce the supply of dollars. However, as long as the negatively sloped supply curve is steeper than the demand curve, as shown in Exhibit 20.2, the market will achieve a stable equilibrium at the point at which the curves cross.

Exhibit 20.2   Current Account Supply and
Demand with Inelastic Import Demand

If a 1 percent increase in the dollar price of imports
decreases the quantity of imports purchased by less than 1
percent, demand for imports is said to be *inelastic*. In that
case, a reduction in the exchange rate, which increases the
dollar price of imports, will result in a greater quantity of
dollars supplied to the exchange markets. That will result in
a negatively sloped supply curve, as shown here.

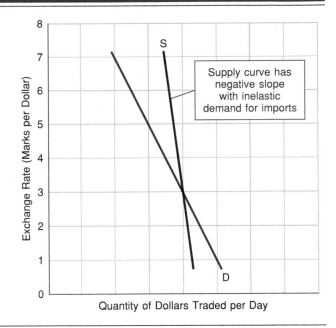

Shifts in Supply and Demand: Current Account

For the time being, we will assume a positive slope for the supply curve, but
this assumption is not always justified in practice. Later we will consider the
implications of different elasticity assumptions.

Changes in economic conditions can cause shifts in the supply and demand
curves for foreign exchange markets. Exhibit 20.3 gives an example. For the
moment, we will continue to focus on current account transactions.

Starting from an equilibrium at point E_1 with an exchange rate of 3 marks
per dollar, suppose that the U.S. Department of Defense places a large order for
armored vehicles made in West Germany. In order to import German goods, it
must trade dollars for marks in the foreign exchange market. The result, as
shown in Exhibit 20.3, is a rightward shift in the dollar supply curve from S_1 to S_2.

At first, the shift in the supply curve creates an excess supply of dollars,
which tends to depress the exchange rate. This surplus reflects an incipient U.S.
balance of payments deficit on current account that would result if the increase
in imports were sustained and there were no change in exports. However, as the
exchange rate falls, U.S. goods become cheaper for Germans to buy, which
increases the number of dollars demanded; this situation is shown by a downward movement along the demand curve. At the same time, German goods
become more expensive for U.S. buyers, which somewhat decreases the number
of dollars supplied; this situation appears as a downward movement along the
new dollar supply curve. In Exhibit 20.3, the supply of and demand for dollars
again come into equilibrium at an exchange rate of 2 marks per dollar. In the
new equilibrium, E_2, the exchange rate is lower than before and both U.S.
imports and U.S. exports have increased. The balance of payments on the current account remains in equilibrium.

Exhibit 20.3   Effects of a Shift in the Current Account Supply Curve for Dollars

This exhibit shows the effects of a shift in the supply curve for dollars in a world limited to current account transactions. The shift in the supply curve is assumed to be caused by a major purchase of German goods by the U.S. government. In order to buy the German goods, the government must first exchange dollars for marks, thereby adding to the supply of dollars offered in the foreign exchange market at the initial exchange rate. To eliminate the excess supply of dollars, the dollar's value must fall (depreciate). Depreciation of the dollar makes U.S. goods cheaper for German buyers. As exports increase, the market moves downward along the demand curve to a point at which supply and demand are brought into balance.

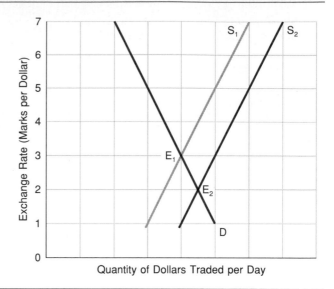

Depreciation (of a currency)
A decline in the value of a country's currency relative to another's.

Appreciation (of a currency)
An increase in the value of a country's currency relative to another's.

Purchasing power parity
A situation in which a given sum of money will buy the same market basket of goods and services when converted from one currency to another at prevailing exchange rates.

In the terminology of foreign exchange markets, the dollar is said to **depreciate** when its price falls in terms of a foreign currency as in the above example. Seen from the German point of view, a fall in the price of the dollar in terms of marks is equivalent to a rise in the price of marks in terms of dollars. At the same time that the dollar depreciates, then, the mark can be said to **appreciate** against the dollar.

According to one theory, in a world limited to current account transactions the dollar would tend to appreciate or depreciate until a point was reached at which a given amount of money, converted at the market exchange rate, would buy the same "market basket" of goods and services in the two countries. This state of affairs is known as **purchasing power parity.** For example, suppose 3 marks per dollar is the exchange rate corresponding to purchasing power parity for Germany and the United States. That would mean that a typical market basket of goods and services (so many raincoats, so many airline tickets, so many apples, and so on) that cost $1,000 in the United States would cost 3,000 marks in Germany so that a person would be no better off, on the average, by purchasing the whole market basket in one country rather than the other. Purchasing power parity provides an interesting reference point in discussing exchange rates. However, as "Applying Economic Ideas 20.1" shows, in practice exchange rates do not correspond to purchasing power parity at any given time.

The Capital Account Net Demand Curve

Now that we have discussed the current account supply and demand curves for dollars, it is time to consider the capital account. First we will look at the capital account by itself; then we will combine it with the current account.

Capital account net demand curve
A graph that shows the net demand for a country's currency that results at various exchange rates from capital account transactions.

A graphical representation of the capital account is given in Exhibit 20.4. It contains a downward-sloping line, which we will call the **capital account net demand curve,** that shows the net demand for dollars arising from capital account transactions. If capital inflows to the United States exceed capital outflows, the net demand for dollars on capital account will be positive. If capital

Exchange Rates and Purchasing Power Parity

Is the dollar, at any moment, overvalued, undervalued, or about right? In one sense, the answer is always "just right": The dollar is worth whatever people are willing to pay for it in exchange for marks, yen, pounds, or whatever. However, according to another view, the dollar tends, in the long run, to move toward the level of *purchasing power parity*. Under the purchasing power parity theory, the dollar's exchange rate is said to be appropriate when it is possible to buy the same basket of goods and services in various countries for the same amount of money when that money is converted at the prevailing exchange rates.

To illustrate, we can first apply the purchasing power parity concept to individual goods. As shown in the accompanying chart, in the spring of 1987 it was possible to buy a dozen eggs in the United States for about $1. In London, a dozen eggs would have cost 1.23 British pounds, the equivalent of $1.89 at the then current exchange rate. Thus, in terms of eggs the dollar could be said to have been below the purchasing power parity level at that time. As the chart shows, by the purchasing power parity standard, the dollar in early 1987 was undervalued relative to the currencies of six major U.S. trading partners in terms of several common goods and services.

A closer look at the chart reveals, however, that the degree of undervaluation relative to a given foreign currency differs from one good to another because of differences in relative prices. For example, at that time a dozen eggs cost about twice as much in Tokyo as in the United States, whereas a pound of beef cost about four times as much. Further, in terms of toothpaste in London and Seoul and beef in Rome, the dollar was actually above the parity level. To allow for variations in relative prices, economists commonly base purchasing power parity calculations on the average price of a broad-based market basket of goods and services. For example, a study conducted in late 1986 by the Organization for European Cooperation and Development confirmed undervaluation relative to purchasing power parity for a broad-based market basket of goods and services. According to that study, at that time the purchasing power parity exchange rate for the Japanese yen would have been 223 to the dollar compared with a market rate of 169. For West Germany, the purchasing power parity rate would have been 2.48 marks per dollar compared with a market rate of 2.17 marks. For France, the purchasing power parity rate would have been 7.48 francs per dollar compared with a market rate of 6.93. At

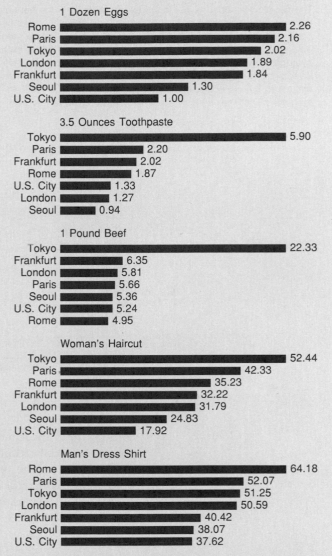

Five common items in a typical major U.S. city versus six cities abroad. Prices abroad in foreign currencies converted into dollars at recent exchange rates.

that time, however, the broad-based comparison showed the dollar to be slightly overvalued relative to purchasing power parity in the case of the Italian lira and the British pound.

The purchasing power parity concept does not allow for capital flows, transportation costs, or international differences in buying habits. However, it provides an interesting, if rough, benchmark for interpreting movements of market exchange rates.

Exhibit 20.4   The Capital Account Net Demand Curve

The negatively sloped curve in this graph represents the net demand for dollars on capital account. This demand can be either positive (indicating a net capital inflow) or negative (indicating a net capital outflow). Assuming interest rates in the two countries to be equal, the curve crosses the vertical axis at the level of the future exchange rate expected by the average investor. The capital account net demand curve has a negative slope because investors are attracted to assets denominated in currencies that they think are undervalued relative to the expected future exchange rate and tend to avoid assets denominated in currencies that they believe are overvalued relative to that rate.

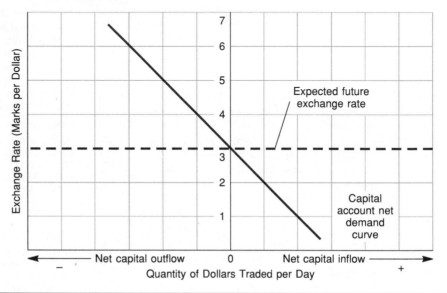

outflows from the United States exceed capital inflows, the net demand for dollars on capital account will be negative. To allow for both positive and negative net demand, the vertical axis is drawn in the middle of the graph.

Several factors affect the slope and position of the capital account net demand curve. The most important of these can be grouped under factors affecting expectations and factors related to interest rates. Let's look at each of these in turn.

Expectations Regarding Future Exchange Rates

We begin by looking at how the capital account net demand for dollars is affected by changes in the exchange relative to that expected to prevail in the future. Put yourself in the position of a person with $1 million to invest. You are trying to decide whether to use the funds to buy bonds issued by the U.S. government or comparable bonds issued by the West German government.

To keep things simple, we will initially assume that the U.S. and German bonds you are considering have identical 10 percent nominal interest rates and mature one year from now. We will also assume for the moment that no change is expected in the average price level for goods and services in either country. Finally, we will assume that you expect the exchange rate one year from now to be 3 marks per dollar.

Given these expectations, suppose that today's exchange rate is 2 marks per dollar. If you trade your $1 million for marks now, you can buy 2 million marks of West German bonds. When the bonds mature a year later, you will have 2.2 million marks, including the interest you have earned at the 10 percent rate assumed in our example. However, you expect the exchange rate to have risen to 3 marks per dollar by then. At that exchange rate, you will get only $733,000 for your 2.2 million marks. You would have done better to buy U.S. government bonds; then you would have come out with $1.1 million at the end of the year, including interest.

Suppose, however, that today's exchange rate is 4 marks per dollar but you expect it to fall to 3 marks per dollar over the next year. In that case, you will come out better buying 4 million marks of German bonds for your $1 million. At 3 marks per dollar, the 4.4 million marks you will have at the end of the year will get you $1,466,666 in the foreign exchange market—more than the $1.1 million you would have had you invested in U.S. bonds.

The moral of the story is: Given the same interest rates in two countries, you should invest in assets of the country whose currency you think is more likely to appreciate and avoid those of the country whose currency is likely to depreciate. The same reasoning applies in reverse if you are a borrower: If interest rates on loans are the same in two countries, you will want to borrow from the one whose exchange rate you expect to fall. That way you will be able to repay the loan in "cheap" marks, dollars, or whatever when the loan comes due.

The effects of expected changes in exchange rates account for the negative slope of the capital account net demand curve. In Exhibit 20.4, the curve intersects the vertical axis at the future rate of 3 marks per dollar that is, on the average, expected by participants in foreign exchange markets. In this example, the exchange rate that the average investor expects one year hence is 3 marks per dollar. As the current exchange rate falls below the benchmark, other things being equal, more investors will expect it to move up over the lives of their investments. Given this majority expectation of a rising exchange rate, those investors will want to switch their mark-denominated assets to dollar-denominated ones. At the same time, borrowers who expect the dollar to appreciate over the lives of their loans will want to switch their borrowing from U.S. to German sources. The actions of both investors and borrowers will increase the net quantity of dollars demanded on capital account. The further the exchange rate of the dollar falls in the present, the greater the proportion of investors who will expect it to rise later and switch to dollar-denominated assets and the greater the proportion of borrowers who will switch out of dollar-denominated borrowing. In Exhibit 20.4, the result is shown as a movement downward and to the right along the capital account net demand curve.

When the current exchange rate rises above the 3-mark-per-dollar average expected rate, the reactions will be reversed. As the dollar rises, more and more investors and borrowers will anticipate that the dollar will fall back toward the average expected rate over the lives of their investments or loans. Hence, they will switch their investments out of dollar-denominated assets and their borrowing into dollar-denominated loans. The net quantity of dollars demanded on capital account will then become negative, moving them upward and to the right along the capital account net demand curve.

Real versus Nominal Exchange Rates

If we relax the assumption of no change in price levels, things become a bit more complicated. In a world in which inflation takes place and at different rates in different countries, it becomes necessary to distinguish between nominal and

Nominal exchange rate
The exchange rate expressed in the usual way: in terms of current units of foreign currency per current dollar.

Real exchange rate
The nominal exchange rate adjusted for changes in the price levels of both countries relative to a chosen base year.

real exchange rates. The **nominal exchange rate** is the exchange rate expressed in the usual way: in terms of current currency units. The **real exchange rate** is adjusted to allow for changes in the price levels of both countries relative to a chosen base year. The nominal rate can be converted to the real rate by applying the formula

$$E_r = E_n \left(\frac{P_d}{P_f} \right),$$

where E_r is the real exchange rate, E_n is the nominal exchange rate, P_d is the domestic price level, and P_f is the foreign price level, with both price levels expressed in terms of the same base year.

For example, suppose that in the base year, 1980, a given market basket of goods costs $1,000 in the United States and 3,000 marks in Germany. The 1980 nominal exchange rate is 3 marks per dollar. By 1987, the price level in the United States has risen by 50 percent—from 1.0 to 1.5—while the price level in Germany is unchanged at 1.0. This means that the market basket now costs $1,500 in the United States. In order to maintain a constant real exchange rate, the 1987 nominal exchange rate must fall to 2 marks per dollar (2 marks per dollar nominal × 1.5/1.0 = 3 marks per dollar real). If the nominal rate had remained unchanged at 3 marks per dollar, the real rate would have risen to 4.5 marks per dollar (3 marks per dollar nominal × 1.5/1.0 = 4.5).

Other things being equal, nominal exchange rates tend to respond to inflation in a way that keeps real exchange rates constant. If the capital account net demand curve were expressed in terms of real exchange rates, changes in expected future nominal exchange rates that matched differences in inflation rates would have no effect on the volume of capital inflows or outflows.

Differences in Real Interest Rates

Now that we have seen how changes in the current exchange rate relative to its expected future value cause movements along the capital account net demand curve, let us return to the subject of interest rates. Exhibit 20.5 sets the stage. As before, we will assume that nominal interest rates initially are equal in the United States and Germany and that there is no inflation. We will also assume that the initial exchange rate of 3 marks per dollar is equal to the average expected future rate. This puts the capital account in balance at E_1.

Now suppose that the nominal interest rate rises in the United States and falls in West Germany. Other things being equal, this difference in nominal interest rates will encourage people to buy U.S. assets and discourage them from borrowing from U.S. sources. The resulting increase in the net demand for dollars on capital account is shown by an upward and rightward shift in the capital account net demand curve from D_1 to D_2.

The shift in the demand curve that results from the relative increase in U.S. interest rates creates an excess demand for dollars in the foreign exchange markets. The excess demand causes the exchange rate to rise above the average expected future level. As it does, investors must begin to consider the possibility that it will fall again at some time during their investments' lives. Leaving any effects on current account imports and exports out of the picture for the moment, the market will reach a new equilibrium at E_2. At that point, the appeal of the relatively higher U.S. interest rate for the marginal investor will be exactly

Exhibit 20.5   A Shift in the Capital Account Net Demand Curve

This exhibit shows the effects of a rise in the U.S. interest rate relative to the West German interest rate. An increase in the U.S. interest rate makes dollar-denominated assets more attractive to investors, shifting the curve upward. This causes the exchange rate to rise. At a higher exchange rate, some investors become unwilling to buy dollar-denominated assets because they think the dollar is overvalued relative to the exchange rate they expect in the future. Leaving effects on current account transactions out of the picture, the shift in the demand curve moves the market from its equilibrium at E_1 to a new equilibrium at E_2.

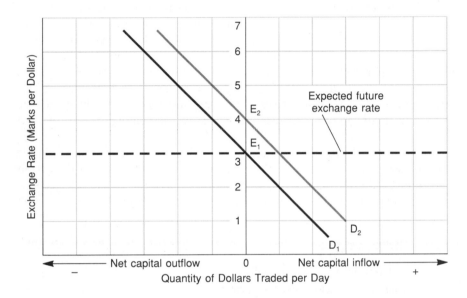

offset by the expectation that the exchange rate will fall. The capital account will be restored to balance.

The example just given is simplified by the assumption of fixed price levels in both countries, but the model can be extended to the case in which inflation is possible at various rates in different countries. To make this extension, we can express both exchange rates and interest rates in real terms. In principle, a stable relationship prevails between real interest rates and real exchange rates even when inflation rates differ from one country to another. For example, beginning from the case illustrated in Exhibit 20.5, consider no change in Germany but an increase in the nominal interest rate that is associated with an equal increase in the expected U.S. inflation rate, thus leaving the expected real U.S. interest rate unchanged. This development would make dollar-denominated assets neither more nor less attractive to German investors. The reason is that the anticipated increase in the U.S. price level will be expected to cause a proportional depreciation in the nominal mark-dollar exchange rate. The higher nominal return on U.S. assets will thus be exactly offset by the expectation of a lower future nominal exchange rate and will be associated with an unchanged net quantity of dollars demanded on capital account.

However, a full development of real exchange rate determination under conditions of differential inflation is beyond the scope of this book. To keep things simple, we will now return to the assumption of fixed price levels in both countries. Under these conditions, real exchange rates are equal to nominal exchange rates and real interest rates to nominal interest rates.

Combining the Current and Capital Accounts

Having looked at the current and capital accounts separately, we will now combine them. Exhibit 20.6 shows how this is done. Part a shows the current account supply and demand curves; as we have seen, these reflect imports and exports of goods and services, plus transfer payments. Part b shows the capital account net demand curve, which reflects international purchases and sales of assets and international borrowing and lending. In this exhibit, the net quantity of dollars demanded in capital account transactions is positive when the exchange rate is below the expected future rate of 3 marks per dollar, indicating a net capital inflow. Above 3 marks per dollar, the net quantity of dollars demanded in capital account transactions is negative, indicating a net capital outflow.

Part c combines the two demand curves. The horizontal distance from the vertical axis to the total demand curve for dollars equals the sum of the current and capital account demands. The total demand curve for dollars intersects the current account demand curve at the exchange rate for which the capital account

Exhibit 20.6   Combining the Current and Capital Account Demand Curves

This graph shows how the current account demand curve for dollars and the capital account net demand curve can be added together to get a total demand curve for dollars. Total demand at each exchange rate equals current account demand plus the net capital inflow to the United States. If there is a net capital outflow from the United States, the total demand curve will lie to the left of the current account demand curve. Here the market is assumed to be in equilibrium at an exchange rate of 3 marks per dollar, which is also the average exchange rate expected in the future. At that point, both the current and capital accounts are in balance.

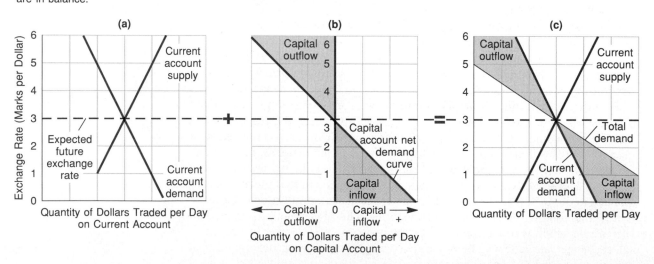

is in balance, that is, at the point where the capital account net demand curve in part b intersects its vertical axis. Thus, at exchange rates below 3 marks per dollar, the total demand curve for dollars is greater than it would be if only current account transactions were considered. Above 3 marks per dollar, where the total demand curve lies to the left of the current account demand curve, the total demand for dollars is less than it would be if only current account transactions were considered.

In Exhibit 20.6 the market is in equilibrium at 3 marks per dollar, the exchange rate that corresponds to the average expected future rate. At this exchange rate, both the current and capital accounts are in balance. The value of imports plus net transfers equals that of exports, and capital inflows equal capital outflows. This position of the foreign exchange market provides a useful benchmark for discussing policy issues—and, in a general sense, it is a position toward which foreign exchange rates tend. However, in practice exchange rates may depart from expected future rates and the current and capital accounts can show surpluses or deficits, not only in the short run but often over periods of many years. In the next section, we examine some of the reasons for this.

Sources of Changes in Exchange Rates

This section will show that changes in exchange rates cannot be understood in terms of the current account alone but only with respect to the interaction of the current and capital accounts. Even when movements in exchange rates stem from changes in current account supply and demand, the capital account will be affected. Likewise, when movements in exchange rates stem from changes in capital account net demand, the current account will be affected. In the first case, the dog wags the tail; in the second, the tail wags the dog.

Exchange Rates and Economic Growth

Differences among countries in rates of economic growth are a key factor affecting exchange rates. Exhibit 20.7 illustrates this effect. At first, the foreign exchange markets are in equilibrium at point E_1. The exchange rate is at 3 marks per dollar, which corresponds to the average expected future rate. Growth rates and interest rates in West Germany and the United States are assumed to be equal, and both the current and capital accounts are in balance.

Starting from this situation, suppose that the rate of growth of the U.S. economy increases. To keep things simple, we will assume that this happens without affecting interest rates or upsetting the price stability assumed to prevail in both countries. As the economy grows, U.S. households and firms increase their spending on consumer goods, investment goods, and raw materials. Much of this spending is directed toward goods and services produced at home, but a certain fraction goes for goods and services imported from Germany. To get the marks they need to buy these imported goods, U.S. households and firms bring dollars to the foreign exchange market. The result is a rightward shift in the current account supply curve from S_1 to S_2.

Given the position of the total demand curve, the increased supply of dollars puts downward pressure on the exchange rate. As the exchange rate begins to

Exhibit 20.7   Effects of an Increase in the U.S. Rate of Economic Growth

An increase in the rate of growth of the U.S. economy increases the demand for imports by U.S. households, firms, and government units. This shifts the current account supply curve for dollars to the right. In the process, an excess supply causes the dollar to depreciate. As the exchange rate depreciates below the average expected future rate of 3 marks per dollar, some investors shift out of mark-denominated assets into dollar-denominated ones. The resulting net capital inflow, shown as a movement downward and to the right along the total dollar demand curve, brings the market back into equilibrium at E_2. There the United States experiences a current account deficit, which is shown by the arrow between the current account demand curve and the total demand curve for dollars. This deficit is offset by a net capital inflow.

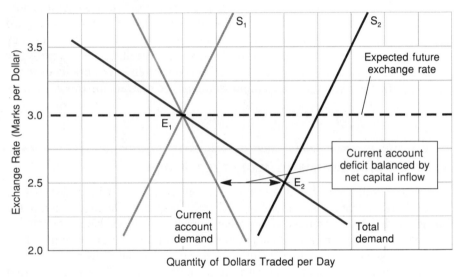

fall, both the current and capital accounts are affected. On the current account, the lower exchange rate makes U.S.-made goods cheaper for buyers in West Germany. U.S. exports increase, as shown by a movement downward and to the right along the current account demand curve. On the capital account, investors see that the dollar has depreciated to a level below the expected future rate. This makes dollar-denominated assets more attractive. We assume that U.S. interest rates remain unchanged and international investors now face better odds that U.S. assets bought with marks now, when the dollar is low, can be converted back into marks later at a profit. Thus, the net quantity of dollars demanded on capital account also increases; this is shown as a widening gap between the current account and total demand curves for dollars as the exchange rate falls.

When the exchange rate falls to 2.5 marks per dollar, the foreign exchange market reaches a new equilibrium at point E_2. Here the total quantity of dollars demanded has increased by enough to equal the quantity of dollars supplied. Note, however, that although the foreign exchange market is back in equilibrium, the current and capital accounts are no longer in balance. As the arrow in Exhibit 20.7 shows, the current account demand for dollars falls short of the current account supply. This indicates that the value of imports exceeds the value of exports—a current account deficit. The remaining supply of dollars is absorbed by the net demand for dollars on capital account. Thus, the current account deficit is just offset by a net inflow of capital.

To summarize, when a country's rate of economic growth increases, other things being equal, its imports increase, its currency depreciates, and a current account deficit develops, offset by a net capital inflow. When a country's growth rate slows down relative to those of its trading partners, the opposite effects take place: Imports fall, the currency appreciates, and a current account surplus develops, offset by a net capital outflow.

Exchange Rates and Interest Rate Differentials

Changing real interest rate differentials among countries are another major factor affecting exchange rates. The relationship between interest rates and exchange rates was discussed in a preliminary way in Chapter 14. Exhibit 20.8 tells the interest rate story using our model of the foreign exchange market.

At first, the market is again in equilibrium at 3 marks per dollar, which corresponds to the expected future rate. Growth rates and interest rates are the same in West Germany and the United States, and both the current and capital accounts are in balance. Now we assume that interest rates increase in the United States but remain unchanged in Germany. To keep things simple, we will assume that this happens with no change in the U.S. or German rates of economic growth and with stable price levels in both countries.

An increase in U.S. interest rates relative to West German rates makes dollar-denominated assets more attractive to investors. At the same time, it

---

Exhibit 20.8   Effects of an Increase in the U.S. Interest Rate

This graph shows the effects of an increase in the U.S. interest rate relative to West Germany's. The increase in the interest rates causes investors to switch to dollar-denominated assets and borrowers to switch to mark-denominated borrowing. The result is an upward shift in the capital account net demand curve for dollars and, hence, a shift in the total demand curve from D_1 to D_2. The shift in the demand curve causes an excess demand for dollars, and the dollar appreciates. As it does, U.S.-made goods become more expensive for German buyers and German-made goods become cheaper for U.S. buyers. The result is a current account deficit, as shown by the arrow. This is offset by a net capital inflow into the United States.

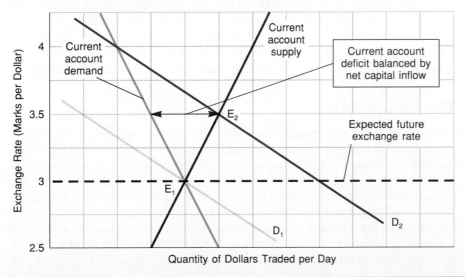

makes borrowing from U.S. sources less attractive. These developments are shown in Exhibit 20.8 by an upward and rightward shift in the total demand curve for dollars from D_1 to D_2. The current account demand curve remains in place, as the entire shift arises from the capital account.

Investors' increased demand for dollars puts upward pressure on the exchange rate. As the exchange rate rises, imports become cheaper for U.S. buyers. They supply more dollars in order to obtain the marks they need to buy additional imports, thereby moving upward and to the right along the current account supply curve. At the same time, U.S. exports become more expensive for German buyers. They demand fewer dollars, thus moving upward and to the left along the current account demand curve.

The capital account is also affected by the rising exchange rate. The higher the rate rises above the average expected future rate of 3 marks per dollar, the more widespread is the expectation that it will fall again during the time period affecting investors and borrowers. If it were to fall, holders of dollar-denominated assets would suffer a loss. This expectation of an exchange rate loss just offsets the attractiveness of relatively high interest rates on dollar-denominated assets for the marginal investor.

As the higher exchange rate reduces the number of dollars demanded on both current and capital account, the market moves upward and to the left along the new total demand curve for dollars. When it reaches point E_2, equilibrium is restored at an exchange rate of 3.5 marks per dollar. Note, however, that neither the current account nor the capital account is in balance. As the arrow in Exhibit 20.8 shows, the current account demand for dollars falls short of the current account supply, indicating a current account deficit. This deficit is offset by an equal net capital inflow.

It is useful to compare the results of an increase in the domestic growth rate (Exhibit 20.7) with those of an increase in domestic interest rates (Exhibit 20.8). In both cases, the United States develops a current account deficit accompanied by a net capital inflow. The effects on the dollar's value are in no way the same, however. In the case of relatively faster U.S. economic growth, a rightward and downward shift in the current account supply curve for dollars produces a current account deficit. It is this deficit that causes the exchange rate to fall. In the case of a higher interest rate, an upward and rightward shift in the capital account net demand curve for dollars causes the exchange rate to rise. It is this change in the exchange rate that causes a current account deficit.

An understanding of the effects of changes in interest rates and growth rates is useful in interpreting the dramatic changes in the international value of the dollar during the 1980s, as "Applying Economic Ideas 20.2" demonstrates.

The J-Curve Effect

The preceding examples suggest that other things being equal, a depreciation of a country's currency will move the current account toward surplus. By "other things being equal" in this case, we mean an appreciation or depreciation that does not arise from a shift in either the current account supply curve or the current account demand curve. This situation is illustrated in part a of Exhibit 20.9. There, beginning from an equilibrium at E_1, a drop in the U.S. interest rate shifts the total demand curve for dollars from D_1 to D_2. The economy moves to a new equilibrium at E_2, where D_2 intersects the current account supply curve. At that point, the exchange rate is 2.5 marks per dollar. Because the

Interest Rates and the Dollar, 1974–1986

According to a standard model of foreign exchange markets, an increase in U.S. interest rates relative to those of trading partners will, other things being equal, cause the dollar to appreciate. Similarly, a fall in U.S. interest rates relative to those abroad will cause the dollar to depreciate.

In the case in which inflation proceeds at different rates in various countries, the underlying relationship predicted by the model is most clearly brought out when expressed in terms of real rather than nominal interest rates and real rather than nominal exchange rates. The accompanying chart confirms that major movements in the real exchange rate of the dollar tended to match movements of

real interest rate differentials over the 1974 to 1986 period. In this chart, the real exchange rate is represented by a weighted average of the dollar's value relative to the currencies of 10 major trading partners, adjusted for movements in consumer prices. The interest rate differential is the real interest rate on long-term U.S. government bonds minus the real rate on a weighted average of comparable long-term bonds issued by the same 10 trading partners' governments. Real interest rates for each country are the country's nominal interest rate minus a moving average of its inflation rate, which serves as a rough measure of the inflation rate that investors on the average expect.

continued

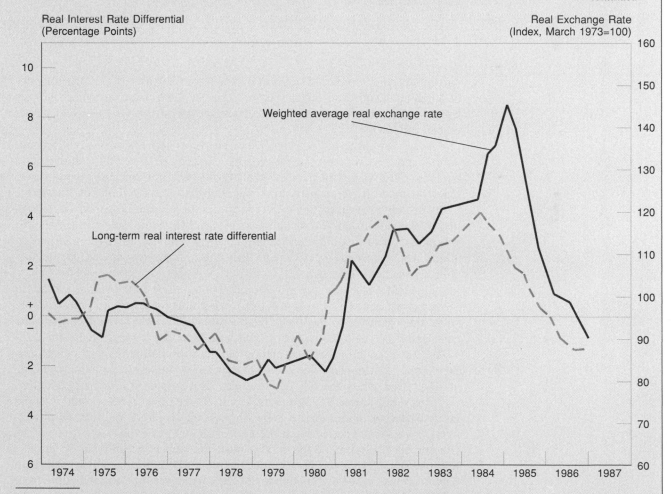

Source: Charles P. Thomas, "U.S. International Transactions in 1986," *Federal Reserve Bulletin* (May 1987): 323.

APPLYING ECONOMIC IDEAS 20.2

continued

In the late 1970s, real interest rates in the United States fell because the U.S. inflation rate rose more rapidly than nominal interest rates. In this situation, foreign investors avoided dollar-denominated assets, and the dollar's real exchange rate hit record lows.

In the early 1980s, the real interest rate differential rose substantially. This happened as nominal U.S. interest rates rose relative to the average rate of inflation. Many economists think that the high U.S. real rates of this period resulted from sizable increases in the federal budget deficit combined with disinflationary monetary policy. During these years, the dollar rose to record highs.

Beginning in early 1984, the real interest rate differential began to slide. For a time, the real dollar exchange rate

continued to rise—in fact, it rose at its most rapid rate of the entire period, perhaps fueled by "safe haven" motives and upward revisions in the expected future real exchange rate. As the real interest rate differential between the United States and its trading partners continued its downward course, however, the dollar began a rapid descent. This descent was consistent with coordinated policy initiatives of major industrial nations that were aimed at reducing the relative value of the dollar, partly with a view to containing the rising U.S. current account deficit. In two years, the dollar's real exchange rate fell as much as it had risen over the previous five years. By early 1987, the interest rate differential was again negative and the dollar had fallen back to the mid-1970s level.

current account supply and demand curves have "normal" slopes, the quantity of dollars demanded on current account exceeds the quantity supplied, indicating a current account surplus. This current account surplus is balanced by a net capital outflow.

As we saw earlier in the chapter, however, the slopes of the current account supply and demand curves depend on the elasticity of demand for imports and exports. For a variety of reasons, demand for both imports and exports is less elastic—that is, less responsive to changes in prices—in the short run than in the long run. One reason is that long order times are required for many industrial goods. Aircraft, machine tools, oil rigs, and the like are not sold "off the shelf"; commitments to buy are made months or even years in advance of shipment. Thus, when exchange rates change, they affect shipments of such goods only after a considerable lag.

Demand is also less responsive to price in the short run than in the long run for consumer goods. One reason is that it takes time for tastes and preferences to shift. For example, in the 1960s relatively few U.S. drivers bought imported cars, and those who did were attracted largely by the low prices. By the mid-1980s, however, imported cars had developed a reputation for quality and styling among U.S. buyers. Thus, after 1985 sales of imported cars fell only a little at first, even when the fall of the dollar drove their prices sharply higher.

Part b of Exhibit 20.9 shows the result. There the current account demand curve is steeper than in part a, reflecting less elastic short-run demand in Germany for goods exported from the United States. As explained earlier in the chapter, inelastic demand for imports gives the current account supply curve a negative slope. However, here, unlike in Exhibit 20.2, the current account supply curve has a slope low enough to cut the current account demand curve from below rather than from above.

Given these curves, we can trace out what happens when falling U.S. interest rates shift the total demand curve downward from D_1 to D_2. The exchange

Exhibit 20.9   The J-Curve Effect

This exhibit shows the effects of a downward shift in the total demand curve for dollars, caused by a decrease in U.S. interest rates, under two elasticity assumptions. If the demand for imported goods is elastic, the current account supply curve for dollars will have a positive slope, as shown in part a. The shift in the demand curve from D_1 to D_2 will then move the economy to a new equilibrium at E_2, where there is a current account surplus balanced by a net capital outflow. In part b, the demand for imports is assumed to be inelastic. The current account supply curve is negatively sloped and cuts the demand curve from below so that the supply curve lies to the right of the current account demand curve below their intersection at E_1. In this case, a downward shift in the total demand curve will move the economy to a new equilibrium in which there is a current account deficit balanced by a net capital inflow. If import demand is inelastic in the short run and more elastic in the long run, a downward shift in the total demand curve will cause the nominal current account to move first toward deficit and then toward surplus. This is known as the *J-curve effect*.

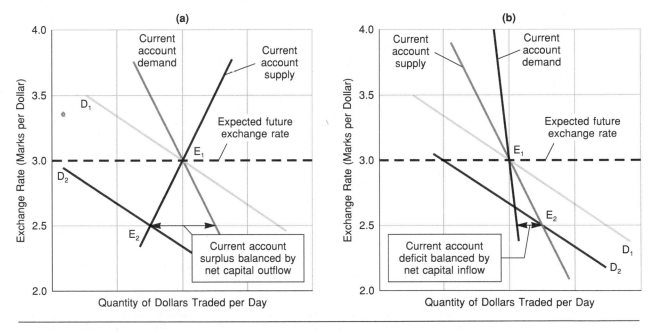

rate, as usual, falls. As it does, the volume of exports rises. Although the increase is only slight, the quantity of dollars demanded on current account increases slightly, indicated by a move downward along the current account demand curve. At the same time, the falling exchange rate raises the dollar prices of imported goods, even though their prices in marks are unchanged. The rising dollar price reduces the physical volume of imports; fewer BMWs, fewer cases of German beer, and so on are imported than before. However, the physical volume of imports falls by a smaller percentage than the dollar prices increase; thus, more dollars than before must be supplied in order to purchase them. Hence, the economy moves down and to the right along the current account supply curve.

As the figure is drawn, the quantity of dollars supplied on current account increases more rapidly than the quantity of dollars demanded on current account. This indicates a deficit in the current account, which must be balanced by a net capital inflow.

The implication for policy is as follows. When a reduction in the domestic real interest rate (or something else) causes the domestic currency to depreciate, the volume of imports and exports will change only slightly in the short run. Thus, the current account balance will move in the direction of deficit, as in part b of Exhibit 20.9. Over time, consumers and firms will adjust more fully to the change in the exchange rate. If the exchange rate remains at its new, lower level, the volume of exports will continue to rise and the volume of imports to shrink. As this happens, the current account will move toward surplus. The final outcome will look more like part a of Exhibit 20.9.

A curve showing the current account balance over time—first falling toward deficit, then rising toward surplus—is somewhat like the letter J. Accordingly, this curve has come to be called the **J-curve effect.** "Applying Economic Ideas 20.3" (pages 506–507) discusses the operation of the J-curve effect as the value of the dollar fell in 1985 and 1986.

J-curve effect
A situation in which a country's nominal current account balance moves at first toward deficit and later toward surplus following a decrease in its currency's exchange rate.

International Monetary Policy

Every change in exchange rates, whether upward or downward, helps some firms and individuals and hurts others, as illustrated by the news item that opened the chapter. When a country's currency appreciates, its export industries suffer, as do industries that compete with imports. However, consumers benefit from the availability of low-cost imports, and they profit from efforts by domestic producers to cut costs and improve quality in response to foreign competition. Also, profits rise and the number of jobs increases in sectors that use imported raw materials and in those devoted to marketing and servicing imported goods.

When a country's currency depreciates, the effects are reversed: Consumers face higher prices; people who sell and service imported goods suffer; but export industries boom, and import-competing industries enjoy a respite from international competition. The former winners become the losers, and vice versa.

These effects insure that exchange rates are a matter of constant concern for policymakers. In previous chapters, we saw several ways in which domestic and international economic policies interact. Now we will use our model of foreign exchange markets to take a closer look at these phenomena.

Effects of Intervention

As we saw in Chapter 13, one option open to governments that wish to raise or lower exchange rates is to intervene in the exchange markets. Suppose, for example, that the Fed sells dollars in an attempt to counter upward pressure on the exchange rate. The immediate impact of the sales of dollars would shift the supply curve for dollars to the right as the dollars sold on official reserve account were added to those sold on current account. The extra supply of dollars would relieve the upward pressure on the exchange rate. Compared with what would have been, the lower exchange rate would eventually cause the value of exports to be higher and the value of imports to be lower, although the nominal deficit might temporarily be higher due to the J-curve effect.

However, as we know, a shift in the supply curve is not the only result of an official reserve account sale of dollars. The dollars sold end up as new reserves in the U.S. banking system. The increase in the U.S. banking system's total reserves, in turn, causes the U.S. money supply to expand.

To the extent that the government's goal is to get the exchange rate down, the increase in the money supply is helpful. An increase in the money supply will depress U.S. interest rates at least temporarily. This, in turn, will cause a downward shift in the capital account net demand curve for dollars. The shift in the net demand curve will reinforce the rightward shift in the supply curve for dollars and add downward pressure on the exchange rate.

However, the change in the money supply resulting from intervention in the foreign exchange market may conflict with the goals of domestic economic policy. In this case, the Fed can *sterilize* by using domestic open market sales of government securities. The sterilization sales of securities will absorb reserves at the same time that intervention purchases of foreign currencies for dollars are creating reserves. Similarly, the Fed can use domestic open market purchases of securities to create reserves at the same time that intervention sales of foreign currencies in exchange for dollars are absorbing reserves. However, sterilized intervention has far less impact on exchange rates than simple, unsterilized intervention. There is still a slight impact on the foreign exchange market supply curve of dollars at the time official sales (or purchases) of dollars are made. However, the effect—if any—of sterilized intervention on the net demand curve for dollars is quite limited. The volume of foreign exchange market transactions and the world stock of dollar-denominated assets are huge. Trying to make a lasting impact on exchange rates with a few billion dollars' worth of sterilized intervention would be like trying to hold back the tide with a teacup.

Other Policies for Affecting the Exchange Rate

Because sterilized intervention gives only limited control over the exchange rate, governments in many countries have looked for alternatives. Pressure to find other means of controlling the exchange rate tends to be especially strong when a country's currency is depreciating and the government lacks the foreign currency reserves necessary for sustained sterilized intervention.

One option is to use tariffs, import quotas, and other *protectionist* methods to restrain imports. If successful, these will shift the current account supply curve to the left, thus limiting downward pressure on the currency. However, this approach, though often tried, has drawbacks. It can raise import prices, contributing to domestic inflation. The inflation, in turn, can create expectations of future depreciation of the nominal exchange rate, thus sparking a capital outflow that will offset any gains on current account. Also, there is a distinct danger that trading partners will retaliate with protectionist measures of their own, thus harming exports.

Another option is to use export subsidies in an attempt to shift the current account demand curve for dollars to the right. Such policies are used by many countries, although only to a limited extent by the United States. They have drawbacks similar to those of import restrictions.

Still another option is to impose **exchange controls,** which are regulations that restrict the right to exchange the domestic currency for foreign currency. For example, countries may restrict the amount of currency that citizens can take abroad as tourists or allow access to the foreign exchange markets only to those with "essential" import needs. If controls become so extensive that they permit no access whatever to exchange markets without government permission, the country's currency is said to be **inconvertible.** The currency of the Soviet

Exchange controls
Restrictions on the freedom of firms and individuals to exchange the domestic currency for foreign currencies at market rates.

Inconvertibility (of a currency)
A situation in which a country's currency can be exchanged for foreign currency only through a government agency or with a government permit.

APPLYING ECONOMIC IDEAS 20.3

The J-Curve Effect and the Decline of the Dollar, 1985–1987

In the mid-1980s, the dollar rose to record highs on foreign exchange markets (see part a of the accompanying chart). As it did, the U.S. balance of trade moved even further into deficit (see part b of the chart). This surprised no one: The dollar's high value had made imported goods very cheap for U.S. buyers while at the same time making it very difficult for U.S. exporters to compete in world markets.

Beginning in the spring of 1985, international investors became less willing to finance the U.S. deficit in view of the country's growing international indebtedness. The dollar's real exchange rate fell sharply. The decline was prompted not only by the growing international indebted-

Source of chart: Federal Reserve Board of Governors.

ness of the United States but also by coordinated policy initiatives of major trading nations. Some observers expected an immediate improvement in the nominal balance of trade. Instead, however, the nominal balance of trade deficit continued to widen during 1985 and 1986. Why was this the case?

As the accompanying chart shows, the J-curve effect appears to be part of the explanation. The fall in the exchange rate made imports more costly for U.S. buyers and lowered the price of U.S. exports in world markets. As a result, by mid-1986 real U.S. exports were rising sharply and real imports were beginning to fall, as shown in parts c and d of the chart. However, the percentage change in import volume was smaller than the percentage increase in import prices brought on by the decline in the dollar's value. Thus, imports rose by more than enough, in nomi-

continued

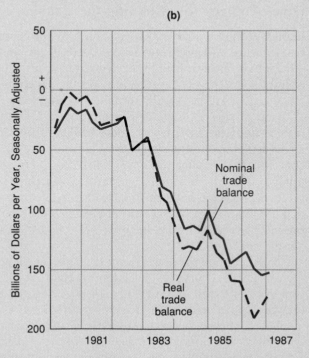

APPLYING ECONOMIC IDEAS 20.3

continued

nal terms, to outweigh the increase in nominal exports. Part b of the chart shows that, as the J-curve model predicts, the balance of trade turns upward in real terms before it turns upward in nominal terms.

However, the different timing of movements in real and nominal imports and exports is not the whole story. If it were, one would have expected the upturn in the real trade balance to have come much sooner after the real exchange rate began to decline, not six quarters later, as was actually the case. Other factors operated to bolster the J-curve effect in 1985 and early 1986, delaying the recovery of the U.S. balance of trade. For one thing, although the value of the dollar fell rapidly during 1985 and 1986 relative to the currencies of the established industrial countries, it changed little relative to the currencies of such newly industrialized nations as Korea and Taiwan or the Canadian dollar. Accordingly, these countries were able to

increase their share of the U.S. market at the expense of Japan, West Germany, and others whose currencies had risen sharply relative to the dollar.

Also, the textbook model of exchange markets assumes that changes in exchange rates are immediately passed on to buyers in the importing country as price changes. This was not what happened in many markets, however. During the early 1980s, when the dollar's value was rising, foreign firms took advantage of the situation to widen their profit margins as well as increase their volume of exports. When the dollar began to fall again, many of these firms at first absorbed the movement in exchange rates through reduced profit margins. This lessened the impact of the falling dollar on relative prices; thus, U.S. import prices in fact rose much less rapidly than would have been expected in view of the sharp drop in the real exchange rate.

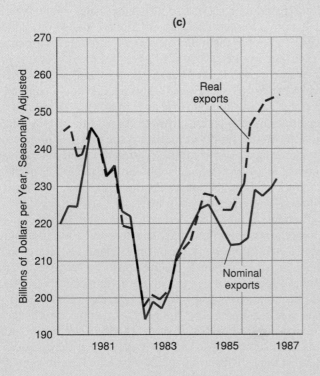

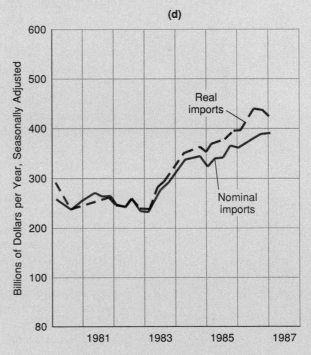

Union and many of its allies, as well as those of many Third World countries, are inconvertible.

All these policies—protectionism, export subsidies, and exchange controls—impose major costs on the domestic economy. They damage efficiency by distorting relative prices and prevent realization of gains from comparative advantage. The fact that these measures are nonetheless frequently employed reflects the political rent-seeking activities of those firms and workers that benefit from the reduction in international competition.

Exchange Rate Management Systems

How should governments use their powers to intervene in foreign exchange markets? This much-debated question has received varying answers in the post–World War II period. Sometimes central banks have actively intervened in the foreign exchange markets on an almost daily basis. In the early 1980s, the U.S. Treasury and the Federal Reserve System followed a largely hands-off strategy. Then, in 1985, the United States joined with Japan, Britain, France, and West Germany (the so-called Group of Five) in a coordinated effort to bring down the value of the dollar. In this section, we will look briefly at various systems for managing foreign exchange rates.

Bretton Woods and the Fixed-Rate System

After World War II, the major trading nations of the world met under United Nations auspices at Bretton Woods, New Hampshire, to forge a new world monetary system. That system, administered by the newly created International Monetary Fund (IMF), was based on a set of fixed exchange rates—four West German marks to the dollar, five French francs to the dollar, and so on. The member nations of the IMF agreed to maintain these rates through systematic intervention in foreign exchange markets.

For example, suppose rapid growth of the French economy caused the value of the franc to fall relative to the dollar. The French central bank would support its currency by buying francs in the foreign exchange markets. To be fully effective, these purchases would have to be unsterilized. As a result, they would drain francs from the domestic money supply at the same time that they propped up the exchange rate. Sooner or later, slower monetary growth would retard the growth of the French economy as a whole, which would remove the source of the downward pressure on the franc. Intervention could then stop, and the franc would be back in equilibrium at the agreed-upon level.

This system had both strengths and weaknesses. On the plus side, it controlled variations in exchange rates. Importers and exporters tended to like this situation, because it created a stable framework for business planning. However, the Bretton Woods system deprived national governments of a great deal of control over economic policy. They could not use domestic monetary policy to expand and contract their economies, control inflation, or create jobs; instead, domestic economic policy was constrained by the need to maintain exchange rates at a fixed level. Countries whose exchange rates tended to fall below the agreed-upon level had to accept lower growth rates than they wanted. Also, those whose currencies tended to push upward could be forced to take unwanted inflationary steps. To avoid these consequences, it was not uncommon for governments to resort to exchange controls, protectionism, and export subsidies.

In the early 1970s, the Bretton Woods system collapsed. Since then, most countries' currencies have been free to fluctuate, or "float," in foreign exchange markets according to supply and demand.[2] What has been the experience with floating rates since 1973?

Experience with Floating Rates

During its lifetime, the fixed-rate Bretton Woods system was criticized by many economists. They viewed it as a brake on world economic growth and free international trade. They especially resented the fact that many countries used protectionist measures and exchange controls, in addition to simple intervention, as a way of keeping their currencies at the agreed-upon exchange rates. The critics thought that if currencies were left free to respond to the forces of supply and demand, they would gravitate toward a set of natural exchange rate relationships. These would remain sufficiently stable over time to provide a basis for an efficient and growing world economy.

For the most part, the international monetary system has worked well since 1973. Few of the former critics of the Bretton Woods system have concluded that floating rates are a mistake. Even so, however, there have been some disappointments.

One of these was the worldwide spread of inflation during the 1970s. Fixed exchange rates help restrain inflation by forcing countries with weak currencies to intervene in foreign exchange markets and thereby slow the growth of their domestic money supplies. Floating rates leave each country's government open to inflationary pressures from within its own political and economic systems. However, inflation among the major industrial countries has moderated since the early 1980s; thus, the worst of this problem may have passed.

The volatility of exchange rates has been another disappointment. In the short run, exchange rates have proven to be highly sensitive to every bit of new information that might bear on the expected future levels of exchange rates. Further, as shown in "Applying Economic Ideas 20.2," the value of the dollar relative to other currencies and the value of other currencies relative to one another have also fluctuated over the longer run in the years since 1973—more widely than many Bretton Woods critics expected. These exchange rate fluctuations have produced boom-and-bust cycles in import and export industries. It is hoped that steps toward greater international policy coordination will damp exchange rate fluctuations in the years ahead—but only time will tell.

Finally, floating rates have not brought an era of free world trade. While it is true that many governments used Bretton Woods as a rationale for pursuing protectionist policies in the early postwar years, since 1973 governments have found many other excuses for doing so. The danger of a slide back into worldwide protectionism, which did so much damage to the world economy during the 1930s, persists despite floating rates.

Presently there is no realistic alternative to a floating-rate system. At every international conference on the subject, some speakers urge a return to a fixed-rate system. But the fact remains that national governments are not inclined to give up the control over their domestic economic policies that fixed rates imply, nor do most economists think that fixed rates are superior to floating rates despite some disappointments with the latter.

---

[2] There are exceptions. A group of countries in Western Europe have attempted to maintain exchange rates within a narrow range for their group. Also, some small countries have pegged their currencies to the U.S. dollar, the French franc, or some other major currency.

The future, then, will almost certainly see a continuation of the present mixed system. The basis for the system is exchange rates that float against one another. However, the system is modified by exchange rate intervention (used more actively by some countries than by others), the existence of some currency blocs within which exchange rates are linked to one another, and protectionist policies that are often inspired by imbalances in current or capital accounts.

Summary

1. **How can supply and demand curves be used to represent foreign exchange market activity arising from current account transactions?** In a world dominated by current account transactions, the demand for dollars arises from foreigners' demand for U.S. exports. The supply of dollars arises from the demand for imports by U.S. firms and households. The supply curve will slope upward provided that the demand for imports is elastic. A shift in either the supply curve or the demand curve will cause the exchange rate of the dollar for foreign currency to rise (*appreciate*) or fall (*depreciate*). In the long run, the exchange rate tends toward *purchasing power parity*—a situation in which it reflects differences in price level between countries. However, at any moment exchange rates may depart substantially from purchasing power parity.

2. **How can the supply and demand framework be extended to incorporate the capital account?** Capital account transactions can be represented by a *capital account net demand curve* for dollars. The negative slope indicates that, other things being equal, investors are attracted to assets denominated in currencies that they think are likely to appreciate and avoid assets denominated in currencies that they believe will depreciate. An increase in the U.S. real interest rate relative to real interest rates abroad will shift the U.S. capital account net demand curve upward. The current and capital account demand curves can be added together to get a total demand curve for dollars in the foreign exchange market.

3. **How do changes in rates of real economic growth affect exchange rates?** Other things being equal, an increase in the U.S. growth rate will increase the demand for imports. This will shift the supply curve for dollars to the right and put downward pressure on the exchange rate. As the exchange rate falls, the number of dollars demanded on both current and capital account will increase, as shown by a movement downward and to the right along the total demand curve for dollars. In the new equilibrium, the exchange rate will be lower and there will be a current account deficit offset by a net capital inflow.

4. **How do changes in interest rates affect exchange rates?** Other things being equal (including fixed price levels), an increase in U.S. interest rates will cause an upward shift in the capital account net demand curve for dollars and, hence, in the total demand curve for dollars. This will put upward pressure on the exchange rate, and the dollar will appreciate. As it does, the value of U.S. imports will increase and the value of U.S. exports will decrease. In the new long-run equilibrium, the exchange rate will be higher and there will be a current account deficit offset by a net capital inflow. Similarly, a drop in U.S. interest rates will result in a lower exchange rate and a current account surplus. However, if the demand for imports and exports is inelastic in the short run, the *J-curve effect* will result in a short-run movement toward a nominal current account deficit following a depreciation of the currency, followed by a longer-run swing toward surplus.

5. **What actions can governments take to affect exchange rates?** Official reserve account transactions by central banks can be used to influence foreign exchange rates. For example, the Federal Reserve System can sell dollars and buy foreign currency in foreign exchange markets, shifting the dollar supply curve to the right and causing the dollar to depreciate. However, intervention can also upset plans for domestic monetary policy. In order to neutralize the impact of intervention on the domestic money supply, the Fed may sterilize the intervention by using domestic open market sales to soak up the dollars created by its official dollar sales in the foreign exchange market. However, sterilized intervention has much less impact on the exchange rate than unsterilized intervention. Governments can also try to affect exchange rates through protectionist measures such as tariffs and import quotas, export subsidies, and *exchange controls*.

6. **How has the international monetary system evolved since World War II?** After World War II, the major trading nations met at Bretton Woods, New Hampshire, to set up a new international monetary system. That system featured fixed exchange rates. If supply and demand tended to push the value of a country's currency above or below the agreed-upon exchange rate, the country was supposed to intervene with official reserve sales or purchases. The Bretton Woods system was abandoned in the early 1970s. Since then, the world has operated with a system of floating exchange rates.

Terms for Review

- depreciation
- appreciation
- purchasing power parity
- capital account net demand curve
- nominal exchange rate
- real exchange rate
- J-curve effect
- exchange controls
- inconvertibility

Questions for Review

1. What determines the slope and position of the demand curve for a country's currency when only current account transactions are considered? What determines the slope and position of the supply curve for its currency? Under what conditions can the supply curve have a negative slope?

2. Why does the capital account net demand curve for a country's currency have a negative slope? How is the curve affected by a change in the interest rate?

3. How does an increase in a country's rate of economic growth, other things being equal, affect its exchange rate, current account balance, and net capital flows?

4. How does an increase in a country's interest rate, other things being equal, affect its exchange rate, current account balance, and net capital flows?

5. How can official reserve transactions be used to affect a country's exchange rate? What is meant by *sterilization* of official reserve account transactions?

6. What kind of exchange rate system was established at the Bretton Woods conference after World War II? What kind of system has prevailed since 1973?

Problems and Topics for Discussion

1. **Examining the lead-off case.** Why does it take several months or more for the exports of Mattison Machine Works to rise following a depreciation of the dollar? What does this have to do with the J-curve effect? In May 1987, the Japanese government announced a program of public works expenditures, tax cuts, and expansionary monetary policy. Would this program help relieve the problems of Hitachi Zosen, or would it worsen them? Explain.

2. **Exchange rates and currency reform.** In the mid-1980s, the Italian lira was trading at an exchange rate of about 2,000 lire per dollar. The Italian government was discussing the possibility of establishing a new unit of currency, a "strong lira," that would be worth 1,000 old lire. New currency would be issued to replace the old; all bank accounts would be changed over to the new unit; and so on. If the Italian currency reform were carried out, how would it affect the purchasing power parity of the dollar compared with the lira? How would it affect the nominal exchange rate? The real exchange rate?

3. **Growth abroad and the exchange rate.** Rework the graph presented in Exhibit 20.7 for a case in which the West German growth rate speeds up while that of the United States stays the same. What happens to the supply curve? The current account, capital account, and total demand curves? The exchange rate? The current account balance? Net capital flows?

4. **Public distress and the value of the dollar.** In the late 1970s, the dollar sank to record lows in the foreign exchange markets. This caused much hand wringing in Washington. Great pressure was put on the government to "do something" about the terrible situation of an undervalued dollar. Five years later, the dollar was soaring to record highs. This too caused much hand wringing and elicited calls to "do something" about the overvalued dollar. Question: If people are distressed when the dollar's value is low, why aren't they pleased when it is high? Discuss.

5. **The J-curve effect.** Using the *Survey of Current Business* or another government statistical source, update the data given in "Applying Economic Ideas 20.3" to cover the second half of 1987 and beyond. Is the pattern you observe consistent with the J-curve effect? Discuss.

The current trade deficit is not a sign of economic weakness.

Leave the Trade Deficit Alone

To say that the United States has a trade deficit is to use a figure of speech. It is like saying that New York won the World Series when we really mean that the New York Mets, a team of young men who mostly live elsewhere, won it.

The fact is that a certain (unknown) number of Americans bought more abroad than they sold abroad and a certain other (unknown) number of Americans sold more than they bought abroad. The trade deficit is the excess of the net foreign purchases of the first group over the net foreign sales of the second group. It is a statistical aggregate.

My interest here is not simply in verbal precision. I am raising the question why any of us should worry about this particular statistic, and why the U.S. government should take any responsibility for it. The people who have the trade deficit—who are buying more abroad than they are selling—are doing so voluntarily. If they were worried much they would stop. I had a trade deficit in 1986 because I took a vacation in France. I didn't worry about it; I enjoyed it.

A cliché of these days is that the trade deficit of the present size cannot go on forever. That is not axiomatically true, but it is probably true. That does not, however, give any guidance. As I have said before, if something cannot go on forever it will stop. Government action to stop it is not required.

The trade deficit will end when Americans are no longer willing to borrow enough or foreigners are no longer willing to lend enough to finance it. These borrowers and lenders have a lot of their own money at stake and are at least as well informed and as well motivated as the government to decide when the deficit has gone too far.

A great source of confusion today is the common association of the term "trade deficit" with the term "competitiveness." The term "competitiveness" raises all kinds of images that give the trade deficit a popular emotional force that the mere economist's term does not have. Competitiveness evokes the spirit of a game, and suggests that the United States is losing. National pride is involved. Politicians are inspired to promise that they will make America "No. 1" again.

But the fact of the trade deficit does not mean that the United States is losing anything, and it is not a sign of economic weakness. Total output in the United States and total per-capita output are both higher now than when we last had a trade surplus (1982). We have a trade deficit because although we produce much, we use more, including what we invest for the future and use for the defense of the entire Free World. The United States can have a trade deficit only because the rest of the world has confidence in the U.S. economy and U.S. policy and is willing to invest here. No one has to hold dollars. Willingness of foreigners to do so is a sign of the strength of the United States, not of its weakness. Taiwan and South Korea have large trade surpluses. That does not make them stronger economies or countries than the United States.

Anyway, the belief that the United States is in economic competition with the other industrial countries that are our principal allies and trading partners is a mistake. To have high real output per capita in the United States is a good thing, but there is no advantage for us in its being higher than that of our friends. This is important to realize, because we cannot expect to have more output per capita than our friends forever.

Knowledge and capital move around the world with increasing ease. There is a strong tendency for levels of output per capita to converge—for the difference between the lowest and the highest to diminish. We will have to get used to living in a world in which we are no longer No. 1 in that sense, or at least not No. 1 by much.

There must be something more serious to worry about.

Source: Herbert Stein, "Leave the Trade Deficit Alone," *The Wall Street Journal*, March 11, 1987, 36. Reprinted by permission of *The Wall Street Journal*, © Dow Jones & Company, Inc. 1987. All Rights Reserved. Photo Source: Courtesy of the International Ladies' Garment Workers Union.

Questions

1. It is common for a balance of payments surplus to be called a "favorable" balance of payments and for a deficit to be called an "unfavorable" balance. In view of the points raised in this editorial, do you think this terminology is appropriate?

2. Suppose that a massive earthquake devastated the Japanese consumer electronics industry. What do you think would happen to the U.S. trade balance as a result? Who in the United States would benefit from this disaster? Who would suffer? In what scnsc, if any, would the United States "as a whole" be made better off?

3. When foreign firms sell goods and services to buyers in the United States, they earn dollars. They can use these dollars either to buy goods and services produced in the United States, make loans to U.S. borrowers, or buy U.S. assets. How does their choice affect the U.S. balance of payments on current account? Who in the United States gains or loses as a result of their choice?

Suggestions for Further Reading

Grennes, Thomas. *International Economics.* Englewood Cliffs, N.J.: Prentice-Hall, 1984.

Chapters 14 through 24 review the economics of foreign exchange markets and the international monetary system.

Melton, William C. *Inside the Fed.* Homewood, Ill.: Dow Jones-Irwin, 1985.

Chapter 11 of this book by a former Federal Reserve System official covers the relationship between domestic and international monetary policy.

President's Council of Economic Advisers. *Economic Report of the President.* Washington, D.C.: Government Printing Office, annually.

Each year's economic report contains a chapter on international economic policy.

Schwartz, Anna J. "Prospects of an International Monetary System Constitution." *Contemporary Policy Issues* (April 1987): 16–30.

Schwartz briefly reviews experience with Bretton Woods and the floating-rate system and then discusses several alternative proposals for a new international monetary system.

Dictionary of Economic Terms

Accelerationist model of inflation
A theory according to which changes in the inflation rate affect unemployment and real output.

Adaptive-expectations hypothesis
The hypothesis that people form their expectations about future economic events mainly on the basis of past economic events.

Aggregate demand
The value of all planned expenditures.

Aggregate demand curve
A graph showing the relationship between the price level and the total level of real planned expenditures.

Aggregate supply
The value of all goods and services produced in the economy; a synonym for national product.

Aggregate supply curve
A graph showing the relationship between the price level and the real output (real national product) supplied by the economy.

Appreciation (of a currency)
An increase in the value of a country's currency relative to another's.

Assets
All the things to which a firm or household holds legal claim.

Automatic fiscal policy
Changes in government purchases or net taxes caused by changes in economic conditions given unchanged tax and spending laws.

Automatic stabilizers
Those elements of automatic fiscal policy that move the federal budget toward deficit during a contraction

and toward surplus during an expansion.

Autonomous
In the context of the Keynesian income-expenditure model, refers to an expenditure that is independent of the level of real national income.

Autonomous consumption
The part of total consumption expenditure that is independent of the level of disposable income; for any given consumption schedule, autonomous consumption equals the level of real consumption associated with zero real disposable income.

Autonomous net taxes
Taxes or transfer payments that do not vary with the level of national income.

Average propensity to consume
Total consumption for any income level divided by total disposable income.

Balance sheet
A financial statement showing a firm's or household's assets, liabilities, and net worth.

Base year
The year chosen as a basis for comparison in calculating a price index or price level.

Bond
A promise, given in return for borrowed funds, to make a fixed annual or semiannual payment over a set number of years plus a larger final payment equal to the amount borrowed.

Business cycle
A pattern of alternating economic growth and contraction.

Capital
All means of production that are created by people, including tools, industrial equipment, and structures.

Capital account
The section of a country's international accounts that consists of purchases and sales of assets and international borrowing and lending.

Capital account balance
The value of net private capital inflows less the value of net private capital outflows.

Capital account net demand curve
A graph that shows the net demand for a country's currency that results at various exchange rates from capital account transactions.

Capital inflows
Borrowing from foreign financial intermediaries and funds earned through sales of real or financial assets to foreign buyers.

Capitalism
An economic system in which control of business firms rests with the owners of capital.

Capital outflows
Lending to foreign borrowers and funds used to purchase real or financial assets from foreign sellers.

Change in demand
A change in the quantity of a good that buyers are willing and able to purchase that results from a change in some condition other than the price of that good; a shift in the demand curve.

Change in quantity demanded
A change in the quantity of a good that buyers are willing and able to purchase that results from a change

in the good's price, other things being equal; a movement from one point to another along a demand curve.

Change in quantity supplied
A change in the quantity of a good that producers are willing and able to sell that results from a change in the good's price, other things being equal; a movement along a supply curve.

Change in supply
A change in the quantity of a good that producers are willing and able to sell that results from a change in some condition other than the good's price; a shift in the supply curve.

Circular flow of income and product
The flow of goods and services between households and firms balanced by the flow of payments made in exchange for them.

Civilian labor force
The sum of the employed and the unemployed; excludes members of the armed forces on active duty.

Civilian unemployment rate
The percentage of the civilian labor force that is unemployed.

Closed economy
An economy having no links to the rest of the world.

Commercial banks
Financial intermediaries that provide a broad range of banking services, including accepting demand deposits and making commercial loans.

Common property
Property to which all members of a community have open access.

Common stock
A certificate of part ownership in a corporation that gives the owner a vote in the selection of the firm's directors and the right to a share of dividends, if any.

Comparative advantage
The ability to produce a good or

service at a lower opportunity cost than another person or country.

Complements
A pair of goods for which an increase in the price of one results in a decrease in demand for the other.

Conditional forecast
A prediction of future economic events, usually stated in the form "If A, then B, other things being equal."

Consumer price index (CPI)
A price index based on the market basket of goods and services purchased by a typical urban household.

Consumer sovereignty
A system under which consumers determine which goods and services will be produced by means of what they decide to buy or not to buy.

Consumption function
See Consumption schedule.

Consumption schedule
A graph that shows how real consumption expenditure varies as real disposable income changes, other things being equal.

Corporation
A firm that takes the form of an independent legal entity with ownership divided into equal shares and each owner's liability limited to his or her investment in the firm.

Cost-push inflation
Inflation that is caused by an upward shift in the aggregate supply curve while the aggregate demand curve remains fixed or shifts upward more slowly.

Crowding-out effect
The tendency of expansionary fiscal policy to raise the interest rate and thereby cause a decrease in the planned-investment level.

Currency
Coins and paper money.

Current account
The section of a country's

international accounts that consists of imports, exports, and unilateral transfers.

Current account balance
The value of a country's exports of goods and services minus the value of its imports of goods and services plus its net transfer receipts from foreign sources.

Cyclical deficit
The difference between the actual federal deficit and the structural deficit.

Cyclical unemployment
The difference between the actual rate of unemployment at a given point in the business cycle and the natural rate of unemployment.

Demand curve
A graphic representation of the relationship between the price of a good and the quantity of it that buyers demand.

Demand-pull inflation
An increase in the price level caused by an increase of aggregate demand relative to natural real output.

Depository institutions
Financial intermediaries, including commercial banks and thrift institutions, that accept deposits from the public.

Depreciation (of a currency)
A decline in the value of a country's currency relative to another's.

Direct financing
The process of raising investment funds directly from savers.

Discount rate
The interest rate the Fed charges on loans of reserves to banks.

Discount window
The department through which the Federal Reserve lends reserves to banks.

Discouraged worker
A person who would work if a suitable job were available but has given up looking.

Discretionary fiscal policy
Changes in the laws setting government purchases and net taxes.

Disposable income
See Disposable personal income.

Disposable personal income
Personal income less personal taxes (particularly income taxes).

Economic efficiency
A state of affairs in which it is not possible, by changing the pattern of either distribution or production, to satisfy one person's wants more fully without causing some other person's wants to be satisfied less fully.

Economic planning
Systematic government intervention in the economy with the goal of improving coordination, efficiency, and growth.

Economic rent
Any payment to a factor of production in excess of its opportunity costs.

Economics
The study of the choices people make and the actions they take in order to make the best use of scarce resources in meeting their wants.

Efficiency in distribution
A situation in which it is not possible, by redistributing existing supplies of goods and services, to satisfy one person's wants more fully without causing some other person's wants to be satisfied less fully.

Efficiency in production
A situation in which it is not possible, given available technology and factors of production, to produce more of one good or service without forgoing the opportunity to produce some of another good or service.

Employed
A person working at least 1 hour a week for pay or 15 hours a week as an unpaid worker in a family business.

Employment rate
The percentage of the working-age population that is employed.

Entitlements
Transfer payments governed by long-term laws that are not subject to annual budget review.

Entrepreneurship
The process of looking for new possibilities—making use of new ways of doing things, being alert to new opportunities, and overcoming old limits.

Equation of exchange
An equation that shows the relationships among the money stock (M), the velocity of money (V), the price level (P), and the level of real income (y); written as $MV = Py$.

Equilibrium
A condition in which buyers' and sellers' plans exactly mesh in the marketplace so that the quantity supplied exactly equals the quantity demanded at a given price.

Excess quantity demanded (shortage)
A condition in which the quantity of a good demanded at a given price exceeds the quantity supplied.

Excess quantity supplied (surplus)
A condition in which the quantity of a good supplied at a given price exceeds the quantity demanded.

Excess reserves
Total reserves minus required reserves.

Exchange controls
Restrictions on the freedom of firms and individuals to exchange the domestic currency for foreign currencies at market rates.

Expenditure multiplier
The ratio of the induced shift in aggregate demand to an initial shift in planned investment (or other expenditure).

Externality
An effect of producing or consuming a good whose impact on third parties other than buyers and sellers of the good is not reflected in prices.

Factors of production
The basic inputs of labor, capital, and natural resources used in producing all goods and services.

Federal funds market
A market in which banks lend reserves to one another for periods as short as 24 hours.

Federal funds rate
The interest rate banks charge for overnight loans of reserves to one another.

Final goods and services
Goods and services that are sold to or are ready for sale to parties that will use them for consumption, investment, government purchases, or export.

Financial intermediaries
Financial firms, including banks, savings and loan associations, insurance companies, pension funds, and mutual funds, that gather funds from net savers and provide funds to net borrowers.

Financial markets
Markets through which borrowers obtain funds from savers.

Fiscal policy
Policy concerning government purchases, taxes, and transfer payments.

Fiscal year
The federal government's budgetary year, which starts on October 1 of the preceding calendar year.

Fixed investment
Purchases by firms of newly produced goods, such as production machinery, office equipment, and newly built structures.

Flow
A process that occurs continuously through time, measured in units per time period.

Foreign exchange market
A market in which the currency of one country is traded for that of another.

Frictional unemployment
The portion of unemployment that is accounted for by short periods of unemployment needed for matching jobs with job seekers within the mainstream of the economy.

GNP deflator
A weighted average of prices of all final goods and services produced in the economy.

Goods
All things that people value.

Government purchases
See Government purchases of goods and services.

Government purchases of goods and services
Purchases of finished goods by government plus the cost of hiring the services of government employees and contractors.

Gross national product (GNP)
A measure of the economy's total output of goods and services; the dollar value at current market prices of all final goods and services produced annually by a nation's factors of production.

Growth recession
A situation in which real output grows, but not quickly enough to keep unemployment from rising.

Hyperinflation
Very rapid inflation.

Income-expenditure model
The Keynesian model in which the equilibrium level of real national income is determined by treating real planned expenditure and real national product as functions of the level of real national income.

Income-product line
A graph showing the level of real planned expenditure (aggregate demand) associated with each level of real national income.

Inconvertibility (of a currency)
A situation in which a country's currency can be exchanged for foreign currency only through a government agency or with a government permit.

Indexing
Adjusting a value or payment automatically in proportion to changes in a specific price index.

Indirect financing
The process of raising investment funds via financial intermediaries.

Inferior good
A good for which an increase in consumer income results in a decrease in demand.

Inflation
A sustained increase in the average prices of all goods and services.

Inflationary recession
An episode in which real output falls below its natural level and unemployment rises above its natural rate while rapid inflation continues.

Inside lag
The delay between the time a policy change is needed and the time a decision is made.

Inventory
Stocks of a finished good awaiting sale or use.

Inventory investment
Changes in the stocks of finished products and raw materials that firms keep on hand; figure is positive if such stocks are increasing and negative if they are decreasing.

Investment
(1) The act of increasing the economy's stock of capital, that is, its stock of means of production made by people; (2) the sum of fixed investment and inventory investment.

J-curve effect
A situation in which a country's nominal current account balance moves at first toward deficit and later toward surplus following a decrease in its currency's exchange rate.

Labor
The contributions to production made by people working with their minds and muscles.

Laffer curve
A graph that shows the connection between the marginal rate at which a tax is imposed and the revenues raised by the tax.

Law of demand
The principle that, other things being equal, the quantity of a good demanded by buyers tends to rise as the price of the good falls and to fall as its price rises.

Liabilities
All the legal claims against a firm by nonowners or against a household by nonmembers.

Liquidity
An asset's ability to be used directly as a means of payment, or readily converted to one, and remain fixed in nominal value.

M1
A measure of the money supply that includes currency and transaction deposits.

M2
A measure of the money supply that includes M1 plus money market mutual fund shares, savings deposits, small time deposits, overnight repurchase agreements, and certain other liquid assets.

Macroeconomics
The branch of economics that deals with large-scale economic phenomena, particularly inflation, unemployment, and economic growth.

Managerial coordination
A means of coordinating economic activity that uses directives from managers to subordinates.

Marginal propensity to consume
The proportion of each added dollar of real disposable income that households devote to real consumption.

Marginal propensity to import
The percentage of each added dollar of real disposable income that is devoted to consumption of imported goods and services.

Marginal tax rate
The percentage of each added dollar of disposable income that must be paid in taxes.

Market
Any arrangement that people have for trading with one another.

Market coordination
A means of coordinating economic activity that uses the price system to transmit information and provide incentives.

Market failure
An instance in which a market fails to meet accepted standards of efficiency or fairness in performing its functions of transmitting information, providing incentives, and distributing income.

Merchandise balance
The value of a country's merchandise exports minus the value of its merchandise imports.

Merit good
A good to which all citizens are entitled regardless of ability to pay.

Microeconomics
The branch of economics that deals with the choices and actions of small economic units—households, business firms, and government units.

Model
A simplified representation of the way in which facts are related.

Monetarism
A school of economics emphasizing the importance of changes in the money stock as determinants of changes in real output and the price level.

Money
An asset that serves as a means of payment, a store of purchasing power, and a unit of account.

Money multiplier
The ratio of the equilibrium money stock to the banking system's total reserves.

Multiplier effect
The tendency for a given shift in planned investment (or another component of aggregate demand) to cause a larger shift in total aggregate demand.

National income
The total income earned by households, including wages, rents, interest payments, and profits.

National product
The total value of all goods and services produced in the economy.

Natural level of real output
The level of real output associated with the natural rate of unemployment.

Natural rate of unemployment
The sum of frictional and structural unemployment; the rate of unemployment that persists when the economy is experiencing neither accelerating nor decelerating inflation.

Natural resources
Anything that can be used as a productive input in its natural state, such as farmland, building sites, forests, and mineral deposits.

Net exports
Exports minus imports.

Net national product (NNP)
Gross national product minus an allowance (called the *capital consumption allowance*) that represents the value of capital equipment used up in the production process.

Net taxes
Taxes paid to government minus transfer payments made by government.

Net tax multiplier
The ratio of an induced shift in aggregate demand to a given change in net taxes.

Net worth (owners' equity)
A firm's or household's assets minus its liabilities.

Neutrality of money
The proposition that in the long run a one-time change in the money stock affects only the price level and not real output, employment, interest rates, or planned investment.

New classical economics
A school of economics stressing the role of rational expectations in shaping the economy's response to policy changes.

Nominal
In economics, a term that refers to data that have not been adjusted for the effects of inflation.

Nominal exchange rate
The exchange rate expressed in the usual way: in terms of current units of foreign currency per current dollar.

Nominal interest rate
The interest rate measured in the usual way: in terms of current dollars of interest paid per current dollar of principal.

Normal good
A good for which an increase in consumer income results in an increase in demand.

Normative economics
The part of economics devoted to making judgments about which economic policies or conditions are good or bad.

Official reserve account
The section of a country's international accounts that consists of changes in central banks' official international reserves.

Okun's law
A rule of thumb according to which each 3 percent by which real output rises above (or falls below) its natural level results in an unemployment rate one percentage point below (or above) the natural rate.

Open economy
An economy linked to the outside world by imports, exports, and financial transactions.

Open market operation
A purchase (sale) by the Fed of government securities from (to) the public.

Operating target
The financial variable—the money stock, the federal funds rate, or whatever—for which the Fed sets a short-term target and uses as a day-to-day guide to the conduct of open market operations.

Opportunity cost
The cost of a good or service measured in terms of the lost opportunity to pursue the best alternative activity with the same time or resources.

Outside lag
The delay between the time a policy decision is made and the time the policy change affects the economy.

Owners' equity
See Net worth.

Partnership
An association of two or more people who operate a business as co-owners by voluntary legal agreement.

Personal income
The total income received by households, including earned income and transfer payments.

Phillips curve
A graph showing the relationship between the inflation rate and the unemployment rate, other things being equal.

Planned-expenditure schedule
A graph showing the level of total real planned expenditure associated with each level of real national income.

Planned-investment schedule
A graph showing the relationship between the total quantity of real planned-investment expenditure and the interest rate.

Portfolio
A person's or firm's collection of assets.

Positive economics
The part of economics concerned with statements about facts and the relationships among them.

Price index
A weighted average of the prices of goods and services expressed in relation to a base year value of 100.

Price level
A weighted average of the prices of goods and services expressed in relation to a base year value of 1.0.

Primary financial markets
Markets in which newly issued stocks, bonds, and other securities are sold.

Privatization
The turning over of government functions to the private sector.

Producer price index (PPI)
A price index based on a sample of goods and services bought by business firms.

Production possibility frontier
A graph showing the possible combinations of goods that can be produced in an economy given the available factors of production and technology.

Public good
A good or service that (1) cannot be provided for one person without also being provided for others and (2) once provided for one person can be provided for others at zero added cost.

Purchasing power parity
A situation in which a given sum of money will buy the same market basket of goods and services when converted from one currency to another at prevailing exchange rates.

Rational-expectations hypothesis
The hypothesis that people form their expectations about future economic events on the basis of not only past events but also their expectations about economic policies and their likely effects.

Real
In economics, a term that refers to data that have been adjusted for the effects of inflation.

Real exchange rate
The nominal exchange rate adjusted for changes in the price levels of both countries relative to a chosen base year.

Real interest rate
The nominal interest rate minus the inflation rate.

Realized expenditure
The sum of all planned and unplanned expenditures.

Realized investment
The sum of planned and unplanned investment.

Recession
A cyclical contraction usually lasting six months or more.

Reflation
An episode in which policy becomes more expansionary while the expected inflation rate is still falling.

Regulation
Government intervention in the market for the purpose of influencing the production and distribution of particular goods and services.

Rent seeking
The activity of obtaining and defending rents.

Repurchase agreement (RP)
A short-term liquid asset that consists of an agreement by a firm or person to buy securities from a financial institution for resale at an agreed-upon price at a later date (often the next business day).

Required-reserve ratio
Required reserves stated as a percentage of the deposits to which reserve requirements apply.

Required reserves
The minimum reserves that the Fed requires depository institutions to hold.

Reserves
Cash in bank vaults and non-interest-bearing deposits of banks with the Federal Reserve System.

Saving
The part of household income that is not used to buy goods and services or to pay taxes.

Saving schedule
A graph showing the relationship between the total quantity of real saving and the interest rate.

Savings deposit
A deposit at a bank or thrift institution from which funds can be withdrawn at any time without payment of a penalty.

Say's law
The proposition that aggregate demand will automatically be sufficient to absorb all of the output that firms and workers are willing to produce with given technology and resources.

Scarcity
A situation in which there is not enough of a resource to meet all of everyone's wants.

Secondary financial markets
Markets in which previously issued bonds, stocks, and other securities are traded among investors.

Services
The valued acts that people perform for one another.

Shortage
See Excess quantity demanded.

Socialism
An economic system in which firms are owned and controlled by the people who work in them or by the government acting in their name.

Sole proprietorship
A firm that is owned and usually operated by one person, who receives all the profits and is responsible for all of the firm's liabilities.

Sterilization
The Fed's use of open market operations to offset the effects of exchange market intervention on domestic reserves and the money stock.

Stock
A quantity that exists at a given point in time, measured in terms of units only.

Structural deficit
The budget surplus or deficit that the federal government would incur given current tax and spending laws and a 6 percent unemployment rate.

Structural unemployment
The portion of unemployment that is accounted for by people who are out of work for long periods because their skills do not match those required for available jobs.

Substitutes
A pair of goods for which an increase in the price of one causes an increase in demand for the other.

Supply curve
A graphic representation of the relationship between the price of a good and the quantity of it supplied.

Supply shock
An event, such as an increase in the price of imported oil, a crop failure, or a natural disaster, that raises input prices for all or most firms and pushes up workers' costs of living.

Supply-side economics
A school of economics that focuses on efforts to increase the growth of natural real output, especially through the incentive of tax cuts.

Surplus
See Excess quantity supplied.

Thrift institutions
A group of financial intermediaries that operate much like commercial banks, including savings and loan associations, savings banks, and credit unions.

Thrifts
See Thrift institutions.

Time deposit
A deposit at a bank or thrift institution from which funds can be withdrawn without payment of a penalty only at the end of an agreed-upon period.

Transaction costs
Incidental costs to buyers and sellers of making a transaction, including the costs of gathering information, making decisions, carrying out trades, writing contracts, and making payments.

Transaction deposit
A deposit from which funds can be freely withdrawn by check in order to make payment to a third party.

Transfer payments
Payments by government to individuals that are not made in return for goods and services currently supplied.

Transmission mechanism
The set of channels through which monetary policy affects real output and the price level.

Unemployed
A person who is not employed but is actively looking for work.

Unemployment rate
The percentage of people in the labor force who are not working but are actively looking for work.

Value added
The dollar value of an industry's sales less the value of intermediate goods purchased for use in production.

Velocity
The ratio of nominal national income to the money stock; a measure of the average number of times each dollar of the money stock is used each year for income-producing purposes.

Index*

---

*Words appearing in boldface type are glossary terms defined in text. The boldface page numbers indicate the pages on which the key terms are defined.